תהלים שטיינזלץ
The Steinsaltz Tehillim

Steinsaltz Center

קוֹרֶן ירושלים

תהלים שטיינזלץ

עם ביאור
הרב עדין אבן-ישראל שטיינזלץ

THE STEINSALTZ TEHILLIM

COMMENTARY BY
RABBI ADIN EVEN-ISRAEL
STEINSALTZ

STEINSALTZ CENTER
KOREN PUBLISHERS JERUSALEM

The Steinsaltz Tehillim

Commentary by
Rabbi Adin Even-Israel Steinsaltz

First Hebrew/English Edition 2018

Koren Publishers Jerusalem Ltd.
POB 4044, Jerusalem 91040, ISRAEL
POB 8531, New Milford, CT 06776, USA
www.korenpub.com

Steinsaltz Center
Steinsaltz Center is the parent organization
of institutions established by Rabbi Adin Even-Israel Steinsaltz
POB 45187, Jerusalem 91450 ISRAEL
Telephone: +972 2 646 0900, Fax +972 2 624 9454
www.steinsaltz-center.org

All rights reserved to Adin Steinsaltz ©2015, 2018
Koren Tanakh Font © 1962, 2018 Koren Publishers Jerusalem Ltd.
Koren Siddur Font and text design © 1981, 2018 Koren Publishers Jerusalem Ltd.

The creation of this book was made possible through the generous support of
Torah Education in Israel.

Considerable research and expense have gone into the creation of this
publication. Unauthorized copying may be considered *geneivat da'at* and breach
of copyright law. No part of this publication (content or design, including
use of the Koren fonts) may be reproduced, stored in a retrieval system or
transmitted in any form or by any means electronic, mechanical, photocopying
or otherwise, without the prior written permission of the publisher, except
in the case of brief quotations embedded in critical articles or reviews.

ISBN 978-965-301-969-0

Printed in USA

Steinsaltz Center

Executive Director,
Steinsaltz Center
Rabbi Meni Even-Israel

Executive Editor
Rabbi Yaakov Blinder

Translator
Gaya Aranoff Bernstein

Editors
Gaya Aranoff Bernstein
Laurie E. Fialkoff

Hebrew Edition Editor
Yehudit Shabta

Technical Staff
Adena Frazer
Shaltiel Shmidman

Editor in Chief
Rabbi Jason Rappoport

Copy Editors
Caryn Meltz, *Manager*
Dvora Rhein, *Senior
  Copy Editor*
Suri Brand
Rachelle Emanuel

Proofreaders
Ilana Brown
Debbie Ismailoff
Ita Olesker

Language Expert
Shira Shmidman, *Aramaic*

KOREN

Design & Typesetting
Avishai Magence, *Production Manager*
Tomi Mager, *Design & Typography*

For Dawne
who is Dina

from her sisters
Lesley, Margot and Serena

Thursday

Dedicated in loving memory of our mother,
grandmother, and great-grandmother,
Edith Kaufthal, Esther bat Mordechai HaKohen,
who said Psalms every day for her family's well-being
and had enormous faith in their redemptive power.

Linda and Ilan Kaufthal   *Judy and Uri Kaufthal*
Abby and Joshua Kaufthal   *Dina and Jonathan Kaufthal*
Lori and David Kaufthal   *Keren and Jeremy Kaufthal*
Laura and Daniel Kaufthal   *Alison and Joshua Kaufthal*

Joseph Leo   Jenna Lily
Sydney Rose   Evan Leo
Jack Ezra   Jacob Asher
Fred   Noah Cory
Ella Julia   Maya Eden
Leo Howard
Maximilian Julius
Bill Abraham

Friday

We are honored to dedicate this section of Rabbi Steinsaltz's
work in honor of our children Judd, Lauren, and Emma.
May their connection to our faith be ever strong.

David & Leslie Fastenberg

Shabbat

Dedicated to Rav Adin Steinsaltz
הרב עדין אבן-ישראל שטיינזלץ שליט״א
with profound respect
for his monumental contribution to the Jewish people

Lewis and Gaya Aranoff Bernstein

Sunday
Dedicated in honor of my beautiful wife, Tatiana,
whose wisdom, humor, warmth,
and love makes our family.

Michael G. Reiff

Monday
In memory of Efraim ben Hilik, Gnesya bat Aaron,
Genya Golda bat Emmanuel, Yosefa bat Boris
and Mark ben Alexander
and in honor of our children
David and Chana Michal Shifra and their children
Sara Nessa, Odelia, Shylie Efrat, and Brielle

Tuesday
In memory of my grandparents Devora and Isaac Glassman
and their journey; my mother, Florence Glassman Carr,
whose kindness, courage, humor, and resilience
supported all around her; and the inspiring lives of
my brothers Robert and Jay.

Daniel B. Carr

Wednesday
Dedicated in honor of
Rose and Lawrence Shaykin
Marilyn and Jack Shechtman
May their memory always be for a blessing
With love from their children

Leonard and Maura Shaykin

Contents

Introduction to the Steinsaltz Tehillim

The book of Psalms is unique among the books of the Bible. Taken as a whole, the Bible depicts the relationship between God and mankind, and more particularly between God and the people of Israel. In the books of the Bible, certainly in the Torah but also in the Prophets, the relationship is primarily portrayed as proceeding from the top down, from God to man. By contrast, Psalms is the only book of the Bible where the relationship flows in the opposite direction, from man to God, in other words, where an individual turns to God and communicates with Him. Psalms is traditionally divided into five books, containing a total of 150 chapters. Some suggest that these are meant to correspond to the five books of the Torah. This parallelism also serves to illustrate that the relationship between God and man runs in both directions. Thus, despite their wide variation in subject matter and tone, the individual chapters comprising Psalms are all narrated from a human perspective, with all the limitations and complexity this entails.

The Hebrew title of the book, *Tehillim*, means "praises," and there is much in the way of praise in its chapters. Yet Psalms is much more than a compendium of ways to praise God. In fact, one can find in it almost any thought or feeling a person might wish to express to God. It includes a wide variety of poetic forms, with personal poetry alongside epic poems, as well as philosophical musings and introspection on matters pertaining to the nation of Israel and to mankind. But what pervades all of the psalms, whether clearly expressed or implicit, is the voice of the individual psalmist.

Just as the topics of the psalms vary, so does the persona of the psalmist. The psalmist is seen as alternately dejected and elated; there are psalms of

◄ defeat

defeat and surrender alongside powerful, exultant victory songs. Moreover, some of the psalms express disquiet, originating in a crisis of faith or a grievance, whereas others bespeak peace and tranquility. To use a musical metaphor, some psalms are staccato, others legato; some largo, others presto. In similar fashion, the psalmist can be compared to a harp, each of whose many strings has its own unique sound while simultaneously working in harmony.

Psalms deals with a number of recurring themes. Many of its chapters contain prayers and supplications that seem to correspond to actual events in the life of King David. But despite their various allusions to historical events, the psalms are not autobiographical. While many of them are attributed to David, neither his private nor his public persona is readily discernible. What emerges from most of the psalms is not the voice of a specific historical figure but rather that of Everyman.

As the bounds of the personal are transcended, the psalms enter the realm of the universal. For instance, from the standpoint of history, we know that King David was surrounded for most of his life by followers, friends, and admirers. Yet what is most striking in the psalms of supplication attributed to David is the loneliness they convey. Only rarely do we get a sense of David as part of a larger "us," for better or for worse. The image is that of a man who feels alone even in the midst of a crowd. This quality, somewhat paradoxically, makes Psalms not only a collection of songs that can be sung aloud in a chorus of voices, but also an expression of many people's most private life experiences, whether joyous or distressing. As the verse says, "The heart alone knows its own bitterness, and no stranger can share in its joy" (Proverbs 14:10). People first feel their own pain and happiness, and only after that can they identify with the feelings and experiences of others.

The logic behind the psalms' arrangement remains unclear. There are no obvious differences between the five books, or sections, of Psalms. And while here and there a group of psalms appears to have certain structural or thematic similarities, these are the exceptions to the rule. It appears likely that the disarray is intentional, reflecting the perspective of a work that above all expresses human emotions. For emotions, like existence itself, have no fixed order; there are no predetermined conditions governing a person's feeling happy, sorrowful, introspective, or grateful. Psalms mirrors life in all its vicissitudes and inconsistencies, demonstrating that despite our most strenuous efforts, life can never be fully organized or controlled.

The chapters of Psalms differ from one another in structure and style as well as content and length. Psalms contains the shortest chapter in the Bible

(two verses) and almost immediately following it, the longest chapter (176 verses). Some of the psalms have the rhythm and tone of epic poetry. Some are simple entreaties, and others are an outpouring of feeling emanating from the depths of the soul. There are many tearful prayers in Psalms, and often no explanation is provided for the psalmist's distress other than that something is wrong. Some psalms are distinctly meditative and deal with a well-defined topic. Others are songs of a historical nature. Also quite a few psalms offer straightforward, moral instruction.

Despite all the differences between them, the psalms share one outstanding characteristic: truth. There is no smoothing of rough edges, no attempt to ignore or gloss over difficult issues in order to create a sense of harmony. Indeed, many of the psalms have a kind of built-in dissonance that results from the psalmist's refusal to relinquish a point of truth even at the expense of disrupting the overall melody. Undoubtedly, this aspect of Psalms is partially why it continues to speak to so many people in all corners of the world. While Psalms very much belongs to a specific place (the Land of Israel) and a specific period (the biblical era), it nonetheless transcends all boundaries of space and time.

Essentially, rather than being a book of poetry expressing the "I" of the poet, Psalms is a book of prayer. To the extent that "I" is present in each psalm, so, too, God is always present as the divine "You." This is the case both when every verse of a given psalm contains some reference to the divine, and when heavenly matters go almost or entirely unmentioned. What we have here, as the psalmist himself notes, is a kind of conversation, or pouring forth of the soul, "before the Lord" (Psalms 102:1). The spiritual world presented in Psalms is neither mysterious nor complicated. Although some of the psalms sound a note of complaint, there is always a sense that here, unlike in other books of the Bible such as Job or Ecclesiastes, these emotions are kept firmly in check. Moreover, even when they raise questions that are essentially unanswerable, the psalms remain a form of prayer.

Like Job and Ecclesiastes, Psalms has a special, unique set of cantillations. The cantillation signs serve to punctuate the verses as well as to indicate specific musical notes. In Psalms, the musical component of the cantillations has been entirely lost. We know that certain psalms were sung in the Temple during the era of the Second Temple and possibly even before that. But beyond this we lack any reliable tradition pertaining to the melodies that were sung.

Until the period of the Sages, Psalms consisted of 147 chapters. Most of these texts have a heading and a clear internal structure. A later, non-Jewish

◄ division

division of Psalms produced the current 150 chapters, a few of which appear to be incomplete or not self-contained. Most of the psalms are attributed to David, as indicated in the psalms themselves, using descriptions such as: "the prayers of David son of Yishai" (Psalms 72:20). Nevertheless, according to the Sages (*Bava Batra* 14b–15a) various psalms were authored by ten others, among them Adam and Moses.

Apart from its literary value, Psalms enjoys an exceptional status in the biblical canon. No book of the Bible has evoked more tears or more words of gratitude and joy. Over the course of Jewish history, Psalms has been utilized more than any other book, not just by poets, but by all who seek to articulate the appropriate words and phrases with which to beseech, express gratitude to, pour out the sorrows of their soul to, or simply have a conversation with God. Whether it is a lonely widow weeping over her travails, a leader grappling with a military or political crisis, or an individual inspired to sing a song of thanksgiving, Psalms provides a mouthpiece for everyone. Indeed, if King David is termed "the sweet singer of Israel" (II Samuel 23:1), it is because he sang the song of an entire people.

Last, in places the book of Psalms contains sparks of mystical inspiration. These are embedded within the text and can be understood as simply poetic expressions of spirituality that are never fully articulated. This, too, accounts for part of the potent appeal of Psalms: Despite the gamut of human experience and emotions it conveys, its underlying melody is never extreme. Penetrating questions, existential doubts, unbearable pain, and unbridled joy as well are all hinted at, but never fully explicated. It is as if, alongside each psalm, the psalmist has left a blank sheet for every reader to inscribe his own poetry.

Rabbi Adin Even-Israel Steinsaltz

Introduction by the Hebrew Editors

The purpose of this commentary is to assist the contemporary reader by bridging the gaps in language, outlook, and culture between us and the world of Psalms. As far as possible, it seeks to clarify ambiguities, elucidate problematic passages, and remove obstacles to understanding while dealing with both explicit and implicit difficulties.

The commentary consists of several parts, which complement but are independent of one another. The literal translation of the verses appears in boldface. Woven into the biblical text in non-bold typeface are brief explanatory comments and elaborations.

The commentary seeks to concisely clarify the language and context at the most basic level, so as not to encumber the reader. Consequently, it is not committed to a particular exegetical method and does not systematically defer to any particular commentator.

Much thought and labor has been invested to ensure that the design of this work is as aesthetically pleasing and convenient for the user as possible. This design is the fruit of an ongoing collaboration between the team at the Institute for Talmudic Publications and Koren Publishers. Our thanks to Rabbi Meir Hanegbi whose wisdom, conviviality, and efficiency contributed greatly to the success of the project. Rabbi Hanokh Ben Arza, may his memory be for a blessing, was the father of the two editors in chief of the Hebrew edition; his spirit and respect for the written word inspired them in their work.

The Editors

Introduction by the Translators

The English translation of the Steinsaltz Tehillim includes a completely new translation of Psalms based on Rabbi Adin Even-Israel Steinsaltz's Hebrew commentary. Translation is necessarily an act of interpretation. We have done our best, at Rabbi Steinsaltz's behest, to stay as close as possible to the original Hebrew verses so that the English reader will encounter the complexities of the text directly. Our goal throughout has been to produce a translation that is true to the original Hebrew text and commentary, yet at the same time is readable and accessible to a broad range of readers, from those who are familiar with Hebrew to those for whom the English translation is the only means by which they will gain access to the text. In the spirit of the Hebrew edition, we have sought to preserve the lofty register of the biblical text while providing a commentary that is relevant and inspiring to our own generation. We hope that the Author of the Torah has aided us in achieving this goal.

We thank Matthew Miller, Avishai Magence, and the devoted and gifted team at Koren Publishers. Special thanks to Gaya Aranoff Bernstein for contributing her insights and knowledge, which greatly enhanced the readability of the text. We are grateful to Rabbi Meni Even-Israel, Executive Director of the Steinsaltz Center, whose wisdom and guidance have made the publication of this Psalms possible.

On behalf of the team of inspired and dedicated translators, editors, and copy editors with whom it has been a great privilege to work, I express my hope that the decisions we have made have produced a translation that is faithful to the Hebrew, readable, accessible, and useful to the reader.

Jason Rappoport
Editor in Chief

תהילים

•

PSALMS

Prayer before the Reading of Psalms

יְהִי רָצוֹן May it be Your will, Lord our God, God of our ancestors, who chooses His servant David and his descendants after him, who chooses song and praise, that You turn, in Your compassion, toward my reading of these Psalms, as if King David, peace be upon him, were reading them himself. And may the merit of the verses of the Psalms, the merit of their words and letters, their vowels and their notes, and of the names found in them, formed of the first letters and last letters of their words, all stand up for us, to bring us atonement for our rebellions and transgressions and sins; to cut down tyrants, to harvest all the thorns and thistles surrounding the heavenly lily, and to join the Bride of His youth with the Beloved, in friendship and in brotherhood and love. And from that place may plenty be drawn down to us, to soul and spirit and higher soul, to purify us of our iniquities and to forgive our sins and atone our transgressions, just as You forgave David, who first spoke these songs before You, as it is said: "The Lord has expunged even your sin; you will not die." And do not *II Sam. 12:13* take us from this world before our time, not before our seventy years are complete; let us live such that we may be able to put right all that we have damaged. And may the merit of King David, peace be upon him, defend us, that You may withhold Your wrath until we return to You in complete repentance. Grace us with gifts undeserved from Your treasury, as it is said, "I will favor whom I will favor, and I will have mercy on whom I will *Ex. 33:19* have mercy." And just as we sing songs in this world, so may we have the merit to sing before You, Lord our God, God of our ancestors, song and praise in the World to Come. And through our speaking these Psalms, may the Rose of Sharon be awakened to sing with a lovely voice, rejoicing, and song, for the glory of Lebanon is given to her. Glory and splendor in *Is. 35:2* the House of our God, speedily in our days. Amen, Selah!

Before reading Psalms it is customary to recite these verses:

Come, let us sing for joy to the Lord, let us make a joyful sound to the rock *Ps. 95:1–3* of our salvation. Let us greet Him with thanksgiving; let us cry out to Him joyfully, with song. For the Lord is a great God, a great King above all gods.

תפילה לפני אמירת תהלים

יְהִי רָצוֹן מִלְּפָנֶיךָ, יהוה אֱלֹהֵינוּ וֵאלֹהֵי אֲבוֹתֵינוּ, הַבּוֹחֵר בְּדָוִד עַבְדּוֹ וּבְזַרְעוֹ
אַחֲרָיו, וְהַבּוֹחֵר בְּשִׁירוֹת וְתִשְׁבָּחוֹת, שֶׁתֵּפֶן בְּרַחֲמִים אֶל קְרִיאַת מִזְמוֹרֵי
תְהִלִּים שֶׁאֶקְרָא כְּאִלּוּ אֲמָרָם דָּוִד הַמֶּלֶךְ עָלָיו הַשָּׁלוֹם בְּעַצְמוֹ, זְכוּתוֹ
תָּגֵן עָלֵינוּ, וְיַעֲמוֹד לָנוּ זְכוּת פְּסוּקֵי תְהִלִּים וּזְכוּת תֵּבוֹתֵיהֶם וְאוֹתִיּוֹתֵיהֶם
וּנְקֻדּוֹתֵיהֶם וְטַעֲמֵיהֶם וְהַשֵּׁמוֹת הַיּוֹצְאִים מֵהֶם מֵרָאשֵׁי תֵבוֹת וּמִסּוֹפֵי
תֵבוֹת לְכַפֵּר פְּשָׁעֵינוּ וַעֲוֹנוֹתֵינוּ וְחַטֹּאתֵינוּ, וּלְזַמֵּר עָרִיצִים וּלְהַכְרִית כָּל
הַחוֹחִים וְהַקּוֹצִים הַסּוֹבְבִים אֶת הַשּׁוֹשַׁנָּה הָעֶלְיוֹנָה וּלְחַבֵּר אֵשֶׁת נְעוּרִים
עִם דּוֹדָהּ בְּאַהֲבָה וְאַחֲוָה וְרֵעוּת, וּמִשָּׁם יִמָּשֵׁךְ לָנוּ שֶׁפַע לְנֶפֶשׁ רוּחַ וּנְשָׁמָה
לְטַהֲרֵנוּ מֵעֲוֹנוֹתֵינוּ וְלִסְלֹחַ חַטֹּאתֵינוּ וּלְכַפֵּר פְּשָׁעֵינוּ, כְּמוֹ שֶׁסָּלַחְתָּ לְדָוִד
שְׁמוּאל ב׳ י״ב:י״ג שֶׁאָמַר מִזְמוֹרִים אֵלּוּ לְפָנֶיךָ, כְּמוֹ שֶׁנֶּאֱמַר, גַּם־יהוה הֶעֱבִיר חַטָּאתְךָ לֹא
תָמוּת: וְאַל תִּקָּחֵנוּ מֵהָעוֹלָם הַזֶּה קֹדֶם זְמַנֵּנוּ עַד מְלֹאת שְׁנוֹתֵינוּ בָּהֶם
שִׁבְעִים שָׁנָה, בְּאוֹפֶן שֶׁנּוּכַל לְתַקֵּן אֶת אֲשֶׁר שִׁחַתְנוּ, וּזְכוּת דָּוִד הַמֶּלֶךְ
עָלָיו הַשָּׁלוֹם תָּגֵן עָלֵינוּ וּבַעֲדֵנוּ, שֶׁתַּאֲרִיךְ אַפְּךָ עַד שׁוּבֵנוּ אֵלֶיךָ בִּתְשׁוּבָה
שְׁמוֹת ל״ג:י״ט שְׁלֵמָה לְפָנֶיךָ, וּמֵאוֹצַר מַתְּנַת חִנָּם חָנֵּנוּ, כְּדִכְתִיב, וְחַנֹּתִי אֶת־אֲשֶׁר אָחֹן
וְרִחַמְתִּי אֶת־אֲשֶׁר אֲרַחֵם: וּכְשֵׁם שֶׁאָנוּ אוֹמְרִים לְפָנֶיךָ שִׁירָה בָּעוֹלָם
הַזֶּה, כָּךְ נִזְכֶּה לוֹמַר לְפָנֶיךָ יהוה אֱלֹהֵינוּ שִׁיר וּשְׁבָחָה לָעוֹלָם הַבָּא. וְעַל
יְדֵי אֲמִירַת תְּהִלִּים, תִּתְעוֹרֵר חֲבַצֶּלֶת הַשָּׁרוֹן וְלָשִׁיר בְּקוֹל נָעִים בְּגִילַת
ישעיה ל״ה:ב וְרַנֵּן, כְּבוֹד הַלְּבָנוֹן נִתַּן־לָהּ: הוֹד וְהָדָר בְּבֵית אֱלֹהֵינוּ בִּמְהֵרָה בְיָמֵינוּ,
אָמֵן סֶלָה.

Before reading Psalms it is customary to recite these verses:

תהלים צ״ה:א־ג

לְכוּ נְרַנְּנָה לַיהוה, נָרִיעָה לְצוּר יִשְׁעֵנוּ:
נְקַדְּמָה פָנָיו בְּתוֹדָה, בִּזְמִרוֹת נָרִיעַ לוֹ:
כִּי אֵל גָּדוֹל יהוה, וּמֶלֶךְ גָּדוֹל עַל־כָּל־אֱלֹהִים:

BOOK ONE
SUNDAY

PSALM 1

A psalm that offers general observations on the joy of an individual who conducts his life in the proper manner, in contrast to the lives of those who are evil and sinful.

אַשְׁרֵי־הָאִישׁ אֲשֶׁר ׀ לֹא
הָלַךְ בַּעֲצַת רְשָׁעִים וּבְדֶרֶךְ
חַטָּאִים לֹא עָמָד וּבְמוֹשַׁב
לֵצִים לֹא יָשָׁב:

1 Happy is the man who has not walked in the counsel of the wicked, has not stood in the path of sinners, and has not sat in the company of scoffers

כִּי אִם בְּתוֹרַת יְהוָֹה חֶפְצוֹ
וּבְתוֹרָתוֹ יֶהְגֶּה יוֹמָם וָלָיְלָה:

2 but whose desire is the Torah of the Lord; he meditates on His Torah day and night.

PSALM 1

1 **Happy is the man who has not walked in the counsel of the wicked, has not stood in the path of sinners.** A person who shuns evil leads a fortunate, happy life. The simplest definition of the word *ashrei*, which is found mainly in Psalms, is "happy," but *ashrei* also connotes the right path, the correct way, that which is true and good. This definition complements the first in that happiness ensues when a person leads his life in the proper manner. Thus, *ashrei* expresses both the subjective, emotional component of good or happiness as well as the objective good of choosing the righteous and honest path. The phrase *atzat resha'im*, "counsel of the wicked," refers to bad advice given by wicked people. The happy man described here has not accepted or followed that advice. Since in other places the word *atzat* can be defined as "company" as well as "counsel," this verse can also be interpreted to mean that a good man does not associate with wicked people, refusing to be considered part of their society. **And has not sat in the company of scoffers.** In modern Hebrew, *letzim*, translated here as "scoffers," are clowns or jokers. But in Psalms, as in Proverbs and other sources, the word has a darker, more pejorative meaning. Scoffers are characterized by their frivolity and lightheartedness toward that which is good. Even if they have no evil intent and do not actually behave in an evil manner, their mode of thinking and speaking opens the door to all manner of forbidden actions. The phrase "has not sat in the company of scoffers" emphasizes that even if someone is not an active participant in such a group, even if he merely sits among them, he is exposing himself to wrongdoing.

2 **But whose desire is the Torah of the Lord.** God's Torah is a guidebook for a way of life, and he, the good and happy person, desires God's Torah. **He meditates on His Torah day and night.**

וְהָיָה כְּעֵץ שָׁתוּל עַל־פַּלְגֵי
מֵיִם אֲשֶׁר פִּרְיוֹ ׀ יִתֵּן בְּעִתּוֹ
וְעָלֵהוּ לֹא־יִבּוֹל וְכֹל אֲשֶׁר־
יַעֲשֶׂה יַצְלִיחַ:

לֹא־כֵן הָרְשָׁעִים כִּי אִם־כַּמֹּץ
אֲשֶׁר־תִּדְּפֶנּוּ רוּחַ:

עַל־כֵּן ׀ לֹא־יָקֻמוּ רְשָׁעִים
בַּמִּשְׁפָּט וְחַטָּאִים בַּעֲדַת
צַדִּיקִים:

3 He is like a tree planted by
streams of water, which brings
forth its fruit in season and
whose leaf does not wither;
whatever he does will prosper.

4 Not so the wicked, who are
like chaff that wind blows away.

5 Therefore the wicked will not
stand up in judgment, nor
evildoers among the righteous.

The pronoun "His" can be said to be referring to the person studying the Torah rather than to God. This phrase, then, emphasizes each specific individual's understanding of Torah, what he knows of it in his mind and heart. The term *yehgeh*, translated here as "meditates," can also mean "utters." In a way, this psalm provides a definition of a righteous person. Such a person's innermost desire is for Torah, not only in the intellectual sense, but intuitively and spiritually as well. His thoughts and speech consist of Torah even when he has no particular task, be it religious or mundane, to undertake at the time. In choosing to spend all his time thinking and speaking of God's Torah, he distances himself from evil and clings to good, and for this he is rewarded as described in the following verse.

3 **He is like a tree planted by streams of water.** The tree described here lacks nothing. Even without rain, it has sufficient water. It is a tree **which brings forth its fruit in season and whose leaf does not wither.** Trees that lack water often bear their fruit late, and their leaves shrivel and fall, but this tree is eternally fresh and thriving. This image is not merely one of blessing but also a concrete promise of ongoing fruitfulness in all its manifestations. The fruit of the righteous person's Torah, as well as that of his everyday labors, will ripen at the right time, bringing benefit both to himself and to others. He will not suffer from premature decline or withering, and **whatever he does will prosper.**

4 By contrast, **not so the wicked, who** are not at all like well-rooted trees but instead **are like chaff that wind blows away.** Chaff is incapable of growth and, lacking a secure place of its own, is scattered by the wind in all directions. The wicked have a similar fate. They have no real place, no plan, but simply conform to shifting influences.

5 **Therefore the wicked will not stand up in judgment.** When the time of judgment comes, the wicked will have no standing, **nor evildoers among the righteous.** Not only will evildoers not be acquitted, but they will not even be able to join the company of the righteous.

כִּי־יוֹדֵעַ יְהוָה דֶּרֶךְ צַדִּיקִים
וְדֶרֶךְ רְשָׁעִים תֹּאבֵד:

6 For the Lord knows the way of the righteous, but the way of the wicked will perish.

PSALM 2

A psalm without a heading in honor of a king who is mentioned several times. From its content and visionary language, it appears that the psalm is not describing a specific king but rather a prophetic vision of the future redeemer, the Messiah.

לָמָּה רָגְשׁוּ גוֹיִם וּלְאֻמִּים
יֶהְגּוּ־רִיק:

1 Why do nations rage and peoples meditate in vain?

יִתְיַצְּבוּ ׀ מַלְכֵי־אֶרֶץ וְרוֹזְנִים
נוֹסְדוּ־יָחַד עַל־יְהוָה וְעַל־
מְשִׁיחוֹ:

2 The kings of the earth have assembled, and rulers are gathered together against the Lord and against His anointed one:

נְנַתְּקָה אֶת־מוֹסְרוֹתֵימוֹ
וְנַשְׁלִיכָה מִמֶּנּוּ עֲבֹתֵימוֹ:

3 Let us snap off their chains and throw off their bonds.

---

6 **For the Lord knows the way of the righteous.** Here, as elsewhere, *yode'a*, translated here as "knows," specifically implies connectedness and love. God loves the righteous, and He therefore guides and assists them on their journey through life. **But** by contrast, **the way of the wicked will perish.** The way of the wicked results not only in the loss of eternal existence but also in an inability to withstand the vicissitudes of life. Their path inevitably ends in ruin.

PSALM 2

1 **Why do nations rage** and stir up a great commotion, **and peoples meditate in vain?** Why do they deliberate and make declarations that, in the end, are no more than empty threats?

2 **The kings of the earth have assembled, and rulers are gathered together against the Lord and against His anointed one.** Those in power consult with one another, gathering together in order to plot against God and His anointed one, as described in the following verse:

3 **Let us snap off their chains,** a metaphor for the rule and control that Israel exerts over them,

יוֹשֵׁב בַּשָּׁמַיִם יִשְׂחָק אֲדֹנָי
יִלְעַג־לָמוֹ:

אָז יְדַבֵּר אֵלֵימוֹ בְאַפּוֹ
וּבַחֲרוֹנוֹ יְבַהֲלֵמוֹ:

וַאֲנִי נָסַכְתִּי מַלְכִּי עַל־צִיּוֹן
הַר־קָדְשִׁי:

אֲסַפְּרָה אֶל חֹק יְהוָה אָמַר
אֵלַי בְּנִי־אַתָּה אֲנִי הַיּוֹם
יְלִדְתִּיךָ:

שְׁאַל מִמֶּנִּי וְאֶתְּנָה גוֹיִם
נַחֲלָתֶךָ וַאֲחֻזָּתְךָ אַפְסֵי־
אָרֶץ:

4 He whose seat is in heaven will laugh; the Lord will ridicule them.

5 Then He will talk to them in His anger; in His wrath He will frighten them:

6 Yet I have anointed My king on Zion, My holy mountain.

7 I will tell of the decree. The Lord said to me: You are My son; today I begat you.

8 Make your request of Me, and I will make nations your inheritance; the ends of earth will be your portion.

---

and throw off their bonds. The main objective of their rebellion against the king is to be free of God, as the king represents the nation's connection to God.

4 **He whose seat is in heaven will laugh; the Lord will ridicule them.** All those rulers' plans will come to naught, for they are void of any true substance. What actually will come to pass is punishment from on high.

5 **Then He will talk to them in His anger; in His wrath He will frighten them:**

6 **Yet I have anointed My king on Zion, My holy mountain.** The continuation of the psalm is spoken by the king himself:

7 **I will tell of the decree.** I will set forth the basic premise of all my actions. **The Lord said to me: You are My son; today I begat you.** The king can be likened to God's beloved son. When he ascends to the throne, it is as if he is being reborn.

8 God has told me: **Make your request of Me,** God has told me, **and I will make nations your inheritance; the ends of earth will be your portion.** You will reign over many nations; your sovereignty will extend to the ends of the earth.

ט תְּרֹעֵם בְּשֵׁבֶט בַּרְזֶל כִּכְלִי
יוֹצֵר תְּנַפְּצֵם:

י וְעַתָּה מְלָכִים הַשְׂכִּילוּ
הִוָּסְרוּ שֹׁפְטֵי אָרֶץ:

יא עִבְדוּ אֶת־יהוה בְּיִרְאָה וְגִילוּ
בִּרְעָדָה:

יב נַשְּׁקוּ־בַר פֶּן־יֶאֱנַף ׀ וְתֹאבְדוּ
דֶרֶךְ כִּי־יִבְעַר כִּמְעַט אַפּוֹ
אַשְׁרֵי כָּל־חוֹסֵי בוֹ:

9 You will smash them with an iron rod, shatter them like a potter's vessel.

10 So now, kings, be wise; accept admonishment, judges of the earth.

11 Serve the Lord with reverence, and rejoice with trembling.

12 Kiss the son, lest He be angry and you lose your way, even if His anger burns only slightly. Happy are all who rely on Him.

---

9 **You will smash them with an iron rod, shatter them like a potter's vessel.** You will destroy all your enemies as easily as one shatters a clay vessel.

10 **So now, kings, be wise; accept admonishment, judges of the earth.** Understand that God has placed the privilege of sovereignty in my hands, and that is why you are powerless against me. For this reason, one should follow the piece of advice given in the next verse:

11 **Serve the Lord with reverence,** aware of the consequences that await you if you do not serve Him, **and rejoice with trembling.** Although you will be able to rejoice under the rule of the king, this joy must be tempered with a trembling awe as a hidden threat will always be present: If you do not serve God, you will be punished in various and sundry ways.

12 **Kiss the son.** Most commentators define *bar* here as "son," which is the meaning of this word in Aramaic, referring to the king to whom God referred when He said: "You are My son" (verse 7). The kiss is an expression of homage and affection. **Lest He be angry and you lose your way, even if His anger burns only slightly.** You cannot withstand God's fury; you cannot weather even His slightest anger. By contrast, **happy are all who rely on Him.** Those who put their faith in God will find the world both beautiful and full of goodness.

PSALM 3

A psalm referring to an episode in which David is surrounded by enemies and considered by everyone to be in a hopeless situation. Notwithstanding, he trusts in God to deliver him from his enemies and lead him to victory and peace.

מִזְמוֹר לְדָוִד בְּבָרְחוֹ מִפְּנֵי ׀
אַבְשָׁלוֹם בְּנוֹ:

1 A psalm by David when he fled from Avshalom his son.

יְהוָה מָה־רַבּוּ צָרָי רַבִּים
קָמִים עָלָי:

2 Lord, how numerous are my tormentors; many rise up against me.

רַבִּים אֹמְרִים לְנַפְשִׁי אֵין
יְשׁוּעָתָה לּוֹ בֵאלֹהִים סֶלָה:

3 Many say of me: There is no salvation for him in God, Selah.

וְאַתָּה יְהוָה מָגֵן בַּעֲדִי כְּבוֹדִי
וּמֵרִים רֹאשִׁי:

4 But You, Lord, protect me. You are my glory; You lift my head.

PSALM 3

1 **A psalm by David when he fled from Avshalom his son.** Although this heading makes reference to a specific episode, the psalm speaks generally of a situation of great distress. It is an entreaty to God, coupled with an expression of faith that He will rescue the psalmist from his dire straits.

2 **Lord, how numerous are my tormentors; many rise up against me.** Not only are they enemies, but they are rebels from within my own ranks.

3 In addition to these enemies and rebels, principally Avshalom's army, there are **many** others who **say of me: There is no salvation for him in God.** Although they were not actively involved in the insurgency, there were those who nonetheless believed that David's reign had ended and his predicament was hopeless. **Selah.** The meaning of the word "Selah," which is found almost exclusively in Psalms, is not entirely clear. According to ancient tradition, the word means "forever, eternally." Though this definition is often acceptable, it sometimes seems forced. There are those who interpret it to be a confirmation of the preceding phrase, akin to "indeed" or "it is so." Others believe the term is a musical notation signifying a type of crescendo, as if to indicate that the volume should be increased. Finally, some commentators are convinced that it is an instruction to prolong the recitation of the preceding word in order to maintain the cadence of the psalm.

4 **But You, Lord, protect me. You are my glory,** or, alternatively, You are the source of my glory, and **You lift my head.** You keep me from being completely cast off and humiliated.

ה קוֹלִי אֶל־יהוה אֶקְרָא וַיַּעֲנֵנִי
מֵהַר קָדְשׁוֹ סֶלָה:

ו אֲנִי שָׁכַבְתִּי וָאִישָׁנָה
הֱקִיצׁוֹתִי כִּי יהוה יִסְמְכֵנִי:

ז לֹא־אִירָא מֵרִבְבׁוֹת עָם
אֲשֶׁר סָבִיב שָׁתוּ עָלָי:

ח קוּמָה יהוה ׀ הוֹשִׁיעֵנִי אֱלֹהַי
כִּי־הִכִּיתָ אֶת־כָּל־אֹיְבַי לֶחִי
שִׁנֵּי רְשָׁעִים שִׁבַּרְתָּ:

ט לַיהוה הַיְשׁוּעָה עַל־עַמְּךָ
בִרְכָתֶךָ סֶּלָה:

5 I cried aloud to the Lord and He answered me from His holy mount, Selah.

6 I lay down and slept; I awoke because the Lord sustains me.

7 I shall have no fear of the myriads that surround me and oppose me.

8 Arise, Lord; save me, my God. For You have smitten my enemies on the cheek; You have broken the teeth of the wicked.

9 Salvation belongs to the Lord. Your blessing is on Your people, Selah.

---

5 **I cried aloud to the Lord and He answered me from His holy mount, Selah.** It is as if I can hear the voice of God speaking to me from the holy mount in Jerusalem.

6 **I lay down and slept,** often dejected and with no expectation that I would live to see the following day. But **I awoke,** I did not succumb to eternal sleep, **because the Lord sustains me** and has given me the strength to carry on.

7 And because God sustains me, **I shall have no fear of the myriads that surround me and oppose me.** I am not afraid of tens of thousands of people, all of whom are poised to attack me.

8 **Arise, Lord.** This is a call for God to reveal Himself in a recognizable way. **Save me, my God. For You have smitten my enemies on the cheek.** You have slapped the faces of all the enemies who surround me. This notion of a painful blow to the enemy's cheek resonates with the succeeding imagery: **You have broken the teeth of the wicked.**

9 In summation, David declares: **Salvation belongs to the Lord.** Even if salvation from God does not appear to be imminent, eventually it becomes apparent that **Your blessing is on Your people, Selah.**

PSALM 4

A psalm of entreaty on the part of one who is being vilified and pursued for no good reason.
The psalmist calls upon God, as He both saves the blameless and foils the schemes of the wicked.

לַמְנַצֵּחַ בִּנְגִינוֹת מִזְמוֹר
לְדָוִד:

בְּקָרְאִי עֲנֵנִי ׀ אֱלֹהֵי צִדְקִי
בַּצָּר הִרְחַבְתָּ לִּי חָנֵּנִי וּשְׁמַע
תְּפִלָּתִי:

¹ For the chief musician, on stringed instruments, a psalm by David.

² When I call, answer me, God of my righteousness. In my distress, You have relieved me; be gracious to me and hear my prayer.

PSALM 4

¹ **For the chief musician, on stringed instruments.** This heading indicates that the psalm is addressed to the person who conducts its musical recital, known as the *menatze'aḥ* or "chief musician." This is one of a number of instructive openings to individual psalms. Some mention the type of musical instruments to be used, whereas others refer to a specific ancient melody. In this psalm, *binginot*, translated here as "on stringed instruments," literally, "in melodies," is interpreted by some commentators to mean that the psalm consists of two melodies. Alternatively, several instruments may have been needed to perform this song. Even the word *mizmor*, translated here as "psalm," apparently serves to identify a particular type of melody. **A psalm by David.** Like the preceding psalm, this is essentially a prayer, though it does not speak of a specific struggle or imminent danger, but rather conveys a more generalized state of distress. It also includes expressions of encouragement for others.

² **When I call, answer me, God of my righteousness. In my distress,** I feel as though I am confined. The word *batzar*, translated here as "distress," literally means "in a narrow place." This implies a feeling of paralysis, that my very existence, whether physical or spiritual, is so pressed that I am unable to even move. **You have relieved me.** The word *hirḥavta*, "you have relieved," literally "you have widened," describes the feeling of relief that comes when redemption follows profound distress; it is as if all the sources of pressure have receded into the background and one can once again breathe and move freely. Now, God, **be gracious to me and hear my prayer.**

בְּנֵי־אִישׁ עַד־מֶה כְבוֹדִי
לִכְלִמָּה תֶּאֱהָבוּן רִיק
תְּבַקְשׁוּ כָזָב סֶלָה:

וּדְעוּ כִּי־הִפְלָה יהוה חָסִיד
לוֹ יהוה יִשְׁמַע בְּקָרְאִי אֵלָיו:

רִגְזוּ וְאַל־תֶּחֱטָאוּ אִמְרוּ
בִלְבַבְכֶם עַל־מִשְׁכַּבְכֶם
וְדֹמּוּ סֶלָה:

3 Sons of man, how long will you put my honor to shame, love emptiness, seek deception? Selah.

4 Know that the Lord has set apart the devoted for Himself; the Lord hears when I call to Him.

5 Tremble and do not sin; say in your heart, upon your bed, and be still, Selah.

---

3 **Sons of man.** The psalmist now turns to *benei ish*, "sons of man," namely, the leaders among his adversaries. Throughout the Bible, the word *ish* usually indicates a person of seniority and status. **How long will you put my honor to shame?** How long, or to what extent, will you continue to denigrate and embarrass me? How long will you **love emptiness?** David's humiliation and the enemies' fight against him are not a consequence of his own deficiencies or mistakes. It is an unfounded war brought about by people who are propagating empty distortions and disseminating lies. How long will you **seek deception?** They go out of their way to seek out lies and deceptions concerning me. **Selah.**

4 Rather than pursuing me for baseless deceptive reasons, **know,** be aware, **that the Lord has set apart the devoted for Himself; the Lord hears when I call to Him.** God has a special relationship with those who are faithful to Him. David's devotion to God and desire to be close to Him were acknowledged by all, even during his lifetime. He repeatedly refers to the special way in which God "sets apart" those who seek Him.

5 **Tremble and do not sin.** In this psalm, the word *rigzu*, defined here as "tremble," connotes agitation, though elsewhere the word refers to anger. The psalmist bids his antagonists to shake off their evil ways. **Say in your heart, upon your bed.** He calls on people to bestir themselves, to change their mind-set, and to transform their outlook on life so that they will not be drawn toward habitual sin. It is as if the psalmist is saying: Consider these matters in private, at a time before bed rather than in the company of other people. While public discussion can lead to distorted thought and convoluted expression, private contemplation facilitates a clearer understanding of the truth. **And be still, Selah.** The psalmist further enjoins individuals to be still, to remain silent. One should not give opinions or be drawn into discussion about matters unrelated to himself or outside the realm of his understanding. In the specific case at hand, rather than focusing on David and his deficiencies, people would be better off examining their own behavior and turning toward God.

זִבְחוּ זִבְחֵי־צֶדֶק וּבִטְחוּ אֶל־ יְהוָה:

6 Offer sacrifices of righteousness, and trust in the Lord.

רַבִּים אֹמְרִים מִי־יַרְאֵנוּ טוֹב נְסָה־עָלֵינוּ אוֹר פָּנֶיךָ יְהוָה:

7 Many are saying: Who will show us any good? Bring forth the light of Your countenance upon us, Lord.

נָתַתָּה שִׂמְחָה בְלִבִּי מֵעֵת דְּגָנָם וְתִירוֹשָׁם רָבּוּ:

8 You put gladness in my heart, more than when their grain and new wine abounded.

בְּשָׁלוֹם יַחְדָּו אֶשְׁכְּבָה וְאִישָׁן כִּי־אַתָּה יְהוָה לְבָדָד לָבֶטַח תּוֹשִׁיבֵנִי:

9 I lie down and sleep, at peace together, for You alone, Lord, allow me to dwell in safety.

---

6 **Offer sacrifices of righteousness, and trust in the Lord.**

7 **Many are saying** in their prayers: **Who will show us any good?** They seek out a source of blessing and goodness. **Bring forth the light of Your countenance upon us, Lord.** They ask God to bring forth His light and shine His countenance upon them. Alternatively, the word *nesa*, can mean "reveal Yourself." The psalmist goes on to say: I myself do not sit and contemplate the wrongs of others. I truly attempt to cleave to God.

8 **You put gladness in my heart, more than when their grain and new wine abounded.** You, God, have brought joy to my heart, a joy greater than that felt by others in possession of abundant grain and wine. I am not jealous of them. My inner joy suffices; it even increases in the face of the great success of others.

9 **I lie down and sleep, at peace together.** The apparent meaning of this expression is that when everything all together is peaceful I will be able to sleep undisturbed. **For You alone, Lord,** even if You are alone in seeking peace for me while all others are against me, this is sufficient for me, for You will **allow me to dwell in safety.**

PSALM 5

A psalm of prayer directed against those wicked individuals who are unworthy of God's kindness.
The psalmist prays for his own righteousness to become apparent, and for him
and those who are found worthy to be granted salvation.

לַמְנַצֵּחַ אֶל־הַנְּחִילוֹת מִזְמוֹר ¹
לְדָוִד:

¹ For the chief musician, for
neḥilot accompaniment, a
psalm by David.

אֲמָרַי הַאֲזִינָה ׀ יהוה בִּינָה ²
הֲגִיגִי:

² Give ear to my words, Lord;
consider my meditation.

הַקְשִׁיבָה ׀ לְקוֹל שַׁוְעִי מַלְכִּי ³
וֵאלֹהָי כִּי־אֵלֶיךָ אֶתְפַּלָּל:

³ Listen to the voice of my cry,
my King and my God, for to
You I pray.

יהוה בֹּקֶר תִּשְׁמַע קוֹלִי בֹּקֶר ⁴
אֶעֱרָךְ־לְךָ וַאֲצַפֶּה:

⁴ In the morning, Lord, You
hear my voice; in the morning
I direct my prayer to You and
await Your response.

PSALM 5

¹ **For the chief musician, for *neḥilot* accompaniment, a psalm by David.** We do not
know exactly what the meaning of *neḥilot* is, but it is reasonable to assume that it was a musical
instrument used to accompany this psalm. Some commentators say that it made a buzzing sound
like that of a swarm [*neḥil*] of bees. Others believe it refers to an ancient melody known as *El
HaNeḥilot* to which the words of this psalm were sung. Like the preceding psalms, this takes the
form of a prayer, though it does not specify the psalmist's troubles. Instead, the psalmist contends
with the various ways in which people go astray, reiterating for himself, as well as for others, the
importance of desiring to be close to God and choosing the right path.

² **Give ear to my words, Lord; consider my meditation.** Please listen, God, to prayers of the
heart as well as to those uttered by one's lips.

³ **Listen to the voice of my cry, my King and my God, for to You I pray.** The emphasis here
is on "to You": I pray only to You, not to others.

⁴ **In the morning,** each morning, day after day, **Lord, You hear my voice. In the morning,**
each morning, **I direct my prayer to You and await Your response.** These are the words of
someone who is wholeheartedly set on choosing the right path to follow, someone who knows
that the choice of any other path would defy the will of God.

כִּי ו לֹא אֵל־חָפֵץ רֶשַׁע ו
אָתָּה לֹא יְגֻרְךָ רָע:

לֹא־יִתְיַצְּבוּ הוֹלְלִים לְנֶגֶד
עֵינֶיךָ שָׂנֵאתָ כָּל־פֹּעֲלֵי אָוֶן:

תְּאַבֵּד דֹּבְרֵי כָזָב אִישׁ־דָּמִים
וּמִרְמָה יְתָעֵב ו יְהוָה:

וַאֲנִי בְּרֹב חַסְדְּךָ אָבוֹא
בֵיתֶךָ אֶשְׁתַּחֲוֶה אֶל־הֵיכַל־
קָדְשְׁךָ בְּיִרְאָתֶךָ:

יְהוָה ו נְחֵנִי בְצִדְקָתֶךָ לְמַעַן
שׁוֹרְרָי הוֹשַׁר לְפָנַי דַּרְכֶּךָ:

הַיְשַׁר

5 For You are not a God who takes pleasure in wickedness; no evil dwells with You.

6 The foolish will not stand before Your eyes; You hate all evildoers.

7 You destroy those who speak falsehood; the Lord abhors a man of bloodshed and deceit.

8 But as for me, through Your abundant kindness, I will enter Your House; I will bow to Your Holy Temple in reverence to You.

9 Lead me, Lord, in Your righteousness, against my foes. Straighten Your path before me.

---

5 **For You are not a God who takes pleasure in wickedness.** God's will is opposed to evil. **No evil dwells with You.**

6 **The foolish,** those who act impulsively, lack direction, and go astray, **will not stand before Your eyes.** You do not want them near You, for **You hate all evildoers.**

7 **You destroy those who speak falsehood; the Lord abhors a man of bloodshed and deceit.**

8 **But as for me, through Your abundant kindness, I will enter Your House.** The psalmist knows full well that he is not perfect. What matters is that he is trying to choose the right path. The fact that he is allowed to enter God's House is an expression of God's kindness toward him. **I will bow to Your Holy Temple in reverence to You.**

9 **Lead me, Lord, in Your righteousness.** Place me on the right path, guide me in Your righteous ways, so that I will be able to choose the appropriate way to stand **against my foes.** When surrounded by enemies, a person does not always have the ability to know how to act. It is precisely then that he needs guidance in how to remain on the proper path. **Straighten Your path before me** so that I will be able to walk easily on the path of righteousness.

כִּי אֵין בְּפִּיהוּ נְכוֹנָה֮ קִרְבָּ֫ם
הַוּוֹת קֶבֶר־פָּת֥וּחַ גְּרֹנָ֑ם
לְשׁוֹנָ֗ם יַחֲלִיקֽוּן׃

יא הַאֲשִׁימֵ֨ם ׀ אֱלֹהִ֗ים יִפְּלוּ֮
מִֽמֹּעֲצֽוֹתֵיהֶם֒ בְּרֹ֣ב פִּ֭שְׁעֵיהֶם
הַדִּיחֵ֑מוֹ כִּי־מָ֥רוּ בָֽךְ׃

יב וְיִשְׂמְח֨וּ כָל־ח֪וֹסֵי בָ֡ךְ לְעוֹלָ֣ם
יְ֭רַנֵּנוּ וְתָסֵ֣ךְ עָלֵ֑ימוֹ וְֽיַעְלְצ֥וּ
בְ֝ךָ֗ אֹהֲבֵ֥י שְׁמֶֽךָ׃

¹⁰ There is no truth in what
they say. Their inner being is
misfortune; their throat is an
open grave; they deceive with
their tongue.

¹¹ Condemn them, God; let
them fall by their own devices.
Cast them out for their many
transgressions, for they have
rebelled against You.

¹² But let all who put their trust
in You rejoice; let them sing for
joy forever, and You will shelter
them. Those who love Your
name will exult in You.

---

¹⁰ **There is no truth in what they say.** In contrast with the divine path mentioned in the previous
verse, that of the enemies is marked by deceit. **Their inner being is misfortune.** All that
is found within them is *havot*, disaster and trouble, which they plot for others. **Their throat
is an open grave.** In a certain sense, their mouths are like open tombs. For one thing, they
exude an inner decay; moreover, they entice and seduce others to fall within. **They deceive with
their tongue.** More often than not, they make use of deceptive accusations rather than honest
argumentation.

¹¹ **Condemn them, God.** Judge them as they deserve to be judged; find them guilty. **Let them
fall by their own devices.** Alternatively, let them fall away from their schemes and conspiracies.
Cast them out for their many transgressions, for they have rebelled against You, and
as such they are deserving of punishment. *Pesha*, translated here as "transgression," indicates a sin
committed deliberately.

¹² The psalmist concludes on a more positive note: **But let all who put their trust in You rejoice;
let them sing for joy forever, and You will shelter them. Those who love Your name
will exult in You.**

כִּי־אַתָּה תְּבָרֵךְ צַדִּיק יהוה ׳ ¹³ For it is You who blesses
בַּצִּנָּה רָצוֹן תַּעְטְרֶנּוּ: the righteous man, Lord,
surrounding him with favor,
like a shield.

PSALM 6

A psalm of entreaty by a man who is both ill and persecuted by his enemies, crying out to God
in his suffering and asking that God have mercy on him and heed his supplications.

לַמְנַצֵּחַ בִּנְגִינוֹת עַל־ א ¹ For the chief musician on
הַשְּׁמִינִית מִזְמוֹר לְדָוִד: stringed instruments, on the
eight-stringed harp, a psalm
יהוה אַל־בְּאַפְּךָ תוֹכִיחֵנִי ׳ by David.
וְאַל־בַּחֲמָתְךָ תְיַסְּרֵנִי: ² Lord, rebuke me not in Your
anger nor chasten me in Your
displeasure.

---

¹³ **For it is You who blesses the righteous man, Lord, surrounding him with favor, like a shield.** *Tzinna* evokes an image of a large shield that covers the entire body like a suit of armor. This is how God loves and is close to the righteous. The word *ratzon*, "favor," has two interconnected meanings; one is desire, a yearning and longing for something, and the other is the satisfaction that ensues with its fulfillment. The righteous are engulfed in God's love and in His willingness to hear and gratify their desires.

PSALM 6

¹ **For the chief musician on stringed instruments, on the eight-stringed harp, a psalm by David.** Most commentators believe that *sheminit* refers to a type of eight-stringed musical instrument, translated here as an eight-stringed harp. Others claim that the phrase *al hasheminit*, literally, "on the eighth," is an instruction for this particular psalm to be sung to the last of the eight melodies typically played on the instrument.

² **Lord, rebuke me not in Your anger nor chasten me in Your displeasure.** The word *tokhiheni* refers to both rebuke and physical punishment. The psalmist entreats God: Do not rebuke me by means of physical punishment; pain can sometimes be unbearable.

חָנֵּנִי יהוה כִּי אֻמְלַל אָנִי
רְפָאֵנִי יהוה כִּי נִבְהֲלוּ
עֲצָמָי:

³ Be gracious to me, Lord, for I
am miserable; heal me, Lord,
for my bones are frightened.

וְנַפְשִׁי נִבְהֲלָה מְאֹד וְאַתְּ
יהוה עַד־מָתָי:

⁴ For I am in great terror. And
You, Lord, how long?

שׁוּבָה יהוה חַלְּצָה נַפְשִׁי
הוֹשִׁיעֵנִי לְמַעַן חַסְדֶּךָ:

⁵ Return, Lord. Rescue my soul;
save me for the sake of Your
kindness.

כִּי אֵין בַּמָּוֶת זִכְרֶךָ בִּשְׁאוֹל
מִי יוֹדֶה־לָּךְ:

⁶ For in death, there is no
memory of You; in the grave,
who can give You thanks?

יָגַעְתִּי ׀ בְּאַנְחָתִי אַשְׂחֶה
בְכָל־לַיְלָה מִטָּתִי בְּדִמְעָתִי
עַרְשִׂי אַמְסֶה:

⁷ I am depleted by my groaning.
Every night I cause my bed to
swim; I melt my couch with
my tears.

---

³ **Be gracious to me, Lord, for I am miserable; heal me, Lord, for my bones are frightened.** The psalmist bases his request not on his own good deeds but rather on his inability to bear the intensity of the pain. The phrase "my bones are frightened" is almost certainly a poetic expression depicting fear and pain that have penetrated to the core.

⁴ **For I am in great terror.** More than just a matter of pain, the psalmist also fears that he will never recover from his illness, that he will die. He asks of God: **And You, Lord, how long** will You leave me in this dire and hopeless situation? When will I be healed?

⁵ **Return, Lord.** Pain and suffering can be understood as signs that one has been abandoned by God. This is why the psalmist beseeches God to return to him. **Rescue my soul.** Rescue me from this state of oppression. **Save me for the sake of Your kindness.** The rationale behind this request, "for the sake of Your kindness," appears frequently in the book of Psalms.

⁶ **For in death, there is no memory of You; in the grave, who can give You thanks?** The psalmist argues that it is not in God's interest to kill him, as he is capable of acknowledging and thanking God only while he is alive.

⁷ **I am depleted by my groaning.** Excessive groaning from pain can further sap the strength of a sick person. Alternatively, his pain is so great that it is difficult even to groan. **Every night I cause my bed to swim.** Because of all his weeping at night, his bed has practically become a pool of water. **I melt my couch with my tears.** I weep so profusely that my tears seem to dissolve my bed.

עָשְׁשָׁה מִכַּעַס עֵינִי עָתְקָה
בְּכָל־צוֹרְרָי:

8 My eye is weakened by anger,
pulled out because of all
my foes.

סוּרוּ מִמֶּנִּי כָּל־פֹּעֲלֵי אָוֶן כִּי־
שָׁמַע יהוה קוֹל בִּכְיִי:

9 Leave me, all you evildoers, for
the Lord has heard the voice of
my weeping.

שָׁמַע יהוה תְּחִנָּתִי יהוה
תְּפִלָּתִי יִקָּח:

10 The Lord has heard my plea;
the Lord will accept my prayer.

יֵבֹשׁוּ ׀ וְיִבָּהֲלוּ מְאֹד כָּל־אֹיְבָי
יָשֻׁבוּ יֵבֹשׁוּ רָגַע:

11 My enemies will be greatly
ashamed and frightened; they
will retreat, immediately be put
to shame.

---

8 In addition, the psalmist's illness is not just his own private matter; it also arouses and encourages his enemies. He suffers not only from the pain of the illness but also from the awareness that his enemies are rejoicing in his misery, hoping daily for his demise. **My eye is weakened by anger, pulled out because of all my foes.** When I think of my adversaries celebrating my misfortune, I feel as if my eyes are falling out of their sockets. My vision has been weakened and clouded by grief. The foes in this psalm are not necessarily mortal flesh and blood; such imagery is rather an expression of the emotional state of a person who is desperately ill. He may feel that many different forces of evil are gathering against him, rejoicing in his misfortune. But when he recovers, all these dark feelings disappear. The concluding verses indicate the psalmist's abrupt shift in mood:

9 **Leave me, all you evildoers, for the Lord has heard the voice of my weeping** and has healed me.

10 **The Lord has heard my plea; the Lord will accept my prayer.** Once He accepts my prayer, I am able to recover.

11 **My enemies will be greatly ashamed and frightened; they will retreat, immediately be put to shame.** And once I recover, my enemies will disappear; they will even feel ashamed that they had been lying in wait for me.

PSALM 7

A psalm that offers the prayer of an individual beset by enemies and falsely accused of wrongdoing,
who asks God to acknowledge his righteousness and requite his foes.

שִׁגָּיוֹן לְדָוִד אֲשֶׁר־שָׁר לַיהוָה
עַל־דִּבְרֵי־כוּשׁ בֶּן־יְמִינִי:

1 A meditation by David, a
song that he sang to the Lord
concerning the words of Kush
the Benjamite.

יהוה אֱלֹהַי בְּךָ חָסִיתִי
הוֹשִׁיעֵנִי מִכָּל־רֹדְפַי
וְהַצִּילֵנִי:

2 Lord, I put my faith in You.
Deliver me from all my
pursuers and rescue me,

פֶּן־יִטְרֹף כְּאַרְיֵה נַפְשִׁי פֹּרֵק
וְאֵין מַצִּיל:

3 lest he tear me like a lion,
rending me in pieces, while
there is no one to be my savior.

יהוה אֱלֹהַי אִם־עָשִׂיתִי זֹאת
אִם־יֶשׁ־עָוֶל בְּכַפָּי:

4 Lord, my God, if I have done
this, if my hands have done any
wrong,

PSALM 7

1 **A meditation by David.** The simplest definition of the word *shiggayon*, translated here as
"meditation," is a specific song or melody,[1] but some commentators note that since it is linguistically
similar to *shegia* or *shegaga*, both meaning "error," it must mean that this is a psalm of remorse
for mistakes that have been made. In any case, since the word stems from the verb root "to
contemplate," it pertains to the realm of thought. **A song that he sang to the Lord concerning
the words of Kush the Benjamite.** We do not know who Kush the Benjamite was. Some of
the Sages suggest that it was another name for King Saul, who was from the tribe of Benjamin.
A simpler explanation is that Kush was an ordinary Benjamite who spoke ill of David, possibly
accusing him of being responsible for a military setback or of not fighting valiantly enough as a
soldier in Saul's army.

2 **Lord, I put my faith in You. Deliver me from all my pursuers and rescue me,**

3 **lest he,** my enemy, **tear me like a lion, rending me in pieces, while there is no one
to be my savior.** The psalmist now apparently addresses the complaint that had been directed
against him:

4 **Lord, my God, if I have done this,** if I have committed the misdeeds of which my enemies
accuse me, **if my hands have done any wrong,**

אִם־גָּמַלְתִּי שׁוֹלְמִי רָע
וָאֲחַלְּצָה צוֹרְרִי רֵיקָם:

יִרַדֹּף אוֹיֵב ׀ נַפְשִׁי וְיַשֵּׂג
וְיִרְמֹס לָאָרֶץ חַיָּי וּכְבוֹדִי ׀
לֶעָפָר יַשְׁכֵּן סֶלָה:

קוּמָה יהוה ׀ בְּאַפֶּךָ הִנָּשֵׂא
בְּעַבְרוֹת צוֹרְרָי וְעוּרָה אֵלַי
מִשְׁפָּט צִוִּיתָ:

וַעֲדַת לְאֻמִּים תְּסוֹבְבֶךָּ
וְעָלֶיהָ לַמָּרוֹם שׁוּבָה:

5 if I have repaid my friend with evil, or despoiled my enemy without cause,

6 then let the enemy pursue me and overtake me; let my life be trampled on the ground and my soul to the dust, Selah.

7 Arise, Lord, in Your anger; lift Yourself up against the wrath of my enemies. Awaken for me the judgment You commanded.

8 A congregation of nations will surround You, and with it return on high.

---

5 **if I have repaid my friend with evil,** referring to someone who had once paid him a kind act, as *sholmi*, "my friend," is linguistically similar to *shalem*, "to pay," **or despoiled my enemy without cause,**

6 **then let the enemy pursue me and overtake me; let my life be trampled on the ground and my soul to the dust, Selah.** The word *kavod*, which usually means "honor," can also connote "being" or "soul." Hence the translation here and elsewhere of *kevodi* as "my life," "my being," or "my soul." Despite having said this, about being overtaken by the enemy and trampled to the ground, the psalmist goes on to say:

7 **Arise, Lord, in Your anger.** It is fitting for You as well to be angered by the evil being done to me. **Lift Yourself up** and display Your power **against the wrath of my enemies. Awaken for me the judgment You commanded** concerning me.

8 **A congregation of nations will surround You, and with it return on high.** This is an image of God surrounded by an honor guard or entourage of the nations, all of whom have come to thank Him and escort Him to heaven, His holy abode on high.

ט יְהוָֹה יָדֵין עַמֵּים שָׁפְטֵנִי
יְהוָֹה כְּצִדְקֵי וּכְתֻמֵּי עָלֵי:

The Lord will be the Judge of
the peoples; judge me, Lord, as
befits my righteousness and as
befits my innocence.

י יִגְמָר־נָֽא רַע ׀ רְשָׁעִים
וּתְכוֹנֵן צַדֵּיק וּבֹחֵן לִבּוֹת
וּכְלָיֹות אֱלֹהֵים צַדֵּיק:

10 Let the evil of the wicked come
to an end, but give strength to
the righteous one; for men's
minds and hearts are probed
by the God of righteousness.

יא מָֽגִנֵּי עַל־אֱלֹהֵים מוֹשֵׁיעַ
יִשְׁרֵי־לֵב:

11 God, the Savior of the upright
of heart, is my shield.

יב אֱלֹהִים שׁוֹפֵט צַדֵּיק וְאֵל
זֹעֵם בְּכָל־יֽוֹם:

12 God is a righteous Judge, and
the Almighty shows His wrath
every day

יג אִם־לֹא יָשׁוּב חַרְבּוֹ יִלְטֵוֹשׁ
קַשְׁתּוֹ דָרַךְ וַֽיְכוֹנְנֶֽהָ:

13 if he does not repent, if he
sharpens his sword and pulls
back his bow in readiness.

---

9 **The Lord will be the Judge of the peoples.** When this time arrives, when God reveals Himself in judgment, I can request of Him as well to **judge me, Lord, as befits my righteousness and as befits my innocence.**

10 At that time, **let the evil of the wicked come to an end, but give strength to the righteous one.** God has no need to examine external testimony in order to execute justice, **for men's minds and hearts are probed by the God of righteousness.** *Kelayot*, translated here as "minds," literally means "kidneys," which are considered the seat of a person's thoughts.

11 **God, the Savior of the upright of heart, is my shield.**

12 **God is a righteous Judge.** Because God is just, He exonerates the righteous. **And** at the same time, **the Almighty** also **shows His wrath** against the evildoers **every day**

13 **if he,** the evildoer, **does not repent** of his threats and evil plans against the righteous, **if he** persists and **sharpens his sword and pulls back his bow in readiness.**

וְלוֹ הֵכִין כְּלֵי־מָוֶת חִצָּיו
לְדֹלְקִים יִפְעָל:

הִנֵּה יְחַבֶּל־אָוֶן וְהָרָה עָמָל
וְיָלַד שָׁקֶר:

בּוֹר כָּרָה וַיַּחְפְּרֵהוּ וַיִּפֹּל
בְּשַׁחַת יִפְעָל:

יָשׁוּב עֲמָלוֹ בְרֹאשׁוֹ וְעַל
קָדְקֳדוֹ חֲמָסוֹ יֵרֵד:

14 But he prepares deadly
weapons against himself; his
arrows are used against those
who pursue.

15 Behold how he conceives evil,
is pregnant with iniquity, and
gives birth to deceit.

16 He has dug a hole deep in the
earth and has fallen into the pit
he made.

17 His wrongdoing will return
to punish him; his violent
behavior will come down on
his head.

---

14 **But** his plans will fail anyway, and the final result will be his own destruction; in the end, **he prepares deadly weapons against himself.** The very weapons the wicked aim at the righteous will instead target and destroy the wicked themselves. **His arrows are used against those who pursue.** The arrows directed against the righteous will instead be used against their pursuers.

15 **Behold how he conceives evil, is pregnant with iniquity, and gives birth to deceit.** This analogy uses images of a developing fetus. First there is the moment of conception, then the pregnancy, and finally the delivery. Whatever the wicked person creates and produces, the plans are undertaken in *aven*, translated here as "evil" but also meaning "nothingness," and *amal*, which is "iniquity" but also connotes toiling in vain. The final result is nothing but an empty lie.

16 **He,** the evildoer, **has dug a hole deep in the earth and has fallen into the pit he made.** Ultimately, the evil person falls into the hole that he dug for others.

17 **His wrongdoing will return to punish him; his violent behavior will come down on his head.** His own sins and evil deeds bring him trouble, suffering, and punitive consequences. He suffers even without the external infliction of punishment; he is essentially punished by his own wrongful deeds.

‫יח 18 אוֹדֶה יהוה כְּצִדְקוֹ וַאֲזַמְּרָה‬
‫שֵׁם־יהוה עֶלְיוֹן:‬

18 I praise the Lord for His righteousness; I sing to the name of the Lord Most High.

PSALM 8

A psalm that begins as a hymn of praise to God
but is also an introspective poem that muses about man's place in the world.

‫א 1 לַמְנַצֵּחַ עַל־הַגִּתִּית מִזְמוֹר‬
‫לְדָוִד:‬

1 For the chief musician on the *gittit*, a psalm by David.

‫ב 2 יהוה אֲדֹנֵינוּ מָה־אַדִּיר שִׁמְךָ‬
‫בְּכָל־הָאָרֶץ אֲשֶׁר תְּנָה‬
‫הוֹדְךָ עַל־הַשָּׁמָיִם:‬

2 Lord, our Master, how mighty is Your name throughout the world! You set Your glory in the heavens.

‫ג 3 מִפִּי עוֹלְלִים ׀ וְיֹנְקִים יִסַּדְתָּ‬
‫עֹז לְמַעַן צוֹרְרֶיךָ לְהַשְׁבִּית‬
‫אוֹיֵב וּמִתְנַקֵּם:‬

3 Out of the mouths of small children and suckling babes You founded strength against Your foes, to stop the enemy and the avenger.

---

18 In conclusion: **I praise the Lord for His righteousness; I sing to the name of the Lord Most High.**

PSALM 8

1 **For the chief musician on the *gittit*,** probably a musical instrument named after Gat, the city in which it was apparently invented, or where it was commonly played, **a psalm by David.** The psalm begins and ends with a proclamation of praise:

2 **Lord, our Master, how mighty is Your name throughout the world! You set Your glory in the heavens.** This verse can be understood to be an observation that God's name is glorified in heaven. Others explain it to mean: It would be befitting for You to bestow Your glory exclusively on the heavens.

3 **Out of the mouths of small children and suckling babes You founded strength.** There is a special kind of praise and worship of God that is unique to little children. Their prayers are lacking

כִּי־אֶרְאֶה שָׁמֶיךָ מַעֲשֵׂה ⁴
אֶצְבְּעֹתֶיךָ יָרֵחַ וְכוֹכָבִים
אֲשֶׁר כּוֹנָנְתָּה:

מָה־אֱנוֹשׁ כִּי־תִזְכְּרֶנּוּ וּבֶן־ ⁵
אָדָם כִּי תִפְקְדֶנּוּ:

וַתְּחַסְּרֵהוּ מְּעַט מֵאֱלֹהִים ⁶
וְכָבוֹד וְהָדָר תְּעַטְּרֵהוּ:

תַּמְשִׁילֵהוּ בְּמַעֲשֵׂי יָדֶיךָ כֹּל ⁷
שַׁתָּה תַחַת־רַגְלָיו:

⁴ When I see Your heavens, the work of Your fingers, the moon and the stars You have made:

⁵ What is a mortal that You remember him, a man that You take him into account?

⁶ For You have made him a little less than divine, crowning him with honor and glory.

⁷ You have made him ruler over the works of Your hands; You placed all things at his feet,

---

in deceit, pretense, or sophistication. It is this kind of prayer that is referred to here as "strength," and it is directed **against Your foes,** in order **to stop the enemy and the avenger.** Sung with childish sincerity, these songs are a positive force in the war against God's enemies. They represent a fundamental, basic strength that cannot be extinguished by adversaries, and they are a buffer against the waves of hatred that recur in every generation.

⁴ **When I see Your heavens, the work of Your fingers, the moon and the stars You have made.** I am thrilled by the enormity of Your all-encompassing greatness. But the sight of Your miraculous creations also raises doubts and uncertainty in my mind:

⁵ **What is a mortal that You remember him, a man that You take him into account?** After seeing the sun, moon, and stars, after contemplating enormous and distant worlds, one might conclude that man is an inconsequential and pitiful creation, fundamentally unworthy of attention from God above. Yet somehow, despite man's insignificance, You, God, have chosen to bestow on him manifold gifts.

⁶ **For You have made him a little less than divine.** You have created him "in the image of God."[2] Consequently, God's spirit resides within man. An alternative interpretation of "divine" in this verse is that it refers to God's angels. Because of the powers bestowed upon him by God, man is only slightly inferior to the divine angels, **crowning him with honor and glory** through the unique powers that You have granted him.

⁷ In addition to creating man to be essentially superior to other beings, as is written in the book of Genesis, **You have made him ruler over the works of Your hands,** giving him the permission, and the power, to rule over Your handiwork. **You placed all things at his feet.** You charged him with reigning over all that exists,

ח ‏8 ‏צֹנֶה וַאֲלָפִים כֻּלָּם וְגַם
‏בַּהֲמוֹת שָׂדָי:

all sheep and cattle, all the
animals of the field,

ט ‏9 ‏צִפּוֹר שָׁמַיִם וּדְגֵי הַיָּם עֹבֵר
‏אָרְחוֹת יַמִּים:

the birds of the air and the fish
of the sea, whatever crosses the
sea's deep waters.

‏10 ‏יְהֹוָה אֲדֹנֵינוּ מָה־אַדִּיר שִׁמְךָ
‏בְּכָל־הָאָרֶץ:

Lord, our Master, how mighty
is Your name throughout the
world!

PSALM 9

A psalm of thanksgiving by one who has been rescued from his enemies and led to victory. The
psalmist prays that God will continue to be at his side against others who wage war against him.

א ‏1 ‏לַמְנַצֵּחַ עַל־מוּת לַבֵּן מִזְמוֹר
‏לְדָוִד:

For the chief musician, on the
death of Laben, a psalm by
David.

---

8 **all sheep and cattle.** Domestic animals have been given over to man, and he also has dominion
over **all the** wild **animals of the field,**

9 and over **the birds of the air and the fish of the sea, whatever crosses the sea's deep
waters.** Man should thank God for giving him power over all the creatures of the land, sea, and sky.
This vast power should be humbling. One might wonder: Is man truly worthy of it? This question
can be instructive, helping one to realize that although man is in charge, his power stems from God
who, in His kindness, relegated it to him. When man considers his own insignificance vis-à-vis the
immensity of the power placed in his hands, he should acknowledge that all this is a God-given
gift. Therefore, he should say again, as in the opening verse of the psalm:

10 **Lord, our Master, how mighty is Your name throughout the world!**

PSALM 9

1 **For the chief musician, on the death of Laben, a psalm by David.** Since this psalm is
generally one of thanksgiving to God and does not appear to be a lament about the loss of a son,
certainly not one of David's own children, most commentators agree that the word *laben*, literally
translated as "for the son," does not have that meaning here. Some commentators argue that Laben
could be the name of an enemy king or commander unknown to us from other sources. Others

אוֹדֶה יְהוָה בְּכָל־לִבִּי
אֲסַפְּרָה כָּל־נִפְלְאוֹתֶיךָ׃

² I will thank You, Lord, with all my heart. I will tell of all Your wonders.

אֶשְׂמְחָה וְאֶעֶלְצָה בָךְ
אֲזַמְּרָה שִׁמְךָ עֶלְיוֹן׃

³ I will be glad and delight in You. I will sing for Your name, Most High.

בְּשׁוּב־אוֹיְבַי אָחוֹר יִכָּשְׁלוּ
וְיֹאבְדוּ מִפָּנֶיךָ׃

⁴ When my enemies are turned back, they stumble and perish before You.

כִּי־עָשִׂיתָ מִשְׁפָּטִי וְדִינִי
יָשַׁבְתָּ לְכִסֵּא שׁוֹפֵט צֶדֶק׃

⁵ For You have performed my judgment and my verdict. You sat on Your throne, Judge of righteousness.

גָּעַרְתָּ גוֹיִם אִבַּדְתָּ רָשָׁע
שְׁמָם מָחִיתָ לְעוֹלָם וָעֶד׃

⁶ You rebuked the nations; You obliterated the wicked. You blotted out their name forever and ever.

---

speculate that *al mut Laben*, translated here as "on the death of Laben," actually has nothing to do with death, but rather was the name of a well-known song, and that this psalm was meant to be sung to its melody. Written mostly in first-person singular, this psalm is intended to be studied and taught. To facilitate its being learned by heart, this Hebrew text, like many others, is arranged in an alphabetical acrostic. The alphabet is not complete, however, and there are sometimes one or more non-alphabetical verses inserted between consecutive letters.

2 **I will thank You, Lord, with all my heart. I will tell of all Your wonders.**

3 **I will be glad and delight in You. I will sing for Your name, Most High.**

4 **When my enemies are turned back, they stumble and perish before You.**

5 This will occur **for You have performed my judgment and my verdict.** When the time came for me to be judged by You, I knew that You would find my enemies guilty. **You sat on Your throne** of justice, **Judge of righteousness.**

6 **You rebuked the nations,** and since God's rebuke manifests itself in the physical world of man, the outcome is that these evil nations are struck down. **You obliterated the wicked** to such an extent that **You blotted out their name forever and ever.**

הָאוֹיֵב ׀ תַּמּוּ חֳרָבוֹת לָנֶצַח
וְעָרִים נָתַשְׁתָּ אָבַד זִכְרָם
הֵמָּה: ^ז

וַיהוה לְעוֹלָם יֵשֵׁב כּוֹנֵן
לַמִּשְׁפָּט כִּסְאוֹ: ^ח

וְהוּא יִשְׁפֹּט־תֵּבֵל בְּצֶדֶק
יָדִין לְאֻמִּים בְּמֵישָׁרִים: ^ט

וִיהִי יהוה מִשְׂגָּב לַדָּךְ
מִשְׂגָּב לְעִתּוֹת בַּצָּרָה: ^י

וְיִבְטְחוּ בְךָ יוֹדְעֵי שְׁמֶךָ כִּי
לֹא־עָזַבְתָּ דֹרְשֶׁיךָ יהוה: ^{יא}

⁷ The enemy is no more, in eternal ruin. You have destroyed their cities; the memory of them is lost.

⁸ But the Lord will endure forever. He has prepared His throne for judgment,

⁹ and He will judge the world in righteousness. He will administer fair judgment to the nations.

¹⁰ The Lord is a fortress for the oppressed, a fortress in times of trouble.

¹¹ And those who know Your name place their trust in You, for You, Lord, do not forsake those who seek You.

---

⁷ **The enemy is no more,** and all that is left of their territory lies **in eternal ruin. You have destroyed their cities.** The word *natashta* is translated here as "You have destroyed," similar to the word *natatzta*, "You have shattered." **The memory of them is lost.** Not only have the cities fallen in conquest, but their memory has been obliterated as well.

⁸ **But** in contrast to the aforementioned enemies, whose end is foretold, **the Lord will endure forever. He has prepared His throne for judgment,**

⁹ **and He will judge the world in righteousness. He will administer fair judgment to the nations.**

¹⁰ **The Lord is a fortress for the oppressed, a fortress in times of trouble.**

¹¹ **And those who know Your name,** who believe in You and recognize You, and are thus close to You, **place their trust in You, for You, Lord, do not forsake those who seek You.**

זַמְּרוּ לַיהוה יֹשֵׁב צִיּוֹן הַגִּידוּ
בָּעַמִּים עֲלִילוֹתָיו:

כִּי־דֹרֵשׁ דָּמִים אוֹתָם זָכָר
לֹא־שָׁכַח צַעֲקַת עֲנִיִּים: עֲנָוִים

חָנְנֵנִי יהוה רְאֵה עָנְיִי
מִשֹּׂנְאָי מְרוֹמְמִי מִשַּׁעֲרֵי־
מָוֶת:

לְמַעַן אֲסַפְּרָה כָּל־תְּהִלָּתֶיךָ
בְּשַׁעֲרֵי בַת־צִיּוֹן אָגִילָה
בִּישׁוּעָתֶךָ:

טָבְעוּ גוֹיִם בְּשַׁחַת עָשׂוּ
בְּרֶשֶׁת־זוּ טָמָנוּ נִלְכְּדָה
רַגְלָם:

12 Sing to the Lord, dweller in Zion; make His deeds known among the peoples.

13 For He avenges blood, He remembers them; He does not forget the cries of the humble.

14 Be gracious to me, Lord; see my deprivation inflicted by my enemies. You lift me up from the gates of death,

15 so I might speak Your praise at the gates of the daughter of Zion. I rejoice in Your salvation.

16 The nations have sunk into the pit they made, their feet trapped in the nets they hid.

---

12 **Sing to the Lord** a song of thanksgiving, **dweller in Zion; make His deeds known among the peoples.** Tell all the nations how He saved you from danger and from the attacks of your enemies.

13 **For He avenges blood.** The word *doresh*, translated here as "avenges," literally means "searches." God investigates, as it were, incidents of bloodshed, and **He remembers them,** the righteous who have been unjustly slain. **He does not forget the cries of the humble,** those who have conducted themselves with righteousness and humility.

14 **Be gracious to me, Lord; see my deprivation inflicted by my enemies. You lift me up from the gates of death,**

15 **so I might speak Your praise** when I experience Your salvation, **at the gates of the daughter of Zion.** The gates of a city were the public spaces, akin to a central plaza. **I rejoice in Your salvation** and tell others about it.

16 In contrast to my joy, **the nations have sunk into the pit they made, their feet trapped in the nets they hid.** The evil nations will fall into the very pits they dug; their feet will be caught in the traps they set for others.

יז נוֹדַ֤ע ׀ יְהֹוָה֮ מִשְׁפָּ֢ט עָ֫שָׂ֥ה בְּפֹ֣עַל כַּ֭פָּיו נוֹקֵ֣שׁ רָשָׁ֑ע הִגָּי֥וֹן סֶֽלָה:

יח יָשׁ֣וּבוּ רְשָׁעִ֣ים לִשְׁא֑וֹלָה כָּל־ גּ֝וֹיִ֗ם שְׁכֵחֵ֥י אֱלֹהִֽים:

יט כִּ֤י לֹ֣א לָ֭נֶצַח יִשָּׁכַ֣ח אֶבְי֑וֹן תִּקְוַ֥ת עֲנָוִ֗ים   תִּקְוַ֥ת עֲ֝נִיִּ֗ים תֹּאבַ֥ד לָעַֽד:

כ ק֘וּמָ֤ה יְהֹוָ֗ה אַל־יָעֹ֥ז אֱנ֑וֹשׁ יִשָּׁפְט֥וּ ג֝וֹיִ֗ם עַל־פָּנֶֽיךָ:

כא שִׁ֘יתָ֤ה יְהֹוָ֨ה ׀ מוֹרָ֗ה לָ֫הֶ֥ם יֵדְע֥וּ גוֹיִ֑ם אֱנ֖וֹשׁ הֵ֣מָּה סֶּֽלָה:

17 The Lord is known through the judgments He executes; the evildoer is snared in the work of his own hands. Reflect upon this, Selah.

18 The wicked will return to the netherworld, all nations who have no memory of God.

19 For the needy will not always be forgotten, the hopes of the poor forever lost.

20 Arise, Lord; let man not be arrogant. Let the nations be judged in Your sight.

21 Place fear in them, Lord, so that nations know they are but mortal men, Selah.

---

17 **The Lord is known through the judgments He executes** throughout the world. **The evildoer is snared in the work of his own hands. Reflect upon this, Selah.** The word *higgayon,* translated here as "reflect upon this," apparently means: This topic deserves consideration; think about it and discuss it with others.

18 **The wicked will return to,** or go in the direction of, **the netherworld.** Alternatively, one might say that, in a certain sense, evildoers are creatures emanating from the netherworld who are forced to go back to where they came from. The same may be said of **all nations who have no memory of God.**

19 **For the needy will not always be forgotten, the hopes of the poor forever lost.** Thus, even if the needy appear to be abandoned, hope is not lost; God turns toward them in the end.

20 **Arise, Lord.** Stir Yourself to action and reveal Yourself through justice. **Let man not be arrogant.** The wicked will not prevail once God's presence is revealed in the world; no one then will dare to be insolent. **Let the nations be judged in Your sight.**

21 **Place fear in them, Lord.** The word *mora,* ending with a *heh,* apparently means "edict." However, there are those who interpret it in the sense of *mora* with an *alef,* which means "fear." Thus, the verse can either mean issue an edict against them or instill fear in them. Either way, this is **so that nations know they are but mortal men, Selah.** The nations must acknowledge that they

PSALM 10

A psalm of prayer that rails against the rule of the wicked.

לְמָה יְהוָה תַּעֲמֹד בְּרָחֹוק
תַּעְלִים לְעִתּוֹת בַּצָּרָה:

בְּגַאֲוַת רָשָׁע יִדְלַק עָנִי
יִתָּפְשׂוּ ׀ בִּמְזִמּוֹת זוּ חָשָׁבוּ:

כִּי־הִלֵּל רָשָׁע עַל־תַּאֲוַת
נַפְשׁוֹ וּבֹצֵעַ בֵּרֵךְ נִאֵץ ׀
יְהוָה:

ב לחודש
2nd day
of month

Why do You stand far off,
Lord? Why do You hide
Yourself in times of trouble?

2 The wicked in their pride
fervently pursue the afflicted,
who are caught in the schemes
they plot.

3 For the wicked one sings
praises about his heart's desire,
and the evil man blesses and
reviles the Lord.

---

are far from invincible; being human, they are *enosh*, "mortal," and both their power and their very lives will inevitably come to an end. The use of the word is significant in this context, as it evokes the similarly spelled word *anush*, someone who is critically ill.

PSALM 10

1 **Why do You stand far off, Lord,** as if You were not here among us? **Why do You hide Yourself in times of trouble?**

2 **The wicked in their pride fervently pursue the afflicted, who are caught in the schemes they plot.**

3 **For the wicked one sings praises about his heart's desire.** If an evil person decides for some reason to praise God, it is only about the attainment of his own desires. **And the evil man blesses and reviles the Lord.** When that evil person blesses God, his blessing is so insincere that it is actually an affront to Him. An alternative translation of *botze'a* is "one who breaks bread." The meaning of this phrase, then, would be that an immoral person who steals bread from another and now sits down to eat it is committing a sacrilege by uttering a blessing over the bread.

רָשָׁע כְּגֹבַהּ אַפּוֹ בַּל־יִדְרֹשׁ אֵין אֱלֹהִים כָּל־מְזִמּוֹתָיו: יָחִילוּ דְרָכָו ׀ בְּכָל־עֵת מָרוֹם מִשְׁפָּטֶיךָ מִנֶּגְדּוֹ כָּל־צוֹרְרָיו יָפִיחַ בָּהֶם: אָמַר בְּלִבּוֹ בַּל־אֶמּוֹט לְדֹר וָדֹר אֲשֶׁר לֹא־בְרָע: אָלָה ׀ פִּיהוּ מָלֵא וּמִרְמוֹת וָתֹךְ תַּחַת לְשׁוֹנוֹ עָמָל וָאָוֶן:

The wicked one, with his proud countenance, does not seek; God is not in his thoughts.

His ways always prosper; Your judgments are on high, out of his sight. As for his foes, he blows at them.

He said in his heart: I will not stumble. Throughout generations I will never be in adversity.

His mouth is full of curses and deceit and intrigue; beneath his tongue are mischief and wickedness.

---

4 **The wicked one, with his proud countenance,** or, alternatively, in his great wrath, **does not seek** God. The greater his pride, or wrath, the less likely he is to seek and find God. **God is not in his thoughts.** A wicked person does not take God into consideration when he plots to do evil.

5 **His ways always prosper; Your judgments are on high, out of his sight.** It seems, especially to the evil people themselves, that Your judgments "on high" cannot affect them, for they seem to remain successful no matter what they do. **As for his foes, he blows at them.** With great ease, as if with a puff of air, the evil people blow away their rivals.

6 **He said in his heart: I will not stumble.** In his heart, the evil person believes himself to be secure, noting: I persist, I am stable; nothing can topple me. **Throughout generations I will never be in adversity.** He believes he can continue to live and do as he pleases, without anything untoward ever happening to him.

7 **His mouth is full of curses and deceit and intrigue; beneath his tongue are mischief and wickedness.**

ח ⁸ יֵשֵׁב ׀ בְּמַאְרַב חֲצֵרִים
בַּמִּסְתָּרִים יַהֲרֹג נָקִי עֵינָיו
לְחֵלְכָה יִצְפֹּנוּ:

ט ⁹ יֶאֱרֹב בַּמִּסְתָּר ׀ כְּאַרְיֵה
בְסֻכֹּה יֶאֱרֹב לַחֲטוֹף עָנִי
יַחְטֹף עָנִי בְּמָשְׁכוֹ בְרִשְׁתּוֹ:

יָדְכֶּה
חֵל כָּ י ¹⁰ ודכה יָשֹׁחַ וְנָפַל בַּעֲצוּמָיו
חֵלְכָּאִים:

יא ¹¹ אָמַר בְּלִבּוֹ שָׁכַח אֵל הִסְתִּיר
פָּנָיו בַּל־רָאָה לָנֶצַח:

יב ¹² קוּמָה יהוה אֵל נְשָׂא יָדֶךָ
עֲנִיִּים
בִּעֲנָיִ אַל־תִּשְׁכַּח עֲנִיִּים:

⁸ He lies in wait in courtyards; in hidden places he kills the innocent. He fixes his eyes on the downtrodden.

⁹ He lurks in a hiding place like a lion in its lair; he lurks to catch the poor man; he catches the poor man and draws him into his net.

¹⁰ He crushes him, forces him to a crouch, and the downtrodden are toppled by his might.

¹¹ He says to himself: The Almighty has forgotten. He has hidden His face, He will never see.

¹² Arise, Lord God, raise Your hand. Do not forget the humble.

---

8 The following is the wicked person's mode of action: **He lies in wait in courtyards; in hidden places he kills the innocent. He fixes his eyes on the downtrodden.** He lies in ambush in unguarded places, on the prowl for his victims.

9 **He lurks in a hiding place like a lion in its lair.** He lies in wait like a lion in the brambles, stalking its prey. **He lurks to catch the poor man; he catches the poor man and draws him into his net.** He is deceptive; he entraps the vulnerable person. He sets obstacles in his path.

10 **He crushes him, forces him to a crouch, and the downtrodden are toppled by his might.** He uses his might to crush and oppress the unfortunate, bringing them down.

11 **He says to himself: The Almighty has forgotten** about our existence. **He has hidden His face, He will never see.** Since God remains mostly unrevealed in His world, the wicked think they can do as they please. They are convinced that God does not see them.

12 Here begins the psalmist's prayer: **Arise, Lord God, raise Your hand,** reveal Your strength. **Do not forget the humble.**

עַל־מֶה ׀ נִאֵץ רָשָׁע ׀ אֱלֹהִים
אָמַר בְּלִבּוֹ לֹא תִדְרֹשׁ: יג

רָאִתָה כִּי־אַתָּה ׀ עָמָל
וָכַעַס ׀ תַּבִּיט לָתֵת בְּיָדֶךָ
עָלֶיךָ יַעֲזֹב חֵלֵכָה יָתוֹם
אַתָּה ׀ הָיִיתָ עוֹזֵר: יד

שְׁבֹר זְרוֹעַ רָשָׁע וָרָע
תִּדְרוֹשׁ־רִשְׁעוֹ בַל־תִּמְצָא: טו

יְהוָה מֶלֶךְ עוֹלָם וָעֶד אָבְדוּ
גוֹיִם מֵאַרְצוֹ: טז

תַּאֲוַת עֲנָוִים שָׁמַעְתָּ יְהוָה
תָּכִין לִבָּם תַּקְשִׁיב אָזְנֶךָ: יז

13 Why has the wicked man mocked God, saying to himself: You will not seek?

14 You have seen it; You have beheld mischief and anger, and You gave it the power to be. The poor rely on You; You have always helped the orphan.

15 Break the arm of the wicked one and evildoer; purge his wickedness until You can find none.

16 The Lord is King forever and ever; nations have perished from His land.

17 Lord, You hear the desire of the humble. You will strengthen their heart, You will incline Your ear,

---

13 **Why has the wicked man mocked God, saying to himself** of God: **You will not seek?** The wicked man believes that God is oblivious, that He has no interest in mankind.

14 But the truth is that **You have seen it; You have beheld mischief and anger.** You do look and You do see all the sins and the fury of the world, **and You gave it the power to be.** You Yourself are the one who makes it possible for evil to flourish in the world. **The poor rely on You; You have always helped the orphan.** Yet now the world appears to be completely abandoned by You. Because of this, the psalmist beseeches God:

15 **Break the arm of the wicked one and evildoer; purge his wickedness until You can find none.** Eradicate evil to such an extent that if You look for it, You will not find it.

16 **The Lord is King forever and ever; nations have perished from His land.** God has banished the wicked and immoral nations from His land.

17 **Lord, You hear the desire of the humble,** which they express in their prayers. **You will strengthen their heart, You will incline Your ear** to their prayers,

לִשְׁפֹּט יָתוֹם וָדָךְ בַּל־יוֹסִיף
עוֹד לַעֲרֹץ אֱנוֹשׁ מִן־הָאָרֶץ:

18 to vindicate the orphan and the oppressed. It will no longer destroy mortals from the earth.

PSALM 11

A contemplative psalm on evil, in which the psalmist depicts the way wicked people lie in ambush, attacking the righteous both secretly and in full view, without realizing that God watches over the world and punishes those who deserve it.

לַמְנַצֵּחַ לְדָוִד בַּיהוָה ׀
חָסִיתִי אֵיךְ תֹּאמְרוּ לְנַפְשִׁי
נוּדוּ הַרְכֶם צִפּוֹר:

נוּדִי

כִּי הִנֵּה הָרְשָׁעִים יִדְרְכוּן
קֶשֶׁת כּוֹנְנוּ חִצָּם עַל־יֶתֶר
לִירוֹת בְּמוֹ־אֹפֶל לְיִשְׁרֵי־
לֵב:

1 For the chief musician, by David. In the Lord I take refuge. How can you say to me: Wander away, bird, to your mountain?

2 For behold, the wicked bend the bow; they have fixed their arrow on the string to shoot, in darkness, at the upright of heart.

---

18 **to vindicate the orphan and the oppressed,** so that **it,** evil, **will no longer destroy mortals,** particularly those who are weak and vulnerable, **from the earth.**

PSALM 11
1 **For the chief musician, by David. In the Lord I take refuge. How can you say to me: Wander away, bird, to your mountain?** How can you speak to me so harshly, with words that seem to say: Take off, bird, fly to the hills, get away from here?
2 The world is full of menace: **For behold, the wicked bend the bow; they have fixed their arrow on the string to shoot, in darkness,** when they cannot be detected, **at the upright of heart,** whom they intend to kill.

כִּי הַשָּׁתוֹת יֵהָרֵסוּן צַדִּיק
מַה־פָּעָל: ³

יהוה ׀ בְּהֵיכַל קָדְשׁוֹ יהוה
בַּשָּׁמַיִם כִּסְאוֹ עֵינָיו יֶחֱזוּ
עַפְעַפָּיו יִבְחֲנוּ בְּנֵי אָדָם: ⁴

יהוה צַדִּיק יִבְחָן וְרָשָׁע
וְאֹהֵב חָמָס שָׂנְאָה נַפְשׁוֹ: ⁵

יַמְטֵר עַל־רְשָׁעִים פַּחִים אֵשׁ
וְגָפְרִית וְרוּחַ זִלְעָפוֹת מְנָת
כּוֹסָם: ⁶

כִּי־צַדִּיק יהוה צְדָקוֹת אָהֵב
יָשָׁר יֶחֱזוּ פָנֵימוֹ: ⁷

³ If the foundations are destroyed, what can the righteous man do?

⁴ The Lord is in His Holy Temple; the Lord's throne is in heaven. His eyes behold; He puts His gaze on the sons of man.

⁵ The Lord attends to the righteous, but He hates the wicked and the lover of violence.

⁶ He will rain burning coal upon the wicked; fire and brimstone and windstorm will be their lot.

⁷ For the Lord is righteous and He loves righteousness. Their faces will behold the Upright One.

---

3 **If the foundations,** the moral and societal foundations of the world, **are destroyed, what can the righteous man do?** When the moral foundations of society are in ruins, what good can possibly come of the individual deeds of a righteous person?

4 And yet, there are grounds for a different kind of contemplation, one imbued with faith and hope: **The Lord is in His Holy Temple.** He has not abandoned His earthly abode. **The Lord's throne is in heaven** and He rules over the world. **His eyes behold** all that occurs on earth; **He puts His gaze on the sons of man.**

5 **The Lord attends to the righteous, but He hates the wicked and the lover of violence.**

6 **He will rain burning coal upon the wicked; fire and brimstone and windstorm will be their lot.**

7 **For the Lord is righteous and He** therefore **loves righteousness. Their faces,** the faces of the virtuous, **will behold the Upright One.**

PSALM 12

A plea against evildoers who seem to have the upper hand in the world,
who speak of righteousness while fomenting evil. It is also a prayer to God
to protect all those who follow the proper path.

לַמְנַצֵּחַ עַל־הַשְּׁמִינִית
מִזְמוֹר לְדָוִד:

הוֹשִׁיעָה יהוה כִּי־גָמַר חָסִיד
כִּי־פַסּוּ אֱמוּנִים מִבְּנֵי אָדָם:

שָׁוְא ׀ יְדַבְּרוּ אִישׁ אֶת־רֵעֵהוּ
שְׂפַת חֲלָקוֹת בְּלֵב וָלֵב
יְדַבֵּרוּ:

יַכְרֵת יהוה כָּל־שִׂפְתֵי
חֲלָקוֹת לָשׁוֹן מְדַבֶּרֶת
גְּדֹלוֹת:

1 For the chief musician, on the eight-stringed harp, a psalm by David.

2 Help, Lord, for the faithful man is no more, for trustworthiness has disappeared from among men.

3 People speak falsehood to one another; they speak with flattering lips and a double heart.

4 May the Lord cut off all flattering lips and the tongue that boasts.

PSALM 12

1 **For the chief musician, on the eight-stringed harp, a psalm by David.**

2 **Help, Lord, for the faithful man is no more, for trustworthiness has disappeared from among men.** There are no more righteous men; they are all gone, lost to mankind. Truth and loyalty have disappeared; all that is left is evil.

3 **People speak falsehood to one another.** Their words mean nothing; their promises are worthless. **They speak with flattering lips and a double heart.** They are duplicitous; they do not say what they are really thinking. They speak falsely, hiding their real intentions.

4 The psalmist pleads: **May the Lord cut off all flattering lips and the tongue that boasts.** Although flattery may be pleasing to those in power, it is indicative of haughtiness and bravado on the part of those who lack influence.

‎ה ‏אֲשֶׁר אָמְרוּ ׀ לִלְשֹׁנֵנוּ נַגְבִּיר
‎שְׂפָתֵינוּ אִתָּנוּ מִי אָדוֹן לָנוּ:

‎ו ‏מִשֹּׁד עֲנִיִּים מֵאֶנְקַת אֶבְיוֹנִים
‎עַתָּה אָקוּם יֹאמַר יהוה
‎אָשִׁית בְּיֵשַׁע יָפִיחַ לוֹ:

‎אִמְרוֹת יהוה אֲמָרוֹת
‎טְהֹרוֹת כֶּסֶף צָרוּף בַּעֲלִיל
‎לָאָרֶץ מְזֻקָּק שִׁבְעָתָיִם:

‎ח ‏אַתָּה־יהוה תִּשְׁמְרֵם תִּצְּרֶנּוּ ׀
‎מִן־הַדּוֹר זוּ לְעוֹלָם:

5 Those who say: With our
tongue we will prevail; our lips
are our own. Who is master
over us?

6 Because of the robbery of
the poor and the groans of
the needy, the Lord says:
Now I will arise. I will bring
deliverance; it will be revealed
to him.

7 The words of the Lord are pure
words, like silver purified in the
furnace of the earth, refined
seven times.

8 You, Lord, will preserve them;
You will keep them secure from
this generation, forever.

---

5 **Those who say: With our tongue we will prevail; our lips are our own. Who is master over us?** Flatterers believe they can continue to deceive and threaten with impunity. What follows is a prayer and a message of good tidings.

6 God will not allow this situation to go on indefinitely. **Because of the robbery of the poor and the groans of the needy, the Lord says: Now I will arise** and reveal Myself to avenge these injustices. **I will bring deliverance; it will be revealed to him.**

7 **The words of the Lord are pure words,** devoid of all pollutants. They are **like silver purified in the furnace of the earth.** *Alil,* translated here as "furnace," can also mean "in plain view." The silver is **refined seven times** so that it is completely free of impurities. That is to say, the words of God are utterly pure and perfect.

8 **You, Lord, will preserve them,** all the unfortunate and afflicted. **You will keep them secure from this generation,** which seems poised to persevere **forever.**

ס ⁹ סָבִיב רְשָׁעִים יִתְהַלָּכוּן כְּרֻם
זֻלּוּת לִבְנֵי אָדָם:

⁹ The wicked roam about,
as lowliness is exalted
among men.

PSALM 13

A psalm of supplication. It seems to the psalmist that God has hidden His face from him and has delivered him into the hands of his enemies. He beseeches God to reveal His kindness and save him.

א ¹ לַמְנַצֵּחַ מִזְמוֹר לְדָוִד:

¹ For the chief musician, a psalm
by David.

ב עַד־אָנָה יְהוָה תִּשְׁכָּחֵנִי נֶצַח
עַד־אָנָה ׀ תַּסְתִּיר אֶת־פָּנֶיךָ
מִמֶּנִּי:

² How long, Lord? Will You
forget me forever? How
long will You hide Your face
from me?

ג עַד־אָנָה אָשִׁית עֵצוֹת
בְּנַפְשִׁי יָגוֹן בִּלְבָבִי יוֹמָם עַד־
אָנָה ׀ יָרוּם אֹיְבִי עָלָי:

³ How long must I devise plans,
have sorrow in my heart all
day? For how long will my
enemies tower over me?

---

⁹ God's protection is needed because **the wicked roam about, as lowliness is exalted among men.** Some translate *kerum zulut* as "leeches," which suck the blood of man. According to this reading, the wicked surround the downtrodden and exploit them, as if sucking their blood.

PSALM 13

¹ **For the chief musician, a psalm by David.**

² **How long, Lord? Will You forget me forever? How long will You hide Your face from me?**

³ **How long must I devise plans** to escape the clutches of the wicked? I seem to be unable to find the right way out. How long must I **have sorrow in my heart** that overwhelms me **all day?** My very existence is devoid of joy; all my thoughts are full of gloom. **For how long will my enemies tower over me?**

הַבִּיטָה עֲנֵנִי יהוה אֱלֹהָי הָאִירָה עֵינַי פֶּן־אִישַׁן הַמָּוֶת:

⁴ Look and answer me, Lord my God; bring light to my eyes lest I will sleep in death.

פֶּן־יֹאמַר אֹיְבִי יְכָלְתִּיו צָרַי יָגִילוּ כִּי אֶמּוֹט:

⁵ Lest my enemy say: I have overcome him, lest my foes rejoice when I stumble.

וַאֲנִי ׀ בְּחַסְדְּךָ בָטַחְתִּי יָגֵל לִבִּי בִּישׁוּעָתֶךָ אָשִׁירָה לַיהוה כִּי גָמַל עָלָי:

⁶ But I trust in Your kindness; my heart rejoices in Your salvation. I sing to the Lord, for He has dealt kindly with me.

PSALM 14

A psalm that contemplates the wicked of the world, who have no belief in God and thus are not afraid of Him, but rather go about their evil ways until the world is full of wrongdoing. The psalmist beseeches God for salvation in his time of trouble. With minor variations in language, the text closely resembles Psalm 53.

לַמְנַצֵּחַ לְדָוִד אָמַר נָבָל בְּלִבּוֹ אֵין אֱלֹהִים הִשְׁחִיתוּ הִתְעִיבוּ עֲלִילָה אֵין עֹשֵׂה־טוֹב:

¹ For the chief musician, a psalm by David. The scoundrel says in his heart: There is no God. They have been corrupted, they have acted abominably; there is no one who does good.

---

⁴ **Look and answer me, Lord my God; bring light to my eyes** to help me to find the path to salvation, **lest I will sleep in** the eternal sleep of **death.**

⁵ **Lest my enemy say: I have overcome him, lest my foes rejoice when I stumble.**

⁶ **But** still **I trust in Your kindness,** my only solace. **My heart rejoices in** anticipation of **Your salvation. I sing to the Lord, for He has dealt kindly with me.**

PSALM 14

¹ **For the chief musician, a psalm by David. The scoundrel,** a mean, arrogant man, **says in**

יְהוָה מִשָּׁמַיִם הִשְׁקִיף עַל־
בְּנֵי־אָדָם לִרְאוֹת הֲיֵשׁ
מַשְׂכִּיל דֹּרֵשׁ אֶת־אֱלֹהִים:

הַכֹּל סָר יַחְדָּו נֶאֱלָחוּ אֵין
עֹשֵׂה־טוֹב אֵין גַּם־אֶחָד:

הֲלֹא יָדְעוּ כָּל־פֹּעֲלֵי אָוֶן
אֹכְלֵי עַמִּי אָכְלוּ לֶחֶם יְהוָה
לֹא קָרָאוּ:

שָׁם ׀ פָּחֲדוּ פָחַד כִּי־אֱלֹהִים
בְּדוֹר צַדִּיק:

2 The Lord looks down from heaven upon the sons of man to see if there is anyone of understanding who seeks God.

3 They have all gone sour, all of them together befouled. There is no one who does good, not even one.

4 Have all the evildoers no knowledge? They, who devour my people as if eating bread, they who do not call out to the Lord,

5 there they are, in great fear, for God is with the righteous generation.

---

his heart: **There is no God.** He does not acknowledge God's existence at all. Hence, **they have been corrupted, they have acted abominably; there is no one who does good.**

2 **The Lord looks down from heaven** into this world **upon the sons of man to see if there is anyone of understanding who seeks God,** and He finds:

3 **They have all gone sour, all of them together befouled. There is no one who does good, not even one.**

4 **Have all the evildoers,** who deny God's existence and consequently have no qualms about their evil actions, **no knowledge? They, who devour my people as if eating bread, they who do not call out to the Lord** under any circumstances,

5 **there they are,** all the people of the generation, **in great fear, for God is** only **with the righteous generation.** In a generation that is not righteous, no one feels that God's salvation is imminent.

עֲצַת־עָנִי תָבִישׁוּ כִּי יהוה
מַחְסֵהוּ: ⁶

מִי יִתֵּן מִצִּיּוֹן יְשׁוּעַת יִשְׂרָאֵל
בְּשׁוּב יהוה שְׁבוּת עַמּוֹ יָגֵל
יַעֲקֹב יִשְׂמַח יִשְׂרָאֵל: ⁷

⁶ You despise the counsel of the poor, for the Lord is their refuge.

⁷ May the salvation of Israel emerge from Zion! When the Lord returns the captives of His people, Jacob will rejoice and Israel will exult.

PSALM 15

A psalm that expresses, in summary form, the positive personality traits of an individual. The Talmud states that King David condensed all the commandments of the Torah into a mere eleven precepts.[3] This psalm does not deal with observance of commandments but rather with personal virtues; the individual described here is not engaged in prayer or other religious rituals, yet he follows the path of the righteous in both demeanor and action.

מִזְמוֹר לְדָוִד יהוה מִי־יָגוּר
בְּאָהֳלֶךָ מִי־יִשְׁכֹּן בְּהַר
קׇדְשֶׁךָ: ¹

¹ A psalm by David. Lord, who may sojourn in Your tent? Who may dwell on Your holy mountain?

⁶ **You despise the counsel of the poor, for the Lord is their refuge.** You, the wicked, shame the poor, discrediting their opinions because God is their only refuge and they depend solely on Him. When God hides Himself and is seemingly absent from this world, the wretched are bereft, with no one to lean on. Following this dire description, the psalmist concludes with a prayer:

⁷ **May the salvation of Israel emerge from Zion! When the Lord returns the captives of His people,** and settles them securely in their land, **Jacob will rejoice and Israel will exult.**

PSALM 15

¹ **A psalm by David. Lord, who may** claim the merit to **sojourn in Your tent? Who may dwell on Your holy mountain?** There is an element of poetic license to this question, since a tent is transported from place to place and those who dwell within it are sojourners, like guests who move on, whereas the Sanctuary on God's holy mountain is permanent and does not move. Some understand this opening question as follows: Who is truly worthy, and not simply permitted

הוֹלֵךְ תָּמִים וּפֹעֵל צֶדֶק
וְדֹבֵר אֱמֶת בִּלְבָבוֹ:

לֹא־רָגַל ׀ עַל־לְשֹׁנוֹ לֹא־
עָשָׂה לְרֵעֵהוּ רָעָה וְחֶרְפָּה
לֹא־נָשָׂא עַל־קְרֹבוֹ:

נִבְזֶה ׀ בְּעֵינָיו נִמְאָס וְאֶת־
יִרְאֵי יהוה יְכַבֵּד נִשְׁבַּע
לְהָרַע וְלֹא יָמִר:

2 He who walks with integrity
and does righteous works, and
speaks the truth in his heart.

3 He who does not gossip with
his tongue, nor does evil to his
neighbor, nor tolerates disgrace
for his friend.

4 In his own eyes he is despised
and repugnant, but he honors
those who fear the Lord. He
abides by his oaths, even if they
cause him harm.

---

from the standpoint of Jewish law, to enter the grounds of the Holy Temple? It seems, however, that the question is meant to be more general and abstract: Who is worthy of being close to God? The psalmist continues by specifying the characteristics that can make a person worthy of such intimacy.

2 **He who walks with integrity,** wholehearted in his honesty, **and does righteous works** toward others, **and speaks the truth in his heart.** He does not delude himself or deceive others; there is no contradiction between what he believes in his heart and what he says with his mouth. His is a world of truth.

3 **He who does not gossip with his tongue, nor does evil to his neighbor, nor tolerates disgrace for his friend.** He not only refrains from doing evil himself; he is also concerned about others. He tries to make sure that no disgrace befalls those who associate with him.

4 **In his own eyes he is despised and repugnant,** he does not view himself as deserving of glory and honor, **but he honors those who fear the Lord.** Alternatively, the righteous man looks upon despicable people with repugnance, but honors those who fear God. In other words, he knows how to differentiate between the deserving and the undeserving. **He abides by his oaths, even if they cause him harm.** He carries out oaths he has made, even if these cause him personal loss or suffering; he does not attempt to modify an oath or evade his responsibility.

הֵ כַּסְפּוֹ ׀ לֹא־נָתַן בְּנֶשֶׁךְ וְשֹׁחַד
עַל־נָקִי לֹא־לָקָח עֹשֵׂה אֵלֶּה
לֹא יִמּוֹט לְעוֹלָם:

5 He does not lend with usury,
nor does he take bribes
against the innocent. Whoever
behaves in this manner will
never stumble.

PSALM 16

A psalm of thanksgiving to God for having guided the psalmist
on a righteous path and for granting him the bliss of being close to Him.

א מִכְתָּם לְדָוִד שָׁמְרֵנִי אֵל כִּי־
חָסִיתִי בָךְ:

ב אָמַרְתְּ לַיהוה אֲדֹנָי אָתָּה
טוֹבָתִי בַּל־עָלֶיךָ:

1 An instruction by David.
Almighty, protect me, for I take
refuge in You.

2 You said to the Lord: You are
my Lord. I have no goodness
but from You.

---

5 **He does not lend with usury,** he does not derive benefit from forbidden practices. **Nor,** if he is a judge or a person of influence, **does he take bribes against the innocent** to unjustly condemn them. **Whoever behaves in this manner,** consistent with all the good practices described above, **will never stumble.** It is he who is truly worthy of standing in God's Sanctuary.

PSALM 16
1 **An instruction by David.** Several chapters in Psalms open with the word *mikhtam*, translated here as "instruction." Its meaning is unclear. Some claim it is the name of a melody or a musical instruction specific to this kind of psalm. Others believe that the term ascribes a special significance to the psalm, as it is related to the biblical word *ketem*, which means "gold." According to the latter interpretation, this psalm is a magnificent work of gold. **Almighty, protect me, for I take refuge in You.**
2 **You,** my soul, **said to the Lord: You are my Lord. I have no goodness but from You.** The literal meaning of this last phrase is "My goodness is not upon You," an obscure expression. It might mean the following: It is not incumbent upon You to bestow on me goodness. That is, I cannot consider myself virtuous and deserving of reward from You for having chosen to cling to You, for the goodness You have already bestowed upon me is boundless.

לִקְדוֹשִׁים אֲשֶׁר־בָּאָרֶץ הֵמָּה
וְאַדִּירֵי כָּל־חֶפְצִי־בָם:

יִרְבּוּ עַצְּבוֹתָם אַחֵר מָהָרוּ
בַּל־אַסִּיךְ נִסְכֵּיהֶם מִדָּם
וּבַל־אֶשָּׂא אֶת־שְׁמוֹתָם עַל־
שְׂפָתָי:

יְהוָה מְנָת־חֶלְקִי וְכוֹסִי אַתָּה
תּוֹמִיךְ גּוֹרָלִי:

חֲבָלִים נָפְלוּ־לִי בַּנְּעִמִים
אַף־נַחֲלָת שָׁפְרָה עָלָי:

אֲבָרֵךְ אֶת־יהוה אֲשֶׁר יְעָצָנִי
אַף־לֵילוֹת יִסְּרוּנִי כִלְיוֹתָי:

³ With the holy of the earth and the majestic ones, all my wishes are with them.

⁴ They are engaged in many matters, they who have dealings with strange things. I will not pour their libations of blood or carry their names on my lips.

⁵ The Lord is my lot and my portion; You sustain my fate.

⁶ The lots that have fallen to me are pleasant; my estate is lovely.

⁷ I bless the Lord who counsels me, even on nights when my thoughts are anguished.

---

3   I join myself **with the holy of the earth,** righteous men, as opposed to the holy beings in heaven, the angels. **And the majestic ones, all my wishes are** to be counted **with them.** In contrast, the psalmist now notes those things he wishes to have no part of:

4   **They are engaged in many** mundane **matters, they who have dealings with strange things,** literally, "other things," meaning idols, which are often termed "other gods." **I will not pour their libations of blood or** even **carry their names on my lips.** The psalmist desires to thoroughly distance himself from anything to do with idol worship.

5   Unlike them, **the Lord is my lot and my portion; You sustain my fate.**

6   With regard to his choice of acknowledging God, the psalmist says: **The lots [havalim],** which can refer to portions of land, lottery slips, or the actual winnings of a lottery, **that have fallen to me are pleasant.** Since "You sustain my fate" (verse 5), I am assured that the portions that have fallen to me are the best. **My estate,** all that I have been fortunate to receive, **is lovely.**

7   **I bless the Lord who counsels me,** whose guidance has prevented me from choosing the wrong path. **Even on nights when my thoughts are anguished,** I am continually focused on finding the right path, and I regret the bad choices I have made in the past.

שִׁוִּ֬יתִי יהוה לְנֶגְדִּ֣י תָמִ֑יד כִּ֥י ח
מִ֝ימִינִ֗י בַּל־אֶמּֽוֹט׃

לָכֵ֤ן ׀ שָׂמַ֣ח לִ֭בִּי וַיָּ֣גֶל כְּבוֹדִ֑י ט
אַף־בְּ֝שָׂרִ֗י יִשְׁכֹּ֥ן לָבֶֽטַח׃

כִּ֤י ׀ לֹא־תַעֲזֹ֣ב נַפְשִׁ֣י לִשְׁא֑וֹל י
חֲסִידֶ֔ךָ   לֹֽא־תִתֵּ֥ן חֲ֝סִידְךָ֗ לִרְא֥וֹת
שָֽׁחַת׃

תּֽוֹדִיעֵנִי֮ אֹ֤רַח חַ֫יִּ֥ים שֹׂ֣בַע יא
שְׂמָח֣וֹת אֶת־פָּנֶ֑יךָ נְעִמ֖וֹת
בִּימִינְךָ֣ נֶֽצַח׃

8 I set the Lord before me always. He is on my right; I will not stumble.

9 Because of this my heart is glad. My being is joyous; my body rests securely.

10 For You will not abandon me to the netherworld; You will not allow Your devoted one to see the grave.

11 May You show me the path of life, abundance and joy in Your presence. Eternal pleasure is by Your right hand.

---

8 **I set the Lord before me always. He is on my right,** always coming to my assistance; **I will not stumble.**

9 **Because of this,** because of God's help, **my heart is glad. My being is joyous; my body rests securely.**

10 **For You will not abandon me to the netherworld; You will not allow Your devoted one to see the grave.**

11 **May You show me the path of life,** through which I may attain **abundance and joy in Your presence. Eternal pleasure is by Your right hand.** As you are my portion (verse 5), I forever merit the good and pleasure that result from being with you.

PSALM 17

A prayer to God to guard those who go in His path, saving them from their enemies
and granting them joy and the merit of drawing close to Him.

תְּפִלָּה לְדָוִד שִׁמְעָה יהוה ׀
צֶדֶק הַקְשִׁיבָה רִנָּתִי הַאֲזִינָה
תְפִלָּתִי בְּלֹא שִׂפְתֵי מִרְמָה:

מִלְּפָנֶיךָ מִשְׁפָּטִי יֵצֵא עֵינֶיךָ
תֶּחֱזֶינָה מֵישָׁרִים:

בָּחַנְתָּ לִבִּי ׀ פָּקַדְתָּ לַּיְלָה
צְרַפְתַּנִי בַל־תִּמְצָא זַמֹּתִי
בַּל־יַעֲבָר־פִּי:

לִפְעֻלּוֹת אָדָם בִּדְבַר שְׂפָתֶיךָ
אֲנִי שָׁמַרְתִּי אָרְחוֹת פָּרִיץ:

¹ A prayer by David. Hear, Lord,
what is just; heed my cry. Give
ear to my prayer, which does
not come from deceitful lips.

² Let my judgment come forth
from Your presence; let Your
eyes see what is right.

³ You have examined my heart,
taken an account at night.
You inspected me and found
nothing; I pondered and
nothing passed my lips.

⁴ In the doings of men, I follow
Your instruction; I have
avoided the ways of trespassers.

PSALM 17

¹ **A prayer by David. Hear, Lord, what is just,** that which is sincere and true; **heed my cry. Give ear to my** earnest **prayer, which does not come from deceitful lips.**

² **Let my judgment come forth from Your presence,** as I am confident that there will be a favorable outcome when God judges me. **Let Your eyes see what is right,** see if there is any fault that lies within me.

³ **You have examined my heart, taken an account at night.** Your examination of me is applied not only to deeds, usually performed during the day, but also to the thoughts of the heart, which are just as active at night as by day. **You inspected me and found nothing.** The term *tzeraftani*, translated as "You inspected me," literally means "You refined me" as a silversmith refines silver by inspecting it and removing any impurities that he finds. But even at this level of scrutiny, You found nothing. **I pondered,** I examined my thoughts to ascertain that I had no unworthy musings, **and nothing passed my lips,** and I certainly did not utter anything unworthy aloud.

⁴ **In the doings of men,** in all my mundane actions, in everything that I do in this world, **I follow Your instruction. I have avoided the ways of trespassers,** those whose evil respects no boundaries.

ה תְּמֹךְ אֲשֻׁרַי בְּמַעְגְּלוֹתֶיךָ
בַּל־נָמוֹטוּ פְעָמָי:

ו אֲנִי־קְרָאתִיךָ כִי־תַעֲנֵנִי אֵל
הַט־אָזְנְךָ לִי שְׁמַע אִמְרָתִי:

ז הַפְלֵה חֲסָדֶיךָ מוֹשִׁיעַ
חוֹסִים מִמִּתְקוֹמְמִים
בִּימִינֶךָ:

ח שָׁמְרֵנִי כְּאִישׁוֹן בַּת־עָיִן בְּצֵל
כְּנָפֶיךָ תַּסְתִּירֵנִי:

ט מִפְּנֵי רְשָׁעִים זוּ שַׁדּוּנִי אֹיְבַי
בְּנֶפֶשׁ יַקִּיפוּ עָלָי:

י חֶלְבָּמוֹ סָגְרוּ פִּימוֹ דִּבְּרוּ
בְגֵאוּת:

5 Secure my steps on Your paths, so my feet will not stumble.

6 I call upon You that You answer me, Almighty. Incline Your ear to me; hear my speech.

7 Reveal Your kindness, Redeemer of those who take refuge from the enemies who rise up, sheltering in Your right hand.

8 Guard me like the pupil of an eye, hide me in the shadow of Your wings,

9 from the wicked who rob me, my mortal enemies who encircle me.

10 They are encased in their fat; their mouths speak with haughtiness.

---

5 **Secure my steps on Your paths, so my feet will not stumble.**

6 **I call upon You** in the hope **that You answer me, Almighty,** because I know You can help me. **Incline Your ear to me; hear my speech.**

7 **Reveal Your kindness, Redeemer of those who take refuge** in You, protecting them **from the enemies who rise up** against You, whom I consider to be my own enemies as well, **sheltering in Your right hand.**

8 **Guard me like the pupil of an eye, hide me in the shadow of Your wings,**

9 **from the wicked who rob me, my mortal enemies who encircle me.**

10 **They are encased in their fat.** In ancient times, obesity was a sign of wealth and power. **Their mouths speak with haughtiness.**

יא אַשֻּׁרֵנוּ עַתָּה סבבוני עֵינֵיהֶם סבב
יָשִׁיתוּ לִנְטוֹת בָּאָרֶץ:

יב דִּמְיֹנוֹ כְּאַרְיֵה יִכְסוֹף לִטְרֹף
וְכִכְפִיר יֹשֵׁב בְּמִסְתָּרִים:

יג קוּמָה יהוה קַדְּמָה פָנָיו
הַכְרִיעֵהוּ פַּלְּטָה נַפְשִׁי
מֵרָשָׁע חַרְבֶּךָ:

יד מְמְתִים יָדְךָ ׀ יהוה מְמְתִים וצפו
מֵחֶלֶד חֶלְקָם בַּחַיִּים וּצְפִינְךָ
תְּמַלֵּא בִטְנָם יִשְׂבְּעוּ בָנִים
וְהִנִּיחוּ יִתְרָם לְעוֹלְלֵיהֶם:

טו אֲנִי בְּצֶדֶק אֶחֱזֶה פָנֶיךָ
אֶשְׂבְּעָה בְהָקִיץ תְּמוּנָתֶךָ:

11 I see them now surrounding us.
They cast their eyes, spreading
them over the land.

12 He is akin to a lion yearning to
tear at his prey, like a lion cub
lurking in hidden lairs.

13 Arise, Lord, confront him and
subdue him. Rescue me from
the wicked with Your sword.

14 Among those people under
Your hand, Lord, those people
in the land whose portion is
life. Fill their bellies with Your
hidden treasures; sate their
sons, too, and let them leave
what is left to their offspring.

15 Truly, I shall see Your face;
Your image will fill my waking
vision.

---

11 **I see them now surrounding us. They cast their eyes, spreading them over the land.**
The psalmist sees his enemies surrounding him, looking about in search of prey.

12 **He is akin to a lion yearning to tear at his prey, like a lion cub lurking in hidden lairs.**

13 The psalmist prays: **Arise, Lord, confront him and subdue him. Rescue me from the wicked with Your sword.** Reveal Yourself, God, declare war on the enemy.

14 Furthermore, he asks for God's protection to be **among those people,** among those who are **under Your hand, Lord,** protected by God, **those people in the land whose portion,** thanks to Your assistance to them, **is life. Fill their bellies with Your hidden treasures; sate their sons, too, and let them leave what is left to their offspring.**

15 The psalmist concludes with a prayer and a request: **Truly, I shall see Your face; Your image will fill my waking vision.** Find me worthy of seeing Your presence revealed, as the prophets did, even while awake.

PSALM 18

A hymn of thanksgiving by David to God, replete with imagery of God's might.

ג לחודש

3rd day
of month

לַמְנַצֵּחַ לְעֶבֶד יהוה לְדָוִד ׀ אֲשֶׁר דִּבֶּר ׀ לַיהוה אֶת־ דִּבְרֵי הַשִּׁירָה הַזֹּאת בְּיוֹם ׀ הִצִּיל־יהוה אוֹתוֹ מִכַּף כָּל־ אֹיְבָיו וּמִיַּד שָׁאוּל׃

וַיֹּאמַר אֶרְחָמְךָ יהוה חִזְקִי׃

יהוה ׀ סַלְעִי וּמְצוּדָתִי וּמְפַלְּטִי אֵלִי צוּרִי אֶחֱסֶה־בּוֹ מָגִנִּי וְקֶרֶן־יִשְׁעִי מִשְׂגַּבִּי׃

1 To the chief musician, by David servant of the Lord, who spoke the words of this song to the Lord on the day the Lord saved him from the hands of all his enemies and from the hand of Saul.

2 And he said: I love You, Lord, my strength.

3 The Lord is my rock and my fortress, my redeemer, my Almighty, my mighty rock. I take refuge in Him, my shield, the horn of my salvation, my stronghold.

PSALM 18

1 **To the chief musician, by David servant of the Lord, who spoke the words of this song to the Lord on the day the Lord saved him from the hands of all his enemies and from the hand of Saul.** The opening verse of this psalm describes its content beautifully. It addresses a specific period in David's life, not his youth but rather the time when he reached the height of his powers and his reign was secure. For this reason, David is able to draw conclusions about his life that are mostly optimistic. Saul is mentioned because he represented the greatest danger to David's life by far, equal to all the dangers that followed. It should be noted that this psalm also appears in II Samuel 22, with various minor linguistic differences. Psalm 18 is apparently a slightly revised version of the more ancient text found in Samuel, which contains archaic language and a number of expressions whose meanings remain unclear.

2 **And he said: I love You, Lord, my strength.** *Raḥamu* means "love" in Aramaic, though generally the root of this word connotes "mercy" in Hebrew. This is also the meaning of the root in ancient Hebrew, and is the sense of *erḥamkha* here, "I love you." David expresses his love for God, then continues with detailed words of praise:

3 **The Lord is my rock and my fortress, my redeemer.** Several levels of protection are mentioned here. A rock is something one can lean on or climb onto in order to escape various

מְהֻלָּל אֶקְרָא יהוה וּמִן־
אֹיְבַי אִוָּשֵׁעַ:

אֲפָפוּנִי חֶבְלֵי־מָוֶת וְנַחֲלֵי
בְלִיַּעַל יְבַעֲתוּנִי:

חֶבְלֵי שְׁאוֹל סְבָבוּנִי קִדְּמוּנִי
מוֹקְשֵׁי מָוֶת:

בַּצַּר־לִי ׀ אֶקְרָא יהוה וְאֶל־
אֱלֹהַי אֲשַׁוֵּעַ יִשְׁמַע מֵהֵיכָלוֹ
קוֹלִי וְשַׁוְעָתִי לְפָנָיו ׀ תָּבוֹא
בְאָזְנָיו:

⁴ I call in praise to the Lord, and I am delivered from my enemies.

⁵ Cords of death were wrapped around me; floods of wickedness terrified me.

⁶ Cords of the grave surrounded me; snares of death confronted me.

⁷ In my distress I called to the Lord, cried out to my God. From His dwelling place He heard my voice, and my cry reached His ears.

---

troubles. A fortress is a protective physical structure. "My redeemer" describes God as being actively involved in the rescue. **My Almighty, my mighty rock. I take refuge in Him, my shield, the horn of my salvation, my stronghold.** The verse describes God's continually increasing support.

⁴ **I call in praise to the Lord, and I am delivered from my enemies.**

⁵ **Cords of death were wrapped around me.** "Cords of death" [hevlei mavet] is a poetic phrase that has a double meaning. The simple meaning is that death is like a cord that ultimately binds and ropes in all men. But hevlei can also mean "pains," indicating physical suffering or connoting troubles and distress that envelop a person as though he were bound by cords. **Floods of wickedness terrified me.**

⁶ **Cords of the grave surrounded me; snares of death,** traps from which escape is all but impossible, **confronted me.**

⁷ **In my distress I called to the Lord, cried out to my God. From His dwelling place He heard my voice, and my cry reached His ears.**

וַתִּגְעַשׁ וַתִּרְעַשׁ ׀ הָאָרֶץ
וּמוֹסְדֵי הָרִים יִרְגָּזוּ וַיִּתְגָּעֲשׁוּ
כִּי־חָרָה לֽוֹ:

עָלָה עָשָׁן ׀ בְּאַפּוֹ וְאֵשׁ־מִפִּיו
תֹּאכֵל גֶּחָלִים בָּעֲרוּ מִמֶּֽנּוּ:

וַיֵּט שָׁמַיִם וַיֵּרַד וַעֲרָפֶל
תַּחַת רַגְלָֽיו:

וַיִּרְכַּב עַל־כְּרוּב וַיָּעֹף וַיֵּדֶא
עַל־כַּנְפֵי־רֽוּחַ:

יָשֶׁת חֹשֶׁךְ ׀ סִתְרוֹ סְבִיבוֹתָיו
סֻכָּתוֹ חֶשְׁכַת־מַיִם עָבֵי
שְׁחָקִֽים:

8 The earth shook and quaked. Foundations of mountains trembled, shaken because of His anger.

9 Smoke arose from His nostrils, a consuming fire from His mouth; burning coals emerged from Him.

10 He bent the heavens and came down, a dense cloud beneath His feet.

11 He mounted a cherub and flew, and He soared on wings of wind.

12 He engulfed His secret place in darkness, His sheltered surroundings, the darkness of waters, clouds of the skies.

---

8 The second part of this psalm depicts the glory and power of God's revelation. It is not directly related to events in David's life. It is, rather, a general description of revelation, reminiscent of songs depicting the revelation at Mount Sinai and the like. **The earth shook and quaked. Foundations of mountains trembled, shaken because of His anger.**

9 **Smoke arose from His nostrils, a consuming fire from His mouth; burning coals emerged from Him.** These are descriptions of God's revelation in fire and smoke.

10 **He bent the heavens and came down.** It is not as if the Master of the Universe descends from the heavens, not even metaphorically; rather, He lowers the heavens toward earth.[4] **A dense cloud** is **beneath His feet.**

11 **He mounted a cherub and flew.** Cherubs are symbolic of the divine chariot, as described in Ezekiel, as well as the Divine Presence, as in the Holy of Holies in the Temple.[5] **And He soared on wings of wind.**

12 **He engulfed His secret place in darkness, His sheltered surroundings, the darkness of waters.** This apparently refers to the darkness of black rainclouds, **clouds of the skies.**

מִנֹּגַהּ נֶגְדּוֹ עָבָיו עָבְרוּ בָּרָד
וְגַחֲלֵי־אֵשׁ:

^{יג}

¹³ From the radiance before Him, hail and coals of fire passed through His clouds.

וַיַּרְעֵם בַּשָּׁמַיִם ׀ יְהֹוָה וְעֶלְיוֹן
יִתֵּן קֹלוֹ בָּרָד וְגַחֲלֵי־אֵשׁ:

^{יד}

¹⁴ And the Lord thundered in the heavens, the voice of the Most High spewing forth hail and coals of fire.

וַיִּשְׁלַח חִצָּיו וַיְפִיצֵם וּבְרָקִים
רָב וַיְהֻמֵּם:

^{טו}

¹⁵ He shot His arrows and dispersed them; many bolts of lightning confounded them.

וַיֵּרָאוּ ׀ אֲפִיקֵי מַיִם וַיִּגָּלוּ
מוֹסְדוֹת תֵּבֵל מִגַּעֲרָתְךָ
יְהֹוָה מִנִּשְׁמַת רוּחַ אַפֶּךָ:

^{טז}

¹⁶ Streams of water appeared, and the foundations of the world were laid bare at Your rebuke, Lord, from the blast of the breath of Your nostrils.

יִשְׁלַח מִמָּרוֹם יִקָּחֵנִי יַמְשֵׁנִי
מִמַּיִם רַבִּים:

^{יז}

¹⁷ He sent from above and He took me; He drew me out of surging waters.

---

¹³ Though engulfed in darkness, **from the radiance** that is **before Him,** behind all that concealment, **hail and coals of fire passed through His clouds.** Revelation is depicted here using imagery of hail and coals of fire breaking through the clouds of concealment.

¹⁴ **And the Lord thundered in the heavens, the voice of the Most High spewing forth hail and coals of fire.** The combination of ice and fire is an expression of divine power.

¹⁵ **He shot His arrows and dispersed them,** His enemies. **Many bolts of lightning confounded them.**

¹⁶ In the midst of all this, **streams of water appeared.** The world was shaken up, causing sources of water to be displaced, as during the splitting of the Red Sea. **And the foundations of the world were laid bare.** The lower foundations of the world were exposed; unknown depths could be seen. All this occurred as a consequence of God's wrath: **At Your rebuke, Lord, from the blast of the breath of Your nostrils.**

¹⁷ Until this point, the psalm describes God's power over the world. Yet His greatness also has a more intimate, personal aspect: **He sent** His hand, through various agents, **from above and He took me** to lift me out of trouble. **He drew me out of surging waters.**

יח יַצִּילֵנִי מֵאֹיְבִי עָז וּמִשֹּׂנְאַי
כִּי־אָמְצוּ מִמֶּנִּי:

יט יְקַדְּמוּנִי בְיוֹם־אֵידִי וַיְהִי־
יהוה לְמִשְׁעָן לִי:

כ וַיּוֹצִיאֵנִי לַמֶּרְחָב יְחַלְּצֵנִי כִּי
חָפֵץ בִּי:

כא יִגְמְלֵנִי יהוה כְּצִדְקִי כְּבֹר יָדַי
יָשִׁיב לִי:

כב כִּי־שָׁמַרְתִּי דַּרְכֵי יהוה וְלֹא־
רָשַׁעְתִּי מֵאֱלֹהָי:

כג כִּי כָל־מִשְׁפָּטָיו לְנֶגְדִּי
וְחֻקֹּתָיו לֹא־אָסִיר מֶנִּי:

18 He rescued me from my mighty enemy, from those who hated me, when they were too strong for me.

19 They confronted me on the day of my calamity, but the Lord was my support.

20 He brought me out into an open space; He rescued me because He delighted in me.

21 God has rewarded me for my righteousness; for the purity of my hands He has requited me.

22 For I have kept the ways of the Lord and have not wickedly departed from my God.

23 For all His judgments were before me, and I did not dismiss His statutes.

---

18 Or, in more concrete terms, without metaphor, **He rescued me from my mighty enemy, from those who hated me, when they were too strong for me.**

19 **They confronted me on the day of my calamity, but** at a time when enemies were poised and ready to attack, **the Lord was my support.**

20 **He brought me out into an open space.** He moved me from a place of distress to one of relief. **He rescued me because He delighted in me.**

21 There is a reason that God rescued me from adversity and attack: **God has rewarded me for my righteousness; for the purity of my hands He has requited me.**

22 **For I have kept the ways of the Lord and have not wickedly departed from my God.**

23 **For all His judgments were before me;** I was always aware of His laws, **and I did not dismiss His statutes.**

כד וָאֱהִי תָמִים עִמּוֹ וָאֶשְׁתַּמֵּר מֵעֲוֹנִי:

24 I was blameless with Him and guarded myself from iniquity.

כה וַיָּשֶׁב־יְהוָה לִי כְצִדְקִי כְּבֹר יָדַי לְנֶגֶד עֵינָיו:

25 And the Lord requited me for my righteousness, for the purity of my hands in His eyes.

כו עִם־חָסִיד תִּתְחַסָּד עִם־גְּבַר תָּמִים תִּתַּמָּם:

26 With the pious, You act mercifully; with a guileless man, You behave without guile.

כז עִם־נָבָר תִּתְבָּרָר וְעִם־עִקֵּשׁ תִּתְפַּתָּל:

27 You are pure with the purehearted; with the crooked, You are devious.

כח כִּי־אַתָּה עַם־עָנִי תוֹשִׁיעַ וְעֵינַיִם רָמוֹת תַּשְׁפִּיל:

28 For You rescue the poor and abase those with haughty looks.

כט כִּי־אַתָּה תָּאִיר נֵרִי יהוה אֱלֹהַי יַגִּיהַּ חָשְׁכִּי:

29 For You light my lamp, Lord my God, illuminating my darkness.

ל כִּי־בְךָ אָרֻץ גְּדוּד וּבֵאלֹהַי אֲדַלֶּג־שׁוּר:

30 For with You I can shatter a battalion; with my God, I can leap over walls.

---

24 **I was blameless with Him and guarded myself from iniquity.**

25 **And the Lord requited me for my righteousness, for the purity of my hands in His eyes.** God, in His mercy, acknowledges my innocence. This attribute of mercy is the way of God, and it is not limited to a particular person with whom He has a special relationship.

26 **With the pious, You act mercifully; with a guileless man, You behave without guile.**

27 **You are pure with the purehearted; with the crooked, You are devious.** You behave forthrightly with the innocent, but You are cunning with those who take devious paths.

28 **For You rescue the poor, and,** on the other hand, You **abase those with haughty looks.**

29 Once again, the psalm takes on a personal tone: **For You light my lamp** to shine before me and lead the way, **Lord my God, illuminating my darkness.**

30 **For with You,** with Your help, **I can shatter a battalion. With my God,** with His help, **I can leap over walls.** This is an allusion to the cities captured by King David; it was as if he flew over their walls.

לא הָאֵל תָּמִים דַּרְכּוֹ אִמְרַת־
יהוה צְרוּפָה מָגֵן הוּא לְכֹל ׀
הַחוֹסִים בּוֹ:

לב כִּי מִי אֱלוֹהַּ מִבַּלְעֲדֵי יהוה
וּמִי צוּר זוּלָתִי אֱלֹהֵינוּ:

לג הָאֵל הַמְאַזְּרֵנִי חָיִל וַיִּתֵּן
תָּמִים דַּרְכִּי:

לד מְשַׁוֶּה רַגְלַי כָּאַיָּלוֹת וְעַל
בָּמֹתַי יַעֲמִידֵנִי:

לה מְלַמֵּד יָדַי לַמִּלְחָמָה וְנִחֲתָה
קֶשֶׁת־נְחוּשָׁה זְרוֹעֹתָי:

לו וַתִּתֶּן־לִי מָגֵן יִשְׁעֶךָ וִימִינְךָ
תִסְעָדֵנִי וְעַנְוַתְךָ תַרְבֵּנִי:

31 The Almighty's way is blameless; the word of the Lord is purity. He is a shield for all who take refuge in Him.

32 For who is a god but the Lord? And who is a mighty rock except our God?

33 The Almighty girds me with strength and shows me a straight path.

34 He makes my feet as swift as deer and sets me in high places.

35 He trains my hands for battle, and my arms are made as a bow of bronze.

36 You have given me the shield of Your salvation and Your right hand assists me; Your humility makes me grow great.

---

31 **The Almighty's way is blameless,** bestowing upon each individual the reward or punishment that exactly suits his deeds. **The word of the Lord is purity.** *Tzerufa*, translated as "purity," literally refers to the process of refinement of precious metals, purging them of impurities. **He is a shield for all who take refuge in Him.**

32 **For who is a god but the Lord? And who is a mighty rock except our God?**

33 The psalmist, relying on God, benefits from His protection: **The Almighty girds me with strength and shows me a straight path.**

34 **He makes my feet as swift as deer and sets me in high places.**

35 **He trains my hands for battle, and my arms are made as** unbreakable as **a bow of bronze.**

36 **You have given me the shield of Your salvation,** Your protection, and the success it helps me achieve; **and Your right hand,** Your power and Your support, **assists me. Your humility,** Your willingness to descend to my aid, **makes me grow great.**

תַּרְחִיב צַעֲדִי תַחְתָּי וְלֹא מָעֲדוּ קַרְסֻלָּי: לז

אֶרְדּוֹף אוֹיְבַי וְאַשִּׂיגֵם וְלֹא־ אָשׁוּב עַד־כַּלּוֹתָם: לח

אֶמְחָצֵם וְלֹא־יֻכְלוּ קוּם יִפְּלוּ תַּחַת רַגְלָי: לט

וַתְּאַזְּרֵנִי חַיִל לַמִּלְחָמָה תַּכְרִיעַ קָמַי תַּחְתָּי: מ

וְאֹיְבַי נָתַתָּה לִּי עֹרֶף וּמְשַׂנְאַי אַצְמִיתֵם: מא

37 You lengthen my strides beneath me, and my feet do not stumble.

38 I pursue my enemies and overtake them, and I will not turn back until they are utterly destroyed.

39 I crush them so they are unable to rise; they fall beneath my feet.

40 You girded me with strength for battle. You brought down beneath me those who rose against me.

41 And You have made my enemies turn their backs to me; I destroyed those who hated me.

---

37 Metaphorically, **You lengthen my strides beneath me, and my feet do not stumble.** You have enabled me to advance rapidly, without falling.

38 Because of Your help in enabling me to stride broadly and swiftly, **I pursue my enemies and overtake them, and I will not turn back until they are utterly destroyed.**

39 **I crush them so they are unable to rise; they fall beneath my feet.**

40 **You girded me with strength for battle. You brought down beneath me those who rose against me.**

41 **And you have made my enemies turn their backs to me** in flight; **I destroyed those who hated me.**

מב יְשַׁוְּע֥וּ וְאֵין־מוֹשִׁ֑יעַ עַל־
יְ֝הֹוָ֗ה וְלֹ֣א עָנָֽם׃

מג וְֽאֶשְׁחָקֵ֗ם כְּעָפָ֥ר עַל־פְּנֵי־
ר֑וּחַ כְּטִ֖יט חוּצ֣וֹת אֲרִיקֵֽם׃

מד תְּפַלְּטֵנִי֮ מֵרִ֪יבֵ֫י עָ֥ם תְּ֭שִׂימֵנִי
לְרֹ֣אשׁ גּוֹיִ֑ם עַ֖ם לֹא־יָדַ֣עְתִּי
יַֽעַבְדֽוּנִי׃

מה לְשֵׁ֣מַֽע אֹ֭זֶן יִשָּׁ֣מְעוּ לִ֑י בְּנֵֽי־
נֵ֝כָ֗ר יְכַחֲשׁוּ־לִֽי׃

מו בְּנֵי־נֵכָ֥ר יִבֹּ֑לוּ וְֽ֝יַחְרְג֗וּ
מִֽמִּסְגְּרֽוֹתֵיהֶֽם׃

42 They cried out for help, but there was no savior; they turned to the Lord, who did not answer them.

43 Then I beat them as fine as dust in the wind; I poured them out like mud in the streets.

44 You delivered me from the strife of peoples; You placed me at the head of nations. A people whom I have not known serve me.

45 As soon as they hear, they obey me; foreigners submit to me.

46 Foreigners, exhausted, emerge from their fortresses.

---

42 **They cried out for help, but there was no savior** for them; **they turned to the Lord, who did not answer them.**

43 **Then I beat them as fine as dust in the wind;** nothing at all was left of them. **I poured them out like mud in the streets.**

44 **You delivered me from the strife of** other **peoples; You placed me at the head of nations.** My success was so great that I ruled not only over nations neighboring the Land of Israel but also over faraway places, and **a people whom I have not known serve me.** The king's reputation of great power was such that even nations he did not know submitted to his sovereignty.

45 **As soon as they hear, they obey me; foreigners submit to me.** Foreigners who know me only by reputation are willing to submit to my commands. The word *yekhaḥashu*, translated here as "submit," literally means "to act with deceit." My enemies feign loyalty to me so they can benefit from my goodwill. The fact that his enemies feel obliged to conceal their adversarial status, and lie and abase themselves before him, is a clear manifestation of the ruler's power.

46 **Foreigners, exhausted, emerge** defeated **from their fortresses.**

מה חַי־יְהוָה וּבָרוּךְ צוּרִי וְיָרוּם
אֱלוֹהֵי יִשְׁעִי:

מח הָאֵל הַנּוֹתֵן נְקָמוֹת לִי וַיַּדְבֵּר
עַמִּים תַּחְתָּי:

מט מְפַלְּטִי מֵאֹיְבָי אַף מִן־
קָמַי תְּרוֹמְמֵנִי מֵאִישׁ חָמָס
תַּצִּילֵנִי:

נ עַל־כֵּן ׀ אוֹדְךָ בַגּוֹיִם ׀ יְהוָה
וּלְשִׁמְךָ אֲזַמֵּרָה:

נא מַגְדִּל יְשׁוּעוֹת מַלְכּוֹ וְעֹשֶׂה
חֶסֶד ׀ לִמְשִׁיחוֹ לְדָוִד וּלְזַרְעוֹ
עַד־עוֹלָם:

47 The Lord lives; blessed is my mighty rock. Exalted be the God of my salvation.

48 The Almighty who executes vengeance for me and destroys nations beneath me,

49 rescues me from my enemies, lifts me above those who rise against me, saves me from men of violence.

50 For this I give thanks to You among the nations, Lord, and sing praises to Your name.

51 He increases deliverance to His king, shows kindness to His anointed, to David and to his descendants, eternally.

---

47 The psalmist concludes: **The Lord lives; blessed is my mighty rock. Exalted be the God of my salvation.**

48 **The Almighty who executes vengeance for me and destroys nations beneath me,** alternatively the word *yadber*, translated here as "destroys," can mean "leads" or "brings": The Almighty brings nations under my rule,

49 He **rescues me from my enemies, lifts me above those who rise against me, saves me from men of violence.**

50 **For this I give thanks to You among the nations, Lord, and sing praises to Your name.**

51 **He increases deliverance to His king.** God continually increases the support He gives to David, the king He chose. He **shows kindness to His anointed, to David and to his descendants,** to whom the kingship of Israel was promised **eternally.**

PSALM 19

A psalm about creation, Torah, and man, comprising three seemingly unconnected parts, which are revealed, ultimately, to be interrelated.

לַמְנַצֵּחַ מִזְמוֹר לְדָוִד׃ א

הַשָּׁמַיִם מְסַפְּרִים כְּבוֹד־אֵל ב
וּמַעֲשֵׂה יָדָיו מַגִּיד הָרָקִיעַ׃

יוֹם לְיוֹם יַבִּיעַ אֹמֶר וְלַיְלָה ג
לְּלַיְלָה יְחַוֶּה־דָּעַת׃

אֵין־אֹמֶר וְאֵין דְּבָרִים בְּלִי ד
נִשְׁמָע קוֹלָם׃

1 To the chief musician, a psalm by David.

2 The heavens declare the glory of God, and the sky tells the work of His hands.

3 Day to day gives utterance; night to night renders understanding.

4 There is no talk, nor are there words; their voice is not heard.

PSALM 19

1 **To the chief musician, a psalm by David.**

2 **The heavens declare the glory of God, and the sky tells the work of His hands.** This verse is not a depiction of God as Creator of the world. It expresses a more introspective idea, that mere observation of the world makes man aware of God's presence. It is not a miracle or the act of creation that is spoken of here; rather, it is the wonder that accompanies one's awareness of the world's existence. This is how "the sky tells the work of His hands"; its very presence speaks volumes. When a man looks at the sky, he is seeing, in some sense, God's glory revealed. The heavens, the planetary orbits, the order of the universe, all are evidence of God's handiwork. The psalmist is not searching for God's presence in the world; for him, the world itself is an expression of divine revelation.

3 **Day to day gives utterance; night to night renders understanding.** Every day expresses God's glory; every night elicits new understanding. Daylight hours are inherently active; time itself is dynamic and declarative. The stories told by day speak of the glory of God, whereas the night is quieter, allowing for introspection. Its peace and tranquility also "speak," but with a broader and possibly deeper understanding.

4 **There is no talk, nor are there words; their voice is not heard.** This verse clarifies the words of the previous verse, "Day to day gives utterance." Obviously, the days do not actually talk; the fact of their existence makes them heard.

בְּכָל־הָאָ֗רֶץ ׀ יָצָ֬א קַוָּ֗ם
וּבִקְצֵ֣ה תֵ֭בֵל מִלֵּיהֶ֑ם לַ֝שֶּׁ֗מֶשׁ
שָׂם־אֹ֥הֶל בָּהֶֽם׃

וְה֗וּא כְּ֭חָתָן יֹצֵ֣א מֵחֻפָּת֑וֹ
יָשִׂ֥ישׂ כְּ֝גִבּ֗וֹר לָר֥וּץ אֹֽרַח׃

מִקְצֵ֤ה הַשָּׁמַ֨יִם ׀ מֽוֹצָא֗וֹ
וּתְקוּפָת֥וֹ עַל־קְצוֹתָ֑ם וְאֵ֥ין
נִ֝סְתָּ֗ר מֵֽחַמָּתֽוֹ׃

תּ֘וֹרַ֤ת יְהֹוָ֣ה תְּ֭מִימָה מְשִׁ֣יבַת
נָ֑פֶשׁ עֵד֥וּת יְהֹוָ֥ה נֶ֝אֱמָנָ֗ה
מַחְכִּ֥ימַת פֶּֽתִי׃

5 Their influence encompasses the earth; their words reach to the end of the world. In a tent within, He placed the sun,

6 which, like a bridegroom leaving his bridal chamber, rejoices like a warrior running his course.

7 It rises from one end of the heavens, coursing the sky to the other edge; nothing escapes its heat.

8 The Torah of the Lord is perfect, restoring the soul; the testimony of the Lord can be trusted, making the simpleton wise.

---

5 **Their influence encompasses the earth; their words reach to the end of the world.** Even though the declarations of the sky and of time have no voice and cannot actually be heard, they are transmitted to the ends of the earth. Their "words" are powerful enough to resound throughout the world. **In a tent within, He placed the sun.** The sky appears to serve as a dwelling place or tent for the sun, its most prominent object.

6 In describing his experience of observing the sun as it makes its way across the sky, the psalmist portrays the sunrise, **which** is **like a bridegroom leaving his bridal chamber;** the sun is blushing a little, but very happy. As it continues across the sky, it **rejoices like a warrior running his course,** not letting up its powerful run for a moment.

7 **It rises from one end of the heavens, coursing the sky to the other edge; nothing escapes its heat.** The sun begins its run at one end of the sky, completes its arc, and concludes at the other end. All the while, as it shines and illuminates the earth, it evokes the full power of a warrior racing across the sky. No one is able to stop it.

8 The preceding verses describe the ways in which the skies, by their very existence, speak to someone who is able to hear them. The second part of this psalm is a hymn in praise of the Torah and its commandments. It is composed of six phrases, each of which describes a specific aspect of the Torah, followed by a quality inherently related to that aspect. A similar structure is found in Psalm 119. **The Torah of the Lord is perfect, restoring the soul,** bringing inner

פְּקוּדֵי יהוה יְשָׁרִים
מְשַׂמְּחֵי־לֵב מִצְוַת יהוה
בָּרָה מְאִירַת עֵינָיִם:

יִרְאַת יהוה ׀ טְהוֹרָה
עוֹמֶדֶת לָעַד מִשְׁפְּטֵי־יהוה
אֱמֶת צָדְקוּ יַחְדָּו:

9 The precepts of the Lord are upright, gladdening the heart; the commandments of the Lord are clear, enlightening the eyes.

10 Fear of the Lord is pure and endures forever; the judgments of the Lord are true and altogether righteous.

---

peace, a quality that is pure and unblemished. The reality of our world is replete with defects, dishonesty, cheating, and plotting; all result in spiritual exhaustion. The act of becoming absorbed in the Torah, which is whole and unblemished, soothes and restores the soul. **The testimony,** or Torah, **of the Lord can be trusted, making the simpleton,** one who lacks knowledge and understanding, **wise.** When the simpleton opens his mouth to explain something, his reasoning is usually distorted or inaccurate. However, when one states true, incontrovertible facts without elaboration, he speaks words of wisdom. This form of faithfulness can make even a simpleton wise.

9 **The precepts of the Lord,** namely, the commandments, **are upright, gladdening the heart.** A connection between uprightness and joy is found in several other places, for example, in Psalms 97:11: "Light is sown for the righteous, and joy for the upright of heart." Uprightness of heart is a state of being that leaves no room for deviation or circumvention, no way of getting around the truth. A man who is not honest at heart is preoccupied with doubts and accountings; he is unable to enjoy anything, even good times. But one who is true to his heart is unencumbered by such complications. He is able to see things as they are and to accept them with joy. For this reason, God's commandments bring joy to the heart; they are devoid of fraudulence. **The commandments of the Lord are clear, enlightening the eyes.** The commandments are described as "clear" in the sense of being pristine, pure. Although it is possible to see through something that is fogged or polluted by impurities, the eyes are strained in the process. By contrast, God's commandments, which are clear, spotless, and devoid of any impurities, brighten the eyes and clarify vision.

10 **Fear of the Lord is pure and endures forever.** "Fear of the Lord" does not merely describe a relationship with God. In this context, it is also almost synonymous with the Torah, which is pure and eternal. The more complex something is, the more likely it is to change and eventually wear out. Complicated machinery is apt to malfunction when any of its interconnected parts are faulty. In contrast, something that is completely and intrinsically pure, even in the simplest physical sense, is more stable, as it contains no foreign matter, nothing liable to break down. This is also true of fear of God, which is pure in the most absolute sense; It endures forever because nothing can possibly damage it. **The judgments of the Lord are true and altogether righteous.** This verse, as with those preceding it, deals with a definition of truth. Something is "altogether" true when its

הַנֶּחֱמָדִים מִזָּהָב וּמִפַּז רָב
וּמְתוּקִים מִדְּבַשׁ וְנֹפֶת
צוּפִים:

11 They are more desirable than gold, than quantities of fine gold, and sweeter than honey and the juices of ripe fruit.

גַּם־עַבְדְּךָ נִזְהָר בָּהֶם
בְּשָׁמְרָם עֵקֶב רָב:

12 Your servant as well is mindful of them, heeding them to the utmost.

שְׁגִיאוֹת מִי־יָבִין מִנִּסְתָּרוֹת
נַקֵּנִי:

13 Who can discern his errors? Acquit me of hidden faults.

גַּם מִזֵּדִים ׀ חֲשֹׂךְ עַבְדֶּךָ אַל־
יִמְשְׁלוּ־בִי אָז אֵיתָם וְנִקֵּיתִי
מִפֶּשַׁע רָב:

14 And keep Your servant far from sinners; let them not have dominion over me. Then I will be blameless and cleansed of great transgression.

---

separate parts are not contradictory when combined with one another; they remain true whether the components are seen individually or as a whole.

11 A more emotional description of the Torah follows: **They,** words of Torah and the commandments, **are more desirable than gold, than quantities of fine gold.** They are objects of desire, more precious than the finest gold. **And** they are **sweeter than honey and the juices of ripe fruit.** Moreover, while gold has no taste, words of Torah are sweet. These figurative definitions of Torah and the commandments serve as an appropriate transition to the third, most personal part of the psalm:

12 **Your servant,** I, the psalmist, **as well is mindful of them,** the commandments, **heeding them to the utmost.** The psalmist avows that even in places where observance of the commandments is difficult, he is always conscientious in following God's precepts. The phrase *ekev rav*, translated here as "to the utmost," can also be understood to mean "crooked places." Despite his vigilance, the psalmist goes on to acknowledge that there are obstacles to perfect observance:

13 **Who can discern his errors?** At times, an individual is apt to err unknowingly. Who can possibly be certain that his actions are faultless? **Acquit me of hidden faults.** The psalmist beseeches God: I need You to absolve me of misdeeds carried out unwittingly. Man cannot know what is hidden from him.[6]

14 There is an additional factor that can lead to a person's downfall, namely, other people. **And keep Your servant far from sinners.** Protect me from the spiritually malevolent influence of evildoers. **Let them not have dominion over me,** for if they have me in their control they will be able to negatively impact my behavior. If You absolve me of mistakes I have made due to lack of knowledge or lack of understanding, and if You acquit me concerning matters I have done

טו יִהְיֽוּ לְרָצֽוֹן ׀ אִמְרֵי־פִֿי וְהֶגְיֽוֹן
לִבִּֿי לְפָנֶֽיךָ יהוה צוּרִי וְגֹאֲלִֽי:

15 Let the words of my mouth
and the meditation of my heart
be acceptable before you, Lord,
my rock and my redeemer.

PSALM 20

A psalm of intermingled prayer, supplication, and praise.

א לַמְנַצֵּחַ מִזְמֽוֹר לְדָוִֽד:

ב יַֽעַנְךָ יהוה בְּיֽוֹם צָרָה יְשַׂגֶּבְךָ
שֵׁם ׀ אֱלֹהֵי יַעֲקֹב:

ג יִשְׁלַח־עֶזְרְךָ מִקֹּֽדֶשׁ וּמִצִּיּֽוֹן
יִסְעָדֶֽךָ:

1 To the chief musician, a psalm
by David.

2 May the Lord answer you at a
time of trouble; may the name
of the God of Jacob fortify you.

3 May He send you help from
the Sanctuary and support you
from Zion.

---

as a result of external factors beyond my control, **then I will be blameless and cleansed of great transgression.**

15 The psalm concludes with a prayer: **Let the words of my mouth and the meditation of my heart,** sentiments that were not expressed verbally, **be acceptable before you, Lord, my rock and my redeemer.** In summary, it may be said that this psalm expresses a parallel between the glory of God as it is perceived by contemplating the heavens and the glory of God as revealed through Torah study. The third section of the psalm, then, is a kind of specific, personal conclusion that derives from the general sentiments expressed in the first two sections.

PSALM 20

1 **To the chief musician, a psalm by David.** This psalm appears to be a request on behalf of the king rather than a prayer of the king as a private individual. Therefore, some commentators interpret the word *leDavid* in this verse to mean "on behalf of David" and his reign.

2 **May the Lord answer you at a time of trouble; may the name of the God of Jacob fortify you.**

3 **May He send you help from the Sanctuary,** from His dwelling place on earth, **and support you from Zion,** the Temple Mount.

יִזְכֹּר כָּל־מִנְחֹתֶיךָ וְעוֹלָתְךָ
יְדַשְּׁנֶה סֶלָה:

⁴ May He remember all your
offerings and accept your burnt
offering, Selah.

יִתֶּן־לְךָ כִלְבָבֶךָ וְכָל־עֲצָתְךָ
יְמַלֵּא:

⁵ May He grant you your heart's
desire and fulfill all your plans.

נְרַנְּנָה ׀ בִּישׁוּעָתֶךָ וּבְשֵׁם־
אֱלֹהֵינוּ נִדְגֹּל יְמַלֵּא יְהוָה
כָּל־מִשְׁאֲלוֹתֶיךָ:

⁶ We will sing with joy at your
salvation and raise banners in
the name of our God. May the
Lord fulfill all your wishes.

עַתָּה יָדַעְתִּי כִּי הוֹשִׁיעַ ׀
יְהוָה מְשִׁיחוֹ יַעֲנֵהוּ מִשְּׁמֵי
קָדְשׁוֹ בִּגְבוּרוֹת יֵשַׁע יְמִינוֹ:

⁷ Now I know that the Lord
has rescued His anointed one;
He will answer him from His
holy heavens, with the mighty
strength of His right hand.

אֵלֶּה בָרֶכֶב וְאֵלֶּה בַסּוּסִים
וַאֲנַחְנוּ ׀ בְּשֵׁם־יְהוָה אֱלֹהֵינוּ
נַזְכִּיר:

⁸ Some come on chariots and
some on horses, but we invoke
the name of the Lord our God.

---

4 **May He remember** favorably **all your offerings** that you have brought to Him in the past, **and accept your burnt offering, Selah.** The word *yedashne*, translated here as "accept," is related to *deshen*, referring to fatness and choice quality. The psalmist prays: May your burnt offerings be accepted as the choicest of gifts.

5 **May He grant you your heart's desire and fulfill all your plans.**

6 **We will sing with joy at your salvation and raise banners in the name of our God,** in glorification of God's name; we will glorify His name as if waving it above us like a flag. **May the Lord fulfill all your wishes.**

7 **Now,** when victory comes, **I know that the Lord has rescued His anointed one,** the king of Israel; **He will answer him** and his prayers **from His holy heavens, with the mighty strength of His right hand,** which represents God's attributes of strength and beneficence. God provides the power to subdue the enemy, and He bestows the gift of redemption on the righteous.

8 **Some** of our adversaries **come** to wage war riding **on chariots,** the most formidable tool of war in ancient times, **and some on horses,** adding the elements of strength and swiftness to the attacking army, **but we invoke the name of the Lord our God.** We may not be armed with the most sophisticated weaponry, but we know that weapons do not determine the outcome of the battle; we derive our strength from God.

ט הֵ֣מָּה כָּרְע֣וּ וְנָפָ֑לוּ וַאֲנַ֥חְנוּ
קַ֗מְנוּ וַנִּתְעוֹדָֽד׃

יְהֹוָ֥ה הוֹשִׁ֑יעָה הַמֶּ֥לֶךְ יַעֲנֵ֖נוּ
בְיֽוֹם־קׇרְאֵֽנוּ׃

9 They collapse and fall; we rise and take heart.

10 Deliver us, Lord. The King will answer us on the day we call.

PSALM 21

A psalm in which the righteous king exalts and gives thanks to God;
he trusts in God to overcome his enemies.

א לַמְנַצֵּ֗חַ מִזְמ֥וֹר לְדָוִֽד׃

יְהֹוָ֗ה בְּעׇזְּךָ֥ יִשְׂמַח־מֶ֑לֶךְ
וּ֝בִישׁ֥וּעָ֣תְךָ֗ מַה־יָּ֥גֶל מְאֹֽד׃

תַּאֲוַ֣ת לִ֭בּוֹ נָתַ֣תָּה לּ֑וֹ
וַאֲרֶ֥שֶׁת שְׂ֝פָתָ֗יו בַּל־מָנַ֥עְתָּ
סֶּֽלָה׃

כִּֽי־תְקַדְּמֶ֗נּוּ בִּרְכ֣וֹת ט֑וֹב
תָּשִׁ֥ית לְ֝רֹאשׁ֗וֹ עֲטֶ֥רֶת פָּֽז׃

1 To the chief musician, a psalm by David.

2 The king has joy in Your strength, Lord; how greatly he rejoices in Your salvation.

3 You gave him his heart's desire. You did not deny the request of his lips, Selah.

4 You greet him with blessings of goodness; You set a crown of pure gold upon his head.

---

9 **They collapse and fall; we rise and take heart.**
10 **Deliver us, Lord. The King** of the Universe **will answer us on the day we call.**

PSALM 21
1 **To the chief musician, a psalm by David.**
2 **The king has joy in Your strength, Lord; how greatly he rejoices in Your salvation.**
3 **You gave him his heart's desire. You did not deny** his prayers, **the request of his lips, Selah.**
4 **You greet him with blessings of goodness,** literally, "You precede him with blessings"; even before he approaches You, You bestow Your blessings on him. **You set a crown of pure gold upon his head.**

חַיִּים ׀ שָׁאַל מִמְּךָ נָתַתָּה לּוֹ
אֹרֶךְ יָמִים עוֹלָם וָעֶד:

גָּדוֹל כְּבוֹדוֹ בִּישׁוּעָתֶךָ הוֹד
וְהָדָר תְּשַׁוֶּה עָלָיו:

כִּי־תְשִׁיתֵהוּ בְרָכוֹת לָעַד
תְּחַדֵּהוּ בְשִׂמְחָה אֶת־פָּנֶיךָ:

כִּי־הַמֶּלֶךְ בֹּטֵחַ בַּיהוָה
וּבְחֶסֶד עֶלְיוֹן בַּל־יִמּוֹט:

תִּמְצָא יָדְךָ לְכָל־אֹיְבֶיךָ
יְמִינְךָ תִּמְצָא שֹׂנְאֶיךָ:

5 He asked You for life; You gave him length of days, forevermore.

6 His honor is great in Your salvation; You bestow splendor and glory upon him.

7 For You set blessings upon him continually; You make him exceedingly joyous in Your presence.

8 For the king trusts in the Lord; in the kindness of the Most High he will not stumble.

9 Your hand will find all your enemies; your right hand will find those who hate you.

---

5 **He asked You for life; You gave him** not only life for the moment but great longevity and **length of days.** May it be Your will that this continue **forevermore.**

6 **His honor is great in Your salvation.** The help You give him to win battles increases his honor and majesty. **You bestow splendor and glory upon him.**

7 **For You set** him as a recipient of **blessings** bestowed **upon him continually; You make him exceedingly joyous in Your presence.**

8 **For the king trusts in the Lord; in the kindness of the Most High he will not stumble.**

9 The psalmist now addresses the king: **Your hand will find,** reach, **all your enemies; your right hand will find those who hate you.**

תְּשִׁיתֵמוֹ ׀ כְּתַנּוּר אֵשׁ לְעֵת
פָּנֶיךָ יְהוָה בְּאַפּוֹ יְבַלְּעֵם
וְתֹאכְלֵם אֵשׁ:

פִּרְיָמוֹ מֵאֶרֶץ תְּאַבֵּד וְזַרְעָם
מִבְּנֵי אָדָם:

כִּי־נָטוּ עָלֶיךָ רָעָה חָשְׁבוּ
מְזִמָּה בַּל־יוּכָלוּ:

כִּי תְּשִׁיתֵמוֹ שֶׁכֶם בְּמֵיתָרֶיךָ
תְּכוֹנֵן עַל־פְּנֵיהֶם:

רוּמָה יְהוָה בְּעֻזֶּךָ נָשִׁירָה
וּנְזַמְּרָה גְּבוּרָתֶךָ:

10 You will make them like a fiery oven at the time of your anger; the Lord will consume them with His wrath and let fire devour them.

11 You will destroy their offspring from the earth, and their descendants from among the sons of man.

12 Though they were inclined to evil against you, devising plots, they will not succeed.

13 For You make them turn back; You aim Your bowstring at their faces.

14 Be exalted, Lord, in Your strength; we will sing and praise Your might.

---

10 **You will make them like a fiery oven at the time of your anger; the Lord will consume them with His wrath and let fire devour them.** When you direct your anger at your enemies, they will burn as if in a furnace. The fire of God's fury will consume them.

11 **You will destroy their offspring from the earth, and their descendants from among the sons of man.**

12 **Though they were inclined to evil against you, devising plots, they will not succeed.**

13 **For You make them turn back.** *Teshitemo shekhem* might also mean "You make them into targets," as **You aim Your bowstring at their faces.** You shoot them with arrows from Your bow.

14 In conclusion: **Be exalted, Lord, in Your strength.** Let the greatness of Your power be revealed to us, and then **we will sing and praise Your might.**

PSALM 22

A psalm that begins as a psalm of entreaty, a cry for help by someone who is isolated
and surrounded by numerous enemies. It ends as a hymn of praise for the psalmist's salvation,
which can be a source of hope for others.

לַמְנַצֵּחַ עַל־אַיֶּלֶת הַשַּׁחַר
מִזְמוֹר לְדָוִד:

אֵלִי אֵלִי לָמָה עֲזַבְתָּנִי רָחוֹק
מִישׁוּעָתִי דִּבְרֵי שַׁאֲגָתִי:

אֱלֹהַי אֶקְרָא יוֹמָם וְלֹא
תַעֲנֶה וְלַיְלָה וְלֹא־דוּמִיָּה לִי:

וְאַתָּה קָדוֹשׁ יוֹשֵׁב תְּהִלּוֹת
יִשְׂרָאֵל:

בְּךָ בָּטְחוּ אֲבֹתֵינוּ בָּטְחוּ
וַתְּפַלְּטֵמוֹ:

1 To the chief musician on *ayelet hashaḥar*, a psalm by David.

2 My God, my God, why have You forsaken me? So far from my deliverance are the words of my anguished cry.

3 My God, I call You by day, but You do not answer; by night I have no solace.

4 Yet You are holy, enthroned in the praises of Israel.

5 In You our fathers placed their trust; they trusted, and You rescued them.

PSALM 22

1 **To the chief musician on *ayelet hashaḥar*, a psalm by David.** *Ayelet hashaḥar*, literally, "morning star" in Hebrew, refers to the first light visible long before sunrise. It was probably the name of the melody used for this psalm.

2 **My God, my God, why have You forsaken me?** This verse describes how the psalmist feels: Alone, pursued by adversaries, and abandoned by God. **So far from my deliverance are the words of my anguished cry.** In this context, "my deliverance" may refer to God. The psalmist feels that his cries are so distant from God that it seems as if they cannot reach Him.

3 **My God, I call You by day, but You do not answer; by night I have no solace.** I pray day and night, but my soul is not at peace.

4 **Yet You are holy, enthroned in the praises of Israel.** God is portrayed by the psalmist as sitting on a throne made of songs of praise sung to Him by generations of the people of Israel.

5 **In You our fathers placed their trust; they trusted, and You rescued them.** You delivered them from their sufferings.

אֵלֶיךָ זָעֲקוּ וְנִמְלָטוּ בְּךָ
בָטְחוּ וְלֹא־בֽוֹשׁוּ:

וְאָנֹכִי תוֹלַעַת וְלֹא־אִישׁ
חֶרְפַּת אָדָם וּבְזוּי עָם:

כָּל־רֹאַי יַלְעִגוּ לִי יַפְטִירוּ
בְשָׂפָה יָנִיעוּ רֹאשׁ:

גֹּל אֶל־יהוה יְפַלְּטֵהוּ יַצִּילֵהוּ
כִּי חָפֵץ בּוֹ:

כִּי־אַתָּה גֹחִי מִבָּטֶן מַבְטִיחִי
עַל־שְׁדֵי אִמִּי:

עָלֶיךָ הָשְׁלַכְתִּי מֵרָחֶם מִבֶּטֶן
אִמִּי אֵלִי אָתָּה:

6 They cried out to You and escaped, trusted in You and were not disappointed.

7 But I am a worm and not a man; an object of disgrace, scorned by the masses.

8 All who see me revile me, rejecting me with curled lip and wagging head.

9 Let him turn toward the Lord; let Him rescue him, let Him save him, for He delights in him.

10 For You brought me forth from the womb; You made me secure at my mother's breast.

11 I have been cast upon You from the womb; from my mother's belly, You have been my God.

---

6 **They cried out to You and escaped** from their precarious situations, **trusted in You and were not disappointed.**

7 **But I am a worm and not a man** in the eyes of my detractors; **an object of disgrace, scorned by the masses.**

8 **All who see me revile me, rejecting me with curled lip and wagging head.** Their insults are not even fully articulated; they consist of half-phrases accompanied by contemptuous snarls and head-shaking gesticulations, whether of contempt or pity.

9 **Let him turn toward the Lord; let Him rescue him, let Him save him, for He delights in him.** These are the words of the psalmist, voicing his inner feelings toward others.

10 **For You brought me forth from the womb; You made me secure at my mother's breast.**

11 **I have been cast upon You** to be dependent upon You **from the womb; from my mother's belly, You have been my God.** From earliest childhood, I have relied on You.

אַל־תִּרְחַק מִמֶּנִּי כִּי־צָרָה
קְרוֹבָה כִּי־אֵין עוֹזֵר:

סְבָבוּנִי פָּרִים רַבִּים אַבִּירֵי
בָשָׁן כִּתְּרוּנִי:

פָּצוּ עָלַי פִּיהֶם אַרְיֵה טֹרֵף
וְשֹׁאֵג:

כַּמַּיִם נִשְׁפַּכְתִּי וְהִתְפָּרְדוּ
כָּל־עַצְמוֹתָי הָיָה לִבִּי כַּדּוֹנָג
נָמֵס בְּתוֹךְ מֵעָי:

יָבֵשׁ כַּחֶרֶשׂ ׀ כֹּחִי וּלְשׁוֹנִי
מֻדְבָּק מַלְקוֹחָי וְלַעֲפַר־מָוֶת
תִּשְׁפְּתֵנִי:

כִּי סְבָבוּנִי כְּלָבִים עֲדַת
מְרֵעִים הִקִּיפוּנִי כָּאֲרִי יָדַי
וְרַגְלָי:

12 Be not far from me, for trouble is near and there is no one to help.

13 I am surrounded by many bulls, encircled by the mighty bulls of Bashan.

14 They open their mouths at me like a rapacious, roaring lion.

15 I am spilled out like water; all my bones are disjointed. My heart is like wax, melting within me.

16 My vitality is parched like clay; my tongue cleaves to my palate. You have consigned me to the dust of death.

17 For dogs have surrounded me, a band of evildoers have encircled me, like a lion at my hands and feet.

---

12 **Be not far from me, for trouble is near and there is no one** else **to help.**

13 **I am surrounded by** enemies that are like **many bulls,** large and dangerous animals, **encircled by the mighty bulls of Bashan,** an unusually large kind of cattle.

14 **They open their mouths at me like a rapacious, roaring lion.**

15 **I am spilled out like water.** I feel depleted and vulnerable. **All my bones are disjointed. My heart is like wax, melting within me.** I have no inner strength to draw on.

16 **My vitality is parched like clay; my tongue cleaves to my palate. You have consigned me to the dust of death.** I feel barely alive; You have brought me to the brink of death.

17 **For dogs have surrounded me.** The psalmist compares his enemies to hungry dogs. **A band of evildoers have encircled me, like a lion at my hands and feet.** I am surrounded by hordes of terrifying, evil foes. I am devastated and broken.

יח אֲסַפֵּר כָּל־עַצְמוֹתָי הֵמָּה
יַבִּיטוּ יִרְאוּ־בִי:

יט יְחַלְּקוּ בְגָדַי לָהֶם וְעַל־
לְבוּשִׁי יַפִּילוּ גוֹרָל:

כ וְאַתָּה יהוה אַל־תִּרְחָק
אֱיָלוּתִי לְעֶזְרָתִי חוּשָׁה:

כא הַצִּילָה מֵחֶרֶב נַפְשִׁי מִיַּד־
כֶּלֶב יְחִידָתִי:

כב הוֹשִׁיעֵנִי מִפִּי אַרְיֵה וּמִקַּרְנֵי
רֵמִים עֲנִיתָנִי:

כג אֲסַפְּרָה שִׁמְךָ לְאֶחָי בְּתוֹךְ
קָהָל אֲהַלְלֶךָּ:

18 I count all my bones; they gaze and look at me.

19 They divide my garments among them and cast lots for my clothing.

20 But You, Lord, be not far off. My Strength, hasten to help me.

21 Rescue me from the sword, my soul from the grasp of the dog.

22 Save me from the lion's mouth, from the horns of the oryx; answer me.

23 I will tell of Your name to my brothers; in the midst of the assembly I will praise You.

---

18 **I count all my bones,** because I feel that they are shattered. **They gaze and look at me.** My enemies are on the alert, waiting for my final downfall.

19 Even while I am still alive, **they divide my garments among them and cast lots for my clothing,** to decide who will get each garment.

20 **But You, Lord, be not far off. My Strength, hasten to help me.**

21 **Rescue me from the sword, my soul from the grasp of the dog** that stands ready to attack me. The word *yeḥidati*, which means something singular and unique, is used here as a synonym for "my soul."

22 **Save me from the lion's mouth, from the horns of the oryx; answer me,** rescue me from these vicious animals.

23 The concluding verses of the psalm may have been composed at a later date, after the psalmist had been rescued from danger: **I will tell of Your name to my brothers; in the midst of the assembly I will praise You.** I will tell my kinsmen that You have rescued me from danger.

כד יִרְאֵי יְהוָֹה ׀ הַלְלוּהוּ כָּל־זֶרַע
יַעֲקֹב כַּבְּדוּהוּ וְגוּרוּ מִמֶּנּוּ
כָּל־זֶרַע יִשְׂרָאֵל:

כה כִּי לֹא־בָזָה וְלֹא שִׁקַּץ עֱנוּת
עָנִי וְלֹא־הִסְתִּיר פָּנָיו מִמֶּנּוּ
וּבְשַׁוְּעוֹ אֵלָיו שָׁמֵעַ:

כו מֵאִתְּךָ תְּהִלָּתִי בְּקָהָל רָב
נְדָרַי אֲשַׁלֵּם נֶגֶד יְרֵאָיו:

כז יֹאכְלוּ עֲנָוִים ׀ וְיִשְׂבָּעוּ יְהַלְלוּ
יְהוָֹה דֹּרְשָׁיו יְחִי לְבַבְכֶם
לָעַד:

²⁴ You who fear the Lord, praise Him; may the progeny of Jacob honor Him, and may the progeny of Israel fear Him.

²⁵ For He did not despise or abhor the plea of the poor person, nor did He hide His face from him; when he cried to Him, He heard.

²⁶ My praise will be of You in the great assembly; I will fulfill my vows in the presence of those who fear Him.

²⁷ The humble will eat and be satiated. Those who seek Him will praise the Lord; may your hearts be forever alive.

---

²⁴ **You who fear the Lord, praise Him; may the progeny of Jacob honor Him, and may the progeny of Israel fear Him.**

²⁵ **For** I, by my very survival, am testimony to the fact that **He did not despise or abhor the plea of the poor person, nor did He hide His face from him; when he cried to Him, He heard.**

²⁶ **My praise will be of You in the great assembly.** I will praise You now in public, and **I will fulfill,** also in public, **my vows** that I made in my time of distress, **in the presence of those who fear Him.**

²⁷ **The humble will eat and be satiated. Those who seek Him will praise the Lord; may your hearts be forever alive** due to your hope for God and His salvation.

כח יִזְכְּרוּ ׀ וְיָשֻׁבוּ אֶל־יהוה כָּל־
אַפְסֵי־אָרֶץ וְיִשְׁתַּחֲווּ לְפָנֶיךָ
כָּל־מִשְׁפְּחוֹת גּוֹיִם:

כט כִּי לַיהוה הַמְּלוּכָה וּמֹשֵׁל
בַּגּוֹיִם:

ל אָכְלוּ וַיִּשְׁתַּחֲווּ ׀ כָּל־דִּשְׁנֵי־
אֶרֶץ לְפָנָיו יִכְרְעוּ כָּל־יוֹרְדֵי
עָפָר וְנַפְשׁוֹ לֹא חִיָּה:

לא זֶרַע יַעַבְדֶנּוּ יְסֻפַּר לַאדֹנָי
לַדּוֹר:

לב יָבֹאוּ וְיַגִּידוּ צִדְקָתוֹ לְעַם
נוֹלָד כִּי עָשָׂה:

[28] The ends of the earth will all remember and return to the Lord; all families of nations will bow down before You.

[29] For kingship belongs to the Lord; He rules over nations.

[30] The well-fed of the earth have all eaten and bowed down before Him; all who return to the dust kneel before Him; is there a soul to whom He has not given life?

[31] Posterity will serve Him; coming generations will be told of the Lord.

[32] They will come and declare His righteousness to a nation yet to be born, for so He has done.

---

[28] **The ends of the earth will all remember and return to the Lord; all families of nations will bow down before You.**

[29] **For kingship belongs to the Lord; He rules over nations.**

[30] **The well-fed of the earth have all eaten and bowed down before Him; all who return to the dust,** that is, all men, **kneel before Him; is there a soul to whom He has not given life?** Everyone alive is sustained by God. Every living, mortal soul, both privileged, prosperous people and those who are impoverished, should bow down in gratitude before God.

[31] **Posterity will serve Him; coming generations will be told of the Lord.**

[32] **They will come and declare His righteousness to a nation yet to be born,** to future generations, **for so He has done.** He has granted salvation to men in their times of distress.

PSALM 23

A psalm of devotion, in which the psalmist envisions himself as a lamb, wholly reliant
on his devoted shepherd. The lamb trusts that the shepherd will lead him on a secure path
and provide him with a dwelling in a good and happy place. Although it likely contains allusions
to specific events in King David's life, the simple eloquence of this psalm has universal appeal,
and it is therefore frequently recited in public as well as in private prayer.

מִזְמוֹר לְדָוִד יהוה רֹעִי לֹא
אֶחְסָר:

א

¹ A psalm by David. The Lord is
my shepherd; I lack nothing.

ד לחודש
4th day
of month

בִּנְאוֹת דֶּשֶׁא יַרְבִּיצֵנִי עַל־מֵי
מְנֻחוֹת יְנַהֲלֵנִי:

ב

² He has me lie down in green
pastures; He leads me beside
still waters.

נַפְשִׁי יְשׁוֹבֵב יַנְחֵנִי בְמַעְגְּלֵי־
צֶדֶק לְמַעַן שְׁמוֹ:

ג

³ He restores my soul; He leads
me in paths of righteousness
for His name's sake.

PSALM 23

¹ **A psalm by David. The Lord is my shepherd.** Taking on the perspective of the lamb, the
psalmist expresses gratitude to the shepherd for all he does. The meaning of this metaphor, which
is maintained throughout much of the psalm, is self-evident. Because God watches over me, **I
lack nothing.**

² **He has me lie down in green pastures.** Wherever I go, He provides me with resources that
offer food and rest. **He leads me beside still,** gently flowing **waters,** streams that provide water
in abundance without the danger that a strong current could pose to a lamb.

³ **He restores my soul.** The root of the Hebrew word *yeshovev*, translated here as "He restores,"
sometimes means "to grant rest," but its basic meaning is "to return." When a man's soul is troubled
or worried, it is not at peace; it is as if it is not in its natural place, but rather it is distanced and
dislocated. When the soul returns to its true place, the result is inner peace. **He leads me in paths
of righteousness.** *Maglei tzedek*, translated as "paths of righteousness," can also mean "correct
paths," ones that are fitting for the occasion. In the metaphor of the lamb and the shepherd, they
represent paths suitable for a lamb to tread. In human terms, the phrase refers to one's course in
life, a pathway that enables a person to maintain his righteousness and does not provide negative
influences that contradict that goal. **For His name's sake.** God cares for us for His own sake, not
necessarily because we are deserving of His protection. Whatever God's motivation, we, like the
lamb, benefit from His tender care, as through it we attain serenity.

גַּם כִּי־אֵלֵךְ בְּגֵיא צַלְמָוֶת
לֹא־אִירָא רָע כִּי־אַתָּה
עִמָּדִי שִׁבְטְךָ וּמִשְׁעַנְתֶּךָ
הֵמָּה יְנַחֲמֻנִי:

תַּעֲרֹךְ לְפָנַי ׀ שֻׁלְחָן נֶגֶד
צֹרְרָי דִּשַּׁנְתָּ בַשֶּׁמֶן רֹאשִׁי
כּוֹסִי רְוָיָה:

Even when I walk through the valley of the shadow of death, I fear no evil, for You are with me; Your rod and Your staff, they comfort me.

You prepare a table before me in the presence of my enemies. You anoint my head with oil; my cup is full.

---

4 **Even when I walk through the valley of the shadow of death;** this phrase apparently refers to a vale that is accessed by a dangerous path, surrounded by pitfalls or perilous cliffs. Even when I traverse such a place, **I fear no evil.** I walk with confidence, **for You are with me. Your rod and Your staff,** instruments used by the shepherd to guide the flock, gently prodding those that stray back to the proper path, **they comfort me.** From the perspective of the lamb, these implements are an integral part of the shepherd's image and are a source of comfort and security. The rod gives the shepherd the power to fend off enemies; the staff enables him to rescue the lamb from danger. For humans, however, a rod often represents a means of punishment. This gives the phrase a second, deeper meaning: Both Your rod, Your instrument of punishment, and Your staff, literally, "Your support stick," are a source of comfort to me, because I know that whatever You do for me is ultimately in my best interest.

5 The images in this verse belong more to the human realm, but they too have a dual meaning: **You prepare a table before me in the presence of my enemies.** "Table" is used here in the broad sense of a place to eat. Even though enemies of all kinds may be lying in wait for me, I can sit and eat in peace because You are with me, just as when the trusted shepherd is close by, the lamb can graze, unafraid of predators. **You anoint my head with oil,** referring to a practice that was meant to impart comfort, as well as cosmetic value, to one's head. **My cup is full.** Literally, this expression means "my cup is one of saturation." That is, there is enough wine in the cup to enable me to drink my fill and adequately quench my thirst.

אַךְ ׀ ט֤וֹב וָחֶ֨סֶד יִרְדְּפ֗וּנִי כָּל־
יְמֵ֥י חַיָּ֑י וְשַׁבְתִּ֥י בְּבֵית־יְ֝הֹוָ֗ה
לְאֹ֣רֶךְ יָמִֽים׃

6 May only goodness and kindness pursue me all the days of my life, and I will dwell in the House of the Lord forever.

PSALM 24

A hymn depicting two different modes of entrance to the Holy Temple:
That of man versus the majestic arrival of God.

לְדָוִ֗ד מִ֫זְמ֥וֹר לַ֭יהֹוָה הָאָ֣רֶץ
וּמְלוֹאָ֑הּ תֵּ֝בֵ֗ל וְיֹ֣שְׁבֵי בָֽהּ׃

1 By David, a psalm. The earth is the Lord's, and all that it holds, the world and all its inhabitants.

כִּי־ה֭וּא עַל־יַמִּ֣ים יְסָדָ֑הּ
וְעַל־נְ֝הָר֗וֹת יְכוֹנְנֶֽהָ׃

2 For He founded it upon the seas and established it upon the rivers.

---

6 **May only goodness and kindness pursue me all the days of my life.** The literal meaning is that the psalmist wishes for his entire life to be composed of experiences that are good and pleasant. Yet the phrase "pursue me" would seem somewhat inappropriate in this context. It might be explained as follows: At times, a person does not recognize the path in life that will bring him happiness and therefore does not follow it. In such a case, he feels grateful when this path of goodness and kindness actively "pursues" him, as it were, and finds him despite his own lack of initiative. **And I will dwell in the House of the Lord forever.** Relieved of fear of adversity, my happiness complete, I will be able to spend my time in the House of God, singing His praises without want or worry.

PSALM 24

1 **By David, a psalm. The earth is the Lord's, and all that it holds,** namely, **the world and all its inhabitants.**

2 **For He founded it upon the seas.** The terrain of the earth towers over the ocean below, as a building rises above its foundations. **And established it upon the rivers.** The water flowing in the rivers has its origin in subterranean springs, upon which the earth is situated.

מִי־יַעֲלֶ֥ה בְהַר־יְהוָ֑ה וּמִי־
יָ֝ק֗וּם בִּמְק֥וֹם קָדְשֽׁוֹ׃

נְקִ֥י כַפַּ֗יִם וּֽבַר־לֵ֫בָ֥ב אֲשֶׁ֤ר
לֹא־נָשָׂ֣א לַשָּׁ֣וְא נַפְשׁ֑וֹ וְלֹ֖א נַפְשִׁ֑י
נִשְׁבַּ֣ע לְמִרְמָֽה׃

יִשָּׂ֣א בְ֭רָכָה מֵאֵ֣ת יְהוָ֑ה
וּ֝צְדָקָ֗ה מֵאֱלֹהֵ֥י יִשְׁעֽוֹ׃

3 Who may ascend the mountain
of the Lord? Who may stand in
His holy place?

4 He who has clean hands and
a pure heart, he who has not
raised up his soul for falsehood,
nor sworn deceitfully.

5 He will receive the blessing of
the Lord, righteousness from
the God of his deliverance.

---

3 The focal point of the earth, its spiritual apex, is the Temple Mount, concerning which the psalmist asks: **Who may** be considered worthy to **ascend the mountain of the Lord? Who may stand in His holy place?** In this verse, and throughout the psalm, the "mountain of the Lord" refers both to the visible, physical Temple and to the concept of spiritual holiness on high, something that is beyond the physical world.

4 The psalmist answers the question posed in the preceding verse: **He who has clean hands and a pure heart,** that is, one who is beyond reproach both in his deeds and in his thoughts; **he who has not raised up his soul for falsehood.** He does not yearn for the attainment of false, corrupt goals. The word *nafshi*, which appears in most texts, translated here as "his soul," literally means "my soul," which is a difficult phrase in our context. There are some who reinterpret the entire psalm in order to accommodate this unusual expression. However, it may be that the psalmist, in a sudden emotional outburst, inserts his own soul into the discussion of the righteous man's virtues. **Nor** has he **sworn deceitfully.** In its plain sense, "sworn deceitfully" refers to a person who is not engaged in actual evil deeds but does allow himself to sin through false speech, even swearing a false oath. The phrase can also be translated more literally as "nor sworn for deceit." Not only is the virtuous man pure in deed and thought, as mentioned above, but he does not get involved in deceit practiced by others, through supporting them or obligating himself to ally with them through a covenantal oath.

5 **He,** the virtuous man described above, **will receive the blessing of the Lord, righteousness from the God of his deliverance.**

זֶה דּוֹר דֹּרְשָׁו מְבַקְשֵׁי פָנֶיךָ
יַעֲקֹב סֶלָה:

שְׂאוּ שְׁעָרִים ׀ רָאשֵׁיכֶם
וְהִנָּשְׂאוּ פִּתְחֵי עוֹלָם וְיָבוֹא
מֶלֶךְ הַכָּבוֹד:

מִי זֶה מֶלֶךְ הַכָּבוֹד יהוה
עִזּוּז וְגִבּוֹר יהוה גִּבּוֹר
מִלְחָמָה:

שְׂאוּ שְׁעָרִים ׀ רָאשֵׁיכֶם
וּשְׂאוּ פִּתְחֵי עוֹלָם וְיָבֹא
מֶלֶךְ הַכָּבוֹד:

מִי הוּא זֶה מֶלֶךְ הַכָּבוֹד
יהוה צְבָאוֹת הוּא מֶלֶךְ
הַכָּבוֹד סֶלָה:

6 This is the generation who seeks Him out, who seek Your countenance, the people of Jacob, Selah.

7 Lift up your heads, gates; be raised up, infinite portals, so the King of glory may enter.

8 Who is the King of glory? The Lord, strong and mighty; the Lord, mighty in battle.

9 Lift up your heads, gates; raise yourselves up, infinite portals, so the King of glory may enter.

10 Who is He, this King of glory? The Lord of hosts, He is the King of glory, Selah.

---

6 Of such people it may be said: **This is the generation who seeks Him out,** who desire to follow His ways, **who seek Your countenance, the people of Jacob, Selah.**

7 Until this point, the psalm has described those worthy of entering and worshipping in the Holy Temple; among their characteristics are modesty and humility. The psalmist now depicts God's entrance to His Holy Temple, in grandeur and majesty. He addresses the gates of the Temple: **Lift up your heads, gates; be raised up, infinite portals,** as befits the entrance of a visitor of great stature, **so the King of glory may enter.**

8 **Who is the King of glory** that I refer to? Not a human warrior or a mortal of great renown; I refer rather to **the Lord, strong and mighty; the Lord,** who enters His palace in the manner of a warrior **mighty in battle,** entering in triumphal procession.

9 The psalmist repeats his stirring call to the gates of entry to the Temple: **Lift up your heads, gates; raise yourselves up, infinite portals, so the King of glory may enter.**

10 **Who is He, this King of glory? The Lord of hosts,** the Ruler over all forces on earth and in the heavens, **He is the King of glory, Selah.**

PSALM 25

A prayer that does not deal with a specific topic but is rather the expression of one individual's
desire to go in the path of God. Like other psalms offering moral instruction, its verses are arranged,
for the most part, in alphabetical order. The final verse begins with the letter *peh*,
which may signify the end of a chapter [*perek*] or paragraph [*piska*].

א לְדָוִד אֵלֶיךָ יהוה נַפְשִׁי
אֶשָּׂא:

ב אֱלֹהַי בְּךָ בָטַחְתִּי אַל־
אֵבוֹשָׁה אַל־יַעַלְצוּ אֹיְבַי
לִי:

ג גַּם כָּל־קֹוֶיךָ לֹא יֵבֹשׁוּ יֵבֹשׁוּ
הַבּוֹגְדִים רֵיקָם:

ד דְּרָכֶיךָ יהוה הוֹדִיעֵנִי
אֹרְחוֹתֶיךָ לַמְּדֵנִי:

ה הַדְרִיכֵנִי בַאֲמִתֶּךָ ׀ וְלַמְּדֵנִי
כִּי־אַתָּה אֱלֹהֵי יִשְׁעִי אוֹתְךָ
קִוִּיתִי כָּל־הַיּוֹם:

1 By David. To You, Lord, I lift
up my soul.

2 My God, in You do I trust; do
not let me be shamed, nor let
my enemies exult over me.

3 Indeed, all those who place
their hope in You will not be
ashamed; ashamed will be
those who deal treacherously
without cause.

4 Show me Your ways, Lord;
teach me Your path.

5 Lead me in Your truth and
instruct me, for You are the
God of my salvation; in You do
I hope all day long.

PSALM 25

1 **By David. To You, Lord, I lift up my soul.** "Lifting the soul" means elevating it to a higher level,
bringing it closer to God.

2 **My God, in You do I trust,** and because I trust in You, **do not let me be shamed, nor let my
enemies exult over me.**

3 **Indeed, all those who place their hope in You will not be ashamed,** for You will come to
their aid; **ashamed will be those who deal treacherously without cause,** for no particular
gain, but out of pure malice.

4 **Show me Your ways, Lord; teach me Your path.**

5 **Lead me in Your truth and instruct me, for You are the God of my salvation; in You do
I hope all day long.**

זְכֹר־רַחֲמֶיךָ יְהוָה וַחֲסָדֶיךָ כִּי
מֵעוֹלָם הֵמָּה:

חַטֹּאות נְעוּרַי ׀ וּפְשָׁעַי אַל־
תִּזְכֹּר כְּחַסְדְּךָ זְכָר־לִי־אַתָּה
לְמַעַן טוּבְךָ יְהוָה:

טוֹב־וְיָשָׁר יְהוָה עַל־כֵּן יוֹרֶה
חַטָּאִים בַּדָּרֶךְ:

יַדְרֵךְ עֲנָוִים בַּמִּשְׁפָּט וִילַמֵּד
עֲנָוִים דַּרְכּוֹ:

כָּל־אָרְחוֹת יְהוָה חֶסֶד
וֶאֱמֶת לְנֹצְרֵי בְרִיתוֹ וְעֵדֹתָיו:

לְמַעַן־שִׁמְךָ יְהוָה וְסָלַחְתָּ
לַעֲוֹנִי כִּי רַב־הוּא:

6 Remember, Lord, Your mercy and kindness, for they are eternal.

7 Do not recall the sins of my youth nor my transgressions; remember me with Your kindness, for the sake of Your goodness, Lord.

8 Good and upright is the Lord; therefore He instructs sinners in the way.

9 He guides the humble with justice, and He teaches the humble His way.

10 All the paths of the Lord are kindness and truth, for those who keep His covenant and His precepts.

11 For the sake of Your name, Lord, and pardon my iniquity, for it is great.

---

6 **Remember, Lord, Your mercy and kindness, for they are eternal.**

7 But **do not recall the sins of my youth nor my transgressions,** committed out of impetuous, youthful desire. **Remember** for **me** my good deeds **with Your kindness, for the sake of Your goodness, Lord.**

8 **Good and upright is the Lord; therefore He instructs sinners in the** proper **way,** in order to help them find the path of goodness and integrity.

9 **He guides the humble with justice, and He teaches the humble His way.**

10 **All the paths of the Lord are kindness and truth, for those who keep His covenant and His precepts.**

11 Act **for the sake of Your name, Lord, and pardon my iniquity, for it is great.**

מִי־זֶה הָאִישׁ יְרֵא יהוה יוֹרֶנּוּ
בְּדֶרֶךְ יִבְחָר:

נַפְשׁוֹ בְּטוֹב תָּלִין וְזַרְעוֹ יִירַשׁ
אָרֶץ:

סוֹד יהוה לִירֵאָיו וּבְרִיתוֹ
לְהוֹדִיעָם:

עֵינַי תָּמִיד אֶל־יהוה כִּי
הוּא־יוֹצִיא מֵרֶשֶׁת רַגְלָי:

פְּנֵה־אֵלַי וְחָנֵּנִי כִּי־יָחִיד וְעָנִי
אָנִי:

12 Who is the man who fears the Lord, whom He instructs in the way that He chooses?

13 His soul will rest in good, and his descendants will inherit the earth.

14 The secret of the Lord is to those who fear Him; He will give them knowledge of His covenant.

15 My eyes are ever toward the Lord, for He draws my feet out of the net.

16 Turn to me and be gracious to me, for I am lonely and afflicted.

---

12 **Who is the man,** how great is the man, **who fears the Lord, whom He instructs in the way that He chooses?**

13 **His soul will rest in good.** "Rest" here can refer both to ordinary sleep and to death; the righteous man's sleep, in both senses of the word, will be peaceful. **And his descendants will inherit the earth.**

14 **The secret of the Lord is** revealed **to those who fear Him. He will give them knowledge of His covenant** expressed in the words of the Torah.

15 **My eyes are ever toward the Lord, for He draws my feet out of the net.** He rescues me from traps and pitfalls that surround me even when I am unaware that they are there.

16 **Turn to me and be gracious to me, for I am lonely and afflicted** and in need of Your help.

יז צָרוֹת לְבָבִי הִרְחִיבוּ
מִמְּצוּקוֹתַי הוֹצִיאֵנִי:

יח רְאֵה עָנְיִי וַעֲמָלִי וְשָׂא לְכָל־
חַטֹּאותָי:

יט רְאֵה־אֹיְבַי כִּי־רָבּוּ וְשִׂנְאַת
חָמָס שְׂנֵאוּנִי:

כ שָׁמְרָה נַפְשִׁי וְהַצִּילֵנִי אַל־
אֵבוֹשׁ כִּי־חָסִיתִי בָךְ:

כא תֹּם־וָיֹשֶׁר יִצְּרוּנִי כִּי קִוִּיתִיךָ:

כב פְּדֵה אֱלֹהִים אֶת־יִשְׂרָאֵל
מִכֹּל צָרוֹתָיו:

17 The troubles of my heart are widespread; free me from my distresses.

18 See my affliction and my toil and forgive all my sins.

19 Regard my enemies, for they are many; they hate me with a hatred of injustice.

20 Protect me and deliver me; do not let me be ashamed, for I take refuge in You.

21 Let integrity and uprightness preserve me, for I place my hope in You.

22 God, redeem Israel from all its troubles.

---

17 **The troubles of my heart are widespread; free me from my distresses.**
18 **See my affliction and my toil and forgive all my sins.**
19 **Regard my enemies, for they are many; they hate me with a hatred of injustice,** a hatred that is driven by their desire to unjustly rob me of my possessions.
20 **Protect me and deliver me; do not let me be ashamed, for I take refuge in You.**
21 **Let** Your **integrity and uprightness preserve me, for I place my hope in You.**
22 In conclusion, a general request on behalf of the entire nation: **God, redeem Israel from all its troubles.**

PSALM 26

A psalm in which the psalmist prays for God's help, basing his request
on his continual efforts to be as close to God as possible.

א לְדָוִד ׀ שָׁפְטֵנִי יהוה כִּי־
אֲנִי בְּתֻמִּי הָלַכְתִּי וּבַיהוה
בָּטַחְתִּי לֹא אֶמְעָד:

צְרֻפָה
צָרְפָה

ב בְּחָנֵנִי יהוה וְנַסֵּנִי צרופה
כִלְיוֹתַי וְלִבִּי:

ג כִּי־חַסְדְּךָ לְנֶגֶד עֵינָי
וְהִתְהַלַּכְתִּי בַּאֲמִתֶּךָ:

ד לֹא־יָשַׁבְתִּי עִם־מְתֵי־שָׁוְא
וְעִם נַעֲלָמִים לֹא אָבוֹא:

ה שָׂנֵאתִי קְהַל מְרֵעִים וְעִם־
רְשָׁעִים לֹא אֵשֵׁב:

1 By David. Judge me, Lord, for I have walked in innocence. I have trusted in the Lord and shall not falter.

2 Examine me, Lord, and try me; purify my mind and my heart.

3 For Your kindness is before my eyes, and I walk in Your truth.

4 I do not sit with worthless men, nor do I go with those who hide themselves.

5 I abhor the assembly of evildoers and will not sit with the wicked.

PSALM 26

1 **By David. Judge me** for my thoughts and deeds, **Lord, for I have walked in innocence. I have trusted in the Lord, and** as I have chosen to follow a path of integrity and trust in God, I trust that I **shall not falter.**

2 **Examine me, Lord, and try me,** and You will see that I truly am devoted to following Your way. **Purify my mind and my heart.**

3 **For Your kindness is before my eyes;** I set my direction toward Your acts of kindness, **and I walk in** the path of **Your truth.**

4 **I do not sit with worthless men, nor do I go with those who** must **hide themselves** because of their nefarious activities.

5 **I abhor the assembly of evildoers and will not sit with the wicked.**

אֶרְחַץ בְּנִקָּיוֹן כַּפָּי וַאֲסֹבְבָה
אֶת־מִזְבַּחֲךָ יְהוָה:

לַשְׁמִעַ בְּקוֹל תּוֹדָה וּלְסַפֵּר
כָּל־נִפְלְאוֹתֶיךָ:

ח יְהוָה אָהַבְתִּי מְעוֹן בֵּיתֶךָ
וּמְקוֹם מִשְׁכַּן כְּבוֹדֶךָ:

ט אַל־תֶּאֱסֹף עִם־חַטָּאִים
נַפְשִׁי וְעִם־אַנְשֵׁי דָמִים חַיָּי:

אֲשֶׁר־בִּידֵיהֶם זִמָּה וִימִינָם
מָלְאָה שֹּׁחַד:

יא וַאֲנִי בְּתֻמִּי אֵלֵךְ פְּדֵנִי וְחָנֵּנִי:

יב רַגְלִי עָמְדָה בְמִישׁוֹר
בְּמַקְהֵלִים אֲבָרֵךְ יְהוָה:

6 I wash my hands in purity, and I circle Your altar, Lord,

7 proclaiming thankfulness, and telling of all Your wonders.

8 Lord, I love the abode of Your House, the place where Your glory dwells.

9 Do not gather in my soul with sinners, my life with men of bloodshed,

10 who have intrigue in their hands, whose right hand is full of bribes,

11 while I go in my innocence. Redeem me and be gracious to me.

12 My foot stands on a straight path. I will bless the Lord among congregations.

---

6 Rather, **I wash my hands in purity.** This may be understood both literally and figuratively. Literally, I wash my hands in preparation for prayer to You; figuratively, I keep my hands clean of evildoing. **And I circle Your altar, Lord,** in the manner of worshippers who come to pray at the Temple,

7 **proclaiming thankfulness** there, **and telling of all Your wonders.**

8 The psalmist concludes: **Lord, I love the abode of Your House** and I frequent it, **the place where Your glory dwells.**

9 Therefore, I beseech You: **Do not gather in my soul with sinners** when You punish them; do not take **my life** along **with men of bloodshed,**

10 **who have intrigue** and evil plans **in their hands, whose right hand is full of bribes,**

11 **while I go in my innocence.** Therefore, **redeem me and be gracious to me.**

12 **My foot stands on a straight path. I will bless the Lord among** the **congregations** of the righteous who pray to Him.

PSALM 27

A psalm that combines gratitude for the past and
supplication for the future, essentially a hymn of closeness to God.

לְדָוִד ׀ יְהֹוָה ׀ אוֹרִי וְיִשְׁעִי
מִמִּי אִירָא יְהֹוָה מָעוֹז־חַיַּי
מִמִּי אֶפְחָד:

בִּקְרֹב עָלַי ׀ מְרֵעִים לֶאֱכֹל
אֶת־בְּשָׂרִי צָרַי וְאֹיְבַי לִי
הֵמָּה כָשְׁלוּ וְנָפָלוּ:

אִם־תַּחֲנֶה עָלַי ׀ מַחֲנֶה לֹא־
יִירָא לִבִּי אִם־תָּקוּם עָלַי
מִלְחָמָה בְּזֹאת אֲנִי בוֹטֵחַ:

אַחַת ׀ שָׁאַלְתִּי מֵאֵת־יְהֹוָה
אוֹתָהּ אֲבַקֵּשׁ שִׁבְתִּי בְּבֵית־
יְהֹוָה כָּל־יְמֵי חַיַּי לַחֲזוֹת
בְּנֹעַם־יְהֹוָה וּלְבַקֵּר בְּהֵיכָלוֹ:

By David. The Lord is my
light and my salvation; whom
shall I fear? The Lord is the
stronghold of my life; of whom
shall I be afraid?

2 When evildoers come upon
me to devour my flesh, my foes
and my adversaries, it is they
who stumble and fall.

3 If an army besieges me, my
heart will not fear. If war comes
upon me, I will put my trust
in this.

4 One request have I made of
the Lord; this is what I ask for:
That I may dwell in the House
of the Lord all the days of my
life, to behold the goodness
of the Lord and to visit
His Temple.

PSALM 27

1 **By David. The Lord is my light and my salvation.** Consequently, **whom shall I fear? The Lord is the stronghold of my life; of whom shall I be afraid?**

2 **When evildoers come upon me to devour my flesh, my foes and my adversaries, it is they who stumble and fall.**

3 **If an army besieges me, my heart will not fear. If war comes upon me, I will put my trust in this,** in the realization that God is my light and my salvation.

4 The psalmist is aware that God is his Protector and he is grateful for that. But his foremost desire and wish is in a different direction altogether. **One request have I made of the Lord; this**

כִּי יִצְפְּנֵנִי ׀ בְּסֻכֹּה בְּיוֹם רָעָה יַסְתִּרֵנִי בְּסֵתֶר אָהֳלוֹ בְּצוּר יְרוֹמְמֵנִי׃

5 For in time of trouble He shelters me in His pavilion. He conceals me in the secret of His tent; He sets me high upon a mighty rock,

וְעַתָּה יָרוּם רֹאשִׁי עַל אֹיְבַי סְבִיבוֹתַי וְאֶזְבְּחָה בְאָהֳלוֹ זִבְחֵי תְרוּעָה אָשִׁירָה וַאֲזַמְּרָה לַיהוָה׃

6 so that now my head rises above my enemies around me. I will offer victory sacrifices in His tent; I will sing songs of praise to the Lord.

שְׁמַע־יְהוָה קוֹלִי אֶקְרָא וְחָנֵּנִי וַעֲנֵנִי׃

7 Hear, Lord, when I cry out. Be gracious to me and answer me.

לְךָ ׀ אָמַר לִבִּי בַּקְּשׁוּ פָנָי אֶת־פָּנֶיךָ יְהוָה אֲבַקֵּשׁ׃

8 For You my heart said: Seek Me. Your presence, Lord, I do seek.

---

is what I ask for: **That I may dwell in the House of the Lord all the days of my life, to behold the goodness of the Lord and to visit His Temple.** This entreaty, especially when expressed by someone who, as neither priest nor Levite, has no tasks to perform in the daily Temple service, is not to be taken as a literal request to stay in the Temple to participate in its religious rituals. Rather, it is an ecstatic exclamation of devotion to God made by a person who enters His Temple and experiences the sheer joy of being close to God there.

5 **For in time of trouble He shelters me in His pavilion. He conceals me in the secret of His tent** to protect me from adversity. **He sets me high upon a mighty rock,** where no harm can come to me,

6 **so that now my head rises above my enemies around me. I will offer victory sacrifices in His tent.** The unusual Hebrew phrase *zivḥei terua* literally means "sacrifices with shofar blasts." It refers to thanksgiving sacrifices that are offered in the wake of a victory or triumph. **I will sing songs of praise to the Lord.**

7 Now, again, are words of prayer: **Hear, Lord, when I cry out** to You. **Be gracious to me and answer me.**

8 **For You,** on Your behalf, **my heart said: Seek Me.** When my heart says, "seek Me," it is quoting God, who is asking of me, and all others, to seek Him. To this divine call I can honestly respond: **Your presence, Lord, I do seek.**

ט אַל־תַּסְתֵּר פָּנֶיךָ ׀ מִמֶּנִּי
אַל תַּט־בְּאַף עַבְדֶּךָ עֶזְרָתִי
הָיִיתָ אַל־תִּטְּשֵׁנִי וְאַל־
תַּעַזְבֵנִי אֱלֹהֵי יִשְׁעִי:

י כִּי־אָבִי וְאִמִּי עֲזָבוּנִי וַיהוָה
יַאַסְפֵנִי:

יא הוֹרֵנִי יְהוָה דַּרְכֶּךָ וּנְחֵנִי
בְּאֹרַח מִישׁוֹר לְמַעַן שׁוֹרְרָי:

יב אַל־תִּתְּנֵנִי בְּנֶפֶשׁ צָרָי כִּי
קָמוּ־בִי עֵדֵי־שֶׁקֶר וִיפֵחַ
חָמָס:

9 Do not hide Your face from me; do not turn Your servant away in anger. You have been my succor; do not abandon me or forsake me, God of my salvation.

10 For my father and my mother may abandon me, but the Lord will gather me up.

11 Teach me Your way, Lord, and lead me on a level path, because of my foes.

12 Do not deliver me to my foes, as is their desire, for they have risen against me as false witnesses testifying unjustly.

---

9 **Do not hide Your face from me,** do not withhold Your assistance and abandon me to the vicissitudes of life. **Do not turn Your servant away in anger,** even if Your wrath is justified. **You have been my succor** until now; **do not abandon me or forsake me** now or in the future, **God of my salvation.**

10 **For my father and my mother may abandon me.** The bond between parent and child is one that endures almost unconditionally. For this reason, there is no greater sense of isolation than that felt by an abandoned child. **But the Lord will gather me up.** God's protection, however, covers everyone, even those who have been completely and utterly deserted. This verse is, therefore, a most powerful expression of trust in God and God alone.

11 **Teach me Your way,** the way of righteousness, **Lord, and lead me on a level path,** a correct and tranquil path in both the physical and the moral sense, **because of my foes,** in order for me to escape my foes.

12 **Do not deliver me to my foes, as is their desire, for they have risen against me as false witnesses,** making untrue accusations against me, **testifying unjustly.** An alternative interpretation is that *yafe'aḥ*, translated here as "testify," may be related to *yifrah*, to make something blossom or grow. The translation would then be "and they foment injustice."

לוּלֵא הֶאֱמַנְתִּי לִרְאוֹת
בְּטוּב־יהוה בְּאֶרֶץ חַיִּים: ^{יג}

13 Had I not believed that I would see the goodness of the Lord in the land of the living.

קַוֵּה אֶל־יהוה חֲזַק וְיַאֲמֵץ
לִבֶּךָ וְקַוֵּה אֶל־יהוה: ^{יד}

14 Put your hope in the Lord; be strong and let your heart take courage, and hope in the Lord.

PSALM 28

A psalm that begins as a prayer for God's help and concludes
with the psalmist's expression of gratitude for his salvation.

לְדָוִד אֵלֶיךָ יהוה ׀ אֶקְרָא
צוּרִי אַל־תֶּחֱרַשׁ מִמֶּנִּי פֶּן־
תֶּחֱשֶׁה מִמֶּנִּי וְנִמְשַׁלְתִּי עִם־
יוֹרְדֵי בוֹר: ^א

1 By David. To You, Lord, I call. My rock, do not be deaf to me, for if You are silent, I will be like those descending into the pit.

---

13 If I survive unharmed, it is only because of my faith and prayers; I would have been vanquished **had I not believed that I would see the goodness of the Lord in the land of the living.** It was this faith that enabled me to continue fighting against my adversaries.

14 In conclusion, the psalmist offers words of encouragement to himself and to others: **Put your hope in the Lord; be strong and let your heart take courage, and** continue to **hope in the Lord** even if you do not see immediate results.

PSALM 28

1 **By David. To You, Lord, I call. My rock,** my strength, **do not be deaf to me** by ignoring my plea, **for if You are silent, I will be like those descending into the pit,** the grave. The psalmist's plea is for God's attentiveness, which is not only a source of strength but the very wellspring of his life.

שְׁמַ֤ע ק֣וֹל תַּ֭חֲנוּנַי בְּשַׁוְּעִ֣י
אֵלֶ֑יךָ בְּנָשְׂאִ֥י יָ֝דַ֗י אֶל־דְּבִ֥יר
קָדְשֶֽׁךָ:

אַל־תִּמְשְׁכֵ֣נִי עִם־רְשָׁעִים֮
וְעִם־פֹּ֪עֲלֵ֫י אָ֥וֶן דֹּבְרֵ֣י שָׁ֭לוֹם
עִם־רֵעֵיהֶ֑ם וְ֝רָעָ֗ה בִּלְבָבָֽם:

תֶּן־לָהֶ֣ם כְּפׇעֳלָם֮ וּכְרֹ֤עַ
מַ֫עַלְלֵיהֶ֥ם כְּמַעֲשֵׂ֣ה יְ֭דֵיהֶם
תֵּ֣ן לָהֶ֑ם הָשֵׁ֖ב גְּמוּלָ֣ם לָהֶֽם:

כִּ֤י לֹ֤א יָבִ֡ינוּ אֶל־פְּעֻלֹּ֣ת יְהֹוָה֮
וְאֶל־מַעֲשֵׂ֪ה יָ֫דָ֥יו יֶ֭הֶרְסֵם
וְלֹ֣א יִבְנֵֽם:

2 Hear the sound of my pleas
when I cry to You for help,
when I lift up my hands toward
Your holy shrine.

3 Do not drag me away with
the wicked and with evildoers,
who speak peaceably with their
neighbors while malice is in
their hearts.

4 Requite them according to
their actions and wicked deeds,
pay them back for what they
have done; render to them
what they deserve.

5 For they do not regard the
works of the Lord, nor the
deeds of His hands. He will
tear them down and not build
them up.

---

2 **Hear the sound of my pleas when I cry to You for help, when I lift up my hands toward Your holy shrine.**

3 **Do not drag me away with the wicked,** do not include me in the ranks of wicked people, **and with evildoers,** those **who speak peaceably with their neighbors while malice is in their hearts.** Such people are even more dangerous than overt adversaries.

4 **Requite them according to their actions and wicked deeds, pay them back for what they have done; render to them what they deserve.** My prayer is only that they receive just punishment, no more.

5 **For they do not regard the works of the Lord, nor the deeds of His hands.** They do not understand that God is actively involved in His world; they would prefer not to think about the matter. In this way, they are able to carry on with their wrongdoing. However, **He will tear them down and not build them up.** Intrigue and scheming will not save them from being destroyed.

בָּרוּךְ יהוָה כִּי־שָׁמַע קוֹל
תַּחֲנוּנָי:

⁶ Blessed be the Lord, for He has heard the sound of my pleas.

יהוָה ׀ עֻזִּי וּמָגִנִּי בּוֹ בָטַח
לִבִּי וְנֶעֱזָרְתִּי וַיַּעֲלֹז לִבִּי
וּמִשִּׁירִי אֲהוֹדֶנּוּ:

⁷ The Lord is my strength and my shield; my heart trusts in Him, and I am helped. My heart exults, and with my song I give thanks to Him.

יהוָה עֹז־לָמוֹ וּמָעוֹז יְשׁוּעוֹת
מְשִׁיחוֹ הוּא:

⁸ The Lord is their strength; He is a stronghold of salvation for His anointed one.

הוֹשִׁיעָה ׀ אֶת־עַמֶּךָ וּבָרֵךְ
אֶת־נַחֲלָתֶךָ וּרְעֵם וְנַשְּׂאֵם
עַד־הָעוֹלָם:

⁹ Deliver Your people and bless Your possession; shepherd them and raise them up forever.

---

⁶ **Blessed be the Lord, for He has heard the sound of my pleas.**

⁷ **The Lord is my strength and my shield; my heart trusts in Him, and I am helped** by Him. **My heart exults** in His salvation, **and with my song I give thanks to Him.** Alternatively, with my song I glorify Him.

⁸ **The Lord is their strength,** the strength of those who trust in Him; **He is a stronghold of salvation for His anointed one,** the king of Israel.

⁹ **Deliver Your people and bless Your possession,** a reference either to the people of Israel or the Land of Israel. **Shepherd them,** lead them as a shepherd leads his flock, **and raise them up forever.**

PSALM 29

A hymn about God's greatness and His revelation in the world, in which each different kind of revelation is termed "the voice of the Lord."

א מִזְמוֹר לְדָוִד הָבוּ לַיהוה בְּנֵי אֵלִים הָבוּ לַיהוה כָּבוֹד וָעֹז:

ב הָבוּ לַיהוה כְּבוֹד שְׁמוֹ הִשְׁתַּחֲווּ לַיהוה בְּהַדְרַת־קֹדֶשׁ:

ג קוֹל יהוה עַל־הַמָּיִם אֵל־הַכָּבוֹד הִרְעִים יהוה עַל־מַיִם רַבִּים:

ד קוֹל־יהוה בַּכֹּחַ קוֹל יהוה בֶּהָדָר:

ה קוֹל יהוה שֹׁבֵר אֲרָזִים וַיְשַׁבֵּר יהוה אֶת־אַרְזֵי הַלְּבָנוֹן:

¹ A psalm by David. Give to the Lord, sons of the mighty, give to the Lord glory and strength.

² Give to the Lord the glory due His name; bow down to the Lord in holy splendor.

³ The voice of the Lord is on the waters; God of glory thunders; the Lord is upon surging waters.

⁴ The voice of the Lord is mighty; the voice of the Lord is majestic.

⁵ The voice of the Lord breaks cedars; the Lord splinters the cedars of Lebanon.

PSALM 29

¹ **A psalm by David. Give to the Lord, sons of the mighty.** Some commentators understand "sons of the mighty" to be angels; others say this represents the heavenly bodies. But the context of the verse implies that it is addressing human beings of great strength and stature; it is they who are best able to praise God in the most fitting manner. **Give to the Lord,** that is, praise Him, for His **glory and strength.**

² **Give to the Lord the glory due His name; bow down to the Lord in holy splendor.**

³ From this point on, the psalmist elaborates on the various manifestations of God's revelation, which He terms "the voice of the Lord": **The voice of the Lord is on the waters; God of glory thunders; the Lord is** heard **upon surging waters.**

⁴ **The voice of the Lord is mighty; the voice of the Lord is** also **majestic.** He is also revealed in majestic beauty.

⁵ **The voice of the Lord** with its might **breaks cedars,** the strongest of trees; **the Lord splinters**

וַיַּרְקִידֵם כְּמוֹ־עֵגֶל לְבָנוֹן
וְשִׂרְיֹן כְּמוֹ בֶן־רְאֵמִים:

6 He makes them skip like calves,
Lebanon and Siryon like young
oryxes.

קוֹל־יהוה חֹצֵב לַהֲבוֹת אֵשׁ:

7 The voice of the Lord hews
flames of fire.

קוֹל יהוה יָחִיל מִדְבָּר יָחִיל
יהוה מִדְבַּר קָדֵשׁ:

8 The voice of the Lord makes
the desert tremble; the Lord
makes the desert of Kadesh
tremble.

קוֹל יהוה ׀ יְחוֹלֵל אַיָּלוֹת
וַיֶּחֱשֹׂף יְעָרוֹת וּבְהֵיכָלוֹ כֻּלּוֹ
אֹמֵר כָּבוֹד:

9 The voice of the Lord causes
deer to calve and strips the
forests bare. In His abode all
proclaim His glory.

יהוה לַמַּבּוּל יָשָׁב וַיֵּשֶׁב
יהוה מֶלֶךְ לְעוֹלָם:

10 The Lord sat enthroned at the
flood; the Lord sits as King
forever.

---

the cedars of Lebanon. In essence, the revelation of God makes the entire world tremble.

6 **He makes them,** the trees and all the creations in the world, jump from their place and **skip like calves,** the great mountains, such as Mount **Lebanon and** Mount **Siryon,** which is Mount Hermon,[7] skip **like young oryxes.**

7 **The voice of the Lord hews flames of fire.** It draws forth fire from the shattering mountains.

8 **The voice of the Lord makes the desert tremble** in awe. **The Lord makes the desert of Kadesh tremble.** This particular desert is mentioned to allude to the events that accompanied the revelation at Sinai, near Kadesh, as they are portrayed in several other psalms.[8]

9 **The voice of the Lord causes deer to calve.** The very same revelatory powers, the same voice that splinters forests, can also be a voice of gentleness, bringing fertility and fruitfulness to the world. **And strips the forests bare** by felling all their trees. **In His abode,** which is close to Him, as it were, the "voices of God" manifest themselves not in a display of power but rather in a tranquil manner, as **all proclaim His glory.**

10 **The Lord sat enthroned at the flood.** Some commentators say that *mabul,* "the flood," refers to the time when God sat in judgment and sentenced the earth to annihilation. It exemplifies how terrifying God's power can be. Others, however, believe that it is a name for God's throne of judgment. **The Lord sits as King forever,** as builder and creator upon earth, not as its destroyer.

יא יְהוָֹה עֹז לְעַמּוֹ יִתֵּן יְהוָֹה ׀
יְבָרֵךְ אֶת־עַמּוֹ בַשָּׁלוֹם:

11 The Lord gives strength to His people; the Lord will bless His people with peace.

MONDAY

PSALM 30

A psalm of thanks by one who, at a calm and peaceful period in his life, has suddenly been beset with great distress, a serious illness that has darkened his life. After turning to God in prayer, he regains his health and expresses his gratitude.

א מִזְמוֹר שִׁיר־חֲנֻכַּת הַבַּיִת
לְדָוִד:

ב אֲרוֹמִמְךָ יהוה כִּי דִלִּיתָנִי
וְלֹא־שִׂמַּחְתָּ אֹיְבַי לִי:

1 A psalm, a song for the dedication of the house, by David.

2 I extol You, Lord, for You lifted me up and did not let my enemies rejoice over me.

---

11 **The Lord gives strength to His people,** so that they may be able to praise Him suitably; this requires strength, as the opening verse of the psalm stated. But at the same time, the **Lord will bless His people with peace.** He will grant a double blessing, combining physical strength and power with peace and tranquility.

PSALM 30

1 **A psalm, a song for the dedication of the house, by David.** "The house" here is generally understood to be the Temple in Jerusalem. However, the text offers thanks for something completely different, namely, David's recovery from a grave illness or danger that suddenly befell him. It is possible, then, that he composed this hymn of praise to celebrate his recovery at the dedication of his private dwelling in Jerusalem.

2 **I extol You, Lord, for You lifted me up** out of the depths of despair, infirmity, and weakness, **and did not let my enemies rejoice over me,** gloating at my downfall.

יהוה אֱלֹהָי שִׁוַּעְתִּי אֵלֶיךָ
וַתִּרְפָּאֵנִי:

מְיָ

יהוה הֶעֱלִיתָ מִן־שְׁאוֹל
נַפְשִׁי חִיִּיתַנִי מִיּוֹרְדִי־בוֹר:

זַמְּרוּ לַיהוה חֲסִידָיו וְהוֹדוּ
לְזֵכֶר קָדְשׁוֹ:

כִּי רֶגַע ׀ בְּאַפּוֹ חַיִּים בִּרְצוֹנוֹ
בָּעֶרֶב יָלִין בֶּכִי וְלַבֹּקֶר רִנָּה:

וַאֲנִי אָמַרְתִּי בְשַׁלְוִי בַּל־
אֶמּוֹט לְעוֹלָם:

3 Lord my God, I cried out to You, and You healed me.

4 Lord, You lifted up my soul from the grave; You kept me alive, kept me from going down to the pit.

5 Sing to the Lord, His devoted ones, and give thanks in remembrance of His holy name.

6 For His anger is but a moment; in His desire there is life. At night he goes to sleep weeping; in the morning there is joy.

7 I had said in my tranquility: I will never stumble.

---

3 **Lord my God, I cried out to You, and You healed me.**

4 **Lord, You lifted up my soul from the grave,** so close was I to death. **You kept me alive, kept me from going down to the pit,** another reference to the grave.

5 In his joy over his recovery, David calls upon others to join him in praising God: **Sing to the Lord, His devoted ones, and give thanks in remembrance of His holy name.**

6 **For His anger is but a moment.** An instant of God's anger can be devastating: Success, and life itself, can end in a heartbeat. But **in His desire, there is life.** If God wills it, man can live a long, full life. **At night he goes to sleep weeping.** Night represents gloom and despair; it is also a time when sickness intensifies. **In the morning,** however, **there is** relief and optimism, and, in their wake, **joy.**

7 **I had said in my tranquility,** when all was going well for me: **I will never stumble.** I was certain things would remain that way.

ח יְהֹוָה בִּרְצוֹנְךָ הֶעֱמַדְתָּה לְהַרְרִי עֹז הִסְתַּרְתָּ פָנֶיךָ הָיִיתִי נִבְהָל:

8 Lord, by Your will, You put in place mighty mountains; You hid Your face, and I was terrified.

ט אֵלֶיךָ יְהֹוָה אֶקְרָא וְאֶל־אֲדֹנָי אֶתְחַנָּן:

9 To You, Lord, I called; I prayed to my Lord:

י מַה־בֶּצַע בְּדָמִי בְּרִדְתִּי אֶל שָׁחַת הֲיוֹדְךָ עָפָר הֲיַגִּיד אֲמִתֶּךָ:

10 What gain is in my blood, in my descending into the pit? Can the dust thank You? Can it declare Your truth?

יא שְׁמַע־יְהֹוָה וְחָנֵּנִי יְהֹוָה הֱיֵה־עֹזֵר לִי:

11 Hear me, Lord, and be gracious to me; Lord, be my savior.

יב הָפַכְתָּ מִסְפְּדִי לְמָחוֹל לִי פִּתַּחְתָּ שַׂקִּי וַתְּאַזְּרֵנִי שִׂמְחָה:

12 You transformed my mourning into dancing; You loosened my sackcloth and girded me with joy,

---

8 **Lord, by Your will, You put in place mighty mountains,** metaphorically, to obscure Your presence; **You hid Your face, and I was terrified.** When God "hides His face," that is, withdraws His providence and protection, man is left vulnerable to all the forces of evil wreaking havoc in the world.

9 In that dire hour, **to You, Lord, I called; I prayed to my Lord** with the words of one who fears imminent death:

10 **What gain is** there **in** the shedding of **my blood, in my descending into the pit** of the grave, turning there to dust? **Can the dust thank You? Can it declare Your truth?**

11 The psalmist's plea continues: **Hear me, Lord, and be gracious to me; Lord, be my savior.**

12 When help from God does appear, David's prayer turns joyous: **You transformed my mourning** over my dismal fate **into** joyous **dancing; You loosened my sackcloth and girded me with joy.**

לְמַעַן ׀ יְזַמֶּרְךָ כָבוֹד וְלֹא
יִדֹּם יהוה אֱלֹהַי לְעוֹלָם
אוֹדֶךָ:

13 so that he may sing unceasing praises of glory to You. Lord my God, I will give thanks to You forever.

PSALM 31

A psalm of entreaty and gratitude. Apparently written during a period of relative calm, it addresses the psalmist's past trials and fears alongside his present salvation.

לַמְנַצֵּחַ מִזְמוֹר לְדָוִד:

1 For the chief musician, a psalm by David.

בְּךָ־יהוה חָסִיתִי אַל־
אֵבוֹשָׁה לְעוֹלָם בְּצִדְקָתְךָ
פַלְּטֵנִי:

2 In You, Lord, I place my trust. May I never be put to shame; rescue me in Your righteousness.

הַטֵּה אֵלַי ׀ אָזְנְךָ מְהֵרָה
הַצִּילֵנִי הֱיֵה לִי ׀ לְצוּר־מָעוֹז
לְבֵית מְצוּדוֹת לְהוֹשִׁיעֵנִי:

3 Incline Your ear to me; make haste to save me. Be my rock of refuge, a stronghold to deliver me.

---

13 A person who has survived a nearly fatal experience, who has once again been given the gift of life, knows full well how to use this precious gift; it is **so that he may sing unceasing praises of glory to You. Lord my God, I will give thanks to You forever.**

PSALM 31

1 **For the chief musician, a psalm by David.**

2 **In You, Lord, I place my trust,** and therefore I pray: **May I never be put to shame; rescue me in Your righteousness.**

3 **Incline Your ear to me,** to hear my prayer; **make haste to save me** from imminent danger. **Be my rock of refuge, a stronghold to deliver me.**

כִּי־סַלְעִי וּמְצוּדָתִי אָתָּה
וּלְמַעַן שִׁמְךָ תַּנְחֵנִי
וּתְנַהֲלֵנִי:

תּוֹצִיאֵנִי מֵרֶשֶׁת זוּ טָמְנוּ לִי
כִּי־אַתָּה מָעוּזִּי:

בְּיָדְךָ אַפְקִיד רוּחִי פָּדִיתָה
אוֹתִי יהוה אֵל אֱמֶת:

שָׂנֵאתִי הַשֹּׁמְרִים הַבְלֵי־
שָׁוְא וַאֲנִי אֶל־יהוה בָּטָחְתִּי:

אָגִילָה וְאֶשְׂמְחָה בְּחַסְדֶּךָ
אֲשֶׁר רָאִיתָ אֶת־עָנְיִי יָדַעְתָּ
בְּצָרוֹת נַפְשִׁי:

וְלֹא הִסְגַּרְתַּנִי בְּיַד־אוֹיֵב
הֶעֱמַדְתָּ בַמֶּרְחָב רַגְלָי:

4 For You are my rock and my fortress, and for the sake of Your name, You guide me and lead me.

5 Draw me out of the net they laid for me, for You are my stronghold.

6 Into Your hand I commit my spirit; You redeem me, Lord, Almighty God of truth.

7 I hate those who rely on the vanities of falsehood; as for me, I trust in the Lord.

8 I rejoice and am happy in Your kindness, for You have seen my affliction. You know my soul's distress,

9 and You did not deliver me into the hand of the enemy; You planted my feet in open space.

---

4 **For You are my rock and my fortress, and for the sake of Your name, You guide me and lead me.**

5 **Draw me out of the net they laid for me, for You are my stronghold.**

6 **Into Your hand I commit my spirit.** I entrust my life to You, depending on You to guard it. And indeed, **You redeem me, Lord, Almighty God of truth.**

7 **I hate those who rely on the vanities of falsehood,** namely, false gods. **As for me, I trust** only **in the Lord.**

8 **I rejoice and am happy in Your kindness, for You have seen my affliction. You know my soul's distress,**

9 **and** because of this, **You did not deliver me into the hand of the enemy; You planted my feet in open space,** whereas I had previously been in a situation of confinement, as it were, unable to escape my desperate situation.

חָנֵּנִי יהוה כִּי צַר לִי עָשְׁשָׁה
בְכַעַס עֵינִי נַפְשִׁי וּבִטְנִי:

כִּי כָלוּ בְיָגוֹן חַיַּי וּשְׁנוֹתַי
בַּאֲנָחָה כָּשַׁל בַּעֲוֹנִי כֹחִי
וַעֲצָמַי עָשֵׁשׁוּ:

מִכָּל־צֹרְרַי הָיִיתִי חֶרְפָּה
וְלִשְׁכֵנַי ׀ מְאֹד וּפַחַד לִמְיֻדָּעָי
רֹאַי בַּחוּץ נָדְדוּ מִמֶּנִּי:

נִשְׁכַּחְתִּי כְּמֵת מִלֵּב הָיִיתִי
כִּכְלִי אֹבֵד:

¹⁰ Be gracious to me, Lord, for I am in distress; my eyes are weakened from vexation, my soul and my belly.

¹¹ For my life is withered away in anguish and my years in sighing. In my iniquity, my strength fails; my bones have decayed.

¹² For all my foes I have become a disgrace, and greatly so for my acquaintances. I am an object of dread to my well-wishers. Those who see me in the street flee from me.

¹³ I am as forgotten from men's hearts as a dead man; I am like a discarded tool.

---

¹⁰ **Be gracious to me, Lord, for I am in distress; my eyes are weakened from vexation,** as are **my soul and my belly.** It seems as if all the parts of my body are unable to function properly because of my distress.

¹¹ **For my life is withered away in anguish and my years in sighing. In my iniquity, my strength fails; my bones have decayed.**

¹² **For all my foes I have become a disgrace,** an object of scorn, **and greatly so for my acquaintances.** I am scorned greatly by my acquaintances as well. **I am an object of dread to my well-wishers,** who fear for my well-being when they witness my deteriorating state. My acquaintances see things in me that cause them to keep their distance. **Those who see me in the street flee from me.** They avoid coming in contact with me because of my ill and miserable appearance.

¹³ **I am as forgotten from men's hearts as a dead man,** whose memory fades away with time. **I am** forgotten **like a discarded tool.**

יד כִּי שָׁמַעְתִּי ׀ דִּבַּת רַבִּים
מָגוֹר מִסָּבִיב בְּהִוָּסְדָם יַחַד
עָלַי לָקַחַת נַפְשִׁי זָמָמוּ:

טו וַאֲנִי ׀ עָלֶיךָ בָטַחְתִּי יהוה
אָמַרְתִּי אֱלֹהַי אָתָּה:

טז בְּיָדְךָ עִתֹּתָי הַצִּילֵנִי מִיַּד־
אוֹיְבַי וּמֵרֹדְפָי:

יז הָאִירָה פָנֶיךָ עַל־עַבְדֶּךָ
הוֹשִׁיעֵנִי בְחַסְדֶּךָ:

יח יהוה אַל־אֵבוֹשָׁה כִּי
קְרָאתִיךָ יֵבֹשׁוּ רְשָׁעִים יִדְּמוּ
לִשְׁאוֹל:

יט תֵּאָלַמְנָה שִׂפְתֵי שָׁקֶר
הַדֹּבְרוֹת עַל־צַדִּיק עָתָק
בְּגַאֲוָה וָבוּז:

14 For I have heard the slander of many. There is terror all around; they have gathered together, scheming to take my life.

15 But as for me, I trust in You, Lord. I say: You are my God.

16 My fate is in your hand; save me from my enemies and from those who pursue me.

17 Shine Your countenance upon Your servant; deliver me in Your kindness.

18 Lord, let me not be shamed, for I have called upon You. Let the wicked be shamed; let them go silent to the grave.

19 Mute the lying lips that speak falsehood against the righteous with arrogance and contempt.

---

14 **For I have heard the slander of many. There is** nothing but **terror all around** me; **they have gathered together, scheming to take my life.**

15 **But as for me, I trust** only **in You, Lord. I say: You are my God.**

16 **My fate is in Your hand.** *Itotai*, literally "my times," denotes my life or my fate. **Save me from my enemies and from those who pursue me.**

17 **Shine your countenance upon Your servant; deliver me in Your kindness.**

18 **Lord, let me not be shamed, for I have called upon You. Let** it be **the wicked** who will **be shamed; let them go silent to the grave.**

19 **Mute the lying lips that speak falsehood against the righteous with arrogance and contempt.**

מָה רַב־טוּבְךָ אֲשֶׁר־צָפַנְתָּ
לִירֵאֶיךָ פָּעַלְתָּ לַחוֹסִים בָּךְ
נֶגֶד בְּנֵי אָדָם:

כא תַּסְתִּירֵם ו בְּסֵתֶר פָּנֶיךָ
מֵרֻכְסֵי אִישׁ תִּצְפְּנֵם בְּסֻכָּה
מֵרִיב לְשֹׁנוֹת:

כב בָּרוּךְ יהוה כִּי הִפְלִיא חַסְדּוֹ
לִי בְּעִיר מָצוֹר:

כג וַאֲנִי ו אָמַרְתִּי בְחָפְזִי נִגְרַזְתִּי
מִנֶּגֶד עֵינֶיךָ אָכֵן שָׁמַעְתָּ קוֹל
תַּחֲנוּנַי בְּשַׁוְּעִי אֵלֶיךָ:

20 How great is the goodness You have in store for those who fear You, which You have created for those taking refuge in You, to be bestowed openly.

21 Conceal them in the secret place of Your presence; shelter them from man's intrigues in Your pavilion, away from the strife of tongues.

22 Blessed is the Lord, for He showed me wondrous kindness in a besieged city.

23 I had said in my anxious haste: I am cut off from Your view. But You heard the voice of my pleas when I cried out to You.

---

20 The psalmist now turns from decrying the wicked to extolling the righteous and the salvation destined for them: **How great is the goodness You have in store for those who fear You.** They will be the beneficiaries of Your hidden gifts, which previously had not been bestowed upon man and **which You have created for those taking refuge in You, to be bestowed openly.**

21 **Conceal them in the secret place of Your presence; shelter them from man's intrigues in Your pavilion, away from the strife of** the slanderous **tongues** that are aimed against them.

22 **Blessed is the Lord, for He showed me wondrous kindness in a besieged city,** referring to either a literal or figurative siege.

23 **I had said in my anxious haste** while I was in distress: **I am cut off from Your view,** and You are no longer concerned about me. **But,** in fact, **You heard the voice of my pleas when I cried out to You.**

כד אֶהֱבוּ אֶת־יהוה כָּל־חֲסִידָיו
אֱמוּנִים נֹצֵר יהוה וּמְשַׁלֵּם
עַל־יֶתֶר עֹשֵׂה גַאֲוָה:

²⁴ Love the Lord, all His devoted ones. The Lord is faithful, and He requites the arrogant with the bowstring.

כה חִזְקוּ וְיַאֲמֵץ לְבַבְכֶם כָּל־
הַמְיַחֲלִים לַיהוה:

²⁵ Be strong and let your hearts take courage, all of you who hope in the Lord.

PSALM 32

A contemplative prayer that requests God's forgiveness and expresses hope for salvation.

א לְדָוִד מַשְׂכִּיל אַשְׁרֵי נְשׂוּי־
פֶּשַׁע כְּסוּי חֲטָאָה:

¹ By David, a contemplation. Happy is he whose transgression is forgiven, whose sin is pardoned.

---

²⁴ **Love the Lord, all His devoted ones,** for **the Lord is faithful** to reward those who trust in Him **and He requites the arrogant with the bowstring,** punishing them with His arrows, as it were.

²⁵ In conclusion, the psalmist proclaims: **Be strong and let your hearts take courage, all of you who hope in the Lord.** This verse can be seen not only as sound advice, but as a summation of the psalm. Evoking his own life experience as evidence, the psalmist concludes that God comes to the aid of those who rely on Him.

PSALM 32

¹ **By David, a contemplation.** The word *maskil*, translated here as a "contemplation," apparently describes a thought-provoking psalm that is primarily introspective in nature and is to be pondered, rather than a psalm of prayer. Some commentators, however, suggest that it refers to the name of a particular melody. **Happy is he whose transgression is forgiven, whose sin is pardoned.** The phrase *kesui ḥata'a*, translated here as "whose sin is pardoned," literally means "who is covered up from sin"; it is as if he is protected from any connection with sin.

אַשְׁרֵי־אָדָם לֹא יַחְשֹׁב יהוה
לוֹ עָוֺן וְאֵין בְּרוּחוֹ רְמִיָּה:

כִּי־הֶחֱרַשְׁתִּי בָּלוּ עֲצָמָי
בְּשַׁאֲגָתִי כָּל־הַיּוֹם:

כִּי ׀ יוֹמָם וָלַיְלָה תִּכְבַּד עָלַי
יָדֶךָ נֶהְפַּךְ לְשַׁדִּי בְּחַרְבֹנֵי
קַיִץ סֶלָה:

חַטָּאתִי אוֹדִיעֲךָ וַעֲוֺנִי לֹא־
כִסִּיתִי אָמַרְתִּי אוֹדֶה עֲלֵי
פְשָׁעַי לַיהוה וְאַתָּה נָשָׂאתָ
עֲוֺן חַטָּאתִי סֶלָה:

² Happy is the man in whom the
Lord sees no iniquity, and in
whose spirit there is no deceit.

³ When I kept silent, my bones
wasted away; so too when I
roared throughout the day.

⁴ For day and night Your
hand weighed upon me; my
moisture has left me as if by
summer heat, Selah.

⁵ I acknowledged my sin
to You; I did not hide my
iniquity. I said: I will confess
my transgressions to the Lord.
And You forgave the guilt of my
sin, Selah.

---

2 **Happy is the man in whom the Lord sees no iniquity, and in whose spirit there is no deceit.** The psalmist admits: I do not always feel that I have attained the spiritual height of being without iniquity, but at least I honestly try to achieve repentance.

3 His sins have caused him physical suffering: **When I kept silent, my bones wasted away; so too when I roared** in prayer **throughout the day.** Whether I am silent or I cry out in prayer, my suffering does not abate.

4 **For day and night Your hand weighed upon me.** As I endured painful experiences and physical punishments, I felt as if a heavy hand was putting pressure on me. **My moisture,** my vitality, **has left me as if by summer heat, Selah.**

5 **I acknowledged my sin to You; I did not hide my iniquity. I said: I will confess my transgressions to the Lord. And You forgave the guilt of my sin, Selah.**

עַל־זֹאת יִתְפַּלֵּל כָּל־חָסִיד ׀
אֵלֶיךָ לְעֵת מְצֹא רַק לְשֵׁטֶף
מַיִם רַבִּים אֵלָיו לֹא יַגִּיעוּ:

אַתָּה ׀ סֵתֶר לִי מִצַּר תִּצְּרֵנִי
רָנֵּי פַלֵּט תְּסוֹבְבֵנִי סֶלָה:

אַשְׂכִּילְךָ ׀ וְאוֹרְךָ בְּדֶרֶךְ־זוּ
תֵלֵךְ אִיעֲצָה עָלֶיךָ עֵינִי:

אַל־תִּהְיוּ ׀ כְּסוּס כְּפֶרֶד
אֵין הָבִין בְּמֶתֶג־וָרֶסֶן עֶדְיוֹ
לִבְלוֹם בַּל קְרֹב אֵלֶיךָ:

6 Therefore, everyone who is devoted to You should pray at the time of searching, so the torrent of mighty waters does not reach him.

7 You are my hiding place; protect me from enemies. Surround me with songs of deliverance, Selah.

8 I will instruct you and direct you in the path you should take. I will advise you; My eye is upon you.

9 Do not be like a horse or a mule without understanding, whose wildness must be restrained with bit and bridle lest it approach you.

---

6 **Therefore, everyone who is devoted to You should pray at the time of searching,** in times of crisis or when he is at a crossroads in life, **so the torrent of mighty waters does not reach him,** so that he does not end up in a situation where he is drowning, as it were, in a torrent of surging water, hopelessly overwhelmed by troubles.

7 **You are my hiding place; protect me from enemies. Surround me with songs of deliverance** and gratitude, which will come in the wake of Your salvation, **Selah.**

8 In this next verse, the psalmist apparently quotes what would be God's response to him: **I will instruct you and direct you in the path you should take. I will advise you,** as **My eye is upon you.**

9 This verse, shifting from singular to plural, is directed not just to the psalmist, but to all people: **Do not be like a horse or a mule,** who, as mere animals, are **without understanding, whose wildness must be restrained with bit and bridle lest it approach you** and injure you.

רַבִּ֤ים מַכְאוֹבִ֗ים לָ֫רָשָׁ֥ע וְהַבּוֹטֵ֥חַ בַּיהֹוָ֑ה חֶ֝֗סֶד יְסֽוֹבְבֶֽנּוּ׃

10 There are many maladies for the wicked, but one trusting in the Lord is enveloped in kindness.

שִׂמְח֬וּ בַֽיהֹוָ֣ה וְ֭גִילוּ צַדִּיקִ֑ים וְ֝הַרְנִ֗ינוּ כׇּל־יִשְׁרֵי־לֵֽב׃

11 Rejoice in the Lord and be glad, you righteous ones; sing out with joy, all you whose hearts are upright.

PSALM 33

A psalm in praise of the greatness of God. Although it contains some instructive material, it focuses on God's beneficence on behalf of the world in general and humanity in particular.

רַנְּנ֣וּ צַדִּיקִ֣ים בַּֽיהֹוָ֑ה לַ֝יְשָׁרִ֗ים נָאוָ֥ה תְהִלָּֽה׃

1 Rejoice in the Lord, righteous ones; it is comely for the upright to offer praise.

הוֹד֣וּ לַיהֹוָ֣ה בְּכִנּ֑וֹר בְּנֵ֥בֶל עָ֝שׂ֗וֹר זַמְּרוּ־לֽוֹ׃

2 Give thanks to the Lord with the lyre; sing praises to Him with a ten-stringed harp.

שִֽׁירוּ־ל֭וֹ שִׁ֣יר חָדָ֑שׁ הֵיטִ֥יבוּ נַ֝גֵּ֗ן בִּתְרוּעָֽה׃

3 Sing Him a new song; play beautifully with loud sound.

---

10 In summation: **There are many maladies for the wicked, but one trusting in the Lord is enveloped in kindness.**

11 **Rejoice in the Lord and be glad, you righteous ones; sing out with joy, all you whose hearts are upright.**

PSALM 33

1 **Rejoice in the Lord, righteous ones; it is comely for the upright to offer praise.**

2 **Give thanks to the Lord with the lyre; sing praises to Him with a ten-stringed harp.**

3 **Sing Him a new song.** It is a greater tribute to God to sing new songs and praises than it is to

כִּי־יָשָׁר דְּבַר־יהוה וְכָל־
מַעֲשֵׂהוּ בָּאֱמוּנָה:

אֹהֵב צְדָקָה וּמִשְׁפָּט חֶסֶד
יהוה מָלְאָה הָאָרֶץ:

בִּדְבַר יהוה שָׁמַיִם נַעֲשׂוּ
וּבְרוּחַ פִּיו כָּל־צְבָאָם:

כֹּנֵס כַּנֵּד מֵי הַיָּם נֹתֵן
בְּאוֹצָרוֹת תְּהוֹמוֹת:

יִירְאוּ מֵיהוה כָּל־הָאָרֶץ
מִמֶּנּוּ יָגוּרוּ כָּל־יֹשְׁבֵי תֵבֵל:

⁴ For the word of the Lord is upright, all His deeds faithfully wrought.

⁵ He loves righteousness and justice; the Lord's kindness fills the world.

⁶ By the word of the Lord were the heavens made; by the breath of His mouth, all their hosts.

⁷ He heaps together the waters of the sea, storing in vaults the waters of the deep.

⁸ Let the entire world be in awe of the Lord; let all earth's inhabitants fear Him.

---

repeat tributes that have been sung before. **Play beautifully with loud sound.** The word *terua*, translated as "loud sound," usually refers to music made with a trumpet or horn.

⁴ And this is the song they should sing: **For the word of the Lord is upright, all His deeds faithfully wrought.** God's deeds are characterized as "upright" and "faithful"; these are also attributes He seeks in the world.

⁵ **He loves righteousness and justice; the Lord's kindness fills the world.** The entire world is an expression of God's beneficence and generosity. From this we can learn that God values these qualities in us as well.

⁶ **By the word of the Lord were the heavens made; by the breath of His mouth, all their hosts.**

⁷ **He heaps together the waters of the sea, storing in vaults the waters of the deep.** God has designated special places for the concentrations of water found beneath the earth.

⁸ **Let the entire world be in awe of the Lord; let all earth's inhabitants fear Him** as they contemplate His immense power in creation.

כִּי הוּא אָמַר וַיֶּהִי הוּא־צִוָּה
וַיַּעֲמֹד׃

9 For He spoke, and it was done; He commanded, and it took form.

יְהוָה הֵפִיר עֲצַת־גּוֹיִם הֵנִיא
מַחְשְׁבוֹת עַמִּים׃

10 The Lord overturns the counsel of nations, annuls the schemes of peoples.

עֲצַת יְהוָה לְעוֹלָם תַּעֲמֹד
מַחְשְׁבוֹת לִבּוֹ לְדֹר וָדֹר׃

11 The Lord's counsel endures forever, the plans of His heart for all generations.

אַשְׁרֵי הַגּוֹי אֲשֶׁר־יְהוָה
אֱלֹהָיו הָעָם ׀ בָּחַר לְנַחֲלָה
לוֹ׃

12 Happy is the nation whose God is the Lord, the people whom He chose as His possession.

מִשָּׁמַיִם הִבִּיט יְהוָה רָאָה
אֶת־כָּל־בְּנֵי הָאָדָם׃

13 The Lord looks from heaven; He sees all mankind.

מִמְּכוֹן־שִׁבְתּוֹ הִשְׁגִּיחַ אֶל
כָּל־יֹשְׁבֵי הָאָרֶץ׃

14 From His dwelling place He observes all the inhabitants of the earth.

---

9 **For He spoke, and it was done.** The world's creation was accomplished through God's mere utterance. **He commanded, and it,** referring to all the creations of the world, **took form.**

10 God's power manifests itself in creation in general, but particularly in His interaction with mankind: **The Lord overturns the counsel of nations, annuls the schemes of peoples.**

11 In contrast to the futility of man's grand designs: **The Lord's counsel endures forever; the plans of His heart** remain **for all generations.**

12 But God not only created the world; He also chose a particular people to be His: **Happy is the nation whose God is the Lord, the people whom He chose as His possession.**

13 **The Lord looks from heaven; He sees all mankind.**

14 **From His dwelling place** in the heavens, **He observes all the inhabitants of the earth.**

טו הַיֹּצֵר יַחַד לִבָּם הַמֵּבִין אֶל־
כָּל־מַעֲשֵׂיהֶם:

טז אֵין־הַמֶּלֶךְ נוֹשָׁע בְּרָב־חָיִל
גִּבּוֹר לֹא־יִנָּצֵל בְּרָב־כֹּחַ:

יז שֶׁקֶר הַסּוּס לִתְשׁוּעָה וּבְרֹב
חֵילוֹ לֹא יְמַלֵּט:

יח הִנֵּה עֵין יְהוָה אֶל־יְרֵאָיו
לַמְיַחֲלִים לְחַסְדּוֹ:

יט לְהַצִּיל מִמָּוֶת נַפְשָׁם
וּלְחַיּוֹתָם בָּרָעָב:

כ נַפְשֵׁנוּ חִכְּתָה לַיהוָה עֶזְרֵנוּ
וּמָגִנֵּנוּ הוּא:

כא כִּי־בוֹ יִשְׂמַח לִבֵּנוּ כִּי בְשֵׁם
קָדְשׁוֹ בָטָחְנוּ:

15 He who fashions all their hearts, who understands all their deeds.

16 The king is not saved by a mighty army, the warrior not rescued by great strength.

17 A horse is false hope for victory; even in its great power, it cannot offer escape.

18 Truly, the eye of the Lord is on those who fear Him, on those who await His kindness

19 to deliver them from death, to sustain them in famine.

20 Our soul longs for the Lord; He is our help and our shield.

21 For our heart rejoices in Him, for we trust in His holy name.

---

15 **He who fashions all their hearts,** and **who** consequently **understands all their deeds.**

16 Since God observes and controls all, it follows that all outcomes are determined by Him: **The king is not saved by** the fact that he has **a mighty army** at his disposal; **the warrior** is **not rescued by** virtue of his **great strength.**

17 In ancient times, armies relied on horses and chariots both for defense and for attack. However, **a horse is false hope for victory** if God does not will it; **even in its great power, it cannot offer escape.**

18 If not horses and chariots, on what can one rely? **Truly, the eye of the Lord is on those who fear Him, on those who await His kindness**

19 **to deliver them from death** in battle, **to sustain them in famine.**

20 **Our soul longs for the Lord; He is our help and our shield.**

21 **For our heart rejoices in Him, for we trust in His holy name** that He will come to our aid.

כב יְהִי־חַסְדְּךָ יהוה עָלֵינוּ
כַּאֲשֶׁר יִחַלְנוּ לָךְ:

22 Let Your kindness, Lord, be upon us, as we have put our hope in You.

PSALM 34

A psalm relating to a specific incident in King David's life. Its verses are arranged alphabetically.

א לְדָוִד בְּשַׁנּוֹתוֹ אֶת־טַעְמוֹ
לִפְנֵי אֲבִימֶלֶךְ וַיְגָרְשֵׁהוּ
וַיֵּלַךְ:

1 By David, when he feigned madness before Avimelekh, who drove him away; and he left.

ב אֲבָרְכָה אֶת־יהוה בְּכָל־עֵת
תָּמִיד תְּהִלָּתוֹ בְּפִי:

2 I will bless the Lord at all times; His praise will always be in my mouth.

---

22 The psalm ends with a request: **Let Your kindness, Lord, be upon us, as we have put our hope in You.**

PSALM 34

1 **By David, when he feigned madness before Avimelekh, who drove him away; and he left.** When David fled from Saul, he found himself approaching the territory of Avimelekh king of the Philistines. Fearing that the Philistines would murder him in revenge for the many battles he had waged against them, David pretended to be mad, since madmen are generally regarded as being harmless. The ruse succeeded. David was not attacked but rather banished from Avimelekh's kingdom.[9] There appears to be no connection between the content of this psalm and the encounter with Avimelekh. David may have written the psalm, which is didactic rather than emotive in tone, in order to demonstrate that he was indeed rational and in full control of his faculties. It is also possible that the alphabetical acrostic is employed as additional evidence that, despite his feigning madness, David was capable of clearly ordered thinking.

2 **I will bless the Lord at all times,** in times of glory and redemption as well as times of sorrow and trouble. **His praise will always be in my mouth.** External circumstances, be they good or bad, will not interfere with the psalmist's continual blessing of God.

בַּיהוה תִּתְהַלֵּל נַפְשִׁי
יִשְׁמְעוּ עֲנָוִים וְיִשְׂמָחוּ:

ג

3 I will have glory in the Lord;
the humble will hear and
rejoice.

גַּדְּלוּ לַיהוה אִתִּי וּנְרוֹמְמָה
שְׁמוֹ יַחְדָּו:

ד

4 Declare the greatness of the
Lord with me; let us exalt His
name together.

דָּרַשְׁתִּי אֶת־יהוה וְעָנָנִי
וּמִכָּל־מְגוּרוֹתַי הִצִּילָנִי:

ה

5 I sought the Lord and He
answered me; He delivered me
from all the things I dreaded.

הִבִּיטוּ אֵלָיו וְנָהָרוּ וּפְנֵיהֶם
אַל־יֶחְפָּרוּ:

ו

6 Those who look to Him are
illuminated, and their faces will
never be ashamed.

זֶה עָנִי קָרָא וַיהוה שָׁמֵעַ
וּמִכָּל־צָרוֹתָיו הוֹשִׁיעוֹ:

ז

7 A poor man cried out, and the
Lord heard him and saved him
from all his troubles.

---

3 **I will have glory in the Lord.** Here the psalmist explains how he is able to praise God at all times. If he dwells on his own problems, he is liable to feel anguish and doubt. However, by thinking about God, he invariably comes to an awareness of God's greatness and glory, which are eternally present. **The humble will hear and rejoice.** Praising God has nothing to do with the state of man's glory; it is about the glory of God Himself. Even the humble, who regard themselves as unworthy, are able to rejoice and to sing God's praises.

4 Consequently, the psalmist calls on everyone to extol God: **Declare the greatness of the Lord with me; let us exalt His name together.**

5 **I sought the Lord and He answered me; He delivered me from all the things I dreaded.**

6 **Those who look to Him are illuminated, and their faces will never be ashamed.** The centrality of God's presence in their lives is a primary source of blessing and strength.

7 In addition, the psalmist affirms that God listens to them and comes to their aid: **A poor man cried out, and the Lord heard him and saved him from all his troubles.**

חֹנֶ֤ה מַלְאַךְ־יְהֹוָ֓ה סָבִ֖יב
לִֽירֵאָ֣יו וַֽיְחַלְּצֵֽם:

טַעֲמ֣וּ וּ֭רְאוּ כִּי־ט֣וֹב יְהֹוָ֑ה
אַֽשְׁרֵ֥י הַ֝גֶּ֗בֶר יֶֽחֱסֶה־בּֽוֹ:

יְר֣אוּ אֶת־יְהֹוָ֣ה קְדֹשָׁ֑יו כִּֽי־
אֵ֥ין מַ֝חְס֗וֹר לִֽירֵאָֽיו:

כְּפִירִ֣ים רָשׁ֣וּ וְרָעֵ֑בוּ וְדֹֽרְשֵׁ֥י
יְ֝הֹוָ֗ה לֹֽא־יַחְסְר֥וּ כׇל־טֽוֹב:

לְֽכוּ־בָ֭נִים שִׁמְעוּ־לִ֑י יִרְאַ֥ת
יְ֝הֹוָ֗ה אֲלַמֶּדְכֶֽם:

8 The angel of the Lord encamps around those who fear Him, and rescues them.

9 Taste and see that the Lord is good; happy is the man who takes refuge in Him.

10 Fear the Lord, His holy ones, for those who fear Him lack nothing.

11 Young lions may suffer from want and hunger, but those who seek the Lord will lack no good.

12 Come, children, listen to me; I will teach you to fear the Lord.

---

8 God's salvation is not always noticed by its beneficiary, but **the angel of the Lord encamps around those who fear Him, and rescues** and protects **them.**

9 **Taste and see that the Lord is good.** In order to come close to God, one needs to experience, or "taste," Him on some level so as to appreciate that "the Lord is good." **Happy is the man who takes refuge in Him.** Closeness to God, in and of itself, is the essence of good fortune, even when it is not rewarded by material gain.

10 Nonetheless, the psalmist offers assurance that closeness to God does bring tangible reward: **Fear the Lord, His holy ones,** those who dedicate themselves to serving Him. **For those who fear Him** are under His protection, and He sees to it that they **lack nothing.**

11 Even **young lions,** at the height of their physical power, **may suffer from want and hunger** at times for lack of prey, **but those who seek the Lord,** though they do not have the physical strength of lions, **will lack no good,** as God will see to it that their needs are met.

12 The psalmist continues with words of advice: **Come, children, listen to me; I will teach you to fear the Lord.** The following verses, addressed to students or young people, do not supply practical instruction for material success, but are intended to define the proper behavior of God-fearing people.

מִי־הָאִישׁ הֶחָפֵץ חַיִּים אֹהֵב
יָמִים לִרְאוֹת טוֹב:

^{יד} נְצֹר לְשׁוֹנְךָ מֵרָע וּשְׂפָתֶיךָ
מִדַּבֵּר מִרְמָה:

^{טו} סוּר מֵרָע וַעֲשֵׂה־טוֹב בַּקֵּשׁ
שָׁלוֹם וְרָדְפֵהוּ:

^{טז} עֵינֵי יְהוָה אֶל־צַדִּיקִים וְאָזְנָיו
אֶל־שַׁוְעָתָם:

^{יז} פְּנֵי יְהוָה בְּעֹשֵׂי רָע לְהַכְרִית
מֵאֶרֶץ זִכְרָם:

13 Who is the man who desires life, loving his days to see good?

14 Guard your tongue from evil and your lips from speaking deceit.

15 Turn away from evil and do good; seek peace and pursue it.

16 The eyes of the Lord are on the righteous, and His ears are open to their cry.

17 The face of the Lord turns against evildoers to excise their memory from the earth.

---

13 **Who is the man who desires life, loving his days** of his life in order **to see good** during his lifetime?

14 One piece of advice for such a person: **Guard your tongue from evil,** do not speak derogatively and refrain from using coarse language or shouting in anger even if you are justifiably upset, **and** guard **your lips from speaking** any words of **deceit.**

15 **Turn away from evil.** It is not always necessary to confront evil and fight against it; it is better to avoid contact with it from the outset. **And do good.** Actively pursuing good deeds is preferable to fighting off negative influences. In your dealings with your fellow man, **seek peace,** for there is always a way to resolve differences peacefully, **and pursue it.** Sometimes the peaceful approach is not conveniently available, and one must go out of his way to actively pursue it.

16 The psalmist now speaks of promises made by God to the righteous: **The eyes of the Lord are on the righteous;** He watches over them, never abandoning them, **and His ears are open to their cry.**

17 **The face of the Lord,** displaying His anger, **turns against evildoers.** He also attends to those who do evil; He does not allow their evil schemes to succeed, but turns **to excise their memory from the earth.**

יח צָעֲקוּ וַיהוה שָׁמֵעַ וּמִכָּל־
צָרוֹתָם הִצִּילָם:

יט קָרוֹב יהוה לְנִשְׁבְּרֵי־לֵב
וְאֶת־דַּכְּאֵי־רוּחַ יוֹשִׁיעַ:

כ רַבּוֹת רָעוֹת צַדִּיק וּמִכֻּלָּם
יַצִּילֶנּוּ יהוה:

כא שֹׁמֵר כָּל־עַצְמוֹתָיו אַחַת
מֵהֵנָּה לֹא נִשְׁבָּרָה:

כב תְּמוֹתֵת רָשָׁע רָעָה וְשֹׂנְאֵי
צַדִּיק יֶאְשָׁמוּ:

18 They cry out and the Lord hears them, delivering them from all their troubles.

19 The Lord is near to the brokenhearted and saves those whose spirit is crushed.

20 Many evils may afflict a righteous man, but the Lord delivers him from them all.

21 He preserves all his bones; not one of them will be broken.

22 Evil causes the death of the wicked, and those who hate the righteous will be condemned.

---

18 **They,** the righteous, **cry out and the Lord hears them, delivering them from all their troubles.**

19 God does not limit His attention to well-known righteous and God-fearing individuals; He also hearkens to the cries of the humblest and most downtrodden people: **The Lord is near to the** people whose suffering is so intense that they are **brokenhearted and saves those whose spirit is crushed.**

20 **Many evils may afflict a righteous man, but** ultimately, **the Lord delivers him from them all.**

21 Even if the righteous man may fall, **He preserves all his bones** and ensures that **not one of them will be broken,** so extensive is God's protection of him.

22 **Evil causes the death of the wicked.** This is not necessarily referring to divine punishment; rather, evil by its very nature is essentially noxious and deadly. **And those who hate the righteous will be condemned** to failure and destroyed by their own actions.

כב פּוֹדֶה יהוה נֶפֶשׁ עֲבָדָיו וְלֹא יֶאְשְׁמוּ כָּל־הַחֹסִים בּוֹ:

23 The Lord redeems the souls of His servants, and none are condemned who take refuge in Him.

PSALM 35

A psalm of prayer in which the psalmist beseeches God to actively protect and defend him against his many enemies.

א לְדָוִד ו רִיבָה יהוה אֶת־יְרִיבַי לְחַם אֶת־לֹחֲמָי:

ב הַחֲזֵק מָגֵן וְצִנָּה וְקוּמָה בְּעֶזְרָתִי:

ג וְהָרֵק חֲנִית וּסְגֹר לִקְרַאת רֹדְפָי אֱמֹר לְנַפְשִׁי יְשֻׁעָתֵךְ אָנִי:

ולחודש
6th day
of month

1 By David. Strive, Lord, against my rivals. Fight on my behalf.

2 Take hold of shield and armor and rise up to help me,

3 and unsheathe the spear to block my pursuers; say to me: I am your salvation.

---

23 This last verse, beginning with the letter *peh*, the significance of which is explained in the introduction to Psalm 25, is connected to the previous one. In contrast to the fate of the evildoers, whom God abandons to the natural consequences of their sinful deeds, **the Lord redeems the souls of His servants,** sparing them from harm emanating from themselves or from others, **and none are condemned who take refuge in Him.**

PSALM 35
1 By David. Strive, Lord, against my rivals. Fight on my behalf.
2 Take hold of shield and armor and rise up to help me,
3 and unsheathe the spear to block my pursuers; say to me: I am your salvation.

יֵבֹ֓שׁוּ וְיִכָּלְמוּ֮ מְבַקְשֵׁ֪י נַ֫פְשִׁ֥י ד
יִסֹּ֣גוּ אָ֭חוֹר וְיַחְפְּר֑וּ חֹ֝שְׁבֵ֗י
רָעָתִֽי׃

⁴ Let those who seek my life be ashamed and dishonored; may those devising evil against me be turned back and humiliated.

יִֽהְי֗וּ כְּמֹ֥ץ לִפְנֵי־ר֑וּחַ וּמַלְאַ֖ךְ ה
יהוה דּוֹחֶֽה׃

⁵ Let them be like chaff in the wind, with an angel of the Lord scattering them.

יְֽהִי־דַרְכָּ֗ם חֹ֥שֶׁךְ וַחֲלַקְלַקֹּ֑ת ו
וּמַלְאַ֥ךְ יהוה רֹדְפָֽם׃

⁶ Let their way be dark and slippery, with an angel of the Lord pursuing them.

כִּֽי־חִנָּ֣ם טָֽמְנוּ־לִ֭י שַׁ֣חַת ז
רִשְׁתָּ֑ם חִ֝נָּ֗ם חָפְר֥וּ לְנַפְשִֽׁי׃

⁷ For without cause they have hidden ditches and nets against me; without cause they have dug pits for my soul.

תְּבוֹאֵ֣הוּ שׁוֹאָה֮ לֹֽא־יֵ֫דָ֥ע ח
וְרִשְׁתּ֣וֹ אֲשֶׁר־טָמַ֣ן תִּלְכְּד֑וֹ
בְּ֝שׁוֹאָ֗ה יִפָּל־בָּֽהּ׃

⁸ Let calamity come upon him unawares; let the net that he laid ensnare him. Let him plunge into that very calamity.

וְ֭נַפְשִׁי תָּגִ֣יל בַּיהוה תָּ֝שִׂ֗ישׂ ט
בִּישׁוּעָתֽוֹ׃

⁹ As for me, I will rejoice in the Lord, happy in His salvation.

---

⁴ **Let those who seek my life be ashamed and dishonored; may those devising evil against me be turned back and humiliated.**

⁵ **Let them be like chaff in the wind, with an angel of the Lord scattering them.**

⁶ **Let their way be dark and slippery,** two factors that are likely to cause one to lose footing and fall, **with an angel of the Lord pursuing them.**

⁷ **For without cause they have hidden ditches and nets against me** with which to trap me; **without cause they have dug pits for** the purpose of harming me or taking **my soul.**

⁸ **Let calamity come upon him,** upon my enemy, **unawares,** without him even understanding what it was that brought him down. **Let the net that he laid** for me actually **ensnare him** instead. **Let him plunge into that very calamity** that he had planned for me.

⁹ **As for me, I will rejoice in the Lord, happy in His salvation.**

כָּל עַצְמֹתַי ׀ תֹּאמַרְנָה יהוה
מִי כָמוֹךָ מַצִּיל עָנִי מֵחָזָק
מִמֶּנּוּ וְעָנִי וְאֶבְיוֹן מִגֹּזְלוֹ:

יא יָקוּמוּן עֵדֵי חָמָס אֲשֶׁר לֹא־
יָדַעְתִּי יִשְׁאָלוּנִי:

יב יְשַׁלְּמוּנִי רָעָה תַּחַת טוֹבָה
שְׁכוֹל לְנַפְשִׁי:

יג וַאֲנִי ׀ בַּחֲלוֹתָם לְבוּשִׁי שָׂק
עִנֵּיתִי בַצּוֹם נַפְשִׁי וּתְפִלָּתִי
עַל־חֵיקִי תָשׁוּב:

יד כְּרֵעַ־כְּאָח לִי הִתְהַלָּכְתִּי
כַּאֲבֶל־אֵם קֹדֵר שַׁחוֹתִי:

10 All my bones will say: Lord, who is like You, who delivers the poor from those who are stronger, the poor and the needy from their despoiler?

11 Malicious witnesses arise, asking me concerning things about which I know nothing.

12 They repay me evil for good, causing me grief.

13 Whereas I, when they were sick, my garb was sackcloth. I afflicted my soul in fasting, but my prayer returned to my breast.

14 As if with a beloved friend or brother I walked along, bowed in gloom, as if grieving for a mother.

---

10 **All my bones will say,** my entire body, as it were, will join with my mouth in praising God: **Lord, who is like You, who delivers the poor from those who are stronger, the poor and the needy from their despoiler?**

11 The psalmist describes some of the evil plans his enemies have employed against him: **Malicious,** false **witnesses arise** to accuse me, **asking me concerning things about which I know nothing,** imputing to me baseless claims.

12 What hurts most is that some of my accusers are people whom I used to help out in their times of need. **They repay me evil for good, causing me grief.**

13 **Whereas I, when they were sick,** felt genuine sympathy for them, and **my garb was sackcloth** as an expression of my distress over their troubles. **I afflicted my soul in fasting, but my prayer returned to my breast.** They did not appreciate my commiseration and actions on their behalf; to them it is as if my prayers were being uttered for myself.

14 **As if with a beloved friend or brother I walked along** with them, sharing their burden, **bowed in gloom, as if grieving for a** deceased **mother.**

וּבְצַלְעִי שָׂמְחוּ וְנֶאֱסָפוּ ט
נֶאֶסְפוּ עָלַי נֵכִים וְלֹא יָדַעְתִּי
קָרְעוּ וְלֹא־דָמּוּ:

בְּחַנְפֵי לַעֲגֵי מָעוֹג חָרֹק עָלַי ט
שִׁנֵּימוֹ:

אֲדֹנָי כַּמָּה תִּרְאֶה הָשִׁיבָה ז
נַפְשִׁי מִשֹּׁאֵיהֶם מִכְּפִירִים
יְחִידָתִי:

אוֹדְךָ בְּקָהָל רָב בְּעַם עָצוּם ח
אֲהַלְלֶךָּ:

אַל־יִשְׂמְחוּ־לִי אֹיְבַי שֶׁקֶר ט
שֹׂנְאַי חִנָּם יִקְרְצוּ־עָיִן:

15 But when I was limping, they rejoiced and gathered together; my attackers congregated without my knowing, tearing at me without pause.

16 In their hypocrisy they made contemptuous gestures; they gnashed their teeth at me.

17 My Lord, how long will You look on? Rescue me from their ravages; save my soul from young lions.

18 I will thank You in a great assembly; I will praise You among a mighty throng.

19 Do not allow my false enemies to gloat over me, or those who hate me without cause to wink with their eyes.

---

15 **But,** in marked contrast, **when I was limping** and hurting, **they rejoiced and gathered together** to gloat and taunt me. **My attackers congregated without my knowing** what it was that caused them to turn against me, **tearing at me,** at my clothing and my flesh, **without pause.**

16 **In their hypocrisy they made contemptuous gestures; they gnashed their teeth at me** in contempt and enmity.

17 In the face of such hatred, the psalmist prays to God: **My Lord, how long will You look on** without coming to my aid? **Rescue me from their ravages** that they have devised for me; **save my soul from** these enemies, who may be compared to **young lions** in their ferocity.

18 After You heed my prayer and save me, **I will thank You in a great assembly; I will praise You among a mighty throng.**

19 **Do not allow my false enemies,** enemies who pretended all along to be my friends, **to gloat over me, or those who hate me without cause,** people who had no reason to hate me and hence remained unsuspected by me, **to wink with their eyes** toward me in contempt.

כ כִּי לֹא שָׁלוֹם יְדַבֵּרוּ וְעַל
רִגְעֵי־אֶרֶץ דִּבְרֵי מִרְמוֹת
יַחֲשֹׁבוּן:

כא וַיַּרְחִיבוּ עָלַי פִּיהֶם אָמְרוּ
הֶאָח ׀ הֶאָח רָאֲתָה עֵינֵנוּ:

כב רָאִיתָה יְהוָה אַל־תֶּחֱרַשׁ
אֲדֹנָי אַל־תִּרְחַק מִמֶּנִּי:

כג הָעִירָה וְהָקִיצָה לְמִשְׁפָּטִי
אֱלֹהַי וַאדֹנָי לְרִיבִי:

כד שָׁפְטֵנִי כְצִדְקְךָ יְהוָה אֱלֹהָי
וְאַל־יִשְׂמְחוּ־לִי:

כה אַל־יֹאמְרוּ בְלִבָּם הֶאָח
נַפְשֵׁנוּ אַל־יֹאמְרוּ בִּלַּעֲנוּהוּ:

²⁰ For they do not speak of peace; they devise deceitful plans against those living serenely in the land.

²¹ They open their mouths wide against me, saying: Hurrah, hurrah! Our eyes have seen it.

²² You have seen this, Lord; do not keep silent. Lord, do not be far from me.

²³ Be bestirred and awaken to justice for me, my God and my Lord to my struggle.

²⁴ Vindicate me, Lord my God, as befits Your righteousness; do not let them rejoice over me.

²⁵ Do not let them say in their heart: Hurrah for us! Do not let them say: We have devoured him.

---

20 **For they do not speak of peace** toward me; **they devise deceitful plans against those living serenely in the land,** who harbor no malice toward anyone.

21 And when they believe that they have witnessed my downfall, **they** mockingly **open their mouths wide against me, saying: Hurrah, hurrah! Our eyes have** finally **seen it,** his defeat.

22 **You have seen this, Lord; do not keep silent. Lord, do not be far from me.**

23 **Be bestirred and awaken to** do **justice for me; my God and my Lord,** come **to** aid me in **my struggle.**

24 **Vindicate me, Lord my God, as befits Your righteousness; do not let them rejoice over me.**

25 **Do not let them say in their heart: Hurrah for us,** for he has finally fallen! **Do not let them say: We have devoured** and destroyed **him.**

כו יֵבֹ֤שׁוּ וְיַחְפְּר֨וּ ׀ יַחְדָּו֮ שְׂמֵחֵ֪י
רָעָ֫תִ֥י יִֽלְבְּשׁוּ־בֹ֥שֶׁת וּכְלִמָּ֑ה
הַֽמַּגְדִּילִ֥ים עָלָֽי׃

כז יָרֹ֣נּוּ וְיִשְׂמְחוּ֮ חֲפֵצֵ֪י צִ֫דְקִ֥י
וְיֹאמְר֣וּ תָ֭מִיד יִגְדַּ֣ל יְהֹוָ֑ה
הֶ֝חָפֵ֗ץ שְׁל֣וֹם עַבְדּֽוֹ׃

כח וּ֭לְשׁוֹנִי תֶּהְגֶּ֣ה צִדְקֶ֑ךָ כׇּל־
הַ֝יּ֗וֹם תְּהִלָּתֶֽךָ׃

26 May those who rejoice at my distress be altogether ashamed and humiliated; may those who glorify themselves about me be clothed in shame and dishonor.

27 May those who desire my vindication sing out and rejoice, always saying: Great is the Lord who delights in the well-being of His servant.

28 And my tongue will utter Your righteousness, Your praises all day long.

PSALM 36

A psalm that contrasts the wicked person, who from lack of faith is drawn deeper and deeper into evil, with the righteous person, whose chief happiness is to cleave to God. The psalmist prays for the downfall of the wicked and the salvation of the righteous.

א לַמְנַצֵּ֬חַ ׀ לְעֶבֶד־יְהֹוָ֬ה לְדָוִֽד׃

1 For the chief musician, by David servant of the Lord.

---

26 **May those who rejoice at my distress be altogether ashamed and humiliated; may those who glorify themselves about me,** about my misfortune, **be clothed in shame and dishonor.**

27 The psalmist ends on a positive note: **May those who desire my vindication sing out and rejoice, always saying: Great is the Lord who delights in the well-being of His servant** and has therefore granted him salvation.

28 **And** then **my tongue will utter Your righteousness, Your praises all day long.**

PSALM 36

1 **For the chief musician, by David servant of the Lord.** The unique phrasing of this

נְאֻם־פֶּשַׁע לָרָשָׁע בְּקֶרֶב
לִבִּי אֵין־פַּחַד אֱלֹהִים לְנֶגֶד
עֵינָיו:

כִּי־הֶחֱלִיק אֵלָיו בְּעֵינָיו
לִמְצֹא עֲוֹנוֹ לִשְׂנֹא:

דִּבְרֵי־פִיו אָוֶן וּמִרְמָה חָדַל
לְהַשְׂכִּיל לְהֵיטִיב:

אָוֶן ׀ יַחְשֹׁב עַל־מִשְׁכָּבוֹ
יִתְיַצֵּב עַל־דֶּרֶךְ לֹא־טוֹב רָע
לֹא יִמְאָס:

יהוה בְּהַשָּׁמַיִם חַסְדֶּךָ
אֱמוּנָתְךָ עַד־שְׁחָקִים:

2 Sinfulness speaks to the wicked one, in my heart. There is no fear of God before him.

3 For in his eyes he glides past Him to find his iniquity, to hate.

4 The words of his mouth are wickedness and deceit; he has ceased to learn to do what is good.

5 He plots wickedness in his bed; he sets himself on a path of no good; he does not abhor evil.

6 Your kindness, Lord, extends to the heavens; Your faithfulness reaches the skies.

---

introductory verse, "David servant of the Lord," is an expression of David's love and fear of God. Although the psalm addresses issues that are relevant to people in general, its personal expressions of devotion are based on the psalmist's life experience.

2 **Sinfulness speaks to the wicked one.** This dialogue sometimes takes place **in my** own **heart;** it is an internal dialogue that is known to me personally. The central attribute of the wicked person is that **there is no fear of God before him.** He may acknowledge God's existence, but, lacking fear of Him, such a person finds ways to rationalize his behavior and continue to sin.

3 **For in his eyes,** in his own misguided opinion, **he glides past Him.** The sinner thinks that he can somehow evade God's attention **to** thereby **find,** commit, **his iniquity, to hate** others.

4 **The words of his mouth are wickedness and deceit; he has ceased to learn to do what is good.** He no longer tries to mend his ways, instead allowing his evil impulses to go unrestrained.

5 **He plots wickedness in his bed** as he goes to sleep, and when he arises, **he sets himself on a path of no good; he does not abhor evil.** This is a description of a person going through an internal spiritual crisis or breakdown. Even if he has not completely lost his faith in God, such faith no longer serves to block his negative thoughts or behavior. He is on a road spiraling downward.

6 But there is an alternative path, one that leads to enlightenment. For those who contemplate the matter, know that **Your kindness, Lord, extends to the heavens; Your faithfulness reaches the skies.**

צִדְקָתְךָ ׀ כְּהַרְרֵי־אֵל
מִשְׁפָּטֶיךָ תְּהוֹם רַבָּה אָדָם
וּבְהֵמָה תוֹשִׁיעַ ׀ יְהֹוָה:

מַה־יָּקָר חַסְדְּךָ אֱלֹהִים וּבְנֵי
אָדָם בְּצֵל כְּנָפֶיךָ יֶחֱסָיוּן:

יִרְוְיֻן מִדֶּשֶׁן בֵּיתֶךָ וְנַחַל
עֲדָנֶיךָ תַשְׁקֵם:

כִּי־עִמְּךָ מְקוֹר חַיִּים בְּאוֹרְךָ
נִרְאֶה־אוֹר:

מְשֹׁךְ חַסְדְּךָ לְיֹדְעֶיךָ
וְצִדְקָתְךָ לְיִשְׁרֵי־לֵב:

7 Your righteousness is like mighty mountains; Your judgments are a fathomless deep. Lord, You save man and beast.

8 How precious is Your kindness, God; men take refuge in the shadow of Your garment.

9 They are sated by the rich fare of Your House; You give them drink from the stream of Your delights.

10 For the source of life is with You; through Your light we see light.

11 Extend Your kindness to those who know You, and Your righteousness to the upright of heart.

---

7 **Your righteousness,** Your beneficence, **is** steadfast, **like mighty mountains,** and **Your judgments are** like **a fathomless deep. Lord, You save man and beast.** God's righteousness and faithfulness extend to everything He has created, man and beast alike.

8 Some expressions of the psalmist's personal experience follow: **How precious is Your kindness, God; men take refuge in the shadow of Your garment.** Those who seek God's intimacy feel protected by Him, as if enveloped in His cloak.

9 **They are sated by the rich fare of Your House; You give them drink from the stream of Your delights.** The experience of being close to God is comparable to having one's hunger satiated and thirst slaked.

10 **For the source of life is with You,** and those who are close to You benefit from that life. **Through Your light we see light.** Closeness to God supplies one with a sense of satisfaction and enlightenment.

11 **Extend Your kindness to those who know You,** those who love You and therefore strive to know You, **and** show **Your righteousness to the upright of heart,** those whose internal compass always points toward God, and who are therefore devoid of crookedness and deception.

אַל־תְּבוֹאֵנִי רֶגֶל גַּאֲוָה וְיַד־ ¹² Let no arrogant foot come to
רְשָׁעִים אַל־תְּנִדֵנִי: me; let no hand of the wicked
drive me away.

שָׁם נָפְלוּ פֹּעֲלֵי אָוֶן דֹּחוּ ¹³ There the evildoers have fallen,
וְלֹא־יָכְלוּ קוּם: cast down and unable to rise.

PSALM 37

An instructive psalm, much of which is organized alphabetically, whose main theme is that the
wicked, in all their varieties, are fated for destruction, despite any temporary success they may
enjoy. In contrast, those who love and trust in God eventually flourish and endure.

לְדָוִד ׀ אַל־תִּתְחַר בַּמְּרֵעִים ¹ By David. Contend not with
אַל־תְּקַנֵּא בְּעֹשֵׂי עַוְלָה: the wicked, nor be envious of
evildoers.

כִּי כֶחָצִיר מְהֵרָה יִמָּלוּ וּכְיֶרֶק ² They will soon be cut down
דֶּשֶׁא יִבּוֹלוּן: like grass, wither like the
green herb.

---

¹² The psalmist concludes with a request: **Let no arrogant foot come to me.** Do not let my
actions be spoiled by arrogance, whether coming from others or from within myself. **Let no hand
of the wicked drive me away** from You.

¹³ **There,** in the proximity of God, **the evildoers have fallen, cast down and unable to rise.**

PSALM 37

¹ **By David. Contend not with the wicked.** Do not compare your situation with that of evildoers.
Do not compete with them nor emulate them, **nor be envious of evildoers.** A person who is
not evil is harmed by putting himself in the same arena as the wicked; his image is damaged and
his desires are corrupted. In addition, while it may appear that bad people always seem to succeed,
their success is fleeting:

² **They will soon be cut down like grass** that is cut while still green and used for animal feed;
they will **wither like the green herb.** They are like fields that turn a vibrant green after the
rains begin, but, as experience shows, quickly dry out and turn brown.

בְּטַח בַּיהוה וַעֲשֵׂה־טוֹב
שְׁכָן־אֶרֶץ וּרְעֵה אֱמוּנָה:

וְהִתְעַנַּג עַל־יהוה וְיִתֶּן־לְךָ
מִשְׁאֲלֹת לִבֶּךָ:

גּוֹל עַל־יהוה דַּרְכֶּךָ וּבְטַח
עָלָיו וְהוּא יַעֲשֶׂה:

וְהוֹצִיא כָאוֹר צִדְקֶךָ
וּמִשְׁפָּטֶךָ כַּצָּהֳרָיִם:

דּוֹם ׀ לַיהוה וְהִתְחוֹלֵל לוֹ
אַל־תִּתְחַר בְּמַצְלִיחַ דַּרְכּוֹ
בְּאִישׁ עֹשֶׂה מְזִמּוֹת:

³ Trust in the Lord and do good; dwell in the land and cultivate faithfulness.

⁴ Take pleasure in the Lord, and He will grant you the desires of your heart.

⁵ Cast the path of your life onto the Lord; trust in Him and He will act.

⁶ He will bring your righteousness to light, your vindication bright as noon.

⁷ Be silent before the Lord and wait for Him; do not contend with one who prospers or the man who is busy with intrigue.

---

3 **Trust in the Lord and do good; dwell in the land.** Avoid self-aggrandizement by associating with the humbler people of the land, **and cultivate faithfulness.** The literal meaning of the verb *re'eh*, which is translated here as "cultivate," is "to herd," "to graze," or "to feed oneself." A person who "grazes in faithfulness" is nourished and sustained by his faith in God. The phrase is thus a call to live modestly, subsisting on faithfulness, rather than seeking to attain material affluence.

4 **Take pleasure in the Lord** from being close to Him, **and** in the end, **He will grant you the desires of your heart.**

5 **Cast the path of your life onto the Lord.** *Gol*, translated here as "cast," literally means to roll something. The psalmist here encourages us to roll over, or transfer, the burdens of our daily life onto God and rely solely on Him. **Trust in Him and He will act** in response to this by assisting you.

6 Even if others behave toward you with deceit, maintain your own goodness and innocence, and **He will bring your righteousness to light, your vindication bright as noon.**

7 **Be silent before the Lord and wait for Him; do not contend with one who prospers** through unjust means **or the man who is busy with intrigue.**

הֶ֣רֶף מֵ֭אַף וַעֲזֹ֣ב חֵמָ֑ה אַל־
תִּ֝תְחַ֗ר אַךְ־לְהָרֵֽעַ: ח

כִּֽי־מְ֭רֵעִים יִכָּרֵת֑וּן וְקֹוֵ֥י יְהֹוָ֗ה
הֵ֣מָּה יִֽירְשׁוּ־אָֽרֶץ: ט

וְע֣וֹד מְ֭עַט וְאֵ֣ין רָשָׁ֑ע
וְהִתְבּוֹנַ֖נְתָּ עַל־מְקוֹמ֣וֹ
וְאֵינֶֽנּוּ: י

וַעֲנָוִ֥ים יִֽירְשׁוּ־אָ֑רֶץ וְֽהִתְעַנְּג֗וּ
עַל־רֹ֥ב שָׁלֽוֹם: יא

זֹמֵ֣ם רָ֭שָׁע לַצַּדִּ֑יק וְחֹרֵ֖ק
עָלָ֣יו שִׁנָּֽיו: יב

אֲדֹנָ֥י יִשְׂחַק־ל֑וֹ כִּֽי־רָ֝אָ֗ה כִּֽי־
יָבֹ֥א יוֹמֽוֹ: יג

8 Leave off anger and forsake wrath. Do not contend merely to make things go badly.

9 For evildoers will be cut off, while those who place their hope in the Lord will inherit the earth.

10 Soon the wicked man will be no more; you will gaze at his place and he will be gone,

11 while the humble inherit the earth, delighting in abundant peace.

12 The wicked man plots against the righteous man, gnashing his teeth at him.

13 The Lord laughs at him; He sees his day coming.

---

8 Maintain your righteousness not only in the realm of action but also in your emotions: **Leave off anger and forsake wrath,** both of which often cause a person to stray from the proper path. **Do not contend** and compete with the wicked, even if **merely to make things go badly** for them, to avenge misdeeds they may have committed against you.

9 It is unnecessary for you to take revenge or punish those who have wronged you, **for evildoers will be cut off** even without your efforts, **while those who place their hope in the Lord will inherit the earth,** including the portions owned by those evildoers.

10 **Soon the wicked man will be no more; you will gaze at his** former **place and he will be gone.** This can mean that he will no longer be alive, or that he will no longer be enjoying his former state of power and prosperity,

11 **while the humble,** as opposed to those sinners, will enjoy stability and **inherit the earth, delighting in abundant peace** and well-being.

12 **The wicked man plots against the righteous man,** menacingly **gnashing his teeth at him.**

13 But **the Lord laughs at him** and his evil schemes; **He sees his day** of downfall **coming.**

יד חֶ֤רֶב ׀ פָּתְח֣וּ רְשָׁעִים֮ וְדָרְכ֪וּ קַ֫שְׁתָּ֥ם לְהַפִּ֥יל עָנִ֥י וְאֶבְי֑וֹן לִ֝טְב֗וֹחַ יִשְׁרֵי־דָֽרֶךְ׃

טו חַ֭רְבָּם תָּב֣וֹא בְלִבָּ֑ם וְ֝קַשְּׁתוֹתָ֗ם תִּשָּׁבַֽרְנָה׃

טז טֽוֹב־מְ֭עַט לַצַּדִּ֑יק מֵ֝הֲמ֗וֹן רְשָׁעִ֥ים רַבִּֽים׃

יז כִּ֤י זְרוֹע֣וֹת רְ֭שָׁעִים תִּשָּׁבַ֑רְנָה וְסוֹמֵ֖ךְ צַדִּיקִ֣ים יְהֹוָֽה׃

יח יוֹדֵ֣עַ יְ֭הֹוָה יְמֵ֣י תְמִימִ֑ם וְ֝נַחֲלָתָ֗ם לְעוֹלָ֥ם תִּהְיֶֽה׃

יט לֹֽא־יֵ֭בֹשׁוּ בְּעֵ֣ת רָעָ֑ה וּבִימֵ֖י רְעָב֣וֹן יִשְׂבָּֽעוּ׃

14 The wicked draw their swords and stretch their bows to cast down the poor and the needy, to slaughter those who are upright in conduct.

15 Their swords will come into their own hearts, and their bows will be broken.

16 Better a little for the righteous man than abundance for many wicked people,

17 for the arms of the wicked will be broken, while the Lord supports the righteous.

18 The Lord knows the days of the blameless; their portion will last forever.

19 They are not put to shame in difficult times; in days of famine they eat their fill.

---

14 **The wicked draw their swords and stretch their bows** in order **to cast down the poor and the needy, to slaughter those who are upright in conduct.**

15 But in the end, **their swords will come into their own hearts, and their bows will be broken.**

16 **Better a little for the righteous man than abundance for many wicked people.** The goods and property possessed by the wicked are ephemeral.

17 **For the arms of the wicked will be broken, while the Lord supports the righteous.**

18 **The Lord knows** and loves **the days** and ways of life **of the blameless;** consequently, **their portion will last forever.**

19 **They are not put to shame** even **in difficult times;** in days of famine they eat their fill.

כ כִּי רְשָׁעִים ׀ יֹאבֵדוּ וְאֹיְבֵי
יְהֹוָה כִּיקַר כָּרִים כָּלוּ בֶעָשָׁן
כָּלוּ:

כא לֹוֶה רָשָׁע וְלֹא יְשַׁלֵּם וְצַדִּיק
חוֹנֵן וְנוֹתֵן:

כב כִּי מְבֹרָכָיו יִירְשׁוּ אָרֶץ
וּמְקֻלָּלָיו יִכָּרֵתוּ:

כג מֵיְהֹוָה מִצְעֲדֵי־גֶבֶר כּוֹנָנוּ
וְדַרְכּוֹ יֶחְפָּץ:

כד כִּי־יִפֹּל לֹא־יוּטָל כִּי־יְהֹוָה
סוֹמֵךְ יָדוֹ:

כה נַעַר ׀ הָיִיתִי גַּם־זָקַנְתִּי וְלֹא־
רָאִיתִי צַדִּיק נֶעֱזָב וְזַרְעוֹ
מְבַקֶּשׁ־לָחֶם:

20 But the wicked will perish, and the enemies of the Lord will be like the fat of rams; they will utterly vanish in smoke.

21 The wicked one borrows and does not repay; the righteous one is gracious and gives.

22 Those whom he blesses inherit the earth; those whom he curses are cut off.

23 The Lord sets the footsteps of man; He desires his path.

24 When he stumbles, he will not fall down, because the Lord takes his hand.

25 I was once a youth, now I have grown old, and I have never seen a righteous man forsaken, nor his children seeking bread.

---

20 **But the wicked will perish, and the enemies of the Lord will be like the fat of rams,** consumed by others; **they will utterly vanish in smoke.**

21 **The wicked one borrows and does not repay.** It is typical of bad people to take whatever they can and not give to others, even what is owed them. **The righteous one,** in contrast, **is gracious and gives** of his possessions to others, either as a loan or, if needed, as an outright gift.

22 **Those whom he,** the righteous man, **blesses inherit the earth; those whom he curses are cut off.**

23 **The Lord sets the footsteps of man; He desires his path,** the upright path of the righteous man.

24 **When he,** the righteous man, **stumbles, he will not fall down, because the Lord takes his hand.** The image here is of a father holding his child's hand; even if the child trips, he does not fall to the ground, since his father is supporting him.

25 **I was once a youth, now I have grown old, and I have never seen a righteous man forsaken, nor his children seeking bread.** Even if a righteous person may not be counted

כו כָּל־הַיּוֹם חוֹנֵן וּמַלְוֶה וְזַרְעוֹ
לִבְרָכָה:

כז סוּר מֵרָע וַעֲשֵׂה־טוֹב וּשְׁכֹן
לְעוֹלָם:

כח כִּי יְהֹוָה ׀ אֹהֵב מִשְׁפָּט וְלֹא־
יַעֲזֹב אֶת־חֲסִידָיו לְעוֹלָם
נִשְׁמָרוּ וְזֶרַע רְשָׁעִים נִכְרָת:

כט צַדִּיקִים יִירְשׁוּ־אָרֶץ וְיִשְׁכְּנוּ
לָעַד עָלֶיהָ:

ל פִּי־צַדִּיק יֶהְגֶּה חָכְמָה
וּלְשׁוֹנוֹ תְּדַבֵּר מִשְׁפָּט:

לא תּוֹרַת אֱלֹהָיו בְּלִבּוֹ לֹא
תִמְעַד אֲשֻׁרָיו:

26 All day long he is gracious and lending, and his children become a blessing.

27 Turn from evil and do good, and dwell securely forever,

28 for the Lord loves justice and does not forsake His pious ones. They are guarded forever, while the seed of the wicked is cut off.

29 The righteous will inherit the earth and dwell on it forever.

30 The mouth of the righteous utters wisdom, and his tongue speaks justice.

31 The teaching of his God is in his heart; his steps do not falter.

---

among the prominent, wealthy people of his time, he is never entirely forsaken, nor are his children. This is in contrast to the wicked, who ultimately experience utter ruin.

26 **All day long he is gracious and lending, and his children become a blessing.** The children of the righteous "become a blessing," not only in the sense of God rewarding them for their father's beneficence, but also, more practically, because people who benefited from their father's generosity will look after them.

27 **Turn from evil and do good, and** thereby **dwell securely forever,**

28 **for the Lord loves justice and does not forsake His pious ones. They are guarded forever, while the seed of the wicked is cut off.**

29 **The righteous will inherit the earth and dwell on it forever.**

30 The psalmist now describes the behavior of the righteous: **The mouth of the righteous utters wisdom, and his tongue speaks justice,** voicing proper and just statements.

31 **The teaching of his God is in his heart; his steps do not falter.**

צוֹפֶה רָשָׁע לַצַּדִּיק וּמְבַקֵּשׁ
לַהֲמִיתוֹ:

יהוה לֹא־יַעַזְבֶנּוּ בְיָדוֹ וְלֹא
יַרְשִׁיעֶנּוּ בְּהִשָּׁפְטוֹ:

קַוֵּה אֶל־יהוה ׀ וּשְׁמֹר
דַּרְכּוֹ וִירוֹמִמְךָ לָרֶשֶׁת אָרֶץ
בְּהִכָּרֵת רְשָׁעִים תִּרְאֶה:

רָאִיתִי רָשָׁע עָרִיץ וּמִתְעָרֶה
כְּאֶזְרָח רַעֲנָן:

וַיַּעֲבֹר וְהִנֵּה אֵינֶנּוּ
וָאֲבַקְשֵׁהוּ וְלֹא נִמְצָא:

שְׁמָר־תָּם וּרְאֵה יָשָׁר כִּי־
אַחֲרִית לְאִישׁ שָׁלוֹם:

32 The wicked man spies out the righteous man and seeks to kill him,

33 but the Lord will not leave him in his hand or let him be condemned when judged.

34 Put your hope in the Lord and follow His ways, and He will raise you up to inherit the earth; when the wicked are cut off, you will see it.

35 I have seen a cruel and wicked man firmly rooted like a well-watered tree in its native soil.

36 He passed away and was gone; I looked for him, but he was no longer to be found.

37 Maintain innocence, seek integrity, for there is a future for the man of peace.

---

32 To be sure, **the wicked man spies out the righteous man and seeks to kill him,**

33 **but the Lord will not leave him in his hand.** He will not abandon the righteous to the hands of the wicked **or let him be condemned when judged.**

34 **Put your hope in the Lord and follow His ways and,** if you follow in God's path, **He will** ultimately **raise you up** from your lowly position **to inherit the earth. When the wicked are cut off, you will see it.**

35 **I have seen a cruel and wicked man firmly rooted like a well-watered tree in its native soil.**

36 Yet sometime later, I saw that despite his apparent sturdiness and robustness, **he passed away and was gone; I looked for him but he was no longer to be found.**

37 **Maintain** the path of **innocence, seek** the path of **integrity, for there is a** bright **future for the man of peace.**

וּפֹשְׁעִים נִשְׁמְדוּ יַחְדָּו אַחֲרִית רְשָׁעִים נִכְרָתָה: לח

וּתְשׁוּעַת צַדִּיקִים מֵיהֹוָה מָעוּזָּם בְּעֵת צָרָה: לט

וַיַּעְזְרֵם יְהֹוָה וַיְפַלְּטֵם יְפַלְּטֵם מֵרְשָׁעִים וְיוֹשִׁיעֵם כִּי־חָסוּ בוֹ: מ

38 But transgressors will be altogether destroyed, the future of the wicked cut off.

39 The salvation of the righteous is from the Lord; He is their strength in times of trouble.

40 The Lord helps them and rescues them; He will rescue and deliver them from the wicked, because they took refuge in Him.

PSALM 38

A psalm of supplication by one who suffers calamity and is wracked with physical pain and the anguish of being abandoned by formerly close friends. The psalmist acknowledges his transgressions and pleads to God for salvation, for apart from God, he has nothing.

מִזְמוֹר לְדָוִד לְהַזְכִּיר: א 1 A psalm by David, to remind.

---

38 **But transgressors,** in contrast, **will be altogether destroyed, the future of the wicked cut off.**

39 **The salvation of the righteous is from the Lord; He is their strength in times of trouble.**

40 **The Lord helps them and rescues them; He will rescue and deliver them from the wicked, because they took refuge in Him.**

PSALM 38

1 **A psalm by David, to remind.** This psalm was apparently meant to remind God, as it were,[10] of how the psalmist suffered. It seems to have been written when the psalmist was gravely ill and in great physical pain. At the time, his enemies were convinced that his death was imminent and were hopeful that they would soon be able to celebrate his downfall.

יְהֹוָה אַל־בְּקֶצְפְּךָ תוֹכִיחֵנִי
וּבַחֲמָתְךָ תְיַסְּרֵנִי:

כִּי־חִצֶּיךָ נִחֲתוּ בִי וַתִּנְחַת
עָלַי יָדֶךָ:

אֵין־מְתֹם בִּבְשָׂרִי מִפְּנֵי
זַעְמֶךָ אֵין־שָׁלוֹם בַּעֲצָמַי
מִפְּנֵי חַטָּאתִי:

כִּי עֲוֺנֹתַי עָבְרוּ רֹאשִׁי
כְּמַשָּׂא כָבֵד יִכְבְּדוּ מִמֶּנִּי:

הִבְאִישׁוּ נָמַקּוּ חַבּוּרֹתָי מִפְּנֵי
אִוַּלְתִּי:

נַעֲוֵיתִי שַׁחֹתִי עַד־מְאֹד כָּל־
הַיּוֹם קֹדֵר הִלָּכְתִּי:

2 Lord, do not rebuke me with Your fury and chastise me with Your burning anger.

3 Your arrows have pierced me; Your hand has come down upon me.

4 There is nothing whole in my body because of Your anger, no tranquility in my bones because of my sin.

5 My iniquities have risen above my head; like an onerous burden, they are too heavy for me.

6 My wounds stink and fester because of my folly.

7 I am greatly bent over and bowed; I walk about in gloom the entire day.

---

2 The psalmist begins by pleading to God for relief from his pain: **Lord, do not rebuke me with Your fury and chastise me with Your burning anger.**

3 **Your arrows have pierced me,** a metaphorical description of God punishing him with pain and illness, and **Your hand has come down upon me** with a severe blow.

4 **There is nothing whole in my body,** no part of my body is well, **because of Your anger,** and there is **no tranquility in** any of **my bones because of my sin.** This is not a complaint, but a plea for mercy. The psalmist admits that he is suffering justly because of his sins, but he nevertheless prays for healing.

5 **My iniquities** are so numerous, it is as if they **have** piled up and **risen above my head; like an onerous burden, they are too heavy for me.**

6 **My wounds stink and fester because of my folly.** All this is punishment for my sins.

7 **I am greatly bent over and bowed; I walk about in gloom the entire day** because of my pain.

⁸ My loins are filled with refuse; there is nothing whole in my flesh.

כִּי־כְסָלַי מָלְאוּ נִקְלֶה וְאֵין מְתֹם בִּבְשָׂרִי:

⁹ I am depleted and utterly crushed; I roar from my heart's agitation.

נְפוּגֹתִי וְנִדְכֵּיתִי עַד־מְאֹד שָׁאַגְתִּי מִנַּהֲמַת לִבִּי:

¹⁰ My Lord, all my desires are before You, and my sighs are not hidden from You.

אֲדֹנָי נֶגְדְּךָ כָל־תַּאֲוָתִי וְאַנְחָתִי מִמְּךָ לֹא־נִסְתָּרָה:

¹¹ My heart races, my strength fails me; even the light of my eyes has left me.

לִבִּי סְחַרְחַר עֲזָבַנִי כֹחִי וְאוֹר־עֵינַי גַּם־הֵם אֵין אִתִּי:

¹² My friends and companions stand aloof from my affliction, and those who are close to me keep their distance.

אֹהֲבַי וְרֵעַי מִנֶּגֶד נִגְעִי יַעֲמֹדוּ וּקְרוֹבַי מֵרָחֹק עָמָדוּ:

¹³ Those who seek my life lay snares for me; those who wish me ill speak of devastation, uttering deceit all day long.

וַיְנַקְשׁוּ מְבַקְשֵׁי נַפְשִׁי וְדֹרְשֵׁי רָעָתִי דִּבְּרוּ הַוּוֹת וּמִרְמוֹת כָּל־הַיּוֹם יֶהְגּוּ:

---

⁸ **My loins** can barely support me. I feel as if they **are filled with refuse; there is nothing whole** and healthy **in** all **my flesh.**

⁹ **I am depleted and utterly crushed; I roar from my heart's agitation.**

¹⁰ Yet the psalmist immediately realizes that there is no reason for him to cry out in pain: **My Lord, all my desires are** known **before You, and** even my muffled **sighs are not hidden from You.**

¹¹ **My heart races,** my heartbeat is irregular, and **my strength fails me;** in my sickness and weakness it seems that **even the light of my eyes has left me.**

¹² I suffer not only physically but also from lack of support: **My friends and companions stand aloof from my affliction, and those who are close to me keep their distance.** They do not come forward to help.

¹³ Moreover, **those who seek my life lay snares for me.** Assuming that my situation is hopeless, they feel free to plot against me. **Those who wish me ill speak of devastation** against me, **uttering deceit** about me **all day long.**

יד וַאֲנִי כְחֵרֵשׁ לֹא אֶשְׁמֵע
וּכְאִלֵּם לֹא יִפְתַּח־פִּיו:

טו וָאֱהִי כְּאִישׁ אֲשֶׁר לֹא־שֹׁמֵעַ
וְאֵין בְּפִּיו תּוֹכָחוֹת:

טז כִּי־לְךָ יְהוָה הוֹחָלְתִּי אַתָּה
תַעֲנֶה אֲדֹנָי אֱלֹהָי:

יז כִּי־אָמַרְתִּי פֶּן־יִשְׂמְחוּ־לִי
בְּמוֹט רַגְלִי עָלַי הִגְדִּילוּ:

יח כִּי־אֲנִי לְצֶלַע נָכוֹן וּמַכְאוֹבִי
נֶגְדִּי תָמִיד:

יט כִּי־עֲוֹנִי אַגִּיד אֶדְאַג
מֵחַטָּאתִי:

14 And I, like one who is deaf, do not hear. I am like a mute who does not open his mouth.

15 Indeed, I am like a man who does not hear, a man with no power to rebuke.

16 For in You, Lord, I place my hope; Lord my God, You will answer.

17 For I said: Lest they rejoice and become exalted over me when my leg falters.

18 For I am poised to stumble; my pain is always before me.

19 I will tell of my iniquity; I am anxious because of my sin.

---

14 **And I,** out of weakness, **like one who is deaf, do not hear. I am like a mute who does not open his mouth.**

15 **Indeed, I am like a man who does not hear, a man with no power to rebuke** in response to their affronts.

16 My silence is not only a result of my weakness; it also stems from my faith, **for in You, Lord, I place my hope; Lord my God,** in my stead **You will answer** those who taunt me, since I am unable to do so.

17 **For I said: Lest they rejoice and become exalted over me when my leg falters.**

18 **For I am poised to stumble; my pain is always before me.**

19 **I will tell of my iniquity** and openly admit it; **I am anxious because of my sin.** For this reason, I do not complain that my punishment and suffering are unjustified.

כ וְאֹיְבַי חַיִּים עָצֵמוּ וְרַבּוּ שֹׂנְאַי
שָׁקֶר:

כא וּמְשַׁלְּמֵי רָעָה תַּחַת טוֹבָה
יִשְׂטְנוּנִי תַּחַת רדופי־טוֹב:

כב אַל־תַּעַזְבֵנִי יְהֹוָה אֱלֹהַי אַל־
תִּרְחַק מִמֶּנִּי:

כג חוּשָׁה לְעֶזְרָתִי אֲדֹנָי
תְּשׁוּעָתִי:

20 My enemies grow mighty; many are those who hate me without cause.

21 Those rendering evil for good despise me because I pursue goodness.

22 Do not forsake me, Lord. My God, do not distance Yourself from me.

23 Make haste to help me, Lord, my salvation.

PSALM 39

A psalm of prayer dealing with illness, pain, and the suffering inflicted by enemies.
It also ponders the fate of humanity in a more general sense.

א לַמְנַצֵּחַ לִידִיתוּן מִזְמוֹר
לְדָוִד:

1 For the chief musician, for *Yedutun*, a psalm by David.

---

20 **My enemies grow mighty; many are those who hate me without cause.**

21 **Those rendering evil for good,** who repay the good I have done for them in the past with hostility, **despise me because I pursue goodness.** The word *yistenuni* encompasses both hatred and accusation. It is not uncommon behavior for beneficiaries of aid to turn against their benefactors rather than show gratitude.

22 **Do not forsake me, Lord. My God, do not distance Yourself from me.**

23 **Make haste to help me, Lord, my salvation.**

PSALM 39

1 **For the chief musician, for *Yedutun*.** *Yedutun* was one of the Temple's chief musicians.[11] David gave this song over to him either to set it to music or to sing it. Some commentators are of the opinion that *yedutun* is the name of an existing melody to which this psalm was meant to be sung, or, alternatively, the name of a musical instrument. **A psalm by David.**

אָמַ֗רְתִּי אֶשְׁמְרָ֣ה דְרָכַי֮ ²
מֵחֲט֪וֹא בִלְשׁ֫וֹנִ֥י אֶשְׁמְרָ֥ה
לְפִ֥י מַחְס֑וֹם בְּעֹ֖ד רָשָׁ֣ע
לְנֶגְדִּֽי:

נֶאֱלַ֣מְתִּי דּ֭וּמִיָּה הֶחֱשֵׁ֣יתִי ³
מִטּ֑וֹב וּכְאֵבִ֥י נֶעְכָּֽר:

חַם־לִבִּ֨י ׀ בְּקִרְבִּ֗י בַּהֲגִיגִ֥י ⁴
תִבְעַר־אֵ֑שׁ דִּ֝בַּ֗רְתִּי בִּלְשׁוֹנִֽי:

הוֹדִ֘יעֵ֤נִי יְהֹוָ֨ה ׀ קִצִּ֗י וּמִדַּ֣ת ⁵
יָמַ֣י מַה־הִ֑יא אֵ֝דְעָ֗ה מֶה־
חָדֵ֥ל אָֽנִי:

² I have said: I will guard my ways lest I sin with my tongue; I will muzzle my mouth while the wicked are in my presence.

³ I was mute and silent; I refrained even from speaking good, but my pain worsened.

⁴ My heart was hot within me while I was musing; the fire burned, and my tongue gave utterance.

⁵ Lord, let me know my end and what will be the measure of my days. Let me know when I will cease to be.

---

² **I have said: I will guard my ways lest I sin with my tongue** by saying improper things. **I will muzzle my mouth while the wicked are in my presence.**

³ **I was mute and silent; I refrained even from speaking good,** lest I end up saying something inappropriate, **but my pain worsened.**

⁴ **My heart was hot within me while I was musing; the fire burned, and my tongue gave utterance,** not with complaints against God over my predicament but with meditations about matters of deeper significance:

⁵ **Lord, let me know my end and what will be the measure of my days.** This is primarily the psalmist's request to be granted true awareness and appreciation of the transience of life, that we are here on earth only temporarily. It is also an expression of the psalmist's desire to know when he will die so that he can prepare for his death in a fitting manner. **Let me know when I will cease to be,** when all my suffering will come to an end; it is sometimes comforting to know this. In addition, the knowledge of man's mortality generates a different perspective on assessing one's life.

הִנֵּה טְפָחוֹת ׀ נָתַתָּה יָמַי
וְחֶלְדִּי כְאַיִן נֶגְדֶּךָ אַךְ־כָּל־
הֶבֶל כָּל־אָדָם נִצָּב סֶלָה:

אַךְ־בְּצֶלֶם ׀ יִתְהַלֶּךְ־אִישׁ
אַךְ־הֶבֶל יֶהֱמָיוּן יִצְבֹּר וְלֹא־
יֵדַע מִי־אֹסְפָם:

וְעַתָּה מַה־קִּוִּיתִי אֲדֹנָי
תּוֹחַלְתִּי לְךָ הִיא:

מִכָּל־פְּשָׁעַי הַצִּילֵנִי חֶרְפַּת
נָבָל אַל־תְּשִׂימֵנִי:

6 Behold, You have given me days as handbreadths; my existence is as nothing in Your sight. Indeed, everyone is like nothingness, every standing man, Selah.

Surely man walks about as a shadow; indeed, he is in turmoil for naught, amassing riches and not knowing who will gather them.

8 And now, Lord, on what do I rely? My hope resides in You.

9 Deliver me from all my transgressions; do not disgrace me among the scoundrels.

---

6 **Behold, You have given me days as handbreadths.** My life is so short that it is as if it could be quantified in handbreadths, a small unit of measurement. **My existence,** my world and everything in it, **is as nothing in Your sight. Indeed, everyone is like nothingness, every standing man, Selah.** Even when man is alive and standing, he has no significance before You.

7 **Surely man walks about as a shadow,** living in a world of illusion and false images. **Indeed, he is in turmoil for naught, amassing riches and not knowing who will gather them** and benefit from them after his death. Life is short and not particularly meaningful; all of man's endeavors lack real consequence.

8 Although the psalmist acknowledges that man is essentially insignificant, he still turns to God in prayer: **And now, Lord, on what do I rely? My hope resides** only **in You.** He does not expect help from anyone else.

9 I confess that I have sinned, but I beseech You to **deliver me from all my transgressions; do not disgrace me among the scoundrels.** Do not allow my enemies to overtake and shame me. Punishing me, besides being painful for me, would be a reward for them, and they are unworthy.

נֶאֱלַמְתִּי לֹא אֶפְתַּח־פִּי כִּי
אַתָּה עָשִֽׂיתָ:

הָסֵר מֵעָלַי נִגְעֶךָ מִתִּגְרַת
יָדְךָ אֲנִי כָלִֽיתִי:

בְּתוֹכָחוֹת עַל־עָוֺן ׀ יִסַּ֫רְתָּ
אִישׁ וַתֶּ֣מֶס כָּעָ֣שׁ חֲמוּדוֹ אַ֤ךְ
הֶ֖בֶל כָּל־אָדָ֣ם סֶֽלָה:

שִׁמְעָ֬ה תְפִלָּתִ֨י ׀ יְהֹוָ֡ה
וְשַׁוְעָתִ֨י ׀ הַאֲזִ֗ינָה אֶֽל־
דִּמְעָתִ֮י אַֽל־תֶּ֫חֱרַ֥שׁ כִּ֤י גֵ֣ר
אָנֹכִ֣י עִמָּ֑ךְ תּ֝וֹשָׁ֗ב כְּכָל־
אֲבוֹתָֽי:

הָשַׁ֣ע מִמֶּ֣נִּי וְאַבְלִ֑יגָה בְּטֶ֖רֶם
אֵלֵ֣ךְ וְאֵינֶֽנִּי:

10 I have become mute; I do not open my mouth, for it is Your doing.

11 Remove Your plague from me; I am perishing from the blows of Your hand.

12 You chastise a man with punishments for his sin, consuming, like a moth, what is precious to him. Surely man is mere nothingness, Selah.

13 Hear my prayer, Lord, and heed my cry; do not be silent at my tears. For I am a stranger with You, a sojourner, as were all my fathers.

14 Let me be, so I may have relief, before I depart and am no more.

---

10 **I have become mute; I do not open my mouth** to argue or complain to You, **for,** regarding my suffering, I am aware that **it is Your doing.**

11 Nevertheless, I entreat God: **Remove Your plague from me; I am perishing from the blows of Your hand.**

12 **You chastise a man with punishments for his sin, consuming, like a moth, what is precious to him.** His possessions and his loved ones perish before him. **Surely man is mere nothingness, Selah.**

13 **Hear my prayer, Lord, and heed my cry; do not be silent at my tears. For I am a stranger with You, a sojourner, as were all my fathers.** Precisely because I am such a fragile and transient being, perhaps I could be granted a respite from suffering. The reference to "all my fathers" indicates that the psalmist's plea does not pertain specifically to his own individual circumstances but is on behalf of all humanity. When compared with God's infinite existence, human life in this world is but an ephemeral interlude.

14 Therefore I pray: **Let me be, so I may have relief, before I depart and am no more.** If You do not give respite to a creature as short-lived and lowly as I am, my life will consist only of suffering and I will not have experienced what the world had in store for me.

PSALM 40

A psalm that contains an intermingling of praise and supplication and moves between
past, present, and future. The concluding five verses of this psalm
appear in almost identical form in Psalm 70.

לַמְנַצֵּחַ לְדָוִד מִזְמוֹר:

קַוֹּה קִוִּיתִי יהוה וַיֵּט אֵלַי
וַיִּשְׁמַע שַׁוְעָתִי:

וַיַּעֲלֵנִי ׀ מִבּוֹר שָׁאוֹן מִטִּיט
הַיָּוֵן וַיָּקֶם עַל־סֶלַע רַגְלַי
כּוֹנֵן אֲשֻׁרָי:

וַיִּתֵּן בְּפִי ׀ שִׁיר חָדָשׁ תְּהִלָּה
לֵאלֹהֵינוּ יִרְאוּ רַבִּים וְיִירָאוּ
וְיִבְטְחוּ בַּיהוה:

1. For the chief musician, a psalm by David.

2. I greatly hoped for the Lord, and He turned to me and heard my cry.

3. He brought me out of the pit of destruction, out of the swampy mud, and He set my feet upon a rock, making my footsteps firm.

4. He placed a new song in my mouth, a song of praise for our God. Many will see, and they will fear and trust in the Lord.

PSALM 40

1 **For the chief musician, a psalm by David.**

2 **I greatly hoped for the Lord, and He turned to me and heard my cry.**

3 **He brought me out of the pit of destruction, out of the swampy mud.** "Pit of destruction" apparently refers to a pit whose bottom is not firm but rather is full of slime and mud. This image is reinforced by the next phrase, "swampy mud," which describes a person who feels that he has nothing to lean on; the very ground beneath him does not support him, and he feels that he is liable at any moment to slip away and drown. But, continues the psalmist, God rescued me from this slippery peril, **and He set my feet upon a rock, making my footsteps firm.** Once he is rescued from the pit, the psalmist is grateful to God not only for his narrow escape from death but also for the opportunity to set himself on a new, more secure path.

4 **He placed a new song in my mouth, a song of praise for our God. Many will see** what happened to me, **and they will fear,** realizing just how far a man can slip and fall into peril, **and** they will also **trust in the Lord.** They will understand that God can be relied upon to rescue man from such dire straits.

ה ‏אַשְׁרֵי־הַגֶּבֶר אֲשֶׁר־שָׂם
יְהוָה מִבְטַחוֹ וְלֹא־פָנָה אֶל־
רְהָבִים וְשָׂטֵי כָזָב:

ו ‏רַבּוֹת עָשִׂיתָ ׀ אַתָּה ׀ יְהוָה
אֱלֹהַי נִפְלְאֹתֶיךָ וּמַחְשְׁבֹתֶיךָ
אֵלֵינוּ אֵין ׀ עֲרֹךְ אֵלֶיךָ
אַגִּידָה וַאֲדַבֵּרָה עָצְמוּ
מִסַּפֵּר:

ז ‏זֶבַח וּמִנְחָה ׀ לֹא־חָפַצְתָּ
אׇזְנַיִם כָּרִיתָ לִּי עוֹלָה
וַחֲטָאָה לֹא שָׁאָלְתָּ:

ח ‏אָז אָמַרְתִּי הִנֵּה־בָאתִי
בִּמְגִלַּת־סֵפֶר כָּתוּב עָלָי:

5 Happy is the man who makes the Lord his trust, not turning to the proud and those who have strayed into falsehood.

6 Many things, Lord my God, have You done; Your wondrous works and thoughts are for us. No one compares to You. Though I declare and speak of Your miraculous deeds, they are too numerous to count.

7 You do not desire sacrifice or meal offerings. You have opened my ears; You do not ask for burnt offerings or sin offerings.

8 So I said: I have come with a written scroll of a book upon me.

---

5 **Happy is the man who makes the Lord his trust, not turning** for help **to the proud,** who boast of their strengths and abilities, **and those who have strayed into falsehood,** whose promises are worthless.

6 **Many things, Lord my God, have You done; Your wondrous works and thoughts are for us.** Often it is only in retrospect that one can understand how certain situations that appeared to be incomprehensible or problematic actually worked out for the best. **No one compares to You** in comprehending all the hidden solutions to the problems and complications of life. **Though I declare and speak of Your miraculous deeds, they are too numerous to count.**

7 When one comes to give thanks to You, he realizes that **You do not desire sacrifice or meal offerings** as expressions of gratitude. Rather, **You have opened my ears** and given them the ability to hear and understand this: **You do not ask for burnt offerings or sin offerings.**

8 **So,** having contemplated all this, **I said: I have come with a written scroll of a book upon me.** I understand that I need to express my gratitude with words, both spoken and written.

לַעֲשׂוֹת־רְצוֹנְךָ אֱלֹהַי
חָפַצְתִּי וְתוֹרָתְךָ בְּתוֹךְ מֵעָי:

בִּשַּׂרְתִּי צֶדֶק ׀ בְּקָהָל רָב
הִנֵּה שְׂפָתַי לֹא אֶכְלָא יהוה
אַתָּה יָדָעְתָּ:

צִדְקָתְךָ לֹא־כִסִּיתִי ׀ בְּתוֹךְ
לִבִּי אֱמוּנָתְךָ וּתְשׁוּעָתְךָ
אָמַרְתִּי לֹא־כִחַדְתִּי חַסְדְּךָ
וַאֲמִתְּךָ לְקָהָל רָב:

אַתָּה יהוה לֹא־תִכְלָא
רַחֲמֶיךָ מִמֶּנִּי חַסְדְּךָ וַאֲמִתְּךָ
תָּמִיד יִצְּרוּנִי:

⁹ I delight in doing Your will,
my God; Your teaching is in
my belly.

¹⁰ I proclaimed righteousness
in a great assembly; I will not
restrain my lips, my Lord, as
You know.

¹¹ I did not conceal Your
righteousness within my heart;
I spoke of Your faithfulness and
Your salvation. I did not hide
Your kindness and Your truth
from a great assembly.

¹² You, Lord, will not withhold
Your compassion from me;
Your kindness and Your truth
will always preserve me.

---

9 **I delight in doing Your will, my God; Your teaching is in my belly.** It pervades my very core and informs everything I have to say.

10 **I proclaimed** the **righteousness** of Your deeds **in a great assembly,** so that everyone might hear of the mercies You showed me. **I will not restrain my lips, my Lord, as You know.**

11 **I did not conceal Your righteousness within my heart** by refraining to share knowledge of it with others; **I spoke of Your faithfulness and Your salvation. I did not hide Your kindness and Your truth from a great assembly.** In other words, rather than offering sacrifices, it is psalms such as this, made public in their being transcribed and sung before "a great assembly," that properly express gratitude to God.

12 In turn, may it be that **You, Lord, will not withhold Your compassion from me; Your kindness and Your truth will always preserve me.**

כִּי אָפְפוּ־עָלַי ׀ רָעוֹת עַד־ ‏
אֵין מִסְפָּר הִשִּׂיגוּנִי עֲוֺנֹתַי ‏
וְלֹא־יָכֹלְתִּי לִרְאוֹת עָצְמוּ ‏
מִשַּׂעֲרוֹת רֹאשִׁי וְלִבִּי עֲזָבָנִי: ‏

רְצֵה יהוה לְהַצִּילֵנִי יהוה ‏
לְעֶזְרָתִי חוּשָׁה: ‏

יֵבֹשׁוּ וְיַחְפְּרוּ ׀ יַחַד מְבַקְשֵׁי ‏
נַפְשִׁי לִסְפּוֹתָהּ יִסֹּגוּ אָחוֹר ‏
וְיִכָּלְמוּ חֲפֵצֵי רָעָתִי: ‏

יָשֹׁמּוּ עַל־עֵקֶב בָּשְׁתָּם ‏
הָאֹמְרִים לִי הֶאָח ׀ הֶאָח: ‏

13 For innumerable evils surrounded me. My iniquities, more numerous than the hairs on my head, overtook me. I was unable to see; my heart failed me.

14 Please, Lord, deliver me; make haste to help me.

15 Let those who seek to destroy my life be utterly ashamed and humiliated. Let those who delight in my misfortune retreat in disgrace.

16 May those who say to me: Hurrah, hurrah! be confounded and turn on their heels in shame.

---

13 The psalmist describes the dire situation he had faced before God's salvation: **For innumerable evils surrounded me.** But I realize that it is ultimately my fault, as **my iniquities, more numerous than the hairs on my head, overtook me. I was unable to see.** When my suffering afflicted me, it sapped my strength and my ability to see and understand that it was well deserved. **My heart,** my hope for deliverance, **failed me.**

14 At that time, I was only able to plead: **Please, Lord, deliver me; make haste to help me.**

15 **Let those who seek to destroy my life be utterly ashamed and humiliated. Let those who delight in my misfortune retreat in disgrace.**

16 **May those who say to me: Hurrah, hurrah! be confounded and turn on their heels in shame.** The word *yashomu* can mean both "may they be confounded" and "may they be destroyed."

יְשִׂישׂוּ וְיִשְׂמְחוּ ׀ בְּךָ כָּל־
מְבַקְשֶׁיךָ יֹאמְרוּ תָמִיד יִגְדַּל
יהוה אֹהֲבֵי תְּשׁוּעָתֶךָ:

יז 17 Let all who seek You be happy and rejoice in You; let those who love Your salvation always say: Great is the Lord.

וַאֲנִי ׀ עָנִי וְאֶבְיוֹן אֲדֹנָי יַחֲשָׁב
לִי עֶזְרָתִי וּמְפַלְטִי אַתָּה
אֱלֹהַי אַל־תְּאַחַר:

יח 18 As for me, poor and destitute, my Lord takes me into account; You are my Help and my Savior. My God, do not tarry.

PSALM 41

A psalm about illness and the suffering it causes.

לַמְנַצֵּחַ מִזְמוֹר לְדָוִד:

א 1 For the chief musician, a psalm by David.

אַשְׁרֵי מַשְׂכִּיל אֶל־דָּל בְּיוֹם
רָעָה יְמַלְּטֵהוּ יהוה:

ב 2 Happy is one who attends to the helpless; the Lord will deliver him in times of trouble.

---

17 Conversely, **let all who seek You be happy and rejoice in You; let those who love Your salvation always say: Great is the Lord.**

18 **As for me, poor and destitute,** having no importance on my own, **my Lord** nevertheless **takes me into account,** and because of that, **You are my Help and my Savior. My God, do not tarry** with Your assistance to me.

PSALM 41

1 **For the chief musician, a psalm by David.**

2 **Happy is one who attends to the helpless.** *Maskil,* translated here as "attends to," more literally means "shows understanding for." The psalmist speaks of a person who not only aids the sick but does so with sensitivity, in a way that maximizes benefit and minimizes embarrassment and shame. **The Lord will deliver him in times of trouble.**

יְהֹוָה ׀ יִשְׁמְרֵהוּ וִיחַיֵּהוּ
וְאֶשֶׁר יֻאשַׁר בָּאָרֶץ וְאַל־תִּתְּנֵהוּ
בְּנֶפֶשׁ אֹיְבָיו:

יְהֹוָה יִסְעָדֶנּוּ עַל־עֶרֶשׂ דְּוָי
כָּל־מִשְׁכָּבוֹ הָפַכְתָּ בְחָלְיוֹ:

אֲנִי־אָמַרְתִּי יְהֹוָה חָנֵּנִי
רְפָאָה נַפְשִׁי כִּי־חָטָאתִי לָךְ:

אוֹיְבַי יֹאמְרוּ רַע לִי מָתַי
יָמוּת וְאָבַד שְׁמוֹ:

3 The Lord will preserve him and sustain him, and he will be made happy on earth. You will not give him over to the will of his enemies.

4 The Lord will support him on his sickbed; You change his bedding during his illness.

5 As for me, I said: Lord, be gracious to me; heal my soul, for I have sinned against You.

6 My enemies speak evil against me, saying: When will he die, and his name be lost?

---

3 **The Lord will preserve him and sustain him, and he will be made happy on earth. You will not give him over to the will** and evil desires **of his enemies.**

4 **The Lord will support him on his sickbed; You change his bedding during his illness.** God will see to it that he is cared for in his own illness. Changing the bed linens is just one example of how to aid a sick person.

5 **As for me, I said: Lord, be gracious to me; heal my soul, for I have sinned against You.** This statement seems to mean the following: Although I have sinned against You and realize that I deserve to be punished for my sins, I still pray to You to grant me recovery.

6 **My enemies,** under the impression that I am mortally ill, **speak evil against me, saying: When will he die, and his name be lost?**

וְאִם־בָּא לִרְא֗וֹת ׀ שָׁ֤וְא יְדַבֵּ֗ר לִבּ֗וֹ יִקְבָּץ־אָ֥וֶן ל֑וֹ יֵצֵ֖א לַח֣וּץ יְדַבֵּֽר׃

7 And if someone comes to see me, he speaks falsely. His heart gathers wickedness; when he goes outside, he speaks of it.

יַ֗חַד עָלַ֣י יִֽתְלַחֲשׁ֣וּ כָּל־שֹׂנְאָ֑י עָלַ֓י ׀ יַחְשְׁב֖וּ רָעָ֣ה לִֽי׃

8 Together, all my enemies are whispering about me, considering the evil that has befallen me.

דְּבַר־בְּלִיַּ֗עַל יָצ֥וּק בּ֑וֹ וַאֲשֶׁ֥ר שָׁ֝כַ֗ב לֹא־יוֹסִ֥יף לָקֽוּם׃

9 An incurable evil has taken hold of him; now that he is bedridden, he will never rise again.

גַּם־אִ֤ישׁ שְׁלוֹמִ֨י ׀ אֲשֶׁר־בָּטַ֣חְתִּי ב֭וֹ אוֹכֵ֣ל לַחְמִ֑י הִגְדִּ֖יל עָלַ֣י עָקֵֽב׃

10 Even my ally, whom I trusted, he who partook of my bread, has lifted his heel against me.

וְאַתָּ֤ה יְהֹוָ֗ה חָנֵּ֥נִי וַהֲקִימֵ֑נִי וַאֲשַׁלְּמָ֥ה לָהֶֽם׃

11 But may You, Lord, be gracious to me and raise me up, so I might pay them back.

---

7 **And if someone comes to see me,** ostensibly for a thoughtful visit, **he speaks** his words of encouragement **falsely.** For in reality, **his heart gathers wickedness** that he does not speak out loud; only **when he goes outside, he speaks of it** to others.

8 **Together, all my enemies are whispering about me** and my dire situation, **considering the evil that has befallen me.**

9 This is what they are saying: **An incurable evil** illness **has taken hold of him; now that he is bedridden, he will never rise again.**

10 **Even my ally, whom I trusted, he who partook of my bread,** even he who was graciously sustained by me, **has lifted his heel against me,** as if ready to trample me.

11 **But may You, Lord, be gracious to me and raise me up** from this sickbed, **so I might pay them back.**

בְּזֹאת יָדַעְתִּי כִּי־חָפַצְתָּ בִּי ^{יב}
כִּי לֹא־יָרִיעַ אֹיְבִי עָלָי:

וַאֲנִי בְּתֻמִּי תָּמַכְתָּ בִּי ^{יג}
וַתַּצִּיבֵנִי לְפָנֶיךָ לְעוֹלָם:

בָּרוּךְ יהוה ׀ אֱלֹהֵי יִשְׂרָאֵל ^{יד}
מֵהָעוֹלָם וְעַד־הָעוֹלָם אָמֵן ׀
וְאָמֵן:

¹² Then I will know You have favored me, for my enemy will not shout in triumph over me.

¹³ And I, in my innocence, You have supported me; You have kept me upright before You always.

¹⁴ Blessed is the Lord, God of Israel, from eternity to eternity, amen and amen.

---

¹² **Then I will know You have favored me, for** then **my enemy will not** have occasion to **shout in triumph over me** any longer.

¹³ **And I, in my innocence, You have supported me; You have kept me upright before You always.**

¹⁴ This verse concludes the first of the five books of Psalms: **Blessed is the Lord, God of Israel, from eternity to eternity,** in all times, **amen and amen.**

BOOK TWO

PSALM 42

A psalm of prayer and yearning in which the psalmist describes himself in exile,
hunted, despised, and alone. He knows that only God can deliver him from all his troubles.

אֲ לַמְנַצֵּחַ מַשְׂכִּיל לִבְנֵי־קֹרַח:

בּ כְּאַיָּל תַּעֲרֹג עַל־אֲפִיקֵי־
מָיִם כֵּן נַפְשִׁי תַעֲרֹג אֵלֶיךָ
אֱלֹהִים:

גּ צָמְאָה נַפְשִׁי ׀ לֵאלֹהִים לְאֵל
חָי מָתַי אָבוֹא וְאֵרָאֶה פְּנֵי
אֱלֹהִים:

דּ הָיְתָה־לִּי דִמְעָתִי לֶחֶם יוֹמָם
וָלַיְלָה בֶּאֱמֹר אֵלַי כָּל־הַיּוֹם
אַיֵּה אֱלֹהֶיךָ:

1 For the chief musician, a contemplation, by the sons of Korah.

2 As a deer longs for brooks of water, so my soul longs for You, God.

3 My soul thirsts for God, the living God Almighty. When will I come and appear before God's countenance?

4 My tears have been my bread day and night, when they say to me all day long: Where is your God?

PSALM 42

1 **For the chief musician, a contemplation, by the sons of Korah.** An alternative translation is "for the sons of Korah," meaning that the song was composed by someone else and given to them to sing.

2 **As a deer longs for brooks of water, so my soul longs for You, God.** The rare verb *ta'arog*, translated here as "longs," can also refer to the craving sound made by a deer. In either case the sense is the same.

3 **My soul thirsts for God, the living God Almighty. When will I come** to God's Temple **and appear before God's countenance?** The Torah refers to a visit to the House of God as "appearing before God's presence."[1]

4 The psalmist describes his feelings when he is distant from God's Temple, or even in exile in a foreign land: **My tears have been my bread,** they are as common to me as my daily food, **day and night, when they,** my enemies, **say to me all day long: Where is your God?**

ה אֵלֶּה אֶזְכְּרָה ׀ וְאֶשְׁפְּכָה עָלַי ׀ נַפְשִׁי כִּי אֶעֱבֹר ׀ בַּסָּךְ אֶדַּדֵּם עַד־בֵּית אֱלֹהִים בְּקוֹל־רִנָּה וְתוֹדָה הָמוֹן חוֹגֵג:

ו מַה־תִּשְׁתּוֹחֲחִי ׀ נַפְשִׁי וַתֶּהֱמִי עָלָי הוֹחִלִי לֵאלֹהִים כִּי־עוֹד אוֹדֶנּוּ יְשׁוּעוֹת פָּנָיו:

ז אֱלֹהַי עָלַי נַפְשִׁי תִשְׁתּוֹחָח עַל־כֵּן אֶזְכָּרְךָ מֵאֶרֶץ יַרְדֵּן וְחֶרְמוֹנִים מֵהַר מִצְעָר:

ח תְּהוֹם־אֶל־תְּהוֹם קוֹרֵא לְקוֹל צִנּוֹרֶיךָ כָּל־מִשְׁבָּרֶיךָ וְגַלֶּיךָ עָלַי עָבָרוּ:

5 These things I remember, and pour out my soul, when I used to go with a throng of people in a procession to the House of God, a celebrating multitude with voice of song and thanksgiving.

6 Why, my soul, are you stooped over? Why do you sigh for me? Have hope in God, for I will yet thank Him for the salvation of His presence.

7 My God, my soul is stooped over; thus I recall You from the lands of Jordan and the Hermons, from Mount Mitzar.

8 Deep calls to deep in the sound of your waterways; all your breakers and waves have passed over me.

---

5 These things I remember, and pour out my soul, when I used to go with a throng of people in a procession to the House of God, a celebrating multitude with voice of song and thanksgiving.

6 The psalmist returns to speaking of his feelings while in exile. Addressing himself, he asks: Why, my soul, are you stooped over, downcast? Why do you sigh for me? Have hope in God, for I will yet be saved by Him and thank Him for the salvation of His presence.

7 My God, my soul is stooped over, downcast; thus I recall You from the lands of Jordan and the Hermons, the territories where the sources of the Jordan River are located, near Mount Hermon, from Mount Mitzar, apparently a mountain in that northern area.

8 Deep calls to deep, one body of abundant water calls to another, as it were, in the sound of Your waterways. For the psalmist, the sound of cascading water is evocative of sadness. All Your breakers and waves have passed over me, as if signifying my being overrun with torrents of troubles.

יוֹמָם ׀ יְצַוֶּה יְהֹוָה ׀ חַסְדּוֹ
וּבַלַּיְלָה שִׁירֹה עִמִּי תְּפִלָּה
לְאֵל חַיָּי:

אוֹמְרָה ׀ לְאֵל סַלְעִי לָמָה
שְׁכַחְתָּנִי לָמָּה־קֹדֵר אֵלֵךְ
בְּלַחַץ אוֹיֵב:

בְּרֶצַח ׀ בְּעַצְמוֹתַי חֵרְפוּנִי
צוֹרְרָי בְּאָמְרָם אֵלַי כָּל־הַיּוֹם
אַיֵּה אֱלֹהֶיךָ:

מַה־תִּשְׁתּוֹחֲחִי ׀ נַפְשִׁי וּמַה־
תֶּהֱמִי עָלָי הוֹחִילִי לֵאלֹהִים
כִּי־עוֹד אוֹדֶנּוּ יְשׁוּעֹת פָּנַי
וֵאלֹהָי:

⁹ The Lord commands His kindness by day. His song remains with me by night, a prayer to the Almighty God of my life.

¹⁰ I will say to the Almighty, my rock: Why have You forgotten me? Why do I walk in gloom, oppressed by the enemy?

¹¹ I feel murder in my bones, as my foes ridicule me with their taunts, saying to me all day long: Where is your God?

¹² Why, my soul, are you stooped over? Why do you sigh for me? Have hope in God, for I will thank Him again, my salvation and my God.

---

9 The psalmist expresses his devotion and hope: **The Lord commands His kindness** to me **by day,** so that **His song,** the song of prayer that I sing to Him, **remains with me by night, a prayer to the Almighty God of my life.**

10 In that prayer, **I will say to the Almighty,** who is **my rock: Why have You forgotten me? Why do I walk in gloom, oppressed by the enemy?**

11 **I feel murder in my bones,** as if I were actually being stabbed in my bones, **as my foes ridicule me with their taunts, saying to me all day long: Where is your God?** There is nothing more painful to me than this scornful question.

12 The psalmist again addresses his soul: **Why, my soul, are you stooped over,** downcast? **Why do you sigh for me?** Rather, **have hope in God, for I will** be saved by Him and **thank Him again;** I will thank Him, **my salvation and my God,** even before He redeems me, and again when He comes to my aid.

PSALM 43

Unquestionably a continuation of the preceding psalm.
It is unclear why this psalm was made into a separate chapter.

שָׁפְטֵנִי אֱלֹהִים ׀ וְרִיבָה רִיבִי
מִגּוֹי לֹא־חָסִיד מֵאִישׁ־
מִרְמָה וְעַוְלָה תְפַלְּטֵנִי:

כִּי־אַתָּה ׀ אֱלֹהֵי מָעוּזִּי לָמָה
זְנַחְתָּנִי לָמָה־קֹדֵר אֶתְהַלֵּךְ
בְּלַחַץ אוֹיֵב:

שְׁלַח־אוֹרְךָ וַאֲמִתְּךָ הֵמָּה
יַנְחוּנִי יְבִיאוּנִי אֶל־הַר־
קָדְשְׁךָ וְאֶל־מִשְׁכְּנוֹתֶיךָ:

וְאָבוֹאָה ׀ אֶל־מִזְבַּח אֱלֹהִים
אֶל־אֵל שִׂמְחַת גִּילִי וְאוֹדְךָ
בְכִנּוֹר אֱלֹהִים אֱלֹהָי:

1 Vindicate me, God, and plead my cause against an unkind nation. Rescue me from a deceitful and unjust man.

2 For You are God of my stronghold. Why have You neglected me? Why must I walk about in gloom, oppressed by the enemy?

3 Send Your light and Your truth; they will lead me. They will bring me to Your holy mountain and Your dwelling place.

4 Then I will come to the altar of God, to the Almighty God of my abundant joy, and I will praise You on the lyre, God, my God.

PSALM 43

1 Vindicate me, God, and plead my cause against an unkind nation. Rescue me from a deceitful and unjust man.

2 For You are God of my stronghold. Why have You neglected me? Why must I walk about in gloom, oppressed by the enemy?

3 Send me Your light and Your truth; they will lead me. They will bring me back to Your holy mountain and Your dwelling place.

4 Then I will come to the altar of God, to the Almighty God of my abundant joy, and I will praise You on the lyre, God, my God.

מַה־תִּשְׁתּוֹחֲחִי ׀ נַפְשִׁי וּמַה־
תֶּהֱמִי עָלָי הוֹחִילִי לֵאלֹהִים
כִּי־עוֹד אוֹדֶנּוּ יְשׁוּעֹת פָּנַי
וֵאלֹהָי:

5 Why, my soul, are you stooped
over? Why do you sigh for me?
Have hope in God, for I will
yet thank Him, my salvation
and my God.

PSALM 44

A psalm of prayer, entreaty, and complaint whose subject is the difficulties faced by Israel
because it is God's nation. The psalmist contrasts the glorious days of the nation's past
with the harsh reality of its present situation.

לַמְנַצֵּחַ לִבְנֵי־קֹרַח מַשְׂכִּיל:

אֱלֹהִים ׀ בְּאָזְנֵינוּ שָׁמַעְנוּ
אֲבוֹתֵינוּ סִפְּרוּ־לָנוּ פֹּעַל־
פָּעַלְתָּ בִימֵיהֶם בִּימֵי קֶדֶם:

1 To the chief musician, a
contemplation by the sons
of Korah.

2 God, we have heard with our
ears, our fathers have told us, of
the deeds You did in their time,
in days of old.

ח לחודש
8th day
of month

---

5 The psalmist concludes with the refrain from the previous psalm: **Why, my soul, are you
stooped over,** downcast? **Why do you** only **sigh for me? Have hope in God. For I will yet**
be saved by Him and **thank Him,** for He is **my salvation and my God.**

PSALM 44

1 **To the chief musician, a contemplation by the sons of Korah.** The contemplative aspect
of this psalm deals with Israel's devotion to God as the cause of its present suffering. Thus, there is
an element of complaint in the psalm, not with regard to the psalmist's personal woes but rather
those of the nation. Containing both pleas and reminiscence, it has become ever more relevant
with the passage of time.

2 **God, we have heard with our ears, our fathers have told us, of the deeds You did in
their time, in days of old,** such as the conquest of the Land of Israel.

אַתָּה ׀ יָדְךָ גּוֹיִם הוֹרַ֫שְׁתָּ
וַתִּטָּעֵ֥ם תָּרַ֥ע לְאֻמִּ֗ים
וַתְּשַׁלְּחֵֽם׃

כִּ֤י לֹ֪א בְחַרְבָּ֡ם יָ֥רְשׁוּ אָ֗רֶץ
וּזְרוֹעָם֮ לֹא־הוֹשִׁ֪יעָ֫ה לָּ֥מוֹ
כִּֽי־יְמִֽינְךָ֣ וּ֭זְרוֹעֲךָ וְא֥וֹר פָּנֶ֗יךָ
כִּ֣י רְצִיתָֽם׃

אַתָּה־ה֣וּא מַלְכִּ֣י אֱלֹהִ֑ים
צַ֝וֵּ֗ה יְשׁוּע֥וֹת יַעֲקֹֽב׃

בְּ֭ךָ צָרֵ֣ינוּ נְנַגֵּ֑חַ בְּ֝שִׁמְךָ֗ נָב֥וּס
קָמֵֽינוּ׃

כִּ֤י לֹ֣א בְקַשְׁתִּ֣י אֶבְטָ֑ח וְ֝חַרְבִּ֗י
לֹ֣א תוֹשִׁיעֵֽנִי׃

כִּ֣י ה֭וֹשַׁעְתָּנוּ מִצָּרֵ֑ינוּ
וּמְשַׂנְאֵ֥ינוּ הֱבִישֽׁוֹת׃

3 You, with Your hand, drove
out nations, and planted them;
You crushed peoples and sent
them away.

4 For not by their own sword
did they inherit the land;
their own arm did not deliver
them. It was Your right hand
and Your arm and the light
of Your countenance, for You
favored them.

5 You are my King, God;
command victories for Jacob.

6 Through You we gore our foes;
through Your name we subdue
those who rise against us.

7 For I do not put trust in
my bow, nor will my sword
save me.

8 For You delivered us from our
foes and shamed those who
hate us.

---

3 **You, with Your hand, drove out nations, and** You **planted them,** the people of Israel, in
their stead; **You crushed peoples and sent them away.**

4 **For not by their own sword did they,** our ancestors, **inherit the land; their own arm did
not deliver them.** Rather, **it was Your right hand and Your arm and the light of Your
countenance** that accomplished this for them, **for You favored them.**

5 **You are my King, God; command** once again **victories for Jacob,** as You did in the past.

6 **Through You we gore our foes; through Your name we subdue those who rise
against us.**

7 **For I do not put trust in my bow, nor will my sword save me.**

8 **For** it is **You** who **delivered us from our foes and shamed those who hate us.**

בֵּאלֹהִים הִלַּלְנוּ כָל־הַיּוֹם וְשִׁמְךָ ׀ לְעוֹלָם נוֹדֶה סֶלָה: ^ט

אַף־זָנַחְתָּ וַתַּכְלִימֵנוּ וְלֹא־תֵצֵא בְּצִבְאוֹתֵינוּ: ^י

תְּשִׁיבֵנוּ אָחוֹר מִנִּי־צָר וּמְשַׂנְאֵינוּ שָׁסוּ לָמוֹ: ^{יא}

תִּתְּנֵנוּ כְּצֹאן מַאֲכָל וּבַגּוֹיִם זֵרִיתָנוּ: ^{יב}

תִּמְכֹּר־עַמְּךָ בְלֹא־הוֹן וְלֹא־רִבִּיתָ בִּמְחִירֵיהֶם: ^{יג}

תְּשִׂימֵנוּ חֶרְפָּה לִשְׁכֵנֵינוּ לַעַג וָקֶלֶס לִסְבִיבוֹתֵינוּ: ^{יד}

9 In God we gloried all day long; we acknowledge Your name forever, Selah.

10 Yet You neglected and disgraced us, and do not go forth with our armies.

11 You have made us turn back from our foes; our enemies took spoils for themselves.

12 You made us like sheep that are eaten, and scattered us among the nations.

13 You sold Your people for a pittance; You did not set their value high.

14 You disgraced us among our neighbors, scorn and mockery to those around us.

---

9 **In God we gloried all day long** in light of all of our triumphs, and for this **we acknowledge** the fact that it was **Your name** that enabled our successes, **forever, Selah.**

10 The present reality, however, is completely different: **Yet You** have since then **neglected and disgraced us, and do not go forth** any longer **with our armies.** We no longer enjoy Your support.

11 **You have made us turn back** in retreat **from our foes; our enemies took spoils** of war from us **for themselves.**

12 **You made us like** helpless **sheep that are eaten, and scattered us among the nations.**

13 **You sold Your people** to their enemies as captives **for a pittance; You did not set their value high.** We are enslaved and subjugated with very little cost to our oppressors.

14 **You disgraced us among our neighbors;** we have become objects of **scorn and mockery to those around us.**

טו תְּשִׂימֵנוּ מָשָׁל בַּגּוֹיִם מְנוֹד־
רֹאשׁ בַּלְאֻמִּים:

טז כָּל־הַיּוֹם כְּלִמָּתִי נֶגְדִּי וּבֹשֶׁת
פָּנַי כִּסָּתְנִי:

יז מִקּוֹל מְחָרֵף וּמְגַדֵּף מִפְּנֵי
אוֹיֵב וּמִתְנַקֵּם:

יח כָּל־זֹאת בָּאַתְנוּ וְלֹא
שְׁכַחֲנוּךָ וְלֹא־שִׁקַּרְנוּ
בִּבְרִיתֶךָ:

יט לֹא־נָסוֹג אָחוֹר לִבֵּנוּ וַתֵּט
אֲשֻׁרֵינוּ מִנִּי אָרְחֶךָ:

כ כִּי דִכִּיתָנוּ בִּמְקוֹם תַּנִּים
וַתְּכַס עָלֵינוּ בְצַלְמָוֶת:

15 You made an example of us among the nations, a cause for head shaking among the peoples.

16 All day long my dishonor is before me, shame covering my face

17 from the voices of revilers and blasphemers, because of enemies and avengers.

18 All this befell us, but we did not forget You; we did not deal falsely with Your covenant.

19 Our hearts did not turn back, though You caused our steps to stray from Your path,

20 when You crushed us in a place of jackals, covering us over in a place of the shadow of death.

---

15 **You made an example of us,** turning us into paradigms of degradation and disgrace, **among the nations, a cause for head shaking,** a gesture of pity and contempt, **among the peoples.**

16 **All day long my dishonor is before me, shame covering my face** because of the scorn and contempt that are heaped on me

17 **from the voices of revilers and blasphemers, because of enemies and avengers.**

18 Words of prayer and complaint to God follow: **All this befell us, but we did not forget** our devotion to **You,** despite having been subjected to such humiliation and tragedy. **We did not deal falsely with Your covenant.** We still observe Your commandments.

19 **Our hearts did not turn back** from worshipping You, **though You caused our steps to stray from Your path,** from the path of Your assistance and salvation,

20 **when You crushed us in a place of** howling **jackals,** in a situation comparable to a desolate wilderness, **covering us over in a place of the shadow of death,** in a dark and terrifying place.

כא אִם־שָׁכַחְנוּ שֵׁם אֱלֹהֵינוּ
וַנִּפְרֹשׂ כַּפֵּינוּ לְאֵל זָר:

כב הֲלֹא אֱלֹהִים יַחֲקָר־זֹאת כִּי־
הוּא יֹדֵעַ תַּעֲלֻמוֹת לֵב:

כג כִּי־עָלֶיךָ הֹרַגְנוּ כָל־הַיּוֹם
נֶחְשַׁבְנוּ כְּצֹאן טִבְחָה:

כד עוּרָה ׀ לָמָּה תִישַׁן ׀ אֲדֹנָי
הָקִיצָה אַל־תִּזְנַח לָנֶצַח:

כה לָמָּה־פָנֶיךָ תַסְתִּיר תִּשְׁכַּח
עָנְיֵנוּ וְלַחֲצֵנוּ:

כו כִּי שָׁחָה לֶעָפָר נַפְשֵׁנוּ דָּבְקָה
לָאָרֶץ בִּטְנֵנוּ:

21 Had we forgotten the name of our God and stretched out our palms to a strange god,

22 would not God have discovered it, since He knows the secrets of the heart?

23 For we are killed all day long for You; we are accounted as sheep for slaughter.

24 Arouse Yourself; why do You sleep, Lord? Awaken, do not neglect us forever.

25 Why do You conceal Your face and forget our affliction and oppression?

26 Our soul is stooped over into the dust; our belly cleaves to the earth.

---

21 **Had we** at times **forgotten the name of our God and stretched out our palms** in prayer **to a strange god,**

22 **would not God have discovered it, since He knows the secrets of the heart?** You therefore know the truth, that we have in fact remained loyal to You.

23 **For we are killed all day long for You.** The enemies of God express their enmity toward Him by persecuting the people of Israel. **We are accounted as sheep for slaughter,** seen as easy prey.

24 **Arouse Yourself; why do You sleep, Lord?** Your disregard for our fate makes it appear as if You are asleep. **Awaken, do not neglect us forever.**

25 **Why do You conceal Your face and forget our affliction and oppression?**

26 **Our soul is stooped over into the dust.** We are dejected and of low spirits. It is as if **our belly cleaves to the earth,** so low have we sunk.

קוּמָה עֶזְרָתָה לָּנוּ וּפְדֵנוּ
לְמַעַן חַסְדֶּךָ:

²⁷ Rise up, be our savior; redeem us for the sake of Your kindness.

PSALM 45

A psalm in honor of the marriage of a warrior king. With a bit of poetic license, it can be applied to all bridegrooms, since a bridegroom on his wedding day is considered like a king.

לַמְנַצֵּחַ עַל־שֹׁשַׁנִּים לִבְנֵי־
קֹרַח מַשְׂכִּיל שִׁיר יְדִידֹת:

רָחַשׁ לִבִּי ׀ דָּבָר טוֹב אֹמֵר
אָנִי מַעֲשַׂי לְמֶלֶךְ לְשׁוֹנִי
עֵט ׀ סוֹפֵר מָהִיר:

¹ For the chief musician, on *shoshanim*, a contemplation by the sons of Korah, a song of affection.

² My heart abounds with good words; I address my works to the king. My tongue is the pen of a swift transcriber.

---

²⁷ **Rise up, be our savior; redeem us for the sake of Your kindness.**

PSALM 45

¹ **For the chief musician, on *shoshanim*.** The meaning of *shoshanim* (see also 69:1, 80:1) is not known with certainty. It is likely that it is the name of a musical instrument, possibly one with six strings, as the Hebrew word for six, *shesh*, is contained within the word *shoshanim*. Alternatively, it may be the name of an ancient melody to which this psalm was to be sung. **A contemplation by the sons of Korah, a song of affection.** Unlike other psalms that have the word "contemplation" in their introductory verse, this psalm contains no incisive admonitions or discussions of lofty topics; rather, it contains advice and good wishes for the bride and groom. Some commentators suggest that the psalm was written in praise of King Solomon, or possibly the messianic king.

² By way of introduction, the psalmist declares his noble intentions and his hope that his work will be of excellent quality: **My heart abounds with good words; I address my works to the king.** This verse restates the main purpose of the psalm, namely, to honor the king. **My tongue,** while reciting this song, **is** like **the pen of a swift transcriber.**

יְפְיָפִ֫יתָ מִבְּנֵ֬י אָדָ֗ם ה֣וּצַק חֵ֭ן
בְּשִׂפְתוֹתֶ֑יךָ עַל־כֵּ֤ן בֵּרַכְךָ֖
אֱלֹהִ֣ים לְעוֹלָֽם:

חֲגֽוֹר־חַרְבְּךָ֣ עַל־יָרֵ֣ךְ גִּבּ֑וֹר
הֽוֹדְךָ֗ וַהֲדָרֶֽךָ:

וַהֲדָֽרְךָ֨ ׀ צְלַ֡ח רְכַ֗ב עַֽל־
דְּבַר־אֱ֭מֶת וְעַנְוָה־צֶ֑דֶק
וְתוֹרְךָ֖ נֽוֹרָא֣וֹת יְמִינֶֽךָ:

חִצֶּ֗יךָ שְׁנ֫וּנִ֥ים עַ֭מִּים תַּחְתֶּ֣יךָ
יִפְּל֑וּ בְּ֝לֵ֗ב אוֹיְבֵ֥י הַמֶּֽלֶךְ:

כִּסְאֲךָ֣ אֱ֭לֹהִים עוֹלָ֣ם וָעֶ֑ד
שֵׁ֥בֶט מִ֝ישֹׁ֗ר שֵׁ֣בֶט מַלְכוּתֶֽךָ:

3 You are fairer than sons of
men; grace flows from your
lips. Thus God has blessed you
forever.

4 Gird your sword upon your
thigh, mighty one, for your
majesty and glory.

5 Ride forth in your glory upon
the word of truth, humility,
and righteousness. Let your
right hand guide you along a
wondrous path.

6 Your arrows are sharp,
piercing the hearts of the
king's enemies; nations fall
before you.

7 Your throne is of God forever;
the staff of righteousness is the
scepter of your kingship.

---

3 **You are fairer than** all the other **sons of men; grace flows from your lips.** You express
yourself gracefully, in a manner that is pleasant to hear. **Thus God has blessed you forever.**

4 As the king is also a warrior, the psalmist describes his military aspect: **Gird your sword upon
your thigh, mighty one,** as this would be **for your majesty and glory.**

5 **Ride forth in your glory upon the word of truth.** The king's chariot, in a metaphorical sense,
is the word of truth, **humility, and righteousness.** In addition to his role as warrior, the king
serves as a judge. Here the military expressions acquire an additional, metaphorical meaning: The
glory and might of a king are manifest in his pursuit of truth in a manner that is both just and
self-effacing. In similar fashion: **Let your right hand,** the symbol of both power and uprightness,
guide you along a wondrous path that leads you to victory.

6 **Your arrows are sharp, piercing the hearts of the king's enemies; nations fall
before you.**

7 **Your throne is** the throne **of God forever.** It is said of King Solomon that he "sat on the throne
of God."[2] **The staff of righteousness is the scepter of your kingship.**

אָהַ֘בְתָּ צֶּ֤דֶק וַתִּשְׂנָ֫א רֶ֥שַׁע
עַל־כֵּ֤ן ׀ מְשָׁחֲךָ֡ אֱלֹהִ֣ים
אֱ֭לֹהֶיךָ שֶׁ֥מֶן שָׂשׂ֗וֹן מֵֽחֲבֵרֶֽךָ׃

מֹר־וַאֲהָל֣וֹת קְ֭צִיעוֹת כָּל־
בִּגְדֹתֶ֑יךָ מִֽן־הֵ֥יכְלֵי שֵׁ֝֗ן מִנִּ֥י
שִׂמְּחֽוּךָ׃

בְּנ֣וֹת מְ֭לָכִים בְּיִקְּרוֹתֶ֑יךָ
נִצְּבָ֥ה שֵׁגַ֥ל לִֽ֝ימִינְךָ֗ בְּכֶ֥תֶם
אוֹפִֽיר׃

שִׁמְעִי־בַ֣ת וּ֭רְאִי וְהַטִּ֣י אָזְנֵ֑ךְ
וְשִׁכְחִ֥י עַ֝מֵּ֗ךְ וּבֵ֥ית אָבִֽיךְ׃

וְיִתְאָ֣ו הַמֶּ֣לֶךְ יָפְיֵ֑ךְ כִּי־ה֥וּא
אֲ֝דֹנַ֗יִךְ וְהִשְׁתַּֽחֲוִי־לֽוֹ׃

8 You love righteousness and
abhor wickedness. Because
of this, God, your God, has
anointed you over your fellows
with the oil of joy.

9 Myrrh, aloes, and cassia were
on all your garments as you
went from ivory halls, since
they began to rejoice for you.

10 The daughters of kings are
among those who honor you;
at your right hand stands
the consort, attired in gold
from Ofir.

11 Listen, daughter, and take note;
incline your ear. Forget your
people and your father's house.

12 The king will desire your
beauty, as he is your master;
bow to him.

---

8 **You love righteousness and abhor wickedness. Because of this, God, your God, has anointed you,** the King Messiah, **over your fellows with the oil of joy,** a reference to the oil used to anoint the king, as his rise to power, culminating in his coronation, is an occasion of great joy.

9 The psalmist now describes the king as a bridegroom: **Myrrh, aloes, and cassia were on all your garments as you went from ivory halls.** This was so ever **since they began to rejoice for you,** starting from when the wedding festivities began.

10 **The daughters of kings are among those who honor you; at your right hand stands the consort,** the queen, **attired in gold from** faraway **Ofir,** a land known for its fine gold.[3]

11 The psalmist now addresses the bride: **Listen, daughter, and take note** of all the splendor you will enjoy after your marriage; **incline your ear. Forget your people and your father's house** after you become the king's wife.

12 **The king will desire your beauty, as he is your master,** as your king as well as your husband. **Bow to him.**

וּבַת־צֹר ׀ בְּמִנְחָה פָּנַיִךְ יְחַלּוּ
עֲשִׁירֵי עָם:

כָּל־כְּבוּדָּה בַת־מֶלֶךְ פְּנִימָה
מִמִּשְׁבְּצוֹת זָהָב לְבוּשָׁהּ:

לִרְקָמוֹת תּוּבַל לַמֶּלֶךְ
בְּתוּלוֹת אַחֲרֶיהָ רֵעוֹתֶיהָ
מוּבָאוֹת לָךְ:

תּוּבַלְנָה בִּשְׂמָחֹת וָגִיל
תְּבֹאֶינָה בְּהֵיכַל מֶלֶךְ:

תַּחַת אֲבֹתֶיךָ יִהְיוּ בָנֶיךָ
תְּשִׁיתֵמוֹ לְשָׂרִים בְּכָל־
הָאָרֶץ:

13 The populace of Tyre will come with gifts seeking your favor, the wealthiest of the people.

14 All of the glory of the princess is within, her dress interwoven with gold.

15 In embroidered clothing, she is led to the king; her virgin companions follow her, escorting her to you.

16 They are brought forth in gladness and rejoicing, entering the palace of the king.

17 May your sons follow in the wake of your fathers. You will appoint them as ministers throughout the land.

---

13 **The populace of Tyre will come with gifts** for the future queen, **seeking your favor, the wealthiest of the people.**

14 **All of the glory of the princess is within.** She does not appear in public; people honor her from a distance. **Her dress** is **interwoven with gold.**

15 **In embroidered clothing, she is led to the king; her virgin companions follow her, escorting her to you,** the king.

16 **They,** the bride and her attendants and companions, **are brought forth in gladness and rejoicing, entering the palace of the king.**

17 A blessing for the groom follows: **May your sons follow in the wake of your fathers.** May the dynasty remain unbroken, with your sons continuing to reign after you. **You will appoint them as ministers throughout the land.**

יח אַזְכִּירָה שִׁמְךָ בְּכָל־דֹּר וָדֹר
עַל־כֵּן עַמִּים יְהוֹדוּךָ
לְעוֹלָם וָעֶד:

18 I commemorate your name for all generations to come; thus nations will praise you forever.

PSALM 46

A song of praise and thanksgiving to God in the wake of a victory.
This triumph has been preceded by a period of great distress, but following God's intervention,
there ensues a period of peace and tranquility.

א לַמְנַצֵּחַ לִבְנֵי־קֹרַח עַל־
עֲלָמוֹת שִׁיר:

1 For the chief musician, by the sons of Korah, a song on *alamot*.

ב אֱלֹהִים לָנוּ מַחֲסֶה וָעֹז עֶזְרָה
בְצָרוֹת נִמְצָא מְאֹד:

2 God is our refuge and our strength, our ever-present help in times of trouble.

ג עַל־כֵּן לֹא־נִירָא בְּהָמִיר
אָרֶץ וּבְמוֹט הָרִים בְּלֵב
יַמִּים:

3 And so we will not fear during earth's upheaval, when mountains tumble into the heart of the sea,

---

18 **I commemorate your name for all generations to come; thus nations will praise you forever.**

PSALM 46

1 **For the chief musician, by the sons of Korah, a song on *alamot*.** *Alamot*, literally, "young women," may have been the name of a musical instrument played mostly by women. Alternatively, it may have been the name of the melody used for this psalm.

2 **God is our refuge and our strength, our ever-present help in times of trouble.**

3 **And so,** because God shelters us, **we will not fear during earth's upheaval,** apparently a reference to an actual earthquake, or perhaps geopolitical turmoil, **when mountains topple into the heart of the sea,**

יֶהֱמ֣וּ יֶחְמְר֣וּ מֵימָ֑יו יִרְעֲשֽׁוּ־
הָרִ֣ים בְּגַאֲוָת֣וֹ סֶֽלָה׃

נָהָ֗ר פְּלָגָ֗יו יְשַׂמְּח֥וּ עִיר־
אֱלֹהִ֑ים קְ֝דֹ֗שׁ מִשְׁכְּנֵ֥י עֶלְיֽוֹן׃

אֱלֹהִ֣ים בְּ֭קִרְבָּהּ בַּל־תִּמּ֑וֹט
יַעְזְרֶ֥הָ אֱ֝לֹהִ֗ים לִפְנ֥וֹת בֹּֽקֶר׃

הָמ֣וּ ג֭וֹיִם מָ֣טוּ מַמְלָכ֑וֹת נָתַ֥ן
בְּ֝קוֹל֗וֹ תָּמ֥וּג אָֽרֶץ׃

יְהוָ֣ה צְבָא֣וֹת עִמָּ֑נוּ מִשְׂגָּֽב־
לָ֝֗נוּ אֱלֹהֵ֖י יַעֲקֹ֣ב סֶֽלָה׃

לְֽכוּ־חֲ֭זוּ מִפְעֲל֣וֹת יְהוָ֑ה
אֲשֶׁר־שָׂ֖ם שַׁמּ֣וֹת בָּאָֽרֶץ׃

4 though waters roar and foam,
though mountains quake
before His grandeur, Selah.

5 There is a river whose streams
gladden the city of God, the
holy dwelling place of the
Most High.

6 God is in its midst; it will not
topple. God will help it toward
morning.

7 Nations raged, kingdoms
tottered; He raised His voice
and the earth melted.

8 The Lord of hosts is with
us; the God of Jacob is our
stronghold, Selah.

9 Come behold the works of the
Lord, who made desolations
on the earth.

---

4 **though waters roar and foam, though mountains quake before His grandeur,** as manifestations of God's great power, **Selah.**

5 **There is a river whose streams gladden the city of God, the holy dwelling place of the Most High.** As with the previous description, the river and its streams are not necessarily to be understood in a literal sense, but as a metaphor for spiritual inspiration.

6 **God is in its midst,** in the midst of Jerusalem; therefore, **it will not topple. God will help it toward morning,** not only during daylight hours, but also in the darkness that precedes the dawn.

7 **Nations raged, kingdoms tottered; He raised His voice and the earth melted.**

8 **The Lord of hosts is with us; the God of Jacob is our stronghold, Selah.**

9 **Come behold the works of the Lord,** His actions against the enemies, the Lord **who made desolations,** total devastation of them, **on the earth.**

מַשְׁבִּ֥ית מִלְחָמוֹת֮ עַד־קְצֵ֢ה
הָ֫אָ֥רֶץ קֶ֣שֶׁת יְ֭שַׁבֵּר וְקִצֵּ֣ץ
חֲנִ֑ית עֲ֝גָל֗וֹת יִשְׂרֹ֥ף בָּאֵֽשׁ׃

הַרְפּ֣וּ וּ֭דְעוּ כִּֽי־אָנֹכִ֣י אֱלֹהִ֑ים
אָר֥וּם בַּ֝גּוֹיִ֗ם אָר֥וּם בָּאָֽרֶץ׃

יְהוָ֣ה צְבָא֣וֹת עִמָּ֑נוּ מִשְׂגָּֽב־
לָ֝֗נוּ אֱלֹהֵ֖י יַעֲקֹ֣ב סֶֽלָה׃

10 He makes wars cease
throughout the earth; He
breaks bows and severs spears.
He burns wagons in fire.

11 Desist, and know that I am
God. I tower above nations,
tower above the land.

12 The Lord of hosts is with
us; the God of Jacob is our
stronghold, Selah.

PSALM 47

A psalm devoted entirely to praising God's sovereignty over the universe.
For this reason, it is associated with Rosh HaShana, the day of God's coronation;
it is recited before the shofar is blown.

לַמְנַצֵּ֬חַ לִבְנֵי־קֹ֬רַח מִזְמֽוֹר׃

1 For the chief musician, a psalm
by the sons of Korah.

---

10 **He makes wars,** the enemies' attacks against us, **cease throughout the earth; He breaks** the **bows** of the enemies **and severs** their **spears. He burns** their **wagons,** used to transport soldiers or supplies to the battlefront, **in fire.**

11 God now speaks to those enemies: **Desist** from your attempts to wage war, **and know that I am God. I tower above nations, tower above the land.**

12 The psalm repeats, as a kind of refrain: **The Lord of hosts is with us; the God of Jacob is our stronghold, Selah.**

PSALM 47

1 **For the chief musician, a psalm by the sons of Korah.**

כָּל־הָעַמִּים תִּקְעוּ־כָף הָרִיעוּ
לֵאלֹהִים בְּקוֹל רִנָּה:

כִּי־יְהוָה עֶלְיוֹן נוֹרָא מֶלֶךְ
גָּדוֹל עַל־כָּל־הָאָרֶץ:

יַדְבֵּר עַמִּים תַּחְתֵּינוּ וּלְאֻמִּים
תַּחַת רַגְלֵינוּ:

יִבְחַר־לָנוּ אֶת־נַחֲלָתֵנוּ
אֶת גְּאוֹן יַעֲקֹב אֲשֶׁר־אָהֵב
סֶלָה:

עָלָה אֱלֹהִים בִּתְרוּעָה יְהוָה
בְּקוֹל שׁוֹפָר:

זַמְּרוּ אֱלֹהִים זַמֵּרוּ זַמְּרוּ
לְמַלְכֵּנוּ זַמֵּרוּ:

כִּי מֶלֶךְ כָּל־הָאָרֶץ אֱלֹהִים
זַמְּרוּ מַשְׂכִּיל:

² All people, clap your hands; shout to God with a joyous voice.

³ For the Lord is most high and awesome, a great King over all the earth.

⁴ He subdues peoples beneath us, nations under our feet.

⁵ He has chosen our portion for us, the pride of Jacob, whom He loves, Selah.

⁶ God ascends with a clarion cry, the Lord with the sound of a shofar.

⁷ Sing praises to God, sing praises. Sing praises to our King, sing praises.

⁸ For God is King of all the earth; sing thoughtful praises.

---

2 **All people, clap your hands; shout to God with a joyous voice.**

3 **For the Lord is most high and awesome, a great King over all the earth.**

4 **He subdues peoples beneath us, nations under our feet.** This verse and the next are references to the conquest of the Land of Israel.

5 **He has chosen our portion,** the Land of Israel, **for us, the pride of Jacob, whom He loves, Selah.**

6 **God ascends,** He is elevated and glorified, **with a clarion cry,** which evokes majesty and glory, **the Lord with the sound of a shofar.**

7 **Sing praises to God, sing praises. Sing praises to our King, sing praises.**

8 **For God is King of all the earth; sing thoughtful praises** in His honor.

מֶלֶךְ אֱלֹהִים עַל־גּוֹיִם ⁹
אֱלֹהִים יָשַׁב ׀ עַל־כִּסֵּא
קָדְשׁוֹ:

נְדִיבֵי עַמִּים ׀ נֶאֱסָפוּ עַם ¹⁰
אֱלֹהֵי אַבְרָהָם כִּי לֵאלֹהִים
מָגִנֵּי־אֶרֶץ מְאֹד נַעֲלָה:

⁹ God reigns over the nations;
God sits on His holy throne.

¹⁰ Ministers of the peoples have
assembled, joining with the
people of the God of Abraham.
For the shields of the earth
belong to God; He is greatly
elevated.

PSALM 48

A psalm in praise and honor of Jerusalem in all its glory.

שִׁיר מִזְמוֹר לִבְנֵי־קֹרַח: ¹
גָּדוֹל יהוה וּמְהֻלָּל מְאֹד ²
בְּעִיר אֱלֹהֵינוּ הַר־קָדְשׁוֹ:

¹ A song, a psalm by the sons
of Korah.

² The Lord is great and
exceedingly praised in the
city of our God, on His holy
mountain.

---

⁹ **God reigns over** all **the nations; God sits on His holy throne.**
¹⁰ **Ministers of the peoples have assembled, joining with the people of the God of Abraham.** Noble leaders of all nations gather to join the people of Israel in honoring God. Abraham is mentioned here specifically, because he was not only Israel's forefather but also the propagator of monotheism in the world. **For the shields of the earth,** the power and ability to safeguard the world, **belong to God;** in this, **He is greatly elevated.** These words are a fitting conclusion to the psalm, which is both a song of praise and a song of coronation for God as King.

PSALM 48
¹ **A song, a psalm by the sons of Korah.**
² **The Lord is great and exceedingly praised** when He appears **in the city of our God,** Jerusalem, and particularly when He appears **on His holy mountain,** the Temple Mount.

יְפֵה נוֹף מְשׂוֹשׂ כָּל־הָאָרֶץ
הַר־צִיּוֹן יַרְכְּתֵי צָפוֹן קִרְיַת
מֶלֶךְ רָב:

³ Beautiful in its views, joy of all the world. Mount Zion, the northern summit, the city of the great king.

אֱלֹהִים בְּאַרְמְנוֹתֶיהָ נוֹדַע
לְמִשְׂגָּב:

⁴ God, through its palaces, is known as its stronghold.

כִּי־הִנֵּה הַמְּלָכִים נוֹעֲדוּ
עָבְרוּ יַחְדָּו:

⁵ Behold, the kings assembled, passing through together.

הֵמָּה רָאוּ כֵּן תָּמָהוּ נִבְהֲלוּ
נֶחְפָּזוּ:

⁶ They saw it and were amazed. They were terrified; they hastened.

רְעָדָה אֲחָזָתַם שָׁם חִיל
כַּיּוֹלֵדָה:

⁷ A fearful trembling seized them there, like the pangs of a woman giving birth,

---

³ **Beautiful in its views, joy of all the world.** *Nof*, translated here as "views," literally refers to the foliage of a tree. But the expression "beautiful foliage" is expanded to allude to the beauty of the entire city. The entire world sees Jerusalem as a paradigm of magnificence. **Mount Zion,** apparently a reference to the Temple Mount, as well as **the northern summit.** The northern summit contained palaces and, later, defense fortifications. It is **the city of the great king.** The "great king" may be a reference to King Solomon, whose palace was apparently situated in this northern part of the city.

⁴ **God, through its palaces,** referring to Jerusalem's largest and most exquisite structures, not only the homes of the wealthy and powerful but also public buildings and fortifications, **is known as its stronghold.** For these structures are testimony to the greatness and strength of the city of God.

⁵ **Behold, the kings,** who had gone to visit Jerusalem, **assembled, passing through** the city **together.**

⁶ **They saw it** in all its splendor **and were amazed. They were terrified** by its strength; **they hastened** to leave the city, feeling overwhelmed and even threatened by its might.

⁷ **A fearful trembling seized them there, like the pangs of a woman giving birth,**

ח בְּרֵוּחַ קָדֵים תְּשַׁבֵּר אֲנִיְּוֹת תַּרְשִׁישׁ:

8 or an east wind that breaks the ships of Tarshish.

ט כַּאֲשֶׁר שָׁמַעְנוּ ׀ כֵּן רָאִינוּ בְּעִיר־יהוה צְבָאוֹת בְּעִיר אֱלֹהֵינוּ אֱלֹהִים יְכוֹנְנֶהָ עַד־עוֹלָם סֶלָה:

9 As we have heard, so we have seen in the city of the Lord of hosts, in the city of our God; may God establish it forever, Selah.

י דִּמִּינוּ אֱלֹהִים חַסְדֶּךָ בְּקֶרֶב הֵיכָלֶךָ:

10 We envisage Your kindness, God, in the midst of Your Sanctuary.

יא כְּשִׁמְךָ ׀ אֱלֹהִים כֵּן תְּהִלָּתְךָ עַל־קַצְוֵי־אֶרֶץ צֶדֶק מָלְאָה יְמִינֶךָ:

11 As with Your name, God, so Your praise reaches to the ends of the earth; Your right hand is filled with righteousness.

---

8 **or** like the terror of a seafarer who experiences **an east wind that breaks the ships of Tarshish.** Although the east wind is rarely dangerous, it can acquire gale force during a severe storm, becoming powerful enough to destroy large ships. Tarshish was a faraway port. Some say it was in Spain; others place its location in the eastern Mediterranean. In any event, "ships of Tarshish" were large, sturdy vessels built for long voyages.

9 Those people who visit Jerusalem exclaim: **As we have heard** about Jerusalem in our home countries, **so we have seen** with our own eyes **in the city of the Lord of hosts, in the city of our God.** "Lord of hosts" is one of the names of God, depicting Him as ruler over all the creations of the world. **May God establish it forever, Selah.**

10 Having witnessed the splendor of Jerusalem, **we envisage** a very different aspect of Godliness in Jerusalem, namely, **Your kindness, God,** which we do not see here, but is revealed **in the midst of Your Sanctuary.**

11 **As with Your name, God, so Your praise,** which people declare, is widespread and **reaches to the ends of the earth. Your right hand is filled with righteousness.** The image of God's "right hand" represents His power as well as His upright justice, an allusion to His faithfulness to His covenant.

יב יִשְׂמַח ׀ הַר־צִיּוֹן תָּגֵלְנָה
בְּנוֹת יְהוּדָה לְמַעַן
מִשְׁפָּטֶיךָ:

יג סֹבּוּ צִיּוֹן וְהַקִּיפוּהָ סִפְרוּ
מִגְדָּלֶיהָ:

יד שִׁיתוּ לִבְּכֶם ׀ לְחֵילָה פַּסְּגוּ
אַרְמְנוֹתֶיהָ לְמַעַן תְּסַפְּרוּ
לְדוֹר אַחֲרוֹן:

טו כִּי זֶה ׀ אֱלֹהִים אֱלֹהֵינוּ עוֹלָם
וָעֶד הוּא יְנַהֲגֵנוּ עַל־מוּת:

12 Let Mount Zion be glad; let the daughters of Judah rejoice because of Your judgments.

13 Go about Zion and encircle it; count its towers.

14 Pay attention to its ramparts; climb up to its palaces, so you may tell of it to the next generation.

15 For this is God, our God, forever and ever. He will guide us beyond death.

---

12 **Let Mount Zion be glad; let the daughters of Judah rejoice because of Your judgments.**

13 What follows is a call directed to those coming to Jerusalem: **Go about Zion,** the Temple Mount, which was surrounded by its own wall, **and encircle it; count** all **its towers,** the towers of the city as a whole.

14 **Pay attention to its ramparts; climb up to its palaces, so you may tell of it to the next generation.** Go from place to place so that you will be able to describe fully Jerusalem's greatness and glory.

15 Because Jerusalem is "the city of our God" and not merely the capital of a small country, the psalmist concludes with the following words: **For this is God, our God, forever and ever. He will guide us** forever, even **beyond death.**

PSALM 49

A psalm dealing with death. It is recited nowadays in a house of mourning;
it is possible that it was actually composed for such a purpose.

א לַמְנַצֵּחַ לִבְנֵי־קֹרַח מִזְמוֹר:

1 For the chief musician, a psalm
by the sons of Korah.

ב שִׁמְעוּ־זֹאת כָּל־הָעַמִּים
הַאֲזִינוּ כָּל־יֹשְׁבֵי חָלֶד:

2 Hear this, all peoples; listen, all
inhabitants of the world,

ג גַּם־בְּנֵי אָדָם גַּם־בְּנֵי־אִישׁ
יַחַד עָשִׁיר וְאֶבְיוֹן:

3 people and sons of man as well,
rich and poor together.

ד פִּי יְדַבֵּר חָכְמוֹת וְהָגוּת לִבִּי
תְבוּנוֹת:

4 My mouth will speak wisdom,
understanding from my heart's
meditation.

ה אַטֶּה לְמָשָׁל אָזְנִי אֶפְתַּח
בְּכִנּוֹר חִידָתִי:

5 I incline my ear for an allegory,
opening with the lyre to state
my sayings.

PSALM 49

1 **For the chief musician, a psalm by the sons of Korah.**

2 The psalm begins with a call for attention: **Hear this, all peoples; listen, all inhabitants of the world.** The word *ḥaled*, translated here as "the world," is usually defined more narrowly as land or soil. Given the similarities of sound, *ḥaled* also evokes a sense of termination or ending, as in the verb *ḥadal*, "to cease."

3 As noted in the previous verse, this psalm is directed to people in general, as its subject matter is universal, to **people and sons of man as well, rich and poor together.** Apparently, *benei adam*, translated here as "people," refers to the common folk, whereas *benei ish*, "sons of man," refers to people of prominence, since the word *ish* is often used to indicate specifically men of stature.

4 **My mouth will speak wisdom, understanding from my heart's meditation.** From this verse it is apparent that the psalm is introspective in nature.

5 **I incline my ear for an allegory, opening with the lyre to state my sayings.** *Mashal*, translated here as "allegory," means a pithy or poetic utterance; in biblical Hebrew the word does not refer to a parable, a meaning it began to take on in the talmudic era. *Ḥidati*, translated here as "my sayings," refers to a kind of eloquent, clever statement, derived from the root *ḥad*, sharp. It does not necessarily denote a riddle or enigma, as it does elsewhere.

לָמָּה אִירָא בִּימֵי רָע עֲוֹן
עֲקֵבַי יְסוּבֵּנִי:

הַבֹּטְחִים עַל־חֵילָם וּבְרֹב
עָשְׁרָם יִתְהַלָּלוּ:

אָח לֹא־פָדֹה יִפְדֶּה אִישׁ
לֹא־יִתֵּן לֵאלֹהִים כָּפְרוֹ:

וְיֵקַר פִּדְיוֹן נַפְשָׁם וְחָדַל
לְעוֹלָם:

וִיחִי־עוֹד לָנֶצַח לֹא יִרְאֶה
הַשָּׁחַת:

6 Why should I fear, in days of evil, though the iniquity of my feet surrounds me?

7 Those who trust in their wealth and boast about their great riches.

8 A man can neither redeem his brother nor give God a ransom for him.

9 The redemption of their lives is too costly and can never be attained.

10 Can one live forever, never seeing the grave?

---

6 **Why should I fear, in days of evil,** since all adversity eventually comes to an end, **though the iniquity of my feet surrounds me?** "Iniquity of my feet," literally, "of my heels," refers to sins committed as one walks along the path of life; alternatively, it indicates sins committed intentionally. I may be punished for my sins, but ultimately everything comes to an end.

7 The same may be said of **those who** are tranquil and comfortable in life, who **trust in their wealth and boast about their great riches.** In the end, death claims these people as well.

8 **A man can neither redeem his brother** from death **nor give God a ransom for him** to save him from that fate, nor can anyone else. When death calls, there is no escape.

9 **The redemption of their lives is too costly.** Even if it were possible to speak of a ransom from death, the price would be far too high **and can never be attained,** exceeding the value of everything in existence.

10 **Can one live forever, never seeing the grave?** Most people have illusions of immortality. They go about their daily lives, deluding themselves that they will live forever.

יא כִּי יִרְאֶה ׀ חֲכָמִים יָמוּתוּ יַחַד
כְּסִיל וָבַעַר יֹאבֵדוּ וְעָזְבוּ
לַאֲחֵרִים חֵילָם:

יב קִרְבָּם בָּתֵּימוֹ ׀ לְעוֹלָם
מִשְׁכְּנֹתָם לְדֹר וָדֹר קָרְאוּ
בִשְׁמוֹתָם עֲלֵי אֲדָמוֹת:

יג וְאָדָם בִּיקָר בַּל־יָלִין נִמְשַׁל
כַּבְּהֵמוֹת נִדְמוּ:

יד זֶה דַרְכָּם כֵּסֶל לָמוֹ
וְאַחֲרֵיהֶם ׀ בְּפִיהֶם יִרְצוּ
סֶלָה:

11 For he sees that wise men
die; the foolish and the
simpleminded all perish and
leave their wealth to others.

12 Deep within them, their
houses will endure forever;
their dwelling places will
remain for all generations.
They name their lands after
themselves.

13 Yet man cannot abide in his
splendor; he is like the beasts
that perish.

14 This is their way of folly; so, too,
those who follow speak the
same desires, Selah.

---

11 A man should realize that death is inevitable, **for he sees that** even the **wise men die. The foolish and the simpleminded** as well **all perish and leave** behind **their wealth to others.**

12 **Deep within them,** in their minds, **their houses will endure** in their possession **forever; their dwelling places will remain** theirs **for all generations. They name their lands after themselves,** expecting that their legacy will endure along with them.

13 **Yet man cannot abide** indefinitely **in his splendor.** In the end, all individuals are taken from this world. Worldly possessions, no matter how splendid, cannot save them from this fate. He is like the beasts that perish, dying just as animals do.

14 **This is their way of folly,** building their hopes and dreams on what they possess in this world, even though possessions are ephemeral and annulled by death. **So, too, those who follow,** subsequent generations, **speak the same desires** about indefinite continuation of life in this world, **Selah.**

כַּצֹּאן ׀ לִשְׁאוֹל שַׁתּוּ מָוֶת ‏15‏
יִרְעֵם וַיִּרְדּוּ בָם יְשָׁרִים ׀
לַבֹּקֶר וְצִירָם לְבַלּוֹת שְׁאוֹל
מִזְּבֻל לֽוֹ:

אַךְ־אֱלֹהִים יִפְדֶּה נַפְשִׁי מִיַּד ‏16‏
שְׁאוֹל כִּי יִקָּחֵנִי סֶֽלָה:

אַל־תִּירָא כִּי־יַעֲשִׁר אִישׁ כִּי־ ‏17‏
יִרְבֶּה כְּבוֹד בֵּיתֽוֹ:

15 Like sheep, they are destined for the grave; death will shepherd them. The upright will rule over them in the morning; their form will be consumed in the abode of the grave.

16 But God will redeem my soul from the grip of Sheol; He will take me in, Selah.

17 Do not fear when a man becomes wealthy, increasing the honor of his house,

---

15 **Like sheep, they are destined for the grave; death will shepherd them.** All of humanity is like a flock of sheep being led by a shepherd to inevitable death. Some commentators interpret *yirem* as "will consume them" rather than "will shepherd them." **The upright will rule over them,** will take control of their property, **in the morning,** in the future, after their death, while **their form,** their bodies, **will be consumed in the abode of the grave.**

16 In one of the few places in the Bible in which the continuing existence of the soul after death is mentioned, the psalmist now inserts a verse on a more positive note: **But God will redeem my soul from the grip of Sheol.** Usually *sheol* is translated as "the grave," a place one goes to after death. But sometimes, as here, it refers to a place of suffering and misery after death, a hell, where the souls of those who dedicated their lives exclusively to worldly matters go. As such, elsewhere this word is translated as the "netherworld." The righteous, however, will be redeemed from this fate by God. **He will take me in, Selah.** True redemption, real deliverance from Sheol, occurs when a soul reaches a level in which it is bound to God, a situation referred to in I Samuel 25:28 as the "bond of life with the Lord your God."

17 The psalmist now turns to those people who choose to walk a righteous path, but feel that the world does not value their choice: **Do not fear,** do not be concerned, **when a man becomes wealthy** and powerful, **increasing the honor of his house.** All this is ultimately of no consequence,

יח כִּי לֹא בְמוֹתוֹ יִקַּח הַכֹּל לֹא־
יֵרֵד אַחֲרָיו כְּבוֹדוֹ:

יט כִּי־נַפְשׁוֹ בְּחַיָּיו יְבָרֵךְ וְיוֹדֻךָ
כִּי־תֵיטִיב לָךְ:

כ תָּבוֹא עַד־דּוֹר אֲבוֹתָיו עַד־
נֵצַח לֹא יִרְאוּ־אוֹר:

כא אָדָם בִּיקָר וְלֹא יָבִין נִמְשַׁל
כַּבְּהֵמוֹת נִדְמוּ:

18 for he will take nothing when he dies; his honor will not descend with him.

19 Rather, he should bring blessing upon himself during his life; people will praise you, and you will benefit.

20 Or it will return to the generations of his fathers, who forever will not behold the light.

21 Man, in his splendor, does not understand; he is like the beasts that perish.

---

18 **for he will take nothing when he dies; his honor will not descend** to the grave **with him.** Wealth and honor have no meaning in the grave.

19 **Rather** than a person seeking out riches, **he should bring blessing upon himself during his life,** by doing good deeds that are seen as a blessing. Turning to such a person, the psalmist declares: Thereupon, **people will praise you** for your upright behavior, **and you** yourself **will benefit** from this. Good deeds are of benefit to the soul. People who are good to others are actually helping themselves; indeed, all that remains with one's soul in eternity is the good that it has done.

20 **Or** if not, **it,** man's soul, **will return to the generations of his fathers.** It will experience the same fate is the souls of his ancestors, who did not follow this advice and **who forever will not behold the light.** All their material accomplishments will dim and fade after death.

21 The psalmist concludes with a summary of man's attitude toward his life: A **man** who is preoccupied with material life and basks **in his splendor does not understand** which things in life are truly meaningful and beneficial for his soul; **he is like the beasts that perish.** In life he is like an animal, devoid of understanding, and in death as well, he is like a beast in that there remains no memory of him and there is no hope for his soul.

PSALM 50

A psalm providing perspective about the offering of sacrifices in general. According to tradition,
it was recited on one of the days of the Sukkot festival during the daily sacrifice.

מִזְמוֹר לְאָסָף אֵל ׀ אֱלֹהִים
יְהֹוָה דִּבֶּר וַיִּקְרָא־אָרֶץ
מִמִּזְרַח־שֶׁמֶשׁ עַד־מְבֹאוֹ:

1 A psalm by Asaf. The Almighty God, the Lord, has spoken, addressing the earth from the rising of the sun to its setting.

מִצִּיּוֹן מִכְלַל־יֹפִי אֱלֹהִים
הוֹפִיעַ:

2 Out of Zion, the perfection of beauty, God shines forth.

יָבֹא אֱלֹהֵינוּ וְאַל־יֶחֱרַשׁ
אֵשׁ־לְפָנָיו תֹּאכֵל וּסְבִיבָיו
נִשְׂעֲרָה מְאֹד:

3 Our God arrives and is not silent. Before Him a fire consumes, and surrounding Him it is exceedingly stormy.

יִקְרָא אֶל־הַשָּׁמַיִם מֵעָל
וְאֶל־הָאָרֶץ לָדִין עַמּוֹ:

4 He summons the heavens above, and the earth, to judge His people.

אִסְפוּ־לִי חֲסִידָי כֹּרְתֵי
בְרִיתִי עֲלֵי־זָבַח:

5 Gather My devoted ones, those who make a covenant with Me by sacrifice.

PSALM 50

1 **A psalm by Asaf. The Almighty God, the Lord, has spoken, addressing** all people of **the earth from the rising of the sun to its setting,** from east to west.

2 **Out of Zion,** the Temple Mount, **the perfection of beauty, God shines forth.** The focal point of God's revelation is the Temple in Jerusalem.

3 **Our God arrives and is not silent;** His words will be heard. **Before Him a fire consumes, and surrounding Him it is exceedingly stormy.** Divine revelation is accompanied by stormy winds and fire.[4]

4 **He summons the heavens above, and** He also calls upon **the earth,** in order **to judge His people.**

5 This is what He says to the earth: **Gather My devoted ones, those who make a covenant with Me by sacrifice.**

וַיַּגִּ֣ידוּ שָׁמַ֣יִם צִדְק֑וֹ כִּֽי־
אֱלֹהִ֓ים ׀ שֹׁפֵ֖ט ה֣וּא סֶֽלָה׃

שִׁמְעָ֤ה עַמִּ֨י ׀ וַאֲדַבֵּ֗רָה
יִ֖שְׂרָאֵל וְאָעִ֣ידָה בָּ֑ךְ אֱלֹהִ֖ים
אֱלֹהֶ֣יךָ אָנֹֽכִי׃

לֹ֣א עַל־זְ֭בָחֶיךָ אוֹכִיחֶ֑ךָ
וְעוֹלֹתֶ֖יךָ לְנֶגְדִּ֣י תָמִֽיד׃

לֹא־אֶקַּ֣ח מִבֵּיתְךָ֣ פָ֑ר
מִ֝מִּכְלְאֹתֶ֗יךָ עַתּוּדִֽים׃

כִּי־לִ֥י כָל־חַיְתוֹ־יָ֑עַר בְּ֝הֵמ֗וֹת
בְּהַרְרֵי־אָֽלֶף׃

יָ֭דַעְתִּי כָּל־ע֣וֹף הָרִ֑ים וְזִ֥יז
שָׂ֝דַ֗י עִמָּדִֽי׃

6 The heavens declare His righteousness, for God Himself is Judge, Selah.

7 Hear, My people, and I will speak; Israel, I will bear witness to you. I am God, your God.

8 I do not rebuke you for your sacrifices, nor are your burnt offerings always before Me.

9 I will not take a young bull from your house, nor he-goats from your pens.

10 For every beast of the forest is Mine, as are the cattle on thousands of hills.

11 I know every bird of the mountains; so too the large fowl of the field are with Me.

---

6 In parallel: **The heavens declare His righteousness, for God Himself is Judge, Selah.**

7 God now directs His speech to His people in general, and more specifically, to those who fear Him: **Hear, My people, and I will speak;** hear, **Israel,** and **I will bear witness to you.** Remember that **I am God, your God.** This is an allusion to the first of the Ten Precepts: "I am the Lord your God."[5]

8 Although the Torah encourages animal sacrifices and gives extensive instructions concerning them, **I do not rebuke you for** not having offered **your sacrifices** to Me. **Nor are your burnt offerings always before Me.** They are not the focus of My attention. I do not need any of your sacrifices for My own sake. This point is clarified further in the following verses.

9 **I will not take** for Myself **a young bull from your house, nor he-goats from your pens.**

10 I have no need of your animals, **for every beast of the forest is Mine, as are the cattle on thousands of hills.**

11 **I know every bird of the mountains; so too the large fowl of the field are with Me.** *Ziz,* translated here as "large fowl," is of uncertain meaning, but appears to refer to a species of giant bird.[6]

אִם־אֶרְעַב לֹא־אֹמַר לָךְ כִּי־ ^{יב}
לִי תֵבֵל וּמְלֹאָהּ:

הַאוֹכַל בְּשַׂר אַבִּירִים וְדַם ^{יג}
עַתּוּדִים אֶשְׁתֶּה:

זְבַח לֵאלֹהִים תּוֹדָה וְשַׁלֵּם ^{יד}
לְעֶלְיוֹן נְדָרֶיךָ:

וּקְרָאֵנִי בְּיוֹם צָרָה אֲחַלֶּצְךָ ^{טו}
וּתְכַבְּדֵנִי:

וְלָרָשָׁע ׀ אָמַר אֱלֹהִים מַה־ ^{טז}
לְךָ לְסַפֵּר חֻקָּי וַתִּשָּׂא בְרִיתִי
עֲלֵי־פִיךָ:

וְאַתָּה שָׂנֵאתָ מוּסָר וַתַּשְׁלֵךְ ^{יז}
דְּבָרַי אַחֲרֶיךָ:

¹² If I were hungry, I would not tell you, for the world and all it contains is Mine.

¹³ Do I eat the flesh of bulls or drink the blood of he-goats?

¹⁴ Offer God a thanksgiving sacrifice, and pay your vows to the Most High.

¹⁵ Call upon Me in times of trouble; I will rescue you, and you will honor Me.

¹⁶ But to the wicked one God says: What right have you to speak of My statutes or to invoke My covenant?

¹⁷ For you hate reproof, and you cast My words behind you.

---

¹² Even **if** it were possible to imagine that **I were hungry, I would not tell you** and ask you to fulfill My need, **for the world and all it contains is Mine.**

¹³ Of course, the scenario in the preceding verse is an absurdity, expressed ironically, for **do I eat the flesh of bulls or drink the blood of he-goats?** To believe that would be ludicrous.

¹⁴ It is clear, then, that God does not need the sacrifices we offer. Rather, they are a means by which man can express his relationship with God. **Offer God a thanksgiving sacrifice, and pay your** sacrificial **vows to the Most High** if you have pledged to bring a sacrifice in His honor.

¹⁵ And if you do fulfill your vows faithfully, you can always **call upon Me in times of trouble**, situations in which people are most inclined to make vows; **I will** accept your vow and **rescue you, and you will** subsequently **honor Me** by fulfilling the sacrificial vow.

¹⁶ All the foregoing relates to ordinary or specifically God-fearing individuals. **But to the wicked one God says: What right have you to speak of My statutes or to invoke My covenant** with Israel? Why do you profess to be a member of the holy nation of Israel and a party to their covenant with God?

¹⁷ **For** despite your claims, **you hate reproof, and you cast My words behind you,** following various paths of evil, as described in the following verses.

אִם־רָאִיתָ גַּנָּב וַתִּרֶץ עִמּוֹ יח
וְעִם מְנָאֲפִים חֶלְקֶךָ:

פִּיךָ שָׁלַחְתָּ בְרָעָה וּלְשׁוֹנְךָ יט
תַּצְמִיד מִרְמָה:

תֵּשֵׁב בְּאָחִיךָ תְדַבֵּר בְּבֶן־ כ
אִמְּךָ תִּתֶּן־דֹּפִי:

אֵלֶּה עָשִׂיתָ ׀ וְהֶחֱרַשְׁתִּי כא
דִּמִּיתָ הֱיוֹת־אֶהְיֶה כָמוֹךָ
אוֹכִיחֲךָ וְאֶעֶרְכָה לְעֵינֶיךָ:

בִּינוּ־נָא זֹאת שֹׁכְחֵי אֱלוֹהַּ כב
פֶּן־אֶטְרֹף וְאֵין מַצִּיל:

18 When you see a thief, you run with him; you join in with adulterers.

19 You let your mouth spew out evil and affix your tongue to deceit.

20 You sit and speak against your brother; you slander your own mother's son.

21 You have done these things, and I kept silent. Did you think I was like you, that I would reprove you and set it before your eyes?

22 Ponder this well, you who have forgotten God, lest I tear you to pieces, with no one to rescue you.

---

18 **When you see a thief, you run** to participate **with him** in his crime; **you join in with adulterers.**

19 **You let your mouth spew out evil and affix your tongue to deceit.**

20 **You sit and speak** even **against your brother** when in the company of others. **You slander your own mother's son.**

21 **You have done these** evil **things, and I kept silent,** not immediately responding to them. **Did you think I was like you, that I would** lower Myself to your level and come to **reprove you and set it,** your nefarious behavior, **before your eyes?**

22 God does not respond to evil in that way. But in the end, He does judge man: **Ponder this well, you who have forgotten God,** who believe that God has overlooked their sins entirely. Ponder and realize that the time of punishment will ultimately arrive, **lest I tear you to pieces, with no one to rescue you.**

‫כב ‬ ‫זֹבֵחַ תּוֹדָה יְכַבְּדָנְנִי וְשָׂם‬
‫דֶּרֶךְ אַרְאֶנּוּ בְּיֵשַׁע אֱלֹהִים:‬

²³ He who offers a thanksgiving
sacrifice honors Me; and as
for he who sets his path, I will
show him the salvation of God.

TUESDAY

PSALM 51

A psalm that is the classic text of confession and contrition,
containing a plea for forgiveness and expressing hope for absolution.

‫א ‬ ‫לַמְנַצֵּחַ מִזְמוֹר לְדָוִד:‬

¹ For the chief musician, a psalm
by David,

‫ב ‬ ‫בְּבוֹא־אֵלָיו נָתָן הַנָּבִיא‬
‫כַּאֲשֶׁר־בָּא אֶל־בַּת־שָׁבַע:‬

² when Natan the prophet came
to him after he had been with
Bathsheba.

---

23 Speaking in God's voice, the psalmist addresses his concluding verse to people who heed His
word: **He who offers a thanksgiving sacrifice,** acting on his desire to show his gratitude to
Me, **honors Me.** Such a sacrifice, made out of personal devotion, as opposed to one who thinks
that he is doing Me a favor, is a means of honoring Me. **And as for he who sets his path,** who
consciously chooses to follow the paths of righteousness and propriety, **I will show him the
salvation of God.**

PSALM 51
1 **For the chief musician, a psalm by David,**
2 **when Natan the prophet came to him** to rebuke him **after he had been with Bathsheba.**
Natan informed David that the consequences of his sin would be felt not only in his lifetime but
also in the lives of his descendants. As recounted in the book of Samuel,[7] David acknowledged and
deeply regretted his actions, and God accepted David's repentance, though he was not yet granted
full atonement. This psalm offers David's perspective.

חָנֵּנִי אֱלֹהִים כְּחַסְדֶּךָ כְּרֹב
רַחֲמֶיךָ מְחֵה פְשָׁעָי:

הֶרֶב

הֶרֶב כַּבְּסֵנִי מֵעֲוֹנִי
וּמֵחַטָּאתִי טַהֲרֵנִי:

כִּי־פְשָׁעַי אֲנִי אֵדָע וְחַטָּאתִי
נֶגְדִּי תָמִיד:

לְךָ לְבַדְּךָ ׀ חָטָאתִי וְהָרַע
בְּעֵינֶיךָ עָשִׂיתִי לְמַעַן תִּצְדַּק
בְּדָבְרֶךָ תִּזְכֶּה בְשָׁפְטֶךָ:

הֵן־בְּעָווֹן חוֹלָלְתִּי וּבְחֵטְא
יֶחֱמַתְנִי אִמִּי:

Be gracious to me, God, as befits Your kindness; in the greatness of Your mercy, blot out my transgressions.

Thoroughly wash my iniquity from me; purify me from my sin.

For I know my transgressions; my sin is always before me.

Against You alone I have sinned. I have done that which is evil in Your eyes, so You are just in Your words and right in Your verdict.

I was formed in iniquity; in sin my mother conceived me.

---

3 **Be gracious to me, God, as befits Your kindness; in the greatness of Your mercy, blot out my transgressions.** I offer no excuses; I plead only for compassion and mercy.

4 **Thoroughly wash my iniquity from me.** The word *kabseni* refers to an intense and thorough scrubbing to remove deeply ingrained dirt. **Purify me from my sin.**

5 **For I know my transgressions.** David is saying that he "knows" his transgressions, in the sense that he recognizes the severity of the sins he committed deliberately. **My sin is always before me,** always on my mind; I am unable to forget what I have done.

6 **Against You alone I have sinned.** David does not mean to say that his sin was against God, not affecting other individuals; clearly his sin harmed others as well: Bathsheba, Uriya, and other people who were involved. What David means is the following: My sin is so severe, so grave, that I cannot deal with it in any way other than by placing it before God to judge. In other words, his transgression was not only a crime and a violation of societal norms, but also a manifestation of a deeply ingrained flaw in his relationship with God. **I have done that which is evil in Your eyes, so** I understand and accept that **You are just in your words and right in Your verdict,** whatever punishment it may involve.

7 At the same time, David offers an explanation that might mitigate his culpability. He notes that sin is not a onetime, exceptional occurrence in man's life but rather an intrinsic part of his existence: **I was formed in iniquity; in sin my mother conceived me.** The very process of conception

^ה הֵן־אֱמֶת חָפַצְתָּ בַטֻּחוֹת
וּבְסָתֻם חָכְמָה תוֹדִיעֵנִי:

^ט תְּחַטְּאֵנִי בְאֵזוֹב וְאֶטְהָר
תְּכַבְּסֵנִי וּמִשֶּׁלֶג אַלְבִּין:

^י תַּשְׁמִיעֵנִי שָׂשׂוֹן וְשִׂמְחָה
תָּגֵלְנָה עֲצָמוֹת דִּכִּיתָ:

^{יא} הַסְתֵּר פָּנֶיךָ מֵחֲטָאָי וְכָל־
עֲוֹנֹתַי מְחֵה:

^{יא} לֵב טָהוֹר בְּרָא־לִי אֱלֹהִים
וְרוּחַ נָכוֹן חַדֵּשׁ בְּקִרְבִּי:

8 You desire truth in the innermost parts; show me wisdom in the hidden place within.

9 Purify me with hyssop, and I will be clean; cleanse me, so I will be whiter than snow.

10 Make me hear joy and gladness; let the bones that You crushed rejoice.

11 Hide Your face from my sins and blot out all my iniquities.

12 Create in me a pure heart, God, and renew a steadfast spirit within me.

---

involves actions that are not necessarily driven by the purest impulses. Thus, from the beginning of man's existence, he is imbued with drives and passions, and this becomes part of human nature.

8 **You desire truth in the innermost parts.** The word *tuḥot*, translated here as "the innermost parts," literally means "the kidneys," regarded as the seat of counsel and decision within man. You desire that truth should penetrate the innermost recesses of man's mind, and it is with this degree of sincerity that I confess my sin. **Show me wisdom,** the ability to understand the depth of my sin, **in the hidden place within** my soul, where my private thoughts reside.

9 David now beseeches God to purify him of his sin, alluding to methods described in the Torah to remove ritual impurity: **Purify me** as if **with hyssop, and I will be clean.** Hyssop was used in the procedure of purification from the ritual impurity of leprosy,[8] as well as in the procedure of purification from contamination by contact with a corpse.[9] **Cleanse me, so I will be whiter than snow.** As mentioned previously, the word *tekhabseni* refers to an intense cleansing. David is willing to accept the concomitant pain involved in this process.

10 And when you purify me from my sin, this will **make me hear,** or experience, **joy and gladness** in the knowledge that my sin has been expiated. **Let the bones that You crushed rejoice.** The bones represent the essential, innermost part of me that have been damaged by sins and guilt.

11 **Hide Your face from my sins,** do not keep them constantly in mind, **and blot out all my iniquities** in light of my repentance.

12 **Create in me a pure heart, God.** Replace my heart that has been damaged by my sins with a new heart. Grant me new understanding and feeling, **and renew a steadfast spirit within me.**

יג אַל־תַּשְׁלִיכֵנִי מִלְּפָנֶיךָ וְרוּחַ
קָדְשְׁךָ אַל־תִּקַּח מִמֶּנִּי:

יד הָשִׁיבָה לִּי שְׂשׂוֹן יִשְׁעֶךָ וְרוּחַ
נְדִיבָה תִסְמְכֵנִי:

טו אֲלַמְּדָה פֹשְׁעִים דְּרָכֶיךָ
וְחַטָּאִים אֵלֶיךָ יָשׁוּבוּ:

טז הַצִּילֵנִי מִדָּמִים אֱלֹהִים
אֱלֹהֵי תְשׁוּעָתִי תְּרַנֵּן לְשׁוֹנִי
צִדְקָתֶךָ:

יז אֲדֹנָי שְׂפָתַי תִּפְתָּח וּפִי יַגִּיד
תְּהִלָּתֶךָ:

13 Do not cast me away from Your presence, and do not take Your holy spirit from me.

14 Restore the joy of Your salvation to me; sustain me with a generous spirit.

15 I will teach Your ways to transgressors; sinners will return to You.

16 Save me from bloodshed, God, the God of my salvation. My tongue will sing of Your righteousness.

17 Lord, open my lips so my mouth may declare Your praise.

---

13 **Do not cast me away from Your presence** because of my sin, **and do not take** away **Your holy spirit from me.** Leave the holiness that is within me intact. David was not only a man of greatness; in many ways he was also a holy man.

14 **Restore the joy of Your salvation to me** by forgiving my sins. **Sustain me with a generous spirit** of divine grace.

15 Your acceptance of my repentance will be significant not only for me, but also for others who can learn from my experience, for **I will teach** about **Your ways** of forgiveness **to transgressors,** and thereupon **sinners will return to You** once they realize the potential of repentance.

16 **Save me from** the guilt of **bloodshed,** referring to David's causing of the death of Uriya, Bathsheba's husband, **God, the God of my salvation.** Save me from death for this sin, and then **my tongue will sing of Your righteousness** before others, who will learn from me the power of repentance.

17 **Lord, open my lips,** assist me in formulating these words, **so my mouth may declare Your praise.**

יח כִּי ׀ לֹא־תַחְפֹּץ זֶבַח וְאֶתֵּנָה
עוֹלָה לֹא תִרְצֶה:

18 For You do not desire me to offer a sacrifice; You are not pleased by a burnt offering.

יט זִבְחֵי אֱלֹהִים רוּחַ נִשְׁבָּרָה
לֵב־נִשְׁבָּר וְנִדְכֶּה אֱלֹהִים לֹא
תִבְזֶה:

19 Sacrifices to God are a broken spirit; You, God, will not reject a broken and crushed heart.

כ הֵיטִיבָה בִרְצוֹנְךָ אֶת־צִיּוֹן
תִּבְנֶה חוֹמוֹת יְרוּשָׁלָ͏ִם:

20 Show Your favor to Zion; build the walls of Jerusalem.

כא אָז תַּחְפֹּץ זִבְחֵי־צֶדֶק עוֹלָה
וְכָלִיל אָז יַעֲלוּ עַל־מִזְבַּחֲךָ
פָרִים:

21 Then You will delight in righteous sacrifices, in burnt offerings and whole burnt offerings; then young bulls will be offered on Your altar.

---

18 It is only the concepts discussed above that grant man atonement for his sins: the admission of wrongdoing, acceptance of punishment, and asking for forgiveness. Atonement cannot be achieved through sacrificial offerings, **for You do not desire me to offer a sacrifice; You are not pleased by a burnt offering.**

19 True **sacrifices to God are** not animal offerings, but **a broken,** contrite **spirit; You, God, will not reject a broken and crushed heart.**

20 Since David is the king of Israel as well as a private individual, he beseeches God to prevent his personal sins from being detrimental for the people of Israel as a whole: **Show Your favor to Zion; build the walls of Jerusalem.**

21 **Then,** after atonement and forgiveness have been granted, **You will delight in righteous sacrifices,** sacrifices offered not for expiation but voluntary offerings that are expressive of our love, **in burnt offerings and whole burnt offerings. Then,** after true, heartfelt repentance, **young bulls will be offered on Your altar.**

PSALM 52

A prayer directed against liars and informers. At times they appear to attain their devious goals, but ultimately both the lie and the liar are discredited, while their innocent victim, with God's help, attains peace and tranquility.

א לַמְנַצֵּחַ מַשְׂכִּיל לְדָוִד:

ב בְּבוֹא ׀ דּוֹאֵג הָאֲדֹמִי וַיַּגֵּד
לְשָׁאוּל וַיֹּאמֶר לוֹ בָּא דָוִד
אֶל־בֵּית אֲחִימֶלֶךְ:

ג מַה־תִּתְהַלֵּל בְּרָעָה הַגִּבּוֹר
חֶסֶד אֵל כָּל־הַיּוֹם:

ד הַוּוֹת תַּחְשֹׁב לְשׁוֹנֶךָ כְּתַעַר
מְלֻטָּשׁ עֹשֵׂה רְמִיָּה:

ה אָהַבְתָּ רָּע מִטּוֹב שֶׁקֶר ׀
מִדַּבֵּר צֶדֶק סֶלָה:

1 For the chief musician, a contemplation by David,

2 when Doeg the Edomite came and informed Saul, saying to him: David has come to the house of Ahimelekh.

3 Why do you boast of evil, you warrior? The kindness of the Almighty is all day long.

4 Your tongue contemplates wickedness. Like a honed razor, it works deceit.

5 You love evil more than good, falsehood more than honest speech, Selah.

PSALM 52

1 **For the chief musician, a contemplation by David,**

2 composed **when Doeg the Edomite came and informed Saul, saying to him: David has come to the house of Ahimelekh.** As a result of what Doeg told Saul,[10] almost all the people of the house of Ahimelekh were killed for having harbored the fugitive David, despite their being innocent of any wrongdoing.

3 **Why do you boast of evil, you warrior?** Doeg was one of Saul's senior ministers and warriors. **The kindness of the Almighty,** which counteracts your evil deeds, **is all day long.**

4 **Your tongue contemplates wickedness. Like a honed razor, it works deceit.** A very sharp razor often "works deceit" by causing unintended scrapes and cuts.

5 **You love evil more than good, falsehood more than honest speech, Selah.**

אָהַבְתָּ כָל־דִּבְרֵי־בָלַע לְשׁוֹן
מִרְמָה:

גַּם־אֵל יִתָּצְךָ לָנֶצַח יַחְתְּךָ
וְיִסָּחֲךָ מֵאֹהֶל וְשֵׁרֶשְׁךָ
מֵאֶרֶץ חַיִּים סֶלָה:

וְיִרְאוּ צַדִּיקִים וְיִירָאוּ וְעָלָיו
יִשְׂחָקוּ:

הִנֵּה הַגֶּבֶר לֹא יָשִׂים אֱלֹהִים
מָעוּזוֹ וַיִּבְטַח בְּרֹב עָשְׁרוֹ יָעֹז
בְּהַוָּתוֹ:

וַאֲנִי כְּזַיִת רַעֲנָן בְּבֵית
אֱלֹהִים בָּטַחְתִּי בְחֶסֶד־
אֱלֹהִים עוֹלָם וָעֶד:

6 You love all slanderous words,
   a deceiving tongue.

7 The Almighty will also shatter
   you forever; He will snatch you
   up and drag you from your tent,
   and uproot you from the land
   of the living, Selah.

8 And the righteous will see and
   be awed, and will laugh at him,
   saying:

9 Here is the man who did not
   make God his stronghold,
   relying on his great riches,
   fortifying himself in his
   wickedness.

10 But as for me, I am like a
   verdant olive tree in the
   House of God; I trusted in the
   kindness of God forevermore.

---

6 **You love all slanderous words, a deceiving tongue.**

7 As punishment for this, **the Almighty will also shatter you forever; He will snatch you up and drag you from your tent, and uproot you from the land of the living, Selah.**

8 **And** when **the righteous will see** Doeg's downfall, they will have a twofold reaction: They will take note of the harshness of his punishment **and be awed, and** they **will laugh** and scoff **at him, saying:**

9 **Here is the man who did not make God his stronghold, relying** instead **on his great riches, fortifying himself in his wickedness.**

10 **But as for me,** one of the intended victims of Doeg's malevolent speech, **I am** thriving **like a verdant olive tree in the House of God; I trusted in the kindness of God forevermore** and emerged from the ordeal unscathed.

אֽוֹדְךָ לְעוֹלָם כִּי עָשִׂיתָ
וַאֲקַוֶּה שִׁמְךָ כִי־טוֹב נֶגֶד
חֲסִידֶיךָ׃

11 I will give thanks to You forever
for what You have done, and
I will place my hope in Your
name, for it is good, in the
presence of Your devoted ones.

PSALM 53

This psalm, a *maskil*,[11] is an introspective psalm about the deeds of the wicked,
which sees the source of their evil in their lack of faith in divine providence and their misguided
assumption that the world has been abandoned to those who are strong and lawless.
Psalm 14 is a slightly different version of this psalm.

לַמְנַצֵּחַ עַל־מָחֲלַת מַשְׂכִּיל
לְדָוִד׃

אָמַר נָבָל בְּלִבּוֹ אֵין אֱלֹהִים
הִשְׁחִיתוּ וְהִתְעִיבוּ עָוֶל אֵין
עֹשֵׂה־טוֹב׃

1 For the chief musician, on
the *maḥalat*, a contemplation
by David.

2 The scoundrel says in his heart:
There is no God. They have
been corrupted and have acted
abominably; there is no one
who does good.

---

11 I will give thanks to You forever for what You have done, and I will place my hope in
Your name, for it is good, in the presence of Your devoted ones.

PSALM 53

1 **For the chief musician, on the *maḥalat*, a contemplation by David.** It is unclear what
maḥalat refers to. It was probably a type of musical instrument, or perhaps the name of a specific
melody.

2 **The scoundrel says in his heart,** even if he does not declare it audibly: **There is no God.** It is
evident from his behavior that this is what he thinks in his heart. **They have been corrupted
and have acted abominably; there is no one who does good.** This belief, to some extent,
underlies his abominable behavior.

אֱלֹהִים מִשָּׁמַיִם הִשְׁקִיף
עַל־בְּנֵי־אָדָם לִרְאוֹת הֲיֵשׁ
מַשְׂכִּיל דֹּרֵשׁ אֶת־אֱלֹהִים:

כֻּלּוֹ סָג יַחְדָּו נֶאֱלָחוּ אֵין
עֹשֵׂה־טוֹב אֵין גַּם־אֶחָד:

הֲלֹא יָדְעוּ פֹּעֲלֵי אָוֶן אֹכְלֵי
עַמִּי אָכְלוּ לֶחֶם אֱלֹהִים לֹא
קָרָאוּ:

שָׁם ׀ פָּחֲדוּ־פַחַד לֹא־הָיָה
פָחַד כִּי־אֱלֹהִים פִּזַּר עַצְמוֹת
חֹנָךְ הֱבִשֹׁתָה כִּי־אֱלֹהִים
מְאָסָם:

³ God looks down from heaven upon the sons of man to see if there is anyone of understanding who seeks God.

⁴ It has all gone sour, all of them together befouled; there is no one who does good, not even one.

⁵ Have the evildoers no knowledge? They, who devour my people as if eating bread, they who do not call out to God.

⁶ There they were in great fear. But there was no fear, for God has scattered the bones of those who encamped against you. You were put to shame, because God despised them.

---

3 **God looks down from heaven upon the sons of man to see if there is anyone of understanding who seeks God.**

4 The results of God's examination of mankind are discouraging. He finds that **it,** the entire generation, **has all gone sour** in the spiritual sense, **all of them together befouled; there is no one who does good, not even one.**

5 **Have the evildoers no knowledge? They, who devour my people as if eating bread, they who do not call out to God.** This verse depicts a world devoid of holiness. Evil people are present everywhere, attacking and harming those who are good.

6 **There they,** the few virtuous people, the victims of the evildoers, **were in great fear** of being swallowed up by the wicked. Turning to the righteous, the psalmist declares: **But,** in fact, **there was no** reason for you to **fear, for God has scattered the bones of those who** beset you and **encamped against you.** The psalmist addresses himself to the evildoers themselves: **You were put to shame!** And this is **because God despised them,** the evildoers.

מִי יִתֵּן מִצִּיּוֹן יְשׁוּעוֹת יִשְׂרָאֵל בְּשׁוּב אֱלֹהִים שְׁבוּת עַמּוֹ יָגֵל יַעֲקֹב יִשְׂמַח יִשְׂרָאֵל:

7 May the salvation of Israel emerge from Zion! When God restores the captives of His people, Jacob will rejoice and Israel will exult.

PSALM 54

A prayer against the wicked in which the psalmist expresses his faith that God will save him from his enemies and mete out just punishment for their misdeeds.

א לַמְנַצֵּחַ בִּנְגִינֹת מַשְׂכִּיל לְדָוִד:

1 For the chief musician on stringed instruments, a contemplation by David,

ב בְּבֹא הַזִּיפִים וַיֹּאמְרוּ לְשָׁאוּל הֲלֹא דָוִד מִסְתַּתֵּר עִמָּנוּ:

2 when the Zifites came and said to Saul: David is hiding among us.

---

7 The psalm closes with words of prayer: **May the salvation of Israel emerge from Zion! When God restores the captives of His people, Jacob will rejoice and Israel will exult.**

PSALM 54

1 **For the chief musician on stringed instruments, a contemplation by David.** Although this psalm was written during a time in David's life that was not particularly good, as detailed in the following verse, he still expresses gratitude for a temporary reprieve from his troubles. This is probably why it is termed a *maskil*, a "contemplation." Even in the midst of suffering or difficult times, a person should take a moment to offer thanks to God for any relief He provides.

2 It was composed **when the Zifites came and said to Saul: David is hiding among us,** whereupon Saul sent his men to capture him. Warned in advance, however, David managed to escape,[12] a turn of events for which he offers his thanks here.

אֱלֹהִים בְּשִׁמְךָ הוֹשִׁיעֵנִי
וּבִגְבוּרָתְךָ תְדִינֵנִי:

3 God, by Your name save me and vindicate me by Your might.

אֱלֹהִים שְׁמַע תְּפִלָּתִי
הַאֲזִינָה לְאִמְרֵי־פִי:

4 God, hear my prayer; listen to the words of my mouth.

כִּי זָרִים ׀ קָמוּ עָלַי וְעָרִיצִים
בִּקְשׁוּ נַפְשִׁי לֹא שָׂמוּ
אֱלֹהִים לְנֶגְדָּם סֶלָה:

5 For strangers have risen against me and violent foes have sought my life; they have not set God before them, Selah.

הִנֵּה אֱלֹהִים עֹזֵר לִי אֲדֹנָי
בְּסֹמְכֵי נַפְשִׁי:

6 Behold, God is my helper; the Lord is counted among those who support me.

יָשׁוּב הָרַע לְשֹׁרְרָי בַּאֲמִתְּךָ
הַצְמִיתֵם:

7 He will repay evil to my foes. Destroy them by Your truth.

בִּנְדָבָה אֶזְבְּחָה־לָּךְ אוֹדֶה
שִּׁמְךָ יְהוָה כִּי־טוֹב:

8 I will bring a freewill sacrifice to You; I will give thanks to Your name, Lord, for it is good.

כִּי מִכָּל־צָרָה הִצִּילָנִי וּבְאֹיְבַי
רָאֲתָה עֵינִי:

9 For He delivered me from all trouble, and my eyes have gazed upon my enemies.

---

3 **God, by Your name save me and vindicate me by Your might.**

4 **God, hear my prayer; listen to the words of my mouth.**

5 **For strangers,** people who do not even know me and should have no reason to wish me ill, **have risen against me and violent foes have sought my life.** They are acting unjustly toward me, demonstrating that **they have not set God before them, Selah.**

6 **Behold, God is my helper; the Lord is counted among those who support me.**

7 **He will repay evil to my foes.** Turning to God, David prays: **Destroy them by Your truth.**

8 **I will** then **bring a freewill sacrifice to You** for Your salvation; **I will give thanks to Your name, Lord, for it is good.**

9 **For He delivered me from all trouble, and my eyes have gazed upon** the downfall of **my enemies.**

PSALM 55

A psalm of prayer and supplication, relating to a time when the psalmist was beset by enemies, including traitors from among his own camp. According to some, the text alludes to the insurgency of Avshalom and the treachery of Ahitofel and others in supporting it.

א לַמְנַצֵּחַ בִּנְגִינֹת מַשְׂכִּיל לְדָוִד:

¹ For the chief musician on stringed instruments, a contemplation by David.

ב הַאֲזִינָה אֱלֹהִים תְּפִלָּתִי וְאַל־תִּתְעַלַּם מִתְּחִנָּתִי:

² Listen to my prayer, God; do not ignore my plea.

ג הַקְשִׁיבָה לִּי וַעֲנֵנִי אָרִיד בְּשִׂיחִי וְאָהִימָה:

³ Heed me and answer me as I lament with my speech and cry out

ד מִקּוֹל אוֹיֵב מִפְּנֵי עָקַת רָשָׁע כִּי־יָמִיטוּ עָלַי אָוֶן וּבְאַף יִשְׂטְמוּנִי:

⁴ at the enemy's voice, the oppression of the wicked, casting evil upon me and hating me with wrath.

ה לִבִּי יָחִיל בְּקִרְבִּי וְאֵימוֹת מָוֶת נָפְלוּ עָלָי:

⁵ My heart is fearful within me; terrors of death descend upon me.

PSALM 55

¹ **For the chief musician on stringed instruments, a contemplation by David.**

² **Listen to my prayer, God; do not ignore my plea.** The psalmist's request that God heed his prayer is followed by a more modest request, that God not ignore him.

³ **Heed me and answer me as I lament with my speech,** as I speak of my pain and suffering, **and cry out**

⁴ **at the enemy's voice, the oppression of the wicked, casting** their **evil upon me and hating me with wrath.**

⁵ **My heart is fearful within me; terrors of death descend upon me** because of their threats.

יִרְאָה וָרַעַד יָבֹא בִי וַתְּכַסֵּנִי
פַּלָּצוּת:

וָאֹמַר מִי־יִתֶּן־לִי אֵבֶר כַּיּוֹנָה
אָעוּפָה וְאֶשְׁכֹּנָה:

הִנֵּה אַרְחִיק נְדֹד אָלִין
בַּמִּדְבָּר סֶלָה:

אָחִישָׁה מִפְלָט לִי מֵרוּחַ
סֹעָה מִסָּעַר:

בַּלַּע אֲדֹנָי פַּלַּג לְשׁוֹנָם כִּי־
רָאִיתִי חָמָס וְרִיב בָּעִיר:

יוֹמָם וָלַיְלָה יְסוֹבְבֻהָ
עַל־חוֹמֹתֶיהָ וְאָוֶן וְעָמָל
בְּקִרְבָּהּ:

הַוּוֹת בְּקִרְבָּהּ וְלֹא־יָמִישׁ
מֵרְחֹבָהּ תֹּךְ וּמִרְמָה:

6 Fear and trembling enter me; I am enveloped in horror.

7 I said: Would that I had wings like a dove, I would fly away and come to rest.

8 I would wander far away to reside in the wilderness, Selah.

9 I would hasten to a place of refuge, away from the stormy wind and tempest.

10 Confound them, Lord, confuse their tongue, for I see injustice and strife in the city.

11 Day and night they encircle its walls, and there is iniquity and mischief within,

12 disasters within, intrigue and deceit not quitting its streets.

---

6 **Fear and trembling enter me; I am enveloped in horror.**

7 **I said: Would that I had wings like a dove, I would fly away** to another place, anywhere else but here, **and come to rest.**

8 **I would wander far away to reside in the wilderness,** where I might be isolated, but at least I would be safe, **Selah.**

9 **I would hasten to** seek out **a place of refuge, away from the stormy wind and tempest.**

10 The psalmist now shifts his attention to his foes, asking God for aid: **Confound them, Lord, confuse their tongue,** bring an end to their calumnies, **for I see injustice and strife in the city** when they are in control.

11 **Day and night they encircle its walls** with injustice, **and there is iniquity and mischief within,**

12 **disasters within, intrigue and deceit not quitting its streets.**

כִּי לֹא־אוֹיֵב יְחָרְפֵנִי וְאֶשָּׂא
לֹא־מְשַׂנְאִי עָלַי הִגְדִּיל
וְאֶסָּתֵר מִמֶּנּוּ:

וְאַתָּה אֱנוֹשׁ כְּעֶרְכִּי אַלּוּפִי
וּמְיֻדָּעִי:

אֲשֶׁר יַחְדָּו נַמְתִּיק סוֹד
בְּבֵית אֱלֹהִים נְהַלֵּךְ בְּרָגֶשׁ:

יַשִּׁימָוֶת ׀ עָלֵימוֹ יַרְדוּ שְׁאוֹל
חַיִּים כִּי־רָעוֹת בִּמְגוּרָם
בְּקִרְבָּם:

אֲנִי אֶל־אֱלֹהִים אֶקְרָא
וַיהוָה יוֹשִׁיעֵנִי:

13 For it is not an enemy who taunts me, which I could bear. Nor is it one of my foes who has grown threatening, from whom I could hide.

14 But rather it is you, a man who was my equal, my guide and companion.

15 We shared confidences; we walked with great feeling in the House of God.

16 May He bring up death upon them; let them go down, still living, to the netherworld, for evil is in their dwelling place, inside them.

17 I call upon God; the Lord will save me.

---

13 The psalmist now turns to a particularly painful matter: **For it is not an enemy who taunts me, which I could bear.** It would not be so bad if a known enemy would be scorning me. **Nor is it one of my foes who has grown threatening, from whom I could hide.**

14 David addresses his antagonist: **But rather it is you,** the one who is assailing me, **a man who was** always considered by me to be **my equal,** and moreover **my guide and companion.**

15 In our friendship **we shared confidences** with each other; **we walked** together **with great feeling in the House of God.** The pain is so much greater, then, that my betrayal comes from one who had been a close friend.

16 David prays: **May He bring up death upon them; let them go down, still living, to the netherworld.** This alludes to the rebellion of Korah,[13] in which this was the fate of those who instigated an internal insurrection against Moses' leadership. **For evil is in their dwelling place,** that is, it is **inside them.**

17 **I call upon God; the Lord will save me.**

יח עֶ֤רֶב וָבֹ֣קֶר וְ֭צָהֳרַיִם אָשִׂ֣יחָה וְאֶהֱמֶ֑ה וַיִּשְׁמַ֥ע קוֹלִֽי׃

יט פָּדָ֬ה בְשָׁל֣וֹם נַ֭פְשִׁי מִקֲּרָב־לִ֑י כִּֽי־בְ֝רַבִּ֗ים הָי֥וּ עִמָּדִֽי׃

כ יִשְׁמַ֤ע ׀ אֵ֨ל ׀ וְֽיַעֲנֵם֮ וְיֹ֤שֵׁ֥ב קֶ֗דֶם סֶ֥לָה אֲשֶׁ֤ר אֵ֣ין חֲלִיפ֣וֹת לָ֑מוֹ וְלֹ֖א יָרְא֣וּ אֱלֹהִֽים׃

כא שָׁלַ֣ח יָ֭דָיו בִּשְׁלֹמָ֗יו חִלֵּ֥ל בְּרִיתֽוֹ׃

כב חָלְק֤וּ ׀ מַחְמָאֹ֬ת פִּ֗יו וּֽקֲרָב־לִ֫בּ֥וֹ רַכּ֖וּ דְבָרָ֥יו מִשֶּׁ֗מֶן וְהֵ֣מָּה פְתִחֽוֹת׃

18 Evening and morning and noon, I speak and cry aloud, and He hears my voice.

19 He redeemed me unharmed from the battle waged against me, for there were many with me.

20 The Almighty, He who abides from days of yore, will hear, and He will answer them, Selah. They do not change; they do not fear God.

21 He raised his arms against his comrades, violating his covenant.

22 His speech was smoother than cream, but war was in his heart. His words were softer than oil, yet they were drawn swords.

---

18 **Evening and morning and noon, I speak** in prayer **and cry aloud, and He hears my voice.**

19 At this point, there is a shift in the psalm's tone, evidently describing events that occurred at a later time: **He redeemed me unharmed from the battle waged against me, for there were many with me** supporting me, and for their sake God saved me from harm. It is also possible that this verse is describing occasions in the past in which David was rescued by God.

20 **The Almighty, He who abides from days of yore, will hear and He will answer them,** those who have remained loyal to me, **Selah.** Referring now to the enemies: **They do not change;** as always, they **do not fear God.**

21 **He,** my antagonist, **raised his arms against his** erstwhile **comrades, violating his covenant** with them.

22 **His speech was smoother than cream, but war was** actually **in his heart. His words were softer than oil, yet they,** those words, **were** like **drawn swords** or, alternatively, like snares.

‏כג הַשְׁלֵךְ עַל־יהוה ׀ יְהָבְךָ
וְהוּא יְכַלְכְּלֶךָ לֹא־יִתֵּן
לְעוֹלָם מוֹט לַצַּדִּיק:‎

‏כד וְאַתָּה אֱלֹהִים ׀ תּוֹרִדֵם
לִבְאֵר שַׁחַת אַנְשֵׁי דָמִים
וּמִרְמָה לֹא־יֶחֱצוּ יְמֵיהֶם
וַאֲנִי אֶבְטַח־בָּךְ:‎

23 Cast your burden upon the Lord, and He will sustain you. He will never let the righteous slip.

24 You, God, will bring them down to the pit of destruction. Men of bloodshed and deceit will not live out half their days, but I shall trust in You.

PSALM 56

Another psalm of prayer and supplication, which also contains expressions of faith and hope.

‏א לַמְנַצֵּחַ ׀ עַל־יוֹנַת אֵלֶם
רְחֹקִים לְדָוִד מִכְתָּם בֶּאֱחֹז
אֹתוֹ פְלִשְׁתִּים בְּגַת:‎

‏ב חָנֵּנִי אֱלֹהִים כִּי־שְׁאָפַנִי
אֱנוֹשׁ כָּל־הַיּוֹם לֹחֵם
יִלְחָצֵנִי:‎

1 For the chief musician, on *yonat elem reḥokim*, an instruction by David, when the Philistines seized him in Gat.

2 Be gracious to me, God, for men seek to devour me; fighters harass me all day long.

---

23 The psalmist now offers general words of encouragement: **Cast your burden upon the Lord, and He will sustain you. He will never let the righteous slip.**

24 As for his enemies, however: **You, God, will bring them down to the pit of destruction. Men of bloodshed and deceit will not live out** even **half their days, but I shall trust in You.**

PSALM 56

1 **For the chief musician, on *yonat elem reḥokim*.** The heading of this psalm is, in all likelihood, the name of a melody to be used for this particular text. **An instruction by David,** composed **when the Philistines seized him in Gat.**[14] David fled from Saul, seeking shelter with the Philistines in Gat, where he was beset by further troubles.

2 **Be gracious to me, God, for men seek to devour me; fighters harass me all day long.**

שָׁאֲפוּ שׁוֹרְרַי כָּל־הַיּוֹם כִּי־
רַבִּים לֹחֲמִים לִי מָרוֹם:

יוֹם אִירָא אֲנִי אֵלֶיךָ אֶבְטָח:

בֵּאלֹהִים אֲהַלֵּל דְּבָרוֹ
בֵּאלֹהִים בָּטַחְתִּי לֹא אִירָא
מַה־יַּעֲשֶׂה בָשָׂר לִי:

כָּל־הַיּוֹם דְּבָרַי יְעַצֵּבוּ עָלַי
כָּל־מַחְשְׁבֹתָם לָרָע:

יָגוּרוּ ׀ יִצְפּוֹנוּ הֵמָּה עֲקֵבַי
יִשְׁמֹרוּ כַּאֲשֶׁר קִוּוּ נַפְשִׁי:

עַל־אָוֶן פַּלֶּט־לָמוֹ בְּאַף
עַמִּים ׀ הוֹרֵד אֱלֹהִים:

3 My foes seek to devour me all day long, but many on high are fighting for me.

4 On a day when I am afraid, I put my trust in You.

5 I praise the word of God. In God I trust; I shall not be afraid. What can mere flesh do to me?

6 All day long they ponder my doings, their thoughts of evil directed against me.

7 They lie in wait in their dwelling places; they watch my footsteps in hopes of taking my life.

8 Cast them out for their iniquity; bring down nations, God, in anger.

---

3 **My foes seek to devour me all day long. But** despite the enemy's relentless pressure, there is reason for hope, for **many on high,** angels in heaven, **are fighting for me.**

4 **On a day when I am afraid, I put my trust in You.**

5 **I praise the word of God. In God I trust; I shall not be afraid. What,** then, **can** a mortal man of **mere flesh do to me?**

6 **All day long they ponder my doings, their thoughts of evil directed against me.**

7 **They lie in wait in their dwelling places, they watch my footsteps in hopes of taking my life.**

8 **Cast them out for their iniquity; bring down nations, God, in anger.**

נְדִ֮י סָפַ֪רְתָּ֫ה אָ֥תָּה שִׂ֫ימָה
דִמְעָתִ֥י בְנֹאדֶ֑ךָ הֲ֝לֹ֗א
בְּסִפְרָתֶֽךָ׃

9 You have taken account of my wandering. Put my tears in Your flask; indeed, keep them in Your reckoning.

אָ֤ז יָ֘שׁ֤וּבוּ אֽוֹיְבַ֣י אָ֭חוֹר בְּי֣וֹם
אֶקְרָ֑א זֶה־יָ֝דַ֗עְתִּי כִּֽי־אֱלֹהִ֥ים
לִֽי׃

10 Then, on the day that I call, my enemies will turn back. This I know, that God is with me.

בֵּֽ֭אלֹהִים אֲהַלֵּ֣ל דָּבָ֑ר בַּֽ֝יהֹוָ֗ה
אֲהַלֵּ֥ל דָּבָֽר׃

11 I praise the word of God; I praise the word of the Lord.

בֵּֽאלֹהִ֣ים בָּ֭טַחְתִּי לֹ֣א אִירָ֑א
מַה־יַּעֲשֶׂ֖ה אָדָ֣ם לִֽי׃

12 In God I trust; I shall not be afraid. What can man do to me?

עָלַ֣י אֱלֹהִ֣ים נְדָרֶ֑יךָ אֲשַׁלֵּ֖ם
תּוֹדֹ֣ת לָֽךְ׃

13 I will fulfill the vows I made to You; I will offer thanksgiving sacrifices to You.

כִּ֤י הִצַּ֪לְתָּ נַפְשִׁ֡י מִמָּוֶת֮ הֲלֹ֥א
רַגְלַ֗י מִ֫דֶּ֥חִי לְ֭הִֽתְהַלֵּךְ לִפְנֵ֣י
אֱלֹהִ֑ים בְּ֝א֗וֹר הַֽחַיִּֽים׃

14 For You have delivered me from death, indeed kept my feet from stumbling, so that I might walk before God in the light of the living.

---

9 **You have taken** an **account of my** numerous places of **wandering. Put my tears in Your flask,** that is, take note of them and value them. There is a play on words here: The Hebrew word for both "wandering" and "flask" is *nod*. **Indeed, keep them in Your reckoning.**

10 **Then, on the day that I call** out to You in prayer, I trust that **my enemies will turn back** in retreat. But in any event, **this I know, that God is with me.**

11 **I praise the word of God; I praise the word of the Lord.** This verse invokes two of God's names, "God" referring to His attribute of justice and "the Lord" alluding to His attribute of mercy. The psalmist declares his praise of God whatever the situation, whether He manifests Himself as stern Judge or merciful Protector.

12 **In God I trust; I shall not be afraid. What can man do to me?**

13 **I will fulfill the vows I made to You; I will offer thanksgiving sacrifices to You.**

14 **For You have delivered me from death, indeed kept my feet from stumbling, so that I might walk before God in the light of the living.**

PSALM 57

A psalm in which, in a time of great distress, the psalmist turns to God. Although surrounded by enemies, he is confident that he will be rescued; indeed, he already thanks God for His assistance.

לַמְנַצֵּחַ אַל־תַּשְׁחֵת לְדָוִד
מִכְתָּם בְּבָרְחוֹ מִפְּנֵי־שָׁאוּל
בַּמְּעָרָה:

1 For the chief musician, *al tashḥet*, an instruction by David, when he was in the cave, fleeing from Saul.

חָנֵּנִי אֱלֹהִים ׀ חָנֵּנִי כִּי בְךָ
חָסָיָה נַפְשִׁי וּבְצֵל־כְּנָפֶיךָ
אֶחְסֶה עַד יַעֲבֹר הַוּוֹת:

2 Be gracious to me, God, be gracious to me. For in You I take refuge; in the shadow of Your wings I will shelter, until calamity passes.

אֶקְרָא לֵאלֹהִים עֶלְיוֹן לָאֵל
גֹּמֵר עָלָי:

3 I cry out to God Most High, to the Almighty who completes for me.

PSALM 57

1 **For the chief musician, *al tashḥet*,** apparently a reference to an ancient poem or melody on which this psalm is based. **An instruction by David,** written **when he was in the cave, fleeing from Saul,** an incident described elsewhere.[15]

2 **Be gracious to me, God, be gracious to me. For in You I take refuge; in the shadow of Your wings I will shelter, until calamity passes.**

3 **I cry out to God Most High, to the Almighty who completes for me.** The word *gomer*, translated here as "completes," is interpreted by some commentators as if it were written *gomel*, meaning "who repays me for my good deeds." If *gomer* is understood literally, it seems that David is asking God to bring his rescue to a successful conclusion. David's situation in the meantime remains precarious; he has found no more than a temporary shelter.

יִשְׁלַח מִשָּׁמַיִם ׀ וְיוֹשִׁיעֵנִי
חֵרֵף שֹׁאֲפִי סֶלָה יִשְׁלַח
אֱלֹהִים חַסְדּוֹ וַאֲמִתּוֹ:

נַפְשִׁי ׀ בְּתוֹךְ לְבָאִם אֶשְׁכְּבָה
לֹהֲטִים בְּנֵי־אָדָם שִׁנֵּיהֶם
חֲנִית וְחִצִּים וּלְשׁוֹנָם חֶרֶב
חַדָּה:

רוּמָה עַל־הַשָּׁמַיִם אֱלֹהִים
עַל כָּל־הָאָרֶץ כְּבוֹדֶךָ:

רֶשֶׁת ׀ הֵכִינוּ לִפְעָמַי כָּפַף
נַפְשִׁי כָּרוּ לְפָנַי שִׁיחָה נָפְלוּ
בְתוֹכָהּ סֶלָה:

נָכוֹן לִבִּי אֱלֹהִים נָכוֹן לִבִּי
אָשִׁירָה וַאֲזַמֵּרָה:

4. May He send forth from heaven and deliver me, and put to shame those who desire my destruction, Selah. May God dispatch His kindness and His truth.

5. I lie amid lions, anxious beasts, among men whose teeth are spears and arrows, whose tongues are a honed sword.

6. Rise above the heavens, God; let Your glory extend over all the earth.

7. They prepared a net for me to step onto, to bend my spirit; they dug a pit before me but fell into it, Selah.

8. My heart is ready, God, my heart is ready. I will sing and give praise.

---

4 **May He send forth from heaven and deliver me, and put to shame those who desire my destruction, Selah. May God dispatch His kindness and His truth.**

5 **I lie amid** men who are as ferocious as **lions, anxious beasts, among men whose teeth are spears and arrows, whose tongues are a honed sword.** The people surrounding me are even more dangerous than beasts, because they are armed. Moreover, their mouths, through their slander and disparagement, are as perilous as actual weapons.

6 The psalmist turns to God in prayer: **Rise above the heavens, God; let Your glory extend over all the earth.**

7 **They prepared a net for me to step onto, to bend my spirit; they dug a pit before me but** in the end, they themselves **fell into it, Selah.**

8 From here, the psalm concludes with words of praise and gratitude: **My heart is ready, God, my heart is ready. I will sing and give praise.**

עֽוּרָה כְבוֹדִי עֽוּרָה הַנֵּ֫בֶל
וְכִנּ֑וֹר אָעִ֥ירָה שָּֽׁחַר:

אֽוֹדְךָ בָֽעַמִּ֥ים ׀ אֲדֹנָ֑י אֲזַמֶּרְךָ֗
בַּלְאֻמִּֽים:

כִּֽי־גָדֹ֣ל עַד־שָׁמַ֣יִם חַסְדֶּ֑ךָ
וְֽעַד־שְׁחָקִ֥ים אֲמִתֶּֽךָ:

ר֣וּמָה עַל־שָׁמַ֣יִם אֱלֹהִ֑ים עַ֖ל
כָּל־הָאָ֣רֶץ כְּבוֹדֶֽךָ:

9 Awaken, my soul! Awaken, harp and lyre; I will wake the dawn.

10 I will give thanks to You, my Lord, among the peoples; I will sing Your praise among the nations.

11 For Your kindness is great, reaching to the heavens, Your truth to the sky.

12 Rise above the heavens, God; let Your glory extend over all the earth.

PSALM 58

A prayer against the wicked, who are full of evil thoughts.
The psalmist beseeches God to destroy them.

לַמְנַצֵּ֣חַ אַל־תַּשְׁחֵ֑ת לְדָוִ֥ד
מִכְתָּֽם:

1 For the chief musician, *al tashḥet*, an instruction by David.

---

9 **Awaken, my soul! Awaken,** my **harp and lyre** with which I sing God's praises; **I will wake the dawn.** Even before daybreak I will begin to sing this psalm.

10 **I will give thanks to You, my Lord, among the peoples; I will sing Your praise among the nations.**

11 **For Your kindness is great, reaching to the heavens, Your truth,** in fulfillment of Your promise to protect me, **to the sky.**

12 The psalm ends by repeating verse 6 as a kind of refrain: **Rise above the heavens, God; let Your glory extend over all the earth.**

PSALM 58

1 **For the chief musician,** *al tashḥet.* This expression is explained above, in 57:1. **An instruction by David.**

הַאֻמְנָם אֵלֶם צֶדֶק תְּדַבֵּרוּן
מֵישָׁרִים תִּשְׁפְּטוּ בְּנֵי אָדָם:

אַף־בְּלֵב עוֹלֹת תִּפְעָלוּן
בָּאָרֶץ חֲמַס יְדֵיכֶם תְּפַלֵּסוּן:

זֹרוּ רְשָׁעִים מֵרָחֶם תָּעוּ
מִבֶּטֶן דֹּבְרֵי כָזָב:

חֲמַת־לָמוֹ כִּדְמוּת חֲמַת־
נָחָשׁ כְּמוֹ־פֶתֶן חֵרֵשׁ יַאְטֵם
אָזְנוֹ:

אֲשֶׁר לֹא־יִשְׁמַע לְקוֹל
מְלַחֲשִׁים חוֹבֵר חֲבָרִים
מְחֻכָּם:

אֱלֹהִים הֲרָס־שִׁנֵּימוֹ בְּפִימוֹ
מַלְתְּעוֹת כְּפִירִים נְתֹץ ׀
יְהֹוָה:

2 Do you violent men really speak with righteousness? Do you judge men honestly?

3 You plan wrongful deeds in your heart; with your hands you mete out injustice in the land.

4 The wicked are corrupt from the womb; from birth, liars go astray.

5 They have poison like the venom of a serpent, like a deaf viper blocking its ear,

6 which does not hear the voice of charmers, skillful casters of spells.

7 God, break their teeth in their mouths; shatter the fangs of the young lions, Lord.

---

2 The psalmist begins by addressing his enemies: **Do you violent men really speak with righteousness? Do you judge men honestly?**

3 No, **you plan wrongful deeds in your heart; with your hands you mete out injustice in the land.**

4 **The wicked are corrupt from the womb; from birth, liars go astray.**

5 **They have poison like the venom of a serpent, like a deaf viper blocking its ear,**

6 **which does not hear** or react to **the voice of charmers, skillful casters of spells.** Most snakes can be calmed by charmers, but the "deaf viper" is resistant to such pacification. The wicked are compared to such serpents, incapable of being swayed by words.

7 The psalmist continues with a prayer that is more like a curse: **God, break their teeth in their mouths; shatter the fangs of the young lions, Lord.**

יִמָּאֲסוּ כְמוֹ־מַיִם יִתְהַלְּכוּ־ ⁸
לָמוֹ יִדְרֹךְ חִצָּו כְּמוֹ יִתְמֹלָלוּ:

כְּמוֹ שַׁבְּלוּל תֶּמֶס יַהֲלֹךְ נֵפֶל ⁹
אֵשֶׁת בַּל־חָזוּ שָׁמֶשׁ:

בְּטֶרֶם יָבִינוּ סִּירֹתֵיכֶם אָטָד ¹⁰
כְּמוֹ־חַי כְּמוֹ־חָרוֹן יִשְׂעָרֶנּוּ:

יִשְׂמַח צַדִּיק כִּי־חָזָה נָקָם ¹¹
פְּעָמָיו יִרְחַץ בְּדַם הָרָשָׁע:

וְיֹאמַר אָדָם אַךְ־פְּרִי לַצַּדִּיק ¹²
אַךְ יֵשׁ־אֱלֹהִים שֹׁפְטִים
בָּאָרֶץ:

⁸ Let them melt away like the runoff of water; when he aims his arrows, let them be crushed.

⁹ Let them be like snails that melt away as they go along, like a stillborn of a woman, which has never seen the sun.

¹⁰ Before reaching understanding, your shoots will become a bramble, and you will be like a plant, swept away by a whirlwind of wrath.

¹¹ The righteous one will rejoice in seeing vengeance; he will wash his feet in the blood of the wicked.

¹² And man will say: Surely there is a reward for the righteous; surely there is a God who judges on earth.

---

8 **Let them melt away like the runoff of water,** dispersing in all different directions; **when he aims his arrows, let them be crushed** and broken before they hit their targets.

9 **Let them be like snails that melt away as they go along.** Snails leave a trail of mucus behind them, giving the appearance that they are disintegrating as they move forward. **Like a stillborn of a woman, which has never seen the sun.**

10 The psalmist now addresses the evildoers directly: **Before reaching** the age of **understanding, your shoots will become** hardened like **a bramble** bush, **and** then, when **you will be** solidified **like a** discrete **plant,** you will be **swept away by a whirlwind of wrath.**

11 In the end, **the righteous one will rejoice in seeing vengeance; he will wash his feet in the blood of the wicked.**

12 **And** then **man will say: Surely there is a reward for the righteous;** and even if this reward is not always immediately evident, we nevertheless realize that **surely there is a God who judges on earth.**

PSALM 59

A psalm in which David prays to be rescued from foes who are gathering to attack him
for no justifiable reason. He expresses his faith that those foes will not only be defeated
but will also acknowledge their wrongdoing. In addition, he prays that he will be able
to offer his wholehearted thanks to God.

לַמְנַצֵּחַ אַל־תַּשְׁחֵת לְדָוִד ×
מִכְתָּם בִּשְׁלֹחַ שָׁאוּל
וַיִּשְׁמְרוּ אֶת־הַבַּיִת לַהֲמִיתוֹ:

הַצִּילֵנִי מֵאֹיְבַי ׀ אֱלֹהָי ב
מִמִּתְקוֹמְמַי תְּשַׂגְּבֵנִי:

הַצִּילֵנִי מִפֹּעֲלֵי אָוֶן וּמֵאַנְשֵׁי ג
דָמִים הוֹשִׁיעֵנִי:

כִּי הִנֵּה אָרְבוּ לְנַפְשִׁי יָגוּרוּ ד
עָלַי עַזִּים לֹא־פִשְׁעִי וְלֹא־
חַטָּאתִי יְהוָה:

1 For the chief musician, *al
tashḥet,* an instruction by
David, when Saul sent men to
watch the house in order to
kill him.

2 Rescue me from my enemies,
my God; secure me from those
rising against me.

3 Rescue me from evildoers; save
me from men of bloodshed.

4 For they lie in wait against
me; fierce men have gathered
against me for no transgression
or sin of mine, Lord.

PSALM 59

1 **For the chief musician,** *al tashḥet*.[16] **An instruction by David, when Saul sent men to
watch the house in order to kill him.** This psalm relates to a specific event in David's life, when
Saul sent messengers to David's house with orders to kill him. David succeeded in escaping with
his life at the last moment.[17] In the verses that follow, he prays to be rescued from the continuing
danger posed by those seeking his life.

2 **Rescue me from my enemies, my God; secure me from those rising against me.**

3 **Rescue me from evildoers; save me from men of bloodshed.**

4 **For they lie in wait against me; fierce men have gathered against me for no
transgression or sin of mine, Lord.**

בְּלִי־עָוֹן יָרֻצוּן וְיִכּוֹנָנוּ עוּרָה ה
לִקְרָאתִי וּרְאֵה:

וְאַתָּה יהוה־אֱלֹהִים ׀ ו
צְבָאוֹת אֱלֹהֵי יִשְׂרָאֵל
הָקִיצָה לִפְקֹד כָּל־הַגּוֹיִם
אַל־תָּחֹן כָּל־בֹּגְדֵי אָוֶן סֶלָה:

יָשׁוּבוּ לָעֶרֶב יֶהֱמוּ כַכָּלֶב ו
וִיסוֹבְבוּ עִיר:

הִנֵּה ׀ יַבִּיעוּן בְּפִיהֶם חֲרָבוֹת ה
בְּשִׂפְתוֹתֵיהֶם כִּי־מִי שֹׁמֵעַ:

וְאַתָּה יהוה תִּשְׂחַק־לָמוֹ ט
תִּלְעַג לְכָל־גּוֹיִם:

5 They run and prepare themselves, through no fault of my own. Bestir Yourself for me, and see!

6 As for You, Lord, God of hosts, God of Israel, arouse Yourself to make reckoning with all the nations. Do not pardon all the treacherous evildoers, Selah.

7 They return toward evening, barking like dogs and roaming the city.

8 Here they are, making declarations with their mouths, swords in their lips; for who hears?

9 But You, Lord, laugh at them; You mock all the nations.

---

5 **They run** toward me **and prepare themselves** to do me harm, **through no fault of my own. Bestir Yourself for me, and see!**

6 **As for You, Lord, God of hosts, God of Israel, arouse Yourself** and reveal Yourself, **to make reckoning with all the nations.** The mention of "all the nations" might be a reference to the fact that Saul, for a variety of reasons, made use of foreign mercenaries in his effort to rid himself of David. **Do not pardon all the treacherous evildoers, Selah.**

7 David offers a description of those trying to capture him: **They return toward evening,** as they are nowhere to be found during the day, **barking like dogs and roaming the city.** Like wild dogs, they wander through the city mostly at night.

8 **Here they are, making** threatening **declarations with their mouths,** as if they had **swords in their lips.** They feel that they can speak and act as they please, **for** they say to themselves: **Who hears?** They do not believe that God hears them and will hold them to account.

9 **But You, Lord, laugh at them; You mock all the nations,** knowing that none of their schemes will be realized.

עֻזּוֹ אֵלֶיךָ אֶשְׁמֹרָה כִּי־
אֱלֹהִים מִשְׂגַּבִּי:

¹⁰ His strength! I will wait for You, for God is my fortress.

אֱלֹהֵי חַסְדּוֹ יְקַדְּמֵנִי אֱלֹהִים חַסְדִּי
יַרְאֵנִי בְשֹׁרְרָי:

¹¹ My merciful God will come toward me; God will let me look upon my foes.

אַל־תַּהַרְגֵם ׀ פֶּן־יִשְׁכְּחוּ עַמִּי
הֲנִיעֵמוֹ בְחֵילְךָ וְהוֹרִידֵמוֹ
מָגִנֵּנוּ אֲדֹנָי:

¹² Do not slay them, lest my people forget; scatter them by Your power and bring them down, our shield, my Lord.

חַטַּאת־פִּימוֹ דְּבַר־שְׂפָתֵימוֹ
וְיִלָּכְדוּ בִגְאוֹנָם וּמֵאָלָה
וּמִכַּחַשׁ יְסַפֵּרוּ:

¹³ There is sin in their mouths, the words of their lips. Let them be trapped by their pride, by the curses and lies that they utter.

כַּלֵּה בְחֵמָה כַּלֵּה וְאֵינֵמוֹ
וְיֵדְעוּ כִּי־אֱלֹהִים מֹשֵׁל
בְּיַעֲקֹב לְאַפְסֵי הָאָרֶץ סֶלָה:

¹⁴ Destroy in wrath, destroy so they are no more, and they will know to the ends of the earth that God rules over Jacob, Selah.

---

¹⁰ **His strength!** This is a call to God's power. **I will** hope and **wait for You, for God is my fortress.**

¹¹ **My merciful God will come toward me;** He will grant me consideration and come to protect me. **God will let me look upon** the downfall of **my foes.**

¹² The psalmist prays to God to deal with his pursuers: **Do not** simply **slay them, lest my people forget.** If you kill them, their nefarious deeds will be forgotten along with them. I pray that in their punishment they will remain alive, so that their people will be reminded of their misdeeds. **Scatter them by Your power and bring them down, our shield, my Lord.**

¹³ **There is sin in their mouths** and in **the words of their lips. Let them be trapped** and then led to defeat **by their** own **pride, by the curses and lies that they utter.**

¹⁴ **Destroy** them **in wrath, destroy so they are no more, and they,** everyone in the world, **will know to the ends of the earth that God rules over Jacob, Selah.**

טו וְיָשֻׁבוּ לָעֶרֶב יֶהֱמוּ כַכָּלֶב וִיסוֹבְבוּ עִיר:

טז הֵמָּה יְנוּעוּן לֶאֱכֹל אִם־לֹא יִשְׂבְּעוּ וַיָּלִינוּ:

יז וַאֲנִי ׀ אָשִׁיר עֻזֶּךָ וַאֲרַנֵּן לַבֹּקֶר חַסְדֶּךָ כִּי־הָיִיתָ מִשְׂגָּב לִי וּמָנוֹס בְּיוֹם צַר־לִי:

יח עֻזִּי אֵלֶיךָ אֲזַמֵּרָה כִּי־אֱלֹהִים מִשְׂגַּבִּי אֱלֹהֵי חַסְדִּי:

¹⁵ And they return toward evening, barking like dogs and roaming the city.

¹⁶ They wander about to eat; if they are not sated, they stay to sleep.

¹⁷ But as for me, I will sing of Your strength, I will joyfully sing of Your kindness in the morning, for You were my fortress and a refuge on the day of my distress.

¹⁸ My Strength! To You I sing praises. For God is my fortress, my merciful God.

---

15 The psalmist now reiterates and expands upon his previous description of his foes: **And they return toward evening, barking like dogs and roaming the city.**

16 **They,** the dogs, **wander about,** searching for food **to eat; if they are not sated, they stay to sleep.** So too, Saul's mercenaries prowl about in an unfamiliar city, searching for me everywhere.

17 The psalmist ends with words of praise to God: **But as for me, I will sing of Your strength, I will joyfully sing of Your kindness in the morning, for You were my fortress and a refuge on the day of my distress.**

18 **My Strength,** God! **To You I sing praises. For God is my fortress, my merciful God.**

PSALM 60

A song of praise and thanksgiving in the wake of a military victory. It opens with a description of previous difficult times of setback and defeat, and continues with an expression of gratitude for the ultimate triumph, conveying the message that everything is in the hands of God.

יא לחודש

11th day
of month

לַמְנַצֵּחַ עַל־שׁוּשַׁן עֵדוּת
מִכְתָּם לְדָוִד לְלַמֵּד:

בְּהַצּוֹתוֹ ׀ אֶת אֲרַם נַהֲרַיִם
וְאֶת־אֲרַם צוֹבָה וַיָּשָׁב יוֹאָב
וַיַּךְ אֶת־אֱדוֹם בְּגֵיא־מֶלַח
שְׁנֵים עָשָׂר אָלֶף:

אֱלֹהִים זְנַחְתָּנוּ פְרַצְתָּנוּ
אָנַפְתָּ תְּשׁוֹבֵב לָנוּ:

1 For the chief musician, on *shushan edut*, an instruction by David to teach,

2 when he contended with Aram Naharayim and with Aram Tzova, and Yoav returned and smote twelve thousand Edomites in the Valley of Salt.

3 God, You abandoned us, You sundered us. You were angry with us. Restore us.

PSALM 60

1 **For the chief musician, on *shushan edut*,** literally, "lily of testimony." This psalm, like those immediately preceding it, was apparently accompanied by an ancient melody. The psalm was written in celebration of major victories in a war, and though the war may not yet have reached its decisive conclusion, there was already ample reason to give thanks. The psalm is called **an instruction by David to teach** because in addition to being a prayer, it also teaches of past events.

2 David wrote this psalm **when** his armies were engaged in active combat on several distant fronts: **He contended with Aram Naharayim,** at the northernmost border of David's kingdom, **and with Aram Tzova,** to the northwest, **and Yoav returned and smote twelve thousand Edomites in the Valley of Salt,**[18] apparently adjacent to the Dead Sea, or Salt Sea as it is known in Hebrew, to the south. In effect, then, David and his armies were fighting two major wars and won battles on both fronts. The psalm is thus a combination of praise, thanks, and remembrance.

3 **God,** it appeared to us that **You** had **abandoned us, You** had **sundered us. You were angry with us,** and we beseeched You to **restore us.**

הִרְעַשְׁתָּה אֶרֶץ פְּצַמְתָּהּ
רְפָה שְׁבָרֶיהָ כִי־מָטָה:

הִרְאִיתָ עַמְּךָ קָשָׁה
הִשְׁקִיתָנוּ יַיִן תַּרְעֵלָה:

נָתַתָּה לִּירֵאֶיךָ נֵּס לְהִתְנוֹסֵס
מִפְּנֵי קֹשֶׁט סֶלָה:

לְמַעַן יֵחָלְצוּן יְדִידֶיךָ
הוֹשִׁיעָה יְמִינְךָ וַעֲנֵנוּ:

אֱלֹהִים ׀ דִּבֶּר בְּקָדְשׁוֹ
אֶעְלֹזָה אֲחַלְּקָה שְׁכֶם וְעֵמֶק
סֻכּוֹת אֲמַדֵּד:

וַעֲנֵנִי

4 You made the land quake, You shattered it. Heal its broken pieces, for it has toppled.

5 You showed Your people harshness; You gave us poison wine to drink.

6 You have given those who fear You a banner to wave, because of Your truth, Selah.

7 So that Your beloved ones be saved, deliver us with Your right hand; answer me.

8 God spoke in His holiness; I exulted. I divided Shekhem and measured out the Valley of Sukot.

---

4 **You** had **made the land quake, You shattered it**, and we prayed: **Heal its broken pieces, for it has toppled.**

5 **You showed Your people harshness; You gave us poison wine to drink,** so to speak. The years prior to the current victories were characterized by difficulties and defeats, with enemies pressing on all sides.

6 Now, however, **You have given those who fear You a banner** of victory **to wave** proudly, **because of Your truth,** Your faithfulness in keeping the ancient covenant that You made with our forefathers, **Selah.**

7 **So that Your beloved ones,** the people of Israel, **be saved, deliver us with Your right hand; answer me.**

8 The psalmist now describes the victories: **God spoke** to me **in His holiness,** assuring me of victory; **I** therefore **exulted. I divided Shekhem and measured out the Valley of Sukot.** Until this point, these regions had been only partially under the rule of Israel; other nations had occupied and fortified portions of them. After David's victories, however, they fell completely under Israelite control, and he was now able to divide these areas among the people.

ט לִי גִלְעָד ׀ וְלִי מְנַשֶּׁה וְאֶפְרַיִם מָעוֹז רֹאשִׁי יְהוּדָה מְחֹקְקִי:

 י מוֹאָב ׀ סִיר רַחְצִי עַל־אֱדוֹם אַשְׁלִיךְ נַעֲלִי עָלַי פְּלֶשֶׁת הִתְרֹעָעִי:

יא מִי יֹבִלֵנִי עִיר מָצוֹר מִי נָחַנִי עַד־אֱדוֹם:

יב הֲלֹא־אַתָּה אֱלֹהִים זְנַחְתָּנוּ וְלֹא־תֵצֵא אֱלֹהִים בְּצִבְאוֹתֵינוּ:

יג הָבָה־לָּנוּ עֶזְרָת מִצָּר וְשָׁוְא תְּשׁוּעַת אָדָם:

יד בֵּאלֹהִים נַעֲשֶׂה־חָיִל וְהוּא יָבוּס צָרֵינוּ:

9 Gilad is mine, and Manasseh is mine, and Ephraim is my stronghold, Judah my lawgiver.

10 Moav is my washbasin; I will fling my shoe at Edom. Philistia will be crushed because of me.

11 Who leads me to besiege the city, who guides me to Edom?

12 Is it not You, God, who had abandoned us; You, God, who would not go forth with our armies?

13 Give us help against the foe, for deliverance by man is in vain.

14 With God we will triumph, and He will rout our foes.

---

9 Israel's victory in battle was made possible by the fact that the people of Israel were now united behind a single leader: **Gilad is mine, and Manasseh,** who dwelled in Gilad and Bashan, **is also mine, and Ephraim is my stronghold, Judah my lawgiver,** the one who decides and sets the laws. All of the tribes, even those who had not been on friendly terms with one another, were unified under David's rule.

10 **Moav is my washbasin,** an expression of contempt; **I will fling my shoe at Edom**, an insulting gesture recognized throughout the Middle East. **Philistia will be crushed because of me.**

11 **Who leads me to besiege the city, who guides me to Edom?**

12 **Is it not You, God, who had** previously **abandoned us; You, God, who would not go forth with our armies?**

13 But now that You have once again come to our aid, **give us help against the foe, for deliverance by man** alone **is in vain.**

14 And if You come to our assistance, we will require no other form of salvation, for **with God we will triumph, and He will rout our foes.**

PSALM 61

A song of thanksgiving to God for His providing aid and shelter at a time of distress.
It is possible that it was written on the occasion of a great military victory.

לַמְנַצֵּחַ ׀ עַל־נְגִינַת לְדָוִד׃

שִׁמְעָה אֱלֹהִים רִנָּתִי הַקְשִׁיבָה תְּפִלָּתִי׃

מִקְצֵה הָאָרֶץ ׀ אֵלֶיךָ אֶקְרָא בַּעֲטֹף לִבִּי בְּצוּר־יָרוּם מִמֶּנִּי תַנְחֵנִי׃

כִּי־הָיִיתָ מַחְסֶה לִי מִגְדַּל־עֹז מִפְּנֵי אוֹיֵב׃

אָגוּרָה בְאָהָלְךָ עוֹלָמִים אֶחֱסֶה בְסֵתֶר כְּנָפֶיךָ סֶּלָה׃

¹ For the chief musician, upon *neginat*, by David.

² Hear my singing, God; attend to my prayer.

³ From the end of the earth, I call to You when my heart is faint; guide me against a rock that is high above me.

⁴ For You have been a refuge for me, a tower of strength against the enemy.

⁵ Let me dwell in Your tent forever; let me take refuge in the shelter of Your wings, Selah.

PSALM 61

1 **For the chief musician, upon *neginat*,** the name of a musical instrument or a type of melody, **by David.**

2 **Hear my singing, God; attend to my prayer,** in which I wish to praise You and also to request an additional blessing from You.

3 **From the end of the earth, I call to You when my heart is faint.** It seems that this psalm was written when David was on a military campaign in a land far from the borders of Israel. **Guide me** to victory **against** an enemy so formidable that he is like **a rock that is** towering **high above me.**

4 **For You have been a refuge for me, a tower of strength against the enemy.**

5 **Let me dwell in Your tent forever; let me** always **take refuge in the shelter of Your wings, Selah.**

כִּי־אַתָּה אֱלֹהִים שָׁמַעְתָּ
לִנְדָרָי נָתַתָּ יְרֻשַּׁת יִרְאֵי
שְׁמֶךָ:

יָמִים עַל־יְמֵי־מֶלֶךְ תּוֹסִיף
שְׁנוֹתָיו כְּמוֹ־דֹר וָדֹר:

יֵשֵׁב עוֹלָם לִפְנֵי אֱלֹהִים
חֶסֶד וֶאֱמֶת מַן יִנְצְרֻהוּ:

כֵּן אֲזַמְּרָה שִׁמְךָ לָעַד
לְשַׁלְּמִי נְדָרַי יוֹם ׀ יוֹם:

6 For You, God, have heard my
vows; You granted the portion
of those who fear Your name.

7 May You add years to the life
of the king, so that his days
extend over generations.

8 May he abide before the Lord
forever. Make his portion
kindness and truth, that they
might preserve him.

9 So I will sing praise to Your
name forever, every day as I
pay my vows.

---

6 **For You, God, have heard my vows** that I undertook to fulfill if You helped me survive and
win this war. **You granted the portion of those who fear Your name.** You rewarded them
with what they deserve, namely, possession of the land that they retook from the enemy.

7 This is followed by David's additional request: **May you add years to the life of the king,**
apparently a reference to himself, **so that his days extend over generations.**

8 **May he abide before the Lord forever. Make his portion kindness and truth;** bless the
king with gifts of kindness and truth, **that they might preserve him.** In this translation, the
word *man* is related to *mana*, "portion." The phrase can also be rendered: "Kindness and truth are
what will preserve him."

9 **So I will sing praise to Your name forever, every day as I pay my vows,** expressing my
gratitude to You for Your salvation.

PSALM 62

An introspective psalm that contrasts the lives of the wicked, whose apparent success
is temporary, with those of individuals who embrace God and are thus bound to eternity.
It describes David's many enemies, as well as his hope to be rescued from them.

לַמְנַצֵּחַ עַל־יְדוּתוּן מִזְמוֹר
לְדָוִד:

For the chief musician, for
Yedutun, a psalm by David.

אַךְ אֶל־אֱלֹהִים דּוּמִיָּה נַפְשִׁי
מִמֶּנּוּ יְשׁוּעָתִי:

For God alone does my soul
wait silently; my salvation is
from Him.

אַךְ־הוּא צוּרִי וִישׁוּעָתִי
מִשְׂגַּבִּי לֹא־אֶמּוֹט רַבָּה:

He alone is my rock and my
salvation, my stronghold; I will
not stumble greatly.

עַד־אָנָה ׀ תְּהוֹתְתוּ עַל־אִישׁ
תְּרָצְּחוּ כֻלְּכֶם כְּקִיר נָטוּי
גָּדֵר הַדְּחוּיָה:

For how long will you terrorize
a man? You are murderers, all
of you, like a leaning wall or a
tottering fence.

PSALM 62

1 **For the chief musician, for *Yedutun*, a psalm by David.**

2 **For God alone does my soul wait silently** and anxiously, for **my salvation is from Him.**

3 **He alone is my rock and my salvation, my stronghold; I will not stumble** during times
when adversity **greatly** besets me. An alternative understanding of *rabba*, "greatly," in this phrase
is: Even if I stumble a bit, I will not fall "greatly," all the way down to the ground.

4 The psalmist addresses his foes: **For how long will you terrorize a man?** This is the only time
that the word *tehotetu*, translated as "terrorize," is used in the Bible. Its meaning is derived from
the context of the verse. **You are murderers,** whether actual or potential killers, **all of you;** it is
dangerous to be in your environs, **like** near **a leaning wall or a tottering fence.**

אַךְ מִשְּׂאֵתוֹ ׀ יָעֲצ֣וּ לְהַדִּ֗יחַ
יִרְצ֬וּ כָזָ֗ב בְּפִ֥יו יְבָרֵ֑כוּ
וּֽבְקִרְבָּ֗ם יְקַֽלְלוּ־סֶֽלָה׃

אַ֣ךְ לֵ֭אלֹהִים דּ֣וֹמִּי נַפְשִׁ֑י כִּי־
מִ֝מֶּ֗נּוּ תִּקְוָתִֽי׃

אַךְ־ה֣וּא צ֭וּרִי וִישׁוּעָתִ֑י
מִ֝שְׂגַּבִּ֗י לֹ֣א אֶמּֽוֹט׃

עַל־אֱ֭לֹהִים יִשְׁעִ֣י וּכְבוֹדִ֑י
צוּר־עֻזִּ֥י מַ֝חְסִ֗י בֵּֽאלֹהִֽים׃

בִּטְח֪וּ ב֡וֹ בְכָל־עֵ֤ת ׀ עָ֗ם
שִׁפְכֽוּ־לְפָנָ֥יו לְבַבְכֶ֑ם אֱלֹהִ֖ים
מַֽחֲסֶה־לָּ֣נוּ סֶֽלָה׃

5 They scheme to bring down
a man from his lofty position.
They speak falsehood. They
bless with their mouths, but
inwardly they curse, Selah.

6 For God alone wait silently, My
soul, for my hope is from Him.

7 He alone is my rock and my
salvation, my stronghold; I will
not stumble.

8 My salvation and my glory are
with God, rock of my strength;
my refuge is in God.

9 Trust in Him at all times,
people. Pour out your heart
before Him; God is a refuge for
us, Selah.

---

5 **They scheme to bring down a man,** any man who has gained prominence, **from his lofty position.** And when they cannot attack that person directly, **they** resort to slander and lies and **speak falsehood** against him. **They bless** him **with their mouths, but inwardly they curse, Selah.**

6 The psalmist repeats a variation of verse 2: **For God alone wait silently, My soul, for my hope is from Him.**

7 **He alone is my rock and my salvation, my stronghold; I will not stumble.**

8 **My** hope for **salvation and my** source of **glory are with God, rock of my strength; my refuge is in God.**

9 Speaking to members of the nation at large, the psalmist admonishes them: **Trust** only **in Him at all times, people,** for you can fully rely only on Him. **Pour out your heart before Him;** tell Him of all your troubles, for only **God is a refuge for us, Selah.**

אַךְ ׀ הֶבֶל בְּנֵי־אָדָם כָּזָב בְּנֵי אִישׁ בְּמֹאזְנַיִם לַעֲלוֹת הֵמָּה מֵהֶבֶל יָחַד:

אַל־תִּבְטְחוּ בְעֹשֶׁק וּבְגָזֵל אַל־תֶּהְבָּלוּ חָיִל ׀ כִּי־יָנוּב אַל־תָּשִׁיתוּ לֵב:

אַחַת ׀ דִּבֶּר אֱלֹהִים שְׁתַּיִם־זוּ שָׁמָעְתִּי כִּי עֹז לֵאלֹהִים:

וּלְךָ־אֲדֹנָי חָסֶד כִּי־אַתָּה תְשַׁלֵּם לְאִישׁ כְּמַעֲשֵׂהוּ:

10 Men are nothingness; men of rank are an illusion. They rise together on the scales, lighter than nothingness.

11 Do not trust in fraud; do not delude yourselves by stealing. If wealth increases, do not pay it heed.

12 God has spoken once; I have heard it twice. Might belongs to God.

13 Kindness is Yours, my Lord, for You render to every man according to his deeds.

---

10 One should not put his trust in human beings, for **men are nothingness,** inconsequential and ephemeral; **men of rank are an illusion.** If one could weigh their worth, **they** would **rise together on the scales, lighter than nothingness.**

11 **Do not trust in** obtaining wealth through **fraud; do not delude yourselves by stealing.** Not only is it dishonest and sinful, but practically speaking, if you steal money, your wealth will prove to be elusive and short-lived. **If wealth** built on deception and theft **increases, do not pay it heed,** for it will not last.

12 All these matters are decreed from on high; we are commanded by God to follow a path of proper behavior: **God has spoken once,** commanding us to follow in the path He has set for us, but **I have heard it twice.** This verse refers to the two aspects of God's commandments: to follow God's will, and to refrain from doing what opposes that will. The Torah, in essence, can be summed up in one phrase: "Turn from evil and do good" (34:15). **Might belongs to God,** and therefore we must be guided by His words.

13 Moreover, **kindness is Yours, my Lord, for You render to every man according to his deeds,** whether they are bad or good.

PSALM 63

A psalm of devotion composed in the desert, a place of scarcity, thirst, and danger.
The psalmist discovers that there is a yearning more powerful than thirst for water,
namely, the yearning for closeness to God.

מִזְמוֹר לְדָוִד בִּהְיוֹתוֹ
בְּמִדְבַּר יְהוּדָה:

¹ A psalm by David, when he was in the Judean Desert.

אֱלֹהִים ׀ אֵלִי אַתָּה אֲשַׁחֲרֶךָּ
צָמְאָה לְךָ ׀ נַפְשִׁי כָּמַהּ לְךָ
בְשָׂרִי בְּאֶרֶץ־צִיָּה וְעָיֵף בְּלִי־
מָיִם:

² God, You are my Almighty; I search for You. My soul thirsts for You; my flesh yearns for You, in a parched and thirsty land without water.

כֵּן בַּקֹּדֶשׁ חֲזִיתִךָ לִרְאוֹת
עֻזְּךָ וּכְבוֹדֶךָ:

³ Indeed, in holiness I have seen You, beholding Your power and Your glory.

כִּי־טוֹב חַסְדְּךָ מֵחַיִּים שְׂפָתַי
יְשַׁבְּחוּנְךָ:

⁴ For Your kindness is better than life; my lips praise You.

PSALM 63

¹ **A psalm by David, when he was in the Judean Desert.** This psalm depicts David's plight in the Judean Desert as he was fleeing from Saul, surrounded by enemies on all sides, and suffering from constant deprivation. It is essentially a psalm of yearning for intimacy with God. The physical hardships of the desert only intensify rather than diminish his desire for spirituality.

² **God, You are my Almighty; I search for You. My soul thirsts for You; my flesh yearns for You, in a parched and thirsty land without water.** The psalmist's spiritual thirst for God is expressed against the backdrop of an arid desert in which man's physical needs are immediate and urgent. And yet, the psalmist's most intense thirst is not for water but for intimacy with God. It is precisely when his physical deprivation and isolation are most extreme that David realizes that his foremost longing in life is for spirituality.

³ **Indeed, in holiness I have seen You,** I imagine myself being enveloped in holiness, in a situation in which I am **beholding Your power and Your glory.** This is my dream and my desire.

⁴ **For Your kindness is better than life.** The realization that God's kindness is the source of all the goodness of the world means more to me than life itself. The mere recollection of Your kindness causes **my lips** to **praise You.**

כֵּן אֲבָרֶכְךָ בְחַיָּי בְּשִׁמְךָ אֶשָּׂא כַפָּי:

5 So I will bless You as long as I live. I will lift up my hands in Your name.

כְּמוֹ חֵלֶב וָדֶשֶׁן תִּשְׂבַּע נַפְשִׁי וְשִׂפְתֵי רְנָנוֹת יְהַלֶּל־פִּי:

6 I am sated as with fat and rich fare; my mouth offers praises with joyful lips.

אִם־זְכַרְתִּיךָ עַל־יְצוּעָי בְּאַשְׁמֻרוֹת אֶהְגֶּה־בָּךְ:

7 Even on my bed I remember You; I meditate on You during the night watches.

כִּי־הָיִיתָ עֶזְרָתָה לִי וּבְצֵל כְּנָפֶיךָ אֲרַנֵּן:

8 For You have been my help, and in the shadow of Your wings I sing for joy.

דָּבְקָה נַפְשִׁי אַחֲרֶיךָ בִּי תָּמְכָה יְמִינֶךָ:

9 My soul clings to You; Your right hand has supported me.

---

5 **So I will bless You as long as I live.** My very life, the fact that I am alive, can be regarded as a means of blessing You. **I will lift up my hands** in prayer **in Your name.**

6 **I am sated as with fat and rich fare.** My thoughts about You and the praises that I sing to You suffice to make me happy and fulfilled, providing gratification in the way that good food satisfies one who eats to his heart's content. **My mouth offers praises with joyful lips,** not because of God's beneficence to me, but because I am filled with joy at sensing His presence.

7 **Even on my bed,** when it is time to relax and fall asleep, **I remember You. I meditate on You during the night watches.** A portion of the night, consisting of several hours, is called a "watch." People are sometimes roused from their sleep between one watch and the next, but they are not fully awake and immediately fall back asleep. The psalmist explains: I, however, use these opportunities to meditate further upon You, which clearly indicates that You are central to all my thoughts. There is nothing more meaningful to me than awareness of God's presence; it occupies my heart and mind more than anything else.

8 **For You have been my help, and in the shadow of Your wings I sing for joy.** The psalmist here is thankful to God not only because He has kept him alive and relatively free, avoiding capture by Saul, but, more importantly, because of the feeling that he knows that God is always with him, providing him with protection.

9 **My soul clings to You;** it desires Your closeness, for **Your right hand has supported me.**

וְהֵמָּה לְשׁוֹאָה יְבַקְשׁוּ נַפְשִׁי יָבֹאוּ בְּתַחְתִּיּוֹת הָאָרֶץ:

יַגִּירֻהוּ עַל־יְדֵי־חָרֶב מְנָת שֻׁעָלִים יִהְיוּ:

וְהַמֶּלֶךְ יִשְׂמַח בֵּאלֹהִים יִתְהַלֵּל כָּל־הַנִּשְׁבָּע בּוֹ כִּי יִסָּכֵר פִּי דוֹבְרֵי־שָׁקֶר:

10 But they seek my annihilation. May they descend into the depths of the earth.

11 They will shed his blood by the sword. May they become prey to the foxes.

12 And may the king rejoice in God, and everyone who swears by him be glorified, when the mouths of liars are stopped.

PSALM 64

A plea for protection by one who is pursued by enemies both visible and covert, all of whom use every means available in order to cause him harm.

לַמְנַצֵּחַ מִזְמוֹר לְדָוִד:

1 For the chief musician, a psalm by David.

---

10 After describing his physical and spiritual state, the psalmist addresses the matter of his pursuers: **But they** who pursue me **seek my annihilation. May they descend into the depths of the earth.**

11 My enemies say that **they will shed his,** David's, **blood by the sword. May they become prey to the foxes** that prowl in the desert looking for dead animals and corpses.

12 **And may the king rejoice in God.** It is unclear whether the "king" refers to David himself, who had already been anointed by Saul at this point, or to Saul, whom David saw as still being the legitimate king. David did not regard Saul as an enemy but rather as a man hounded by phantom terrors, driven to madness by his jealousy of David. David's hope is that if Saul finds happiness in God, he will no longer have cause to hate and pursue him. **And** may **everyone who swears by him,** one of the basic indicators of one's allegiance to the monarch, **be glorified, when the mouths of liars,** who have goaded Saul into jealousy of David, **are stopped.**

PSALM 64
1 **For the chief musician, a psalm by David.**

שְׁמַע־אֱלֹהִים קוֹלִי בְשִׂיחִי
מִפַּחַד אוֹיֵב תִּצֹּר חַיָּי:

² Hear my voice, God, in my prayer; preserve my life from the terror of the enemy.

תַּסְתִּירֵנִי מִסּוֹד מְרֵעִים
מֵרִגְשַׁת פֹּעֲלֵי אָוֶן:

³ Hide me from the counsel of the wicked, from the tumult of evildoers,

אֲשֶׁר שָׁנְנוּ כַחֶרֶב לְשׁוֹנָם
דָּרְכוּ חִצָּם דָּבָר מָר:

⁴ who whet their tongues like a sword, aiming their arrows with venomous words,

לִירוֹת בַּמִּסְתָּרִים תָּם פִּתְאֹם
יֹרֻהוּ וְלֹא יִירָאוּ:

⁵ to shoot furtively at the innocent. They shoot him suddenly and without fear.

יְחַזְּקוּ־לָמוֹ ׀ דָּבָר רָע יְסַפְּרוּ
לִטְמוֹן מוֹקְשִׁים אָמְרוּ מִי
יִרְאֶה־לָּמוֹ:

⁶ They bolster themselves with evil matters. They speak of laying hidden snares, saying: Who will see them?

יַחְפְּשׂוּ־עוֹלֹת תַּמְנוּ חֵפֶשׂ
מְחֻפָּשׂ וְקֶרֶב אִישׁ וְלֵב
עָמֹק:

⁷ They thoroughly seek out iniquities, to the very depths of a man's heart.

---

² **Hear my voice, God, in my prayer; preserve my life from the terror of the enemy.**

³ **Hide me from the counsel of the wicked,** from the plans they have against me, **from the tumult of evildoers,**

⁴ **who whet their tongues like a sword, aiming their arrows,** a metaphor for their tongues, **with venomous words,**

⁵ **to shoot furtively at the innocent. They shoot him suddenly,** with no warning, **and without fear,** since they perform their nefarious acts in secret.

⁶ **They bolster themselves with** engaging in **evil matters. They speak** among themselves **of laying hidden snares, saying: Who will see them?** Because they act furtively, they assume they will never be discovered.

⁷ **They thoroughly seek out iniquities** to commit, **to the very depths of a man's heart,** another reference to the clandestine nature of their plans and actions.

ה וַיֹּרֵם אֱלֹהִים חֵץ פִּתְאוֹם הָיוּ
מַכּוֹתָם:

ט וַיַּכְשִׁילֻהוּ עָלֵימוֹ לְשׁוֹנָם
יִתְנֹדֲדוּ כָּל־רֹאֵה בָם:

י וַיִּירְאוּ כָּל־אָדָם וַיַּגִּידוּ פֹּעַל
אֱלֹהִים וּמַעֲשֵׂהוּ הִשְׂכִּילוּ:

יא יִשְׂמַח צַדִּיק בַּיהוה וְחָסָה
בוֹ וְיִתְהַלְלוּ כָּל־יִשְׁרֵי־לֵב:

8 May God shoot them with an unexpected arrow, smiting them.

9 Their own tongues will cause them to stumble. All those who behold them will shudder.

10 And all men will be in awe; they will declare it the work of God, understanding it as His doing.

11 The righteous will rejoice in the Lord and trust in Him, and all the upright in heart will be glorified.

---

8 In this kind of situation, a person can only pray to God for help: **May God shoot them with an unexpected arrow, smiting them.**

9 **Their own** vicious **tongues will** backfire and **cause them,** instead of me, **to stumble.** May the tongues they used against me become the instrument of their own downfall. **All those who behold them** in defeat **will shudder** in revulsion and shock.

10 **And all men** who witness the downfall of the evildoers **will be in awe; they will declare it the work of God, understanding it as His doing.** When people see how the wicked are trapped and devastated by their own evil schemes, they will understand that the world is orchestrated by God's will.

11 **The righteous will** then **rejoice in the Lord and trust in Him, and all the upright in heart will be glorified.**

PSALM 65

A psalm of praise to God, who forgives sinners and embraces those who repent,
and fills the world with bounteous goodness and tranquility.

לַמְנַצֵּחַ מִזְמוֹר לְדָוִד שִׁיר:

לְךָ דֻמִיָּה תְהִלָּה אֱלֹהִים
בְּצִיּוֹן וּלְךָ יְשֻׁלַּם־נֶדֶר:

שֹׁמֵעַ תְּפִלָּה עָדֶיךָ כָּל־בָּשָׂר
יָבֹאוּ:

דִּבְרֵי עֲוֹנֹת גָּבְרוּ מֶנִּי
פְּשָׁעֵינוּ אַתָּה תְכַפְּרֵם:

אַשְׁרֵי ׀ תִּבְחַר וּתְקָרֵב יִשְׁכֹּן
חֲצֵרֶיךָ נִשְׂבְּעָה בְּטוּב בֵּיתֶךָ
קְדֹשׁ הֵיכָלֶךָ:

1 For the chief musician, a psalm
by David, a song.

2 For You, God of Zion, silence
is praise, and a vow to You will
be paid.

3 You, who hear prayer, all flesh
comes to You.

4 Iniquities overwhelm me, but
You forgive our transgressions.

5 Happy is the one You choose
to bring near You to dwell
in Your Sanctuary. May we
be sated by the bounty of
Your House, the holiness of
Your Temple.

PSALM 65

1 **For the chief musician, a psalm by David, a song.** This is a psalm of gratitude that depicts a time of spiritual tranquility and bounty.

2 **For You, God of Zion, silence is praise, and a vow to You will be paid.** While this verse can be interpreted in many ways, its central message is that all words in praise of God are insufficient. Words of praise can actually be shamefully inadequate; silence, on the other hand, includes all that can and cannot be verbalized. Instead of composing lengthy poems or songs in praise of God, we should praise Him with our deeds, by fulfilling the obligations we have undertaken to serve Him.

3 **You, who hear prayer, all flesh comes to You** to pray for their needs and to give thanks.

4 **Iniquities overwhelm me** and threaten to crush me with their weight, **but** despite the enormity of my sins, I trust in You that **You forgive our transgressions**.

5 **Happy is the one You choose to bring near You, to dwell in Your Sanctuary. May we** be among their number, and **be sated by the bounty of Your House, the holiness of Your Temple.**

נוֹרָאוֹת ׀ בְּצֶדֶק תַּעֲנֵנוּ
אֱלֹהֵי יִשְׁעֵנוּ מִבְטָח כָּל־
קַצְוֵי־אֶרֶץ וְיָם רְחֹקִים:

מֵכִין הָרִים בְּכֹחוֹ נֶאְזָר
בִּגְבוּרָה:

מַשְׁבִּיחַ ׀ שְׁאוֹן יַמִּים שְׁאוֹן
גַּלֵּיהֶם וַהֲמוֹן לְאֻמִּים:

וַיִּירְאוּ ׀ יֹשְׁבֵי קְצָוֹת
מֵאוֹתֹתֶיךָ מוֹצָאֵי־בֹקֶר
וָעֶרֶב תַּרְנִין:

פָּקַדְתָּ הָאָרֶץ ׀ וַתְּשֹׁקְקֶהָ
רַבַּת תַּעְשְׁרֶנָּה פֶּלֶג אֱלֹהִים
מָלֵא מָיִם תָּכִין דְּגָנָם כִּי־כֵן
תְּכִינֶהָ:

6 Answer us justly with awesome deeds, God of our salvation and our shelter to the ends of the earth and the farthest sea,

7 who sets mountains with His strength, girded with might,

8 who stills the roaring of the seas, the roaring of their waves, and the tumult of nations.

9 Those who live at the ends of the earth are in awe of Your signs. You make the place of dawn and dusk sing out.

10 You remember the earth and fulfill its desire, enriching it with abundance; the streams of God are full of water. You prepare their grain; indeed, You set it firmly in place.

---

6 **Answer us justly with awesome deeds, God of our salvation and our shelter to the ends of the earth and the farthest sea.**

7 The following verses provide a fuller description of some of God's deeds: It is He **who sets mountains with His strength, girded with might.** God's divine might is expressed here by the image of a great mountain being set in place by Him, layer by layer, rock by rock.

8 God's power can also be portrayed in other ways. It is God **who stills the roaring of the seas, the roaring of their waves, and** He also stills **the tumult of nations.** Here, God's power is depicted not only with regard to the natural world but also vis-à-vis the hubbub of human affairs.

9 Even **those who live at the ends of the earth are in awe of Your signs.** Your signs are everywhere, and through those signs and miracles, **You make the place of dawn and dusk,** a poetic way of saying "east and west," **sing out.**

10 Beyond depicting God's power and grandeur, the psalmist acknowledges His blessings: **You remember the earth and fulfill its desire, enriching it with abundance.** The earth's "desire" refers here, as in many other places, to water. **The streams of God are full of water.** Once the earth has been watered, it is ready to be cultivated: **You prepare their grain,** causing it

תְּלָמֶיהָ רַוֵּה נַחֵת גְּדוּדֶהָ ‏¹¹
בִּרְבִיבִים תְּמֹגְגֶנָּה צִמְחָהּ
תְּבָרֵךְ׃

עִטַּרְתָּ שְׁנַת טוֹבָתֶךָ ‏¹²
וּמַעְגָּלֶיךָ יִרְעֲפוּן דָּשֶׁן׃

יִרְעֲפוּ נְאוֹת מִדְבָּר וְגִיל ‏¹³
גְּבָעוֹת תַּחְגֹּרְנָה׃

לָבְשׁוּ כָרִים ׀ הַצֹּאן וַעֲמָקִים ‏¹⁴
יַעַטְפוּ־בָר יִתְרוֹעֲעוּ אַף־
יָשִׁירוּ׃

11 Saturate its furrows, satisfy its hollows, soften it with showers. Bless its vegetation.

12 You crown the year with Your bounty, and Your paths drip with rich abundance.

13 Oases in the desert overflow; the hills gird themselves with joy.

14 The meadows are covered with flocks of sheep; the valleys are wrapped in grain. They shout for joy, and they sing.

---

to sprout and grow. **Indeed, You set it firmly in place,** allowing it to continue its growth until it ripens. There is some wordplay here in the Hebrew. The same Hebrew verb *takhin* is employed to mean both "You prepare" and "You set firmly"; moreover, the second use of the verb is alliterative with the word for "indeed," *ken*.

11 **Saturate its furrows, satisfy its hollows, soften it with showers. Bless its vegetation.**

12 **You crown the year with Your bounty;** may these blessings continue all year round, "crowning" the year with plenty, **and Your paths drip with rich abundance.** The word *ma'agalekha*, translated here as "Your paths," also refers to a recurring cycle of events.

13 **Oases in the desert overflow.** Ordinarily, oases are barely able to sustain themselves in their endless battle with the surrounding harshness of the desert. But You cause them, through an abundance of rain, to actually flow over to the surrounding arid terrain. **The hills gird themselves with joy.** The normally dry hills become covered with greenery and appear overjoyed by all the growth.

14 **The meadows are covered with flocks of sheep; the valleys**, the most fertile type of terrain, **are wrapped in grain. They shout for joy.** The word *yitroa'u* has a second meaning as well: "They become friends." When there is widespread abundance, all the earth and all that it produces appear to complement each other and join together in harmony, **and they sing.**

PSALM 66

A psalm of praise to God for His revelation, both in general and in connection with specific historical events, beginning with the exodus from Egypt and the giving of the Torah at Mount Sinai, and continuing throughout the generations. The psalm concludes with a personal prayer by an individual who perceives divine providence in his own life.

יב לחודש
12th day
of month

א לַמְנַצֵּחַ שִׁיר מִזְמוֹר הָרִיעוּ לֵאלֹהִים כָּל־הָאָרֶץ:

ב זַמְּרוּ כְבוֹד־שְׁמוֹ שִׂימוּ כָבוֹד תְּהִלָּתוֹ:

ג אִמְרוּ לֵאלֹהִים מַה־נּוֹרָא מַעֲשֶׂיךָ בְּרֹב עֻזְּךָ יְכַחֲשׁוּ־לְךָ אֹיְבֶיךָ:

ד כָּל־הָאָרֶץ ׀ יִשְׁתַּחֲווּ לְךָ וִיזַמְּרוּ־לָךְ יְזַמְּרוּ שִׁמְךָ סֶלָה:

1 For the chief musician, a song, a psalm. Shout out to God, all the earth.

2 Sing the glory of His name; make His praise glorious.

3 Say to God: How awesome are Your works! Because of Your great power, Your enemies feign obedience to You.

4 The entire earth will bow down to You and sing praises to You; they will sing praises to Your name, Selah.

PSALM 66

1 **For the chief musician, a song, a psalm.** This psalm seems to allude to some kind of military victory, as it speaks of former obstacles and enemies who have now passed from existence. It is a hymn of gratitude to God. Its main theme is expressed in the opening verse: **Shout out** with joy and thanks **to God, all the earth.**

2 **Sing the glory of His name; make His praise glorious.**

3 **Say to God: How awesome are Your works! Because of Your great power, Your enemies feign obedience to You.** God's enemies have been vanquished, subjugated; they are compelled to act with obedience, even if it is insincere.

4 **The entire earth will bow down to You and sing praises to You; they will sing praises to Your name, Selah.**

לְכוּ וּרְאוּ מִפְעֲלוֹת אֱלֹהִים
נוֹרָא עֲלִילָה עַל־בְּנֵי אָדָם:

5 Come and see the works of
God, the awesome acts for the
sons of men.

הָפַךְ יָם ׀ לְיַבָּשָׁה בַּנָּהָר
יַעַבְרוּ בְרָגֶל שָׁם נִשְׂמְחָה־
בּוֹ:

6 He turned the sea into dry
land; they passed through the
river on foot. There we rejoiced
in Him.

מֹשֵׁל בִּגְבוּרָתוֹ ׀ עוֹלָם עֵינָיו
בַּגּוֹיִם תִּצְפֶּינָה הַסּוֹרְרִים ׀
אַל־יָרִימוּ לָמוֹ סֶלָה:

ירומ

7 He rules the world with His
might; His eyes keep watch on
the nations. The rebellious will
not be exalted, Selah.

בָּרְכוּ עַמִּים ׀ אֱלֹהֵינוּ
וְהַשְׁמִיעוּ קוֹל תְּהִלָּתוֹ:

8 Bless our God, you nations;
raise a voice in His praise,

הַשָּׂם נַפְשֵׁנוּ בַּחַיִּים וְלֹא־נָתַן
לַמּוֹט רַגְלֵנוּ:

9 to Him who keeps us alive,
and does not allow our feet
to stumble.

כִּי־בְחַנְתָּנוּ אֱלֹהִים צְרַפְתָּנוּ
כִּצְרָף־כָּסֶף:

10 Though You have tested us,
God; You refined us as silver
is refined.

---

5 The psalmist now expresses praises of God: **Come and see the works of God, the awesome acts** that He has done **for the sons of men.**

6 **He turned the** Red **Sea into dry land** for the children of Israel; afterwards **they passed through the** Jordan **River on foot. There we rejoiced in Him.**

7 **He rules the world with His might; His eyes keep watch on the nations,** ensuring that they are accorded their proper place. **The** people who are **rebellious** against God **will not be exalted,** for He will subdue them, **Selah.**

8 **Bless our God, you nations;** God's kindness toward Israel benefits all nations, and it is therefore fitting for all to praise Him. **Raise a voice in His praise,**

9 **to Him who keeps us alive, and does not allow our feet to stumble.** This is the case even though, as described in the following verses, there have been many periods of struggle and testing.

10 **Though You have tested us, God; You refined us as silver is refined.** You have put us through many ordeals, similar to the harsh conditions of the refinement process.

יא הֲבֵאתָנוּ בַמְּצוּדֶה שַׂמְתָּ
מוּעָקָה בְמָתְנֵינוּ:

יב הִרְכַּבְתָּ אֱנוֹשׁ לְרֹאשֵׁנוּ
בָּאנוּ־בָאֵשׁ וּבַמַּיִם וַתּוֹצִיאֵנוּ
לָרְוָיָה:

יג אָבוֹא בֵיתְךָ בְעוֹלוֹת אֲשַׁלֵּם
לְךָ נְדָרָי:

יד אֲשֶׁר־פָּצוּ שְׂפָתָי וְדִבֶּר־פִּי
בַּצַּר־לִי:

טו עֹלוֹת מֵחִים אַעֲלֶה־לָּךְ עִם־
קְטֹרֶת אֵילִים אֶעֱשֶׂה בָקָר
עִם־עַתּוּדִים סֶלָה:

11 You brought us into the net, placed a tight belt around our loins.

12 You let people ride over our heads. We went through fire and water, but You drew us out to relief.

13 I will come to Your House with burnt offerings; I will pay You my vows,

14 those uttered by my lips and spoken by my mouth when I was in distress.

15 I will offer You burnt offerings of fattened animals, with the smoking of rams; I will sacrifice bulls and he-goats, Selah.

---

11 **You brought us into the net, placed a tight belt around our loins.** These are all metaphors for situations of difficulty and distress.

12 **You let people ride over our heads;** that is, You have allowed us to be subjugated by others. **We went through fire and water,** both literally and figuratively. **But** in the end, **You drew us out** of these situations of pressure and anxiety **to** a situation of **relief.** The word *revaya*, translated here as "relief," literally refers to the slaking of thirst. Here it conveys the sense of relief felt by those who have been rescued and are now able to rest.

13 The psalmist continues on a personal note: **I will come to Your House with burnt offerings; I will pay You my vows,**

14 **those uttered by my lips and spoken by my mouth when I was in distress.** It is usually during difficult times that people make such vows.

15 **I will offer You burnt offerings of fattened animals, with the smoking of rams,** that is, rams that are completely burned on the altar. **I will sacrifice bulls and he-goats, Selah.**

טז לְכוּ־שִׁמְעוּ וַאֲסַפְּרָה כָּל־
יִרְאֵי אֱלֹהִים אֲשֶׁר עָשָׂה
לְנַפְשִׁי:

יז אֵלָיו פִּי־קָרָאתִי וְרוֹמַם
תַּחַת לְשׁוֹנִי:

יח אָוֶן אִם־רָאִיתִי בְלִבִּי לֹא
יִשְׁמַע ׀ אֲדֹנָי:

יט אָכֵן שָׁמַע אֱלֹהִים הִקְשִׁיב
בְּקוֹל תְּפִלָּתִי:

כ בָּרוּךְ אֱלֹהִים אֲשֶׁר לֹא־
הֵסִיר תְּפִלָּתִי וְחַסְדּוֹ מֵאִתִּי:

16 Come and hear, all who fear God, and I will tell of what He has done for me.

17 I called to Him with my mouth, and He was extolled with my tongue.

18 Even if I sense wickedness in my heart, the Lord does not take notice.

19 Indeed, God listens and attends to the sound of my prayer.

20 Blessed be God, who has not turned away my prayer nor withheld His kindness from me.

---

16 **Come and hear, all who fear God, and I will tell of what He has done for me.** I can personally attest to what God has done for me.

17 **I called to Him with my mouth, and He was extolled with my tongue.**

18 **Even if I sense wickedness in my heart, the Lord does not take notice.** Even if, like most people, I occasionally have wicked thoughts, God does not judge me harshly. He does not take my aberrant thoughts into consideration.

19 **Indeed, God listens and attends to the sound of my prayer.**

20 The psalmist concludes: **Blessed be God, who has not turned away my prayer nor withheld His kindness from me.**

PSALM 67

On the surface, this is a simple hymn of praise, consisting mainly of expressions of gratitude
and a request for God's continued beneficence. A more insightful reading reveals
a sophisticated structure to this brief psalm. Especially in kabbalistic literature, it has been
interpreted as containing veiled references to higher realms. Apart from its heading, the psalm
has seven verses and a total of forty-nine words. The seven verses correspond to the seven
branches of the Temple's menora; in some prayer books the psalm is even printed in the shape
of such a menora. On a deeper level, the psalm can be understood as a kind of road map
marking the journey from the lowest world to the higher realms.

א לַמְנַצֵּחַ בִּנְגִינֹת מִזְמוֹר שִׁיר:

ב אֱלֹהִים יְחָנֵּנוּ וִיבָרְכֵנוּ יָאֵר
פָּנָיו אִתָּנוּ סֶלָה:

ג לָדַעַת בָּאָרֶץ דַּרְכֶּךָ בְּכָל־
גּוֹיִם יְשׁוּעָתֶךָ:

ד יוֹדוּךָ עַמִּים ׀ אֱלֹהִים יוֹדוּךָ
עַמִּים כֻּלָּם:

1 For the chief musician, with
instrumental music, a psalm,
a song.

2 May God be gracious to us
and bless us; may He shine His
countenance upon us, Selah,

3 so that Your way is known on
earth, Your salvation among all
the nations.

4 Let the peoples praise You,
God; let all the peoples
praise You.

PSALM 67

1 **For the chief musician, with instrumental music, a psalm, a song.** It appears that this
psalm was meant to be sung in the Temple.

2 **May God be gracious to us and bless us; may He shine His countenance upon us,
Selah.** There is an allusion here to the priestly blessing, which contains similar wording.

3 **So that Your way is known on earth.** May God show us His guidance concerning which path
to follow, and may He show everyone that He paves the way forward for those who love Him. May
Your salvation be revealed **among all the nations.**

4 **Let the peoples praise You, God; let all the peoples praise You.** This psalm is directed not
only to Israel but to all peoples of the world. It invites all nations to praise God for His kindness in
general; it does not refer specifically to God's salvation of Israel.

יִשְׂמְחוּ וִירַנְּנוּ לְאֻמִּים ה 5 Let the nations be glad and
כִּי־תִשְׁפֹּט עַמִּים מִישֹׁר   sing for joy, for You judge all
וּלְאֻמִּים ׀ בָּאָרֶץ תַּנְחֵם   peoples fairly and guide the
סֶלָה: nations of the earth, Selah.

יוֹדוּךָ עַמִּים ׀ אֱלֹהִים יוֹדוּךָ ו 6 Let the peoples praise you,
עַמִּים כֻּלָּם: God; let all the peoples
                               praise You.

אֶרֶץ נָתְנָה יְבוּלָהּ יְבָרְכֵנוּ ז 7 The earth has yielded its crop.
אֱלֹהִים אֱלֹהֵינוּ:   May God, our God, bless us.

יְבָרְכֵנוּ אֱלֹהִים וְיִירְאוּ אוֹתוֹ ח 8 May God bless us, and may all
כָּל־אַפְסֵי־אָרֶץ: the ends of the earth fear Him.

---

5 **Let the nations be glad and sing for joy, for You judge all peoples fairly.** You provide
   a straight path for all nations to follow, one that is devoid of conflict or war; **and** You **guide the
   nations of the earth** to achieve that path and appropriate goals, **Selah.**

6 **Let the peoples praise You, God; let all the peoples praise You.** This refrain emphasizes
   the psalm's universal relevance.

7 The following simple blessing is a further expression of the psalm's all-embracing theme: **The
   earth has yielded its crop** with sufficient produce to meet the needs of all. **May God, our
   God, bless us.** We beseech God to supplement the crops that grow naturally in the field with His
   divine blessing.

8 **May God bless us, and may** the people living at **all the ends of the earth fear Him.**

PSALM 68

An epic hymn in praise of the might of God, as manifested not only in military victories
but also in the epitome of divine revelation that occurred at Mount Sinai. The text is noteworthy for
its archaic and obscure Hebrew phrasing. It contains a number of words that are otherwise
not found in the Bible, along with some esoteric verses and expressions
that have been subject to a variety of interpretations.

א לַמְנַצֵּחַ לְדָוִד מִזְמוֹר שִׁיר:

ב יָקוּם אֱלֹהִים יָפוּצוּ אוֹיְבָיו
וְיָנוּסוּ מְשַׂנְאָיו מִפָּנָיו:

ג כְּהִנְדֹּף עָשָׁן תִּנְדֹּף כְּהִמֵּס
דּוֹנַג מִפְּנֵי־אֵשׁ יֹאבְדוּ
רְשָׁעִים מִפְּנֵי אֱלֹהִים:

ד וְצַדִּיקִים יִשְׂמְחוּ יַעַלְצוּ לִפְנֵי
אֱלֹהִים וְיָשִׂישׂוּ בְשִׂמְחָה:

1 For the chief musician, a psalm by David, a song.

2 May God arise and His enemies scatter; may those who hate Him flee before Him.

3 Blow them away as smoke is wafted away, as wax melts before fire; let the wicked perish before God.

4 But let the righteous be happy. May they exult before God; may they revel in happiness.

PSALM 68

1 **For the chief musician, a psalm by David, a song.** This is a psalm for times of war and other momentous historic events.

2 **May God arise and His enemies scatter; may those who hate Him flee before Him.** This verse is an allusion to Numbers 10:35.

3 **Blow them away as smoke is wafted away** by the hand or a fan, **as wax melts before fire. Let the wicked perish before God;** may they disappear completely.

4 **But let the righteous be happy. May they exult before God; may they revel in happiness.** The apparently redundant phrase indicates that *sason*, which means "reveling," is the outward manifestation of *simḥa*, an internal feeling of happiness.

שִׁירוּ ׀ לֵאלֹהִים זַמְּרוּ שְׁמוֹ
סֹלּוּ לָרֹכֵב בָּעֲרָבוֹת בְּיָהּ
שְׁמוֹ וְעִלְזוּ לְפָנָיו:

אֲבִי יְתוֹמִים וְדַיַּן אַלְמָנוֹת
אֱלֹהִים בִּמְעוֹן קָדְשׁוֹ:

אֱלֹהִים ׀ מוֹשִׁיב
יְחִידִים ׀ בַּיְתָה מוֹצִיא
אֲסִירִים בַּכּוֹשָׁרוֹת אַךְ
סוֹרְרִים שָׁכְנוּ צְחִיחָה:

אֱלֹהִים בְּצֵאתְךָ לִפְנֵי עַמֶּךָ
בְּצַעְדְּךָ בִישִׁימוֹן סֶלָה:

⁵ Sing to God; sing hymns to His name. Praise Him who rides in the highest heavens, with His name the Lord. Be joyous before Him.

⁶ The Father of orphans, the Judge of widows, God is in His holy dwelling.

⁷ God settles the lonely in a home; He joyously leads forth prisoners. But the rebellious dwell in a parched land.

⁸ God, when You went forth before Your people, when You marched through the desolate land, Selah,

---

5 **Sing to God; sing hymns to His name. Praise Him who rides in the highest heavens;** praise Him **with His name the Lord.** The Hebrew uses the name *Yah*, which is an abbreviated form of God's four-letter ineffable name, used occasionally in biblical songs of war and victory. **Be joyous before Him.**

6 God's greatness and revelation are manifested in various ways: He is **the Father of orphans, the Judge of widows, God is in His holy dwelling.** God, in His majestic dwelling, watches over the meek.

7 This verse illustrates God's attention to every individual. **God settles the lonely in a home;** He brings isolated people together to marry and build a home for themselves. **He joyously leads forth prisoners.** The word *bakosharot*, translated here as "joyously," appears only here, and from the context it seems to indicate a deeply felt joy. **But the rebellious** are thrust aside to **dwell in a parched land.**

8 The exodus from Egypt and the giving of the Torah at Sinai are powerful examples of God's revelation: **God, when You went forth before Your people,** leading them out of Egypt, **when You marched through the desolate land, Selah,**

אֶרֶץ רָעָשָׁה ׀ אַף־שָׁמַיִם
נָטְפוּ מִפְּנֵי אֱלֹהִים זֶה סִינַי
מִפְּנֵי אֱלֹהִים אֱלֹהֵי יִשְׂרָאֵל:

גֶּשֶׁם נְדָבוֹת תָּנִיף אֱלֹהִים
נַחֲלָתְךָ וְנִלְאָה אַתָּה
כוֹנַנְתָּהּ:

חַיָּתְךָ יָשְׁבוּ־בָהּ תָּכִין
בְּטוֹבָתְךָ לֶעָנִי אֱלֹהִים:

אֲדֹנָי יִתֶּן־אֹמֶר הַמְבַשְּׂרוֹת
צָבָא רָב:

מַלְכֵי צְבָאוֹת יִדֹּדוּן יִדֹּדוּן
וּנְוַת־בַּיִת תְּחַלֵּק שָׁלָל:

9 the earth quaked, the heavens rained before God, this Sinai, before God, the God of Israel.

10 You scatter abundant rain, God; You secure your portion and the weary.

11 Those You sustain have settled in it. In Your goodness, God, secure it for the needy.

12 My Lord gives the word, and the women herald the great armies.

13 The kings of armies flee again and again, while the women at home divide the spoils.

---

9 **the earth quaked.** Physical manifestations of fear and awe in the presence of God included the trembling of Mount Sinai. **The heavens rained before God,** out of fear of Him. The quaking took place at **this** mountain, **Sinai,** which trembled **before God, the God of Israel.**[19]

10 Manifestations of divine revelation can also be calm and reassuring: **You scatter abundant rain upon the earth, God; You secure Your portion,** referring to the people and Land of Israel, **and** You also secure **the weary** people.

11 **Those You sustain have settled in it,** in the portion mentioned above, the Land of Israel. **In Your goodness, God, secure it for the needy,** for the needs of the people of Israel.

12 **My Lord gives the word, and the women herald the great armies.** The apparent meaning of this verse is that when God gives the order, female choruses sing out in acclaim of the returning victorious armies.

13 And this is what those heralds proclaim: **The kings of armies flee again and again,** abandoning their possessions as spoils of war, **while the women at home divide the spoils.** Even housewives, who may symbolically represent the people of Israel, who now live peacefully in their homes, go out to reap the spoils of war.

יד אִם־תִּשְׁכְּבוּן בֵּין שְׁפַתָּיִם כַּנְפֵי יוֹנָה נֶחְפָּה בַכֶּסֶף וְאֶבְרוֹתֶיהָ בִּירַקְרַק חָרוּץ:

טו בְּפָרֵשׂ שַׁדַּי מְלָכִים בָּהּ תַּשְׁלֵג בְּצַלְמוֹן:

טז הַר־אֱלֹהִים הַר־בָּשָׁן הַר גַּבְנֻנִּים הַר־בָּשָׁן:

יז לָמָּה ׀ תְּרַצְּדוּן הָרִים גַּבְנֻנִּים הָהָר חָמַד אֱלֹהִים לְשִׁבְתּוֹ אַף־יְהוָֹה יִשְׁכֹּן לָנֶצַח:

14 Now you may lie within the sheepfolds, wings of the dove covered with silver, its pinions with green and gold.

15 When the Almighty crushed the kings, then it snowed in Tzalmon.

16 A mountain of God is Mount Bashan; a mountain of ridges is Mount Bashan.

17 Why do you shudder, ridged mountains? The mount that God desired for His abode, there the Lord will surely dwell forever.

---

14 **Now you may lie within the sheepfolds.** This verse describes Israel in a time of tranquility, a time peaceful enough for a person to rest secure in a pasture where sheep graze. The following is a metaphorical depiction of the people of Israel: **Wings of the dove covered with silver, its pinions with green and gold.** Caught in the light of the sun, the dove's white feathers gleam like polished silver and its wing tips sparkle with colors of green and gold.

15 **When the Almighty crushed the kings,** when powerful kings are brought down, God's glory is manifest. **Then it snowed in Tzalmon,** in the desert. The reversal of the existing political order is as stunning as snowfall in the desert.

16 **A mountain of God,** a mountain of vast proportions, **is Mount Bashan; a mountain of ridges is Mount Bashan.**

17 **Why do you shudder, ridged mountains,** Bashan and others like it? Your shuddering is due to the fact that **the mount that God desired for His abode** is Mount Sinai, mentioned in verse 9, or, according to others, Mount Moriah, the site of the Temple. Mount Moriah seems to be the more likely interpretation, given the conclusion of the verse: **There the Lord will surely dwell forever.**

יח רֶ֣כֶב אֱ֭לֹהִים רִבֹּתַ֣יִם אַלְפֵ֣י
שִׁנְאָ֑ן אֲדֹנָ֥י בָ֝֗ם סִינַ֥י בַּקֹּֽדֶשׁ:
יט עָ֘לִ֤יתָ לַמָּר֨וֹם ׀ שָׁבִ֬יתָ שֶּׁ֗בִי
לָקַ֣חְתָּ מַ֭תָּנוֹת בָּאָדָ֑ם וְאַ֥ף
סֽוֹרְרִ֗ים לִשְׁכֹּ֤ן ׀ יָ֬הּ אֱלֹהִֽים:
כ בָּ֘ר֤וּךְ אֲדֹנָ֙י י֤וֹם ׀ י֗וֹם יַעֲמׇס־
לָ֝֗נוּ הָאֵ֥ל יְֽשׁוּעָתֵ֥נוּ סֶֽלָה:
כא הָ֤אֵ֣ל ׀ לָנוּ֮ אֵ֤ל לְֽמוֹשָׁ֫ע֥וֹת
וְלֵיהֹוִ֥ה אֲדֹנָ֑י לַ֝מָּ֗וֶת
תּוֹצָאֽוֹת:

18 The chariots of God are myriad, thousands upon thousands of companies. My Lord is among them, at Sinai, in holiness.

19 You ascended on high; You took captives. You received tributes among men; even the rebellious You captured to dwell over, Lord God.

20 Blessed be the Lord, who provides for us day by day, the Almighty of our deliverance, Selah.

21 The Almighty for us is the Almighty of deliverance; the Lord, my Lord, holds power over death.

---

18 The following verse returns to the revelation at Sinai: **The chariots of God,** though of course incorporeal, **are** compared in their might to a human camp of a **myriad, thousands upon thousands of companies.** The word *shinan*, translated here as "companies," may also mean "angels" or "tents." **My Lord is among them, at Sinai, in holiness.**

19 The psalmist describes God as a victorious warrior: **You ascended on high; You took captives. You received tributes among men.** This may mean "tributes taken from men," or it may mean "tributes made up of men," that is, human captives. **Even the rebellious You captured to dwell over, Lord God.**

20 **Blessed be the Lord, who provides for us day by day, the Almighty of our deliverance, Selah.**

21 **The Almighty for us is the Almighty of deliverance** who comes to our aid; as for those who refuse to submit to Him, **the Lord, my Lord, holds power over death** and will subject them to it.

כב אַךְ־אֱלֹהִים יִמְחַץ רֹאשׁ
אֹיְבָיו קׇדְקֹד שֵׂעָר מִתְהַלֵּךְ
בַּאֲשָׁמָיו:

> 22 Indeed, God will shatter the heads of His enemies, hairy skulls of those walking in their guilt.

כג אָמַר אֲדֹנָי מִבָּשָׁן אָשִׁיב
אָשִׁיב מִמְּצֻלוֹת יָם:

> 23 The Lord said: I will bring them back from Bashan, I will bring them back from the depths of the sea.

כד לְמַעַן ׀ תִּמְחַץ רַגְלְךָ בְּדָם
לְשׁוֹן כְּלָבֶיךָ מֵאוֹיְבִים מִנֵּהוּ:

> 24 So that your foot might wade in blood, so your dogs' tongues might lick their portion of the enemy.

כה רָאוּ הֲלִיכוֹתֶיךָ אֱלֹהִים
הֲלִיכוֹת אֵלִי מַלְכִּי בַקֹּדֶשׁ:

> 25 They saw Your ways, God, the ways of my Almighty, my King in holiness.

כו קִדְּמוּ שָׁרִים אַחַר נֹגְנִים
בְּתוֹךְ עֲלָמוֹת תּוֹפֵפוֹת:

> 26 First the singers, followed by musicians, amid the young women playing timbrels.

---

22 **Indeed, God will shatter the heads of His enemies, hairy skulls of those walking in their guilt.**

23 At the same time, God seeks those of Israel who have lost their way, in order to bring them back: **The Lord said: I will bring them back from Bashan,** and **I will bring them back from the depths of the sea.** This last phrase may be an allusion to the splitting of the Red Sea.

24 The psalmist addresses the Israelites: God will bring you back **so that your foot might wade in** the **blood** of your enemies, **so your dogs' tongues might lick their portion** of the blood **of the enemy.**

25 What follows is a description of God's grandeur from the perspective of His people who honor Him in public ceremony: **They saw Your ways, God, the ways of my Almighty, my King in holiness.**

26 **First the singers, followed by musicians, amid the young women playing timbrels.** All of these people come out to greet the victorious King.

בְּמַקְהֵלוֹת בָּרְכוּ אֱלֹהִים
אֲדֹנָי מִמְּקוֹר יִשְׂרָאֵל: כז

שָׁם בִּנְיָמִן ׀ צָעִיר רֹדֵם שָׂרֵי
יְהוּדָה רִגְמָתָם שָׂרֵי זְבֻלוּן
שָׂרֵי נַפְתָּלִי: כח

צִוָּה אֱלֹהֶיךָ עֻזֶּךָ עוּזָּה
אֱלֹהִים זוּ פָּעַלְתָּ לָּנוּ: כט

מֵהֵיכָלֶךָ עַל־יְרוּשָׁלִָם לְךָ
יוֹבִילוּ מְלָכִים שָׁי: ל

27 Bless God among the great assemblies; the Lord, from the fount of Israel.

28 There is Benjamin, the youngest, leading them; the chieftains of Judah in their throng, the chieftains of Zebulun, the chieftains of Naphtali.

29 Your God has decreed strength for you. Reveal Your strength, God, that You have employed on our behalf,

30 from Your Temple above Jerusalem. Kings bring gifts to You.

---

27 **Bless God among the great assemblies; the Lord, from the fount of Israel.**

28 **There,** at this musical tribute, **is** the tribe of **Benjamin,** who was **the youngest** of Jacob's sons, as well as the least populous tribe, **leading them; the chieftains of Judah in their throng, the chieftains of Zebulun, the chieftains of Naphtali.** In short, all the tribes of Israel, from one end to the other, were present.

29 The psalmist addresses Israel and its king: **Your God has decreed strength for you.** Then turning to God, he says: **Reveal Your strength, God, that You have employed on our behalf** in the past.

30 This strength that I speak of emanates **from Your Temple,** which is situated on Mount Zion, **above Jerusalem. Kings** of all nations **bring gifts** and offerings **to You** there.

גְּעַר חַיַּת קָנֶה עֲדַת אַבִּירִים וּ לֹא
בְּעֶגְלֵי עַמִּים מִתְרַפֵּס בְּרַצֵּי־
כֶסֶף בִּזַּר עַמִּים קְרָבוֹת
יֶחְפָּצוּ:

יֶאֱתָיוּ חַשְׁמַנִּים מִנִּי מִצְרָיִם לֹב
כּוּשׁ תָּרִיץ יָדָיו לֵאלֹהִים:

מַמְלְכוֹת הָאָרֶץ שִׁירוּ לֹג
לֵאלֹהִים זַמְּרוּ אֲדֹנָי סֶלָה:

לָרֹכֵב בִּשְׁמֵי שְׁמֵי־קֶדֶם הֵן לֹד
יִתֵּן בְּקוֹלוֹ קוֹל עֹז:

31 Strike fear in the beasts among the reeds, and in the herd of cavalry horses going among the calves of the people, those who grovel for pieces of silver. He scatters the nations who desire battle.

32 Noblemen will arrive from Egypt; Kush will hasten to stretch out her hands to God.

33 Kingdoms of the earth, sing to God; sing praises to my Lord, Selah.

34 To Him who rides on the expanses of the highest, farthest heavens, who speaks with His voice, a mighty voice.

---

31 **Strike fear in the beasts among the reeds,** the wild animals lurking among the reeds near the water,[20] **and in the herd of cavalry horses going among the calves of the people.** The image is one of powerful war horses that cause the enemy to flee like small calves caught in a stampede. The calves represent **those** vanquished people **who grovel** and seek to buy their safety from their invaders **for pieces of silver. He scatters the nations who desire battle.** The belligerent nations are dispersed by God; only those who have surrendered remain.

32 **Noblemen will arrive from Egypt; Kush,** in Africa, **will hasten to stretch out her hands** with gifts **to God.**

33 **Kingdoms of the earth, sing to God; sing praises to my Lord, Selah.**

34 Sing those praises **to Him who rides on the expanses of the highest, farthest heavens, who speaks with His voice, a mighty voice,** referring to the sound of thunder.

לה תְּנ֤וּ עֹ֨ז לֵֽאלֹהִ֗ים עַֽל־יִשְׂרָאֵ֥ל
גַּאֲוָת֑וֹ וְ֝עֻזּ֗וֹ בַּשְּׁחָקִֽים׃

לו נ֤וֹרָ֥א אֱלֹהִ֨ים ׀ מִֽמִּקְדָּשֶׁ֗יךָ
אֵ֥ל יִשְׂרָאֵ֗ל ה֤וּא נֹתֵ֨ן ׀
עֹ֖ז וְתַֽעֲצֻמ֥וֹת לָעָ֗ם בָּר֥וּךְ
אֱלֹהִֽים׃

[35] Ascribe strength to God,
whose majesty is over Israel,
whose strength is in the
heavens.

[36] You are awesome, God, from
Your Sanctuary; the Almighty
of Israel gives strength and
power to the nation. Blessed
be God.

PSALM 69

A psalm of prayer and supplication. It is also the anguished cry of an individual caught in a vise of
personal distress and attacks by an array of enemies. It ends on a hopeful note, which may reflect
the psalmist's faith that God will come to his aid; alternatively, the ending may have been added
at a later date, after the psalmist had been delivered from danger.

א לַמְנַצֵּ֥חַ עַל־שֽׁוֹשַׁנִּ֗ים לְדָוִֽד׃

ב הוֹשִׁיעֵ֥נִי אֱלֹהִ֑ים כִּ֤י בָ֖אוּ
מַ֣יִם עַד־נָֽפֶשׁ׃

[1] For the chief musician, on
shoshanim, by David.

[2] Rescue me, God, for the waters
have come up to my soul.

---

[35] **Ascribe strength to God,** that is, praise Him for His strength, **whose majesty is over Israel.**
God's power and greatness are made manifest through the people of Israel, **whose strength is
in the heavens.**

[36] **You are awesome,** feared, **God, from Your Sanctuary,** the source of God's revelation in the
world; **the Almighty of Israel gives strength and power to the nation** of Israel. **Blessed
be God.**

PSALM 69

[1] **For the chief musician, on *shoshanim,* by David.**

[2] The psalm begins with a plea from an individual who is in great peril: **Rescue me, God, for the
waters have come up to my soul,** up to the point where they threaten my life.

טָבַעְתִּי ׀ בִּיוֵן מְצוּלָה וְאֵין
מָעֳמָד בָּאתִי בְמַעֲמַקֵּי־מַיִם
וְשִׁבֹּלֶת שְׁטָפָתְנִי:

יָגַעְתִּי בְקָרְאִי נִחַר גְּרוֹנִי כָּלוּ
עֵינַי מְיַחֵל לֵאלֹהָי:

רַבּוּ ׀ מִשַּׂעֲרוֹת רֹאשִׁי שֹׂנְאַי
חִנָּם עָצְמוּ מַצְמִיתַי אֹיְבַי
שֶׁקֶר אֲשֶׁר לֹא־גָזַלְתִּי אָז
אָשִׁיב:

אֱלֹהִים אַתָּה יָדַעְתָּ לְאִוַּלְתִּי
וְאַשְׁמוֹתַי מִמְּךָ לֹא־נִכְחָדוּ:

3 I am sinking in muddy depths without a foothold. I am in deep water, and a whirlpool is sweeping me away.

4 I am weary from calling out; my throat is parched. My eyes are failing as I hope for my God.

5 More numerous than the hairs on my head are those who hate me without cause. Those who would destroy me, my deceitful enemies, have grown powerful. I am made to give back what I never stole.

6 God, You know my folly; my wrongs are not hidden from You.

---

3 **I am sinking in muddy depths without a foothold,** with no solid ground underneath to stop me from going under. **I am in deep water, and** I am unable to swim my way out of it because **a whirlpool is sweeping me away.**

4 **I am weary from calling out** for help; **my throat is parched. My eyes are failing,** constantly looking out for the slightest sign of encouragement, **as I hope for my God.**

5 **More numerous than the hairs on my head are those who hate me without cause.** I am surrounded by enemies, many of whom have no justifiable reason to hate me. **Those who would destroy me, my deceitful enemies, have grown powerful.** The most evil among them have fabricated accusations against me for the sole purpose of bringing me down. Because of their false accusations, **I am made to give back** to them **what** in actuality **I never stole.**

6 The psalmist, as one who has dedicated himself completely to God, notes that although he is far from perfect, the hatred against him is not connected to his personal shortcomings: **God, You know my folly,** the sins that I have committed, which emanated from foolishness on my part; **my wrongs,** sins I have committed knowingly, **are** also **not hidden from You.** I am unable to hide these sins from You, and I do not desire to do so.

אַל־יֵבֹשׁוּ בִי ׀ קֹוֶיךָ אֲדֹנָי
יֱהֹוִה צְבָאוֹת אַל־יִכָּלְמוּ בִי
מְבַקְשֶׁיךָ אֱלֹהֵי יִשְׂרָאֵל:

כִּי־עָלֶיךָ נָשָׂאתִי חֶרְפָּה
כִּסְּתָה כְלִמָּה פָנָי:

מוּזָר הָיִיתִי לְאֶחָי וְנָכְרִי
לִבְנֵי אִמִּי:

כִּי־קִנְאַת בֵּיתְךָ אֲכָלָתְנִי
וְחֶרְפּוֹת חוֹרְפֶיךָ נָפְלוּ עָלָי:

וָאֶבְכֶּה בַצּוֹם נַפְשִׁי וַתְּהִי
לַחֲרָפוֹת לִי:

7 May those who place their hope in You not be dismayed because of me, my Lord, Lord of hosts. May those who seek You not be shamed because of me, God of Israel.

8 For I have borne disgrace for Your sake, shame covering my face.

9 I have been considered a stranger by my brothers, an alien to my mother's sons.

10 For zealotry for Your House has consumed me; the insults of those who revile You fall on me.

11 I cry while fasting and become the object of abuse.

---

7 **May those who place their hope in You not be dismayed because of me, my Lord, Lord of hosts.** I am regarded by others as a paradigm of a devoted servant of God. If I am allowed to perish, others will be discouraged from following my example. **May those who seek You not be shamed because of me, God of Israel.**

8 I have shown my complete dedication to You all my life, **for I have borne disgrace for Your sake, shame covering my face.** I have become an object of disdain and contempt because I am so closely bound with You. The path that I follow is not particularly popular, and it has set me apart from others.

9 The psalmist continues to describe the scorn to which he has been subjected: **I have been considered a stranger** even **by my brothers, an alien to my mother's sons.** Shunned even by my close family, I feel totally isolated.

10 **For zealotry for Your House has consumed me;** I have exhibited great passion and zeal for Your name and Your Temple. Therefore, **the insults of those who revile You fall on me.** Because I am so closely identified with You, those who revile You see me as an appropriate target of attack.

11 **I cry while fasting and** thereby **become the object of abuse.**

יב וָאֶתְּנָה לְבוּשִׁי שָׂק וָאֱהִי
לָהֶם לְמָשָׁל:

יג יָשִׂיחוּ בִי יֹשְׁבֵי שָׁעַר וּנְגִינוֹת
שׁוֹתֵי שֵׁכָר:

יד וַאֲנִי תְפִלָּתִי־לְךָ ׀ יְהֹוָה עֵת
רָצוֹן אֱלֹהִים בְּרׇב־חַסְדֶּךָ
עֲנֵנִי בֶּאֱמֶת יִשְׁעֶךָ:

טו הַצִּילֵנִי מִטִּיט וְאַל־אֶטְבָּעָה
אִנָּצְלָה מִשֹּׂנְאַי וּמִמַּעֲמַקֵּי־
מָיִם:

טז אַל־תִּשְׁטְפֵנִי ׀ שִׁבֹּלֶת מַיִם
וְאַל־תִּבְלָעֵנִי מְצוּלָה וְאַל־
תֶּאְטַר־עָלַי בְּאֵר פִּיהָ:

12 And when I garb myself in sackcloth, I am made an example.

13 Those who sit at the gate talk about me; I am the subject of songs by ale drinkers.

14 But as for me, let my prayer come to You, Lord, at a time of favor. God, in the greatness of Your kindness, answer me with the truth of Your deliverance.

15 Save me from the mire, lest I sink. May I be delivered from my foes and from the deep waters.

16 Do not let the whirlpool wash me away, nor the deep swallow me up, nor the well close its mouth over me.

---

12 **And when I garb myself in sackcloth,** as a gesture of mourning or self-abnegation, **I am made an example** for derision.

13 **Those who sit at the gate,** the elders and prominent people of the city, **talk** derisively **about me; I am the subject of** mocking **songs by ale drinkers,** the common folk at the tavern.

14 **But as for me, let my prayer come to You, Lord, at a time of favor.** I pray that this may be a time of favor, when You will be receptive to my prayers. **God, in the greatness of Your kindness, answer me with the truth of Your deliverance;** uphold faithfully that which You have promised, to come to my aid.

15 **Save me from the mire, lest I sink. May I be delivered from my foes and from the deep waters.** The psalmist returns to the imagery presented above, expressing his feeling of drowning.

16 **Do not let the whirlpool wash me away, nor the deep swallow me up, nor the well** in which I am drowning **close its mouth over me,** preventing my escape.

עֲנֵנִי יהוה כִּי־טוֹב חַסְדֶּךָ
כְּרֹב רַחֲמֶיךָ פְּנֵה אֵלָי:

וְאַל־תַּסְתֵּר פָּנֶיךָ מֵעַבְדֶּךָ
כִּי־צַר־לִי מַהֵר עֲנֵנִי:

קָרְבָה אֶל־נַפְשִׁי גְאָלָהּ
לְמַעַן אֹיְבַי פְּדֵנִי:

אַתָּה יָדַעְתָּ חֶרְפָּתִי וּבָשְׁתִּי
וּכְלִמָּתִי נֶגְדְּךָ כָּל־צוֹרְרָי:

חֶרְפָּה ׀ שָׁבְרָה לִבִּי וָאָנוּשָׁה
וָאֲקַוֶּה לָנוּד וָאַיִן וְלַמְנַחֲמִים
וְלֹא מָצָאתִי:

17 Answer me, Lord, for Your kindness is good. Turn to me in the abundance of Your mercy.

18 Do not hide Your face from Your servant, for I am in distress; make haste to answer me.

19 Draw near to me and redeem me; ransom me from my enemies.

20 You know of my humiliation, my shame, and my disgrace; all my foes are before You.

21 Humiliation has broken my heart, and I have become desperately ill. I seek consolation, but there is none; I look for comforters but do not find any.

---

17 **Answer me, Lord, for Your kindness is good. Turn to me** and save me **in the abundance of Your mercy.**

18 **Do not hide Your face,** or remove Your attention, **from Your servant, for I am in distress** and in imminent danger, and I plead that You **make haste to answer me.**

19 **Draw near to me and redeem me; ransom me,** rescue me, **from my enemies,** who are in essence Your foes as well.

20 **You know of my humiliation, my shame, and my disgrace,** because **all** the actions of **my foes are before You.**

21 **Humiliation has broken my heart, and I have become desperately ill** from it. **I seek consolation, but there is none; I look for comforters** to treat me with compassion, **but do not find any.**

כב וַיִּתְּנוּ בְּבָרוּתִי רֹאשׁ וְלִצְמָאִי
יַשְׁקוּנִי חֹמֶץ:

כג יְהִי־שֻׁלְחָנָם לִפְנֵיהֶם לְפָח
וְלִשְׁלוֹמִים לְמוֹקֵשׁ:

כד תֶּחְשַׁכְנָה עֵינֵיהֶם מֵרְאוֹת
וּמָתְנֵיהֶם תָּמִיד הַמְעַד:

כה שְׁפָךְ־עֲלֵיהֶם זַעְמֶךָ וַחֲרוֹן
אַפְּךָ יַשִּׂיגֵם:

כו תְּהִי־טִירָתָם נְשַׁמָּה
בְּאָהֳלֵיהֶם אַל־יְהִי יֹשֵׁב:

כז כִּי־אַתָּה אֲשֶׁר־הִכִּיתָ רָדָפוּ
וְאֶל־מַכְאוֹב חֲלָלֶיךָ יְסַפֵּרוּ:

22 They put hemlock in my food, and for my thirst they give me vinegar to drink.

23 May their table become a trap, their tranquility a snare.

24 May their eyes grow dim so they cannot see; make their loins continuously unsteady.

25 Pour out Your wrath on them; let the fierceness of Your anger overtake them.

26 May their fortress be desolate; may none dwell in their tents.

27 For they have pursued the one You have smitten, and they tell of the pain of Your wounded.

---

22 Not only do they lack compassion, but they seek to harm me, as **they put hemlock in my food, and for my thirst they give me vinegar to drink,** which only intensifies my thirst and increases my suffering.

23 In his misery, the psalmist curses his foes: **May their table become a trap;** may they be entrapped when they are sitting equably at their table. May **their** time of **tranquility** prove to be **a snare** for them.

24 **May their eyes grow dim so they cannot see; make their loins continuously unsteady** so that they will not be able to stand.

25 **Pour out Your wrath on them; let the fierceness of Your anger overtake them** and punish them.

26 **May their fortress be desolate; may none dwell in their tents**.

27 The psalmist offers justification for his harsh words: **For they have pursued** me, **the one You have smitten.** God punished me for my personal sins and deficiencies, as God alone determines who suffers and who dies. **And** yet **they tell** with delight **of the pain of Your wounded;** the psalmist's foes take pleasure in speaking of my misery.

כח תְּנָה־עָוֹן עַל־עֲוֹנָם וְאַל־
יָבֹאוּ בְּצִדְקָתֶךָ:

כט יִמָּחוּ מִסֵּפֶר חַיִּים וְעִם
צַדִּיקִים אַל־יִכָּתֵבוּ:

ל וַאֲנִי עָנִי וְכוֹאֵב יְשׁוּעָתְךָ
אֱלֹהִים תְּשַׂגְּבֵנִי:

לא אֲהַלְלָה שֵׁם־אֱלֹהִים בְּשִׁיר
וַאֲגַדְּלֶנּוּ בְתוֹדָה:

לב וְתִיטַב לַיהוה מִשּׁוֹר פָּר
מַקְרִן מַפְרִיס:

לג רָאוּ עֲנָוִים יִשְׂמָחוּ דֹּרְשֵׁי
אֱלֹהִים וִיחִי לְבַבְכֶם:

28 Add iniquity to their iniquities; let them not be accorded Your righteousness.

29 May they be blotted out of the book of life; may they not be inscribed with the righteous.

30 As for me, afflicted and in pain, may Your salvation, God, strengthen me.

31 I will praise the name of God in song and magnify Him with thanksgiving,

32 and may it please the Lord more than a bull with horns and hoofs.

33 The humble will see it and be glad. You who seek God, let your hearts revive.

---

28 **Add** this **iniquity to their** other **iniquities;** when You judge them for their transgressions, **let them not be accorded Your righteousness,** which You normally extend to everyone.

29 When the time comes for You to record the fate of all men, **may they be blotted out of the book of life. May they not be inscribed** for good **with the righteous;** record them instead among the wicked.

30 **As for me, afflicted and in pain, may Your salvation, God, strengthen me.**

31 And then **I will praise the name of God in song and magnify Him with thanksgiving,**

32 **and may it,** my meager tribute of song, **please the Lord more than** the sacrifice of **a** full-grown **bull with horns and hoofs.**

33 **The humble will see it,** Your salvation of me, **and be glad,** as I am an example to them of one who is fully devoted to God. **You who seek God** and witness His salvation of me, **let your hearts revive;** let this salvation provide you with hope and consolation.

לד כִּי־שֹׁמֵעַ אֶל־אֶבְיוֹנִים יְהוָה
וְאֶת־אֲסִירָיו לֹא בָזָה:

לה יְהַלְלוּהוּ שָׁמַיִם וָאָרֶץ יַמִּים
וְכָל־רֹמֵשׂ בָּם:

לו כִּי אֱלֹהִים ׀ יוֹשִׁיעַ צִיּוֹן
וְיִבְנֶה עָרֵי יְהוּדָה וְיָשְׁבוּ שָׁם
וִירֵשׁוּהָ:

לז וְזֶרַע עֲבָדָיו יִנְחָלוּהָ וְאֹהֲבֵי
שְׁמוֹ יִשְׁכְּנוּ־בָהּ:

34 For the Lord hears the needy and does not despise His prisoners.

35 Let Him be praised by heaven and earth, the seas and everything swarming within.

36 For God will save Zion and build the cities of Judah, and people will settle there and possess it.

37 The descendants of His servants will inherit it, and those who love His name will dwell in it.

---

34 **For the Lord hears the needy,** though they lack the means to vow sacrificial tributes to Him, **and does not despise His prisoners,** who lack not only material possessions but even freedom. He hears the prayers of the lowly people as well and comes to their rescue.

35 **Let Him be praised by heaven and earth, the seas and everything,** all the living creatures, **swarming within.**

36 And this is the praise all of them will declare to Him: **For God will save Zion and build** anew **the cities of Judah** that have been destroyed, **and people will settle there and possess it.**

37 **The descendants of His servants,** namely Israel, **will inherit it, and those who love His name,** as opposed to foreigners or enemies, **will dwell in it.**

PSALM 70

A short psalm of prayer, very similar in wording to the concluding verses of Psalm 40, in which David beseeches God to relieve him of his trials and tribulations.

לַמְנַצֵּחַ לְדָוִד לְהַזְכִּיר: ^א

אֱלֹהִים לְהַצִּילֵנִי יהוה ^ב
לְעֶזְרָתִי חוּשָׁה:

יֵבֹשׁוּ וְיַחְפְּרוּ מְבַקְשֵׁי נַפְשִׁי ^ג
יִסֹּגוּ אָחוֹר וְיִכָּלְמוּ חֲפֵצֵי
רָעָתִי:

יָשׁוּבוּ עַל־עֵקֶב בָּשְׁתָּם ^ד
הָאֹמְרִים הֶאָח הֶאָח:

יָשִׂישׂוּ וְיִשְׂמְחוּ בְּךָ ^ה
כָּל־מְבַקְשֶׁיךָ וְיֹאמְרוּ
תָמִיד יִגְדַּל אֱלֹהִים אֹהֲבֵי
יְשׁוּעָתֶךָ:

¹ For the chief musician, by David, for remembrance.

² God, hasten to deliver me, Lord, make haste to come to my aid.

³ Let those who seek my life be ashamed and humiliated. Let those who delight in my misfortune retreat in disgrace.

⁴ May those who say: Hurrah, hurrah! retreat on their heels in shame.

⁵ Let all who seek You be happy and rejoice in You; let those who love Your salvation always say: May God be magnified.

PSALM 70

¹ **For the chief musician, by David, for remembrance.** This psalm is apparently meant to remind God, as it were, of David's existence.

² **God, hasten to deliver me.** The verb "hasten" is missing in the original Hebrew text, and is understood from the second half of the verse. **Lord, make haste to come to my aid.**

³ **Let those who seek my life be ashamed and humiliated. Let those who delight in my misfortune retreat in disgrace.**

⁴ **May those who say,** upon witnessing my misfortune: **Hurrah, hurrah! retreat on their heels in shame.**

⁵ **Let all who seek You be happy and rejoice in You; let those who love Your salvation always say: May God be magnified.**

וַאֲנִי ׀ עָנִי וְאֶבְיוֹן אֱלֹהִים
חוּשָׁה לִּי עֶזְרִי וּמְפַלְטִי
אַתָּה יְהֹוָה אַל־תְּאַחַר:

⁶ As for me, poor and destitute, God, make haste. You are my Help and my Savior; Lord, do not tarry.

PSALM 71

A psalm of request and thanksgiving. It begins with the psalmist beseeching God to rescue him from his enemies, and concludes with words of praise for his salvation. The psalm lacks a heading; it may have originally been a part of Psalm 70 and separated at a later time.

בְּךָ־יְהֹוָה חָסִיתִי אַל־
אֵבוֹשָׁה לְעוֹלָם:

¹ In You, Lord, I have taken refuge; I shall never be ashamed.

בְּצִדְקָתְךָ תַּצִּילֵנִי וּתְפַלְּטֵנִי
הַטֵּה־אֵלַי אָזְנְךָ וְהוֹשִׁיעֵנִי:

² Save me and rescue me in Your righteousness; incline Your ear to me and deliver me.

הֱיֵה לִי ׀ לְצוּר מָעוֹן לָבוֹא
תָּמִיד צִוִּיתָ לְהוֹשִׁיעֵנִי כִּי־
סַלְעִי וּמְצוּדָתִי אָתָּה:

³ Be a fortified dwelling for me, where I may enter at all times. You have ordained my rescue, for You are my rock and my fortress.

---

⁶ In conclusion, the psalmist returns to his own personal situation: **As for me, poor and destitute, God, make haste,** for I am in urgent need of Your aid. **You are my Help and my Savior; Lord, do not tarry;** save me from my misfortune.

PSALM 71
¹ **In You, Lord, I have taken refuge;** therefore, **I shall never be ashamed.**
² **Save me** from my enemies **and rescue me** from my troubles **in Your righteousness; incline Your ear to me and deliver me.**
³ **Be** like **a fortified dwelling for me, where I may enter at all times,** as **You have ordained my rescue, for You are my rock and my fortress.**

אֱלֹהַי פַּלְּטֵנִי מִיַּד רָשָׁע מִכַּף מְעַוֵּל וְחוֹמֵץ: ד

כִּי־אַתָּה תִקְוָתִי אֲדֹנָי יֱהֹוִה מִבְטַחִי מִנְּעוּרָי: ה

עָלֶיךָ ׀ נִסְמַכְתִּי מִבֶּטֶן מִמְּעֵי אִמִּי אַתָּה גוֹזִי בְּךָ תְהִלָּתִי תָמִיד: ו

כְּמוֹפֵת הָיִיתִי לְרַבִּים וְאַתָּה מַחֲסִי־עֹז: ז

יִמָּלֵא פִי תְּהִלָּתֶךָ כָּל־הַיּוֹם תִּפְאַרְתֶּךָ: ח

4 My God, rescue me from the hand of the wicked, from the grasp of the wrongdoer and the violent man.

5 For You are my hope, my Lord God, my trust from the days of my youth.

6 I have relied on You from birth; You brought me out of my mother's womb. I praise You always.

7 I have been an example for many, and You are my mighty refuge.

8 Let my mouth be filled with praise for You, for Your glory, all day long.

---

4 **My God, rescue me from the hand of the wicked, from the grasp of the wrongdoer and the violent man.** The word *ḥometz* is similar in meaning to *ḥomes*, "violent man" or "robber." It is also found in talmudic literature with a similar meaning.

5 **For You are my hope, my Lord God, my trust from the days of my youth.**

6 **I have relied on You from birth,** literally "from the belly," that is, since emerging from the womb; **You brought me out of my mother's womb,** and I have been with You ever since. **I praise You always.**

7 **I have been an example for many.** David is aware that, as king, his deeds and acts of courage are not private matters; people admire him as a symbol and role model. **And You are my mighty refuge.**

8 **Let my mouth be filled with praise for You;** enable me to praise You with completion and perfection, and may I be able to praise You **for Your glory all day long.**

ט אַל־תַּשְׁלִיכֵנִי לְעֵת זִקְנָה
כִּכְלוֹת כֹּחִי אַל־תַּעַזְבֵנִי:

י כִּי־אָמְרוּ אוֹיְבַי לִי וְשֹׁמְרֵי
נַפְשִׁי נוֹעֲצוּ יַחְדָּו:

יא לֵאמֹר אֱלֹהִים עֲזָבוֹ רִדְפוּ
וְתִפְשׂוּהוּ כִּי־אֵין מַצִּיל:

יב אֱלֹהִים אַל־תִּרְחַק מִמֶּנִּי
חֻיּ אֱלֹהַי לְעֶזְרָתִי חִישָׁה:

יג יֵבֹשׁוּ יִכְלוּ שֹׂטְנֵי נַפְשִׁי יַעֲטוּ
חֶרְפָּה וּכְלִמָּה מְבַקְשֵׁי
רָעָתִי:

יד וַאֲנִי תָּמִיד אֲיַחֵל וְהוֹסַפְתִּי
עַל־כָּל־תְּהִלָּתֶךָ:

9 Do not cast me off in old age;
do not forsake me when my
strength fails.

10 For my enemies have spoken
against me; those who keep
watch over my soul have
conspired and are of one mind,

11 saying: God has forsaken him;
pursue and seize him, for there
is no one to rescue him.

12 God, do not be distant from
me; my God, hasten to my aid.

13 May those who hate me be
humiliated; may they perish.
May those who seek my harm
be wrapped in shame and
disgrace.

14 But as for me, I will hope
continually, and I will add to
Your praises.

---

9 The psalmist makes an additional request: **Do not cast me off in old age; do not forsake me when my strength fails.**

10 **For my enemies have spoken against me; those who keep watch over my soul,** those who await an opportunity to take my life, **have conspired and are of one mind,**

11 **saying: God has forsaken him;** he no longer enjoys divine protection. Therefore, **pursue and seize him, for there is no one to rescue him.**

12 **God, do not be distant from me,** as my enemies would like; **my God, hasten to my aid.**

13 **May those who hate me be humiliated; may they perish. May those who seek my harm be wrapped in shame and disgrace.**

14 **But as for me, I will hope continually** for Your kindness and salvation, **and** when You do rescue me, **I will add to Your praises** that I have expressed in the past.

טו פִּי ׀ יְסַפֵּר צִדְקָתֶךָ כָּל־הַיּוֹם
תְּשׁוּעָתֶךָ כִּי לֹא יָדַעְתִּי
סְפֹרוֹת:

טז אָבוֹא בִּגְבֻרוֹת אֲדֹנָי יֱהֹוִה
אַזְכִּיר צִדְקָתְךָ לְבַדֶּךָ:

יז אֱלֹהִים לִמַּדְתַּנִי מִנְּעוּרָי
וְעַד־הֵנָּה אַגִּיד נִפְלְאוֹתֶיךָ:

יח וְגַם עַד־זִקְנָה ׀ וְשֵׂיבָה
אֱלֹהִים אַל־תַּעַזְבֵנִי עַד־
אַגִּיד זְרוֹעֲךָ לְדוֹר לְכָל־יָבוֹא
גְּבוּרָתֶךָ:

יט וְצִדְקָתְךָ אֱלֹהִים עַד־מָרוֹם
אֲשֶׁר־עָשִׂיתָ גְדֹלוֹת אֱלֹהִים
מִי כָמוֹךָ:

15 My mouth will tell of Your righteousness, of Your salvation all day long, for they are beyond what I know to count.

16 If I come into strength, my Lord God, I will invoke only Your righteousness.

17 God, You have taught me from my youth, and until now I have told of Your wondrous deeds.

18 Also until I am old and gray, God, do not forsake me, until I tell of Your strength to generations, of Your might to all who come.

19 For Your righteousness, God, reaches the heavens. For the great deeds you have done, God, who is comparable to You?

---

15 **My mouth will tell of Your righteousness, of Your salvation all day long, for they,** all Your acts of salvation toward me, **are beyond what I know to count.**

16 **If I come into** a position of **strength, my Lord God, I will invoke only Your righteousness,** for anything else that may have enabled me to achieve that power was only a tool in Your hands.

17 **God, You have taught me** everything that I know **from my youth, and until now I have told of Your wondrous deeds.**

18 **Also until I am old and gray,** as my strength diminishes, **God, do not forsake me, until I tell of Your strength to generations,** and until I tell **of Your might to all who come** into this world.

19 **For Your righteousness, God, reaches the heavens. For the great deeds you have done** for me, **God, who is comparable to You?**

^כ אֲשֶׁר הִרְאִיתַנוּ ׀ צָרוֹת רַבּוֹת וְרָעוֹת תָּשׁוּב תְּחַיֵּינוּ וּמִתְּהֹמוֹת הָאָרֶץ תָּשׁוּב תַּעֲלֵנוּ:

²⁰ Though You brought upon me many severe troubles, You come back and revive me; from the depths of the earth You come back and raise me up.

^{כא} תֶּרֶב ׀ גְּדֻלָּתִי וְתִסֹּב תְּנַחֲמֵנִי:

²¹ You increase my greatness; You turn to comfort me.

^{כב} גַּם־אֲנִי ׀ אוֹדְךָ בִכְלִי־נֶבֶל אֲמִתְּךָ אֱלֹהַי אֲזַמְּרָה לְךָ בְכִנּוֹר קְדוֹשׁ יִשְׂרָאֵל:

²² And I, I will give thanks to You with a harp; I will sing praises of Your truth, my God, on a lyre, Holy One of Israel.

^{כג} תְּרַנֵּנָּה שְׂפָתַי כִּי אֲזַמְּרָה־לָּךְ וְנַפְשִׁי אֲשֶׁר פָּדִיתָ:

²³ My lips will sing out joyfully, along with my very soul that You redeemed.

^{כד} גַּם־לְשׁוֹנִי כָּל־הַיּוֹם תֶּהְגֶּה צִדְקָתֶךָ כִּי־בֹשׁוּ כִי־חָפְרוּ מְבַקְשֵׁי רָעָתִי:

²⁴ My tongue will also utter Your righteousness all day long, for those who sought to harm me have been confounded and brought to shame.

---

20 **Though You brought upon me many severe troubles, You** always **come back and revive me; from the depths of the earth You come back and raise me up.**

21 **You** not only rescue me but even **increase my greatness; You turn** Your attention to me **to comfort me.**

22 **And I, I will give thanks to You with a harp; I will sing praises of Your truth, my God, on a lyre, Holy One of Israel.**

23 **My lips will sing out joyfully, along with my very soul that You redeemed** from peril.

24 **My tongue will also utter Your righteousness all day long, for those who sought to harm me have been confounded and brought to shame.** I can now express my gratitude, for You have indeed come to my rescue.

PSALM 72

A song and prayer regarding King Solomon. It also appears to contain words of prophecy
concerning the future redeemer, the Messiah, who will be a descendant of Solomon.

יד לחודש
14th day
of month

א לִשְׁלֹמֹה ׀ אֱלֹהִים מִשְׁפָּטֶיךָ
לְמֶלֶךְ תֵּן וְצִדְקָתְךָ לְבֶן־
מֶלֶךְ:

ב יָדִין עַמְּךָ בְצֶדֶק וַעֲנִיֶּיךָ
בְמִשְׁפָּט:

ג יִשְׂאוּ הָרִים שָׁלוֹם לָעָם
וּגְבָעוֹת בִּצְדָקָה:

ד יִשְׁפֹּט ׀ עֲנִיֵּי־עָם יוֹשִׁיעַ לִבְנֵי
אֶבְיוֹן וִידַכֵּא עוֹשֵׁק:

1 For Solomon. Endow the king with Your justice, God, and the king's son with Your righteousness.

2 May he judge Your people with righteousness, and Your poor with justice.

3 The mountains will bear peace for the people, and the hills, righteousness.

4 He will bring justice to the afflicted of the people, save the destitute, and crush the oppressor.

PSALM 72

1 **For Solomon.** It appears likely that the psalm was written by David and dedicated to his son Solomon. **Endow the king,** apparently referring to David himself, **with Your justice, God;** enable me to carry out God's laws in the land. **And** endow **the king's son with Your righteousness;** may the king's son, his successor, be granted the ability to apply God's righteousness in the world.

2 **May he judge Your people with righteousness, and Your poor with justice.** *Tzedek,* "righteousness," is objective and absolute, and it is administered to the "people" at large, while *mishpat,* "justice," though not deviating from fairness, can take into account subjective factors such as financial hardship, and it should be applied to the "poor."

3 When justice reigns supreme, there is tranquility in the land. **The mountains will bear peace for the people.** Mountains often provide cover for ominous enemies who may lurk there, but in his day, the mountains will bear within them only peace, **and the hills** will bear **righteousness.**

4 **He will bring justice to the afflicted of the people,** as is his proper function. But beyond that, he will **save the destitute;** he will actively intervene to extend assistance to the most unfortunate, those whose needs go beyond fair justice. **And** he will **crush the oppressor** of

יִירָא֡וּךָ עִם־שָׁ֑מֶשׁ וְלִפְנֵ֥י יָרֵ֗חַ
דּ֣וֹר דּוֹרִֽים׃

5 They will fear You as long as the sun and moon endure, throughout the generations.

יֵ֭רֵד כְּמָטָ֣ר עַל־גֵּ֑ז כִּ֝רְבִיבִ֗ים
זַרְזִ֥יף אָֽרֶץ׃

6 It will descend like rain on fleece, like light showers that water the earth.

יִֽפְרַח־בְּיָמָ֥יו צַדִּ֑יק וְרֹ֥ב שָׁל֗וֹם
עַד־בְּלִ֥י יָרֵֽחַ׃

7 The righteous will flourish in his days; abundant peace until the moon is no more.

וְ֭יֵרְדְּ מִיָּ֣ם עַד־יָ֑ם וּ֝מִנָּהָ֗ר עַד־
אַפְסֵי־אָֽרֶץ׃

8 He will rule from sea to sea, from river to the ends of the land.

לְ֭פָנָיו יִכְרְע֣וּ צִיִּ֑ים וְ֝אֹיְבָ֗יו
עָפָ֥ר יְלַחֵֽכוּ׃

9 Seafarers will kneel before him, and his enemies will lick the dust.

---

the poor man. The king's judgments cannot always involve softheartedness and mercy; at times he must take fierce action to battle oppression.

5 **They will fear You as long as the sun and moon endure.** In this idyllic land, the people will be consistently God-fearing, with the continuity and regularity of the sun and the moon, **throughout the generations.**

6 **It,** the king's righteous administration of justice, **will descend like rain on fleece.** The blessings of justice will never be wasted; they will be fully absorbed, like rain on the woolly fleece of lambs. **Like light showers that** gently **water the earth.**

7 **The righteous will flourish in his days.** The king's virtuous rulership will serve as a kind of shield to protect other righteous people; **abundant peace until the moon is no more,** that is, for all time.

8 In order for the tranquility of this kingdom, initiated by the righteous administration of justice, to be secure, it must also be accompanied by peace with the neighboring peoples: **He will** exert full **rule from sea to sea,** throughout the territory of the Land of Israel, which is surrounded by seas, **from river to the ends of the land.** In the Bible, the word "river," when unspecified, refers to the Euphrates, which was actually a border of Solomon's territory.

9 **Seafarers** from distant lands who come to the Land of Israel **will kneel before him, and his enemies will** be brought so low that they will **lick the dust,** as it were.

מַלְכֵי תַרְשִׁישׁ וְאִיִּים מִנְחָה
יָשִׁיבוּ מַלְכֵי שְׁבָא וּסְבָא
אֶשְׁכָּר יַקְרִיבוּ:

^{יא} וְיִשְׁתַּחֲווּ־לוֹ כָל־מְלָכִים כָּל־
גּוֹיִם יַעַבְדוּהוּ:

^{יב} כִּי־יַצִּיל אֶבְיוֹן מְשַׁוֵּעַ וְעָנִי
וְאֵין־עֹזֵר לוֹ:

^{יג} יָחֹס עַל־דַּל וְאֶבְיוֹן וְנַפְשׁוֹת
אֶבְיוֹנִים יוֹשִׁיעַ:

^{יד} מִתּוֹךְ וּמֵחָמָס יִגְאַל נַפְשָׁם
וְיֵיקַר דָּמָם בְּעֵינָיו:

¹⁰ The kings of Tarshish and of the islands will bring tribute; the kings of Sheba and Seva will offer gifts.

¹¹ And all kings will bow down before him, all nations will serve him.

¹² For he will rescue the needy who cry out, and the poor man with no one to help him.

¹³ He will have compassion on the poor and needy, and the lives of the needy he will save.

¹⁴ He will redeem them from deceit and violence, and their blood will be precious in his sight.

---

¹⁰ But the king's power and influence will extend far beyond the borders of the Land of Israel. **The kings of Tarshish,** a faraway city variously identified, located in Spain according to some, **and of the islands will bring tribute** to the king. **The kings of Sheba and Seva,** in farthest Arabia or Africa, **will offer gifts.**

¹¹ **And all kings,** even from more distant lands than these, **will bow down before him; all nations will serve him** in one way or another.

¹² All this adoration of the king will take place not only because of his military strength but also in appreciation of his wise and compassionate leadership, **for he will rescue,** both in his own realm and abroad, **the needy who cry out** for assistance, **and the poor man with no one to help him.**

¹³ **He will have compassion on the poor and needy, and the lives of the needy he will save.**

¹⁴ **He will redeem them,** those powerless, vulnerable people, **from deceit and violence, and their blood,** their lives, **will be precious in his sight,** unlike typical monarchs, who are indifferent to the suffering of the poor and downtrodden.

טו וִיחִי וְיִתֶּן־לוֹ מִזְּהַב שְׁבָא
וְיִתְפַּלֵּל בַּעֲדוֹ תָמִיד כָּל־
הַיּוֹם יְבָרֲכֶנְהוּ:

טז יְהִי פִסַּת־בַּר ׀ בָּאָרֶץ בְּרֹאשׁ
הָרִים יִרְעַשׁ כַּלְּבָנוֹן פִּרְיוֹ
וְיָצִיצוּ מֵעִיר כְּעֵשֶׂב הָאָרֶץ:

יז יְהִי שְׁמוֹ ׀ לְעוֹלָם לִפְנֵי־
שֶׁמֶשׁ יָנִין שְׁמוֹ וְיִתְבָּרֲכוּ בוֹ   יִנּוֹן
כָּל־גּוֹיִם יְאַשְּׁרֻהוּ:

15 So will he live, and He will give him the gold of Sheba. People will pray for him always; they will bless him all day long.

16 There will be abundance of grain in the land, on the mountain tops. Its fruit will rustle as the Lebanon; there will be sprouting in the city like grass of the earth.

17 May his name endure forever. May his name be praised as long as the sun shines, and may all people bless themselves by him; may all the nations acclaim him.

---

15 **So will he live** well, **and He will give him the gold of Sheba;** God will grant him extreme wealth. **People will pray for him always; they will bless him all day long,** for he will be beloved by all.

16 In addition to the blessing of peace, **there will be abundance of grain in the land,** even **on the mountain tops,** where grain is not normally cultivated. **Its** trees will be so full of **fruit** that they **will rustle as** trees do in **the Lebanon,** a great forest. **There will be sprouting in the city like grass of the earth.** Useful vegetation will spring up like wild grass, in places that are not cultivated and sown.

17 This psalm sums up its prayer in the concluding verse: **May his name endure forever. May his name be praised as long as the sun shines,** that is, forever, **and may all people bless themselves by him;** may they consider him a paradigm of blessing. **May all the nations acclaim him,** or, more literally, may they declare: How fortunate he is! This verse marks the end of the content of the psalm. What follows are verses of conclusion to the second of the five sections that constitute the book of Psalms.

יח בָּרוּךְ ׀ יהוה אֱלֹהִים אֱלֹהֵי יִשְׂרָאֵל עֹשֵׂה נִפְלָאוֹת לְבַדּוֹ:

יט וּבָרוּךְ ׀ שֵׁם כְּבוֹדוֹ לְעוֹלָם וְיִמָּלֵא כְבוֹדוֹ אֶת־כָּל־הָאָרֶץ אָמֵן ׀ וְאָמֵן:

כ כָּלּוּ תְפִלּוֹת דָּוִד בֶּן־יִשָׁי:

18 Blessed be the Lord God, the God of Israel, who alone works wonders.

19 And blessed be His glorious name forever; may the whole earth be filled with His glory, amen and amen.

20 Here end the prayers of David son of Yishai.

---

18 **Blessed be the Lord God, the God of Israel, who alone works wonders.**
19 **And blessed be His glorious name forever; may the whole earth be filled with His glory, amen and amen.** This concept is mirrored, in Aramaic, in the Kaddish prayer.
20 **Here end the prayers of David son of Yishai.** Almost all the psalms up to this point were authored by David. Although some of the psalms that follow were also written by David, most are either unattributed or were authored by others.

BOOK THREE

WEDNESDAY

PSALM 73

A psalm that raises troubling questions about the way the world is run,
but also provides an answer to these questions.

מִזְמוֹר לְאָסָף אַךְ טוֹב
לְיִשְׂרָאֵל אֱלֹהִים לְבָרֵי לֵבָב:

וַאֲנִי כִּמְעַט נָטוּי רַגְלָי כְּאַיִן
שֻׁפְּכָה אֲשֻׁרָי:

כִּי־קִנֵּאתִי בַּהוֹלְלִים שְׁלוֹם
רְשָׁעִים אֶרְאֶה:

כִּי אֵין חַרְצֻבּוֹת לְמוֹתָם
וּבָרִיא אוּלָם:

בַּעֲמַל אֱנוֹשׁ אֵינֵמוֹ וְעִם־
אָדָם לֹא יְנֻגָּעוּ:

1 A psalm by Asaf. Surely God is good to Israel, to those pure of heart.

2 But as for me, my feet came close to swerving, my steps nearly spilling out,

3 for I was jealous of the revelers; I saw the well-being of the wicked.

4 For there are no chains to their death; indeed, they are healthy.

5 Theirs is no mortal toil; no plagues of man afflict them.

PSALM 73

1 **A psalm by Asaf. Surely God is good to Israel, to those pure of heart,** although this is often not evident at all, as the psalmist goes on to describe.

2 **But as for me,** upon pondering this reality, **my feet came close to swerving, my steps nearly spilling out.** Several factors can lead to a person's stumbling from the right path, as described in the coming verses.

3 **For I was jealous of the revelers; I saw the well-being of the wicked.** It seems as if the wicked are enjoying themselves since things are going well for them.

4 **For there are no chains to their death;** they do not seem to be fettered and on their way to death. **Indeed,** on the contrary, **they are** quite **healthy.**

5 **Theirs is no mortal toil;** they are not burdened by hard work as are other people. **No plagues** or illnesses that are normally the lot **of man afflict them.**

לָכֵן עֲנָקַתְמוֹ גַאֲוָה יַעֲטָף־
שִׁית חָמָס לָמוֹ:

יָצָא מֵחֵלֶב עֵינֵמוֹ עָבְרוּ
מַשְׂכִּיּוֹת לֵבָב:

יָמִיקוּ ׀ וִידַבְּרוּ בְרָע עֹשֶׁק
מִמָּרוֹם יְדַבֵּרוּ:

שַׁתּוּ בַשָּׁמַיִם פִּיהֶם וּלְשׁוֹנָם
תִּהֲלַךְ בָּאָרֶץ:

לָכֵן ׀ יָשִׁיב עַמּוֹ הֲלֹם וּמֵי
מָלֵא יִמָּצוּ לָמוֹ:   יָשֻׁב

6 Therefore, they carry pride
as their necklace; lawlessness
envelops them like a mantle.

7 Their eyes bulge from fatness;
the chambers of their hearts
overflow.

8 They are foul, speaking of
wickedness and wrongdoing;
they speak out from their
exalted place.

9 They set their mouth against
heaven; their tongue parades
across the land.

10 Therefore, His people are in
retreat, with only remnants of
the waters of abundance.

---

6 **Therefore,** since their lives go so smoothly, **they carry pride as their necklace;** they display their pride as if it were an ornament. **Lawlessness envelops them like a mantle.**

7 **Their eyes bulge from fatness;** they are so healthy and well fed that that their eyes seem to be protruding. **The chambers of their hearts overflow;** their sense of luxuriant well-being fills their hearts and even overflows into their external appearance.

8 **They are foul, speaking of wickedness and wrongdoing** toward others and toward God**; they speak out from their exalted place.** They have become befouled, continually speaking ill both of others and of God. Encountering no hardships or obstacles in their lives, they allow themselves to say whatever they wish.

9 **They set their mouth against heaven; their tongue,** spreading slander and calumny, **parades across the land.**

10 One of the evil things they say is: **Therefore, His people are in retreat, with only remnants of the waters of abundance.** The wicked believe that the righteous, and everyone else except themselves, receive only scraps of the bounty that they, the wicked, have accrued.

יא וְאָמְרוּ אֵיכָה יָדַע־אֵל וְיֵשׁ
דֵּעָה בְעֶלְיוֹן:

יב הִנֵּה־אֵלֶּה רְשָׁעִים וְשַׁלְוֵי
עוֹלָם הִשְׂגּוּ־חָיִל:

יג אַךְ־רִיק זִכִּיתִי לְבָבִי וָאֶרְחַץ
בְּנִקָּיוֹן כַּפָּי:

יד וָאֱהִי נָגוּעַ כָּל־הַיּוֹם
וְתוֹכַחְתִּי לַבְּקָרִים:

טו אִם־אָמַרְתִּי אֲסַפְּרָה כְמוֹ
הִנֵּה דוֹר בָּנֶיךָ בָגָדְתִּי:

טז וָאֲחַשְּׁבָה לָדַעַת זֹאת עָמָל
הוּא בְעֵינָי:

11 And they say: How does the Almighty know? Is there knowledge in the Most High?

12 Behold, they are wicked, at ease in their worldly attainments.

13 Indeed it is all in vain that I have purified my heart and washed clean my hands.

14 For I have been stricken all day long, and chastised every morning.

15 Had I said: I will speak of this, I would have betrayed generations of Your children.

16 When I sought to understand this, it seemed futile in my eyes,

---

11 **And** since they feel free to speak against heaven, as mentioned in verse 9, **they say: How does the Almighty know** what happens in the world, since He does not involve Himself with people's lives? **Is there knowledge in the Most High?** Their claim is that God neither knows nor cares about what happens in the world.

12 **Behold, they are wicked, at ease in their worldly attainments.**

13 In contrast to the ease and comfort of the wicked, the psalmist feels a sense of despair: **Indeed,** it seems that **it is all in vain that I have purified my heart and washed clean my hands** from wrongdoing.

14 **For** though I have followed the righteous path, **I have been stricken all day long, and chastised** with suffering and hardship **every morning.**

15 **Had I said: I will speak of this,** were I to give a detailed account of the suffering the righteous are made to endure, **I would have betrayed generations of Your children,** as it would cause children of future generations to stray from the right path.

16 **When I sought to understand this,** why there seems to be so much injustice in the world, **it seemed futile in my eyes;** I am at a loss when attempting to make sense of why it is that

עַד־אָבוֹא אֶל־מִקְדְּשֵׁי־אֵל ִ אָבִינָה לְאַחֲרִיתָם:

אַךְ בַּחֲלָקוֹת תָּשִׁית לָמוֹ ִ הִפַּלְתָּם לְמַשּׁוּאוֹת:

אֵיךְ הָיוּ לְשַׁמָּה כְרָגַע סָפוּ ִ תַמּוּ מִן־בַּלָּהוֹת:

כַּחֲלוֹם מֵהָקִיץ אֲדֹנָי בָּעִיר ׀ ִ צַלְמָם תִּבְזֶה:

כִּי יִתְחַמֵּץ לְבָבִי וְכִלְיוֹתַי ִ אֶשְׁתּוֹנָן:

17 until I entered the Temple of God; then I understood what would be their end.

18 Indeed, You set them on smooth paths; You cast them down to destruction.

19 How, in a moment, they are brought to waste, swept away, annihilated by terror.

20 Like a dream after awakening, Lord, in the city You make their image despised.

21 When my heart is embittered, and in my mind I am filled with thoughts,

---

the wicked prosper while the righteous suffer. Until here, the psalmist has described the despair of the righteous man trying to understand why the world operates as it does.

17 The psalmist now considers the matter further: I could not comprehend **until I entered the Temple of God,** where I was granted a greater level of understanding of God's manifestation in the world; **then I understood what would be their end.** I began to understand the true nature of the success of the wicked and the suffering of the righteous.

18 **Indeed, You set them on smooth paths;** God provides the wicked with a smooth path during their lives, and they are enticed to continue in their evil ways. But ultimately this path leads them only to disaster and destruction, as **You cast them down to destruction.**

19 And upon their downfall I see **how, in a moment, they are brought to waste, swept away, annihilated by terror.**

20 **Like a dream after awakening,** when the sleeper realizes that all he has experienced is nothing but a dream, **Lord,** when You reveal Yourself **in the city, You make their image despised.** As stated often in the Bible, all the success and good fortune of the wicked are temporary, and ultimately lead to their undoing.

21 Concerning the fate of the righteous, the psalmist reflects: **When my heart is embittered, and in my mind I am filled with thoughts,** because I do not comprehend their destiny,

כב וַאֲנִי־בַעַר וְלֹא אֵדָע בְּהֵמוֹת הָיִיתִי עִמָּךְ:

22 I am a boor, unknowing; I am like a beast before You.

כג וַאֲנִי תָמִיד עִמָּךְ אָחַזְתָּ בְּיַד־יְמִינִי:

23 Yet I am always with You; You grasp my right hand.

כד בַּעֲצָתְךָ תַנְחֵנִי וְאַחַר כָּבוֹד תִּקָּחֵנִי:

24 You guide me with Your counsel and lead me into honor.

כה מִי־לִי בַשָּׁמָיִם וְעִמְּךָ לֹא־חָפַצְתִּי בָאָרֶץ:

25 Whom else do I have in heaven? With You, I desire nothing on earth.

כו כָּלָה שְׁאֵרִי וּלְבָבִי צוּר־לְבָבִי וְחֶלְקִי אֱלֹהִים לְעוֹלָם:

26 My flesh and my heart may fail, but God is the strength of my heart and my portion forever.

כז כִּי־הִנֵּה רְחֵקֶיךָ יֹאבֵדוּ הִצְמַתָּה כָּל־זוֹנֶה מִמֶּךָּ:

27 Behold, those who are distant from You perish; You destroy all who stray from You.

---

22 I then remind myself that **I am a boor, unknowing** of God's mysterious ways; **I am like a beast before You.** I follow Him like an animal that is led by its master. Although this sort of blind obedience may seem to be lacking substance, it is in fact a tremendous privilege to be with God, as the psalmist acknowledges:

23 **Yet I am always with You; You grasp my right hand.** The fact that I choose to follow You means that You are leading me and giving me support.

24 **You guide me with Your counsel and lead me into honor.** In following God, I am close to Him; He leads me to the right and worthy path. When a person is occupied with yearning to draw close to God and to deepen his love of God, external matters of the world, including deprivation and suffering of the righteous, lose their significance.

25 **Whom else do I have in heaven** in whom I may trust? I recognize only You. I realize that despite all the worldly matters such as wealth, honor, and success that may be attained **with You, I desire nothing on earth;** they are of no real importance to me.

26 **My flesh and my heart may fail, but** that is inconsequential, for **God is the strength of my heart and my portion forever.**

27 **Behold, those who are distant from You** ultimately **perish** from this world, and certainly from the World to Come; **You destroy all who stray from You.**

כח וַאֲנִי ׀ קִרֲבַת אֱלֹהִים לִי טוֹב
שַׁתִּי ׀ בַּאדֹנָי יֱהֹוִה מַחְסִי
לְסַפֵּר כָּל־מַלְאֲכוֹתֶיךָ:

28 As for me, nearness to God
is good; I put my trust in the
Lord God, so I may tell of all
Your works.

PSALM 74

A psalm depicting Israel at a time of crisis, when enemies are prevailing. As in ancient times,
the psalmist entreats God to once again display His miracles and bring about salvation,
both for the sake of His name as God of Israel and for His covenant.

א מַשְׂכִּיל לְאָסָף לָמָה אֱלֹהִים
זָנַחְתָּ לָנֶצַח יֶעְשַׁן אַפְּךָ
בְּצֹאן מַרְעִיתֶךָ:

A contemplation by Asaf. Why,
God, have You abandoned us
forever, Your anger smoldering
against the sheep of Your fold?

ב זְכֹר עֲדָתְךָ ׀ קָנִיתָ קֶּדֶם
גָּאַלְתָּ שֵׁבֶט נַחֲלָתֶךָ הַר־
צִיּוֹן זֶה ׀ שָׁכַנְתָּ בּוֹ:

Remember Your congregation,
which You acquired of old,
which You redeemed as the
tribe of Your portion, this
Mount Zion, where You
dwelled.

---

28 **As for me, nearness to God is good; I put my trust in the Lord God, so I may tell of all
Your works.** This verse expresses the essence of the psalm, namely, the transition from an external
perception of the world, in which evil people appear to be successful and on the ascendant, to the
more introspective understanding that closeness to God is the greatest good.

PSALM 74
1 **A contemplation by Asaf.** The psalmist portrays a dire situation: **Why, God, have You
abandoned us forever, Your anger smoldering against the sheep of Your fold?** To the
psalmist, it appears as if God has abandoned His people in their time of distress.
2 **Remember Your congregation,** Israel, **which You acquired** for Yourself **of old, which You
redeemed as the tribe of Your portion.** And remember **this Mount Zion** as well, **where
You dwelled.**

הָרִימָה פְּעָמֶיךָ לְמַשֻּׁאוֹת
נֶצַח כָּל־הֵרַע אוֹיֵב בַּקֹּדֶשׁ:

שָׁאֲגוּ צֹרְרֶיךָ בְּקֶרֶב מוֹעֲדֶךָ
שָׂמוּ אוֹתֹתָם אֹתוֹת:

יִוָּדַע כְּמֵבִיא לְמָעְלָה
בִּסְבָךְ־עֵץ קַרְדֻּמּוֹת:

וְעַת פִּתּוּחֶיהָ יָּחַד בְּכַשִּׁיל
וְכֵילַפּוֹת יַהֲלֹמוּן:

שִׁלְחוּ בָאֵשׁ מִקְדָּשֶׁךָ לָאָרֶץ
חִלְּלוּ מִשְׁכַּן־שְׁמֶךָ:

אָמְרוּ בְלִבָּם נִינָם יָחַד שָׂרְפוּ
כָל־מוֹעֲדֵי־אֵל בָּאָרֶץ:

3 Lift Your footsteps toward the ongoing destruction, all that the enemy has inflicted on the Sanctuary.

4 Your foes roared within Your meeting place, setting their standards as signs.

5 It has become plainly known, as an axe in a thicket.

6 They smashed all its entrances with axes and hatchets.

7 They burned Your Sanctuary; they defiled the dwelling place of Your name, down to the ground.

8 They said in their heart: Let us utterly destroy them. They burned all the meeting places of God in the land.

---

3 **Lift Your footsteps** and bestir Yourself to action **toward the ongoing destruction** taking place on Mount Zion; see **all that the enemy has inflicted on the Sanctuary** itself.

4 **Your foes roared** with cries of victory **within Your meeting place,** where people once congregated in prayer and service to You, **setting their standards as signs;** their banners are now waving in our camp.

5 **It has become plainly known.** *Kemeivi lemaala,* translated here as "plainly," literally means "as one lifts something up high" to show to all what he is holding. The enemy spreads its destruction wantonly **as an axe** cuts down many branches **in a thicket.**

6 **They smashed all its entrances,** those of Jerusalem, **with axes and hatchets.**

7 **They burned Your Sanctuary; they defiled the dwelling place of Your name,** bringing **down** its glory **to the ground.**

8 **They said in their heart: Let us utterly destroy them. They burned all the meeting places of God in the land.** They destroyed not only Your Sanctuary but also other consecrated places. In later generations, such places would include synagogues and houses of study.

אוֹתֹתֵינוּ לֹא־רָ֠אִ֥ינוּ אֵֽין־ע֥וֹד
נָבִ֑יא וְלֹֽא־אִתָּ֥נוּ יֹדֵ֗עַ עַד־
מָֽה: ^ט

עַד־מָתַ֣י אֱ֭לֹהִים יְחָ֣רֶף צָ֑ר
יְנָ֘אֵ֤ץ אוֹיֵ֖ב שִׁמְךָ֣ לָנֶֽצַח: ^י

לָ֤מָּה תָשִׁ֣יב יָדְךָ֣ וִֽימִינֶ֑ךָ
מִקֶּ֖רֶב חֵיקֶ֣ךָ כַלֵּֽה: ^{יא}
חֵיקְךָ

וֵֽ֭אלֹהִים מַלְכִּ֣י מִקֶּ֑דֶם פֹּעֵ֥ל
יְ֝שׁוּע֗וֹת בְּקֶ֣רֶב הָאָֽרֶץ: ^{יב}

אַתָּ֤ה פוֹרַ֣רְתָּ בְעׇזְּךָ֣ יָ֑ם
שִׁבַּ֥רְתָּ רָאשֵׁ֥י תַ֝נִּינִ֗ים עַל־
הַמָּֽיִם: ^{יג}

9 We cannot see our signs; there is no longer any prophet nor is there any among us who knows for how long.

10 How long, God, will the foe revile? Will the enemy eternally mock Your name?

11 Why do You withhold Your hand? Draw forth Your right hand from Your bosom.

12 For God is my King from times of old, working deliverance in the midst of the land.

13 You shredded the sea with Your strength; You broke the heads of sea creatures on the waters.

---

9 **We cannot see our signs;** we no longer experience the miracles that were performed for us in the past. **There is no longer any prophet** to tell us when the destruction will finally come to an end. **Nor is there any among us who knows for how long** this situation will continue.

10 Therefore, we ask: **How long, God, will the foe revile? Will the enemy eternally mock Your name?**

11 **Why do You withhold Your hand** from sending it out to assist us? **Draw forth Your right hand from Your bosom.** We beseech You to draw forth not one, but both of Your hands, as it were.

12 **For God is my King from times of old,** and in the past You have indeed come to our aid, **working deliverance in the midst of the land.**

13 **You shredded the sea with Your strength; You broke the heads of sea creatures on the waters.** *Tanninim*, translated here as "sea creatures," are giant creatures inhabiting the depths of the seas, as alluded to in Genesis 1 and elsewhere.

יד אַתָּה רִצַּצְתָּ רָאשֵׁי לִוְיָתָן
תִּתְּנֶנּוּ מַאֲכָל לְעָם לְצִיִּים:

טו אַתָּה בָקַעְתָּ מַעְיָן וָנָחַל
אַתָּה הוֹבַשְׁתָּ נַהֲרוֹת אֵיתָן:

טז לְךָ יוֹם אַף־לְךָ לָיְלָה אַתָּה
הֲכִינוֹתָ מָאוֹר וָשָׁמֶשׁ:

יז אַתָּה הִצַּבְתָּ כָּל־גְּבוּלוֹת
אָרֶץ קַיִץ וָחֹרֶף אַתָּה
יְצַרְתָּם:

יח זְכָר־זֹאת אוֹיֵב חֵרֵף ׀ יהוה
וְעַם־נָבָל נִאֲצוּ שְׁמֶךָ:

יט אַל־תִּתֵּן לְחַיַּת נֶפֶשׁ תּוֹרֶךָ
חַיַּת עֲנִיֶּיךָ אַל־תִּשְׁכַּח
לָנֶצַח:

14 You crushed the heads of leviathan; You gave it as food to the nation, to the fleets.

15 You caused springs and streams to break forth; You dried up ever-flowing rivers.

16 The day is Yours, as Yours is the night; You founded light and the sun.

17 You laid down all the boundaries on earth. Summer and winter You created.

18 Remember this: The enemy who reviled the Lord and the base people who mocked Your name.

19 Do not deliver Your dove to the wild beast. Do not eternally forget the lives of Your needy ones.

---

14 **You crushed the heads of leviathan,** a giant sea creature; **You gave it as food to the nation, to the fleets,** feeding its flesh to people who never could have captured it on their own.

15 **You caused springs and streams to break forth** from the earth; **You dried up ever-flowing rivers.**

16 **The day is Yours, as Yours is the night,** for You rule at all times; **You founded** and created **light and the sun.**

17 **You laid down all the boundaries on earth;** You established the natural order of the world. **Summer and winter You created.**

18 And since Your power is so far-reaching, we beseech You: **Remember this: The enemy who reviled the Lord and the base people who mocked Your name.**

19 **Do not deliver Your dove,** the symbol of the people of Israel, **to the wild beast,** their vicious enemy. **Do not eternally forget the lives of Your needy ones.**

כ הַבֵּט לַבְּרִית כִּי־מָלְאוּ
מַחֲשַׁכֵּי־אֶרֶץ נְאוֹת חָמָס:

כא אַל־יָשֹׁב דַּךְ נִכְלָם עָנִי
וְאֶבְיוֹן יְהַלְלוּ שְׁמֶךָ:

כב קוּמָה אֱלֹהִים רִיבָה רִיבֶךָ
זְכֹר חֶרְפָּתְךָ מִנִּי־נָבָל כָּל־
הַיּוֹם:

כג אַל־תִּשְׁכַּח קוֹל צֹרְרֶיךָ
שְׁאוֹן קָמֶיךָ עֹלֶה תָמִיד:

20 Look to the covenant, for the
earth is full of dark places and
habitations of iniquity.

21 Let not the downtrodden one
be turned back and shamed;
let the poor and needy praise
Your name.

22 Arise, God, and strive on
behalf of Your cause. Recall the
abuse of the scoundrels against
You, all day long.

23 Do not forget the voice of Your
foes, the endless tumult of
those rising against You.

---

20 **Look to the covenant** You forged with us, and act to fulfill it, **for the earth is full of dark places and habitations of iniquity.**

21 **Let not the downtrodden one be turned back and shamed** because he has no one to protect him; **let the poor and needy praise Your name** after You have come to their aid.

22 **Arise, God, and strive on behalf of Your** own **cause** because, apart from harming us, the enemy is also desecrating Your name. **Recall the abuse of the scoundrels against You, all day long.**

23 **Do not forget the voice of Your foes, the endless tumult of those rising against You,** through their scorn and desecration of Your name. For all these reasons we beseech You to come to our salvation.

PSALM 75

A psalm mainly expressing gratitude to God, while also voicing the hope
that God will continue to provide deliverance in times of trouble.

לַמְנַצֵּחַ אַל־תַּשְׁחֵת מִזְמוֹר
לְאָסָף שִׁיר:

הוֹדִינוּ לְךָ ׀ אֱלֹהִים
הוֹדִינוּ וְקָרוֹב שְׁמֶךָ סִפְּרוּ
נִפְלְאוֹתֶיךָ:

כִּי אֶקַּח מוֹעֵד אֲנִי מֵישָׁרִים
אֶשְׁפֹּט:

נְמֹגִים אֶרֶץ וְכָל־יֹשְׁבֶיהָ
אָנֹכִי תִכַּנְתִּי עַמּוּדֶיהָ סֶּלָה:

אָמַרְתִּי לַהוֹלְלִים אַל־תָּהֹלּוּ
וְלָרְשָׁעִים אַל־תָּרִימוּ קָרֶן:

1. For the chief musician, *al tashḥet*, a psalm by Asaf, a song.

2. We give thanks to You, God, we give thanks, and Your name is near; they have told of Your wonders.

3. When I set a time, I will judge with equity.

4. The earth and all its inhabitants melt away; I set firm its pillars, Selah.

5. I said to the revelers: Do not revel. And to the wicked: Do not raise a horn.

PSALM 75

1. **For the chief musician, *al tashḥet*, a psalm by Asaf, a song.**

2. **We give thanks to You, God, we give thanks, and Your name is near** to us; it is constantly in our mouths. **They,** our forefathers and teachers, **have told** us **of your wonders.**

3. Here God speaks, as it were: **When I set a time,** when the proper time arrives, **I will judge** the world **with equity.**

4. **The earth and all its inhabitants melt away, I set firm its pillars,** and since I created them, I can either shake the foundations of the earth or keep them standing, **Selah.**

5. Now the psalmist speaks again: **I said to the revelers: Do not revel,** for your joy will not last forever. **And to the wicked I said: Do not raise a horn.** "Raising the horn" in biblical idiom refers to showing off one's pride or status.

אַל־תָּרִ֣ימוּ לַמָּר֣וֹם קַרְנְכֶ֑ם
תְּדַבְּר֖וּ בְצַוָּ֣אר עָתָֽק:

⁶ Do not raise your horn on high,
speaking with insolent pride.

כִּ֤י לֹ֣א מִמּוֹצָ֣א וּמִֽמַּעֲרָ֑ב וְלֹ֝֗א
מִמִּדְבַּ֥ר הָרִֽים:

⁷ For it is not from the east
or the west; not from the
wilderness or the mountains,

כִּֽי־אֱלֹהִ֥ים שֹׁפֵ֑ט זֶ֥ה יַ֝שְׁפִּ֗יל
וְזֶ֥ה יָרִֽים:

⁸ but it is God who is the Judge;
He humbles this one and raises
that one.

כִּ֤י כ֪וֹס בְּֽיַד־יְהֹוָ֡ה וְיַ֤יִן חָמַ֨ר ׀
מָ֥לֵא מֶסֶךְ֮ וַיַּגֵּ֪ר מִ֫זֶּ֥ה אַךְ־
שְׁמָרֶ֗יהָ יִמְצ֥וּ יִשְׁתּ֑וּ כֹּ֝֗ל
רִשְׁעֵי־אָֽרֶץ:

⁹ For a cup is in the hand of the
Lord, with foaming wine, filled
with spices, and He pours from
it. But the dregs are sucked,
drunk by all the wicked of
the earth.

וַ֭אֲנִי אַגִּ֣יד לְעֹלָ֑ם אֲ֝זַמְּרָ֗ה
לֵאלֹהֵ֥י יַעֲקֹֽב:

¹⁰ As for me, I will tell it forever; I
will sing to the God of Jacob.

וְכָל־קַרְנֵ֣י רְשָׁעִ֣ים אֲגַדֵּ֑עַ
תְּ֝רוֹמַ֗מְנָה קַרְנ֥וֹת צַדִּֽיק:

¹¹ All the horns of the wicked I
will cut off, while the horns of
the righteous shall be raised.

---

⁶ **Do not raise your horn on high** in haughtiness and contempt, **speaking with insolent pride,** literally, "with a stiff neck," stretched out as a sign of pride and arrogance.

⁷ **For it is not from the east or the west** that victory and salvation come; **not from the wilderness** of the south **or the mountains** of the north,

⁸ **but it is God who is the Judge; He humbles this one and raises that one.** In the end, it is only God who has the power to determine who will rise and who will fall.

⁹ **For a cup is in the hand of the Lord, with foaming wine, filled with spices, and He pours from it.** The cup of wine may symbolize either deliverance or vengeance. **But the dregs,** which are not fit for proper drinking, **are sucked,** their extract **drunk by all the wicked of the earth.**

¹⁰ **As for me, I will tell it**, God's praise, **forever; I will sing to the God of Jacob.**

¹¹ The last verse is spoken by God: **All the horns of the wicked I will cut off, while the horns of the righteous shall be raised.**

PSALM 76

A psalm of praise over victory and the revelation of God.

א לַמְנַצֵּחַ בִּנְגִינֹת מִזְמוֹר
לְאָסָף שִׁיר:

ב נוֹדָע בִּיהוּדָה אֱלֹהִים
בְּיִשְׂרָאֵל גָּדוֹל שְׁמוֹ:

ג וַיְהִי בְשָׁלֵם סֻכּוֹ וּמְעוֹנָתוֹ
בְצִיּוֹן:

ד שָׁמָּה שִׁבַּר רִשְׁפֵי־קָשֶׁת מָגֵן
וְחֶרֶב וּמִלְחָמָה סֶלָה:

ה נָאוֹר אַתָּה אַדִּיר מֵהַרְרֵי־
טָרֶף:

ו אֶשְׁתּוֹלְלוּ ׀ אַבִּירֵי לֵב נָמוּ
שְׁנָתָם וְלֹא־מָצְאוּ כָל־
אַנְשֵׁי־חַיִל יְדֵיהֶם:

1 For the chief musician, on stringed instruments, a psalm by Asaf, a song.

2 God is known in Judah; His name is great in Israel.

3 His abode is in Shalem, His dwelling place in Zion.

4 There He broke the sparks of the bow, shield and sword, and war, Selah.

5 You are lustrous, mightier than mountains of prey.

6 The stout-hearted ran rampant. They fell into a stupor, and warriors could not find their hands.

PSALM 76

1 **For the chief musician, on stringed instruments, a psalm by Asaf, a song.**

2 **God is known in Judah; His name is great in Israel.**

3 **His abode is in Shalem,** which is another name for Jerusalem, **His dwelling place in Zion.**

4 **There,** near Jerusalem, **He broke the sparks of the** enemy's **bow,** a poetic depiction of arrows; and there he also broke the enemy's **shield and sword, and war, Selah.**

5 **You,** God, **are lustrous, mightier than mountains of prey,** tall and threatening mountains in which beasts of prey roam. All of these are subservient to God.

6 **The stout-hearted** men of the enemy's camp **ran rampant** and were inattentive to what was happening around them. Alternatively, **they fell into a stupor,** and this prevented them from recognizing the impending doom, **and warriors could not find their hands.** The enemies, taken by surprise, were helpless to respond.

מִגַּעֲרָתְךָ אֱלֹהֵי יַעֲקֹב נִרְדָּם וְרֶכֶב וָסוּס: ז

7 At Your rebuke, God of Jacob, it slumbered, along with chariot and horse.

אַתָּה ׀ נוֹרָא אַתָּה וּמִי־יַעֲמֹד לְפָנֶיךָ מֵאָז אַפֶּךָ: ח

8 As for You, You are awesome; who can stand before You at the time of Your anger?

מִשָּׁמַיִם הִשְׁמַעְתָּ דִּין אֶרֶץ יָרְאָה וְשָׁקָטָה: ט

9 From heaven You pronounced judgment. The earth was frightened and became calm,

בְּקוּם־לַמִּשְׁפָּט אֱלֹהִים לְהוֹשִׁיעַ כָּל־עַנְוֵי־אֶרֶץ סֶלָה: י

10 when God arose in judgment, to deliver all the humble of the earth, Selah.

כִּי־חֲמַת אָדָם תּוֹדֶךָּ שְׁאֵרִית חֵמֹת תַּחְגֹּר: יא

11 For wrathful man will praise You; You stem the remnants of wrath.

נִדְרוּ וְשַׁלְּמוּ לַיהוה אֱלֹהֵיכֶם כָּל־סְבִיבָיו יֹבִילוּ שַׁי לַמּוֹרָא: יב

12 Make vows to the Lord your God and fulfill them; let all who are around Him bring gifts to the Awesome One.

---

7 **At Your rebuke, God of Jacob, it,** the enemy's camp, **slumbered, along with** the **chariot** driver **and horse.** In truth, even if they had been awake, they would have been powerless against You.

8 **As for You, You are awesome; who can stand before You at the time of Your anger?**

9 **From heaven You pronounced judgment. The earth was frightened** by God's might, **and** then it **became calm,** after You destroyed the enemy,

10 **when God arose in judgment, to deliver all the humble of the earth, Selah.**

11 **For wrathful man will praise You;** violent aggressors will realize that they are powerless against You, and they will have no choice but to surrender and be grateful for their survival. **You stem the remnants of wrath.** You will rein in what remains of their wrath, allowing it expression only when You wish it.

12 The psalmist closes by imploring everyone to give thanks to God for their salvation: **Make vows to the Lord your God** in thanksgiving for His salvation, **and fulfill them; let all who are around Him bring gifts to the Awesome One.**

יְבַצֹר רוּחַ נְגִידִים נוֹרָא
לְמַלְכֵי־אָרֶץ:

13 He will cut off the spirit of princes, inspiring awe in kings of the earth.

PSALM 77

A psalm describing a time of suffering and calamity, in which the psalmist finds comfort in recalling God's previous deeds on behalf of His people.

יְדוּ

לַמְנַצֵּחַ עַל־יְדִיתוּן לְאָסָף
מִזְמוֹר:

קוֹלִי אֶל־אֱלֹהִים וְאֶצְעָקָה
קוֹלִי אֶל־אֱלֹהִים וְהַאֲזִין
אֵלָי:

בְּיוֹם צָרָתִי אֲדֹנָי דָּרַשְׁתִּי
יָדִי ׀ לַיְלָה נִגְּרָה וְלֹא תָפוּג
מֵאֲנָה הִנָּחֵם נַפְשִׁי:

1 For the chief musician, for *Yedutun*, a psalm by Asaf.

2 I raise my voice to God and cry out; I raise my voice, and He listens to me.

3 On my day of trouble, I beseeched the Lord with my hand; at night it flowed without cease, and my soul refused to be comforted.

טו לחודש
15th day
of month

---

13 **He will cut off the spirit of princes,** and all will admit that His might is great, **inspiring awe in kings of the earth.**

PSALM 77

1 **For the chief musician, for *Yedutun*.** The term *Yedutun* also appears in Psalm 62. It may be the name of a musical instrument, a type of psalm, the name of a poet, or a type of melody. **A psalm by Asaf.**

2 **I raise my voice to God and cry out; I raise my voice, and He listens to me.**

3 **On my day of trouble, I beseeched the Lord with my hand,** raising it up in prayer; **at night it,** my eye, **flowed** with tears **without cease** because of the magnitude of my overwhelming troubles, **and my soul refused to be comforted.**

אֶזְכְּרָה אֱלֹהִים וְאֶהֱמָיָה אָשִׂיחָה ׀ וְתִתְעַטֵּף רוּחִי סֶלָה:

⁴ When I remember God, I moan; I cry out until my spirit becomes faint, Selah.

אָחַזְתָּ שְׁמֻרוֹת עֵינָי נִפְעַמְתִּי וְלֹא אֲדַבֵּר:

⁵ You grasp my eyelids; I am agitated and cannot speak.

חִשַּׁבְתִּי יָמִים מִקֶּדֶם שְׁנוֹת עוֹלָמִים:

⁶ I ponder the days of old, the years of long ago.

אֶזְכְּרָה נְגִינָתִי בַּלָּיְלָה עִם־לְבָבִי אָשִׂיחָה וַיְחַפֵּשׂ רוּחִי:

⁷ I remember my song in the night; I meditate with my heart, and my spirit searches.

הַלְעוֹלָמִים יִזְנַח ׀ אֲדֹנָי וְלֹא־יֹסִיף לִרְצוֹת עוֹד:

⁸ Will the Lord abandon forever? Will He never again find favor?

הֶאָפֵס לָנֶצַח חַסְדּוֹ גָּמַר אֹמֶר לְדֹר וָדֹר:

⁹ Has His kindness forever come to an end? Is His decision final for all generations?

---

⁴ **When I remember God, I moan; I cry out** because of my woes **until my spirit becomes faint, Selah.**

⁵ But I cannot pray or cry out to You at all times, for **You grasp my eyelids,** preventing me from sleeping; moreover, **I am agitated and cannot speak.**

⁶ In my present state of distress, **I ponder** the contrast with **the days of old, the years of long ago.**

⁷ **I remember my song in the night,** when I used to thank God for His kindness; **I meditate with my heart, and my spirit searches.** Alongside these memories, my spirit has many questions that I continually turn over in my mind:

⁸ **Will the Lord abandon forever? Will He never again find favor?** Here and in the next two verses, the psalmist ruminates about God's ongoing relationship with His people.

⁹ **Has His kindness forever come to an end? Is His decision** to punish us **final for all generations?**

הֲשָׁכַח חַנּוֹת אֵל אִם־קָפַץ
בְּאַף רַחֲמָיו סֶלָה: י

וָאֹמַר חַלּוֹתִי הִיא שְׁנוֹת
יְמִין עֶלְיוֹן: יא

אֶזְכִּיר מַעַלְלֵי־יָהּ כִּי־אֶזְכְּרָה אֶזְכּ
מִקֶּדֶם פִּלְאֶךָ: יב

וְהָגִיתִי בְכָל־פָּעֳלֶךָ
וּבַעֲלִילוֹתֶיךָ אָשִׂיחָה: יג

אֱלֹהִים בַּקֹּדֶשׁ דַּרְכֶּךָ מִי־אֵל
גָּדוֹל כֵּאלֹהִים: יד

אַתָּה הָאֵל עֹשֵׂה פֶלֶא
הוֹדַעְתָּ בָעַמִּים עֻזֶּךָ: טו

¹⁰ Has God forgotten to be gracious? Has He in anger closed off His mercy? Selah.

¹¹ Then I said: This is my prayer, the years of the Most High's right hand.

¹² I remember the deeds of the Lord, when I recall Your wonders of old.

¹³ I meditate on all of Your work, telling of Your glorious deeds.

¹⁴ God, Your way is in holiness. What god is as great as God?

¹⁵ You are the Almighty who works wonders; You proclaimed Your strength among the peoples.

---

¹⁰ **Has God forgotten to be gracious** and forgive us? **Has He in anger closed off His mercy** and compassion? **Selah.**

¹¹ **Then I said** to myself: **This is my prayer,** to reflect upon **the years of the Most High's right hand,** a very long span of time that includes periods of divine grace as well as times when God hid His presence. The psalmist prays to be able to perceive and understand this broader view of things.

¹² The psalmist recalls those periods of divine grace: **I remember the deeds of the Lord, when I recall Your wonders of old.**

¹³ **I meditate on all of Your work, telling of Your glorious deeds** of the past.

¹⁴ **God, Your way is in holiness;** when You reveal Yourself, You are perceived with holiness and exaltedness. **What god is as great as God?**

¹⁵ **You are the Almighty who works wonders; You proclaimed Your strength among the peoples.**

^{טז} גָּאַ֣לְתָּ בִּזְר֣וֹעַ עַמֶּ֑ךָ בְּנֵי־
יַעֲקֹ֖ב וְיוֹסֵ֣ף סֶֽלָה׃

^{יז} רָא֘וּךָ֤ מַּ֨יִם ׀ אֱֽלֹהִ֗ים רָא֣וּךָ
מַּ֣יִם יָחִ֑ילוּ אַ֝֗ף יִרְגְּז֥וּ תְהֹמֽוֹת׃

^{יח} זֹ֤רְמוּ מַ֨יִם ׀ עָב֗וֹת ק֖וֹל
נָתְנ֣וּ שְׁחָקִ֑ים אַף־חֲ֝צָצֶ֗יךָ
יִתְהַלָּֽכוּ׃

^{יט} ק֤וֹל רַעַמְךָ֨ ׀ בַּגַּלְגַּ֗ל הֵאִ֣ירוּ
בְרָקִ֣ים תֵּבֵ֑ל רָגְזָ֖ה וַתִּרְעַ֣שׁ
הָאָֽרֶץ׃

^כ בַּיָּ֤ם דַּרְכֶּ֗ךָ וּֽשְׁבִ֖ילְךָ בְּמַ֣יִם
רַבִּ֑ים וְ֝עִקְּבוֹתֶ֗יךָ לֹ֣א נֹדָֽעוּ׃

וּשְׁבִילְךָ

¹⁶ With Your arm, You redeemed
Your people, the sons of Jacob
and Joseph, Selah.

¹⁷ The waters saw you, God;
the waters saw You and were
frightened, and the waters of
the deep trembled.

¹⁸ The clouds poured out water;
the skies gave voice as Your
arrows darted about.

¹⁹ Your thunder was
all-encompassing; lightning
lit up the world. The earth
trembled and quaked.

²⁰ Your way was through the sea,
Your path through the mighty
waters. Your footprints left
no trace.

---

¹⁶ **With Your arm,** Your strength, **You redeemed Your people, the sons of Jacob and Joseph, Selah.**

¹⁷ The psalmist enumerates several instances of God's revelation: **The waters** of the Red Sea **saw you, God; the waters saw You and were frightened,** as it were, into receding and parting, **and the waters of the deep trembled.**

¹⁸ At that time, **the clouds poured out water; the skies gave voice as Your arrows,** bolts of lightning, **darted about.**

¹⁹ **Your thunder was all-encompassing; lightning lit up the world. The earth trembled and quaked.**

²⁰ **Your way was through the** Red **Sea, Your path through the mighty waters,** clearing a trail through it for us to pass; **Your footprints left no trace.** When the splitting of the sea was over, the waters returned to their place, and there was no sign that the event had occurred.

כא נָחִיתָ כַצֹּאן עַמֶּךָ בְּיַד־מֹשֶׁה
וְאַהֲרֹן:

²¹ Like a flock You led Your people in the hands of Moses and Aaron.

PSALM 78

An epic psalm covering the period from the exodus through the establishment of David's kingship, including descriptions of the ten plagues, the Israelites' journeys in the wilderness, and the conquest of the Land of Israel. The psalm focuses on God's continuing redemption of the people despite their many sins.

א מַשְׂכִּיל לְאָסָף הַאֲזִינָה עַמִּי
תּוֹרָתִי הַטּוּ אָזְנְכֶם לְאִמְרֵי־
פִי:

¹ A contemplation by Asaf. Listen, my people, to my teaching. Incline your ears to the words of my mouth.

ב אֶפְתְּחָה בְמָשָׁל פִּי אַבִּיעָה
חִידוֹת מִנִּי־קֶדֶם:

² My mouth will open with a tale; I will recount stories from ancient times

---

²¹ Thereafter, **like a flock You led Your people** to the Land of Israel, **in the hands of Moses and Aaron.** When I consider this, I find that I still have hope, despite all current troubles.

PSALM 78

¹ **A contemplation by Asaf.** As with other psalms containing the heading *maskil*, "contemplation," such as 32, 42, and 44, the focus of this psalm is contemplative and instructive rather than prayerful. It describes historical events with a poetic flair, and for this reason, some of the historical details and order of events differ from the way in which they appear in the Torah. The lengthy psalm begins with several statements of moral instruction. **Listen, my people, to my teaching. Incline your ears to the words of my mouth.**

² **My mouth will open with a tale.** The word *mashal*, which in modern Hebrew pertains to a parable, refers here to a historical story told in poetic fashion. **I will recount stories from ancient times.** Here too, the word *ḥidot* should not be understood in its later sense of "riddles" or "challenging questions"; rather, it refers to artistically worded narratives (see also 49:5).

אֲשֶׁר שָׁמַעְנוּ וַנֵּדָעֵם ‎^ג
וַאֲבוֹתֵינוּ סִפְּרוּ־לָנוּ:

לֹא נְכַחֵד ׀ מִבְּנֵיהֶם לְדוֹר ‎^ד
אַחֲרוֹן מְסַפְּרִים תְּהִלּוֹת
יְהֹוָה וֶעֱזוּזוֹ וְנִפְלְאֹתָיו אֲשֶׁר
עָשָׂה:

וַיָּקֶם עֵדוּת ׀ בְּיַעֲקֹב וְתוֹרָה ‎^ה
שָׂם בְּיִשְׂרָאֵל אֲשֶׁר צִוָּה אֶת־
אֲבוֹתֵינוּ לְהוֹדִיעָם לִבְנֵיהֶם:

לְמַעַן יֵדְעוּ ׀ דּוֹר אַחֲרוֹן ‎^ו
בָּנִים יִוָּלֵדוּ יָקֻמוּ וִיסַפְּרוּ
לִבְנֵיהֶם:

וְיָשִׂימוּ בֵאלֹהִים כִּסְלָם וְלֹא ‎^ז
יִשְׁכְּחוּ מַעַלְלֵי־אֵל וּמִצְוֹתָיו
יִנְצֹרוּ:

3 that we heard and knew, for our fathers told us.

4 We will not conceal it from their children, but will tell a later generation of the praises of the Lord and His might, and the wonders He has done.

5 He set a precept in Jacob and imparted a teaching in Israel, which He commanded our fathers to make known to their children,

6 so that the generation to come, children not yet born, may know; they will arise and tell their own children,

7 so that they place their trust in God and not forget the Almighty's deeds, and keep His commandments,

---

3 **that we heard and knew** from tradition, **for our fathers told us.**

4 The psalmist continues that tradition referred to in the previous verse: **We will not conceal it from their children, but will tell a later generation of the praises of the Lord and His might, and the wonders He has done.**

5 **He set a precept in Jacob and imparted a teaching in Israel,** referring to the Torah in its entirety, among which are precepts commemorating certain historical events, **which He commanded our fathers to make known to their children,**

6 **so that the generation to come, children not yet born, may know** about these events that their fathers witnessed, and **they** in turn **will arise and tell their own children.**

7 Above and beyond historical interest, the lessons have moral benefit, **so that they,** the new generations, will **place their trust in God, and not forget the Almighty's deeds, and keep His commandments,**

ח 8 וְלֹא יִהְיוּ ׀ כַּאֲבוֹתָם דּוֹר
סוֹרֵר וּמֹרֶה דּוֹר לֹא־הֵכִין
לִבּוֹ וְלֹא־נֶאֶמְנָה אֶת־אֵל
רוּחוֹ:

and not be like their fathers, a stubborn and rebellious generation that was not steadfast, and whose spirit was not faithful to God.

ט 9 בְּנֵי־אֶפְרַיִם נוֹשְׁקֵי רוֹמֵי־
קֶשֶׁת הָפְכוּ בְּיוֹם קְרָב:

The sons of Ephraim were archers equipped with bows, yet they turned back on the day of battle.

י 10 לֹא שָׁמְרוּ בְּרִית אֱלֹהִים
וּבְתוֹרָתוֹ מֵאֲנוּ לָלֶכֶת:

They did not keep the covenant of God, and they refused to walk in His law.

יא 11 וַיִּשְׁכְּחוּ עֲלִילוֹתָיו וְנִפְלְאוֹתָיו
אֲשֶׁר הֶרְאָם:

They forgot His deeds and the marvels He had shown them;

יב 12 נֶגֶד אֲבוֹתָם עָשָׂה פֶלֶא
בְּאֶרֶץ מִצְרַיִם שְׂדֵה־צֹעַן:

He had wrought wonders before their fathers in the land of Egypt, in the field of Tzo'an.

---

8 **and** they will **not be like** many of **their fathers,** forefathers, **a stubborn and rebellious generation that was not steadfast, and whose spirit was not faithful to God,** as the psalmist now goes on to elaborate.

9 **The sons of Ephraim were archers equipped with bows, yet they turned back** and fled **on the day of battle.** It is not completely clear to which historical event this verse is referring. Some midrashim speak of an early attempt by the sons of Ephraim to leave Egypt before the time of the exodus.[1] The verse can also be understood as a reference to the kingdom of Ephraim, as the northern Kingdom of Israel is sometimes known, which abandoned the laws of the Torah.

10 **They did not keep the covenant of God, and they refused to walk in His law.**

11 **They forgot His deeds and the marvels He had shown them;**

12 **He had wrought wonders before their fathers in the land of Egypt, in the field of Tzo'an,** a poetic term for Egypt, as Tzo'an was a prominent Egyptian city that once served as its capital.

יג בָּקַע יָם וַיַּעֲבִירֵם וַיַּצֶּב־מַיִם
כְּמוֹ־נֵד:

יד וַיַּנְחֵם בֶּעָנָן יוֹמָם וְכָל־
הַלַּיְלָה בְּאוֹר אֵשׁ:

טו יְבַקַּע צֻרִים בַּמִּדְבָּר וַיַּשְׁקְ
כִּתְהֹמוֹת רַבָּה:

טז וַיּוֹצִא נוֹזְלִים מִסָּלַע וַיּוֹרֶד
כַּנְּהָרוֹת מָיִם:

יז וַיּוֹסִיפוּ עוֹד לַחֲטֹא־לוֹ
לַמְרוֹת עֶלְיוֹן בַּצִּיָּה:

יח וַיְנַסּוּ־אֵל בִּלְבָבָם לִשְׁאָל־
אֹכֶל לְנַפְשָׁם:

[13] He split the sea and led them through; He stood the waters in a heap.

[14] Then He led them with a cloud by day, and throughout the night with the light of fire.

[15] He split boulders in the desert and gave them drink, as from the abundant depths.

[16] And He brought forth streams from the rock, making the water come down like rivers.

[17] Yet they continued to sin against Him, to rebel against the Most High in the parched land.

[18] In their hearts they tested the Almighty, asking food for themselves.

---

[13] The psalmist enumerates the most noteworthy of the wonders wrought in Egypt: **He split the** Red **Sea and led them,** the children of Israel, **through** it; **He stood the waters** of the Red Sea **in a heap,** with walls of water forming on either side of the passing Israelites.

[14] **Then He led them** through the wilderness **with a cloud by day, and throughout the night with the light of fire.**

[15] **He split boulders in the desert and gave them drink,** with water gushing forth from the rocks as plentiful **as** that which springs **from the abundant depths.**

[16] **And He brought forth streams from the rock, making the water come down like rivers** in the middle of the desert.

[17] The psalm goes on to recount the Israelites' response to these miracles: **Yet they continued to sin against Him, to rebel against the Most High in the parched land.**

[18] **In their hearts they tested the Almighty, asking food for themselves,** as described in the Torah.[2]

יט וַיְדַבְּרוּ בֵּאלֹהִים אָמְרוּ
הֲיוּכַל אֵל לַעֲרֹךְ שֻׁלְחָן
בַּמִּדְבָּר:

19 And they spoke against God, saying: Can the Almighty prepare a table in the wilderness?

כ הֵן הִכָּה־צוּר ׀ וַיָּזוּבוּ מַיִם
וּנְחָלִים יִשְׁטֹפוּ הֲגַם־לֶחֶם
יוּכַל תֵּת אִם־יָכִין שְׁאֵר
לְעַמּוֹ:

20 Behold, He struck the rock so that waters gushed out and streams were flowing. Can He provide bread as well? Will He provide meat for His people?

כא לָכֵן ׀ שָׁמַע יהוה וַיִּתְעַבָּר
וְאֵשׁ נִשְּׂקָה בְיַעֲקֹב וְגַם־אַף
עָלָה בְיִשְׂרָאֵל:

21 Thus the Lord was enraged when He heard this, and fire flared against Jacob, and wrath arose against Israel,

כב כִּי לֹא הֶאֱמִינוּ בֵּאלֹהִים וְלֹא
בָטְחוּ בִּישׁוּעָתוֹ:

22 for they did not believe in God and did not trust in His deliverance.

כג וַיְצַו שְׁחָקִים מִמָּעַל וְדַלְתֵי
שָׁמַיִם פָּתָח:

23 He commanded the skies above and opened the doors of heaven,

---

19 **And they spoke against God,** putting Him to the test, **saying: Can the Almighty prepare a table in the wilderness?**

20 **Behold, He struck the rock so that waters gushed out and streams were flowing. Can He provide bread as well? Will He provide meat for His people?**[3]

21 **Thus the Lord was enraged when He heard this, and fire flared against Jacob, and wrath arose against Israel,**

22 **for they did not believe in God and did not trust in His deliverance.** The children of Israel were tested by these experiences in the wilderness, and they were found wanting.

23 Nevertheless, in response to their demands, **He commanded the skies above and opened the doors of heaven,**

^{כד} וַיַּמְטֵ֬ר עֲלֵיהֶ֣ם מָ֣ן לֶאֱכֹ֑ל
וּדְגַן־שָׁ֝מַ֗יִם נָ֣תַן לָֽמוֹ׃

^{כה} לֶ֣חֶם אַ֭בִּירִים אָ֣כַל אִ֑ישׁ
צֵידָ֓ה שָׁלַ֖ח לָהֶ֣ם לָשֹֽׂבַע׃

^{כו} יַסַּ֣ע קָ֭דִים בַּשָּׁמָ֑יִם וַיְנַהֵ֖ג
בְּעֻזּ֣וֹ תֵימָֽן׃

^{כז} וַיַּמְטֵ֬ר עֲלֵיהֶ֣ם כֶּעָפָ֣ר שְׁאֵ֑ר
וּֽכְח֥וֹל יַ֝מִּ֗ים ע֣וֹף כָּנָֽף׃

^{כח} וַ֭יַּפֵּל בְּקֶ֣רֶב מַחֲנֵ֑הוּ סָ֝בִ֗יב
לְמִשְׁכְּנֹתָֽיו׃

^{כט} וַיֹּאכְל֣וּ וַיִּשְׂבְּע֣וּ מְאֹ֑ד
וְ֝תַאֲוָתָ֗ם יָבִ֥א לָהֶֽם׃

24 and He rained down manna for them to eat; grain from heaven He gave them.

25 Men ate the bread of angels; He sent them provisions to satiation.

26 He stirred the east wind in the heavens; He drove the south wind with His might.

27 And He rained meat upon them like dust, winged fowl like sand of the seas.

28 He let it fall in the midst of their camp, encircling their dwellings,

29 so they ate and were exceedingly sated; He brought them their desire.

---

24 **and He rained down manna for them to eat; grain from heaven,** again referring to the manna, **He gave them.**

25 **Men ate the bread of angels; He sent them provisions to satiation.**

26 Having supplied the people with abundant food in the form of manna, He addressed their desire for meat: **He stirred the east wind in the heavens; He drove the south wind with His might.**

27 **And He rained meat upon them like dust, winged fowl like sand of the seas.** Both "meat" and "winged fowl" refer to the quail that God sent to the people to eat.[4]

28 **He let it fall in the midst of their camp, encircling their dwellings,**

29 **so they ate and were exceedingly sated; He brought them their desire** that they had requested.

לֹא־זָרוּ מִתַּאֲוָתָם עֹוד
אָכְלָם בְּפִיהֶם:

וְאַף אֱלֹהִים ׀ עָלָה בָהֶם
וַיַּהֲרֹג בְּמִשְׁמַנֵּיהֶם וּבַחוּרֵי
יִשְׂרָאֵל הִכְרִיעַ:

בְּכָל־זֹאת חָטְאוּ־עֹוד וְלֹא
הֶאֱמִינוּ בְּנִפְלְאוֹתָיו:

וַיְכַל־בַּהֶבֶל יְמֵיהֶם וּשְׁנוֹתָם
בַּבֶּהָלָה:

אִם־הֲרָגָם וּדְרָשׁוּהוּ ׀ וְשָׁבוּ
וְשִׁחֲרוּ־אֵל:

וַיִּזְכְּרוּ כִּי־אֱלֹהִים צוּרָם וְאֵל
עֶלְיוֹן גֹּאֲלָם:

30 They had not yet taken leave of their desire. Their food was still in their mouths

31 when the anger of God rose against them. He slew the best among them; He struck down young warriors of Israel.

32 Nonetheless, they continued to sin and did not believe in His wonders.

33 He ended their days in futility, and their years in terror.

34 When He slew them, then they sought Him out; they returned and searched for the Almighty.

35 They remembered that God was their rock, the Almighty Most High, their Redeemer.

---

30 The psalmist recounts what happened next, reviewing the events as recorded in the Torah:[5] **They had not yet taken leave of their desire. Their food was still in their mouths**

31 **when the anger of God rose against them. He slew the best among them; He struck down young warriors of Israel.**

32 **Nonetheless, they continued to sin and did not believe in His wonders.** Even after the episode of the quail and the plague that came in its wake, they continued to complain and to make various demands.

33 **He ended their days in futility, and their years in terror**. This is an allusion to the Israelites' punishment of wandering in the wilderness instead of being able to enter the Land of Israel.[6]

34 All of their years of wandering were characterized by a recurring pattern of behavior: **When He slew them, then they sought Him out; they returned and searched for the Almighty.**

35 **They remembered** in times of distress **that God was their rock, the Almighty Most High, their Redeemer.**

לו וַיְפַתּוּהוּ בְּפִיהֶם וּבִלְשׁוֹנָם
יְכַזְּבוּ־לוֹ:

לז וְלִבָּם לֹא־נָכוֹן עִמּוֹ וְלֹא
נֶאֶמְנוּ בִּבְרִיתוֹ:

לח וְהוּא רַחוּם ׀ יְכַפֵּר עָוֹן וְלֹא־
יַשְׁחִית וְהִרְבָּה לְהָשִׁיב אַפּוֹ
וְלֹא־יָעִיר כָּל־חֲמָתוֹ:

לט וַיִּזְכֹּר כִּי־בָשָׂר הֵמָּה רוּחַ
הוֹלֵךְ וְלֹא יָשׁוּב:

מ כַּמָּה יַמְרוּהוּ בַמִּדְבָּר
יַעֲצִיבוּהוּ בִּישִׁימוֹן:

מא וַיָּשׁוּבוּ וַיְנַסּוּ אֵל וּקְדוֹשׁ
יִשְׂרָאֵל הִתְווּ:

36 But they beguiled Him with their mouth and lied to Him with their tongue.

37 Their heart was not steadfast toward Him, nor were they faithful to His covenant.

38 Yet He, being merciful, forgave iniquity and did not destroy. He repeatedly restrained His anger and did not kindle all of His wrath.

39 He remembered that they were but flesh, a passing breeze that does not return.

40 How often did they defy Him in the wilderness and distress Him in the desolate land!

41 They continually tested the Almighty; they marked the Holy One of Israel.

---

36 Their turning to God, however, was perfunctory rather than wholehearted: **But they beguiled Him with their mouth and lied to Him with their tongue.** They spoke as if they were faithful to Him, but in fact they were not.

37 **Their heart was not steadfast toward Him, nor were they faithful to His covenant.**

38 **Yet,** though God was aware of their inadequate sincerity, **He, being merciful, forgave iniquity and did not destroy** them for their sins. **He repeatedly restrained His anger and did not kindle all of His wrath.**

39 **He remembered that they were but flesh,** imperfect human beings, **a passing breeze that does not return.** God realizes that, given the frailties of human nature and the shortness of people's lives, one cannot make excessive demands of them.

40 **How often did they defy Him in the wilderness and distress Him in the desolate land!**

41 **They continually tested the Almighty; they marked the Holy One of Israel,** as if to make Him a target for additional provocations.

מב לֹא־זָכְרוּ אֶת־יָדֹו יֹום אֲשֶׁר־פָּדָם מִנִּי־צָר:

מג אֲשֶׁר־שָׂם בְּמִצְרַיִם אֹתֹותָיו וּמֹופְתָיו בִּשְׂדֵה־צֹעַן:

מד וַיַּהֲפֹךְ לְדָם יְאֹרֵיהֶם וְנֹזְלֵיהֶם בַּל־יִשְׁתָּיוּן:

מה יְשַׁלַּח בָּהֶם עָרֹב וַיֹּאכְלֵם וּצְפַרְדֵּעַ וַתַּשְׁחִיתֵם:

מו וַיִּתֵּן לֶחָסִיל יְבוּלָם וִיגִיעָם לָאַרְבֶּה:

מז יַהֲרֹג בַּבָּרָד גַּפְנָם וְשִׁקְמֹותָם בַּחֲנָמַל:

42 They did not remember the strength of His hand on the day He redeemed them from their foes,

43 when He performed His signs in Egypt and His marvels in the field of Tzo'an,

44 and turned their rivers to blood; their waters were unfit to drink.

45 He sent swarms among them, which devoured them, and frogs, which destroyed them,

46 and He gave their crops to grasshoppers, and the product of their labors to locusts.

47 He destroyed their vines with hail and their sycamores with worms,

---

42 **They did not remember the strength of His hand on the day He redeemed them from their foes,**

43 **when He performed His signs in Egypt and His marvels in the field of Tzo'an.**

44 The psalmist now turns to the story of the ten plagues and the exodus from Egypt: **And** He **turned their rivers to blood; their waters were unfit to drink.**

45 **He sent swarms among them, which devoured them, and frogs, which destroyed them,**

46 **and He gave their crops to grasshoppers, and the product of their labors to locusts.** The word *ḥasil*, translated here as "grasshopper," is a synonym for locust, or it refers to a specific kind of locust.

47 **He destroyed their vines with hail and their sycamores with worms,**

מה וַיַּסְגֵּר לַבָּרָד בְּעִירָם
וּמִקְנֵיהֶם לָרְשָׁפִים:

מט יְשַׁלַּח־בָּם ׀ חֲרוֹן אַפּוֹ עֶבְרָה
וָזַעַם וְצָרָה מִשְׁלַחַת מַלְאֲכֵי
רָעִים:

נ יְפַלֵּס נָתִיב לְאַפּוֹ לֹא־חָשַׂךְ
מִמָּוֶת נַפְשָׁם וְחַיָּתָם לַדֶּבֶר
הִסְגִּיר:

נא וַיַּךְ כָּל־בְּכוֹר בְּמִצְרָיִם
רֵאשִׁית אוֹנִים בְּאָהֳלֵי־חָם:

נב וַיַּסַּע כַּצֹּאן עַמּוֹ וַיְנַהֲגֵם
כָּעֵדֶר בַּמִּדְבָּר:

נג וַיַּנְחֵם לָבֶטַח וְלֹא פָחָדוּ
וְאֶת־אוֹיְבֵיהֶם כִּסָּה הַיָּם:

48 and He handed over their livestock to hail, their cattle to bolts of lightning.

49 He sent them His burning anger, fury, indignation, and trouble, a band of destroying angels;

50 He cleared a path for His anger; He did not spare them from death; He delivered their animals to pestilence.

51 And He smote all the firstborn in Egypt, the first fruits of their vigor in the tents of Ham.

52 Then He led forth His people like sheep, and guided them in the wilderness like a flock.

53 He guided them safely and they did not fear; the sea engulfed their enemies.

---

48 **and He handed over their livestock to hail, their cattle to bolts of lightning.**

49 **He sent them His burning anger, fury, indignation, and trouble, a band of destroying angels.** This verse refers to the pestilence that killed all the remaining livestock, which was delivered by angels of destruction.

50 **He cleared a path,** as it were, **for His anger** to reach Egypt; **He did not spare them from death; He delivered their animals to pestilence.**

51 **And He smote all the firstborn in Egypt, the first fruits of their vigor,** another term for "firstborn," **in the tents of Ham,** referring to the Egyptians by the name of their forebear Ham.[7]

52 The aforementioned plagues led to the Israelites' exodus from Egypt, and **then He led forth His people like sheep,** that are led along a designated path by their caring shepherd, **and guided them in the wilderness like a flock.**

53 **He guided them safely and they did not fear; the sea engulfed their enemies.**

נד וַיְבִיאֵם אֶל־גְּבוּל קָדְשׁוֹ הַר־
זֶה קָנְתָה יְמִינוֹ:

נה וַיְגָרֶשׁ מִפְּנֵיהֶם ׀ גּוֹיִם
וַיַּפִּילֵם בְּחֶבֶל נַחֲלָה וַיַּשְׁכֵּן
בְּאָהֳלֵיהֶם שִׁבְטֵי יִשְׂרָאֵל:

נו וַיְנַסּוּ וַיַּמְרוּ אֶת־אֱלֹהִים
עֶלְיוֹן וְעֵדוֹתָיו לֹא שָׁמָרוּ:

נז וַיִּסֹּגוּ וַיִּבְגְּדוּ כַּאֲבוֹתָם נֶהְפְּכוּ
כְּקֶשֶׁת רְמִיָּה:

נח וַיַּכְעִיסוּהוּ בְּבָמוֹתָם
וּבִפְסִילֵיהֶם יַקְנִיאוּהוּ:

⁵⁴ He brought them to the boundary of His holiness, to the mountain owned by His right hand.

⁵⁵ He drove out the nations before them, dividing up their allotments of land. He settled the tribes of Israel in their tents.

⁵⁶ Yet they tested and rebelled against God Most High, and they did not keep His precepts.

⁵⁷ They turned back and acted treacherously, as did their fathers; they became like a crooked bow.

⁵⁸ They provoked Him with their altars in high places, and aroused His jealousy with their graven images.

---

54 In the following verses, the psalmist ends his description of the events of the exodus and recounts the conquest of the land: **He brought them to the boundary of His holiness,** the Land of Israel, **to the mountain owned by His right hand,** the mountain that is God's prized possession, Mount Zion, the choicest portion of the land.

55 **He drove out the nations** of Canaan **before them, dividing up their allotments of land** among the members of each of the twelve tribes. **He settled the tribes of Israel in their tents.**

56 **Yet** even after they were settled in the Land of Israel, the people continued to sin; **they tested and rebelled against God Most High, and they did not keep His precepts.**

57 **They turned back** from the path of propriety **and acted treacherously, as did their fathers** in the wilderness; **they became** unfaithful **like a crooked bow,** whose arrows fly off in all directions, far from the desired destination.

58 **They provoked Him with their altars in high places** dedicated to false gods, **and aroused His jealousy with their graven images.**

נט שָׁמַע אֱלֹהִים וַיִּתְעַבָּר
וַיִּמְאַס מְאֹד בְּיִשְׂרָאֵל:

⁵⁹ God heard and grew angry; He utterly rejected Israel.

ס וַיִּטֹּשׁ מִשְׁכַּן שִׁלוֹ אֹהֶל שִׁכֵּן
בָּאָדָם:

⁶⁰ He abandoned the Sanctuary at Shilo; He pitched a tent among men,

סא וַיִּתֵּן לַשְּׁבִי עֻזּוֹ וְתִפְאַרְתּוֹ
בְיַד־צָר:

and He sent His strength into captivity, His glory into the hand of the foe.

סב וַיַּסְגֵּר לַחֶרֶב עַמּוֹ וּבְנַחֲלָתוֹ
הִתְעַבָּר:

⁶² He delivered His people to the sword; He was filled with anger toward His portion.

סג בַּחוּרָיו אָכְלָה־אֵשׁ
וּבְתוּלֹתָיו לֹא הוּלָּלוּ:

⁶³ Fire devoured His young men, and His virgins were not celebrated with wedding songs.

סד כֹּהֲנָיו בַּחֶרֶב נָפָלוּ וְאַלְמְנֹתָיו
לֹא תִבְכֶּינָה:

⁶⁴ His priests fell by the sword, and His widows could not weep.

---

⁵⁹ **God heard** of these depraved deeds **and grew angry; He utterly rejected Israel.**

⁶⁰ **He abandoned the Sanctuary at Shilo,** which was apparently destroyed by the Philistines;⁸ **He pitched a tent among men.** After the destruction of Shilo, God did not designate a specific alternative location as His dwelling place but instead dwelled among the people.

⁶¹ **And He sent His strength into captivity, His glory into the hand of the foe.** "His strength" and "His glory" refer to the powerful fortresses and cities that were overtaken by the enemy.

⁶² **He delivered His people to the sword; He was filled with anger toward His portion,** the children of Israel.

⁶³ **Fire devoured His young men, and** as a result of their deaths, **His virgins were not celebrated with wedding songs,** as they were left with no potential marriage partners.

⁶⁴ **His priests fell by the sword, and His widows could not weep** for their husbands because they themselves were pursued and killed.

סה וַיִּקַץ כְּיָשֵׁן ׀ אֲדֹנָי כְּגִבּוֹר
מִתְרוֹנֵן מִיָּיִן:

65 Then the Lord awoke as if from sleep, like a warrior rising stridently from his wine.

סו וַיַּךְ־צָרָיו אָחוֹר חֶרְפַּת עוֹלָם
נָתַן לָמוֹ:

66 He drove His foes into retreat, put them to everlasting shame.

סז וַיִּמְאַס בְּאֹהֶל יוֹסֵף וּבְשֵׁבֶט
אֶפְרַיִם לֹא בָחָר:

67 And He rejected the tent of Joseph and did not choose the tribe of Ephraim.

סח וַיִּבְחַר אֶת־שֵׁבֶט יְהוּדָה
אֶת־הַר צִיּוֹן אֲשֶׁר אָהֵב:

68 He chose the tribe of Judah, and Mount Zion, which He loved,

סט וַיִּבֶן כְּמוֹ־רָמִים מִקְדָּשׁוֹ
כְּאֶרֶץ יְסָדָהּ לְעוֹלָם:

69 and He built His holy place in the heights, establishing it, like the earth, for eternity.

ע וַיִּבְחַר בְּדָוִד עַבְדּוֹ וַיִּקָּחֵהוּ
מִמִּכְלְאֹת צֹאן:

70 And He chose David, His servant, and took him from the sheepfolds.

---

65 But after all the defeat and subjugation, there came a time for redemption: **Then the Lord awoke as if from sleep,** after seeming to be indifferent to Israel's suffering for so long, **like a warrior rising stridently from his wine,** after a refreshing reprieve from the battlefield.

66 **He drove His foes into retreat, put them to everlasting shame.**

67 **And He rejected the tent of Joseph and did not choose the tribe of Ephraim.** The tribe of Joseph and its branch Ephraim had been in power mostly during the period of the judges, and God now rejected their leadership.

68 But instead **He chose the tribe of Judah, and Mount Zion** in Judah's territory, **which He loved** and chose as the site of His Temple;

69 **and He built His holy place in the heights, establishing it, like the earth, for eternity.**

70 **And He chose David, His servant,** out of the tribe of Judah, **and took him from the sheepfolds,** where he had worked as a shepherd, to be king of Israel.

עא מֵאַחַר עָלוֹת הֱבִיאוֹ לִרְעוֹת
בְּיַעֲקֹב עַמּוֹ וּבְיִשְׂרָאֵל
נַחֲלָתוֹ:

71 He brought him away from the suckling lambs to be a shepherd among Jacob, His people, and Israel, His portion.

עב וַיִּרְעֵם כְּתֹם לְבָבוֹ וּבִתְבוּנוֹת
כַּפָּיו יַנְחֵם:

72 And He shepherded them with a pure heart and led them with skillful hands.

PSALM 79

A psalm of entreaty, describing the suffering and defeats of the Israelites, ending with a prayer for redemption.

א מִזְמוֹר לְאָסָף אֱלֹהִים בָּאוּ
גוֹיִם ׀ בְּנַחֲלָתֶךָ טִמְּאוּ
אֶת־הֵיכַל קָדְשֶׁךָ שָׂמוּ אֶת־
יְרוּשָׁלַ͏ִם לְעִיִּים:

1 A psalm by Asaf. God, the nations have invaded Your inherited land; they have defiled Your holy Temple. They have laid Jerusalem in ruins.

ב נָתְנוּ אֶת־נִבְלַת עֲבָדֶיךָ
מַאֲכָל לְעוֹף הַשָּׁמָיִם בְּשַׂר
חֲסִידֶיךָ לְחַיְתוֹ־אָרֶץ:

2 They fed the corpses of Your servants to birds of the sky, the flesh of Your devoted ones to the beasts of the earth.

---

71 **He brought him away from the suckling lambs to be a shepherd among Jacob, His people, and Israel, His portion.** The verse notes the apt transition from shepherd of flocks to shepherd of Israel.

72 **And He shepherded them with a pure heart and led them with skillful hands.**

PSALM 79

1 **A psalm by Asaf. God, the nations have invaded Your inherited land; they have defiled Your holy Temple. They have laid Jerusalem in ruins.**

2 **They fed the corpses of Your servants to birds of the sky, the flesh of Your devoted ones to the beasts of the earth.** The people fell in the field, and as they lay there unburied, were picked at by bird and beast.

ג שָׁפְכ֨וּ דָמָ֤ם ׀ כַּמַּ֗יִם סְבִ֬יב֥וֹת
יְֽרוּשָׁלִָ֗ם וְאֵ֣ין קוֹבֵֽר׃

ד הָיִ֣ינוּ חֶ֭רְפָּה לִשְׁכֵנֵ֑ינוּ לַ֥עַג
וָ֝קֶ֗לֶס לִסְבִיבוֹתֵֽינוּ׃

ה עַד־מָ֣ה יְ֭הוָה תֶּאֱנַ֣ף לָנֶ֑צַח
תִּבְעַ֥ר כְּמוֹ־אֵ֝֗שׁ קִנְאָתֶֽךָ׃

ו שְׁפֹ֤ךְ חֲמָתְךָ֗ אֶֽל־הַגּוֹיִם֮
אֲשֶׁ֪ר לֹֽא־יְדָ֫ע֥וּךָ וְעַ֥ל
מַמְלָכ֑וֹת אֲשֶׁ֥ר בְּ֝שִׁמְךָ֗ לֹ֣א
קָרָֽאוּ׃

ז כִּ֭י אָכַ֣ל אֶֽת־יַעֲקֹ֑ב וְֽאֶת־נָוֵ֥הוּ
הֵשַֽׁמּוּ׃

3 They spilled their blood like water around Jerusalem, and there was no one to bury them.

4 We have become a disgrace to our neighbors, an object of scorn and mockery to those around us.

5 How long, Lord? Will You be angry forever, Your jealousy burning like fire?

6 Pour out Your wrath on the nations that do not acknowledge You, and on kingdoms that do not invoke Your name,

7 for they have devoured Jacob and made desolate his habitation.

---

3 **They spilled their blood like water around Jerusalem, and there was no one to bury them.**

4 **We have become a disgrace to our neighbors** as a result of our defeat and downfall, **an object of scorn and mockery to those around us.**

5 **How long, Lord? Will You be angry forever, Your jealousy burning like fire?** Even if we have sinned against You and incurred Your wrath, there has to be a limit to Your anger and to our suffering. This is all the more true if You compare our sins to those of our foes, as the following verse goes on to say:

6 If you are angry, **pour out Your wrath on the nations that do not acknowledge You** at all, rather than on us, **and on kingdoms that do not invoke Your name,** who are unquestionably more distant from You than we are,

7 **for they have devoured Jacob and made desolate his habitation.**

אַל־תִּזְכָּר־לָ֫נוּ עֲוֹנֹ֥ת
רִֽאשֹׁנִ֥ים מַהֵ֖ר יְקַדְּמ֣וּנוּ
רַחֲמֶ֑יךָ כִּ֖י דַלּ֣וֹנוּ מְאֹֽד׃

עָזְרֵ֤נוּ ׀ אֱלֹ֘הֵ֤י יִשְׁעֵ֗נוּ עַל־
דְּבַ֥ר כְּבֽוֹד־שְׁמֶ֑ךָ וְהַצִּילֵ֥נוּ
וְכַפֵּ֥ר עַל־חַטֹּאתֵ֗ינוּ לְמַ֣עַן
שְׁמֶֽךָ׃

לָ֤מָּה ׀ יֹאמְר֣וּ הַגּוֹיִם֮ אַיֵּ֪ה
אֱלֹ֫הֵיהֶ֥ם יִוָּדַ֣ע בַּגֹּיִ֣ים לְעֵינֵ֑ינוּ בַּגּוֹיִם
נִ֝קְמַ֗ת דַּם־עֲבָדֶ֥יךָ הַשָּׁפֽוּךְ׃

תָּ֤בוֹא לְפָנֶ֨יךָ ׀ אֶנְקַ֬ת אָסִ֥יר
כְּגֹ֥דֶל זְרוֹעֲךָ֑ הוֹתֵ֗ר בְּנֵ֥י
תְמוּתָֽה׃

8 Do not hold our former
iniquities against us. Let Your
mercy come to us quickly, for
we are brought very low.

9 Help us, God of our salvation,
for the glory of Your name;
deliver us and forgive us our
sins for the sake of Your name.

10 Why should the nations say:
Where is their God? Let us
witness when there becomes
known among the nations
vengeance for the spilled blood
of Your servants.

11 Let the captive's groaning
come before You. By Your
arm's great power, spare those
doomed to die.

---

8 **Do not hold our former iniquities against us,** though we have indeed sinned. **Let Your mercy come to us quickly, for we are brought very low** and have been punished sufficiently.
9 **Help us, God of our salvation,** at least **for the glory of Your name,** even if we are undeserving; **deliver us and forgive us our sins for the sake of Your name.** We are associated with Your name, so our disgrace is a desecration of Your name.
10 **Why should the nations say: Where is their God?** Why should they say: If He is really their God, why does He not respond to our deeds against them? **Let us witness** it with our own eyes, let it not be in the distant future, **when there becomes known among the nations vengeance for the spilled blood of Your servants.**
11 **Let the captive's groaning come before You,** the cry of those held captive by the enemy. **By Your arm's great power, spare those doomed to die.**

וְהָשֵׁב לִשְׁכֵנֵינוּ שִׁבְעָתַיִם
אֶל־חֵיקָם חֶרְפָּתָם אֲשֶׁר
חֵרְפוּךָ אֲדֹנָי:

12 Pay back our neighbors sevenfold to their bosom for their abuse, for their reviling of You, Lord.

וַאֲנַחְנוּ עַמְּךָ ׀ וְצֹאן
מַרְעִיתֶךָ נוֹדֶה לְּךָ לְעוֹלָם
לְדֹר וָדֹר נְסַפֵּר תְּהִלָּתֶךָ:

13 For we are Your people, the sheep of Your flock; we will give thanks to You forever, from generation to generation recounting Your praise.

PSALM 80

A psalm that begins with recollections of Israel's past power and glory:
First, when the nation left Egypt, and later, when God led the people to capture and settle
the Land of Israel. The psalm goes on to describe the difficult times faced by the nation at present,
ending with a prayer for God to renew His miracles and compassion.

לַמְנַצֵּחַ אֶל־שֹׁשַׁנִּים עֵדוּת
לְאָסָף מִזְמוֹר:

1 For the chief musician, for *shoshanim*, a testimony, a psalm by Asaf.

---

12 **Pay back our neighbors sevenfold to their bosom for their abuse, for their reviling of You, Lord.**
13 **For we are Your people, the sheep of Your flock; we will give thanks to You forever, from generation to generation recounting Your praise.**

PSALM 80
1 **For the chief musician, for *shoshanim*.** As noted earlier,[9] this term refers to a particular melody or to a musical instrument. **A testimony.** Perhaps this psalm is called "a testimony" because it contains elements of remembrance of past events, though it is also a prayer. **A psalm by Asaf.**

רֹעֵה יִשְׂרָאֵל | הַאֲזִינָה נֹהֵג
כַּצֹּאן יוֹסֵף יֹשֵׁב הַכְּרוּבִים
הוֹפִיעָה:

Shepherd of Israel, listen. Appear to us, You who led Joseph like a flock, You who sit enthroned above the cherubs.

לִפְנֵי אֶפְרַיִם | וּבִנְיָמִן וּמְנַשֶּׁה
עוֹרְרָה אֶת־גְּבוּרָתֶךָ וּלְכָה
לִישֻׁעָתָה לָּנוּ:

Rouse Your might before Ephraim, Benjamin, and Manasseh, and come to our rescue.

אֱלֹהִים הֲשִׁיבֵנוּ וְהָאֵר פָּנֶיךָ
וְנִוָּשֵׁעָה:

God, restore us. Shine Your countenance on us and we will be delivered.

יְהֹוָה אֱלֹהִים צְבָאוֹת עַד־
מָתַי עָשַׁנְתָּ בִּתְפִלַּת עַמֶּךָ:

Lord, God of hosts, for how long will You fume against the prayer of Your people?

הֶאֱכַלְתָּם לֶחֶם דִּמְעָה
וַתַּשְׁקֵמוֹ בִּדְמָעוֹת שָׁלִישׁ:

You feed them the bread of tears; You give them tears to drink in a threefold cup.

---

2 **Shepherd of Israel, listen. Appear to us.** This verse entreats God to reveal Himself, as will be explained more fully in the following verses. **You who led Joseph like a flock.** The tribe of Joseph is accorded pride of place in this psalm, to the extent that the name Joseph, like Jacob or Israel, can be understood to represent the entire nation of Israel. **You who sit enthroned above the cherubs.** God, in the Temple and elsewhere, is depicted as riding on the cherubs.

3 **Rouse Your might before Ephraim, Benjamin, and Manasseh, and come to our rescue.** These three tribes, all descended from Rachel, are referred to as a single unit despite the fact that, from various historical perspectives, they did not maintain close ties.

4 **God, restore us.** The word *hashivenu*, literally "return us," in this instance means "turn toward us and save us" rather than being a request to bring us back from other lands. **Shine Your countenance on us and** when You do so **we will be delivered.**

5 **Lord, God of hosts, for how long will You fume against the prayer of Your people?** The expression "fume" is appropriate to depict anger, as in Hebrew the common term for "wrath," *haron af*, is literally "burning anger."

6 **You feed them the bread of tears;** they weep so much and so frequently in their sorrow that it is as if their very bread is soaked with tears. Indeed, **You give them** their **tears to drink in a threefold cup.** *Shalish*, translated here as "threefold cup," is a type of measuring cup.

^ז תְּשִׂימֵנוּ מָדוֹן לִשְׁכֵנֵינוּ
וְאֹיְבֵינוּ יִלְעֲגוּ־לָמוֹ:

^ח אֱלֹהִים צְבָאוֹת הֲשִׁיבֵנוּ
וְהָאֵר פָּנֶיךָ וְנִוָּשֵׁעָה:

^ט גֶּפֶן מִמִּצְרַיִם תַּסִּיעַ תְּגָרֵשׁ
גּוֹיִם וַתִּטָּעֶהָ:

^י פִּנִּיתָ לְפָנֶיהָ וַתַּשְׁרֵשׁ
שָׁרָשֶׁיהָ וַתְּמַלֵּא־אָרֶץ:

^{יא} כָּסּוּ הָרִים צִלָּהּ וַעֲנָפֶיהָ
אַרְזֵי־אֵל:

^{יב} תְּשַׁלַּח קְצִירֶהָ עַד־יָם וְאֶל־
נָהָר יוֹנְקוֹתֶיהָ:

7 You have made us a source of strife to our neighbors; our enemies mock us.

8 God of hosts, restore us. Shine Your countenance on us and we will be delivered.

9 You transported a vine from Egypt, drove out the nations and planted it.

10 You cleared space for it, and it took root and filled the land.

11 The mountains were covered with its shade, its branches like cedars of the Almighty.

12 It sent its boughs to the sea and its shoots to the river.

---

7 **You have made us a source of strife to our neighbors,** who fight with us constantly; and even when we are not the target of physical attack, **our enemies mock us.**

8 The psalmist repeats his entreaty: **God of hosts, restore us. Shine Your countenance on us and we will be delivered.**

9 What follows is a poetical-historical account of the nation of Israel, depicting them as a grapevine, an image found frequently in the words of the prophets: **You transported a vine from Egypt** to the Land of Israel, a reference to the exodus, **drove out the** Canaanite **nations and planted it** there.

10 **You cleared space for it, and it took root and** spread out in all directions until it **filled the land.**

11 **The mountains were covered with its shade,** so tall and widespread was it, **its branches** were giant, **like cedars of the Almighty,** that is, cedars of vast proportions.

12 **It sent its boughs** westward **to the** Mediterranean **Sea, and its shoots** eastward **to the river,** a term that, when unspecified, generally refers to the Euphrates.

לָמָּה פָּרַצְתָּ גְדֵרֶיהָ וְאָרוּהָ
כָּל־עֹבְרֵי דָרֶךְ:

יְכַרְסְמֶנָּה חֲזִיר מִיָּעַר וְזִיז
שָׂדַי יִרְעֶנָּה:

אֱלֹהִים צְבָאוֹת שׁוּב נָא
הַבֵּט מִשָּׁמַיִם וּרְאֵה וּפְקֹד
גֶּפֶן זֹאת:

וְכַנָּה אֲשֶׁר־נָטְעָה יְמִינֶךָ
וְעַל־בֵּן אִמַּצְתָּה לָּךְ:

שְׂרֻפָה בָאֵשׁ כְּסוּחָה מִגַּעֲרַת
פָּנֶיךָ יֹאבֵדוּ:

תְּהִי־יָדְךָ עַל־אִישׁ יְמִינֶךָ
עַל־בֶּן־אָדָם אִמַּצְתָּ לָּךְ:

13 Why have You breached its fences, so that all who pass can pick its fruit?

14 The boar from the forest gnaws at it; the large fowl feed on it.

15 God of hosts, please return. Look from heaven and see, and take note of this vine,

16 and the stock that Your right hand planted, and the son whom You embraced as Your own.

17 It is burned with fire and cut down; they perish at the rebuke of Your countenance.

18 Let Your hand sustain the man of Your right hand, the son of man whom You embraced as Your own,

---

13 The preceding verses depict the era of Israel's greatness. In the verses that follow, the psalmist goes on to describe the darker reality of his time: **Why have You breached its fences,** a vine's only protection from predators, **so that all who pass can pick its fruit?**

14 **The boar from the forest gnaws at it; the large fowl feed on it.**

15 The psalmist repeats his plea: **God of hosts, please return. Look from heaven and see, and take note of this vine,** and nurture it once again.

16 **And** take note of **the stock that Your right hand planted, and the son whom You embraced as Your own,** as the Torah states of the people of Israel, "You are the sons of the Lord."[10]

17 **It,** the vine, **is burned with fire and cut down; they,** the people of Israel, **perish at the rebuke of Your countenance.**

18 **Let Your hand sustain the man of Your right hand,** the one whom You hold with Your right hand, a symbol of honor and affection, **the son of man whom You embraced as Your own,**

יט וְלֹא־נָסוֹג מִמֶּךָ תְּחַיֵּינוּ
וּבְשִׁמְךָ נִקְרָא:

19 who never retreated from You.
Revive us, and we will call in
Your name.

כ יְהֹוָה אֱלֹהִים צְבָאוֹת
הֲשִׁיבֵנוּ הָאֵר פָּנֶיךָ וְנִוָּשֵׁעָה:

20 Lord, God of hosts, restore us.
Shine Your countenance on us
and we will be delivered.

PSALM 81

A psalm that makes reference to Rosh HaShana in the course of recounting miraculous events
that led to the salvation of the Israelites, both collectively and as individuals. It teaches that such
miracles can recur if Israel chooses to acknowledge the sovereignty of God and obey His laws.

א לַמְנַצֵּחַ ׀ עַל־הַגִּתִּית לְאָסָף:

1 For the chief musician, on the
gittit, a psalm by Asaf.

ב הַרְנִינוּ לֵאלֹהִים עוּזֵּנוּ הָרִיעוּ
לֵאלֹהֵי יַעֲקֹב:

2 Sing for joy to God, our
strength; shout with joy to the
God of Jacob.

ג שְׂאוּ־זִמְרָה וּתְנוּ־תֹף כִּנּוֹר
נָעִים עִם־נָבֶל:

3 Take up the song. Sound the
timbrel, a tuneful lyre with
a harp.

---

19 **who never retreated from You. Revive us,** restore us to our past glory, **and we will call in
Your name.**

20 The psalm ends with the plea of refrain: **Lord, God of hosts, restore us. Shine Your
countenance on us and we will be delivered.**

PSALM 81

1 For the chief musician, on the *gittit*; a psalm by Asaf.
2 Sing for joy to God, our strength; shout with joy to the God of Jacob.
3 Take up the song. Sound the timbrel, a tuneful lyre with a harp.

תִּקְעוּ בַחֹדֶשׁ שׁוֹפָר בַּכֶּסֶה
לְיוֹם חַגֵּנוּ:

⁴ Blow the shofar at the showing of the New Moon, at the appointed time of our holiday.

כִּי חֹק לְיִשְׂרָאֵל הוּא מִשְׁפָּט
לֵאלֹהֵי יַעֲקֹב:

⁵ For it is a statute for Israel, a law of the God of Jacob.

עֵדוּת ׀ בִּיהוֹסֵף שָׂמוֹ בְּצֵאתוֹ
עַל־אֶרֶץ מִצְרָיִם שְׂפַת לֹא־
יָדַעְתִּי אֶשְׁמָע:

⁶ He established it as a precept for Joseph when he went out over Egypt; I learned a language I had not known.

הֲסִירוֹתִי מִסֵּבֶל שִׁכְמוֹ כַּפָּיו
מִדּוּד תַּעֲבֹרְנָה:

⁷ I removed a burden from his shoulders, freed his hands from the vat.

בַּצָּרָה קָרָאתָ וָאֲחַלְּצֶךָּ
אֶעֶנְךָ בְּסֵתֶר רַעַם אֶבְחָנְךָ
עַל־מֵי מְרִיבָה סֶלָה:

⁸ When you called in distress, I rescued you; I answered your secret call with thunder. I tested you at the waters of Meriva, Selah.

---

⁴ **Blow the shofar at the showing of the New Moon, at the appointed time of our holiday.** The word *ḥodesh*, related to *ḥadash*, new, refers to the New Moon. Here it refers to the specific New Moon of Rosh HaShana, a holiday marked by the blowing of the shofar.

⁵ **For it,** blowing the shofar on this day, **is a statute for Israel, a law of the God of Jacob.**

⁶ The psalmist now reminds us of times past, when God's kindness toward the Israelites in general, as well as toward specific individuals, was manifest: **He established it as a precept for Joseph when he went out** as ruler **over Egypt.** Speaking in Joseph's words, the psalmist says: **I learned a language I had not known** as a newcomer to Egypt.

⁷ Now the psalmist speaks in God's voice: **I removed a burden from his,** Joseph's, **shoulders,** as he had been imprisoned until I released him, **freed his hands from** working with foodstuffs in **the vat.**

⁸ God speaks to the children of Israel: **When you called in distress,** during your enslavement in Egypt, **I rescued you; I answered your secret call with thunder.** Though you prayed to me silently, I rescued you with great commotion. This may also be an allusion to the giving of the Torah, which was accompanied by lightning and thunder. **I tested you at the waters of Meriva, Selah.** Although it was a test, the result was beneficial to you.

ט שְׁמַע עַמִּי וְאָעִידָה בָּךְ
יִשְׂרָאֵל אִם־תִּשְׁמַע־לִי:

י לֹא־יִהְיֶה בְךָ אֵל זָר וְלֹא
תִשְׁתַּחֲוֶה לְאֵל נֵכָר:

יא אָנֹכִי ׀ יְהֹוָה אֱלֹהֶיךָ הַמַּעַלְךָ
מֵאֶרֶץ מִצְרָיִם הַרְחֶב־פִּיךָ
וַאֲמַלְאֵהוּ:

יב וְלֹא־שָׁמַע עַמִּי לְקוֹלִי
וְיִשְׂרָאֵל לֹא־אָבָה לִי:

יג וָאֲשַׁלְּחֵהוּ בִּשְׁרִירוּת לִבָּם
יֵלְכוּ בְּמוֹעֲצוֹתֵיהֶם:

יד לוּ עַמִּי שֹׁמֵעַ לִי יִשְׂרָאֵל
בִּדְרָכַי יְהַלֵּכוּ:

⁹ Listen, My people; I will warn you, Israel, if you listen to Me.

¹⁰ Let there be no strange god among you; you shall not worship any foreign god.

¹¹ I am the Lord your God who brought you up from the land of Egypt; open your mouth wide, and I will fill it.

¹² But My people did not listen to My voice; Israel did not heed Me.

¹³ So I sent them in the way of their willful hearts, to walk in their own counsel.

¹⁴ If only My people would listen to me, Israel would walk in My ways,

---

9 God addresses the nation: **Listen, My people; I will warn you, Israel, if you listen to Me.**

10 Salvation from God is dependent on obedience to Him and to the laws of His Torah. Such obedience begins with the rejection of false gods: **Let there be no strange god among you; you shall not worship any foreign god.** This, along with the following verse, constitutes the first of the Ten Precepts; it is also the essence of the entire acceptance of God's rule.

11 **I am the Lord your God who brought you up from the land of Egypt.** If you follow these basic precepts, I will provide you with all your needs, as one might say to a child: **Open your mouth wide** as a request for food, **and I will fill it.**

12 **But My people did not listen to My voice; Israel did not heed Me** to keep My commandments.

13 **So I sent them in the way of their willful hearts;** I allowed them to follow their own will and **to walk in their own counsel**, and to suffer the consequences of their choices and their actions, without any assistance from Me.

14 **If only My people would listen to me,** if only **Israel would walk in My ways,** for if they did, the outcome would be a dramatic change for the better in their fate.

טו כִּמְעַט אוֹיְבֵיהֶם אַכְנִיעַ וְעַל־
צָרֵיהֶם אָשִׁיב יָדִי:

15 I would subdue their enemies in an instant; I would turn My hand against their foes.

טז מְשַׂנְאֵי יהוה יְכַחֲשׁוּ־לוֹ וִיהִי
עִתָּם לְעוֹלָם:

16 Those who hate the Lord would feign obedience to Him; their time would last forever,

יז וַיַּאֲכִילֵהוּ מֵחֵלֶב חִטָּה
וּמִצּוּר דְּבַשׁ אַשְׂבִּיעֶךָ:

17 while He would feed them the finest of wheat and sate them with honey drawn from the rock.

PSALM 82

A psalm that both excoriates judges who do not perform their job
in a manner befitting their office, and offers guidelines for the proper meting out of justice.

א מִזְמוֹר לְאָסָף אֱלֹהִים נִצָּב
בַּעֲדַת־אֵל בְּקֶרֶב אֱלֹהִים
יִשְׁפֹּט:

1 A psalm by Asaf. God stands in the assembly of the Almighty; in the midst of the judges He renders judgment.

---

15 **I would subdue their enemies in an instant; I would turn My hand against their foes.**
16 **Those who hate the Lord would feign obedience to Him,** as defeated enemies must do; **their time** of punishment **would last forever,**
17 **while,** after subduing and punishing Israel's enemies, **He would feed them,** the Israelites themselves, **the finest of wheat and sate them with honey drawn from the rock.**

PSALM 82
1 **A psalm by Asaf. God stands,** that is, He is eternally present, **in the assembly of the Almighty,** a reference to a court that decides weighty matters, such as capital crimes; such a court comprises twenty-three judges and is aptly called an assembly; **in the midst of the judges He renders judgment.** The psalmist reminds these judges that whether they sense it or not, God Himself is present among them, keeping a watchful eye over all their decisions.

עַד־מָתַי תִּשְׁפְּטוּ־עָוֶל וּפְנֵי
רְשָׁעִים תִּשְׂאוּ־סֶלָה:

² For how long will you judge wrongly and show favor to the wicked? Selah.

שִׁפְטוּ־דַל וְיָתוֹם עָנִי וָרָשׁ
הַצְדִּיקוּ:

³ Do justice to the lowly and the orphan; vindicate the poor and destitute.

פַּלְּטוּ־דַל וְאֶבְיוֹן מִיַּד
רְשָׁעִים הַצִּילוּ:

⁴ Rescue the lowly and the needy; save them from the hands of the wicked.

לֹא יָדְעוּ ׀ וְלֹא יָבִינוּ בַּחֲשֵׁכָה
יִתְהַלָּכוּ יִמּוֹטוּ כָּל־מוֹסְדֵי
אָרֶץ:

⁵ They neither know nor understand. They walk about in darkness while all the foundations of the earth totter and collapse.

אֲנִי־אָמַרְתִּי אֱלֹהִים אַתֶּם
וּבְנֵי עֶלְיוֹן כֻּלְּכֶם:

⁶ I had said: You are divine, like celestial beings, all of you.

---

2 The judges are now admonished: **For how long will you judge wrongly and show favor to the wicked? Selah.** Your job is to be fair, to make sure that the powerless are defended appropriately, and yet you do the opposite; you show favoritism to the wicked at the expense of the weak.

3 The psalmist reminds the judges what their proper function should be: **Do justice to the lowly and the orphan; vindicate the poor and destitute,** even when they stand accused by powerful, wealthy people.

4 **Rescue the lowly and the needy; save them from the hands of the wicked.**

5 But **they,** the judges to whom the psalmist addresses his admonition, **neither know nor understand,** for they conduct themselves according to their own preconceptions. **They walk about in darkness,** unable to see the light of truth. Whether they act in secret or publicly, they are considered "walking in darkness" due to their unwillingness to see the light, **while all the foundations of the earth totter and collapse.** Their corrupt behavior threatens the very existence of society, which is founded upon the pillars of law and justice.

6 Initially **I had said: You are divine.** The word *elohim*, translated here as "divine," usually means "God," but it is also used to refer to angels, and occasionally to judges.[11] The psalmist admonishes the judges: Since you are called *elohim*, it is expected that you be faithful messengers of God, like angels, executing His will among men. **Like celestial beings,** another term for angels, **all of you.**

אָכֵן כְּאָדָם תְּמוּתְוּן וּכְאַחַד הַשָּׂרִים תִּפְּלוּ:

⁷ Yet as men you will die; as any of the ministers you will fall.

קוּמָה אֱלֹהִים שָׁפְטָה הָאָרֶץ כִּי־אַתָּה תִנְחַל בְּכָל־הַגּוֹיִם:

⁸ Arise, God, and judge the earth, for You possess all nations.

PSALM 83

A psalm of supplication that appears to have been written at a time when all the nations surrounding Israel went on the attack. The text seems to place it in very ancient times, before the military victories of King David.

יז לחודש
17th day
of month

שִׁיר מִזְמוֹר לְאָסָף:

¹ A song, a psalm by Asaf.

אֱלֹהִים אַל־דֳּמִי־לָךְ אַל־תֶּחֱרַשׁ וְאַל־תִּשְׁקֹט אֵל:

² God, do not be silent, do not hold Your peace. Almighty, do not be still.

---

⁷ The psalmist now understands that he has been mistaken and that judges are mortal, not divine: **Yet** now I see that I was mistaken, and I see that you are not angels; **as mortal men you will die; as any of the ministers you will fall.** You do not represent divine power but rather personal ambition, and consequently like all ministers and powerful men, your grandeur will not endure.

⁸ The psalmist, disillusioned, closes with a plea to God: **Arise,** reveal Yourself, **God, and judge the earth** Yourself, Israelite and gentile alike, **for You possess all nations.**

PSALM 83
¹ **A song, a psalm by Asaf.**
² **God, do not be silent, do not hold Your peace. Almighty, do not be still.** I beg of You to act, to come to our aid.

כִּי־הִנֵּה אוֹיְבֶיךָ יֶהֱמָיוּן
וּמְשַׂנְאֶיךָ נָשְׂאוּ רֹאשׁ:

עַל־עַמְּךָ יַעֲרִימוּ סוֹד
וְיִתְיָעֲצוּ עַל־צְפוּנֶיךָ:

אָמְרוּ לְכוּ וְנַכְחִידֵם מִגּוֹי
וְלֹא־יִזָּכֵר שֵׁם־יִשְׂרָאֵל עוֹד:

כִּי נוֹעֲצוּ לֵב יַחְדָּו עָלֶיךָ
בְּרִית יִכְרֹתוּ:

אָהֳלֵי אֱדוֹם וְיִשְׁמְעֵאלִים
מוֹאָב וְהַגְרִים:

גְּבָל וְעַמּוֹן וַעֲמָלֵק פְּלֶשֶׁת
עִם־יֹשְׁבֵי צוֹר:

3 For behold, Your enemies are in an uproar; those who hate You have lifted their heads.

4 They meet to lay devious plots against Your people, and conspire together against Your treasured ones.

5 They said: Come, let us wipe them out as a nation, so that the name of Israel is remembered no more.

6 For in unity they take counsel; against You they have made a pact.

7 The tents of Edom and the Ishmaelites, Moav and the Hagrites,

8 Geval, Amon, and Amalek, Philistia with the inhabitants of Tyre;

---

3 **For behold, Your enemies are in an uproar; those who hate You have lifted their heads** in arrogance.

4 **They meet to lay devious plots against Your people, and conspire together against Your treasured ones.** *Tzefunekha*, translated as "Your treasured ones," more literally means "Your hidden things," that which cannot be seen. They seek to destroy us both physically and spiritually.

5 Their plan is not for mere battle, but for our total annihilation: **They said: Come, let us wipe them out as a nation, so that the name of Israel is remembered no more.**

6 **For in unity they take counsel; against You they have made a pact.** War against Israel is ultimately a war waged against the God of Israel.

7 These enemies who seek our destruction are comprised of many parties: **The tents of Edom and the Ishmaelites, Moav and the Hagrites,** the descendants of Hagar,

8 **Geval,** a small kingdom to the north of Israel, **Amon, and Amalek, Philistia with the inhabitants of Tyre.**

ט גַּם־אַשּׁוּר נִלְוָה עִמָּם הָיוּ
זְרוֹעַ לִבְנֵי־לוֹט סֶלָה:

י עֲשֵׂה־לָהֶם כְּמִדְיָן כְּסִיסְרָא
כְיָבִין בְּנַחַל קִישׁוֹן:

יא נִשְׁמְדוּ בְעֵין־דֹּאר הָיוּ דֹּמֶן
לָאֲדָמָה:

יב שִׁיתֵמוֹ נְדִיבֵמוֹ כְּעֹרֵב
וְכִזְאֵב וּכְזֶבַח וּכְצַלְמֻנָּע כָּל־
נְסִיכֵמוֹ:

יג אֲשֶׁר אָמְרוּ נִירֲשָׁה לָּנוּ אֵת
נְאוֹת אֱלֹהִים:

יד אֱלֹהַי שִׁיתֵמוֹ כַגַּלְגַּל כְּקַשׁ
לִפְנֵי־רוּחַ:

טו כְּאֵשׁ תִּבְעַר־יָעַר וּכְלֶהָבָה
תְּלַהֵט הָרִים:

9 Assyria too has joined them; they give a hand to the sons of Lot, Selah.

10 Deal with them as with Midyan, as with Sisera and Yavin at the stream of Kishon.

11 They were destroyed at Ein Dor; they became dung for the ground.

12 Make their nobles like Orev and Ze'ev, all their princes like Zevah and Tzalmuna,

13 who had said: Let us take the pleasant dwellings of God for ourselves.

14 My God, make them like whirling sand, like chaff before the wind,

15 like fire that consumes the forest, like flames that scorch mountains.

---

9 **Assyria too has joined them,** despite its distance from the Land of Israel; **they give a hand to** the instigators of the conflict, **the sons of Lot,** the Moavites and Amonites, **Selah.**

10 The psalmist prays for God to rout these enemies: **Deal with them as** You did **with Midyan,**[12] **as with Sisera and Yavin at the stream of Kishon.**[13]

11 **They,** Sisera and Yavin, **were destroyed at Ein Dor;** in death **they became** as **dung for the ground.**

12 **Make their nobles like Orev and Ze'ev,** officers of Midyan slain by Gideon,[14] **all their princes like Zevah and Tzalmuna,** kings of Midyan who were also killed by Gideon,[15]

13 **who had said: Let us take the pleasant dwellings of God,** the Land of Israel, **for ourselves.**

14 **My God, make them like whirling sand, like chaff** scattering **before the wind,**

15 **like fire that consumes the forest, like flames that scorch mountains.**

כֵּן תִּרְדְּפֵם בְּסַעֲרֶךָ
וּבְסוּפָתְךָ תְבַהֲלֵם: טו

So may You pursue them with Your tempest, terrify them with Your storm. [16]

מַלֵּא פְנֵיהֶם קָלוֹן וִיבַקְשׁוּ
שִׁמְךָ יְהוָה: טז

Fill their faces with shame until they seek Your name, Lord. [17]

יֵבֹשׁוּ וְיִבָּהֲלוּ עֲדֵי־עַד
וְיַחְפְּרוּ וְיֹאבֵדוּ: יז

May they be ashamed and frightened forever; may they be humiliated and may they perish. [18]

וְיֵדְעוּ כִּי־אַתָּה שִׁמְךָ יְהוָה
לְבַדֶּךָ עֶלְיוֹן עַל־כָּל־הָאָרֶץ: יח

Then they will know that You, Your name alone is the Lord Most High over all of the earth. [19]

PSALM 84

A psalm of prayer, expressing a yearning for intimacy with God
and a desire to pray to Him at the Temple.

לַמְנַצֵּחַ עַל־הַגִּתִּית לִבְנֵי־
קֹרַח מִזְמוֹר: א

For the chief musician, on the *gittit*, a psalm by the sons of Korah. [1]

---

[16] **So may You pursue them with Your tempest, terrify them with Your storm.**

[17] **Fill their faces with shame until** in desperation **they seek Your name** to save their lives, **Lord.**

[18] **May they be ashamed and frightened forever; may they be humiliated and may they perish.**

[19] **Then they will know that You, Your name alone is the Lord.** They will ultimately come to realize that only Your name and Your power are eternal, and that You are the **Most High over all of the earth.**

PSALM 84
[1] **For the chief musician, on the *gittit*, a psalm by the sons of Korah.**

מַה־יְּדִידוֹת מִשְׁכְּנוֹתֶיךָ
יהוה צְבָאוֹת:

נִכְסְפָה וְגַם־כָּלְתָה ׀ נַפְשִׁי
לְחַצְרוֹת יהוה לִבִּי וּבְשָׂרִי
יְרַנְּנוּ אֶל אֵל־חָי:

גַּם־צִפּוֹר ׀ מָצְאָה בַיִת
וּדְרוֹר ׀ קֵן ׀ לָהּ אֲשֶׁר־שָׁתָה
אֶפְרֹחֶיהָ אֶת־מִזְבְּחוֹתֶיךָ
יהוה צְבָאוֹת מַלְכִּי וֵאלֹהָי:

אַשְׁרֵי יוֹשְׁבֵי בֵיתֶךָ עוֹד
יְהַלְלוּךָ סֶּלָה:

אַשְׁרֵי אָדָם עוֹז־לוֹ בָךְ
מְסִלּוֹת בִּלְבָבָם:

עֹבְרֵי ׀ בְּעֵמֶק הַבָּכָא מַעְיָן
יְשִׁיתוּהוּ גַּם־בְּרָכוֹת יַעְטֶה
מוֹרֶה:

² How pleasing are Your dwelling places, Lord of hosts.

³ My soul longs, indeed it yearns for the courtyards of the Lord; my heart and my flesh sing with joy to the living Almighty.

⁴ Even the bird has found a home, the sparrow a nest for herself where she can put her young; at Your altars, Lord of hosts, my King and my God.

⁵ Happy are those who dwell in Your House; they will continually praise You, Selah.

⁶ Happy are those whose strength is in You, and whose hearts follow Your path.

⁷ When they pass through a valley of tears, they make it into a spring. Indeed, blessings cover the guide.

---

2 How pleasing are Your dwelling places, Lord of hosts.

3 My soul longs, indeed it yearns for the courtyards of the Lord; my heart and my flesh sing with joy to the living Almighty.

4 **Even the bird** that travels far and wide **has found a home,** and **the sparrow** too has **a nest for herself where she can put her young;** as for me, I wish my place of rest to be **at Your altars, Lord of hosts, my King and my God.**

5 Happy are those who dwell in Your House; they will continually praise You, Selah.

6 Happy are those whose strength is in You, and whose hearts follow Your path.

7 **When they pass through a valley of tears;** according to an alternative interpretation, the phrase *emek habakha,* translated here as "valley of tears," refers to a valley near Jerusalem where trees called *bakha* grew.[16] **They,** through their prayers and devotion to God, can **make it into a** flowing **spring. Indeed, blessings cover** even **the guide** who leads the way into these places.

יֵלְכוּ מֵחַ֫יִל אֶל־חָ֥יִל יֵרָאֶ֖ה
אֶל־אֱלֹהִ֣ים בְּצִיּֽוֹן:

יְהֹוָ֤ה אֱלֹהִ֣ים צְבָא֣וֹת שִׁמְעָ֣ה
תְפִלָּתִ֑י הַאֲזִ֖ינָה אֱלֹהֵ֣י יַעֲקֹ֣ב
סֶֽלָה:

מָ֭גִנֵּנוּ רְאֵ֣ה אֱלֹהִ֑ים וְֽ֝הַבֵּ֗ט
פְּנֵ֣י מְשִׁיחֶֽךָ:

כִּ֤י טֽוֹב־י֣וֹם בַּ֭חֲצֵרֶיךָ מֵאָ֑לֶף
בָּחַ֗רְתִּי הִ֭סְתּוֹפֵף בְּבֵ֣ית
אֱלֹהַ֑י מִ֝דּ֗וּר בְּאׇהֳלֵי־רֶֽשַׁע:

כִּ֤י שֶׁ֨מֶשׁ ׀ וּמָגֵן֮ יְהֹוָ֪ה אֱלֹ֫הִ֥ים
חֵ֣ן וְ֭כָבוֹד יִתֵּ֣ן יְהֹוָ֑ה לֹ֥א
יִמְנַע־ט֝֗וֹב לַֽהֹלְכִ֥ים בְּתָמִֽים:

יְהֹוָ֥ה צְבָא֑וֹת אַֽשְׁרֵ֥י אָ֝דָ֗ם
בֹּטֵ֥חַ בָּֽךְ:

8 They go from one success to another; they will be seen before God in Zion.

9 Lord, God of hosts, hear my prayer. Listen, God of Jacob, Selah.

10 See our shield, God; look upon the face of Your anointed one.

11 For one day in Your courtyard is better than a thousand; I would rather stand at the threshold of the House of my God than dwell in tents of wickedness.

12 For the Lord God is a sun and a shield; the Lord gives grace and honor. He withholds no good from those who walk uprightly.

13 Lord of hosts, happy is the man who trusts in You.

---

8 **They go from one success to another; they will be seen before God in Zion,** which is where their chosen path leads.

9 **Lord, God of hosts, hear my prayer. Listen, God of Jacob, Selah.**

10 **See** and assist **our shield,** the king who defends us, **God; look** with favor **upon the face of Your anointed one.**

11 **For one day in Your courtyard is better than a thousand** ordinary days; **I would rather stand at the threshold of the House of my God than dwell in tents of wickedness.**

12 **For the Lord God is a sun,** a source of light and strength, **and a shield** and protection; **the Lord gives grace and honor** to those who serve Him. **He withholds no good from those who walk uprightly.**

13 **Lord of hosts, happy is the man who trusts in You.**

PSALM 85

A psalm expressing gratitude to God, acknowledging that things have taken a turn for the better,
though it also notes less auspicious times in the distant and more recent past.

^א לַמְנַצֵּחַ לִבְנֵי־קֹרַח מִזְמֹור:

^ב רָצִיתָ יהוה אַרְצֶךָ שַׁבְתָּ
שְׁבִית שְׁבוּת יַעֲקֹב:

^ג נָשָׂאתָ עֲוֹן עַמֶּךָ כִּסִּיתָ כָל־
חַטָּאתָם סֶלָה:

^ד אָסַפְתָּ כָל־עֶבְרָתֶךָ הֱשִׁיבוֹתָ
מֵחֲרוֹן אַפֶּךָ:

^ה שׁוּבֵנוּ אֱלֹהֵי יִשְׁעֵנוּ וְהָפֵר
כַּעַסְךָ עִמָּנוּ:

¹ For the chief musician, a psalm
by the sons of Korah.

² Lord, You showed favor to
Your land; You returned Jacob
from captivity.

³ You forgave the iniquity of
Your people; You covered all of
their sins, Selah.

⁴ You gathered in all of Your fury;
You turned away from Your
fierce anger.

⁵ Return to us, God of our
salvation, and revoke Your
anger against us.

PSALM 85

¹ **For the chief musician, a psalm by the sons of Korah.**

² **Lord, You showed favor to Your land;** You turned Your attention toward it with favor and love,
You returned Jacob to it **from captivity.**

³ **You forgave the iniquity of Your people; You covered all of their sins,** that is, You have
completely forgiven them (see 32:1), to the extent that their sins are no longer known. A person
who truly repents is called *kesui ḥata'a*, someone whose sins have been completely "covered over."
Selah.

⁴ **You gathered in,** that is, You have taken away, **all of Your fury; You turned away from Your
fierce anger.**

⁵ The following are verses of entreaty: **Return to us, God of our salvation, and revoke Your
anger against us.**

הַלְעוֹלָם תֶּאֱנַף־בָּנוּ תִּמְשֹׁךְ
אַפְּךָ לְדֹר וָדֹר:

הֲלֹא־אַתָּה תָּשׁוּב תְּחַיֵּינוּ
וְעַמְּךָ יִשְׂמְחוּ־בָךְ:

הַרְאֵנוּ יהוה חַסְדֶּךָ וְיֶשְׁעֲךָ
תִּתֶּן־לָנוּ:

אֶשְׁמְעָה מַה־יְדַבֵּר הָאֵל ׀
יְהֹוָה כִּי ׀ יְדַבֵּר שָׁלוֹם אֶל־
עַמּוֹ וְאֶל־חֲסִידָיו וְאַל־יָשׁוּבוּ
לְכִסְלָה:

אַךְ קָרוֹב לִירֵאָיו יִשְׁעוֹ
לִשְׁכֹּן כָּבוֹד בְּאַרְצֵנוּ:

חֶסֶד־וֶאֱמֶת נִפְגָּשׁוּ צֶדֶק
וְשָׁלוֹם נָשָׁקוּ:

6 Will You be enraged with us forever? Will You draw out Your wrath for generations?

7 Surely You will once again revive us, so Your people might rejoice in You.

8 Show us Your mercy, Lord, and grant us Your salvation.

9 I will hear what the Almighty Lord has to say, for He will speak peace to His people and to His devoted ones if they do not return to folly.

10 Indeed, His salvation is near for those who fear Him, so that glory may dwell in our land.

11 Kindness and truth have met; justice and peace have touched.

---

6 **Will You be enraged with us forever? Will You draw out Your wrath for generations?**

7 **Surely You will once again revive us, so Your people might rejoice in You.**

8 **Show us Your mercy, Lord, and grant us Your salvation.**

9 **I will hear what the Almighty Lord has to say** about my plea. The psalmist reveals God's response: **For He will speak peace to His people and to His devoted ones**, but with one condition: **If they do not return to folly,** that is, sinful behavior, which is in essence a form of foolishness.

10 **Indeed, His salvation is near for those who fear Him** and we will once again witness His revelation, **so that glory may dwell in our land.**

11 And God's revelation will bring about a point of contact of all that is good: **Kindness and truth have met; justice and peace have touched.** All these qualities come together when God's revelation is realized. Although kindness and truth do not always lead to the same outcome, and similarly for justice and peace, in a world that has attained a level of wholeness and conciliation, such convergence is possible.

יב אֱמֶת מֵאֶרֶץ תִּצְמָח וְצֶדֶק
מִשָּׁמַיִם נִשְׁקָף:

12 Truth will spring up from the earth as righteousness looks down from heaven.

יג גַּם־יהוה יִתֵּן הַטּוֹב וְאַרְצֵנוּ
תִּתֵּן יְבוּלָהּ:

13 Indeed, the Lord will bestow what is good, and our land will yield its produce.

יד צֶדֶק לְפָנָיו יְהַלֵּךְ וְיָשֵׂם
לְדֶרֶךְ פְּעָמָיו:

14 Justice will go before Him as He sets His footsteps on the path.

PSALM 86

A cry to God for help. The psalmist is vulnerable and threatened from all sides.
He prays to God not only to be saved, but also to have the strength to remain on the right path.

א תְּפִלָּה לְדָוִד הַטֵּה־יהוה
אָזְנְךָ עֲנֵנִי כִּי־עָנִי וְאֶבְיוֹן
אָנִי:

1 A prayer by David. Incline Your ear, Lord, answer me, for I am poor and needy.

---

12 At that time, **truth will spring up from the earth as righteousness looks down from heaven** and will be felt as well by those on earth.

13 **Indeed, the Lord will bestow what is good** to everyone, **and our land will yield its produce.**

14 **Justice will go before Him as He sets His footsteps on the path**. Metaphorically speaking, justice will be witnessed and felt by all as it sets out on the path, and the glory of God follows.

PSALM 86

1 **A prayer by David.** The psalmist begins with a general request: **Incline Your ear, Lord, answer me, for I am poor and needy** and worthy of Your pity like any other unfortunate person.

שָׁמְרָ֣ה נַפְשִׁי֮ כִּֽי־חָסִ֪יד אָ֥נִי
הוֹשַׁ֣ע עַ֭בְדְּךָ אַתָּ֣ה אֱלֹהַ֑י
הַבּוֹטֵ֥חַ אֵלֶֽיךָ׃

2 Watch over me, for I am faithful. You, who are my God, save Your servant who trusts in You.

חָנֵּ֥נִי אֲדֹנָ֑י כִּֽי־אֵלֶ֥יךָ אֶ֝קְרָ֗א
כׇּל־הַיּֽוֹם׃

3 Have mercy on me, Lord, for I call to You all day long.

שַׂ֭מֵּחַ נֶ֣פֶשׁ עַבְדֶּ֑ךָ כִּ֥י־אֵלֶ֥יךָ
אֲ֝דֹנָ֗י נַפְשִׁ֥י אֶשָּֽׂא׃

4 Gladden the soul of Your servant, for to You, Lord, I lift up my soul.

כִּֽי־אַתָּ֣ה אֲ֭דֹנָי ט֣וֹב וְסַלָּ֑ח
וְרַב־חֶ֝֗סֶד לְכׇל־קֹרְאֶֽיךָ׃

5 For You, my Lord, are good and forgiving, abounding in kindness to all who call to You.

הַאֲזִ֣ינָה יְ֭הֹוָה תְּפִלָּתִ֑י
וְ֝הַקְשִׁ֗יבָה בְּק֣וֹל תַּחֲנוּנוֹתָֽי׃

6 Listen, Lord, to my prayer; pay heed to the voice of my pleas.

בְּי֣וֹם צָ֭רָתִי אֶקְרָאֶ֑ךָּ כִּ֣י
תַעֲנֵֽנִי׃

7 In my time of trouble I call to You, for You will answer me.

אֵין־כָּמ֖וֹךָ בָאֱלֹהִ֥ים ׀ אֲדֹנָ֗י
וְאֵ֣ין כְּמַעֲשֶֽׂיךָ׃

8 There is none like You among the gods, Lord, and nothing akin to Your deeds.

---

2 Here the psalmist becomes more specific in his request: **Watch over me, for I am faithful;** I have chosen to follow a good and honest path. **You, who are my God, save Your servant who trusts in You.**

3 **Have mercy on me, Lord, for I call to You all day long.**

4 **Gladden the soul of Your servant, for to You, Lord, I lift up my soul** in prayer, recognizing that You are my only source of strength and hope.

5 **For You, my Lord, are good and forgiving, abounding in kindness to all who call to You.**

6 **Listen, Lord, to my prayer; pay heed to the voice of my pleas.**

7 **In my time of trouble I call to You, for** I know that **You will answer me.**

8 **There is none like You among the gods, Lord, and nothing akin to Your deeds.**

ט כָּל־גּוֹיִם ׀ אֲשֶׁר עָשִׂיתָ
יָבוֹאוּ ׀ וְיִשְׁתַּחֲווּ לְפָנֶיךָ אֲדֹנָי
וִיכַבְּדוּ לִשְׁמֶךָ:

All the nations You made
will come and bow before
You, Lord, and give honor to
Your name.

י כִּי־גָדוֹל אַתָּה וְעֹשֵׂה
נִפְלָאוֹת אַתָּה אֱלֹהִים
לְבַדֶּךָ:

10 For You are great and do
wondrous deeds; You alone
are God.

יא הוֹרֵנִי יהוה ׀ דַּרְכֶּךָ אֲהַלֵּךְ
בַּאֲמִתֶּךָ יַחֵד לְבָבִי לְיִרְאָה
שְׁמֶךָ:

11 Teach me Your way, Lord,
so I may walk in Your truth.
Dedicate my heart to fear
Your name.

יב אוֹדְךָ ׀ אֲדֹנָי אֱלֹהַי בְּכָל־
לְבָבִי וַאֲכַבְּדָה שִׁמְךָ
לְעוֹלָם:

12 I give thanks to You, Lord my
God, with all my heart, and I
honor Your name forever.

יג כִּי־חַסְדְּךָ גָּדוֹל עָלָי וְהִצַּלְתָּ
נַפְשִׁי מִשְּׁאוֹל תַּחְתִּיָּה:

13 For Your kindness to me is
great; You rescued me from the
depths of the netherworld.

יד אֱלֹהִים ׀ זֵדִים קָמוּ־עָלַי
וַעֲדַת עָרִיצִים בִּקְשׁוּ נַפְשִׁי
וְלֹא שָׂמוּךָ לְנֶגְדָּם:

14 God, wicked men have arisen
against me; a band of violent
foes has sought my life. They
have not set You before them.

---

9 Consequently, it is fitting that **all the nations You made will come and bow before You, Lord, and give honor to Your name.**

10 **For You are great and do wondrous deeds; You alone are God.**

11 The psalmist now presents his requests to God: **Teach me Your way, Lord, so I may walk in Your truth,** that is, in the path that is proper and correct before You. **Dedicate my heart** so that it will be involved in nothing else, but only **to fear Your name.**

12 **I give thanks to You, Lord my God, with all my heart, and I honor Your name forever.**

13 **For Your kindness to me is great; You rescued me from the depths of the netherworld.**

14 The psalmist now makes a specific, practical request of God: **God, wicked men have arisen against me; a band of violent foes has sought my life. They have not set You before them;** they do as they please, without taking Your will into consideration.

וְאַתָּה אֲדֹנָי אֵל־רַחוּם וְחַנּוּן ﬞﬞ
אֶרֶךְ אַפַּיִם וְרַב־חֶסֶד וֶאֱמֶת:

פְּנֵה אֵלַי וְחָנֵּנִי תְּנָה־עֻזְּךָ
לְעַבְדֶּךָ וְהוֹשִׁיעָה לְבֶן־
אֲמָתֶךָ:

עֲשֵׂה־עִמִּי אוֹת לְטוֹבָה
וְיִרְאוּ שֹׂנְאַי וְיֵבֹשׁוּ כִּי־אַתָּה
יהוה עֲזַרְתַּנִי וְנִחַמְתָּנִי:

15 But You, Lord, are Almighty, full of mercy and gracious, slow to anger and abundant in kindness and truth.

16 Turn to me and be gracious to me. Give Your strength to Your servant; save the son of Your handmaid.

17 Show me a sign for good, so that those who hate me may see it and be shamed, for You, Lord, have helped and comforted me.

PSALM 87

A psalm of praise with particular emphasis on Jerusalem.

לִבְנֵי־קֹרַח מִזְמוֹר שִׁיר ﬞ
יְסוּדָתוֹ בְּהַרְרֵי־קֹדֶשׁ:

1 A song, a psalm by the sons of Korah; its foundation is in the holy mountains.

---

15 **But You, Lord, are Almighty, full of mercy and gracious, slow to anger and abundant in kindness and truth.**[17]

16 **Turn to me and be gracious to me. Give Your strength to Your servant; save the son of Your handmaid,** an expression indicating a slave born into slavery, who has never known personal independence nor had any other master.

17 **Show me a sign for good,** some indication, to myself and to others, that You indeed intend to come to my aid, **so that those who hate me may see it and be shamed, for** they will realize that **You, Lord, have helped and comforted me.**

PSALM 87

1 **A song, a psalm by the sons of Korah; its foundation is in the holy mountains.** The main subject of this song is the mountains upon which Jerusalem rests, and specifically the Temple Mount.

אֹהֵב יהוה שַׁעֲרֵי צִיּוֹן מִכֹּל
מִשְׁכְּנוֹת יַעֲקֹב:

2 The Lord loves the gates of Zion more than all the dwelling places of Jacob.

נִכְבָּדוֹת מְדֻבָּר בָּךְ עִיר
הָאֱלֹהִים סֶלָה:

3 Glorious things are spoken of you, city of God, Selah.

אַזְכִּיר ׀ רַהַב וּבָבֶל לְיֹדְעָי
הִנֵּה פְלֶשֶׁת וְצוֹר עִם־כּוּשׁ
זֶה יֻלַּד־שָׁם:

4 To those of my acquaintance, I mention Rahav and Babylon. Behold Philistia and Tyre and Kush. This one was born there.

וּלְצִיּוֹן ׀ יֵאָמַר אִישׁ וְאִישׁ
יֻלַּד־בָּהּ וְהוּא יְכוֹנְנֶהָ עֶלְיוֹן:

5 But of Zion it is said: This man and that man were born there. May the Most High establish it firmly.

יהוה יִסְפֹּר בִּכְתוֹב עַמִּים זֶה
יֻלַּד־שָׁם סֶלָה:

6 When the Lord makes account of the peoples: This one was born there, Selah.

---

2 **The Lord loves the gates of Zion more than all the dwelling places of Jacob,** because that is the city that He chose for Himself.

3 **Glorious things are spoken of you, city of God, Selah.**

4 Jerusalem, the city of God, is praiseworthy in comparison not only with other "dwelling places of Jacob" but also with all other places in the world. The psalmist offers a number of examples: **To those of my acquaintance, I mention Rahav,** literally "arrogance," another name for Egypt,[18] **and Babylon,** the two great empires of the time. **Behold Philistia and Tyre,** on the Mediterranean coast, **and Kush,** far to the south. In all these places there may occasionally be found a native who brings pride to his country, and of whom it might be said: **This one was born there.**

5 **But of Zion it is said: This man and that man were born there.** *Ish*, translated as "man," often refers specifically to a person of prominence. It is not necessary to search in Zion for an occasional exceptional person; many great people are found there. **May the Most High establish it firmly.**

6 **When the Lord makes account of the peoples,** there will still be one unique city, Jerusalem, concerning which it will be said of many prominent individuals: **This one was born there, Selah.**

וְשָׁרִים כְּחֹלְלִים כָּל־מַעְיָנַי
בָּךְ:

7 And singers and dancers alike:
All my deepest desires are
in you.

PSALM 88

A psalm of entreaty. The psalmist, suffering from grave illness and shunned by those once close to him, prays to God to rescue him from his suffering and bring about his recovery.

שִׁיר מִזְמוֹר לִבְנֵי קֹרַח
לַמְנַצֵּחַ עַל־מָחֲלַת לְעַנּוֹת
מַשְׂכִּיל לְהֵימָן הָאֶזְרָחִי:

יְהוָה אֱלֹהֵי יְשׁוּעָתִי יוֹם־
צָעַקְתִּי בַלַּיְלָה נֶגְדֶּךָ:

א 1 A song, a psalm by the
sons of Korah for the chief
musician on *maḥalat le'anot*;
a contemplation by Heiman
the Ezrahite.

יח לחודש
18th day
of month

ב 2 Lord, God of my salvation, I
cry out before You by day and
by night.

---

7 **And singers and dancers alike** exclaim in honor of Jerusalem: **All my deepest desires are in you,** Jerusalem.

PSALM 88

1 **A song, a psalm by the sons of Korah for the chief musician on *maḥalat le'anot*.** The word *le'anot* can mean "for response," and may indicate that this psalm is meant to be sung by two groups, the second responding to the first, with either a refrain or a complementary verse, as is the case in songs of lamentation. **A contemplation by Heiman the Ezrahite.** This may be referring to the descendant of Korah by that name, a Levite who lived in the time of King David.[19] Alternatively, he may be identified as one of the descendants of Zerah, from the tribe of Judah.[20] Unlike other psalms entreating God for relief, it does not end on an optimistic note.

2 **Lord, God of my salvation, I cry out before You by day and by night.**

תָּבוֹא לְפָנֶיךָ תְּפִלָּתִי הַטֵּה
אׇזְנְךָ לְרִנָּתִי:

כִּי־שָׂבְעָה בְרָעוֹת נַפְשִׁי וְחַיַּי
לִשְׁאוֹל הִגִּיעוּ:

נֶחְשַׁבְתִּי עִם־יוֹרְדֵי בוֹר
הָיִיתִי כְּגֶבֶר אֵין־אֱיָל:

בַּמֵּתִים חׇפְשִׁי כְּמוֹ חֲלָלִים ׀
שֹׁכְבֵי קֶבֶר אֲשֶׁר לֹא זְכַרְתָּם
עוֹד וְהֵמָּה מִיָּדְךָ נִגְזָרוּ:

שַׁתַּנִי בְּבוֹר תַּחְתִּיּוֹת
בְּמַחֲשַׁכִּים בִּמְצֹלוֹת:

עָלַי סָמְכָה חֲמָתֶךָ וְכׇל־
מִשְׁבָּרֶיךָ עִנִּיתָ סֶּלָה:

3 Let my prayer come before You; incline Your ear to my plea.

4 For I am sated with evils; my life is at the brink of the netherworld.

5 I am reckoned as one who has gone down to the pit; I have become like a man with no strength,

6 set free among the dead, like those slain ones lying in the grave whom You no longer remember, those cut off from Your hand.

7 You put me in the lowest pit, in the dark places of the deep.

8 Your wrath weighs upon me; You torment me with all Your breakers, Selah.

---

3 **Let my prayer come before You; incline Your ear to my plea.**

4 **For I am sated with evils;** I do not have the capacity to bear any further suffering. **My life is at the brink of the netherworld,** on the verge of death.

5 **I am reckoned** by some **as one who has** already died and **gone down to the pit,** buried in my grave; **I have become like a man with no** remaining **strength,**

6 **set free** from earthly concerns, **among the dead, like those slain ones lying in the grave whom You no longer remember,** for You have no reason to be involved with those who are dead, **those cut off from Your hand,** or "by Your hand."

7 **You put me in the lowest pit, in the dark places of the deep;** it is as if I am buried deep in the earth.

8 **Your wrath weighs upon me; You torment me with all Your breakers;** it feels as though all Your tidal waves, all the tribulations of the world, are directed against me, **Selah.**

הִרְחַקְתָּ מְיֻדָּעַי מִמֶּנִּי שַׁתַּנִי
תוֹעֵבוֹת לָמוֹ כָּלֻא וְלֹא
אֵצֵא:

עֵינִי דָאֲבָה מִנִּי עֹנִי קְרָאתִיךָ
יהוה בְּכָל־יוֹם שִׁטַּחְתִּי
אֵלֶיךָ כַפָּי:

הֲלַמֵּתִים תַּעֲשֶׂה־פֶּלֶא אִם־
רְפָאִים יָקוּמוּ ׀ יוֹדוּךָ סֶּלָה:

הַיְסֻפַּר בַּקֶּבֶר חַסְדֶּךָ
אֱמוּנָתְךָ בָּאֲבַדּוֹן:

הֲיִוָּדַע בַּחֹשֶׁךְ פִּלְאֶךָ
וְצִדְקָתְךָ בְּאֶרֶץ נְשִׁיָּה:

וַאֲנִי ׀ אֵלֶיךָ יהוה שִׁוַּעְתִּי
וּבַבֹּקֶר תְּפִלָּתִי תְקַדְּמֶךָּ:

9 You have distanced me from my acquaintances; You have made me an object of loathing to them. I am shut in and cannot go out.

10 My eyes ache from misery. Lord, I call to You daily; I stretch out my hands to You.

11 Do You perform wonders for the dead? Do departed spirits rise and praise You? Selah.

12 Is Your kindness recounted in the grave? Your faithfulness in the place of destruction?

13 Are Your wonders made known in the darkness? Your righteousness in the land of forgetfulness?

14 But I, Lord, I have cried out to You for help, and my prayer greets You in the morning.

---

9 **You have distanced me from my acquaintances; You have made me an object of loathing to them. I am shut in and cannot go out.**

10 **My eyes ache from misery. Lord, I call to You daily; I stretch out my hands to You** in prayer, yet my cries go unanswered.

11 Since I feel dead already, I cannot help but wonder: **Do You perform wonders for the dead? Do departed spirits rise and praise You?** Certainly not; they are beyond all hope, **Selah.**

12 **Is Your kindness recounted in the grave? Your faithfulness in the place of destruction?**

13 **Are Your wonders made known in the darkness? Your righteousness in the land of forgetfulness,** in the world of the dead?

14 **But I, Lord,** though I feel I am in just such a place, close to death, **I have cried out to You for help, and my prayer greets You** early **in the morning,** even before other people begin to pray.

לָמָה יְהֹוָה תִּזְנַח נַפְשִׁי תַּסְתִּיר פָּנֶיךָ מִמֶּנִּי: טו

עָנִי אֲנִי וְגוֵֹעַ מִנֹּעַר נָשָׂאתִי אֵמֶיךָ אָפוּנָה: טז

עָלַי עָבְרוּ חֲרוֹנֶיךָ בִּעוּתֶיךָ צִמְּתוּתֻנִי: יז

סַבּוּנִי כַמַּיִם כָּל־הַיּוֹם הִקִּיפוּ עָלַי יָחַד: יח

הִרְחַקְתָּ מִמֶּנִּי אֹהֵב וָרֵעַ מְיֻדָּעַי מַחְשָׁךְ: יט

15 Lord, why do You neglect my soul, hide Your face from me?

16 From my youth I have been afflicted and near death. I bear Your terrors; my attention is turned to them.

17 Your furies have swept over me; Your horrors have silenced me.

18 They surround me like water, all day long. They encompass me altogether.

19 You have distanced friend and comrade from me; those who know me are in darkness.

---

15 And this is what I say in my prayer: **Lord, why do You neglect my soul, hide Your face from me?**

16 **From my youth I have been afflicted and near death;** suffering is not new to me. **I bear Your terrors; my attention is turned to them,** for they surround me on all sides.

17 **Your furies have swept over me; Your horrors have silenced me** out of fear.

18 **They,** all my troubles and suffering, **surround me like water, all day long,** as a man who has fallen into a large body of water. **They encompass me altogether.**

19 There is no one to come to my aid, for **You have distanced** every **friend and comrade from me; those who know me are** as if **in darkness,** as I cannot see them anywhere.

PSALM 89

A psalm with two distinct parts: Praise for God for all His deeds from the beginning of Creation until the time of the reign of David, followed by entreaty and even protest against Him. Being a psalm of prayer, the tone is not defiant.

מַשְׂכִּיל לְאֵיתָן הָאֶזְרָחִי: א

חַסְדֵי יהוה עוֹלָם אָשִׁירָה ב
לְדֹר וָדֹר ׀ אוֹדִיעַ אֱמוּנָתְךָ
בְּפִי:

כִּי־אָמַרְתִּי עוֹלָם חֶסֶד יִבָּנֶה ג
שָׁמַיִם ׀ תָּכִן אֱמוּנָתְךָ בָהֶם:

כָּרַתִּי בְרִית לִבְחִירִי ד
נִשְׁבַּעְתִּי לְדָוִד עַבְדִּי:

1 A contemplation by Eitan the Ezrahite.

2 I will sing of the Lord's kindness forever. For all generations, my mouth will make known Your faithfulness.

3 For I said: Kindness is forever sustained; You set Your constancy in the heavens.

4 I made a covenant with My chosen one; I made an oath to David, My servant.

PSALM 89

1 **A contemplation.** Like other psalms with the heading *maskil*, this psalm seeks to present a specific idea, woven throughout the text, in a poetic and contemplative manner. **By Eitan the Ezrahite.** The identity of this person is unclear, as he is rarely mentioned in the Bible. Some commentators believe that the term "Ezrahite" indicates that he is Eitan son of Zerah,[21] from the tribe of Judah; others identify him with the Levite by that name who sang in the Temple in its early days.[22] According to one interpretation, Eitan is another name for the patriarch Abraham; if so, the events mentioned in the psalm represent his prophecy regarding incidents that would occur in the distant future, namely, the middle or end of the First Temple era.

2 **I will sing of the Lord's kindness forever. For all generations, my mouth will make known Your faithfulness.** *Emunatkha*, translated here as "Your faithfulness," may also mean "my faith in You"; the psalmist is expressing his unquestioning faith in God.

3 **For I said,** I have come to the conclusion that **kindness is forever sustained; You set Your constancy in the heavens.** The word *emuna* is usually translated as "faith" and refers to the spiritual connection between man and God. However, here and in several other verses of this psalm, the term conveys the notion of steadfastness and stability; hence, "Your constancy."

4 In the next two verses the speaker is God: **I made a covenant with My chosen one; I made an oath to David, My servant.** The psalmist here expresses his faith that God's constancy is

ה עַד־עוֹלָם אָכִין זַרְעֶךָ וּבָנִיתִי
לְדֹר־וָדוֹר כִּסְאֲךָ סֶלָה:

ו וְיוֹדוּ שָׁמַיִם פִּלְאֲךָ יהוה אַף־
אֱמוּנָתְךָ בִּקְהַל קְדֹשִׁים:

ז כִּי מִי בַשַּׁחַק יַעֲרֹךְ לַיהוה
יִדְמֶה לַיהוה בִּבְנֵי אֵלִים:

ח אֵל נַעֲרָץ בְּסוֹד־קְדֹשִׁים
רַבָּה וְנוֹרָא עַל־כָּל־סְבִיבָיו:

ט יהוה ׀ אֱלֹהֵי צְבָאוֹת מִי־
כָמוֹךָ חֲסִין ׀ יָהּ וֶאֱמוּנָתְךָ
סְבִיבוֹתֶיךָ:

5 I will establish your seed forever, and build up your throne for all generations, Selah.

6 The heavens praise Your wonders, Lord, and Your constancy in the assembly of holy ones.

7 For who in the skies compares to the Lord? Who among sons of the mighty is like the Lord?

8 The Almighty is revered in the great assembly of the holy ones, awesome to all who surround Him.

9 Lord, God of hosts, who is like You, mighty Lord? Your constancy surrounds You.

---

also manifest in the everlasting covenant He made with the house of David, as summarized in the next verse.

5 **I will establish your seed forever,** ensuring that your descendants will never cease to be; **and build up your throne for all** those **generations, Selah.**

6 The following are general words in praise of God: **The heavens praise Your wonders, Lord,** by exhibiting Your celestial marvels for all to see, **and Your constancy** is acknowledged **in the assembly of holy ones.**

7 **For who in the skies compares to the Lord? Who among sons of the mighty,** the divine angels, **is like the Lord?**

8 **The Almighty is revered in the great assembly of the holy ones,** the angels, **awesome to all who surround Him.**

9 **Lord, God of hosts,** a term depicting God's might among the hosts of the heavens, **who is like You, mighty Lord? Your constancy surrounds You.**

אַתָּה מוֹשֵׁל בְּגֵאוּת הַיָּם בְּשׂוֹא גַלָּיו אַתָּה תְשַׁבְּחֵם:

¹⁰ You rule the swelling sea; when its waves rise, You still them.

אַתָּה דִכִּאתָ כֶחָלָל רָהַב בִּזְרוֹעַ עֻזְּךָ פִּזַּרְתָּ אוֹיְבֶיךָ:

¹¹ You crushed Rahav like a corpse; with the strength of Your arm, You scattered Your enemies.

לְךָ שָׁמַיִם אַף־לְךָ אָרֶץ תֵּבֵל וּמְלֹאָהּ אַתָּה יְסַדְתָּם:

¹² Yours is the heavens, Yours too is the earth; You founded the world and all it contains.

צָפוֹן וְיָמִין אַתָּה בְרָאתָם תָּבוֹר וְחֶרְמוֹן בְּשִׁמְךָ יְרַנֵּנוּ:

¹³ You created the north and the south. Tavor and Hermon sing with joy in Your name.

לְךָ זְרוֹעַ עִם־גְּבוּרָה תָּעֹז יָדְךָ תָּרוּם יְמִינֶךָ:

¹⁴ Your arm is powerful and Your hand is mighty; Your right hand, exalted.

---

¹⁰ And just as God's rule extends through the heavens, so it is manifest in the world below: **You rule the swelling sea; when its waves rise,** even to great heights, **You still them.** At Your will, the waves become calm, even when they have risen to a point at which they seem to be unstoppable.

¹¹ **You crushed Rahav like a corpse.** According to a number of commentaries, Rahav refers here to the leviathan, one of the "great sea monsters" mentioned in Genesis.[23] Based on this verse, they also say that the original male leviathan was killed by God in ancient times. **With the strength of Your arm, You scattered Your enemies.**

¹² **Yours is the heavens, Yours too is the earth; You founded the world and all it contains.**

¹³ **You created the north and the south.** The great mountains **Tavor and Hermon sing with joy in Your name.** Tavor and Hermon are the two most prominent peaks in Israel, located at either end of the country's mountainous region.

¹⁴ **Your arm is powerful and Your hand is mighty; Your right hand, exalted.** Since the word *yadkha*, translated as "Your hand," is juxtaposed to *yeminekha*, "Your right hand," many commentators maintain that *yadkha* is referring to God's left hand, as it were.

טו צֶדֶק וּמִשְׁפָּט מְכוֹן כִּסְאֶךָ
חֶסֶד וֶאֱמֶת יְקַדְּמוּ פָנֶיךָ:

טז אַשְׁרֵי הָעָם יוֹדְעֵי תְרוּעָה
יהוה בְּאוֹר־פָּנֶיךָ יְהַלֵּכוּן:

יז בְּשִׁמְךָ יְגִילוּן כָּל־הַיּוֹם
וּבְצִדְקָתְךָ יָרוּמוּ:

יח כִּי־תִפְאֶרֶת עֻזָּמוֹ אָתָּה
וּבִרְצוֹנְךָ תָּרִים קַרְנֵנוּ:

יט כִּי לַיהוה מָגִנֵּנוּ וְלִקְדוֹשׁ
יִשְׂרָאֵל מַלְכֵּנוּ:

תָּרוּם

15 Righteousness and justice are
at the base of Your throne;
kindness and truth greet Your
countenance.

16 Happy are the people who
know the clarion call; they
walk, Lord, in the light of Your
countenance.

17 They rejoice in Your name
all day long; they are exalted
through Your righteousness.

18 For You are the glory of their
strength; our horn is raised by
Your favor.

19 For our protection is of the
Lord; our king is of the Holy
One of Israel.

---

15 **Righteousness and justice are at the base of Your throne; kindness and truth greet Your countenance.** Kindness and truth are personified in this verse, depicted as servants of God.

16 **Happy are the people,** Israel, **who know the clarion call,** who know how to praise God and sound the trumpet in His honor; **they walk, Lord, in the light of Your countenance.**

17 **They rejoice in Your name all day long; they are exalted through Your righteousness.** They rely on Your righteousness and are thereby exalted.

18 **For You are the glory of their strength; our horn,** our esteem and power, **is raised by Your favor.** When You favor us, we are exalted.

19 **For our protection is of the Lord; our king is of the Holy One of Israel,** for he rules in God's name.

אָז דִּבַּרְתָּ בְחָזוֹן לַחֲסִידֶיךָ ‎כ

וַתֹּאמֶר שִׁוִּיתִי עֵזֶר עַל־גִּבּוֹר

הֲרִימוֹתִי בָחוּר מֵעָם:

מָצָאתִי דָּוִד עַבְדִּי בְּשֶׁמֶן ‎כא

קָדְשִׁי מְשַׁחְתִּיו:

אֲשֶׁר יָדִי תִּכּוֹן עִמּוֹ אַף־ ‎כב

זְרוֹעִי תְאַמְּצֶנּוּ:

לֹא־יַשִּׁיא אוֹיֵב בּוֹ וּבֶן־עַוְלָה ‎כג

לֹא יְעַנֶּנּוּ:

וְכַתּוֹתִי מִפָּנָיו צָרָיו וּמְשַׂנְאָיו ‎כד

אֶגּוֹף:

וֶאֱמוּנָתִי וְחַסְדִּי עִמּוֹ וּבִשְׁמִי ‎כה

תָּרוּם קַרְנוֹ:

20 You once spoke in a vision to Your devoted ones, saying: I aided the warrior; I raised the one chosen from the people.

21 I found David, My servant; I anointed him with My holy oil,

22 as the one whom My hand will establish; My arm will strengthen him.

23 The enemy will not rule over him; the wicked will not torment him,

24 and I will crush his foes before him and smite those who hate him.

25 My constancy and favor will be with him, and his horn will be raised in My name.

---

20 Until this point, the psalm has focused on the greatness and glory of God, in all of His worlds, and on His particular glory with regard to the Israelites. The following section offers a more specific historical perspective: **You once spoke in a vision to Your devoted ones,** the prophets Samuel, Natan, and Gad, **saying: I aided the warrior; I raised the one chosen from the people.** The next verse identifies this "warrior" and "chosen one" whom God revealed to the prophets.

21 **I found David, My servant.** David was "found" in the sense that he had been an unknown figure, the youngest of Yishai's sons, living in a small town. **I anointed him with My holy oil,** a reference to Samuel's anointment of David as king of Israel,[24]

22 **as the one whom My hand will establish; My arm will strengthen him.**

23 **The enemy will not rule over him; the wicked will not torment him,**

24 **and I will crush his foes before him and smite those who hate him.**

25 **My constancy and favor will be with him, and his horn,** his esteem and power, **will be raised in My name,** because he is protected by the power of God.

כּוֹ וְשַׂמְתִּי בַיָּם יָדוֹ וּבַנְּהָרוֹת
יְמִינוֹ:

כּז הוּא יִקְרָאֵנִי אָבִי אָתָּה אֵלִי
וְצוּר יְשׁוּעָתִי:

כּח אַף־אָנִי בְּכוֹר אֶתְּנֵהוּ עֶלְיוֹן
לְמַלְכֵי־אָרֶץ:

כּט לְעוֹלָם אשמור־לוֹ חַסְדִּי   אֶשְׁמָר־
וּבְרִיתִי נֶאֱמֶנֶת לוֹ:

ל וְשַׂמְתִּי לָעַד זַרְעוֹ וְכִסְאוֹ
כִּימֵי שָׁמָיִם:

לא אִם־יַעַזְבוּ בָנָיו תּוֹרָתִי
וּבְמִשְׁפָּטַי לֹא יֵלֵכוּן:

26 I will set his hand upon the seas, his right hand on the rivers.

27 He will call to Me: You are my Father, my God, and the rock of my salvation.

28 As for Me, I will make him My firstborn, supreme among kings of the earth.

29 I will forever preserve My kindness to him; My covenant with him will be steadfast.

30 I will eternally ensure his seed, and his throne will last as the days of the heavens.

31 If his sons forsake My teaching and do not walk according to My judgments,

---

26 **I will set his hand upon the seas.** He will rule the coastline and the sea, **his right hand on the rivers.** This verse may be a reference to David's future victories, both to the east of the kingdom of Israel, the Jordan River, and to its west, the Mediterranean Sea.

27 **He will call to Me: You are my Father, my God, and the rock of my salvation;** that is, He will remain connected and devoted to God.

28 **As for Me, I will make him My firstborn;** not only will I consider him My son, but I will even regard him as the firstborn, being **supreme among kings of the earth.** King David will see God as his Father, and God in turn will treat David like a favored son.

29 **I will forever preserve My kindness to him; My covenant with him will be steadfast.**

30 This everlasting kindness will be expressed in the fact that **I will eternally ensure his seed, and his throne will last as the days of the heavens,** forever. God's covenant is not only with David personally, but with his family line forever.

31 However, this covenant has conditions that must be met: **If his sons forsake My teaching and do not walk according to My judgments,**

לב אִם־חֻקֹּתַי יְחַלֵּלוּ וּמִצְוֹתַי
לֹא יִשְׁמֹרוּ:

לג וּפָקַדְתִּי בְשֵׁבֶט פִּשְׁעָם
וּבִנְגָעִים עֲוֹנָם:

לד וְחַסְדִּי לֹא־אָפִיר מֵעִמּוֹ וְלֹא
אֲשַׁקֵּר בֶּאֱמוּנָתִי:

לה לֹא־אֲחַלֵּל בְּרִיתִי וּמוֹצָא
שְׂפָתַי לֹא אֲשַׁנֶּה:

לו אַחַת נִשְׁבַּעְתִּי בְקָדְשִׁי אִם־
לְדָוִד אֲכַזֵּב:

לז זַרְעוֹ לְעוֹלָם יִהְיֶה וְכִסְאוֹ
כַשֶּׁמֶשׁ נֶגְדִּי:

32 if they violate My statutes and do not keep My commandments,

33 I shall punish their transgressions with a rod, and their iniquity with plague.

34 But I will not remove My kindness from him or be false to My constancy.

35 I will not violate My covenant, nor alter the utterance of My lips.

36 For I have sworn once by My holiness; I will not be false to David.

37 His seed will endure forever, and his throne will be as the sun before Me,

---

32 if they violate My statutes and do not keep My commandments,

33 I shall punish their transgressions with a rod, and their iniquity with plague.

34 Although David's descendants will not be immune from occasional sinful behavior, they will be punished as individuals, **but I will not remove My kindness from him or be false to My constancy.** Their personal chastisement will not affect God's eternal covenant with the house of David at large.

35 I will not violate My covenant, nor alter the utterance of My lips.

36 For I have sworn once and for all by My holiness; I will not be false to David, and My promise to him was that his dynastic line would continue forever, as the next verse clarifies.

37 His seed will endure forever, and his throne will be as permanent as the sun before Me,

לח כְּיָרֵחַ יִכּוֹן עוֹלָם וְעֵד בַּשַּׁחַק נֶאֱמָן סֶלָה:

לט וְאַתָּה זָנַחְתָּ וַתִּמְאָס הִתְעַבַּרְתָּ עִם־מְשִׁיחֶךָ:

מ נֵאַרְתָּה בְּרִית עַבְדֶּךָ חִלַּלְתָּ לָאָרֶץ נִזְרוֹ:

מא פָּרַצְתָּ כָל־גְּדֵרֹתָיו שַׂמְתָּ מִבְצָרָיו מְחִתָּה:

מב שַׁסֻּהוּ כָּל־עֹבְרֵי דָרֶךְ הָיָה חֶרְפָּה לִשְׁכֵנָיו:

מג הֲרִימוֹתָ יְמִין צָרָיו הִשְׂמַחְתָּ כָּל־אוֹיְבָיו:

---

38 eternal like the moon, a constant witness in the sky, Selah.

39 Yet You abandoned and repulsed, You became wrathful with Your anointed one.

40 You spurned the covenant of Your servant; You profaned his crown on the ground.

41 You breached all his walls, brought his fortresses to a fright.

42 All those passing on the way looted him; he was a disgrace to his neighbors.

43 You raised the right hand of his foes; You made all his enemies rejoice.

---

38 **eternal like the moon,** like the stars that are **a constant witness in the sky, Selah.**

39 Having reiterated the promises made by God to David and his descendants, the psalmist registers his complaint: **Yet You abandoned and repulsed** the house of David, **You became wrathful with Your anointed one,** referring to one or more of the kings who arose among David's descendants.

40 **You spurned the covenant of Your servant; You profaned his crown,** throwing it down, as it were, **on the ground.**

41 **You breached all his walls** that he built, **brought his fortresses to** rubble that is **a fright** to behold.

42 **All those passing on the way looted him,** the king himself as well as his people; **he was a disgrace to his neighbors,** who used his kingdom as a paradigm of disgrace and dishonor.

43 **You raised the right hand of his foes** by giving them strength and power; with this **You made all his enemies rejoice.**

מד אַף־תָּשִׁיב צוּר חַרְבּוֹ וְלֹא
הֲקֵמֹתוֹ בַּמִּלְחָמָה:

מה הִשְׁבַּתָּ מִטְּהָרוֹ וְכִסְאוֹ
לָאָרֶץ מִגַּרְתָּה:

מו הִקְצַרְתָּ יְמֵי עֲלוּמָיו הֶעֱטִיתָ
עָלָיו בּוּשָׁה סֶלָה:

מז עַד־מָה יְהוה תִּסָּתֵר לָנֶצַח
תִּבְעַר כְּמוֹ־אֵשׁ חֲמָתֶךָ:

מח זְכׇר־אֲנִי מֶה־חָלֶד עַל־מַה־
שָּׁוְא בָּרָאתָ כׇל־בְּנֵי־אָדָם:

44 You even turned back the blade of his sword; You did not make him steadfast in battle.

45 You took away from his brightness, cast his throne to the ground.

46 You shortened the days of his youth, cloaked him with shame, Selah.

47 How long, Lord? Will You hide Yourself forever, will Your wrath burn like fire?

48 Remember what I am, what the world is; for what futile purpose did You create all the sons of man?

---

44 **You even turned back the blade of his sword,** making it unreliable and useless; **You did not make him steadfast in battle,** and he was constantly defeated.

45 **You took away,** annulled his eminence **from his** previous **brightness** and pureness, when he was impervious to harm. *Hishbata*, translated as "took away," more literally means "You annulled." You **cast his throne to the ground.**

46 **You shortened the days of his youth,** as he died at a young age and **cloaked him with shame, Selah.** This description of the decline of the kingdom of the house of David expresses the psalmist's complaint and even protest against God for His seemingly broken promise regarding the eternal nature of the Davidic dynasty. It is followed by a concluding section of entreaty:

47 **How long, Lord? Will You hide Yourself forever,** for the defeat and humiliation of Israel and David's line are indications of God hiding His countenance from them. How long **will Your wrath burn like fire?**

48 **Remember what I am, what the world is.** *Ḥaled*, translated here as "world," is related to the root *ḥadal*, meaning "to come to an end." The psalmist calls to God to remember that the world is unstable and finite, and our lives in it are brief. **For what futile purpose did You create all the sons of man?**

מִי גֶבֶר יְחְיֶה וְלֹא יִרְאֶה־ מּט
מָוֶת יְמַלֵּט נַפְשׁוֹ מִיַּד־שְׁאוֹל
סֶלָה:

אַיֵּה ׀ חֲסָדֶיךָ הָרִאשֹׁנִים ׀ נ
אֲדֹנָי נִשְׁבַּעְתָּ לְדָוִד
בֶּאֱמוּנָתֶךָ:

זְכֹר אֲדֹנָי חֶרְפַּת עֲבָדֶיךָ נא
שְׂאֵתִי בְחֵיקִי כָּל־רַבִּים
עַמִּים:

אֲשֶׁר חֵרְפוּ אוֹיְבֶיךָ ׀ יְהֹוָה נב
אֲשֶׁר חֵרְפוּ עִקְּבוֹת מְשִׁיחֶךָ:

בָּרוּךְ יְהֹוָה לְעוֹלָם אָמֵן ׀ נג
וְאָמֵן:

49 Who is the man who can live and not see death, who can save his life from the netherworld? Selah.

50 Where are Your former acts of kindness, Lord, those which You swore to David in Your constancy?

51 Remember, Lord, the humiliation of Your servants. My breast is burdened by all the many nations,

52 for Your enemies revile the Lord. They revile the footsteps of Your anointed one.

53 Blessed be the Lord forever, amen and amen.

---

49 Failure, shame, and hopelessness affect not only the king but the entire kingdom and nation of Israel; we are all mortals. **Who is the man who can live and not see death, who can save his life from the netherworld? Selah.** In the face of each individual's inevitable death, it is still possible to carry on, as long as there remains a sense of hope and a belief in a more certain future. In the present situation, however, the only certainty is death.

50 Therefore, the psalmist turns to God in prayer: **Where are Your former acts of kindness, Lord, those which You swore to David in Your constancy?**

51 **Remember, Lord, the humiliation of** us, **Your servants. My breast is burdened by all the many nations.** It is as if numerous nations were pressing on me, weighing me down, and I am unable to shake them off;

52 **for Your enemies revile the Lord.** In causing us pain and suffering, these nations are also desecrating God, whose name is linked with the nation of Israel and the house of David. **They revile the footsteps of Your anointed one.** The psalm ends on this sad note of entreaty and complaint. There is, however, a final line that concludes the third book of Psalms. It is similar to the conclusion of the other books, but it also relates specifically to the content of this particular psalm:

53 **Blessed be the Lord forever, amen and amen.**

BOOK FOUR

THURSDAY

PSALM 90

A psalm dealing with the human condition and man's relationship with God.
It includes elements of praise, complaint, and entreaty.

תְּפִלָּהֿ לְמֹשֶׁה אִישׁ־
הָאֱלֹהִים אֲדֹנָי מָעוֹן אַתָּה
הָיִיתָ לָּנוּ בְּדֹר וָדֹר:

בְּטֶרֶם ׀ הָרִים יֻלָּדוּ וַתְּחוֹלֵל
אֶרֶץ וְתֵבֵל וּמֵעוֹלָם עַד־
עוֹלָם אַתָּה אֵל:

תָּשֵׁב אֱנוֹשׁ עַד־דַּכָּא
וַתֹּאמֶר שׁוּבוּ בְנֵי־אָדָם:

1 A prayer of Moses, man of God.
Lord, You have been a dwelling
place for us from generation to
generation.

2 Before the birth of mountains,
before You brought forth the
earth and the world, forever
and for eternity have You been
the Almighty.

3 You bring man down until he
is crushed and then You say:
Return, sons of man.

PSALM 90

1 **A prayer of Moses, man of God.** This is the only chapter in Psalms attributed to a person who
lived long before King David. Some of the Sages assert that the ten psalms that follow it were
written by Moses as well. In any case, the content of this psalm, which deals with existential
matters rather than problems of a specific time and place, is certainly appropriate for "Moses,
man of God." The psalm begins with words of praise: **Lord, You have been a dwelling place
for us from generation to generation;** we "dwell" within You forever in the sense that Your
existence is the only thing that is essential and eternal, and all of creation exists only through You.[1]

2 **Before the birth of mountains, before You brought forth the earth and the world,
forever and for eternity have You been the Almighty.**

3 The psalm now presents the crux of the problem: **You bring man down until he is crushed
and then You say: Return,** repent, **sons of man.** Moses is not questioning the need for human
repentance. He is merely stating that as human beings, we cannot measure up to divine standards
of behavior. This argument evokes other prayers by Moses found in the Torah, in which he does not
challenge divine justice but instead highlights the other side of the equation, namely, the human
experience.

כִּי אֶלֶף שָׁנִים בְּעֵינֶיךָ כְּיוֹם
אֶתְמוֹל כִּי יַעֲבֹר וְאַשְׁמוּרָה
בַלָּיְלָה:

זְרַמְתָּם שֵׁנָה יִהְיוּ בַּבֹּקֶר
כֶּחָצִיר יַחֲלֹף:

בַּבֹּקֶר יָצִיץ וְחָלָף לָעֶרֶב
יְמוֹלֵל וְיָבֵשׁ:

כִּי־כָלִינוּ בְאַפֶּךָ וּבַחֲמָתְךָ
נִבְהָלְנוּ:

שַׁתָּ עֲוֹנֹתֵינוּ לְנֶגְדֶּךָ עֲלֻמֵנוּ
לִמְאוֹר פָּנֶיךָ:

⁴ Indeed, a thousand years in Your eyes are like yesterday gone by, like a watch of the night.

⁵ You make them flow past, as if in sleep; in the morning, they pass on like grass,

⁶ sprouting in the morning and then passing on, by evening broken and withered.

⁷ We are consumed by Your wrath, frightened by Your rage.

⁸ You have placed our transgressions before You, our hidden things before the light of Your countenance.

---

⁴ **Indeed, a thousand years in Your eyes are like yesterday gone by.** Time as we know it is irrelevant to God. For Him, a thousand years are like a day gone by, leaving no trace of palpable experience but only memory. **Like a watch of the night.** A portion of the night is known as a "watch." The years pass like a night watch, a period of time that goes unnoticed by mortals, who sleep through it.

⁵ **You make them,** man's days, **flow past, as if in sleep,** like a passing dream, not quite real, and **in the morning,** when this sleep is finished, **they pass on like grass** that dries up and perishes.

⁶ **Sprouting in the morning and then passing on, by evening broken and withered.** Such are the days of our lives compared with divine eternity; our days are ephemeral and inconsequential.

⁷ **We are consumed by Your wrath** even in the midst of our swiftly flowing days, **frightened by Your rage,** distressed and attempting to hide.

⁸ **You have placed our transgressions before You, our hidden things before the light of Your countenance.** Our clandestine acts are all plainly revealed before You; we cannot hide from You.

כִּי כָל־יָמֵינוּ פָּנוּ בְעֶבְרָתֶךָ
כִּלִּינוּ שָׁנֵינוּ כְמוֹ־הֶגֶה:

יְמֵי־שְׁנוֹתֵינוּ בָהֶם שִׁבְעִים
שָׁנָה וְאִם בִּגְבוּרֹת ׀ שְׁמוֹנִים
שָׁנָה וְרָהְבָּם עָמָל וָאָוֶן כִּי־גָז
חִישׁ וַנָּעֻפָה:

מִי־יוֹדֵעַ עֹז אַפֶּךָ וּכְיִרְאָתְךָ
עֶבְרָתֶךָ:

לִמְנוֹת יָמֵינוּ כֵּן הוֹדַע וְנָבִא
לְבַב חָכְמָה:

9 All of our days have passed by in Your fury; we have exhausted our years like an utterance.

10 The days of our lives in it are seventy years, or if with might, eighty years; their pride is toil and emptiness, swiftly passing, and we fly away.

11 Who knows the power of Your wrath? As the fear of You, so is Your fury.

12 Teach us to count each of our days, so we might acquire a heart of wisdom.

---

9 Being human, we sin, and we are punished, and **all of our days have passed by in Your fury; we have exhausted our years** fleetingly, **like an utterance,** which leaves no trace a moment after it is spoken.

10 **The days of our lives in it,** in this world, **are** a mere **seventy years, or if with might, eighty years;** and even **their pride,** the greatest accomplishments of our lives, **is toil** in vain **and emptiness.** *Amal va'aven,* translated here as "toil and emptiness," can also mean "sin and wrongdoing." Our lives are **swiftly passing, and we fly away.** One of the reasons our achievements are so insignificant is that our lives are exceedingly brief. We are so taken up with everyday, mundane matters that we have neither the time nor the strength to consider what is truly important, namely, living in a proper manner and repenting any wrongdoing on our part.

11 **Who** among us **knows the** extent of the **power of Your wrath? As the fear of You, so is Your fury.** On the one hand, we are aware that sins bear consequences, even if we underestimate the severity of the punishment we might incur. On the other hand, we rarely have an opportunity to grasp reality and assess the significance of our lives.

12 **Teach us,** grant us the wisdom **to count each of our days,** to realize that our lives are brief and that each day counts, **so we might** thereby **acquire a heart of wisdom.** If we attain this awareness of the passage of time, we might at least refrain from pursuing matters that are worthless or wrong, things that, while attractive in the short run, have no lasting value and can lead us to incur punishment.

שׁוּבָה יְהוָה עַד־מָתָי וְהִנָּחֵם
עַל־עֲבָדֶיךָ:

שַׂבְּעֵנוּ בַבֹּקֶר חַסְדֶּךָ וּנְרַנְּנָה
וְנִשְׂמְחָה בְּכָל־יָמֵינוּ:

שַׂמְּחֵנוּ כִּימוֹת עִנִּיתָנוּ שְׁנוֹת
רָאִינוּ רָעָה:

יֵרָאֶה אֶל־עֲבָדֶיךָ פָעֳלֶךָ
וַהֲדָרְךָ עַל־בְּנֵיהֶם:

וִיהִי ׀ נֹעַם אֲדֹנָי אֱלֹהֵינוּ
עָלֵינוּ וּמַעֲשֵׂה יָדֵינוּ כּוֹנְנָה
עָלֵינוּ וּמַעֲשֵׂה יָדֵינוּ כּוֹנְנֵהוּ:

13 Return to us, Lord; how long?
Have pity on Your servants.

14 Sate us in the morning with
Your kindness so we may sing
and rejoice all our days.

15 Make us happy as the days You
made us suffer, those years of
evil that we saw.

16 Your deeds will be seen by Your
servants, Your majesty by their
children.

17 May the graciousness of
the Lord our God be upon
us, establishing the work of
our hands for us; indeed,
establishing the work of
our hands.

---

13 The last part of the psalm is an entreaty that is based not so much on man's goodness as on his helplessness and mortality: **Return to us** and show us grace, **Lord; how long** will You remain distanced from us? **Have pity on Your servants.** This expression is used by Moses elsewhere as well;[2] it is an appeal to God to extend His mercy toward us even if we are not worthy of it.

14 **Sate us in the morning,** a reference to the early years of our lives, **with Your kindness, so we may sing and rejoice all our days.** Kindness shown to man in his youth is a source of joy throughout his life, as its memory always remains with him.

15 Alternatively, if You do not shower us with kindness at the beginning of our lives, **make us happy as the days You made us suffer, those years of evil that we saw,** so that the end of our lives, at least, will be good.

16 Once we have a measure of rest and tranquility, **Your deeds will be seen by Your servants;** we will be able to contemplate Your actions. This is also an implied request that God show us His mighty deeds. And let **Your majesty** be witnessed **by their children.**

17 The psalm ends with a general prayer for our lives: **May the graciousness of the Lord our God be upon us,** so that all our difficult, tireless efforts in our endeavors, whose continuity and success we must not take for granted, will prove worthwhile through Your **establishing the work of our hands for us** in our lifetime; indeed, **establishing the work of our hands.**

PSALM 91

A song of encouragement and consolation directed toward one who is under God's protection. The
verses alternate between various voices: That of an individual praying, then a chorus
making general statements, followed by that of the individual, and so on.
At the conclusion are words spoken by God.

א יֹשֵׁב בְּסֵ֫תֶר עֶלְי֑וֹן בְּצֵ֥ל שַׁדַּ֗י
יִתְלוֹנָֽן:

ב אֹמַ֗ר לַֽיהוָה מַחְסִ֥י וּמְצוּדָתִ֑י
אֱלֹהַ֗י אֶבְטַח־בּֽוֹ:

ג כִּ֤י ה֣וּא יַ֭צִּֽילְךָ מִפַּ֥ח יָק֑וּשׁ
מִדֶּ֥בֶר הַוֽוֹת:

ד בְּאֶבְרָת֨וֹ ׀ יָ֥סֶךְ לָ֗ךְ וְתַֽחַת־
כְּנָפָ֥יו תֶּחְסֶ֑ה צִנָּ֖ה וְסֹחֵרָ֣ה
אֲמִתּֽוֹ:

1 He who dwells in the shelter of
the Most High, who abides in
the shadow of the Almighty.

2 I will say of the Lord: He is my
shelter and my fortress, my
God in whom I trust.

3 For He will rescue you from
the ensnaring trap, from
devastating pestilence.

4 He will cover you with His
pinion; you will find refuge
under His wings. His truth is a
shield and armor.

PSALM 91

1 Though it is not an actual heading, this first verse clarifies that the psalm is directed at **he who dwells in the shelter of the Most High, who abides in the shadow of the Almighty,** seeking shelter from the troubles of this world, finding refuge in God, and dwelling under His protection.

2 The psalmist then opens with his prayer: **I will say of the Lord: He is my shelter and my fortress, my God in whom I trust.**

3 The chorus responds: It is indeed good to seek refuge in God, **for He will rescue you from the ensnaring trap, from devastating pestilence.**

4 Or, stated metaphorically: **He will cover you with His pinion; you will find refuge under His wings. His truth is** a source of protection from harm, like **a shield and armor.**

לֹא־תִירָא מִפַּחַד לָיְלָה מֵחֵץ יָעוּף יוֹמָם:

מִדֶּבֶר בָּאֹפֶל יַהֲלֹךְ מִקֶּטֶב יָשׁוּד צָהֳרָיִם:

יִפֹּל מִצִּדְּךָ ׀ אֶלֶף וּרְבָבָה מִימִינֶךָ אֵלֶיךָ לֹא יִגָּשׁ:

רַק בְּעֵינֶיךָ תַבִּיט וְשִׁלֻּמַת רְשָׁעִים תִּרְאֶה:

כִּי־אַתָּה יהוה מַחְסִי עֶלְיוֹן שַׂמְתָּ מְעוֹנֶךָ:

לֹא־תְאֻנֶּה אֵלֶיךָ רָעָה וְנֶגַע לֹא־יִקְרַב בְּאָהֳלֶךָ:

5 You will not fear the terror of night, nor the arrow that flies by day,

6 nor the pestilence that stalks in darkness, nor the destruction that lays waste at noon.

7 A thousand may fall at your side, and ten thousand at your right hand, but you it will not reach.

8 You will just look with your eyes and see the punishment of the wicked.

9 For you, Lord, are my shelter. You have made the Most High your dwelling place.

10 No evil will befall you and no plague will come near your tent,

---

5 **You will not fear the terror of night.** At night, a person is more likely to fear being assaulted directly by an armed attacker. **Nor the arrow that flies by day.** Arrows, on the other hand, are usually shot in the daytime, when their targets are in full sight.

6 **Nor the pestilence that stalks in darkness, nor the destruction that lays waste at noon.**

7 **A thousand may fall** victim to some calamity **at your side, and ten thousand at your right hand, but you it will not reach.**

8 **You will just look with your eyes and see the punishment of the wicked** and how they receive their just rewards.

9 The individual, who finds shelter in God, speaks again: **For You, Lord, are my shelter.** And the chorus responds: It is fitting that you seek shelter in Him, for **you have made the Most High your dwelling place.**

10 As a result of your trust in Him, **no evil will befall you and no plague will come near your tent,**

כִּי מַלְאָכָיו יְצַוֶּה־לָּךְ לִשְׁמָרְךָ
בְּכָל־דְּרָכֶיךָ:

עַל־כַּפַּיִם יִשָּׂאוּנְךָ פֶּן־תִּגֹּף
בָּאֶבֶן רַגְלֶךָ:

עַל־שַׁחַל וָפֶתֶן תִּדְרֹךְ
תִּרְמֹס כְּפִיר וְתַנִּין:

כִּי בִי חָשַׁק וַאֲפַלְּטֵהוּ
אֲשַׂגְּבֵהוּ כִּי־יָדַע שְׁמִי:

יִקְרָאֵנִי וְאֶעֱנֵהוּ עִמּוֹ־אָנֹכִי
בְצָרָה אֲחַלְּצֵהוּ וַאֲכַבְּדֵהוּ:

אֹרֶךְ יָמִים אַשְׂבִּיעֵהוּ
וְאַרְאֵהוּ בִּישׁוּעָתִי:

11 for He will charge His angels on your behalf, to guard you in all your ways.

12 They will carry you on their palms, lest your foot be struck by a stone.

13 You will tread upon lions and vipers; you will trample young lions and serpents.

14 Because he desired Me greatly, I will rescue him; I will be his fortress, for he has known My name.

15 When he calls upon Me, I will answer him. I will be with him in times of trouble; I will deliver him and honor him.

16 I will sate him with length of days, and I will show him My salvation.

---

11 **for He will charge his angels on your behalf, to guard you in all your ways.**

12 **They will carry you on their palms** of their hands, **lest your foot be struck by a stone.** As one lifts up a child and carries him when walking on perilous terrain, the angels will protect you from injury.

13 And because of this protection, **you will** be able to **tread** in complete safety, even **upon lions and vipers; you will** be able to **trample young lions and serpents.**

14 At this point, a third voice is heard, that of God: I grant this extraordinary protection to this individual **because he desired Me greatly,** and therefore **I will rescue him; I will be his fortress, for he has known My name.**

15 **When he calls upon Me, I will answer him. I will be with him in times of trouble; I will deliver him and honor him.** Not only will I rescue him from distress, but I will also help him to achieve greatness and honor.

16 In addition, **I will sate him with length of days, and I will show him My salvation,** sparing him both from personal problems and general misfortunes.

PSALM 92

A psalm dedicated to the Sabbath day. At the same time, it is an all-encompassing meditation on matters of the world, reflecting, as if from on high, on good and evil, success and failure.

א מִזְמוֹר שִׁיר לְיוֹם הַשַּׁבָּת:

ב טוֹב לְהֹדוֹת לַיהוָה וּלְזַמֵּר לְשִׁמְךָ עֶלְיוֹן:

ג לְהַגִּיד בַּבֹּקֶר חַסְדֶּךָ וֶאֱמוּנָתְךָ בַּלֵּילוֹת:

ד עֲלֵי־עָשׂוֹר וַעֲלֵי־נָבֶל עֲלֵי הִגָּיוֹן בְּכִנּוֹר:

A psalm, a song for the Sabbath day.

2 How good it is to give thanks to the Lord, to sing praises to Your name, Most High,

3 to tell of Your kindness in the morning and Your faithfulness in the nights,

4 With a ten-stringed lute and with a harp, with meditative music on the lyre.

PSALM 92

1 **A psalm, a song for the Sabbath day.** Although it was sung in the Temple every Sabbath, this psalm is not really about the Sabbath day as such, but rather what our Sages refer to as "the day that is entirely a Sabbath,"[3] that is, the messianic era, when a final reckoning will enable everything to be understood clearly in hindsight. In essence, the psalm is a reflection and overview of history, in which all the negative events that have transpired will be understood as ephemeral phenomena, and a precursor of evil's ultimate downfall. The righteous, however, will prove to have permanence, stability, and continuous prosperity.

2 **How good it is to give thanks to the Lord.** Gratitude is being expressed in this verse for man's very ability to give thanks to God. **To sing praises to Your name, Most High,**

3 **to tell of Your kindness in the morning.** We express gratitude "in the morning," a metaphor for a period when God's mercy is evident and revealed to us. **And Your faithfulness in the nights.** "The nights" are symbolic of dark times or periods of despondency, when it may appear as if God has withdrawn. At such times, it is faith in God that sustains a person.

4 **With a ten-stringed lute and with a harp, with meditative music on the lyre,** an instrument similar to a harp but with fewer strings. The word *higayon*, translated here as "meditative music," may refer to a certain type of melody or a specific way of playing a tune on the lyre.

כִּי שִׂמַּחְתַּנִי יהוה בְּפָעֳלֶךָ
בְּמַעֲשֵׂי יָדֶיךָ אֲרַנֵּן:

מַה־גָּדְלוּ מַעֲשֶׂיךָ יהוה מְאֹד
עָמְקוּ מַחְשְׁבֹתֶיךָ:

אִישׁ־בַּעַר לֹא יֵדָע וּכְסִיל
לֹא־יָבִין אֶת־זֹאת:

בִּפְרֹחַ רְשָׁעִים ׀ כְּמוֹ
עֵשֶׂב וַיָּצִיצוּ כָּל־פֹּעֲלֵי אָוֶן
לְהִשָּׁמְדָם עֲדֵי־עַד:

וְאַתָּה מָרוֹם לְעֹלָם יהוה:

⁵ For You, Lord, have made me
happy by Your actions; I will
sing for joy at the work of
Your hands.

⁶ How great are Your works,
Lord; how profound Your
thoughts.

⁷ A boor cannot know, a fool
cannot understand this.

⁸ When the wicked sprout like
grass and evildoers flourish, it
is only toward their eternal
destruction.

⁹ And You, Lord, are forever
on high.

---

⁵ Here begins the actual content of the song: **For You, Lord, have made me happy by Your actions** in creating the world; **I will sing for joy at the work of Your hands,** all the creations found in the world.

⁶ **How great are Your works, Lord.** The quantity and quality of Your creations, which are manifest before us, give some indication of Your infinite greatness. **How profound Your thoughts.** Aside from that which we can see ourselves, we realize the depth of Your thoughts, which are beyond our grasp.

⁷ And because of the depth of the divine thoughts, **a boor cannot know** their meaning, **a fool cannot understand this.**

⁸ They cannot understand, for instance, that **when the wicked sprout like grass,** in all places, seemingly with no limitation, **and evildoers flourish, it is only toward their eternal destruction.** In fact, the seeming success of the wicked is nothing more than a means leading to their total destruction. The metaphor is that of ridding a field of weeds: If one waters the ground, the weeds sprout and can be readily identified and eradicated, preparing the field for the sowing of crops.

⁹ **And You, Lord, are forever on high.** You see everything from above, and the apparent rise of the wicked and their subsequent downfall are part of Your plan.

כִּי הִנֵּה אֹיְבֶיךָ יהוה כִּי־הִנֵּה
אֹיְבֶיךָ יֹאבֵדוּ יִתְפָּרְדוּ כָּל־
פֹּעֲלֵי אָוֶן:

יא וַתָּרֶם כִּרְאֵים קַרְנִי בַּלֹּתִי
בְּשֶׁמֶן רַעֲנָן:

יב וַתַּבֵּט עֵינִי בְּשׁוּרָי בַּקָּמִים
עָלַי מְרֵעִים תִּשְׁמַעְנָה אָזְנָי:

יג צַדִּיק כַּתָּמָר יִפְרָח כְּאֶרֶז
בַּלְּבָנוֹן יִשְׂגֶּה:

יד שְׁתוּלִים בְּבֵית יהוה
בְּחַצְרוֹת אֱלֹהֵינוּ יַפְרִיחוּ:

טו עוֹד יְנוּבוּן בְּשֵׂיבָה דְּשֵׁנִים
וְרַעֲנַנִּים יִהְיוּ:

10 For behold Your enemies, Lord, behold Your enemies perish, all evildoers are scattered.

11 And You raise my horn like an oryx. I am anointed with fresh oil.

12 My eye has seen my foes; when the wicked rise against me, my ears will hear.

13 The righteous man flourishes like a palm tree; like a cedar in Lebanon he grows tall.

14 Planted in the House of the Lord, they blossom in the courts of our God.

15 They will continue to yield fruit even in old age; they will remain full and fresh,

---

10 **For behold Your enemies, Lord, behold Your enemies perish** in the end, **all evildoers are scattered.**

11 **And** as for me, the righteous one who serves You faithfully, **You raise my horn,** an expression denoting one's stature and power, **like** the tall, upright horns of **an oryx. I am anointed with fresh oil,** I have achieved a position of greatness.

12 And in my prosperity, I have reached a position in which **my eye has seen** the downfall of **my foes. When the wicked rise against me, my ears will hear** of their defeat.

13 **The righteous man flourishes like a palm tree,** which soars to great heights and bears fruit, even in the arid desert. **Like a** lofty **cedar in Lebanon he grows tall.**

14 **Planted in the House of the Lord** and blessed by Him, **they blossom in the courts of our God.**

15 Even if they experience occasional hardship and adversity, **they will continue to yield fruit, even in old age.** While others wither and fade, **they will remain full and fresh.**

לְהַגִּיד כִּי־יָשָׁר יְהֹוָה צוּרִי טו
וְלֹא־עַלְתָה בּֽוֹ:

עוְי

16 to tell that the Lord is upright. He is my rock, and there is no wrongdoing in Him.

PSALM 93

A hymn about God's revelation in the world, in the wake of which all of existence will be filled with song and all people will witness God's rule of the world and His presence within His Sanctuary.

יְהֹוָה מָלָךְ גֵּאוּת לָבֵשׁ לָבֵשׁ א
יְהֹוָה עֹז הִתְאַזָּר אַף־תִּכּוֹן
תֵּבֵל בַּל־תִּמּֽוֹט:

נָכוֹן כִּסְאֲךָ מֵאָז מֵעוֹלָם ב
אָֽתָּה:

1 The Lord reigns; He is clothed in grandeur. The Lord is clothed, and has girded Himself with strength; the world is firmly established, not to be shaken.

2 Your throne stands firm of old; You are from eternity.

---

16 This serves **to tell** all **that the Lord is upright** and His laws are just and true, even when His justice is concealed from human understanding. **He is my rock, and there is no wrongdoing in Him.** Even if the righteousness of God's justice is not evident to me, I must consider the future time, the End of Days, when it will become apparent that evil has been eradicated from the world while goodness remains permanent, vibrant, and fresh.

PSALM 93

1 **The Lord reigns,** that is, when His reign is revealed to this world, **He is clothed in grandeur. The Lord is clothed** in glory, **and** He **has girded Himself with strength.** He is perceived as a king, cloaked in honor, girded in power. **The world is** then **firmly established, not to be shaken.** The world will be secure; wickedness, which is inherently unstable (see above, 92:8–10), will cease to exist.

2 **Your throne stands firm of old.** God's throne was already established in ancient times. **You are from eternity.**

נָשְׂאוּ נְהָרוֹת ׀ יְהֹוָה נָשְׂאוּ
נְהָרוֹת קוֹלָם יִשְׂאוּ נְהָרוֹת
דָּכְיָם:

מִקֹּלוֹת ׀ מַיִם רַבִּים אַדִּירִים
מִשְׁבְּרֵי־יָם אַדִּיר בַּמָּרוֹם
יְהֹוָה:

עֵדֹתֶיךָ ׀ נֶאֶמְנוּ מְאֹד לְבֵיתְךָ
נַאֲוָה־קֹדֶשׁ יְהֹוָה לְאֹרֶךְ
יָמִים:

3 The rivers raise, Lord, the
rivers raise their voices; the
rivers boost their towering
waves.

4 It is from the sound of many
waters, the mighty breakers
of the sea; the Lord is mighty
on high.

5 Your precepts are completely
true. Holiness adorns Your
House; the Lord is for all
length of days.

PSALM 94

*A psalm of prayer about coping with the wicked. Although mainly descriptive and analytic,
it also contains a personal prayer, as the psalmist is suffering from the evil around him
and is in need of assistance and salvation.*

אֵל־נְקָמוֹת יְהֹוָה אֵל נְקָמוֹת
הוֹפִיעַ:

1 God of vengeance, Lord, God
of vengeance, appear.

---

3 When God's reign is revealed, the world sings in His honor: **The rivers raise, Lord, the rivers
raise their voices; the rivers boost their towering waves,** singing and dancing, as it were,
in honor of God.

4 **It is from the sound of many waters** that God's praises are heard, from **the mighty breakers
of the sea,** singing their song. **The Lord is mighty on high.** God Himself is the mightiest of all.

5 And this is the song they will "sing": **Your precepts,** or alternatively, "Your promises," **are
completely true;** they have now been revealed and fulfilled. **Holiness adorns Your House.
The Lord is for all length of days;** He will abide in that House forever.

PSALM 94

1 **God of vengeance.** Vengefulness is not a positive trait; indeed, the Torah forbids us to seek
revenge.[4] But that is for human beings; the matter is different with regard to God, who has

הִנָּשֵׂא שֹׁפֵט הָאָרֶץ הָשֵׁב
גְּמוּל עַל־גֵּאִים:

2 Rise up, Judge of the earth; bring retribution to the arrogant.

עַד־מָתַי רְשָׁעִים ׀ יְהוָה עַד־
מָתַי רְשָׁעִים יַעֲלֹזוּ:

3 How long will the wicked, Lord, how long will the wicked exult?

יַבִּיעוּ יְדַבְּרוּ עָתָק יִתְאַמְּרוּ
כָּל־פֹּעֲלֵי אָוֶן:

4 They express themselves with arrogance; all the evildoers exalt themselves.

עַמְּךָ יְהוָה יְדַכְּאוּ וְנַחֲלָתְךָ
יְעַנּוּ:

5 They crush Your people, Lord; they afflict Your portion.

אַלְמָנָה וְגֵר יַהֲרֹגוּ וִיתוֹמִים
יְרַצֵּחוּ:

6 They slay the widow and the proselyte, and they murder the orphan.

---

no human weakness and exercises perfect justice. It is entirely appropriate for God to act with vengeance in order to prevent the wicked from carrying out further evil deeds and to punish them for previous wrongdoing. This is the sense in which He is characterized as "a jealous, vengeful God,"[5] and in which the phrase "vengeance and retribution is Mine"[6] should be understood. **Lord, God of vengeance, appear.**

2 Because God's justice is not always manifest in the world, and it can seem as if God hides Himself, withholding His power, the psalmist entreats Him: **Rise up, Judge of the earth;** reveal Yourself as the Ruler and Judge of the world. **Bring retribution to the arrogant.** The word *ge'im*, translated here and elsewhere in Psalms as "the arrogant," most often refers to wicked people who have no regard for others.

3 **How long will the wicked, Lord, how long will** You allow **the wicked** to **exult?**

4 **They express themselves with arrogance; all the evildoers exalt themselves.** How long will all this go on?

5 In addition to their self-aggrandizement, the wicked also cause suffering to others: **They crush Your people, Lord; they afflict Your portion,** those who reside in Your portion, the Land of Israel. Alternatively, the people of Israel themselves are referred to as God's portion.

6 **They slay the widow and the proselyte, and they murder the orphan,** all of whom have no personal protector and are the most vulnerable.

וַיֹּאמְרוּ לֹא יִרְאֶה־יָּהּ וְלֹא־
יָבִין אֱלֹהֵי יַעֲקֹב:

בִּינוּ בֹּעֲרִים בָּעָם וּכְסִילִים
מָתַי תַּשְׂכִּילוּ:

הֲנֹטַע אֹזֶן הֲלֹא יִשְׁמָע אִם־
יֹצֵר עַיִן הֲלֹא יַבִּיט:

הֲיֹסֵר גּוֹיִם הֲלֹא יוֹכִיחַ
הַמְלַמֵּד אָדָם דָּעַת:

יְהוָה יֹדֵעַ מַחְשְׁבוֹת אָדָם
כִּי־הֵמָּה הָבֶל:

7 They say: The Lord does not see; the God of Jacob does not comprehend.

8 Take heed, you boors among the people. Fools, when will you learn?

9 He who sets the ear in place, does He not hear? He who forms the eye, does He not see?

10 He who chastises nations, He who teaches man knowledge, shall He not rebuke?

11 The Lord knows the thoughts of man, that they are vain.

---

7 When God chooses not to intervene, the wicked, unpunished, believe they can do as they please: **They say: The Lord does not see; the God of Jacob does not comprehend** what we are doing. Even if they believe that God exists, they assume that He takes no interest in people or in what they do. In their view, He has distanced Himself from the world to the extent that He is unaware of its affairs.

8 The psalmist responds to this attitude: **Take heed, you boors among the people. Fools, when will you learn?**

9 **He who sets the ear in place, does He not hear? He who forms the eye, does He not see?**

10 **He who chastises nations, He who teaches man knowledge, shall He not rebuke?** Can it be that He who teaches all the nations does not instruct an individual human being? Is it possible that He who confers knowledge is incapable of understanding? On the contrary, when God chooses not to intervene and punish the wicked or reward the good, He does so for reasons that are far beyond our comprehension, as the following verses detail.

11 **The Lord knows the thoughts of man, that they are vain,** transient, and insignificant. He knows that grandiose plans that the wicked make for themselves, trampling others in the process, ultimately come to naught.

יב אַשְׁרֵי הַגֶּבֶר אֲשֶׁר־תְּיַסְּרֶנּוּ
יָּהּ וּמִתּוֹרָתְךָ תְלַמְּדֶנּוּ:

יג לְהַשְׁקִיט לוֹ מִימֵי רָע עַד
יִכָּרֶה לָרָשָׁע שָׁחַת:

יד כִּי ׀ לֹא־יִטֹּשׁ יהוה עַמּוֹ
וְנַחֲלָתוֹ לֹא יַעֲזֹב:

טו כִּי־עַד־צֶדֶק יָשׁוּב מִשְׁפָּט
וְאַחֲרָיו כָּל־יִשְׁרֵי־לֵב:

טז מִי־יָקוּם לִי עִם־מְרֵעִים מִי־
יִתְיַצֵּב לִי עִם־פֹּעֲלֵי אָוֶן:

12 Blessed is the man whom You chastise, Lord, whom You instruct with Your teaching,

13 to grant him respite in days of evil, until a pit is dug for the wicked.

14 Indeed, the Lord will not abandon His people, nor will He forsake His portion.

15 Judgment will return with righteousness, and all the upright of heart will follow it.

16 Who will rise up for me against the wicked? Who will take a stand for me against the evildoers?

---

12 The psalmist, turning his attention to those who suffer from the wicked, suggests an additional perspective: **Blessed is the man whom You chastise, Lord, whom You instruct with Your teaching.** Suffering, both when it serves as atonement for sin and when it is a means of redirecting a person toward a better, loftier path, is not an indication of God's indifference toward the one who is suffering. Rather, it is a form of instruction.

13 **To grant him respite in days of evil.** Even though people do not always perceive God's control in the world through immediate reward and punishment, He nevertheless provides them with a measure of relief that allows them to hold out during more difficult times, **until a pit is dug for the wicked,** into which they will ultimately fall and meet their destruction.

14 **Indeed,** even if it is not always evident, **the Lord will not abandon His people, nor will He forsake His portion.**

15 **Judgment will return with righteousness, and all the upright of heart will follow it.** After this judgment of the wicked, the hopes of the upright will be realized.

16 The psalmist muses: **Who will rise up for me** to assist me to struggle **against the wicked? Who will take a stand for me against the evildoers?**

^{יז} לוּלֵי יְהוָה עֶזְרָתָה לִּי כִּמְעַט ׀
שָׁכְנָה דוּמָה נַפְשִׁי:

^{יח} אִם־אָמַרְתִּי מָטָה רַגְלִי
חַסְדְּךָ יְהוָה יִסְעָדֵנִי:

^{יט} בְּרֹב שַׂרְעַפַּי בְּקִרְבִּי
תַּנְחוּמֶיךָ יְשַׁעַשְׁעוּ נַפְשִׁי:

^כ הַיְחָבְרְךָ כִּסֵּא הַוּוֹת יֹצֵר
עָמָל עֲלֵי־חֹק:

^{כא} יָגוֹדּוּ עַל־נֶפֶשׁ צַדִּיק וְדָם נָקִי
יַרְשִׁיעוּ:

^{כב} וַיְהִי יְהוָה לִי לְמִשְׂגָּב וֵאלֹהַי
לְצוּר מַחְסִי:

¹⁷ Had the Lord not helped me, my soul would soon have dwelled in silence.

¹⁸ When I say: My foot is stumbling, Your kindness, Lord, supports me.

¹⁹ In the midst of my many troubled thoughts, Your consolations soothe me.

²⁰ Can the seat of calamity be associated with You, which creates evil that is above the law?

²¹ They band themselves against the lives of the righteous and convict the blood of the innocent.

²² But the Lord is my stronghold; my God, the rock of my refuge.

---

¹⁷ **Had the Lord not helped me, my soul would soon have dwelled in silence.** I would have died and gone to the grave.

¹⁸ **When I say** to myself: **My foot is stumbling** and I am about to fall, **Your kindness, Lord,** comes to my aid and **supports me.**

¹⁹ **In the midst of my many troubled thoughts, Your consolations soothe me.** The realization that God comes to my aid counteracts the thoughts of desperation and anguish that beset me.

²⁰ **Can the seat of calamity,** the dominion of evil in the world, **be associated with You,** that seat **which creates evil that is above the law?**

²¹ **They,** those evildoers alluded to in the previous verse, **band themselves against the lives of the righteous and convict the blood of the innocent;** in condemning the innocent, they may even sentence them to death and thereby shed their blood.

²² **But the Lord is my stronghold; my God, the rock of my refuge.**

כג וַיָּ֤שֶׁב עֲלֵיהֶ֨ם ׀ אֶת־אוֹנָ֗ם
וּבְרָעָתָ֥ם יַצְמִיתֵ֑ם יַ֝צְמִיתֵ֗ם
יְהֹוָ֥ה אֱלֹהֵֽינוּ׃

23 He will requite them for their wickedness and destroy them in their own evil; the Lord our God will destroy them.

PSALM 95

A hymn in praise of God. It is also a call, based on Israel's history, to refrain from sin.

א לְכ֣וּ נְרַנְּנָ֣ה לַיהֹוָ֑ה נָ֝רִ֗יעָה
לְצ֣וּר יִשְׁעֵֽנוּ׃

ב נְקַדְּמָ֣ה פָנָ֣יו בְּתוֹדָ֑ה
בִּ֝זְמִר֗וֹת נָרִ֥יעַֽ לֽוֹ׃

ג כִּ֤י אֵ֣ל גָּד֣וֹל יְהֹוָ֑ה וּמֶ֥לֶךְ גָּ֝ד֗וֹל
עַל־כׇּל־אֱלֹהִֽים׃

1 Come, let us sing for joy to the Lord; let us make a joyful sound to the rock of our salvation.

2 Let us greet Him with thanksgiving; let us cry out to Him joyfully with song.

3 For the Lord is a great God, a great King, above all gods,

---

23 **He will requite them for their wickedness and destroy them in their own evil;** as noted in several places in the book of Proverbs, the evil done by sinners often serves as their own undoing, the means by which the wicked are punished and ultimately destroyed. **The Lord our God will destroy them.**

PSALM 95

1 **Come, let us sing for joy to the Lord;** moreover, **let us make a joyful sound,** both by raising our voices loudly in song and by playing musical instruments, **to the rock of our salvation.**

2 **Let us greet Him with** verbal declarations and sacrificial offerings of **thanksgiving. Let us cry out to Him joyfully with song.**

3 **For the Lord is a great God, a great King, above all gods,** and therefore deserving of our praises and joyful singing.

אֲשֶׁר בְּיָדוֹ מֶחְקְרֵי־אָרֶץ
וְתוֹעֲפוֹת הָרִים לוֹ:

אֲשֶׁר־לוֹ הַיָּם וְהוּא עָשָׂהוּ
וְיַבֶּשֶׁת יָדָיו יָצָרוּ:

בֹּאוּ נִשְׁתַּחֲוֶה וְנִכְרָעָה
נִבְרְכָה לִפְנֵי־יהוה עֹשֵׂנוּ:

כִּי הוּא אֱלֹהֵינוּ וַאֲנַחְנוּ ׀ עַם
מַרְעִיתוֹ וְצֹאן יָדוֹ הַיּוֹם אִם־
בְּקֹלוֹ תִשְׁמָעוּ:

אַל־תַּקְשׁוּ לְבַבְכֶם כִּמְרִיבָה
כְּיוֹם מַסָּה בַּמִּדְבָּר:

⁴ in whose hand are depths of the earth, and peaks of the mountains are His,

⁵ who owns the sea and made it, and whose hands formed the dry land.

⁶ Come, let us prostrate ourselves and bow down; let us kneel before the Lord our Maker.

⁷ For He is our God, and we are the people of His flock and the sheep under His hand, even today, would you only heed His voice.

⁸ Do not harden your hearts as you did at Meriva, or at Masa in the desert,

---

⁴ In whose hand are depths of the earth, and peaks of the mountains are His,

⁵ who owns the sea and made it, and whose hands formed the dry land.

⁶ Come, let us prostrate ourselves and bow down; let us kneel before the Lord our Maker.

⁷ **For He is our God, and we are the people of His flock,** whom He leads and cares for, **and the sheep under His hand, even today, would you only heed His voice.** To remain protected, we must only obey and follow Him.

⁸ Using historical examples, the psalmist provides a reminder of the suffering that befalls those who do not follow God faithfully. In this verse and the following ones, God speaks to Israel: **Do not harden your hearts as you did at** the waters of **Meriva,** referring to the event described in the Torah,⁷ **or at Masa in the desert,** also described in the Torah.⁸ These two incidents represent all the various trials the Israelites underwent and the punishments they incurred.

אֲשֶׁר נִסּוּנִי אֲבוֹתֵיכֶם בְּחָנוּנִי
גַּם־רָאוּ פָעֳלִֽי׃

אַרְבָּעִים שָׁנָה ׀ אָקוּט בְּדוֹר
וָאֹמַר עַם תֹּעֵי לֵבָב הֵם וְהֵם
לֹא־יָדְעוּ דְרָכָֽי׃

אֲשֶׁר־נִשְׁבַּעְתִּי בְאַפִּי אִם־
יְבֹאוּן אֶל־מְנוּחָתִֽי׃

9 when your fathers tested Me;
they tried Me, and they also
saw My work.

10 For forty years I spurned that
generation. I said: They are a
people who err in their hearts;
they do not know My ways.

11 Thus I swore in My wrath that
they would not come to My
resting place.

PSALM 96

A hymn of praise for God. It is characterized as "a new song"
because it is a novel formulation and expression of God's glory.

שִׁירוּ לַיהוה שִׁיר חָדָשׁ שִׁירוּ
לַיהוה כָּל־הָאָֽרֶץ׃

1 Sing to the Lord a new song;
sing to the Lord, all the earth.

---

9 These were times **when your fathers tested Me; they tried Me, and they also saw My work.** They saw that I fulfilled their requests, and that I punished them for their unfaithfulness.

10 **For forty years I spurned that generation,** the generation of the exodus. **I said: They are a people who err in their hearts; they do not know My ways.**

11 **Thus I swore in My wrath that they would not come to My resting place,** the Land of Israel. It follows, then, that alongside the benefit to be gained from being under God's protection, there is also a threat for not having that benefit: Just as those who trust in God are given all they need, those who deviate from His ways are not treated neutrally but are subjected to punishment in all its severity.

PSALM 96

1 **Sing to the Lord a new song; sing to the Lord, all the earth.**

שִׁ֥ירוּ לַֽיהֹוָ֗ה בָּרְכ֥וּ שְׁמ֑וֹ
בַּשְּׂר֥וּ מִיּֽוֹם־לְ֝י֗וֹם יְשֽׁוּעָתֽוֹ:

סַפְּר֣וּ בַגּוֹיִ֣ם כְּבוֹד֑וֹ בְּכָל־
הָֽ֝עַמִּ֗ים נִפְלְאוֹתָֽיו:

כִּ֥י גָ֘ד֤וֹל יְהֹוָ֣ה וּמְהֻלָּ֣ל מְאֹ֑ד
נוֹרָ֥א ה֝֗וּא עַל־כָּל־אֱלֹהִֽים:

כִּ֤י ׀ כָּל־אֱלֹהֵ֣י הָעַמִּ֣ים
אֱלִילִ֑ים וַֽ֝יהֹוָ֗ה שָׁמַ֥יִם עָשָֽׂה:

הוֹד־וְהָדָ֥ר לְפָנָ֑יו עֹ֥ז
וְ֝תִפְאֶ֗רֶת בְּמִקְדָּשֽׁוֹ:

הָב֣וּ לַֽ֭יהֹוָה מִשְׁפְּח֣וֹת עַמִּ֑ים
הָב֥וּ לַ֝יהֹוָ֗ה כָּב֥וֹד וָעֹֽז:

² Sing to the Lord, bless His name; proclaim the good tidings of His salvation day by day.

³ Tell of His glory among the nations, His wonders among all the peoples.

⁴ For the Lord is great and to be praised exceedingly; He is feared above all gods.

⁵ For all gods of the peoples are idols, but the Lord made the heavens.

⁶ Majesty and glory are before Him; might and splendor are in His Sanctuary.

⁷ Render to the Lord, you families of the peoples; render to the Lord honor and might.

---

2 **Sing to the Lord, bless His name; proclaim the good tidings of His salvation day by day**.

3 **Tell of His glory among the nations,** tell of **His wonders among all the peoples.**

4 **For the Lord is great and to be praised exceedingly; He is feared above all gods.**

5 **For all gods of the peoples are** merely useless, powerless **idols, but the Lord** possesses true power, as He **made the heavens.**

6 **Majesty and glory are** situated **before Him,** in the courtyard of His Temple, and **might and splendor are** found **in His Sanctuary.**

7 **Render to the Lord, you families of the peoples; render to the Lord honor and might.** "Render honor" by showing reverence to Him; "render might" by clinging to Him with all your strength.

הָב֣וּ לַ֭יהוה כְּב֣וֹד שְׁמ֑וֹ שְׂאוּ־
מִ֝נְחָ֗ה וּבֹ֥אוּ לְחַצְרוֹתָֽיו׃

הִשְׁתַּחֲו֣וּ לַ֭יהוה בְּהַדְרַת־
קֹ֑דֶשׁ חִ֥ילוּ מִ֝פָּנָ֗יו כָּל־הָאָֽרֶץ׃

אִמְר֤וּ בַגּוֹיִ֨ם ׀ יְה֘וה מָ֫לָ֥ךְ
אַף־תִּכּ֣וֹן תֵּ֭בֵל בַּל־תִּמּ֑וֹט
יָדִ֥ין עַ֝מִּ֗ים בְּמֵישָׁרִֽים׃

יִשְׂמְח֣וּ הַ֭שָּׁמַיִם וְתָגֵ֣ל הָאָ֑רֶץ
יִֽרְעַ֥ם הַ֝יָּ֗ם וּמְלֹאֽוֹ׃

יַעֲלֹ֣ז שָׂ֭דַי וְכָל־אֲשֶׁר־בּ֑וֹ אָ֥ז
יְ֝רַנְּנ֗וּ כָּל־עֲצֵי־יָֽעַר׃

8 Render to the Lord the glory
due His name; bring an
offering, and come into His
courtyards.

9 Bow down to the Lord in
splendor of holiness; tremble
before Him, all the earth.

10 Say among the nations: The
Lord reigns! The world is
firmly established, not to be
shaken. He will minister fair
judgment to the peoples.

11 The heavens will be happy and
the earth will rejoice. The sea
and all its fullness will thunder.

12 The fields and everything
within them will exult. All the
trees of the forest will then cry
out for joy,

---

8 **Render to the Lord the glory due His name; bring an offering, and come into His courtyards,** to serve Him.

9 And while you are there, **bow down to the Lord in** a mindset of **splendor of holiness,** that is, with the awe of awareness of His supreme holiness. **Tremble before Him, all the earth.**

10 **Say among the nations: The Lord reigns!** And when God's kingship is revealed, **the world is firmly established, not to be shaken;** it will no longer seem shaky and precarious, as it sometimes does now. **He will** then **minister fair judgment to the peoples.**

11 And when God's glory becomes revealed, **the heavens will be happy and the earth will rejoice. The sea and all its fullness will thunder.** The sea will thunder with its roaring waves, and all the creatures that fill it will join in the chorus of praise to God.

12 **The fields and everything within them will exult.** Even **all the trees of the forest,** which, unlike cultivated fields, are not under man's dominion, **will then cry out for joy.**

לִפְנֵי יהוֹה ׀ כִּי בָא כִּי בָא
לִשְׁפֹּט הָאָרֶץ יִשְׁפֹּט־תֵּבֵל
בְּצֶדֶק וְעַמִּים בֶּאֱמוּנָתוֹ:

¹³ before the Lord when He comes, when He comes to judge the earth. He will judge the world with righteousness, and the peoples with His faithfulness.

PSALM 97

A hymn of praise that is essentially about God's revelation, but also concerns His sovereignty over the world.

א יהוה מָלָךְ תָּגֵל הָאָרֶץ
יִשְׂמְחוּ אִיִּים רַבִּים:

¹ The Lord reigns; the earth will rejoice. The many islands will be glad.

ב עָנָן וַעֲרָפֶל סְבִיבָיו צֶדֶק
וּמִשְׁפָּט מְכוֹן כִּסְאוֹ:

² Cloud and fog surround Him; justice and judgment are the base of His throne.

ג אֵשׁ לְפָנָיו תֵּלֵךְ וּתְלַהֵט
סָבִיב צָרָיו:

³ Fire goes before Him and burns around His foes.

---

¹³ All of these will sing out in joy **before the Lord when He comes** and reveals Himself in the world, **when He comes to judge the earth.** This revelation of God will take place when **He will judge the world with righteousness, and the peoples with His faithfulness.**

PSALM 97

¹ **The Lord reigns,** and when He is revealed as Sovereign, **the earth will rejoice. The many islands** all over the world **will be glad.**

² The psalmist describes what this revelation will be like: **Cloud and fog surround Him** to conceal His glory as He sits upon His throne; **justice and judgment are the base of His throne.**

³ **Fire goes before Him,** an expression of His glory; but it is also used as a tool for punishment **and burns around His foes.**

הֵאִירוּ בְרָקָיו תֵּבֵל רָאֲתָה ד
וַתָּחֵל הָאָרֶץ:

הָרִים כַּדּוֹנַג נָמַסּוּ מִלִּפְנֵי ה
יְהוָה מִלִּפְנֵי אֲדוֹן כָּל־
הָאָרֶץ:

הִגִּידוּ הַשָּׁמַיִם צִדְקוֹ וְרָאוּ ו
כָל־הָעַמִּים כְּבוֹדוֹ:

יֵבֹשׁוּ ׀ כָּל־עֹבְדֵי פֶסֶל ז
הַמִּתְהַלְלִים בָּאֱלִילִים
הִשְׁתַּחֲווּ־לוֹ כָּל־אֱלֹהִים:

שָׁמְעָה וַתִּשְׂמַח ׀ צִיּוֹן ח
וַתָּגֵלְנָה בְּנוֹת יְהוּדָה לְמַעַן
מִשְׁפָּטֶיךָ יְהוָה:

כִּי־אַתָּה יְהוָה עֶלְיוֹן עַל־ ט
כָּל־הָאָרֶץ מְאֹד נַעֲלֵיתָ עַל־
כָּל־אֱלֹהִים:

4 His lightning illuminates the world; the earth sees and trembles.

5 Mountains melt like wax at the presence of the Lord, before the Master of all the earth.

6 The heavens declare His righteousness; all peoples behold His glory.

7 All those who worship images, who glorify idols, will be ashamed; all gods will bow down before Him.

8 Zion will hear and be glad, and the daughters of Judah will rejoice because of Your judgments, Lord.

9 For You, Lord, are Most High over all the earth; You are greatly exalted above all gods.

---

4 **His lightning illuminates the world; the earth sees and trembles.**

5 **Mountains melt like wax** in fear **at the presence of the Lord, before the Master of all the earth.**

6 **The heavens declare His righteousness,** which will become apparent to all of creation, all the way up to the heavens; **all peoples behold His glory.**

7 And at this time of revelation, **all those who worship images, who glorify idols, will be ashamed,** realizing the utter inanity of their belief. **All gods,** the heavenly powers, **will bow down before Him.**

8 **Zion will hear and be glad,** for it is the city of God, **and the daughters of Judah will rejoice because of Your judgments** that You will mete out upon this revelation, **Lord.**

9 **For You, Lord, are Most High over all the earth; You are greatly exalted** not only above us, but **above all gods.**

אֹהֲבֵי יהוה שִׂנְאוּ רָע שֹׁמֵר
נַפְשׁוֹת חֲסִידָיו מִיַּד רְשָׁעִים
יַצִּילֵם:

^י You who love the Lord, hate
evil. He guards the lives of His
devoted ones, saving them
from the hand of the wicked.

אוֹר זָרֻעַ לַצַּדִּיק וּלְיִשְׁרֵי־לֵב
שִׂמְחָה:

^{יא} Light is sown for the righteous,
and joy for the upright of heart.

שִׂמְחוּ צַדִּיקִים בַּיהוה וְהוֹדוּ
לְזֵכֶר קׇדְשׁוֹ:

^{יב} Rejoice in the Lord, you
righteous ones, and give
thanks at the mention of His
holy name.

PSALM 98

A psalm of general praise to God that describes
how the world and its inhabitants sing and rejoice in His honor.

מִזְמוֹר שִׁירוּ לַיהוה ׀ שִׁיר חָדָשׁ
כִּי־נִפְלָאוֹת עָשָׂה הוֹשִׁיעָה־
לּוֹ יְמִינוֹ וּזְרוֹעַ קׇדְשׁוֹ:

^א A psalm. Sing to the Lord a new
song, for He has done wonders;
His right hand and His holy arm
have wrought salvation for Him.

---

¹⁰ The psalmist now addresses those who serve God: **You who love the Lord, hate evil.** It is not enough to cleave to God; you must also take a clear stand against evil. And you need not fear a backlash from the evildoers when you denounce them, for **He guards the lives of His devoted ones, saving them from the hand of the wicked**.

¹¹ **Light is sown for the righteous, and joy for the upright of heart.** Light for the righteous exists, even though it is not always evident in the present. It is sown for them like seeds; eventually, their light will grow and be revealed to all.

¹² **Rejoice in the Lord, you righteous ones, and give thanks at the mention of His holy name.**

PSALM 98

¹ **A psalm. Sing to the Lord a new song, for He has done wonders; His right hand,** His might, **and His holy arm have wrought salvation for Him.**

הוֹדִיעַ יְהוָה יְשׁוּעָתוֹ לְעֵינֵי
הַגּוֹיִם גִּלָּה צִדְקָתוֹ׃

זָכַר חַסְדּוֹ ׀ וֶאֱמוּנָתוֹ לְבֵית
יִשְׂרָאֵל רָאוּ כָל־אַפְסֵי־אָרֶץ
אֵת יְשׁוּעַת אֱלֹהֵינוּ׃

הָרִיעוּ לַיהוָה כָּל־הָאָרֶץ
פִּצְחוּ וְרַנְּנוּ וְזַמֵּרוּ׃

זַמְּרוּ לַיהוָה בְּכִנּוֹר בְּכִנּוֹר
וְקוֹל זִמְרָה׃

בַּחֲצֹצְרוֹת וְקוֹל שׁוֹפָר
הָרִיעוּ לִפְנֵי ׀ הַמֶּלֶךְ יְהוָה׃

² The Lord has made known His salvation; before the eyes of the nations He revealed His righteousness.

³ He recalled His kindness and His faithfulness to the house of Israel; all the ends of the earth beheld the salvation of our God.

⁴ Shout with joy to the Lord, all the earth! Break forth and sing for joy; sing praises.

⁵ Sing to the Lord with lyre, with lyre and the melody of song;

⁶ with trumpets and the sound of the shofar make loud sound before the King, the Lord.

---

² **The Lord has made known His salvation; before the eyes of the nations He revealed His righteousness.**

³ One aspect of this revelation is connected specifically to the people of Israel: **He recalled His kindness and His faithfulness to the house of Israel.** When God is revealed in all His power, Israel's greatness also becomes recognized. And then, **all the ends of the earth beheld the salvation of our God** that He wrought for Israel.

⁴ However, the psalmist calls to the people of all nations, not just Israel, to express joy in the divine revelation: **Shout with joy to the Lord, all the earth! Break forth,** or open wide your mouths, **and sing for joy; sing praises.**

⁵ **Sing to the Lord with lyre, with lyre and the melody of song.** The music begins softly, with stringed instruments.

⁶ It then increases in volume: **With trumpets and the sound of the shofar make loud sound before the King, the Lord.**

יִרְעַם הַיָּם וּמְלֹאוֹ תֵּבֵל
וְיֹשְׁבֵי בָהּ:

נְהָרוֹת יִמְחֲאוּ־כָף יַחַד הָרִים
יְרַנֵּנוּ:

לִפְנֵי־יהוה כִּי בָא לִשְׁפֹּט
הָאָרֶץ יִשְׁפֹּט־תֵּבֵל בְּצֶדֶק
וְעַמִּים בְּמֵישָׁרִים:

7 Let the sea and all within it thunder, the world and all who dwell in it.

8 Rivers will clap hands; the mountains, in unison, will sing for joy,

9 before the Lord, when He comes to judge the earth. He will judge the world with righteousness, and peoples with equity.

PSALM 99

A psalm that speaks of God's praise as it is revealed in the course of history through various historical figures.

יהוה מָלָךְ יִרְגְּזוּ עַמִּים יֹשֵׁב
כְּרוּבִים תָּנוּט הָאָרֶץ:

1 The Lord reigns; peoples tremble. He is enthroned on cherubs; the earth shudders.

---

7 And at this point, the forces of nature join in, accompanying the song: **Let the sea and all within it thunder, the world and all who dwell in it.**

8 **Rivers will clap hands.** The rivers join in the chorus of praise, though in a gentler manner than that of the thundering sea. The sound of the flowing rivers resembles that of clapping hands. **The mountains, in unison, will sing for joy.**

9 This great musical tribute is to take place **before the Lord, when He comes** and reveals Himself **to judge the earth.** At that time, **He will judge the world with righteousness, and peoples with equity.**

PSALM 99

1 **The Lord reigns,** and when God's sovereignty is revealed, **peoples tremble.** When **He is** sitting **enthroned on** the **cherubs** that are atop the Holy Ark in the Temple and serve as God's throne on earth, as it were, **the earth shudders.**

יְהוָה בְּצִיּוֹן גָּדוֹל וְרָם הוּא
עַל־כָּל־הָעַמִּים:

יוֹדוּ שִׁמְךָ גָּדוֹל וְנוֹרָא קָדוֹשׁ
הוּא:

וְעֹז מֶלֶךְ מִשְׁפָּט אָהֵב אַתָּה
כּוֹנַנְתָּ מֵישָׁרִים מִשְׁפָּט
וּצְדָקָה בְּיַעֲקֹב ׀ אַתָּה
עָשִׂיתָ:

רוֹמְמוּ יְהוָה אֱלֹהֵינוּ
וְהִשְׁתַּחֲווּ לַהֲדֹם רַגְלָיו
קָדוֹשׁ הוּא:

מֹשֶׁה וְאַהֲרֹן ׀ בְּכֹהֲנָיו
וּשְׁמוּאֵל בְּקֹרְאֵי שְׁמוֹ
קֹרִאים אֶל־יְהוָה וְהוּא
יַעֲנֵם:

² The Lord is great in Zion, and He is above all the peoples.

³ They acknowledge Your great and awesome name; it is holy.

⁴ The might of the King is that He loves justice. You set it straightly in place; You wrought judgment and justice in Jacob.

⁵ Exalt the Lord our God and bow down at His footstool; He is holy.

⁶ Moses and Aaron were among his priests, and Samuel among those who called His name; they called to the Lord and He answered them.

---

2 **The Lord is great in Zion, and He is above all the peoples.**

3 **They acknowledge Your great and awesome name; it is holy.**

4 **The might of the King is that He loves justice.** The manner in which God is seen in all His power is evident in His love of justice, not in arbitrary exercise of power. **You set it straightly in place; You wrought judgment and justice in Jacob.** God's revelation on earth is based on law, order, and fairness, and thus the world is set "straightly in place."

5 **Exalt the Lord our God and bow down at His footstool.** These verses portray God as if He is sitting on His throne, His feet resting on the "footstool" of the Temple, thereby imparting sanctity to it. **He is holy.**

6 The psalmist now describes God's greatness as manifested in history: **Moses and Aaron were among His priests, and Samuel among those who called His name.** Samuel was not only a leader; he was also responsible for the revival of Judaism in his generation. **They called to the Lord and He answered them.**

בְּעַמּוּד עָנָן יְדַבֵּר אֲלֵיהֶם
שָׁמְרוּ עֵדֹתָיו וְחֹק נָתַן־לָמוֹ:

יהוה אֱלֹהֵינוּ אַתָּה עֲנִיתָם
אֵל נֹשֵׂא הָיִיתָ לָהֶם וְנֹקֵם
עַל־עֲלִילוֹתָם:

רוֹמְמוּ יהוה אֱלֹהֵינוּ
וְהִשְׁתַּחֲווּ לְהַר קָדְשׁוֹ כִּי־
קָדוֹשׁ יהוה אֱלֹהֵינוּ:

7 Through a pillar of cloud He spoke to them; they kept His precepts and the statutes He gave them.

8 Lord our God, You answered them. You were a forgiving God to them, but You took vengeance for their misdeeds.

9 Exalt the Lord our God, and bow down at His holy mountain, for the Lord our God is holy.

PSALM 100

A psalm associated with the thanksgiving offering; it may have been sung during the bringing of that offering. It is also a general expression of gratitude to God.

מִזְמוֹר לְתוֹדָה הָרִיעוּ לַיהוה כָּל־הָאָרֶץ:

1 A psalm of thanksgiving. Cry out joyously to the Lord, all the earth.

---

7 **Through a pillar of cloud He spoke to them,** to those mentioned in the previous verse, because **they kept His precepts, and the statutes** of the Torah that **He gave them** as leaders.

8 **Lord our God, You answered them** when they prayed to You. **You were a forgiving God to them, but You** also **took vengeance for their misdeeds.** This is as it must be, since God rules the world with justice.

9 **Exalt the Lord our God, and bow down at His holy mountain,** the site of the Temple. **For the Lord our God is holy,** and it is fitting to show reverence to anything connected with Him.

PSALM 100
1 A psalm of thanksgiving. Cry out joyously to the Lord, all the earth.

עִבְדוּ אֶת־יְהֹוָה בְּשִׂמְחָה
בֹּאוּ לְפָנָיו בִּרְנָנָה:

² Serve the Lord with joy; come
before him with song.

דְּעוּ כִּי־יְהֹוָה הוּא אֱלֹהִים
הוּא עָשָׂנוּ וְלֹא אֲנַחְנוּ עַמּוֹ   וְלוֹ
וְצֹאן מַרְעִיתוֹ:

³ Know that the Lord is God.
It is He who made us, and
we belong to Him; we are
His people and the sheep of
His flock.

בֹּאוּ שְׁעָרָיו ׀ בְּתוֹדָה
חֲצֵרֹתָיו בִּתְהִלָּה הוֹדוּ לוֹ
בָּרְכוּ שְׁמוֹ:

⁴ Enter His gates with
thanksgiving, His courtyards
with praise. Give thanks to
Him; bless His name.

כִּי־טוֹב יְהֹוָה לְעוֹלָם חַסְדּוֹ
וְעַד־דֹּר וָדֹר אֱמוּנָתוֹ:

⁵ For the Lord is good, His
kindness eternal. His
faithfulness is for all
generations.

---

² **Serve the Lord with joy; come before him** and bow to Him in His Temple **with song.**
³ **Know that the Lord is God. It is He who made us, and we belong to Him; we are His people and the sheep of His flock.**
⁴ **Enter His gates with thanksgiving;** bring thanksgiving offerings and, more generally, express gratitude to God. Enter **His courtyards with praise. Give thanks to Him; bless His name.**
⁵ **For the Lord is good, His kindness eternal. His faithfulness** toward those who are dedicated to His service **is for all generations.**

PSALM 101

A psalm about David that speaks of his deeds and intentions,
both as a private individual and as king of Israel.

לְדָוִד מִזְמוֹר חֶסֶד־וּמִשְׁפָּט
אָשִׁירָה לְךָ יהוה אֲזַמֵּרָה:

אַשְׂכִּילָה ׀ בְּדֶרֶךְ תָּמִים מָתַי
תָּבוֹא אֵלָי אֶתְהַלֵּךְ בְּתָם־
לְבָבִי בְּקֶרֶב בֵּיתִי:

לֹא־אָשִׁית ׀ לְנֶגֶד עֵינַי דְּבַר־
בְּלִיָּעַל עֲשֹׂה־סֵטִים שָׂנֵאתִי
לֹא יִדְבַּק בִּי:

לֵבָב עִקֵּשׁ יָסוּר מִמֶּנִּי רָע
לֹא אֵדָע:

מְלָשְׁנִי מְלוֹשְׁנִי בַסֵּתֶר ׀ רֵעֵהוּ אוֹתוֹ
אַצְמִית גְּבַהּ־עֵינַיִם וּרְחַב
לֵבָב אֹתוֹ לֹא אוּכָל:

1. A psalm of David. I sing
kindness and justice; to You,
Lord, I sing praises.

2. I ponder the path of integrity.
When will You come to me? I
walk, in the innocence of my
heart, in my house.

3. I set nothing contemptible
before my eyes. I hate
perversity; it does not cling
to me.

4. A crooked heart stays far away
from me; I know no evil.

5. One who secretly slanders his
neighbor, I will cut him down.
I will not tolerate anyone
with a proud demeanor or a
lustful heart.

PSALM 101

1 **A psalm of David. I sing kindness and justice; to You, Lord, I sing praises.**

2 **I ponder the path of integrity.** As I attempt to understand, to seek the right path and act with integrity, I ask of God: **When will You come** and reveal Yourself **to me?** David begins to describe his virtuous personal life: **I walk, in the innocence of my heart, in my house.**

3 **I set nothing contemptible before my eyes,** attempting to avoid even witnessing anything sinful. **I hate perversity; it does not cling to me.** I have nothing to do with it.

4 **A crooked heart stays far away from me.** I attempt to **know no evil.**

5 **One who secretly slanders his neighbor, I will cut him down.** Not only will I keep such a person out of favor, I will seek to destroy him. **I will not tolerate anyone with a proud demeanor or a lustful heart.**

עֵינַ֤י ׀ בְּנֶאֶמְנֵי־אֶ֨רֶץ֮ לָשֶׁ֪בֶת עִמָּ֫דִ֥י הֹלֵ֗ךְ בְּדֶ֣רֶךְ תָּמִ֑ים ה֝֗וּא יְשָׁרְתֵֽנִי׃

לֹֽא־יֵשֵׁ֨ב ׀ בְּקֶ֥רֶב בֵּיתִי֮ עֹשֵׂ֪ה רְמִ֫יָּ֥ה דֹּבֵ֥ר שְׁקָרִ֑ים לֹֽא־יִ֝כּ֗וֹן לְנֶ֣גֶד עֵינָֽי׃

לַבְּקָרִ֗ים אַצְמִ֥ית כָּל־רִשְׁעֵי־אָ֑רֶץ לְהַכְרִ֥ית מֵעִיר־יְ֝הֹוָ֗ה כָּל־פֹּ֥עֲלֵי אָֽוֶן׃

6 My eyes are on the faithful of the land; they will dwell with me. He who walks in the path of integrity, it is he who will serve me.

7 No deceiver or liar will dwell in my house; he will not stand firm before me.

8 Every morning I cut down all the wicked of the land, ridding the city of the Lord of all evildoers.

PSALM 102

A psalm by one who is suffering greatly, whose prayer to be rescued expresses his deep faith in God's omnipotence and compassion.

תְּפִלָּה֮ לְעָנִ֢י כִֽי־יַ֫עֲטֹ֥ף וְלִפְנֵ֥י יְהֹוָ֗ה יִשְׁפֹּ֥ךְ שִׂיחֽוֹ׃

1 The prayer of a poor man, when he feels overwhelmed and pours out his woes before the Lord.

---

6 **My eyes are** instead **on the faithful** and upright people **of the land,** insisting that only **they will dwell with me.** He who walks in the path of integrity, it is only **he who will serve me.**

7 **No deceiver or liar will dwell in my house; he will not stand firm before me.**

8 **Every morning,** each day, **I cut down all the wicked of the land, ridding the city of the Lord,** Jerusalem, **of all evildoers.**

PSALM 102

1 **The prayer of a poor man,** a weak and powerless man, **when he feels overwhelmed,** enveloped by distress and the sense of the world closing in on him. **And** he **pours out his woes before the Lord** in prayer to Him.

יְהֹוָה שִׁמְעָה תְפִלָּתִי
וְשַׁוְעָתִי אֵלֶיךָ תָבוֹא:

אַל־תַּסְתֵּר פָּנֶיךָ ׀ מִמֶּנִּי בְּיוֹם
צַר לִי הַטֵּה־אֵלַי אָזְנֶךָ בְּיוֹם
אֶקְרָא מַהֵר עֲנֵנִי:

כִּי־כָלוּ בְעָשָׁן יָמָי וְעַצְמוֹתַי
כְּמוֹקֵד נִחָרוּ:

הוּכָּה כָעֵשֶׂב וַיִּבַשׁ לִבִּי כִּי־
שָׁכַחְתִּי מֵאֲכֹל לַחְמִי:

מִקּוֹל אַנְחָתִי דָּבְקָה עַצְמִי
לִבְשָׂרִי:

דָּמִיתִי לִקְאַת מִדְבָּר הָיִיתִי
כְּכוֹס חֳרָבוֹת:

שָׁקַדְתִּי וָאֶהְיֶה כְּצִפּוֹר בּוֹדֵד
עַל־גָּג:

2 Lord, hear my prayer; let my cry for help reach You.

3 Do not hide Your face from me at the time of my distress. Incline Your ear to me on the day that I call; answer me quickly.

4 For my days are consumed in smoke, and my bones, as in a pyre, are burnt hollow.

5 My heart is beaten down like grass, and it withers, for I forget to eat my bread.

6 From my groaning, my bones cling to my flesh.

7 I am like a desert owl; like an owl of the ruins I have become.

8 I am fixed in place, and I am like a lonely bird on a rooftop.

---

2 **Lord, hear my prayer; let my cry for help reach You.**

3 **Do not hide Your face from me at the time of my distress. Incline Your ear to** hear **me on the day that I call; answer me quickly.** My anguish and feeling of imminent destruction are so profound that I beg God for His immediate assistance.

4 **For my days are consumed** as if they are going up **in smoke,** destroyed without purpose, **and my bones, as in a pyre, are burnt hollow.**

5 **My heart is beaten down like** trampled **grass, and it withers, for** I am so overcome with pain and sorrow that I neglect to fulfill even my most basic needs; I even **forget to eat my bread.**

6 **From my groaning,** I feel as though I am shriveling up, that **my bones cling to my flesh.**

7 **I am like a desert owl; like an owl of the ruins I have become.** Both of these nocturnal birds make sounds similar to crying or wailing.

8 **I am fixed in place,** I cannot move from where I am, **and I am like a lonely bird on a rooftop,** with no one coming to my aid.

כָּל־הַיּוֹם חֵרְפוּנִי אוֹיְבָי מְהוֹלָלַי בִּי נִשְׁבָּעוּ:

9 My enemies taunt me all day long; my pursuers swear oaths by me.

כִּי־אֵפֶר כַּלֶּחֶם אָכָלְתִּי וְשִׁקֻּוַי בִּבְכִי מָסָכְתִּי:

10 I eat ashes as if bread, and my drink is mixed with tears,

מִפְּנֵי־זַעַמְךָ וְקִצְפֶּךָ כִּי נְשָׂאתַנִי וַתַּשְׁלִיכֵנִי:

11 because of Your wrath and Your fury. Indeed, You lifted me up and flung me away.

יָמַי כְּצֵל נָטוּי וַאֲנִי כָּעֵשֶׂב אִיבָשׁ:

12 My days are like a cast shadow, and I wither away like grass.

וְאַתָּה יְהוָה לְעוֹלָם תֵּשֵׁב וְזִכְרְךָ לְדֹר וָדֹר:

13 But You, Lord, abide forever, Your remembrance throughout the generations.

אַתָּה תָקוּם תְּרַחֵם צִיּוֹן כִּי־ עֵת לְחֶנְנָהּ כִּי־בָא מוֹעֵד:

14 You will arise and have compassion for Zion; for it is time to be gracious to her, for the appointed time has come,

---

9 **My enemies taunt me all day long; my pursuers swear oaths by me,** using my name as a paradigm of wretchedness.

10 **I eat ashes as if bread.** Placing ashes on the head, or dipping one's food in ashes, is a sign of mourning. In my current state, the psalmist says, instead of just dipping my bread in ashes, the ashes have become my food, in place of bread, **and** all of **my drink is mixed with tears,**

11 **because of Your wrath and Your fury,** which are the ultimate source of my suffering. **Indeed, You lifted me up and flung me away.** You lifted me up as one picks up an object to cast it away.

12 **My days are like a cast shadow,** which has no tangible substance and constantly shifts in accordance with the moving of the sun. **And I wither away like grass** that is not watered.

13 Up to this point, the psalmist has described the pain and affliction of the poor man who is overwhelmed by hardship. But despite his suffering, he has faith and trust in God: **But You, Lord, abide forever,** without interruption or diminishment; **Your remembrance** is recalled **throughout the generations.**

14 And when it is Your will to show us grace, **You will arise** from Your place, as it were, **and have compassion for Zion; for it is time to be gracious to her, for the appointed time has come.**

טו כִּי־רָצְוּ עֲבָדֶיךָ אֶת־אֲבָנֶיהָ
וְאֶת־עֲפָרָהּ יְחֹנֵנוּ:

טז וְיִירְאוּ גוֹיִם אֶת־שֵׁם יהוֹה
וְכָל־מַלְכֵי הָאָרֶץ אֶת־
כְּבוֹדֶךָ:

יז כִּי־בָנָה יהוֹה צִיּוֹן נִרְאָה
בִּכְבוֹדוֹ:

יח פָּנָה אֶל־תְּפִלַּת הָעַרְעָר
וְלֹא־בָזָה אֶת־תְּפִלָּתָם:

יט תִּכָּתֶב זֹאת לְדוֹר אַחֲרוֹן
וְעַם נִבְרָא יְהַלֶּל־יָהּ:

כ כִּי־הִשְׁקִיף מִמְּרוֹם קָדְשׁוֹ
יהוֹה מִשָּׁמַיִם ׀ אֶל־אֶרֶץ
הִבִּיט:

15 for Your servants desire her stones and cherish her dust.

16 May nations fear the name of the Lord, and all kings of the earth, Your glory,

17 when the Lord rebuilds Zion and is seen in His glory.

18 He has heeded the prayer of the juniper; He did not despise their prayer.

19 Let this be recorded for the generation to come, so that those yet to be born may praise the Lord.

20 For He gazed down from His holy height; from heaven, the Lord looked upon the earth,

---

15 Because we are devoted to You, we are determined to remain in Jerusalem, close to Your Temple, rather than flee. **For Your servants desire her** very **stones and cherish her** very **dust,** loving even the inanimate and barren stones and dirt.

16 Therefore we pray: **May nations** also come to **fear the name of the Lord, and** may **all kings of the earth** learn to revere **Your glory,**

17 **when the Lord rebuilds Zion and is seen in His glory.**

18 **He has heeded the prayer of the juniper.** The psalmist depicts one who is alone and without support as an *arar*, a juniper, which is a desert shrub that can survive on very little water but does not bear fruit. The word is related to *ariri*, meaning "childless." **He did not despise their prayer.**

19 **Let this** divine salvation **be recorded for the generation to come, so that those yet to be born may praise the Lord.**

20 **For He gazed down from His holy height** to take note and intervene in the events of this world; **from heaven, the Lord looked upon the earth,**

כא לִשְׁמֹעַ אֶנְקַת אָסִיר לְפַתֵּחַ
בְּנֵי תְמוּתָה:

כב לְסַפֵּר בְּצִיּוֹן שֵׁם יהוה
וּתְהִלָּתוֹ בִּירוּשָׁלָ͏ִם:

כג בְּהִקָּבֵץ עַמִּים יַחְדָּו
וּמַמְלָכוֹת לַעֲבֹד אֶת־יהוה:

כד עִנָּה בַדֶּרֶךְ כֹּחִו קִצַּר יָמָי: כֹּחִי

כה אֹמַר אֵלִי אַל־תַּעֲלֵנִי בַּחֲצִי
יָמָי בְּדוֹר דּוֹרִים שְׁנוֹתֶיךָ:

כו לְפָנִים הָאָרֶץ יָסַדְתָּ וּמַעֲשֵׂה
יָדֶיךָ שָׁמָיִם:

21 to hear the groaning of the captive, to unshackle those doomed to death,

22 so that the name of the Lord in Zion may be told, and His praise in Jerusalem,

23 when the peoples are gathered together and kingdoms come to serve the Lord.

24 Along the way, He has weakened my strength, He has shortened my days.

25 I said: My God, do not take me up in the midst of my days; Your years last for all generations.

26 You laid the foundations of earth in times past; the heavens are the work of Your hands.

---

21 **to hear the groaning of the captive, to unshackle those doomed to death,**

22 **so that the name of the Lord in Zion may be told, and His praise in Jerusalem,**

23 **when the peoples are gathered together** there in Jerusalem, **and kingdoms come** there to serve the Lord.

24 The psalmist believes that this redemption will come, and he prays that he may live to witness it. But in the meantime, his current state remains precarious: **Along the way,** along life's path as we await the future redemption, **He has weakened my strength,** and I feel as if **He has shortened my days.**

25 Therefore **I said** in prayer to Him: **My God, do not take me up,** that is, do not bring an end to my life, **in the midst of my days; Your years last for all generations,** and You can grant me a long life.

26 **You laid the foundations of earth in times past,** at creation; **the heavens are the work of Your hands.**

כז הֵ֤מָּה ׀ יֹאבֵדוּ֮ וְאַתָּ֢ה תַֽעֲ֫מֹ֥ד וְכֻלָּם֮ כַּבֶּ֣גֶד יִבְל֑וּ כַּלְּב֖וּשׁ תַּחֲלִיפֵ֣ם וְיַֽחֲלֹֽפוּ׃

כח וְאַתָּה־ה֑וּא וּ֜שְׁנוֹתֶ֗יךָ לֹ֣א יִתָּֽמּוּ׃

כט בְּנֵֽי־עֲבָדֶ֥יךָ יִשְׁכּ֑וֹנוּ וְ֜זַרְעָ֗ם לְפָנֶ֥יךָ יִכּֽוֹן׃

27 Even they will perish, but You will endure. All of them will wear out, like a garment; You will change them like clothing, and they will be gone.

28 But You are He, Your years never ending.

29 The children of Your servants will dwell safely, their descendants standing firmly before You.

PSALM 103

The first of two psalms beginning with the phrase "Bless the Lord, my soul." It deals mainly with the vicissitudes of human life, in both the physical and the spiritual sense. It also contains words of praise and supplication.

א לְדָוִ֨ד ׀ בָּֽרְכִ֣י נַ֭פְשִׁי אֶת־יְהֹוָ֑ה וְכָל־קְ֜רָבַ֗י אֶת־שֵׁ֥ם קָדְשֽׁוֹ׃

By David. Bless the Lord, my soul, and all that is within me bless His holy name.

---

27 **Even they,** the works of Your hands, **will perish, but You will endure** forever. **All of them will wear out, like a garment; You will change them like clothing, and they will be gone.** All the creations of the world will eventually wear out and be replaced.

28 **But You are He** who exists forever, **Your years never ending.**

29 Since You are eternal and omnipotent, You have the power to ensure that **the children of Your servants will dwell safely** and not be driven from their homes, **their descendants standing firmly before You** for all time.

PSALM 103

1 **By David. Bless the Lord, my soul, and all that is within me bless His holy name.**

בָּרְכִי נַפְשִׁי אֶת־יהוה וְאַל־
תִּשְׁכְּחִי כָּל־גְּמוּלָיו:

הַסֹּלֵחַ לְכָל־עֲוֹנֵכִי הָרֹפֵא
לְכָל־תַּחֲלוּאָיְכִי:

הַגּוֹאֵל מִשַּׁחַת חַיָּיְכִי
הַמְעַטְּרֵכִי חֶסֶד וְרַחֲמִים:

הַמַּשְׂבִּיעַ בַּטּוֹב עֶדְיֵךְ
תִּתְחַדֵּשׁ כַּנֶּשֶׁר נְעוּרָיְכִי:

עֹשֵׂה צְדָקוֹת יהוה
וּמִשְׁפָּטִים לְכָל־עֲשׁוּקִים:

2 Bless the Lord, my soul, and do not forget all His acts of kindness.

3 It is He who forgives all your iniquities, who heals all your diseases,

4 who redeems your life from the pit, who crowns you with kindness and mercy,

5 who sates your spirit with good, your youth renewed like an eagle.

6 The Lord performs righteous deeds and metes out justice to all the oppressed.

---

2 **Bless the Lord, my soul, and do not forget all His acts of kindness.** In times of peace and abundance, man tends to forget God's past acts of beneficence; the psalmist warns against this.

3 **It is He who forgives all your iniquities, who heals all your diseases,** referring to both physical and spiritual ailments;

4 **who redeems your life from the pit** of the grave, from death; **who crowns you,** surrounds you, **with kindness and mercy;**

5 **who sates your spirit with good.** *Edyekh,* translated here as "your spirit," literally means "an ornament, an item of beautification." Here it refers to the beauty of one's life, the spirit. Another interpretation of the word is "your body." **Your youth** is **renewed like an eagle.** Eagles live longer than other birds and also retain their power and strength.

6 The psalmist now turns to another aspect of God's praises: **The Lord performs righteous deeds and metes out justice to all the oppressed.** Although people often undergo suffering, God ultimately delivers justice and rescues them from their enemies. Proof for this can be found not only in the experience of individuals, but also in history:

ז יוֹדִ֣יעַ דְּרָכָ֣יו לְמֹשֶׁ֑ה לִבְנֵ֥י
יִ֝שְׂרָאֵ֗ל עֲלִילֽוֹתָֽיו׃

ח רַח֣וּם וְחַנּ֣וּן יְהֹוָ֑ה אֶ֖רֶךְ אַפַּ֣יִם
וְרַב־חָֽסֶד׃

ט לֹֽא־לָנֶ֥צַח יָרִ֑יב וְלֹ֖א לְעוֹלָ֣ם
יִטּֽוֹר׃

י לֹ֣א כַ֭חֲטָאֵ֣ינוּ עָ֣שָׂה לָ֑נוּ וְלֹ֥א
כַ֝עֲוֺנֹתֵ֗ינוּ גָּמַ֥ל עָלֵֽינוּ׃

יא כִּ֤י כִגְבֹ֣הַּ שָׁ֭מַיִם עַל־הָאָ֑רֶץ
גָּבַ֥ר חַ֝סְדּ֗וֹ עַל־יְרֵאָֽיו׃

יב כִּרְחֹ֣ק מִ֭זְרָח מִֽמַּעֲרָ֑ב
הִרְחִ֥יק מִ֝מֶּ֗נּוּ אֶת־פְּשָׁעֵֽינוּ׃

7 He made His ways known
to Moses, His deeds to the
children of Israel.

8 Merciful and gracious is
the Lord, slow to anger and
abounding in kindness.

9 He will not contend to eternity
or forever keep His anger.

10 He has not dealt with us as
befits our sins; He has not
requited our iniquities in kind.

11 Rather, as high as the heavens
above the earth, so is His
kindness great for those who
fear Him.

12 As far as east from west,
so has He distanced our
transgressions from us.

---

7 **He made His ways known to Moses,** showing him time and time again how He saved Israel from all the perils facing them, and **His deeds to the children of Israel.** The entire nation witnessed firsthand His miraculous deeds, from the exodus from Egypt onward.

8 **Merciful and gracious is the Lord, slow to anger and abounding in kindness.** This is an allusion to God's revelation to Moses by the cleft in the rock,[9] where He revealed His attributes of mercy, which include the words of this verse.

9 Even in times of trouble, we can take comfort in the fact that **He will not contend** with us **to eternity or forever keep His anger;** eventually He will forgive us and once again be our Protector.

10 **He has not dealt with us** as harshly as truly **befits our sins; He has not requited our iniquities in kind.**

11 **Rather, as high as the heavens above the earth, so is His kindness great for those who fear Him.**

12 **As far as east from west, so has He distanced our transgressions from us,** in that He no longer remembers them or associates us with them.

כְּרַחֵם אָב עַל־בָּנִים רִחַם
יְהֹוָה עַל־יְרֵאָיו:

¹³ Just as a father has mercy on
his children, so the Lord has
mercy on those who fear Him.

כִּי־הוּא יָדַע יִצְרֵנוּ זָכוּר כִּי־
עָפָר אֲנָחְנוּ:

¹⁴ For He knows our impulses;
He is mindful that we are
but dust.

אֱנוֹשׁ כֶּחָצִיר יָמָיו כְּצִיץ
הַשָּׂדֶה כֵּן יָצִיץ:

¹⁵ As for man, his days are like
grass; he springs up like a bud
in the field,

כִּי רוּחַ עָבְרָה־בּוֹ וְאֵינֶנּוּ
וְלֹא־יַכִּירֶנּוּ עוֹד מְקוֹמוֹ:

¹⁶ which, when a wind passes
over it, it ceases to be; its own
place knows it no more.

וְחֶסֶד יְהֹוָה ׀ מֵעוֹלָם וְעַד־
עוֹלָם עַל־יְרֵאָיו וְצִדְקָתוֹ
לִבְנֵי בָנִים:

¹⁷ But the kindness of the Lord
is forever, to those who fear
Him; His righteousness for the
children's progeny,

---

¹³ **Just as a father has mercy on his children, so the Lord has mercy on those who fear Him.** God is merciful toward us, not necessarily because we are righteous, but because we are weak and dependent on Him.

¹⁴ God is aware of how powerless we are and how much we need His kindness and mercy, **for He knows** how intense **our** evil! **impulses** are, so likely to cause us to veer from the proper path. **He is mindful that we are but dust,** physical beings, children of the earth, and that because of this, He cannot expect perfection from us.

¹⁵ **As for man, his days are like grass** that dries up and withers; **he springs up like a bud** of a wildflower **in the field,** which wilts shortly after it appears,

¹⁶ **which, when a** hot east **wind passes over it, it** dries out and **ceases to be; its own place knows it no more,** as no trace of it remains.

¹⁷ **But,** in contrast to man's fleeting, ephemeral existence, **the kindness of the Lord is forever, to those who fear Him; His righteousness** extends even **for the children's progeny,**

לְשָׁמְרֵי בְרִיתוֹ וּלְזֹכְרֵי פִקֻּדָיו
לַעֲשׂוֹתָם:

יהוה בַּשָּׁמַיִם הֵכִין כִּסְאוֹ
וּמַלְכוּתוֹ בַּכֹּל מָשָׁלָה:

בָּרְכוּ יהוה מַלְאָכָיו גִּבֹּרֵי
כֹחַ עֹשֵׂי דְבָרוֹ לִשְׁמֹעַ בְּקוֹל
דְּבָרוֹ:

בָּרְכוּ יהוה כָּל־צְבָאָיו
מְשָׁרְתָיו עֹשֵׂי רְצוֹנוֹ:

בָּרְכוּ יהוה ׀ כָּל־מַעֲשָׂיו
בְּכָל־מְקֹמוֹת מֶמְשַׁלְתּוֹ
בָּרְכִי נַפְשִׁי אֶת־יהוה:

18 for those who keep His covenant and remember His precepts, to observe them.

19 The Lord has established His throne in the heavens; His kingship rules over all.

20 Bless the Lord, His angels, mighty in strength, who do His bidding, heeding His word.

21 Bless the Lord, all His hosts, His servants who do His will.

22 Bless the Lord, all of His works, in all places of His dominion. Bless the Lord, my soul.

---

18 **for those who keep His covenant and remember His precepts, to observe them.**

19 **The Lord has established His throne in the heavens; His kingship rules over all,** over every facet of creation.

20 The psalmist now suggests words of praise that we humans, despite our limited power and brief life spans, can offer to God: **Bless the Lord, His angels,** who are truly capable of praising Him properly, for they are **mighty in strength,** and they are the ones **who do His bidding;** the entire reason for their existence is the **heeding** of **His word.**

21 **Bless the Lord, all His hosts, His servants who do His will,** namely, all the creatures of the world, from the most exalted to the lowest.

22 **Bless the Lord, all of His works,** all of His creations, **in all places of His dominion,** throughout the entire universe. **Bless the Lord, my soul.** In reiterating the opening words of the psalm, "Bless the Lord, my soul," the psalmist emphasizes that this personal prayer is part of a universal chorus of praise.

PSALM 104

The second of two consecutive psalms beginning with the phrase "Bless the Lord, my soul."
This is a hymn in praise of everything created by God, and it depicts the grand design of the world,
of which man is but a small part.

בָּרְכִי נַפְשִׁי אֶת־יְהֹוָה יהוה
אֱלֹהַי גָּדַלְתָּ מְּאֹד הוֹד וְהָדָר
לָבָשְׁתָּ:

1 Bless the Lord, my soul. Lord
my God, You are greatly
exalted, You are clothed in
splendor and glory.

עֹטֶה־אוֹר כַּשַּׂלְמָה נוֹטֶה
שָׁמַיִם כַּיְרִיעָה:

2 Enveloping with light as if with
a cloak, He spreads out the
heavens like a tent cloth.

הַמְקָרֶה בַמַּיִם עֲלִיּוֹתָיו
הַשָּׂם־עָבִים רְכוּבוֹ הַמְהַלֵּךְ
עַל־כַּנְפֵי־רוּחַ:

3 He covers His upper chambers
with water, He makes clouds
His chariot, He moves on
wings of wind.

PSALM 104

1 **Bless the Lord, my soul.** This is more than an introductory phrase; it also evokes the spirit of
this psalm, which is an outpouring of praise from an individual's point of view rather than a more
dispassionate or seemingly objective outline of God's creation. The person praising God is central
to this hymn of praise. **Lord my God, You are greatly exalted, You are clothed in splendor
and glory.** The psalm begins with praise of God Himself before shifting to a broader, more detailed
description of the world, which is depicted here as a kind of ornament or apparel for God.

2 **Enveloping** the world **with light as if with a cloak.** The expression *oteh or kasalma* is
interpreted in other contexts as referring to God wrapping Himself, as it were, in a garment of
light. Here, however, the explanation is that He envelops the world with light. **He spreads out
the heavens like a tent cloth.**

3 **He covers His upper chambers with water.** As related in Genesis,[10] the heavens, called here
the "upper chambers," are described as covered with water. **He makes clouds His chariot, He
moves on wings of wind.** God rides, as it were, upon the clouds and through the wind.

ד עֹשֶׂה מַלְאָכָיו רוּחֹות
מְשָׁרְתָיו אֵשׁ לֹהֵט:

He makes the winds His messengers, the flaming fires His servants.

ה יָסַד־אֶרֶץ עַל־מְכוֹנֶיהָ בַּל־
תִּמּוֹט עוֹלָם וָעֶד:

He established the earth on its foundations, never to be shaken.

ו תְּהוֹם כַּלְּבוּשׁ כִּסִּיתוֹ עַל־
הָרִים יַעַמְדוּ־מָיִם:

He covered the depths as with a garment; waters stood above the mountains.

ז מִן־גַּעֲרָתְךָ יְנוּסוּן מִן־קוֹל
רַעַמְךָ יֵחָפֵזוּן:

At Your rebuke they fled; at the sound of Your thunder they hastened away.

ח יַעֲלוּ הָרִים יֵרְדוּ בְקָעוֹת
אֶל־מְקוֹם זֶה ׀ יָסַדְתָּ לָהֶם:

They rose to the mountains, descended in the valleys to the place You established for them.

ט גְּבוּל־שַׂמְתָּ בַּל־יַעֲבֹרוּן בַּל־
יְשֻׁבוּן לְכַסּוֹת הָאָרֶץ:

You set a boundary they could not cross, so they would not come back to cover the earth.

---

4 **He makes the winds His messengers** as they do His bidding, **the flaming fires His servants.**

5 **He established the earth on its foundations, never to be shaken.**

6 **He covered the depths,** the great stores of underground water, with land **as one covers himself with a garment.** But at first, in the early stages of creation, **waters stood above** the entire earth, including **the mountains.**[11]

7 The waters covered the earth until God issued them the command: "Let the waters be gathered to one place and let the dry land appear."[12] Thereupon, **at Your rebuke they fled; at the sound of Your thunder they hastened away.** The next two verses provide further detail of this phenomenon.

8 **They rose to the mountains, descended in the valleys,** until they arrived at the sea, **to the place You established for them.**

9 And after the waters converged into the seas, **You set a boundary,** the seashore, which **they could not cross, so they would not come back to cover the earth.**

הַמְשַׁלֵּחַ מַעְיָנִים בַּנְּחָלִים
בֵּין הָרִים יְהַלֵּכוּן:

יַשְׁקוּ כָּל־חַיְתוֹ שָׂדָי יִשְׁבְּרוּ
פְרָאִים צְמָאָם:

עֲלֵיהֶם עוֹף־הַשָּׁמַיִם יִשְׁכּוֹן
מִבֵּין עֳפָאִים יִתְּנוּ־קוֹל:

מַשְׁקֶה הָרִים מֵעֲלִיּוֹתָיו
מִפְּרִי מַעֲשֶׂיךָ תִּשְׂבַּע
הָאָרֶץ:

מַצְמִיחַ חָצִיר ׀ לַבְּהֵמָה
וְעֵשֶׂב לַעֲבֹדַת הָאָדָם
לְהוֹצִיא לֶחֶם מִן־הָאָרֶץ:

10 He sends forth springs through the valleys; between the mountains they flow.

11 They give drink to all beasts of the field; wild asses quench their thirst.

12 Birds of the sky dwell alongside them, giving voice among the branches.

13 He waters the mountains from His upper chambers; the earth is sated with the product of Your works.

14 He makes grass grow for the cattle, and vegetation for the labor of man, for bringing forth bread from the earth,

---

10 Besides what is found in underground stores and in the sea, there is yet another source of water in the world: **He sends forth springs** that course **through the valleys; between the mountains they flow.**

11 Water is ubiquitous in nature, present in desolate as well as settled areas. But though it is an inanimate part of nature, it is closely linked to living creatures, for these waters sustain life: **They give drink to all beasts of the field; wild asses quench their thirst** with them.

12 **Birds of the sky dwell alongside them,** as well as among the vegetation that grows near the streams, **giving voice among the branches.**

13 **He waters the mountains,** too high to obtain water from the springs, with rain that falls **from His upper chambers,** from the heavens; **the earth is sated with the product of Your works,** that is, the rain.

14 And through that rainfall, **He makes grass grow for the cattle, and vegetation for the labor of man,** for the beasts of burden with which he does his work, as well as ears of grain **for bringing forth bread from the earth** for man to eat.

וְיַיִן ׀ יְשַׂמַּח לְבַב־אֱנוֹשׁ
לְהַצְהִיל פָּנִים מִשָּׁמֶן וְלֶחֶם
לְבַב־אֱנוֹשׁ יִסְעָד:

יִשְׂבְּעוּ עֲצֵי יהוה אַרְזֵי לְבָנוֹן
אֲשֶׁר נָטָע:

אֲשֶׁר־שָׁם צִפֳּרִים יְקַנֵּנוּ
חֲסִידָה בְּרוֹשִׁים בֵּיתָהּ:

הָרִים הַגְּבֹהִים לַיְּעֵלִים
סְלָעִים מַחְסֶה לַשְׁפַנִּים:

עָשָׂה יָרֵחַ לְמוֹעֲדִים שֶׁמֶשׁ
יָדַע מְבוֹאוֹ:

15 and wine, which gladdens man's heart, making the face glisten from oil; and bread, to sustain man's heart.

16 The trees of the Lord sate themselves, the cedars of Lebanon that He planted,

17 where birds make their nests; the stork has its home in the cypresses.

18 The high mountains are for the ibex, the crags a shelter for the hyrax.

19 He made the moon for appointed times; the sun knows its setting.

---

15 **And** in addition to these, He brings forth from the ground grapes for **wine, which gladdens man's heart,** as well as olives, **making the face glisten from** their **oil,** by applying it to the skin as a moisturizer. **And bread, to sustain man's heart.** The three basic staples of life: bread, wine, and oil, all sprout from the earth with the help of the rains.

16 **The trees of the Lord,** that is, trees of vast proportion, **sate themselves** from the rainwater and from the ground's nutrients; **the cedars of Lebanon** are a specific example of very large trees **that He planted.**

17 In those trees is **where birds make their nests; the stork has its home in the cypresses.**

18 **The high mountains are** habitats **for the ibex, the crags a shelter for the hyrax.** The hyrax, also known as the rock badger, lives in the mountains as well, but it cannot leap about and is therefore described as sheltering among the crags.

19 Having provided a geographical description of the world and all that grows in it, the psalmist shifts his attention to another aspect of the world, time: **He made the moon for appointed times,** by which dates of the month are fixed; **the sun knows its setting.** Whereas the movements of the moon are not completely regular, and the times of its rising and setting change over the course of the month, the sun "knows" when to set, following a constant and predictable pattern.

תָּֽשֶׁת־חֹשֶׁךְ וִיהִי לָיְלָה בּֽוֹ־ ²⁰ You bring darkness and it
תִרְמֹשׂ כָּל־חַיְתוֹ־יָֽעַר: becomes night, when all the
beasts of the forest are astir.

הַכְּפִירִים שֹׁאֲגִים לַטָּֽרֶף ²¹ The young lions roar for
וּלְבַקֵּשׁ מֵאֵל אָכְלָֽם: prey, asking the Almighty for
their food.

תִּזְרַח הַשֶּׁמֶשׁ יֵאָסֵפוּן וְאֶל־ ²² When the sun rises they
מְעֽוֹנֹתָם יִרְבָּצֽוּן: withdraw, and crouch in
their dens.

יֵצֵא אָדָם לְפָעֳלוֹ וְלַֽעֲבֹדָתוֹ ²³ Man goes out to his work and
עֲדֵי־עָֽרֶב: to his labor until evening.

מָֽה־רַבּוּ מַעֲשֶׂיךָ ׀ יְהֹוָה ²⁴ Lord, how manifold are Your
כֻּלָּם בְּחָכְמָה עָשִׂיתָ מָלְאָה deeds, in wisdom have You
הָאָרֶץ קִנְיָנֶֽךָ: made them all. The earth is full
of Your possessions.

זֶה ׀ הַיָּם גָּדוֹל וּרְחַב יָדָיִם ²⁵ There is the sea, vast and broad;
שָֽׁם־רֶמֶשׂ וְאֵין מִסְפָּר חַיּוֹת an innumerable swarm is in it,
קְטַנּוֹת עִם־גְּדֹלֽוֹת: creatures both great and small.

---

²⁰ Shifts in time also affect the daily cycle of life: **You bring darkness and it becomes night, when all the beasts of the forest are astir,** as the animals of the forest, especially the predators among them, are active mostly at night.

²¹ **The young lions roar for prey, asking the Almighty for their food.** The roar of a lion sets its prey running in the direction that is most desirable for the lion; moreover, in running, the prey is also easier to spot and pursue. The psalmist poetically sees in the lion's roar not only a means to catch its prey but also as a kind of plea to God for food.

²² **When the sun rises they withdraw** and return to their lairs, **and crouch in their dens.**

²³ At that point, when daylight arrives, **man goes out to his work and to his labor until evening.**

²⁴ The psalmist exclaims his awe and wonder at God's works: **Lord, how manifold are Your deeds, in wisdom have You made them all.** Everything You created has its own unique niche and set of interactions with other creatures and with the environment as a whole. **The earth is full of Your possessions.**

²⁵ Until this point, the psalmist has described the wonders of life on earth; here, he goes on to

שָׁם אֳנִיּוֹת יְהַלֵּכוּן לִוְיָתָן זֶה־
יָצַרְתָּ לְשַׂחֶק־בּוֹ: כו

כֻּלָּם אֵלֶיךָ יְשַׂבֵּרוּן לָתֵת
אָכְלָם בְּעִתּוֹ: כז

תִּתֵּן לָהֶם יִלְקֹטוּן תִּפְתַּח
יָדְךָ יִשְׂבְּעוּן טוֹב: כח

תַּסְתִּיר פָּנֶיךָ יִבָּהֵלוּן תֹּסֵף
רוּחָם יִגְוָעוּן וְאֶל־עֲפָרָם
יְשׁוּבוּן: כט

תְּשַׁלַּח רוּחֲךָ יִבָּרֵאוּן
וּתְחַדֵּשׁ פְּנֵי אֲדָמָה: ל

26 There ships go; and the leviathan, which You created to frolic with.

27 They all fix their hopes on You to give them their food at the proper time.

28 When You give it to them, they gather it; when You open Your hand, they are sated with good.

29 When You hide Your face, they take fright; when You take away their spirit, they die and return to their dust.

30 When You send forth Your spirit, they are created; You renew the face of the land.

---

describe an area that is less visible to the human eye: **There is the sea, vast and broad; an innumerable swarm** of organisms **is in it, creatures both great and small.**

26 The sea is so vast that **there ships go,** traveling great distances; **and the leviathan** as well, a giant sea creature, **which You created to frolic with,** as it were. Although it is massive beyond the dimensions of any other creature, in God's hands even the leviathan is like a plaything.

27 **They all,** all the creatures of the sea, land, and air mentioned earlier, **fix their hopes on You,** their true source of sustenance, **to give them their food at the proper time.**

28 **When You give it to them, they gather it.** At times, the food is available, but the creatures must search for it and gather what they can; at other times, **when You open Your hand** and release all Your bounty, **they are sated** amply **with good.**

29 On the other hand, there are also times **when You hide Your face;** You withhold Your goodness from them, and since they are completely dependent on Your kindness, **they take fright,** distraught from the lack of sustenance. Morcover, eventually all life comes to an end; **when You take away their spirit, they die and return to their dust.**

30 Yet **when You send forth Your spirit, they are created.** Your creative spirit can also renew life, and **You renew the face of the land.**

לא יְהִי כְבוֹד יהוה לְעוֹלָם
יִשְׂמַח יהוה בְּמַעֲשָׂיו:

לב הַמַּבִּיט לָאָרֶץ וַתִּרְעָד יִגַּע
בֶּהָרִים וְיֶעֱשָׁנוּ:

לג אָשִׁירָה לַיהוה בְּחַיָּי אֲזַמְּרָה
לֵאלֹהַי בְּעוֹדִי:

לד יֶעֱרַב עָלָיו שִׂיחִי אָנֹכִי
אֶשְׂמַח בַּיהוה:

לה יִתַּמּוּ חַטָּאִים ׀ מִן־הָאָרֶץ
וּרְשָׁעִים ׀ עוֹד אֵינָם בָּרְכִי
נַפְשִׁי אֶת־יהוה הַלְלוּיָהּ:

31 May the glory of the Lord endure forever; may the Lord rejoice in His works,

32 He who looks at the earth, and it trembles; who touches the mountains, and they smoke.

33 I will sing to the Lord as long as I live; I will sing praise to my God as long as I am able.

34 May my utterance please Him; I rejoice in the Lord.

35 May sinners be removed from the earth, and may the wicked be no more. Bless the Lord, my soul. Halleluya.

---

31 Having completed his description of all the various creatures and their circumstances, the psalmist concludes: **May the glory of the Lord endure forever. May the Lord rejoice in His works.**

32 God's glory is evident in the everyday functioning of the world, but there are also occasions when God reveals His power in a more dramatic fashion: It is **He who looks at the earth, and it trembles** just from His stern gaze, like a servant who quakes at his master's scowl. It is He **who touches the mountains, and they smoke.** At a touch from God, as it were, volcanoes spew fire and smoke.

33 The psalmist now adds his personal note of praise: **I will sing to the Lord as long as I live; I will sing praise to my God as long as I am able.**

34 **May my utterance please Him** and find favor with Him. In any event, **I rejoice in the Lord.**

35 After completing this description of the universe as a single, interconnected, harmonious entity comprised of countless varied parts and life forms, all of which are the work of God's hands, the psalmist cannot refrain from noting that there are those who spoil its beauty and perfection. It is for them that he prays at the end of this hymn: **May sinners be removed from the earth, and may the wicked be no more.** The psalmist concludes with the same words with which he opened the psalm: **Bless the Lord, my soul. Halleluya.** This word can be interpreted in two ways. It may be a composite of two words, *hallelu* and *Ya*, meaning "praise the Lord." Alternatively, it may be understood as a single word, an expansion of the word *hallel*,[13] in which case it means "a praise."

PSALM 105

A song expressing gratitude to God for His kindness throughout the generations.
This psalm comprises an abbreviated account of the history of Israel until after the conquest
of the land. Like Psalm 68, it is written in the form of an epic poem; it differs in that its tone
is peaceful and serene rather than majestic or heroic.

הוֹדוּ לַיהוה קִרְאוּ בִשְׁמוֹ א
הוֹדִיעוּ בָעַמִּים עֲלִילוֹתָיו:

שִׁירוּ־לוֹ זַמְּרוּ־לוֹ שִׂיחוּ ב
בְּכָל־נִפְלְאוֹתָיו:

הִתְהַלְלוּ בְּשֵׁם קָדְשׁוֹ יִשְׂמַח ג
לֵב ׀ מְבַקְשֵׁי יהוה:

דִּרְשׁוּ יהוה וְעֻזּוֹ בַּקְּשׁוּ פָנָיו ד
תָמִיד:

זִכְרוּ נִפְלְאוֹתָיו אֲשֶׁר־עָשָׂה ה
מֹפְתָיו וּמִשְׁפְּטֵי־פִיו:

1 Give thanks to the Lord, proclaim His name. Make His deeds known among the peoples.

2 Sing to Him, sing praises to Him. Speak of all His wonders.

3 Glory in His holy name; let the hearts of those who seek the Lord rejoice.

4 Search out the Lord and His strength; seek His presence always.

5 Remember the wonders He has done, His marvels, and the judgments of His mouth.

PSALM 105

1 The psalm begins with a celebratory proclamation: **Give thanks to the Lord, proclaim His name.** This statement makes it clear from the outset that what follows is a song of thanksgiving to God for all He has done on our behalf. **Make His deeds known among the peoples.**

2 **Sing to Him, sing praises to Him. Speak of all His wonders,** referring not only to specific miraculous events, but also to God's continual care and supervision of us.

3 **Glory in His holy name;** and through recalling the miracles He performed for us, **let the hearts of those who seek the Lord rejoice.**

4 **Search out the Lord and His strength; seek His presence always.**

5 **Remember the wonders He has done, His marvels, and the judgments of His mouth.** Remember not only God's miraculous deeds, but also His commandments.

זֶרַע אַבְרָהָם עַבְדּוֹ בְּנֵי יַעֲקֹב בְּחִירָיו:

⁶ Seed of Abraham, His servant; children of Jacob, His chosen ones,

הוּא יהוה אֱלֹהֵינוּ בְּכָל־הָאָרֶץ מִשְׁפָּטָיו:

⁷ He is the Lord our God; His judgments are throughout the land.

זָכַר לְעוֹלָם בְּרִיתוֹ דָּבָר צִוָּה לְאֶלֶף דּוֹר:

⁸ He remembers His covenant forever, the word that He ordained for a thousand generations,

אֲשֶׁר כָּרַת אֶת־אַבְרָהָם וּשְׁבוּעָתוֹ לְיִשְׂחָק:

⁹ which He made with Abraham, and His oath to Isaac.

וַיַּעֲמִידֶהָ לְיַעֲקֹב לְחֹק לְיִשְׂרָאֵל בְּרִית עוֹלָם:

¹⁰ He set it for Jacob as a statute, for Israel as an everlasting covenant,

לֵאמֹר לְךָ אֶתֵּן אֶת־אֶרֶץ־כְּנָעַן חֶבֶל נַחֲלַתְכֶם:

¹¹ saying: To you I will give the land of Canaan as your allotted portion.

---

⁶ **Seed of Abraham, His servant; children of Jacob, His chosen ones,**

⁷ **He is the Lord our God; His judgments are throughout the land.** His words fill the world, which acts in accordance with His commands.

⁸ **He remembers His covenant** with the patriarchs **forever, the word that He ordained for a thousand generations.** The expression "a thousand generations," which essentially means "forever," is found elsewhere in the Torah as well.[14]

⁹ The covenant referred to in the previous verse is that **which He made with Abraham, and His oath to Isaac.** In this verse, Isaac's Hebrew name is spelled *Yisḥak*, a variant of the usual spelling *Yitzḥak*; both words connote laughter, the basis for Isaac's name.[15]

¹⁰ **He set it,** this covenant, **for** Isaac's son **Jacob as a statute, for Israel as an everlasting covenant.** The name "Israel" here is synonymous with Jacob, but it also alludes more broadly to the nation of Israel, which descended from him.

¹¹ **Saying: To you I will give the land of Canaan as your allotted portion.** In the covenant, God promised Abraham and, by extension, the nation of Israel, that the people would inherit

בִּהְיוֹתָם מְתֵי מִסְפָּר כִּמְעַט ^{יב}
וְגָרִים בָּהּ:

וַיִּתְהַלְכוּ מִגּוֹי אֶל־גּוֹי ^{יג}
מִמַּמְלָכָה אֶל־עַם אַחֵר:

לֹא־הִנִּיחַ אָדָם לְעָשְׁקָם ^{יד}
וַיּוֹכַח עֲלֵיהֶם מְלָכִים:

אַל־תִּגְּעוּ בִמְשִׁיחָי וְלִנְבִיאַי ^{טו}
אַל־תָּרֵעוּ:

12 It was when they were a small number of people, just a few sojourning within it.

13 They wandered from nation to nation, from one kingdom to another people.

14 He let no man oppress them, and He reproved kings on their account.

15 Do not touch My anointed ones; do not harm My prophets.

---

the land of Canaan. The covenant addresses other issues as well, but since the purpose of this psalm is to express thanks to God for gifts bestowed upon Israel, only the promise of the land is mentioned here.

12 **It,** that covenant, **was** made **when they,** the nascent nation of Israel, **were a small number of people, just a few** merely **sojourning within it,** not yet permanently settled in the land.

13 **They wandered from nation to nation.** All the patriarchs, Abraham, Isaac, and Jacob, were forced to wander away from the Land of Israel at one time or another. **From one kingdom to another people.** At times, their travels involved interaction with kings of other nations; in other instances, as when Jacob fled to Haran, they merely took up residence among "another people," the commoners.

14 Because of God's covenant with them, however, **He let no man oppress them** during all their travels, **and He** even **reproved kings on their account,** as related in the Torah regarding Abraham and Isaac, that God intervened to protect them.[16]

15 God told those kings: **Do not touch my anointed ones.** The patriarchs possessed the status of anointed kings, and for this reason they merited special protection on God's part. **Do not harm My prophets.** The patriarchs were also prophets, as it says in Genesis[17] regarding Abraham: "Restore the man's wife, as he is a prophet." Their status was thus far higher than would be indicated by their material possessions or political capacities.

טז וַיִּקְרָ֣א רָ֭עָב עַל־הָאָ֑רֶץ כָּֽל־
מַטֵּה־לֶ֥חֶם שָׁבָֽר׃

יז שָׁלַ֣ח לִפְנֵיהֶ֣ם אִ֑ישׁ לְ֝עֶ֗בֶד
נִמְכַּ֥ר יוֹסֵֽף׃

יח עִנּ֣וּ בַכֶּ֣בֶל רַגְלָ֑יו בַּ֝רְזֶ֗ל בָּ֣אָה
נַפְשֽׁוֹ׃

יט עַד־עֵ֥ת בֹּֽא־דְבָר֑וֹ אִמְרַ֖ת
יְהוָ֣ה צְרָפָֽתְהוּ׃

כ שָׁ֣לַח מֶ֭לֶךְ וַיַּתִּירֵ֑הוּ מֹשֵׁ֥ל
עַ֝מִּ֗ים וַֽיְפַתְּחֵֽהוּ׃

כא שָׂמ֣וֹ אָד֣וֹן לְבֵית֑וֹ וּ֝מֹשֵׁ֗ל
בְּכָל־קִנְיָנֽוֹ׃

16 He proclaimed a famine on the land; He broke every staff of bread.

17 He had sent a man before them, Joseph, who had been sold as a slave.

18 They tortured his legs with chains, his body was placed in iron,

19 until the time His word came to pass; the Lord's utterance purged him.

20 He sent a king to release him, a ruler of a people, who set him free.

21 He made him master of his house and ruler of all his possessions,

---

16 Later, when Jacob was old, **He proclaimed a famine on the land; He broke every staff of bread,** every source of sustenance. The famine was so severe, it affected even Egypt.

17 But to offset the devastating effects of that famine, **He had sent a man** to Egypt **before them,** namely, **Joseph,** to provide them with relief. Only in retrospect did it become evident that God had arranged for Joseph, **who had been sold as a slave,** to rise to power in Egypt to prepare for the arrival of the children of Israel.

18 When Joseph was enslaved, **they tortured his legs with chains, his body was placed in iron,**

19 and he remained in this situation **until the time** for his freedom, as was predetermined by **His word, came to pass. The Lord's utterance purged him.** Joseph's suffering as a prisoner served to rectify his previous unworthy deeds.

20 And when that time ordained by God arrived, **He sent a king,** Pharaoh, **to release him** from his incarceration, **a ruler of a people, who set him free.**

21 **He** then promoted Joseph and **made him master of his,** Pharaoh's, **house and ruler of all his possessions.**

כב לֶאְסֹר שָׂרָיו בְּנַפְשׁוֹ וּזְקֵנָיו
יְחַכֵּם:

כג וַיָּבֹא יִשְׂרָאֵל מִצְרָיִם וְיַעֲקֹב
גָּר בְּאֶרֶץ־חָם:

כד וַיֶּפֶר אֶת־עַמּוֹ מְאֹד
וַיַּעֲצִמֵהוּ מִצָּרָיו:

כה הָפַךְ לִבָּם לִשְׂנֹא עַמּוֹ
לְהִתְנַכֵּל בַּעֲבָדָיו:

כו שָׁלַח מֹשֶׁה עַבְדּוֹ אַהֲרֹן
אֲשֶׁר בָּחַר־בּוֹ:

כז שָׂמוּ־בָם דִּבְרֵי אֹתוֹתָיו
וּמֹפְתִים בְּאֶרֶץ חָם:

22 to imprison ministers at his will. He taught wisdom to his elders.

23 Then Israel came to Egypt, and Jacob sojourned in the land of Ham.

24 He made His people exceedingly fruitful, making them greater than their foes.

25 Their hearts changed to hate His people, to harass His servants.

26 He sent Moses His servant, and Aaron, whom He had chosen.

27 They set before them His signs, marvels in the land of Ham.

---

22 Joseph was granted so much power that he was able **to imprison** even high-ranking **ministers at his will. He,** Joseph, **taught wisdom to his,** Pharaoh's, **elders.** Joseph advised Pharaoh how to avoid the ravages of the impending famine, and this wise counsel was given in the presence of all the elders and royal advisors of Egypt.

23 **Then Israel,** referring to Jacob, but also alluding to the nascent nation of Israel, **came to Egypt, and Jacob sojourned in the land of Ham,** referring to Egypt, as Ham was the father of Mitzrayim, the progenitor of the Egyptians.[18]

24 **He,** God, **made His people** Israel **exceedingly fruitful, making them greater than their** Egyptian **foes.**

25 **Their hearts,** the hearts of the Egyptians, **changed** from sympathy and respect for Israel **to hate His people,** due to jealousy and suspicion, **to harass His servants** with all the oppressive decrees described in the book of Exodus.

26 **He** then **sent Moses His servant, and Aaron, whom He had chosen,** first to be his prophet, and subsequently to be the High Priest.

27 **They,** Moses and Aaron, **set before them,** before the Egyptians, **His signs, marvels in the land of Ham.**

כח שָׁלַח חֹשֶׁךְ וַיַּחְשִׁךְ וְלֹא־מָרוּ
אֶת־דבריו:

28 He sent darkness and made it dark; they did not defy His word.

כט הָפַךְ אֶת־מֵימֵיהֶם לְדָם
וַיָּמֶת אֶת־דְּגָתָם:

29 He turned their waters into blood and killed their fish.

ל שָׁרַץ אַרְצָם צְפַרְדְּעִים
בְּחַדְרֵי מַלְכֵיהֶם:

30 Their land swarmed with frogs, even in the chambers of their kings.

לא אָמַר וַיָּבֹא עָרֹב כִּנִּים בְּכָל־
גְּבוּלָם:

31 He spoke, and wild beasts came; lice within all their borders.

לב נָתַן גִּשְׁמֵיהֶם בָּרָד אֵשׁ
לֶהָבוֹת בְּאַרְצָם:

32 He gave them hail for rain, flames of fire in their land.

לג וַיַּךְ גַּפְנָם וּתְאֵנָתָם וַיְשַׁבֵּר
עֵץ גְּבוּלָם:

33 It struck their vines and their fig trees, and it broke the trees of their borders.

לד אָמַר וַיָּבֹא אַרְבֶּה וְיֶלֶק וְאֵין
מִסְפָּר:

34 He spoke, and locusts came, grasshoppers without number.

---

28 Next comes a short description of the ten plagues, recounted here in a different order from that found in the book of Exodus: **He sent darkness and made it dark** in Egypt; **they,** Moses and Aaron, faithfully executed God's commands and **did not defy His word,** even though Moses initially voiced his misgivings about God's mode of action.[19]

29 **He turned their waters into blood and killed their fish.**

30 **Their land swarmed with frogs,** which found their way to every place in Egypt, **even in the chambers of their kings.**[20]

31 **He spoke, and wild beasts came; lice** appeared **within all their borders.**

32 **He gave them hail for rain,** which was mixed with **flames of fire**[21] **in their land.**

33 **It,** the destructive hail, **struck their vines and their fig trees, and it broke the trees** that grew within all **of their borders.** This was the most significant damage caused by the hail.

34 **He spoke, and locusts came, grasshoppers without number.**

לה וַיֹּאכַל כָּל־עֵשֶׂב בְּאַרְצָם
וַיֹּאכַל פְּרִי אַדְמָתָם:

לו וַיַּךְ כָּל־בְּכוֹר בְּאַרְצָם
רֵאשִׁית לְכָל־אוֹנָם:

לז וַיּוֹצִיאֵם בְּכֶסֶף וְזָהָב וְאֵין
בִּשְׁבָטָיו כּוֹשֵׁל:

לח שָׂמַח מִצְרַיִם בְּצֵאתָם כִּי־
נָפַל פַּחְדָּם עֲלֵיהֶם:

לט פָּרַשׂ עָנָן לְמָסָךְ וְאֵשׁ לְהָאִיר
לָיְלָה:

מ שָׁאַל וַיָּבֵא שְׂלָו וְלֶחֶם שָׁמַיִם
יַשְׂבִּיעֵם:

35 They ate all the vegetation in their land; they ate the fruits of their soil.

36 He struck down every firstborn in their land, the first fruits of all their vigor.

37 And He brought them out with silver and gold; none among His tribes faltered.

38 Egypt rejoiced in their departure, for their dread had fallen upon them.

39 He spread out a cloud like a curtain, and fire to light up the night.

40 He requested, and He brought quail; He sated them with the bread of heaven.

---

35 **They ate all the vegetation in their land; they ate the fruits of their soil.**

36 Then came the final plague: **He struck down every firstborn in their land, the first fruits of all their vigor,** an expression used in the Bible that is synonymous with one's firstborn son.[22]

37 **And** following that final plague, **He brought them,** the Israelites, **out** of Egypt **with silver and gold** that they had despoiled from the Egyptians; **none among His tribes faltered,** and no one was left behind.

38 As related in the Torah,[23] **Egypt rejoiced in their departure,** eager to be relieved of all the misfortunes that had befallen them, **for their dread,** the dread of the Israelites, **had fallen upon them.**

39 The psalmist now describes the people's wanderings in the desert after the exodus: **He spread out a cloud like a curtain** by day, with which to protect the people, **and fire to light up the night.**

40 **He,** Moses, **requested** meat from God on behalf of the people, **and He brought quail. He sated them with** manna, **the bread of heaven.**

מא פָּתַח צוּר וַיָּזוּבוּ מָיִם הָלְכוּ
בַּצִּיּוֹת נָהָר:

מב כִּי־זָכַר אֶת־דְּבַר קָדְשׁוֹ אֶת־
אַבְרָהָם עַבְדּוֹ:

מג וַיּוֹצִא עַמּוֹ בְשָׂשׂוֹן בְּרִנָּה
אֶת־בְּחִירָיו:

מד וַיִּתֵּן לָהֶם אַרְצוֹת גּוֹיִם
וַעֲמַל לְאֻמִּים יִירָשׁוּ:

מה בַּעֲבוּר ׀ יִשְׁמְרוּ חֻקָּיו
וְתוֹרֹתָיו יִנְצֹרוּ הַלְלוּיָהּ:

41 He opened a rock and water gushed forth; they traveled through parched lands with a river.

42 For He remembered His holy word to Abraham His servant.

43 And He brought out His people with joy, His chosen ones with joyous song.

44 And He gave them the lands of nations; they inherited the fruit of the peoples' labor,

45 so that they would keep His statutes and observe His teachings. Halleluya.

---

41 **He opened a rock and water gushed forth** from it.[24] **They traveled through parched lands with a river** of fresh water alongside them.

42 God did all this for the Israelites, **for He remembered His holy word,** the covenant and oath he had made **to Abraham His servant.**

43 **And He brought out His people with joy, His chosen ones with joyous song,** and led them through the wilderness until they arrived at the Land of Israel.

44 **And** there **He gave them the lands of nations,** the Canaanites and the surrounding peoples; **they inherited the fruit of the peoples' labor** during their conquest of the Land of Israel.

45 The gift of the land and all the good within it was given to Israel by God **so that they would keep His statutes and observe His teachings. Halleluya.**

PSALM 106

A psalm similar to the previous one, offering a poetic historical account of the people of Israel.
Unlike Psalm 105, which is written in a tone of peace and serenity, the text here focuses largely
on the sins committed by the people and the various ways in which they violated
their covenant with God.

א הַלְלוּיָהּ ׀ הוֹדוּ לַיהוָה כִּי־
טוֹב כִּי לְעוֹלָם חַסְדּוֹ:

ב מִי יְמַלֵּל גְּבוּרוֹת יְהוָה
יַשְׁמִיעַ כָּל־תְּהִלָּתוֹ:

ג אַשְׁרֵי שֹׁמְרֵי מִשְׁפָּט עֹשֵׂה
צְדָקָה בְכָל־עֵת:

ד זָכְרֵנִי יְהוָה בִּרְצוֹן עַמֶּךָ
פָּקְדֵנִי בִּישׁוּעָתֶךָ:

1 Halleluya. Give thanks to the
Lord for He is good, for His
kindness is everlasting.

2 Who can recount the mighty
deeds of the Lord? Who can
tell all His praises?

3 Happy are those who
heed the law, who act with
righteousness at all times.

4 Remember me, Lord, when
You favor Your people; be
mindful of me in Your
salvation,

PSALM 106

1 The psalm begins on a positive note with an expression of gratitude to God: **Halleluya. Give thanks to the Lord for He is good, for His kindness is everlasting.** This verse is repeated several times throughout the book of Psalms, and was apparently a set formulation of praise to God.

2 **Who can recount the mighty deeds of the Lord, who can tell all His praises?**

3 **Happy are those who heed the law, who act with righteousness at all times.** In a sense, this is a reply to the question posed in the preceding verse. The person who constantly strives to act righteously is the one who deserves to "recount the mighty deeds" and tell all God's praises.

4 The next two verses constitute the only personal note in this psalm: **Remember me, Lord, when You favor Your people.** When the time comes for You to forgive and look favorably upon Your people, remember to count me among them. **Be mindful of me in Your salvation,**

לִרְאוֹת ׀ בְּטוֹבַת בְּחִירֶיךָ
לִשְׂמֹחַ בְּשִׂמְחַת גּוֹיֶךָ
לְהִתְהַלֵּל עִם־נַחֲלָתֶךָ:

חָטָאנוּ עִם־אֲבוֹתֵינוּ הֶעֱוִינוּ
הִרְשָׁעְנוּ:

אֲבוֹתֵינוּ בְמִצְרַיִם ׀ לֹא־
הִשְׂכִּילוּ נִפְלְאוֹתֶיךָ לֹא זָכְרוּ
אֶת־רֹב חֲסָדֶיךָ וַיַּמְרוּ עַל־יָם
בְּיַם־סוּף:

וַיּוֹשִׁיעֵם לְמַעַן שְׁמוֹ לְהוֹדִיעַ
אֶת־גְּבוּרָתוֹ:

וַיִּגְעַר בְּיַם־סוּף וַיֶּחֱרָב
וַיּוֹלִיכֵם בַּתְּהֹמוֹת כַּמִּדְבָּר:

5 so I might see the prosperity
of Your chosen ones, rejoice
in the joy of Your nation, and
glory with Your portion.

6 We have sinned like our
fathers; we have committed
iniquity; we have behaved
wickedly.

7 Our fathers in Egypt did not
contemplate Your wonders;
they did not recall Your
abundant acts of kindness.
They rebelled by the sea, the
Red Sea.

8 He rescued them for the sake
of His name, to proclaim His
might.

9 He rebuked the Red Sea and
it dried up, and He led them
through the depths, as if
through a desert.

---

5 **so I might see the prosperity of Your chosen ones, rejoice in the joy of Your nation**
Israel, **and glory with Your portion,** referring both to the people and to the Land of Israel.

6 The confessional portion of the psalm begins here. It opens with a succinct acknowledgment of
guilt before moving to a broader historical perspective: **We have sinned like our fathers; we
have committed iniquity; we have behaved wickedly.**

7 **Our fathers in Egypt did not contemplate Your wonders** even as they were occurring before
their eyes; **they did not recall Your abundant acts of kindness. They rebelled by the sea,
the Red Sea,** complaining when Pharaoh pursued them to the shores of the Red Sea.[25]

8 But despite their rebelliousness, **He rescued them for the sake of His name,** not for their sake,
as they were undeserving, **to proclaim His might.**

9 **He rebuked the Red Sea and it dried up.** The waters of the Red Sea withdrew as if shamed

וַיּוֹשִׁיעֵם מִיַּד שׂוֹנֵא וַיִּגְאָלֵם
מִיַּד אוֹיֵב:

¹⁰ He saved them from those who hated them, redeemed them from the hand of the enemy.

יא וַיְכַסּוּ־מַיִם צָרֵיהֶם אֶחָד
מֵהֶם לֹא נוֹתָר:

¹¹ Water covered their foes; not one of them remained.

יב וַיַּאֲמִינוּ בִדְבָרָיו יָשִׁירוּ
תְּהִלָּתוֹ:

¹² Then they believed in His words; they sang His praise.

יג מִהֲרוּ שָׁכְחוּ מַעֲשָׂיו לֹא־חִכּוּ
לַעֲצָתוֹ:

¹³ They quickly forgot His deeds; they did not await His counsel.

יד וַיִּתְאַוּוּ תַאֲוָה בַּמִּדְבָּר וַיְנַסּוּ־
אֵל בִּישִׁימוֹן:

¹⁴ They craved with desire in the desert. They tested the Almighty in the wilderness.

טו וַיִּתֵּן לָהֶם שֶׁאֱלָתָם וַיְשַׁלַּח
רָזוֹן בְּנַפְשָׁם:

¹⁵ He gave them their request, but sent leanness into their souls.

---

by God's rebuke, leaving dry land in their wake. **And He led them through the depths** on dry land, **as if** they were walking **through a desert.**

¹⁰ **He saved them from those who hated them,** the pursuing Egyptians, and **redeemed them from the hand of the enemy.**

¹¹ **Water covered their foes.** Beyond preventing the Egyptians from pursuing the Israelites across the sea, the waters of the Red Sea drowned them all, so that **not** even **one of them remained.**

¹² **Then,** after the crossing of the sea, **they believed in His words; they sang His praise,** referring to the Song at the Sea.[26]

¹³ But this reconciliation did not last long: **They quickly forgot His deeds; they did not await His counsel.** Whenever the children of Israel encountered any difficulty, they complained immediately, rather than trusting that God, who was leading them through the desert in a miraculous manner, would provide their needs in due time.

¹⁴ Rather, **they craved with desire in the desert,** yearning for items that they lacked. But worse than that, **they tested the Almighty in the wilderness.** On some occasions, even when they lacked nothing, they complained, solely because they wanted to see if God was able to perform a certain deed, testing His omnipotence. This, too, was considered sinful on their part.

¹⁵ **He** ultimately **gave them their request,** sending them quail to eat, **but sent leanness into their souls,** for this quail led to the deaths of many of the people.[27]

וַיְקַנְא֣וּ לְ֭מֹשֶׁה בַּֽמַּחֲנֶ֑ה לְ֝אַהֲרֹ֗ן קְד֣וֹשׁ יְהֹוָֽה: טז

תִּפְתַּח־אֶ֭רֶץ וַתִּבְלַ֣ע דָּתָ֑ן וַ֝תְּכַ֗ס עַל־עֲדַ֥ת אֲבִירָֽם: יז

וַתִּבְעַר־אֵ֥שׁ בַּעֲדָתָ֑ם לֶ֝הָבָ֗ה תְּלַהֵ֥ט רְשָׁעִֽים: יח

יַעֲשׂוּ־עֵ֥גֶל בְּחֹרֵ֑ב וַ֝יִּשְׁתַּחֲו֗וּ לְמַסֵּכָֽה: יט

וַיָּמִ֥ירוּ אֶת־כְּבוֹדָ֑ם בְּתַבְנִ֥ית שׁ֝֗וֹר אֹכֵ֥ל עֵֽשֶׂב: כ

שָׁ֭כְחוּ אֵ֣ל מוֹשִׁיעָ֑ם עֹשֶׂ֖ה גְדֹל֣וֹת בְּמִצְרָֽיִם: כא

16 They became envious of Moses in the camp, and of Aaron, the Lord's holy one.

17 The earth opened and swallowed Datan, covering over the assembly of Aviram.

18 A fire blazed in their assembly; flames consumed the wicked.

19 They made a calf in Horev, bowing down to a molten image,

20 and they exchanged their Glory for the molded image of a grass-eating bull.

21 They forgot the Almighty, their Savior, who had done great things in Egypt,

---

16 In addition to their testing of God, **they became envious of Moses in the camp,** speaking ill of him, particularly during the uprising of Korah and his followers, **and of Aaron, the Lord's holy one,** questioning his right to the priesthood.[28]

17 **The earth opened and swallowed Datan, covering over the assembly of Aviram.** These two men were among the main instigators of Korah's rebellion.[29]

18 **A fire blazed in their assembly** among those pretenders to the priesthood who had offered incense before the Tabernacle;[30] **flames consumed the wicked** participants in this sin.

19 The psalmist now describes an even more grievous sin committed in the wilderness: **They made a calf in Horev,** another name for Mount Sinai, **bowing down to a molten image,**

20 **and they exchanged their Glory,** the Almighty, **for the molded image of a grass-eating bull,** the Golden Calf.

21 **They forgot the Almighty, their Savior, who had done great things in Egypt,**

כב נִפְלָאוֹת בְּאֶרֶץ חָם נוֹרָאוֹת
עַל־יַם־סֽוּף:

כג וַיֹּאמֶר לְהַשְׁמִידָם לוּלֵי
מֹשֶׁה בְחִירוֹ עָמַד בַּפֶּֽרֶץ
לְפָנָיו לְהָשִׁיב חֲמָתֽוֹ
מֵהַשְׁחִֽית:

כד וַיִּמְאֲסוּ בְּאֶרֶץ חֶמְדָּה לֹא־
הֶאֱמִינוּ לִדְבָרֽוֹ:

כה וַיֵּרָגְנוּ בְאָהֳלֵיהֶם לֹא שָׁמְעוּ
בְּקוֹל יְהֹוָה:

כו וַיִּשָּׂא יָדוֹ לָהֶם לְהַפִּיל אוֹתָם
בַּמִּדְבָּֽר:

22 wonders in the land of Ham,
awesome deeds by the Red Sea.

23 He said He would destroy
them, were it not for Moses,
His chosen one, who stood
before Him in the breach to
turn back His wrath from
destruction.

24 And they despised the
desirable land; they did not
have faith in His word.

25 They grumbled in their tents;
they did not heed the voice of
the Lord.

26 And He raised His hand
concerning them, to cast them
down in the desert,

---

22 **wonders in the land of Ham, awesome deeds by the Red Sea.**

23 In the wake of the sin of the Golden Calf, **He said He would destroy them** and would have done so **were it not for Moses, His chosen one, who stood before Him in the breach** and prayed **to turn back His wrath from destruction.**

24 The next grievous sin recounted here is that of the spies who were sent by Moses to scout out the land prior to the arrival of the children of Israel: **And** because of the frightening report brought back by the spies, **they despised the desirable Land** of Israel, and did not want to proceed to conquer it. **They did not have faith in His word,** by which He promised that they would be able to wage a successful conquest.

25 **They grumbled in their tents; they did not heed the voice of the Lord.**

26 **And He raised His hand** in a gesture of oath **concerning them, to cast them down,** to cause them to perish, **in the desert,**

כ וּלְהַפִּיל זַרְעָם בַּגּוֹיִם
וּלְזָרוֹתָם בָּאֲרָצוֹת:

כח וַיִּצָּמְדוּ לְבַעַל פְּעוֹר וַיֹּאכְלוּ
זִבְחֵי מֵתִים:

כט וַיַּכְעִיסוּ בְּמַעַלְלֵיהֶם
וַתִּפְרָץ־בָּם מַגֵּפָה:

ל וַיַּעֲמֹד פִּינְחָס וַיְפַלֵּל וַתֵּעָצַר
הַמַּגֵּפָה:

לא וַתֵּחָשֶׁב לוֹ לִצְדָקָה לְדֹר וָדֹר
עַד־עוֹלָם:

לב וַיַּקְצִיפוּ עַל־מֵי מְרִיבָה וַיֵּרַע
לְמֹשֶׁה בַּעֲבוּרָם:

27 to cast their seed among the nations and to scatter them among the lands.

28 They clung to Baal Peor and ate sacrifices offered to the dead.

29 They provoked anger with their deeds, and a plague broke out among them.

30 Pinhas stood up to carry out judgment, and the plague was stopped.

31 He was accorded merit for all generations to come, for eternity.

32 They provoked at the waters of Meriva, and Moses suffered on their account,

---

27 **to cast their seed among the nations and to scatter them among the lands.** This verse appears to be the source of the Sages' comment[31] that punishment for the sin of the spies has been continuously meted out throughout history, on the date of this rebellion, the ninth of Av.

28 The last of the grievous sins committed by the Israelites in the wilderness was the worship of the idolatry of the Moavites: **They clung to Baal Peor and ate sacrifices offered to the dead,** a disparaging term for idolatrous offerings.

29 **They provoked anger with their** other **deeds** that they committed on that occasion, **and a plague broke out among them.**

30 **Pinhas stood up to carry out judgment** by killing Zimri, one of the main perpetrators of sin in that incident,[32] **and** thereupon **the plague was stopped.**

31 **He was accorded merit for all generations to come, for eternity.** As a reward for his brave actions, Pinhas became the progenitor of a dynasty of priests who, aside from some brief interruptions, served in the high priesthood throughout the days of the Temple.

32 The psalmist mentions more sins committed by the Israelites. **They provoked** God **at the waters of Meriva, and Moses suffered on their account,** as it was he who was punished by being denied entry into the Promised Land.[33]

לֹג כִּי־הִמְר֥וּ אֶת־ר֑וּחוֹ וַ֝יְבַטֵּ֗א
בִּשְׂפָתָֽיו:

לד לֹֽא־הִ֭שְׁמִידוּ אֶת־הָ֥עַמִּ֑ים
אֲשֶׁ֤ר אָמַ֖ר יְהֹוָ֣ה לָהֶֽם:

לה וַיִּתְעָרְב֥וּ בַגּוֹיִ֑ם וַֽ֝יִּלְמְד֗וּ
מַֽעֲשֵׂיהֶֽם:

לו וַיַּֽעַבְד֥וּ אֶת־עֲצַבֵּיהֶ֑ם וַיִּֽהְי֖וּ
לָהֶ֣ם לְמוֹקֵֽשׁ:

לז וַיִּזְבְּח֣וּ אֶת־בְּ֭נֵיהֶם וְאֶת־
בְּנֽוֹתֵיהֶ֗ם לַשֵּׁדִֽים:

לח וַיִּֽשְׁפְּכ֨וּ דָ֪ם נָקִ֡י דַּם־בְּנֵ֤יהֶ֨ם
וּֽבְנֽוֹתֵיהֶ֗ם אֲשֶׁ֣ר זִ֭בְּחוּ לַֽעֲצַבֵּ֣י
כְנָ֑עַן וַתֶּֽחֱנַ֥ף הָ֝אָ֗רֶץ בַּדָּמִֽים:

³³ for they rebelled against him, and he made an utterance with his lips.

³⁴ They did not destroy the peoples as the Lord told them to do.

³⁵ They mingled with the nations and learned their practices,

³⁶ and served their idols, which became a snare for them.

³⁷ They sacrificed their sons and their daughters to demons,

³⁸ and they shed innocent blood, the blood of their sons and their daughters, whom they sacrificed to the idols of Canaan; and the land became polluted with blood.

---

³³ **For they,** the Israelites, **rebelled against him,** against Moses, accusing him of intentionally seeking to kill them, **and** as a result of their accusations, **he made an** unseemly **utterance with his lips.**³⁴ From this verse it is evident that Moses was punished not for his actions at Meriva, but for what he said.

³⁴ Later, after entering and possessing the Land of Israel, **they did not destroy the** Canaanite **peoples as the Lord told them to do,** to kill or expel all of them.

³⁵ And as a result of leaving the Canaanites to live among them, **they mingled with the nations and learned their practices,**

³⁶ **and served their idols, which became a snare for them.**

³⁷ **They sacrificed their sons and their daughters to demons.** This practice is not known to us from other sources. An implicit reference is found in Leviticus 17:7.

³⁸ **And they shed innocent blood, the blood of their sons and their daughters, whom they sacrificed to the idols of Canaan,** as part of the sacrificial rites to Molekh and other idols. **And the land became polluted with** that spilt **blood.**

לט וַיִּטְמְא֥וּ בְמַעֲשֵׂיהֶ֑ם וַ֝יִּזְנ֗וּ בְּמַעַלְלֵיהֶֽם׃

מ וַיִּֽחַר־אַ֣ף יְהֹוָ֣ה בְּעַמּ֑וֹ וַ֝יְתָעֵ֗ב אֶת־נַחֲלָתֽוֹ׃

מא וַיִּתְּנֵ֥ם בְּיַד־גּוֹיִ֑ם וַֽיִּמְשְׁל֥וּ בָ֝הֶ֗ם שֹׂנְאֵיהֶֽם׃

מב וַיִּלְחָצ֣וּם אֽוֹיְבֵיהֶ֑ם וַ֝יִּכָּנְע֗וּ תַּ֣חַת יָדָֽם׃

מג פְּעָמִ֥ים רַבּ֗וֹת יַצִּ֫ילֵ֥ם וְ֭הֵמָּה יַמְר֣וּ בַעֲצָתָ֑ם וַ֝יָּמֹ֗כּוּ בַּעֲוֺנָֽם׃

מד וַ֭יַּרְא בַּצַּ֣ר לָהֶ֑ם בְּ֝שׇׁמְע֗וֹ אֶת־רִנָּתָֽם׃

39 They were defiled by their practices; they went astray with their deeds.

40 The Lord's fury blazed against His people. He abhorred His portion,

41 and He delivered them into the hands of the nations. Those who hated them ruled over them.

42 Their enemies oppressed them; they were subdued under their power.

43 Many times did He rescue them, but they were defiant in their counsel, sinking low in their iniquity.

44 Yet He saw their distress when He heard their cry.

---

39 **They were defiled by their practices; they went astray** from the service of God **with their deeds.** The description of these sins sums up the era of the Judges.

40 Such abominations did not go unpunished: **The Lord's fury blazed against His people. He abhorred His portion,**

41 **and He delivered them into the hands of the nations** who invaded the Land of Israel periodically. **Those who hated them ruled over them.**

42 **Their enemies oppressed them; they were subdued under their power,** as described in detail in the book of Judges.

43 **Many times did He rescue them** by the hand of the various judges and leaders who led them to victory. **But they were defiant in their counsel;** they took counsel among themselves and decided to rebel against God, **sinking low in their iniquity.**

44 **Yet He saw their distress when,** time after time, they cried out in prayer and **He heard their cry.**

מה וַיִּזְכֹּר לָהֶם בְּרִיתוֹ וַיִּנָּחֵם
כְּרֹב חֲסָדָו:

מו וַיִּתֵּן אוֹתָם לְרַחֲמִים לִפְנֵי
כָּל־שׁוֹבֵיהֶם:

מז הוֹשִׁיעֵנוּ ׀ יהוה אֱלֹהֵינוּ
וְקַבְּצֵנוּ מִן־הַגּוֹיִם לְהֹדוֹת
לְשֵׁם קָדְשֶׁךָ לְהִשְׁתַּבֵּחַ
בִּתְהִלָּתֶךָ:

מח בָּרוּךְ יהוה ׀ אֱלֹהֵי יִשְׂרָאֵל
מִן־הָעוֹלָם ׀ וְעַד הָעוֹלָם
וְאָמַר כָּל־הָעָם אָמֵן
הַלְלוּיָהּ:

45 He remembered for them His covenant and relented, because of His great kindness,

46 and He caused them to be pitied by all their captors.

47 Save us, Lord our God, and gather us in from among the nations so we might give thanks to Your holy name and glory in Your praise.

48 Blessed be the Lord God of Israel, forever and ever. Let the entire nation say: Amen. Halleluya.

---

45 **He remembered for them His covenant and relented** of His intention to punish them severely, **because of His great kindness,**

46 **and He caused them to be pitied by all their captors.** Throughout the ages, groups of people from our nation have been exiled from the Land of Israel, in most cases as captives, often to far-flung places, as may be gathered from this and various other biblical verses.[35] It is a known historical fact that this phenomenon occurred as far back as the beginning of the Second Temple era.

47 The psalm closes with words of prayer: **Save us, Lord our God, and gather us in from among the nations,** where some of our nation are in exile, **so we might give thanks to Your holy name and glory in Your praise.**

48 The final verse of the psalm marks the conclusion of the fourth book of Psalms: **Blessed be the Lord God of Israel, forever and ever. Let the entire nation say: Amen. Halleluya.**

BOOK FIVE

FRIDAY

PSALM 107

A psalm that depicts various perils that people may confront, their deliverance from these difficulties, and their thanks to God for His salvation. It serves as a description of the basic forms of deliverance for which individuals were expected to bring a thanksgiving offering in Temple days and, in later generations, to recite the thanksgiving blessing, known as *Birkat HaGomel*.

הֹדֹוּ לַיהוָה כִּי־טֹוֹב כִּי
לְעֹולָם חַסְדֹּוֹ: א

1 Give thanks to the Lord, for He is good, for His kindness is forever.

יֹאמְרוּ גְּאוּלֵי יהוָה אֲשֶׁר
גְּאָלָם מִיַּד־צָר: ב

2 Let those the Lord redeemed say it, those He redeemed from the hand of the foe

וּמֵאֲרָצֹות קִבְּצָם מִמִּזְרָח
וּמִמַּעֲרָב מִצָּפֹון וּמִיָּם: ג

3 and gathered in from lands of the east, of the west, of the north, and from the sea.

תָּעוּ בַמִּדְבָּר בִּישִׁימֹון דָּרֶךְ
עִיר מֹושָׁב לֹא מָצָאוּ: ד

4 They lost their way on a desolate path in the wilderness, not finding an inhabited place.

PSALM 107

1 The psalm opens with a verse of praise that appears in several other psalms as well: **Give thanks to the Lord, for He is good, for His kindness is forever.**

2 Those who have been redeemed from perilous situations should be especially grateful: **Let those the Lord redeemed say it, those He redeemed from the hand of the foe**

3 **and** whom He **gathered in from lands of the east, of the west, of the north, and from the sea.** The word *yam* often refers to the west, but because that direction has already been mentioned in this verse, it is translated here by its literal meaning of "sea."

4 The psalmist now begins to describe the four groups of people who give thanks to God. The first: **They lost their way on a desolate path in the wilderness, not finding an inhabited place.**

ה רְעֵבִים גַּם־צְמֵאִים נַפְשָׁם
בָּהֶם תִּתְעַטָּף:

ו וַיִּצְעֲקוּ אֶל־יהוה בַּצַּר לָהֶם
מִמְּצוּקוֹתֵיהֶם יַצִּילֵם:

ז וַיַּדְרִיכֵם בְּדֶרֶךְ יְשָׁרָה לָלֶכֶת
אֶל־עִיר מוֹשָׁב:

ח יוֹדוּ לַיהוה חַסְדּוֹ וְנִפְלְאוֹתָיו
לִבְנֵי אָדָם:

ט כִּי־הִשְׂבִּיעַ נֶפֶשׁ שֹׁקֵקָה
וְנֶפֶשׁ רְעֵבָה מִלֵּא־טוֹב:

י יֹשְׁבֵי חֹשֶׁךְ וְצַלְמָוֶת אֲסִירֵי
עֳנִי וּבַרְזֶל:

5 Hungry and thirsty, their souls fainting within them,

6 they cried out to the Lord in their trouble; He rescued them from their distress,

7 and led them on a straight path toward an inhabited place.

8 Let them give thanks to the Lord for His kindness and His wonders on behalf of man.

9 For He satisfied the thirsty soul and filled the hungry soul with goodness.

10 Dwellers in darkness and the shadow of death, fettered with affliction and iron,

---

5 **Hungry and thirsty,** lost in the wilderness, **their souls fainting within them,**

6 **they cried out to the Lord in their trouble; He rescued them from their distress,**

7 **and led them on a straight path toward an inhabited place,** from where they were able to find their way out of the wilderness.

8 **Let them give thanks to the Lord for His kindness and His wonders on behalf of man.**

9 **For He satisfied the thirsty soul and filled the hungry soul with goodness.**

10 The psalmist now refers to the second group of people who give thanks to God: Prisoners, **dwellers in darkness and the shadow of death.** Jails were often dark, underground dungeons where prisoners were **fettered with affliction and iron,** figuratively "fettered" by various forms of physical affliction and sometimes by actual iron chains.

יא כִּי־הִמְרוּ אִמְרֵי־אֵל וַעֲצַת
עֶלְיוֹן נָאָצוּ:

יב וַיַּכְנַע בֶּעָמָל לִבָּם כָּשְׁלוּ
וְאֵין עֹזֵר:

יג וַיִּזְעֲקוּ אֶל־יהוה בַּצַּר לָהֶם
מִמְּצֻקוֹתֵיהֶם יוֹשִׁיעֵם:

יד יוֹצִיאֵם מֵחֹשֶׁךְ וְצַלְמָוֶת
וּמוֹסְרוֹתֵיהֶם יְנַתֵּק:

טו יוֹדוּ לַיהוה חַסְדּוֹ וְנִפְלְאוֹתָיו
לִבְנֵי אָדָם:

טז כִּי־שִׁבַּר דַּלְתוֹת נְחֹשֶׁת
וּבְרִיחֵי בַרְזֶל גִּדֵּעַ:

11 for they had rebelled against the word of the Almighty, reviling the counsel of the Most High.

12 He subdued their hearts with toil; they stumbled, and there was no one to help.

13 They cried out to the Lord in their trouble; He redeemed them from their distress.

14 He brought them out of darkness and the shadow of death, and He severed their chains.

15 Let them give thanks to the Lord for His kindness and His wonders on behalf of man.

16 For He shattered doors of bronze and sundered iron bolts.

---

11 The prisoners described here are not necessarily people who were incarcerated unjustly, **for they had rebelled against the word of the Almighty, reviling the counsel of the Most High.**

12 **He subdued their hearts with toil,** forced labor while in captivity; **they stumbled, and there was no one to help.**

13 **They cried out to the Lord in their trouble; He redeemed them from their distress.**

14 **He brought them out of darkness and the shadow of death, and He severed their chains.**

15 **Let them give thanks to the Lord for His kindness and His wonders on behalf of man.**

16 As in the first example, the psalmist concludes this second section by mentioning the exact reason why these people should express gratitude: **For He shattered doors of bronze,** the mighty doors that lock the prison, **and sundered iron bolts.**

יז אֱוִלִים מִדֶּרֶךְ פִּשְׁעָם
וּמֵעֲוֹנֹתֵיהֶם יִתְעַנּוּ:

יח כָּל־אֹכֶל תְּתַעֵב נַפְשָׁם וַיַּגִּיעוּ
עַד־שַׁעֲרֵי מָוֶת:

יט וַיִּזְעֲקוּ אֶל־יהוה בַּצַּר לָהֶם
מִמְּצֻקוֹתֵיהֶם יוֹשִׁיעֵם:

כ יִשְׁלַח דְּבָרוֹ וְיִרְפָּאֵם וִימַלֵּט
מִשְּׁחִיתוֹתָם:

כא יוֹדוּ לַיהוה חַסְדּוֹ וְנִפְלְאוֹתָיו
לִבְנֵי אָדָם:

כב וְיִזְבְּחוּ זִבְחֵי תוֹדָה וִיסַפְּרוּ
מַעֲשָׂיו בְּרִנָּה: ל

17 Fools, because of their path of sin were afflicted, and because of their transgressions.

18 Abhorring all food, they were at death's door.

19 They cried out to the Lord in their trouble; He delivered them from their distress.

20 He sent His word and healed them, and rescued them from the pit.

21 Let them give thanks to the Lord for His kindness and His wonders on behalf of man.

22 Let them offer thanksgiving sacrifices and tell of His deeds with joyful singing.

---

17 The psalmist goes on to describe the third group of people who should give thanks, those who have recovered from serious illness. Here, too, their illness was often punishment for sins they committed: **Fools, because of their path of sin were afflicted, and because of their transgressions.**

18 **Abhorring all food,** lacking appetite because of their illness, they were in danger of dying; **they were at death's door.**

19 **They cried out to the Lord in their trouble; He delivered them from their distress.**

20 **He sent His word and healed them, and rescued them from the pit.** *Shehitotam,* translated here as "the pit," literally, "their pit," can also mean "their perversions." The term therefore refers both to the pit into which they figuratively fell, meaning their illness, as well as the sinful behavior that brought about their punishment.

21 **Let them give thanks to the Lord for His kindness and His wonders on behalf of man.**

22 **Let them offer thanksgiving sacrifices** after their recovery, **and tell of His deeds with joyful singing.**

יוֹרְדֵי הַיָּם בָּאֳנִיּוֹת עֹשֵׂי
מְלָאכָה בְּמַיִם רַבִּים: כ

²³ Those going to sea on ships,
who do their work in the
mighty waters.

הֵמָּה רָאוּ מַעֲשֵׂי יְהוָה
וְנִפְלְאוֹתָיו בִּמְצוּלָה: כד

²⁴ They saw the deeds of the Lord
and His wonders in the deep,

וַיֹּאמֶר וַיַּעֲמֵד רוּחַ סְעָרָה
וַתְּרוֹמֵם גַּלָּיו: כה

²⁵ how He spoke and produced
a gale of wind, lifting its
waves high.

יַעֲלוּ שָׁמַיִם יֵרְדוּ תְהוֹמוֹת
נַפְשָׁם בְּרָעָה תִתְמוֹגָג: כו

²⁶ They rose to the heavens, went
down to the depths. Their
souls dissolved in misery.

יָחוֹגּוּ וְיָנוּעוּ כַּשִּׁכּוֹר וְכָל־
חָכְמָתָם תִּתְבַּלָּע: כז

²⁷ They reeled and staggered like
drunken men, all their skill
come to naught.

וַיִּצְעֲקוּ אֶל־יְהוָה בַּצַּר לָהֶם
וּמִמְּצוּקֹתֵיהֶם יוֹצִיאֵם: כח

²⁸ They cried out to the Lord in
their trouble, and He brought
them out of their distress.

יָקֵם סְעָרָה לִדְמָמָה וַיֶּחֱשׁוּ
גַּלֵּיהֶם: כט

²⁹ He turned the storm into
silence, hushing its waves.

---

²³ The psalmist turns to the final group of people who should express their gratitude to God: **Those going to sea on ships, who do their work in the mighty waters,** such as sailors.

²⁴ **They saw the deeds of the Lord and His wonders in the deep,**

²⁵ **how He spoke and produced a gale of wind, lifting its waves high.**

²⁶ **They rose to the heavens, went down to the depths** as their ships were tossed with the waves. **Their souls dissolved in misery,** both from the discomfort of the rocking ship and from the terror of possibly sinking.

²⁷ **They reeled and staggered** back and forth **like drunken men, all their skill come to naught.** When faced with the overwhelming power of a mighty storm at sea, the sailors' expertise is of no avail.

²⁸ **They cried out to the Lord in their trouble, and He brought them out of their distress.**

²⁹ **He turned the storm into silence, hushing its waves.**

לֹ וַיִּשְׂמְחוּ כִי־יִשְׁתֹּקוּ וַיַּנְחֵם
אֶל־מְחוֹז חֶפְצָם:

לֹא יוֹדוּ לַיהוה חַסְדּוֹ וְנִפְלְאוֹתָיו
לִבְנֵי אָדָם:

לֹב וִירוֹמְמוּהוּ בִּקְהַל־עָם
וּבְמוֹשַׁב זְקֵנִים יְהַלְלוּהוּ:

לֹג יָשֵׂם נְהָרוֹת לְמִדְבָּר וּמֹצָאֵי
מַיִם לְצִמָּאוֹן:

לֹד אֶרֶץ פְּרִי לִמְלֵחָה מֵרָעַת
יֹשְׁבֵי בָהּ:

לֹה יָשֵׂם מִדְבָּר לַאֲגַם־מַיִם
וְאֶרֶץ צִיָּה לְמֹצָאֵי מָיִם:

30 They rejoiced because they were quieted; He led them to their destination.

31 Let them give thanks to the Lord for His kindness and His wonders on behalf of man.

32 Let them exalt Him in the congregation of people, and praise Him in the company of elders.

33 He turns rivers into desert, turning springs of water into parched land,

34 a fruitful land into a salty wasteland, because of the evil of those dwelling in it.

35 He turns a desert into a lake of water and dry land into springs.

---

30 **They,** the sea travelers, **rejoiced because they,** the storm's waves, **were quieted.** Now they would be able to resume their journey, and **He led them to their destination.**

31 **Let them give thanks to the Lord for His kindness and His wonders on behalf of man.**

32 **Let them exalt Him in the congregation of people, and praise Him in the company of** the **elders** of the community.

33 The psalmist now turns his attention from specific instances of peril and deliverance to the more general vicissitudes of life and God's mastery over nature. There are times when **He turns rivers into desert, turning springs of water into parched land.**

34 He turns **a fruitful land into a salty wasteland.** As the underground water supply dries up, the remaining water becomes saline and unfit for drinking and irrigation. God does this as a punishment for the land, **because of the evil of those dwelling in it.**

35 However, droughts do not last forever, and opposite phenomena also occur: **He turns a desert into a lake of water and dry land into springs.**

לו וַיּ֣וֹשֶׁב שָׁ֣ם רְעֵבִ֑ים וַ֜יְכוֹנְנ֗וּ
עִ֣יר מוֹשָֽׁב׃

לז וַיִּזְרְע֣וּ שָׂ֭דוֹת וַיִּטְּע֣וּ כְרָמִ֑ים
וַ֜יַּֽעֲשׂ֗וּ פְּרִ֣י תְבוּאָֽה׃

לח וַיְבָֽרֲכֵ֣ם וַיִּרְבּ֣וּ מְאֹ֑ד וּ֜בְהֶמְתָּ֗ם
לֹ֣א יַמְעִֽיט׃

לט וַיִּמְעֲט֥וּ וַיָּשֹׁ֑חוּ מֵעֹ֖צֶר רָעָ֣ה
וְיָגֽוֹן׃ ב

מ שֹׁפֵ֣ךְ בּ֭וּז עַל־נְדִיבִ֑ים וַ֜יַּתְעֵ֗ם
בְּתֹ֣הוּ לֹא־דָֽרֶךְ׃

מא וַיְשַׂגֵּ֣ב אֶבְי֣וֹן מֵע֑וֹנִי וַיָּ֥שֶׂם
כַּ֜צֹּ֗אן מִשְׁפָּחֽוֹת׃

³⁶ There He brings hungry people to dwell; they establish an inhabited city.

³⁷ They sow fields and plant vineyards, which bring forth fruits of produce.

³⁸ He blesses them and they multiply greatly; He does not let their cattle dwindle.

³⁹ But then their numbers are diminished and they are brought down with distress, sorrow, and anguish.

⁴⁰ He pours contempt upon the wealthy and has them lose their way in a pathless wasteland.

⁴¹ He gives shelter to the needy from affliction; He turns families into flocks.

---

36 **There,** in this newly fertile land, **He brings hungry people to dwell; they establish an inhabited city.**

37 There **they sow fields and plant vineyards, which bring forth fruits of produce.**

38 **He blesses them and they multiply greatly; He does not let their cattle dwindle.**

39 **But** things can also change for the worse: **Then their numbers are diminished and they are brought down with distress, sorrow, and anguish.** Bad times cause loss and death, along with misery and sorrow for those who remain.

40 In another example of reversal of good fortune, **He pours contempt upon the wealthy,** taking away their wealth and impoverishing them, **and has them lose their way in a pathless wasteland,** a metaphor for their inability to extricate themselves from their difficult situation.

41 At the same time, **He gives shelter to the needy from affliction**. He turns families that had been weak and few in number **into** clans as numerous as **flocks** of sheep.

מב The upright see this and are glad; the mouth of iniquity is stopped.

מב יִרְאוּ יְשָׁרִים וְיִשְׂמָחוּ וְכָל־עַוְלָה קָפְצָה פִּיהָ:

מג He who is wise will heed these matters and ponder the kindness of the Lord.

מג מִי־חָכָם וְיִשְׁמָר־אֵלֶּה וְיִתְבּוֹנְנוּ חַסְדֵי יהוה:

PSALM 108

A psalm whose second half is a repetition, with minor changes, of the end of Psalm 60. Its different beginning, however, makes it a more straightforward song of praise. Unlike Psalm 60, which was written under specific historic circumstances (see 60:2), this psalm discusses more generally the contrast between the troubles of the past and the victories of the present.

כג לחודש
23rd day
of month

א שִׁיר מִזְמוֹר לְדָוִד:

א A song, a psalm by David.

ב נָכוֹן לִבִּי אֱלֹהִים אָשִׁירָה וַאֲזַמְּרָה אַף־כְּבוֹדִי:

ב My heart is ready, God; I will sing and give praise, and my soul as well.

ג עוּרָה הַנֵּבֶל וְכִנּוֹר אָעִירָה שָּׁחַר:

ג Awaken, harp and lyre; I will wake the dawn.

---

42 **The upright see this and are glad** over God's beneficence and mercy; **the mouth of iniquity,** of those who ordinarily speak only base and sinful words, **is stopped** and rendered inactive, as they too join in the praising of God.

43 In conclusion: **He who is wise will heed** and give heart to **these matters,** all these reversals of fortune in life, **and ponder the kindness of the Lord,** realizing that man's destiny is completely in God's hands.

PSALM 108

1 **A song, a psalm by David.**

2 **My heart is ready** to begin this song, **God; I will sing and give praise, and my soul as well.** Not only will I sing to You and praise You with my mouth, but my whole soul and being will join in.

3 The psalmist addresses his musical instruments: **Awake, harp and lyre; I will wake the dawn.** Let us begin to play at the first glimmering of light.

אוֹדְךָ בָעַמִּים ׀ יְהֹוָה
וַאֲזַמֶּרְךָ בַּלְאֻמִּים:

כִּי־גָדֹל מֵעַל־שָׁמַיִם חַסְדֶּךָ
וְעַד־שְׁחָקִים אֲמִתֶּךָ:

רוּמָה עַל־שָׁמַיִם אֱלֹהִים
וְעַל כָּל־הָאָרֶץ כְּבוֹדֶךָ:

לְמַעַן יֵחָלְצוּן יְדִידֶיךָ
הוֹשִׁיעָה יְמִינְךָ וַעֲנֵנוּ: וַעֲנֵ֑

אֱלֹהִים ׀ דִּבֶּר בְּקָדְשׁוֹ
אֶעְלֹזָה אֲחַלְּקָה שְׁכֶם וְעֵמֶק
סֻכּוֹת אֲמַדֵּד:

לִי גִלְעָד ׀ לִי מְנַשֶּׁה וְאֶפְרַיִם
מָעוֹז רֹאשִׁי יְהוּדָה מְחֹקְקִי:

4 I will give thanks to You, Lord, among the peoples; I will sing Your praise among the nations.

5 For Your kindness is greater than the heavens; Your truth reaches the skies.

6 Rise above the heavens, God; let Your glory extend throughout the earth,

7 that Your beloved ones may be saved; deliver me with Your right hand and answer me.

8 God spoke in His holiness; I exulted. I divided Shekhem and measured out the Valley of Sukot.

9 Gilad is mine, Manasseh is mine, and Ephraim is my stronghold, Judah my lawgiver.

---

4 **I will give thanks to You, Lord, among the peoples; I will sing Your praise among the nations.**

5 **For Your kindness is greater than the heavens; Your truth** in fulfillment of Your covenant with us **reaches the skies.**

6 **Rise above the heavens, God,** revealing Your presence in the world; **let Your glory extend throughout the earth,**

7 **that Your beloved ones may be saved; deliver me with Your right hand and answer me.**

8 After an introductory section of supplication, the psalmist begins his song of praise: **God spoke in His holiness** to assure me of victory; **I exulted. I divided Shekhem and measured out the Valley of Sukot.**

9 The psalmist acknowledges those tribes of Israel who came to his aid: **Gilad,** a branch of Manasseh, **is mine,** the rest of **Manasseh is mine, and Ephraim is my stronghold, Judah my lawgiver.**

מוֹאָב ׀ סִיר רַחְצִי עַל־אֱדוֹם אַשְׁלִיךְ נַעֲלִי עָלַי־פְּלֶשֶׁת אֶתְרוֹעָע:

יְ מִי יֹבִלֵנִי עִיר מִבְצָר מִי נָחַנִי עַד־אֱדוֹם:

יְ הֲלֹא־אֱלֹהִים זְנַחְתָּנוּ וְלֹא־ תֵצֵא אֱלֹהִים בְּצִבְאוֹתֵינוּ:

יְ הָבָה־לָּנוּ עֶזְרָת מִצָּר וְשָׁוְא תְּשׁוּעַת אָדָם:

יְ בֵּאלֹהִים נַעֲשֶׂה־חָיִל וְהוּא יָבוּס צָרֵינוּ:

10. Moav is my washbasin; I will throw my shoe at Edom; against Philistia I will deliver a crushing defeat.

11. Who leads me to a fortified city? Who guides me to Edom?

12. Is it not You, God, who had abandoned us? You, God, who would not go forth with our armies?

13. Give us aid against the foe, for deliverance by man is in vain.

14. With God we will triumph, and He will rout our foes.

---

10. Now he mentions the enemies against whom he has fought: **Moav,** whom I have vanquished, I regard with contempt as if it **is** nothing more than **my washbasin; I will throw my shoe** in scorn **at Edom; against Philistia I will deliver a crushing defeat.**

11. **Who leads me to a fortified city? Who guides me to Edom** to conquer it?

12. **Is it not You, God, who had abandoned us** in the past? **You, God, who would not go forth with our armies,** and that is why we were not victorious? However, now that You have come to our aid, we are triumphant.

13. **Give us aid against the foe, for deliverance by man is in vain.** Only God's assistance is of any avail.

14. The point is reiterated here: **With God we will triumph, and He will rout our foes.**

PSALM 109

A psalm in which King David pleads for his life, which is endangered by his many enemies,
and he recounts their harsh words against him. Although the curses of this psalm are understood
by many commentators to be the words of David directed toward his adversaries, it is preferable
to explain that they are David's quotes of his enemies' vilifications of him. This interpretation is
bolstered by the fact that David's enemies are referred to in this psalm in the plural, whereas the
object of the curses is recorded in the singular. The historical context of this psalm appears to be
David's flight from his rebellious son Avshalom, when he endured great hostility from many parties,
particularly in the curses of Shimi son of Gera.[1]

לַמְנַצֵּחַ לְדָוִד מִזְמוֹר אֱלֹהֵי
תְהִלָּתִי אַל־תֶּחֱרַשׁ:

For the mouths of the wicked
כִּי פִי רָשָׁע וּפִי־מִרְמָה עָלַי
פָּתָחוּ דִּבְּרוּ אִתִּי לְשׁוֹן
שָׁקֶר:

וְדִבְרֵי שִׂנְאָה סְבָבוּנִי
וַיִּלָּחֲמוּנִי חִנָּם:

1. To the chief musician, a psalm by David. God of my praise, do not keep silent.

2. For the mouths of the wicked and the mouths of the deceitful have opened against me; they speak of me with a lying tongue.

3. Hateful words surround me. They fought against me without cause.

PSALM 109

1. **To the chief musician, a psalm by David. God of my praise, do not keep silent.** Although I am presently unable to respond to my enemies' taunts, may You not remain silent, but requite them as they deserve.

2. **For the mouths of the wicked and the mouths of the deceitful have opened against me.** Some of the accusations against me are founded on deceit; others are simply malicious. **They speak of me with a lying tongue.**

3. **Hateful words surround me.** In the past, my enemies kept silent; it is only now, when I have fallen from power, that they are able to condemn me and fight against me. **They fought against me without cause.**

תַּחַת־אַהֲבָתִי יִשְׂטְנוּנִי וַאֲנִי
תְפִלָּה:

וַיָּשִׂימוּ עָלַי רָעָה תַּחַת
טוֹבָה וְשִׂנְאָה תַּחַת אַהֲבָתִי:

הַפְקֵד עָלָיו רָשָׁע וְשָׂטָן
יַעֲמֹד עַל־יְמִינוֹ:

בְּהִשָּׁפְטוֹ יֵצֵא רָשָׁע וּתְפִלָּתוֹ
תִּהְיֶה לַחֲטָאָה:

יִהְיוּ־יָמָיו מְעַטִּים פְּקֻדָּתוֹ
יִקַּח אַחֵר:

יִהְיוּ־בָנָיו יְתוֹמִים וְאִשְׁתּוֹ
אַלְמָנָה:

4 In return for my love, they accuse me; I am all prayer.

5 They requited my good with evil, hatred in place of my love.

6 Appoint a wicked one over him; have an adversary stand at his right.

7 When he is judged, may he be found guilty; may his prayer be regarded as sin.

8 May his days be few; may another take his position.

9 May his children be fatherless and his wife a widow.

---

4 **In return for my love** toward them, **they accuse me; I am all prayer.** With this unusual expression, David defines himself not merely as someone who prays but as someone whose whole essence is prayer.

5 **They requited my good with evil, hatred in place of my love.** Assuming that the context of this psalm is Avshalom's rebellion, this verse refers both to a once-beloved son, who had been treated with great compassion by David, and to the king's former friends and deputies who joined the insurrection.

6 David now enumerates the curses cast upon him by his enemies. Addressing God, they said: **Appoint a wicked one,** that is, the forces of evil, administered by an avenging angel, **over him; have an adversary stand at his right.**

7 **When he is judged** before You, **may he be found guilty. May his prayer be regarded as sin,** unaccepted and dismissed with contempt.

8 **May his days be few,** may he die soon, and **may another take his position.**

9 **May his children be fatherless and his wife a widow.**

וְנוֹעַ יָנוּעוּ בָנָיו וְשִׁאֵלוּ
וְדָרְשׁוּ מֵחָרְבוֹתֵיהֶם:

יְנַקֵּשׁ נוֹשֶׁה לְכָל־אֲשֶׁר־לוֹ
וְיָבֹזּוּ זָרִים יְגִיעוֹ:

אַל־יְהִי־לוֹ מֹשֵׁךְ חָסֶד וְאַל־
יְהִי חוֹנֵן לִיתוֹמָיו:

יְהִי־אַחֲרִיתוֹ לְהַכְרִית בְּדוֹר
אַחֵר יִמַּח שְׁמָם:

יִזָּכֵר ׀ עֲוֹן אֲבֹתָיו אֶל־יְהֹוָה
וְחַטַּאת אִמּוֹ אַל־תִּמָּח:

יִהְיוּ נֶגֶד־יְהֹוָה תָּמִיד וְיַכְרֵת
מֵאֶרֶץ זִכְרָם:

¹⁰ May his children wander and beg, scrounging because of their ruin.

¹¹ May creditors seize all that he has; may strangers plunder the fruit of his labor.

¹² May there be no one to offer him kindness, no one to pity his orphans.

¹³ May his legacy be cut off; may their names be blotted out from the coming generations.

¹⁴ May the iniquity of his fathers be remembered by the Lord; may his mother's sin not be erased.

¹⁵ May these be before the Lord continually; may He cut off their memory from the earth.

---

¹⁰ **May his** orphaned **children** have to **wander** from place to place **and beg** for their sustenance, **scrounging because of their ruin,** because nothing will be left of what their father had built up.

¹¹ **May creditors seize all that he has; may strangers plunder the fruit of his labor.**

¹² **May there be no one to offer him kindness** during his lifetime, **no one to pity his orphans** after his death.

¹³ **May his legacy be cut off; may their names,** the names of David and his offspring, **be blotted out from the coming generations.**

¹⁴ With their names blotted out, the only preserved memories of them would be those of sin and iniquity: **May the iniquity of his fathers be remembered by the Lord; may his mother's sin not be erased.** This is not an allusion to any specific sins of David's parents, but to the many misdeeds that all human beings commit throughout their lifetimes.

¹⁵ **May these** sins **be before the Lord continually; may He cut off their memory from the earth.**

טז יַעַן אֲשֶׁר ׀ לֹא זָכַר עֲשׂוֹת
חֶסֶד וַיִּרְדֹּף אִישׁ־עָנִי וְאֶבְיוֹן
וְנִכְאֵה לֵבָב לְמוֹתֵת:

יז וַיֶּאֱהַב קְלָלָה וַתְּבוֹאֵהוּ
וְלֹא־חָפֵץ בִּבְרָכָה וַתִּרְחַק
מִמֶּנּוּ:

יח וַיִּלְבַּשׁ קְלָלָה כְּמַדּוֹ וַתָּבֹא
כַמַּיִם בְּקִרְבּוֹ וְכַשֶּׁמֶן
בְּעַצְמוֹתָיו:

יט תְּהִי־לוֹ כְּבֶגֶד יַעְטֶה וּלְמֵזַח
תָּמִיד יַחְגְּרֶהָ:

כ זֹאת ׀ פְּעֻלַּת שֹׂטְנַי מֵאֵת
יהוה וְהַדֹּבְרִים רָע עַל־
נַפְשִׁי:

16 For he did not remember to practice kindness. He drove to death the poor, the needy, and the brokenhearted.

17 He loved curses, and they will now come upon him. He had no desire for blessings, and they will now be far from him.

18 May he be clothed in curses, as with a garment; may they enter his body like water, like oil into his bones.

19 May he wrap them as a garment around him, like a belt he constantly fastens.

20 This is what those who hate me do, they who speak against me; it is from the Lord.

---

16 David's accusers now explain why they believe he deserves to be cursed in this manner: **For he did not remember to practice kindness. He drove to death the poor, the needy, and the brokenhearted.**

17 **He loved curses.** During his reign he did not concern himself with curses that his detractors might level at him, **and they will now come upon him. He had no desire for blessings, and they will now be far from him.**

18 **May he be clothed in curses, as with a garment; may they enter his body like water** that is imbibed, **like oil** rubbed into the skin, penetrating **into his bones.**

19 **May he wrap them as a garment around him, like a belt he constantly fastens.**

20 Following this recitation of the curses hurled at him when he was downtrodden, pursued, and in a seemingly hopeless situation, curses that are expressive of pent-up hostility and possibly longstanding hatred, David goes on to say: **This is what those who hate me do, they who speak against me; it is from the Lord.** David, being a man of profound faith, understands his enemies' deeds as well as their words against him as being a punishment from God.[2]

וְאַתָּה ׀ יְהֹוִה אֲדֹנָי עֲשֵׂה־
אִתִּי לְמַעַן שְׁמֶךָ כִּי־טוֹב
חַסְדְּךָ הַצִּילֵנִי:

²¹ You, Lord my God, do to me
for the sake of Your name;
rescue me, for Your mercy
is good.

כִּי־עָנִי וְאֶבְיוֹן אָנֹכִי וְלִבִּי
חָלַל בְּקִרְבִּי:

²² For I am poor and needy, my
heart hollow within me.

כְּצֵל כִּנְטוֹתוֹ נֶהֱלָכְתִּי
נִנְעַרְתִּי כָּאַרְבֶּה:

²³ I walk along like a lengthening
shadow, tossed about like
a locust.

בִּרְכַּי כָּשְׁלוּ מִצּוֹם וּבְשָׂרִי
כָּחַשׁ מִשָּׁמֶן:

²⁴ My knees are weak from fasting,
my flesh grown gaunt.

וַאֲנִי ׀ הָיִיתִי חֶרְפָּה לָהֶם
יִרְאוּנִי יְנִיעוּן רֹאשָׁם:

²⁵ I have become a disgrace to
them; they see me and shake
their heads.

עָזְרֵנִי יְהוָה אֱלֹהָי הוֹשִׁיעֵנִי
כְחַסְדֶּךָ:

²⁶ Help me, Lord my God; deliver
me, as befits Your kindness.

וְיֵדְעוּ כִּי־יָדְךָ זֹּאת אַתָּה
יְהוָה עֲשִׂיתָהּ:

²⁷ They will know that it is Your
hand, that You, Lord, have
done it.

---

²¹ Having cited his enemies' deep hatred for him, David turns to God in prayer: **You, Lord my God, do to me for the sake of Your name; rescue me, for Your mercy is good.**

²² **For I am poor and needy, my heart hollow within me,** devoid of feeling, confidence, and strength.

²³ **I walk along,** fading **like a lengthening shadow** as the sun is about to set, **tossed about like a locust** driven from place to place by the wind.

²⁴ **My knees are weak from fasting, my flesh grown gaunt.**

²⁵ **I have become a disgrace to them** in my weakness and desperation; **they see me and shake their heads** in disparagement and contempt.

²⁶ David turns to God with a direct plea for assistance: **Help me, Lord my God; deliver me, as befits Your kindness.**

²⁷ **They will know that** it is not my sins or lack of power that have brought about my vulnerable situation, but **it is Your hand, that You, Lord, have done it,** and consequently You can reverse the situation and restore me to my previously exalted position.

כח יְקַלְלוּ־הֵמָּה וְאַתָּה תְבָרֵךְ
קָמוּ ׀ וַיֵּבֹשׁוּ וְעַבְדְּךָ יִשְׂמָח:

כט יִלְבְּשׁוּ שׂוֹטְנַי כְּלִמָּה וְיַעֲטוּ
כַמְעִיל בָּשְׁתָּם:

ל אוֹדֶה יהוה מְאֹד בְּפִי וּבְתוֹךְ
רַבִּים אֲהַלְלֶנּוּ:

לא כִּי־יַעֲמֹד לִימִין אֶבְיוֹן
לְהוֹשִׁיעַ מִשֹּׁפְטֵי נַפְשׁוֹ:

28 They may curse, but You will bless. They rose against me, but they will be shamed while Your servant will rejoice.

29 My accusers will be clothed in dishonor, wrapped in their shame like a cloak.

30 With my mouth, I will give abundant thanks to the Lord; in the midst of multitudes I will glorify Him.

31 For He stands at the right hand of the needy, to deliver him from those who judge him.

---

28 **They may curse, but You will bless. They rose against me, but they will be shamed while Your servant will rejoice.**

29 **My accusers will be clothed in dishonor, wrapped in their shame like a cloak.** Once I return to power, my enemies will be left with nothing but shame at their having conspired against me.

30 When that time comes, **with my mouth, I will give abundant thanks to the Lord; in the midst of multitudes I will glorify Him.**

31 **For He stands at the right hand of the needy, to deliver him from those who judge him.** Although attempts have been made to falsely convict him of all manner of evil, God will save him.

PSALM 110

Apparently a coronation psalm, which may have been recited at David's formal coronation ceremony in Jerusalem. The introductory statement *leDavid mizmor*, usually translated as "a psalm by David," can also be rendered "a psalm for David," and that is evidently its meaning here.

לְדָוִד מִזְמוֹר נְאֻם יהוה ׀
לַאדֹנִי שֵׁב לִימִינִי עַד־אָשִׁית
אֹיְבֶיךָ הֲדֹם לְרַגְלֶיךָ:

מַטֵּה עֻזְּךָ יִשְׁלַח יהוה מִצִּיּוֹן
רְדֵה בְּקֶרֶב אֹיְבֶיךָ:

עַמְּךָ נְדָבֹת בְּיוֹם חֵילֶךָ
בְּהַדְרֵי־קֹדֶשׁ מֵרֶחֶם מִשְׁחָר
לְךָ טַל יַלְדֻתֶיךָ:

¹ A psalm for David. The utterance of the Lord to my master: Sit on My right until I place your enemies as a stool for your feet.

² The Lord will send your rod of strength from Zion; rule among your enemies.

³ Your people will volunteer on your day of battle in sacred glory; from the womb of the dawn, yours is the dew of youth.

PSALM 110

¹ **A psalm for David. The utterance of the Lord to my master,** the king: **Sit on My right.** As is written with regard to King Solomon, the king in Jerusalem is viewed as sitting "on the throne of the Lord."[3] Sit **until I place your enemies as a stool for your feet.** God tells the king to sit, as it were, and wait while He fights his wars for him.

² **The Lord will send your rod of strength from Zion;** with that rod, or royal scepter, **rule among your enemies.**

³ **Your people will volunteer** to fight for you **on your day of battle in sacred glory,** with great reverence; **from the womb of the dawn,** since the day of your birth, you were destined for this glory; **yours is** and will remain **the dew,** the freshness and vigor, **of youth.**

נִשְׁבַּע יהוֹה ׀ וְלֹא יִנָּחֵם אַתָּה־כֹהֵן לְעוֹלָם עַל־ דִּבְרָתִי מַלְכִּי־צֶדֶק: ד

אֲדֹנָי עַל־יְמִינְךָ מָחַץ בְּיוֹם־ אַפּוֹ מְלָכִים: ה

יָדִין בַּגּוֹיִם מָלֵא גְוִיּוֹת מָחַץ רֹאשׁ עַל־אֶרֶץ רַבָּה: ו

מִנַּחַל בַּדֶּרֶךְ יִשְׁתֶּה עַל־כֵּן יָרִים רֹאשׁ: ז

4 The Lord has sworn, and will not renounce it; you are chief forever by My decree, like Malkitzedek.

5 The Lord is at your right hand; He will crush kings on the day of His wrath.

6 He will judge among the nations and make it full of corpses, crushing heads over a broad land.

7 He will drink from the stream on the way; thus will his head be raised.

---

4 In honor of the coronation, the psalmist declares: **The Lord has sworn, and will not renounce it; you are chief forever by My decree.** The word *kohen*, here "chief," usually means "priest," but the term can also refer to any leader or holder of a senior position of authority,[4] **like Malkitzedek,** the king in Jerusalem in ancient times,[5] who was also described as a *kohen* to God Almighty.[6]

5 **The Lord is at your right hand** to assist you; **He will crush kings** who fight against you **on the day of His wrath.**

6 **He will judge among the nations,** smiting all their warriors, **and make it full of corpses.** God will destroy your enemies in war, to the extent that the enemy camp will be full of corpses, **crushing** the **heads** of the enemies **over a broad land.** The imagery is of maimed warriors strewn across the battlefield.

7 As for the warrior in your camp, **he will drink** peacefully, with no opposition, **from the stream on the way. Thus will his head be raised** confidently when he moves on to the battlefield.

PSALM 111

A song of praise to God for His many acts of kindness. Both this psalm and the next one, which resembles it in format, are instructional texts that are meant to be learned by heart. To facilitate memorization, the Hebrew verses are arranged in alphabetical order, with each verse containing two or three phrases that begin with consecutive Hebrew letters.

הַלְלוּיָהּ ׀ אוֹדֶה יְהוה בְּכָל־לֵבָב בְּסוֹד יְשָׁרִים וְעֵדָה: א

גְּדֹלִים מַעֲשֵׂי יְהוה דְּרוּשִׁים לְכָל־חֶפְצֵיהֶם: ב

הוֹד־וְהָדָר פָּעֳלוֹ וְצִדְקָתוֹ עֹמֶדֶת לָעַד: ג

זֵכֶר עָשָׂה לְנִפְלְאֹתָיו חַנּוּן וְרַחוּם יְהוה: ד

טֶרֶף נָתַן לִירֵאָיו יִזְכֹּר לְעוֹלָם בְּרִיתוֹ: ה

1 Halleluya. I will thank the Lord with all my heart in the assembly and council of the upright.

2 Great are the works of the Lord, ready for all that is desired.

3 Splendid and glorious is His work; His righteousness stands forever.

4 He has made His wonders a lasting memory; the Lord is gracious and merciful.

5 He gives food to those who fear Him; He remembers forever His covenant.

PSALM 111

1 **Halleluya. I will thank the Lord with all my heart in the assembly and council of the upright.**

2 **Great are the works of the Lord, ready for all that is desired.** God's works are finely wrought and perfectly ready to be made operational.

3 **Splendid and glorious is His work; His righteousness stands forever.**

4 **He has made His wonders a lasting memory.** God's wonders are not temporary phenomena but rather endure. **The Lord is gracious and merciful.**

5 **He gives food to those who fear Him; He remembers forever His covenant** with those who cling to Him.

כֹּחַ מַעֲשָׂיו הִגִּיד לְעַמּוֹ לָתֵת
לָהֶם נַחֲלַת גּוֹיִם:

מַעֲשֵׂי יָדָיו אֱמֶת וּמִשְׁפָּט
נֶאֱמָנִים כָּל־פִּקּוּדָיו:

סְמוּכִים לָעַד לְעוֹלָם עֲשׂוּיִם
בֶּאֱמֶת וְיָשָׁר:

פְּדוּת ׀ שָׁלַח לְעַמּוֹ צִוָּה־
לְעוֹלָם בְּרִיתוֹ קָדוֹשׁ וְנוֹרָא
שְׁמוֹ:

רֵאשִׁית חָכְמָה ׀ יִרְאַת יהוה
שֵׂכֶל טוֹב לְכָל־עֹשֵׂיהֶם
תְּהִלָּתוֹ עֹמֶדֶת לָעַד:

6 He tells the power of His deeds to His people, giving them the portion of nations.

7 The works of His hands are truth and justice; steadfast are all His edicts.

8 They are set firmly for all eternity, fashioned in truth and uprightness.

9 He has sent redemption to His people, ordaining His covenant for all time. Holy and awesome is His name.

10 Wisdom begins with fear of the Lord; those who practice it will come to good sense. His praise stands forever.

---

6 **He tells the power of His deeds to His people.** God informs His people what will transpire in the future, as all events that occur are ordained from above. And God does not merely tell them of promises, but He also fulfills them, **giving them the portion of nations.**

7 **The works of His hands are truth and justice; steadfast are all His edicts.**

8 **They are set firmly for all eternity, fashioned in truth and uprightness**.

9 **He has sent redemption to His people, ordaining His covenant** with them **for all time. Holy and awesome is His name.**

10 In light of all that has been said, the psalmist summarizes: **Wisdom begins with fear of the Lord.** Fear of God should be the underlying principle of a person's conception of the world, the foundation upon which he constructs his worldview, for all **those who practice it will come to good sense. His praise stands forever.**

PSALM 112

A psalm in praise of the righteous. Like the preceding psalm, it is didactic
and meant to be memorized, and it is similarly structured in alphabetical order.

הַלְלוּיָהּ ׀ אַשְׁרֵי־אִישׁ יָרֵא
אֶת־יהוה בְּמִצְוֺתָיו חָפֵץ
מְאֹד:

גִּבּוֹר בָּאָרֶץ יִהְיֶה זַרְעוֹ דּוֹר
יְשָׁרִים יְבֹרָךְ:

הוֹן־וָעֹשֶׁר בְּבֵיתוֹ וְצִדְקָתוֹ
עֹמֶדֶת לָעַד:

זָרַח בַּחֹשֶׁךְ אוֹר לַיְשָׁרִים
חַנּוּן וְרַחוּם וְצַדִּיק:

1 Halleluya. Happy is the man who fears the Lord and who greatly delights in His commandments.

2 His descendants will be mighty on earth; he will be blessed with a generation of the upright.

3 Wealth and riches are in his house, and his righteousness stands forever.

4 Light dawns in darkness for the upright, for he is gracious and compassionate and righteous.

PSALM 112

1 **Halleluya. Happy is the man who fears the Lord and who greatly delights in His commandments.**

2 Such a person merits everything good this world has to offer: **His descendants will be mighty on earth;** not only will he be successful himself, but he will also reap the blessing of having heroic and successful descendants. **He will be blessed with a generation of the upright,** that is, with upright descendants.

3 **Wealth and riches are in his house.** But he does not hold on to his wealth for himself; he shares it with others, **and his righteousness,** his benevolence, **stands forever.**

4 **Light dawns in darkness for the upright, for he is gracious and compassionate and righteous.**

טֽוֹב־אִ֭ישׁ חוֹנֵ֣ן וּמַלְוֶ֑ה יְכַלְכֵּ֖ל
דְּבָרָ֣יו בְּמִשְׁפָּֽט׃

כִּֽי־לְעוֹלָ֥ם לֹא־יִמּ֑וֹט לְזֵ֥כֶר
עוֹלָ֗ם יִֽהְיֶ֥ה צַדִּֽיק׃

מִשְּׁמוּעָ֣ה רָ֭עָה לֹ֣א יִירָ֑א
נָכ֥וֹן לִ֝בּ֗וֹ בָּטֻ֥חַ בַּיהֹוָֽה׃

סָמ֣וּךְ לִ֭בּוֹ לֹ֣א יִירָ֑א עַ֖ד
אֲשֶׁר־יִרְאֶ֣ה בְצָרָֽיו׃

פִּזַּ֤ר ׀ נָ֘תַ֤ן לָאֶבְיוֹנִ֗ים צִדְקָת֗וֹ
עֹמֶ֥דֶת לָעַ֑ד קַ֝רְנ֗וֹ תָּר֥וּם
בְּכָבֽוֹד׃

רָ֘שָׁ֤ע יִרְאֶ֨ה ׀ וְכָעָ֗ס שִׁנָּ֣יו
יַחֲרֹ֣ק וְנָמָ֑ס תַּאֲוַ֖ת רְשָׁעִ֣ים
תֹּאבֵֽד׃

5 It is good for a man to
   be gracious and to lend,
   conducting his affairs with
   justice.

6 For He will never stumble; the
   righteous man is remembered
   forever.

7 He fears no evil tidings; his
   heart is steadfast, trusting in
   the Lord.

8 His heart is reliant. He will not
   fear, until he beholds the fall of
   his foes.

9 He gives freely to the needy;
   his righteousness stands
   forever. His horn is raised high
   in honor.

10 The wicked one sees and is
   angered; he gnashes his teeth
   and dissolves. The desire of the
   wicked will come to naught.

---

5 **It is good for a man to be gracious and to lend** to others without interest, **conducting his affairs with justice,** or with appropriateness: When appropriate, the money is given as charity, as in verse 3, and when the situation warrants it, he lends it.

6 **For He will never stumble** in his lifetime, and even after his death **the righteous man is remembered** favorably **forever.**

7 **He fears no evil tidings** because **his heart is steadfast, trusting in the Lord.**

8 **His heart is reliant** on God. **He will not fear** in the face of threats or adversity **until,** ultimately, **he beholds the fall of his foes.**

9 **He gives freely to the needy; his righteousness stands forever. His horn,** that is, his good name or stature, **is raised high in honor.**

10 In contrast to the righteous person, who prospers in all his endeavors, **the wicked one sees and**

PSALM 113

One of the most well-known chapters in Psalms, this is the opening psalm of the Hallel prayer recited on Jewish holidays, which consists of Psalms 113–118. It focuses on manifold and complementary aspects of God's greatness.

הַלְלוּיָהּ ׀ הַלְלוּ עַבְדֵי יהוה
הַלְלוּ אֶת־שֵׁם יהוה:

Halleluya. Praise, you servants of the Lord; praise the name of the Lord.

יְהִי שֵׁם יהוה מְבֹרָךְ מֵעַתָּה
וְעַד־עוֹלָם:

Blessed be the name of the Lord from now until eternity.

מִמִּזְרַח־שֶׁמֶשׁ עַד־מְבוֹאוֹ
מְהֻלָּל שֵׁם יהוה:

From the sun's rising place to the place where it sets, the name of the Lord is praised.

רָם עַל־כָּל־גּוֹיִם ׀ יהוה עַל
הַשָּׁמַיִם כְּבוֹדוֹ:

Exalted above all nations is the Lord; above the heavens is His glory.

כד לחודש
24th day
of month

---

is angered. The mere existence of the righteous individual is vexing to one who is wicked. **He gnashes his teeth** in anger **and dissolves,** as it were, in the realization that he has no recourse to harm the righteous man. **The desire of the wicked,** whether to cause harm to the righteous or to attain any material success, **will come to naught.**

PSALM 113

1 **Halleluya. Praise, you servants of the Lord.** These are not necessarily people of any particular status or position, but simply those people who regard themselves as serving God. **Praise the name of the Lord.**

2 This is what you, the servants of God, should say: **Blessed be the name of the Lord from now until eternity.** This is a general statement of praise for God. This praise consists of two distinct facets, as the psalmist goes on to elaborate.

3 The first facet is God's awesome greatness: **From the sun's rising place** in the east **to the place where it sets** in the west, **the name of the Lord is praised.**

4 **Exalted above all nations is the Lord; above the heavens is His glory.** God rules over the heavens, is above worldly existence, and is beyond the powers and forces of the world.

ה מִי כַּיהוה אֱלֹהֵינוּ הַמַּגְבִּיהִי לָשֶֽׁבֶת:

ו הַמַּשְׁפִּילִי לִרְאוֹת בַּשָּׁמַֽיִם וּבָאָֽרֶץ:

ז מְקִימִי מֵעָפָר דָּל מֵאַשְׁפֹּת יָרִים אֶבְיוֹן:

ח לְהוֹשִׁיבִי עִם־נְדִיבִים עִם נְדִיבֵי עַמּוֹ:

ט מוֹשִׁיבִי ׀ עֲקֶֽרֶת הַבַּֽיִת אֵם־הַבָּנִים שְׂמֵחָה הַֽלְלוּיָֽהּ:

5 Who is like the Lord our God, who sits on high,

6 who looks down to see what is in heaven and earth?

7 He raises the poor from the dust, lifts the needy from the refuse heap,

8 to set them among the rich and noble of His people.

9 He sets the barren woman at home as a joyful mother of children. Halleluya.

---

5 **Who is like the Lord our God, who sits on high,**
6 **who looks down to see what is in heaven and earth?** Here we come to the second facet of God's praise: His awareness of all His creations on earth and His care for them. Because God "sits on high" and is "above the heavens" (verse 4), even when He observes what is in heaven He is looking down, as it were. From His perspective, the heavens and everything within them are no more exalted than the creatures of the earth; He cares for everyone and everything to the same degree.

7 As a result of God's concern for all His creations, **He raises the poor from the dust, lifts the needy from the refuse heap,**

8 **to set them among the rich and noble of His people.** The poor receive divine care and are raised to a higher level, even in this world.

9 **He sets the barren woman at home as a joyful mother of children. Halleluya.**

PSALM 114

A song of praise concerning the exodus from Egypt. Rather than describing the events
of the exodus historically, it depicts emotional responses to the revelation of God.

בְּצֵאת יִשְׂרָאֵל מִמִּצְרָיִם
בֵּית יַעֲקֹב מֵעַם לֹעֵז: א

1 When Israel went out of Egypt,
the house of Jacob from a
foreign-speaking people,

הָיְתָה יְהוּדָה לְקָדְשׁוֹ
יִשְׂרָאֵל מַמְשְׁלוֹתָיו: ב

2 Judah became His holy one;
Israel, His dominion.

הַיָּם רָאָה וַיָּנֹס הַיַּרְדֵּן יִסֹּב
לְאָחוֹר: ג

3 The sea saw and fled. The
Jordan turned back.

4 The mountains danced like
rams, the hills like lambs.

הֶהָרִים רָקְדוּ כְאֵילִים
גְּבָעוֹת כִּבְנֵי־צֹאן: ד

5 What is it, sea, that makes
you flee? The Jordan, that you
turn back?

מַה־לְּךָ הַיָּם כִּי תָנוּס הַיַּרְדֵּן
תִּסֹּב לְאָחוֹר: ה

PSALM 114

1 **When Israel went out of Egypt, the house of Jacob from a foreign-speaking people,**
"foreign," as the Egyptian language was very different from Hebrew,

2 the tribe of **Judah became His holy one.** They became the locus of the manifestation of God's
holiness. And **Israel** became **His dominion.** They were the ones who accepted upon themselves
God's sovereignty and power.

3 After that, the Almighty revealed Himself further to them: **The** Red **Sea saw and fled.** The
verse describes the splitting of the Red Sea from the perspective of the water itself rather than the
perspective of Israel's salvation. After witnessing the revelation of God's glory, the sea retreated
in awe. And later, as the Israelites came to the Land of Israel, **the Jordan** River similarly **turned
back** from its course to allow them to cross into the land.

4 **The mountains danced like rams, the hills like lambs.** The earth quaked, which made it
appear as though the mountains and hills were dancing.

5 The psalmist poetically turns to the inanimate objects involved and asks: **What is it, sea, that
makes you flee? The Jordan, that you turn back?**

הֶהָרִים תִּרְקְדוּ כְאֵילִים
גְּבָעוֹת כִּבְנֵי־צֹאן:

מִלְּפְנֵי אָדוֹן חוּלִי אָרֶץ
מִלְּפְנֵי אֱלוֹהַּ יַעֲקֹב:

הַהֹפְכִי הַצּוּר אֲגַם־מָיִם
חַלָּמִישׁ לְמַעְיְנוֹ־מָיִם:

6 The mountains, that you dance like rams? The hills, like lambs?

7 From before the Master, Creator of the earth, from before the God of Jacob,

8 who turns the rock into a pool of water, flint into a fountain of water.

PSALM 115

A psalm expressing thankfulness for the fact that Israel, as opposed to other nations, had the privilege of choosing God.

לֹא לָנוּ יהוה לֹא לָנוּ כִּי־
לְשִׁמְךָ תֵּן כָּבוֹד עַל־חַסְדְּךָ
עַל־אֲמִתֶּךָ:

1 Not for us, Lord, not for us, but for Your name give glory, for Your kindness, for Your truth.

---

6 **The mountains, that you dance like rams? The hills, like lambs?**
7 They respond: We quake and flee **from before the Master, Creator of the earth, from before the God of Jacob,** who created everything and has the power to change the world as He desires.
8 Just as He can cause the sea to split and the mountains to quake, it is He **who turns the rock into a pool of water,** the **flint into a fountain of water,** an allusion to the events described in Exodus 17 and Numbers 20.

PSALM 115

1 **Not for us, Lord, not for us** do we request the salvation that we pray for, **but for Your name give glory.** Here, and in a number of other places in Psalms, the psalmist expresses the idea that because we are so intimately connected and identified with God, His honor is diminished, as it were, whenever we are humiliated. Conversely, when we are rescued from trouble, this redounds to His honor. We ask of God: Give us honor not for our sake but for the sake of Your name, **for** the sake of **Your kindness** that you promised to show us, and **for** the sake of **Your truth,** Your faithfulness in upholding those promises.

לָמָּה יֹאמְרוּ הַגּוֹיִם אַיֵּה־נָא
אֱלֹהֵיהֶם:

2 Why should the nations say:
Where now is their God?

וֵאלֹהֵינוּ בַשָּׁמָיִם כֹּל אֲשֶׁר־
חָפֵץ עָשָׂה:

3 But our God is in the heavens;
whatever He desires, He does.

עֲצַבֵּיהֶם כֶּסֶף וְזָהָב מַעֲשֵׂה
יְדֵי אָדָם:

4 Their idols are silver and gold,
man's handiwork.

פֶּה־לָהֶם וְלֹא יְדַבֵּרוּ עֵינַיִם
לָהֶם וְלֹא יִרְאוּ:

5 Mouths they have but cannot
speak. Eyes they have but
cannot see.

אָזְנַיִם לָהֶם וְלֹא יִשְׁמָעוּ אַף
לָהֶם וְלֹא יְרִיחוּן:

6 Ears they have but cannot hear.
Noses they have but cannot
smell.

יְדֵיהֶם וְלֹא יְמִישׁוּן רַגְלֵיהֶם
וְלֹא יְהַלֵּכוּ לֹא־יֶהְגּוּ
בִּגְרוֹנָם:

7 Their hands do not feel; their
feet do not walk. No utterance
comes from their throat.

כְּמוֹהֶם יִהְיוּ עֹשֵׂיהֶם כֹּל
אֲשֶׁר־בֹּטֵחַ בָּהֶם:

8 May their makers become like
them; so too, all who put their
faith in them.

---

2 The psalmist expands on this theme: **Why should the nations,** who can actually point to their gods, **say: Where now is their God,** who cannot be seen?

3 **But our God is in the heavens; whatever He desires, He does,** for all power is in His hands.

4 **Their idols,** in contrast, **are silver and gold, man's handiwork,** like inanimate, powerless mannequins, as detailed in the following verses.

5 **Mouths they have but cannot speak. Eyes they have but cannot see.**

6 **Ears they have but cannot hear. Noses they have but cannot smell.**

7 **Their hands do not feel.** *Yemishun* can mean both "move" and "feel." These idols can neither move their hands nor feel anything with them. **Their feet do not walk. No utterance comes from their throat,** for they are incapable of speech. They are useless, inanimate objects.

8 The psalmist beseeches God: **May their makers,** those who crafted these idols, **become** silent and lifeless **like them; so too, all who put their faith in them.**

ט יִשְׂרָאֵל בְּטַח בַּיהוָה עֶזְרָם
וּמָגִנָּם הוּא:

י בֵּית אַהֲרֹן בִּטְחוּ בַיהוָה
עֶזְרָם וּמָגִנָּם הוּא:

יא יִרְאֵי יְהוָה בִּטְחוּ בַיהוָה
עֶזְרָם וּמָגִנָּם הוּא:

יב יְהוָה זְכָרָנוּ יְבָרֵךְ יְבָרֵךְ אֶת־
בֵּית יִשְׂרָאֵל יְבָרֵךְ אֶת־בֵּית
אַהֲרֹן:

יג יְבָרֵךְ יִרְאֵי יְהוָה הַקְּטַנִּים
עִם־הַגְּדֹלִים:

יד יֹסֵף יְהוָה עֲלֵיכֶם עֲלֵיכֶם
וְעַל־בְּנֵיכֶם:

9 Israel, trust in the Lord; He is their help and their shield.

10 House of Aaron, trust in the Lord; He is their help and their shield.

11 You who fear the Lord, trust in the Lord; He is their help and their shield.

12 May the Lord who remembers us give His blessing. May He bless the house of Israel; may He bless the house of Aaron.

13 May He bless those who fear the Lord, the young with the old.

14 May the Lord increase your numbers, yours and your children's.

---

9 The psalmist now addresses the nation in accordance with its different factions: **Israel, trust in the Lord** and do not put your faith in such worthless images; **He is their help and their shield.** The sudden change from direct address to third person, in this verse and the succeeding ones, probably indicates that this ending was meant to be recited by a chorus as a kind of refrain.

10 **House of Aaron, trust in the Lord; He is their help and their shield.**

11 **You who fear the Lord, trust in the Lord; He is their help and their shield.** The phrase "you who fear the Lord," which appears several times in Psalms, may refer in general to any group of individuals conducting a God-fearing way of life. It may also relate to a specific group of people, whose exact identity is unknown to us, who dedicated themselves to worshipping God, spending much of their time in the Temple engaged in prayer.

12 **May the Lord who remembers us** for good **give His blessing** to those who are deserving of it: **May He bless the house of Israel; may He bless the house of Aaron.**

13 **May He bless those who fear the Lord, the young with the old.**

14 **May the Lord increase your numbers, yours and your children's.**

טו בְּרוּכִים אַתֶּם לַיהוָה עֹשֵׂה
שָׁמַיִם וָאָרֶץ:

15 You are blessed by the Lord,
the Maker of heaven and earth.

טז הַשָּׁמַיִם שָׁמַיִם לַיהוָה
וְהָאָרֶץ נָתַן לִבְנֵי־אָדָם:

16 The heavens are the heavens of
the Lord, while the earth He
has given to the sons of man.

יז לֹא הַמֵּתִים יְהַלְלוּ־יָהּ וְלֹא
כָּל־יֹרְדֵי דוּמָה:

17 The dead cannot praise the
Lord, nor can any who go
down into silence,

יח וַאֲנַחְנוּ ׀ נְבָרֵךְ יָהּ מֵעַתָּה
וְעַד־עוֹלָם הַלְלוּיָהּ:

18 but we will bless the Lord from
now until eternity. Halleluya.

PSALM 116

A psalm of thanksgiving offered by one who
has been rescued from great peril, such as serious illness.

א אָהַבְתִּי כִּי־יִשְׁמַע ׀ יְהוָה
אֶת־קוֹלִי תַּחֲנוּנָי:

1 I am happy, for the Lord heard
my voice, my pleas.

---

15 **You are blessed by the Lord, the Maker of heaven and earth.**

16 The psalmist offers an explanation as to why he requests God's blessing: **The heavens are the heavens of the Lord,** and that is where He dwells, as it were, **while the earth He has given to the sons of man.** Our place as humans is here on earth, not in the heavens, and we pray for the strength and ability to carry out our earthly, mundane tasks.

17 **The dead cannot praise the Lord.** Though they are also of the earth, they are no longer able to fulfill any kind of role or task, **nor can any who go down into silence** in the grave,

18 **but we will bless the Lord from now until eternity. Halleluya.**

PSALM 116

1 **I am happy, for the Lord heard my voice, my pleas.** This opening verse summarizes the main theme of the psalm. The psalmist is joyful not only because he was rescued but also because God listened to his prayer.

כִּי־הִטָּה אָזְנוֹ לִי וּבְיָמַי
אֶקְרָא:

אֲפָפוּנִי ׀ חֶבְלֵי־מָוֶת וּמְצָרֵי
שְׁאוֹל מְצָאוּנִי צָרָה וְיָגוֹן
אֶמְצָא:

וּבְשֵׁם־יהוה אֶקְרָא אָנָּה
יהוה מַלְּטָה נַפְשִׁי:

חַנּוּן יהוה וְצַדִּיק וֵאלֹהֵינוּ
מְרַחֵם:

שֹׁמֵר פְּתָאיִם יהוה דַּלּוֹתִי
וְלִי יְהוֹשִׁיעַ:

שׁוּבִי נַפְשִׁי לִמְנוּחָיְכִי כִּי־
יהוה גָּמַל עָלָיְכִי:

2 For He inclined His ear to me, and in all my days I call out to Him.

3 Cords of death were wrapped around me; agonies of the grave assailed me. I encountered distress and sorrow.

4 I called in the name of the Lord: Please, Lord, save my life.

5 The Lord is gracious and righteous, and our God is merciful.

6 The Lord protects the simple. I was brought low, and He saved me.

7 Return, my soul, to restfulness, for the Lord has helped you.

---

2 **For He inclined His ear to me, and in all my days** of hardship and adversity **I call out to Him.**

3 **Cords of death were wrapped around me; agonies of the grave assailed me** when I **encountered distress and sorrow.**

4 In those situations, **I called in the name of the Lord: Please, Lord, save my life.**

5 **The Lord is gracious and righteous, and our God is merciful.**

6 **The Lord protects the simple.** The word *petayim*, translated here as "the simple," refers to people who are inexperienced and therefore likely to be enticed, *mitpateh*, into troublesome situations. Since they do not know how to protect themselves, God protects them so they do not come to too much harm. **I was brought low, and He saved me.**

7 **Return, my soul, to restfulness, for the Lord has helped you.**

ח ‏כִּי חִלַּצְתָּ נַפְשִׁי מִמָּוֶת אֶת־
עֵינִי מִן־דִּמְעָה אֶת־רַגְלִי
מִדֶּחִי:

ט ‏אֶתְהַלֵּךְ לִפְנֵי יהוה בְּאַרְצוֹת
הַחַיִּים:

י ‏הֶאֱמַנְתִּי כִּי אֲדַבֵּר אֲנִי עָנִיתִי
מְאֹד:

יא ‏אֲנִי אָמַרְתִּי בְחָפְזִי כָּל־
הָאָדָם כֹּזֵב:

יב ‏מָה־אָשִׁיב לַיהוה כָּל־
תַּגְמוּלוֹהִי עָלָי:

יג ‏כּוֹס־יְשׁוּעוֹת אֶשָּׂא וּבְשֵׁם
יהוה אֶקְרָא:

8 For You rescued me from death, my eyes from tears, my feet from obstruction.

9 I walk before the Lord in the land of the living.

10 I believed as I spoke, when I was suffering greatly.

11 In my haste, I said: All men are false.

12 What shall I give to the Lord in return for all the good He rendered me?

13 I will lift a cup of salvation, and I will call in the name of the Lord.

---

8 **For You rescued me from death, my eyes from tears, my feet from obstruction.**

9 Now that I have been saved from peril, **I walk before the Lord in the land of the living,** without concern for my survival.

10 **I believed** in You **as I spoke** my words of prayer before You, **when I was suffering greatly.**

11 **In my haste, I said: All men are false.** Suffering is a subjective experience that is often exacerbated by a sense of being alone and abandoned, and many people in distress jump to the mistaken conclusion that they are being deceived and that no one around them cares. In truth, even in the darkest hours, people have at least a few loyal friends who will not abandon them. But this may not be immediately apparent, and the seeming lack of support can lead to despondency.

12 The psalmist now turns to words of praise: **What shall I give to the Lord in return for all the good He rendered me?**

13 **I will lift a cup of salvation,** referring to a cup of wine that is raised in a public toast of thanksgiving. **And I will call in the name of the Lord** with words of thanks for Him.

נְדָרַי לַיהוָה אֲשַׁלֵּם נֶגְדָה־
נָּא לְכָל־עַמּוֹ:

¹⁴ I will fulfill my vows to the Lord in the presence of all His people.

יָקָר בְּעֵינֵי יהוָה הַמָּוְתָה
לַחֲסִידָיו:

¹⁵ Weighty in the eyes of the Lord is the death of His devoted ones.

אָנָּה יהוָה כִּי־אֲנִי עַבְדֶּךָ
אֲנִי־עַבְדְּךָ בֶּן־אֲמָתֶךָ
פִּתַּחְתָּ לְמוֹסֵרָי:

¹⁶ Please, Lord, I am Your servant, the son of Your handmaid; You have loosened my bonds.

לְךָ־אֶזְבַּח זֶבַח תּוֹדָה וּבְשֵׁם
יהוָה אֶקְרָא:

¹⁷ I will offer a thanksgiving offering to You, and I will call in the name of the Lord.

נְדָרַי לַיהוָה אֲשַׁלֵּם נֶגְדָה־
נָּא לְכָל־עַמּוֹ:

¹⁸ I will fulfill my vows to the Lord in the presence of all His people,

---

¹⁴ **I will fulfill my vows to the Lord,** which I undertook in my times of distress, now that I have been delivered from danger and am able to fulfill them. When possible, I will fulfill them **in the presence of all His people,** in order to publicize God's kindness to me and to inspire others.

¹⁵ **Weighty in the eyes of the Lord is the death of His devoted ones.** God does not want to bring death to those who love Him.

¹⁶ With this in mind, the psalmist issues his plea: **Please, Lord,** come to my aid, for **I am Your servant, the son of Your handmaid.** The phrase "I am Your servant, the son of Your handmaid" describes an individual born into a family of slaves, who has never known any personal independence. But in contrast to the demeaning human institution of slavery, servitude to God is uplifting and liberating. In fact, the result has been that **You have loosened my bonds.** You have freed me from all my suffering and pain.

¹⁷ **I will offer a thanksgiving offering to You** for Your having saved me from peril, **and I will call in the name of the Lord** with cries of thanksgiving.

¹⁸ **I will fulfill my** sacrificial **vows to the Lord in the presence of all His people.**

בְּחַצְרוֹת ׀ בֵּית יהוה
בְּתוֹכֵכִי יְרוּשָׁלָםִ הַלְלוּיָהּ:

^{יט} ¹⁹ in the courtyards of the House
of the Lord, in your midst,
Jerusalem. Halleluya.

PSALM 117

The shortest psalm in the book of Psalms. Although it is counted as a separate chapter,
it could easily be regarded as the conclusion of the preceding psalm or as
the beginning of the one that follows.

הַלְלוּ אֶת־יהוה כָּל־גּוֹיִם
שַׁבְּחוּהוּ כָּל־הָאֻמִּים:

^א ¹ Praise the Lord, all nations;
extol Him, all peoples,

כִּי גָבַר עָלֵינוּ ׀ חַסְדּוֹ וֶאֱמֶת־
יהוה לְעוֹלָם הַלְלוּיָהּ:

^ב ² for His kindness toward us is
overwhelming, and the truth of
the Lord is forever. Halleluya.

---

19 These vows, which include thanksgiving sacrifices, will be fulfilled in the main place of public
gathering for the people of Israel, **in the courtyards of the House of the Lord, in your midst,
Jerusalem. Halleluya.**

PSALM 117
1 **Praise the Lord, all nations; extol Him, all peoples.** All nations can see and extol the
greatness of God, even when His miracles occur in other places or to other peoples.
2 **For His kindness toward us is overwhelming.** You, the nations of the world, can witness
the revelation of God's kindness toward His people, His servants. **And the truth of the Lord is
forever. Halleluya.**

PSALM 118

A song of thanksgiving, the concluding psalm of the Hallel prayer. In part, it describes how an individual person was rescued by God, but it is also a model for the nation as a whole, since the individual happens to be their king. It seems that this psalm, too, was written for a chorus, as many of its verses in praise of God are written in responsive form.

א הוֹדוּ לַיהוָה כִּי־טֶוֹב
כִּי לְעוֹלָם חַסְדּוֹ:

¹ Give thanks to the Lord, for He is good, for His kindness is forever.

ב יֹאמַר־נָא יִשְׂרָאֵל
כִּי לְעוֹלָם חַסְדּוֹ:

² Let Israel now say: His kindness is forever.

ג יֹאמְרוּ־נָא בֵית־אַהֲרֹן
כִּי לְעוֹלָם חַסְדּוֹ:

³ Let the house of Aaron now say: His kindness is forever.

ד יֹאמְרוּ־נָא יִרְאֵי יהוָה
כִּי לְעוֹלָם חַסְדּוֹ:

⁴ Let those who fear the Lord now say: His kindness is forever.

ה מִן־הַמֵּצַר קָרָאתִי יָּהּ עָנָנִי
בַמֶּרְחָב יָהּ:

⁵ From the straits I called to the Lord; the Lord answered me with a wide expanse.

PSALM 118

¹ The psalm begins on a festive note, with a verse of thanksgiving for God's benevolence, which is found in a number of other chapters of Psalms as well: **Give thanks to the Lord, for He is good;** He has shown kindness toward us, **for His kindness is forever.**

² **Let Israel now say: His kindness is forever.**

³ **Let the house of Aaron,** the priests who serve in the Temple, **now say: His kindness is forever.**

⁴ **Let those who fear the Lord now say: His kindness is forever.**

⁵ After the introductory declarations of praise, the main theme of the psalm, namely, thanksgiving to God for the deliverance He wrought, begins here. From the context (see verse 10), it appears that the psalmist is referring to a rescue from a difficult military or political situation. **From the straits I called to the Lord.** When I began my prayer, I felt as though I were in a narrow, constricted space, as if the boundaries of my life were closing in on me. But then **the Lord answered me with a wide expanse.** He answered my prayers not with words but with action, placing me in a situation that alleviated my sense of distress and confinement.

יְהֹוָה לִי לֹא אִירָא מַה־
יַּעֲשֶׂה לִי אָדָם:

6 The Lord is with me; I shall not fear. What can man do to me?

יְהֹוָה לִי בְּעֹזְרָי וַאֲנִי אֶרְאֶה
בְשֹׂנְאָי:

7 The Lord is with me, with those who help me; I will gaze upon my enemies.

טוֹב לַחֲסוֹת בַּיהֹוָה מִבְּטֹחַ
בָּאָדָם:

8 It is better to take refuge in the Lord than to trust in man.

טוֹב לַחֲסוֹת בַּיהֹוָה מִבְּטֹחַ
בִּנְדִיבִים:

9 It is better to take refuge in the Lord than to trust in nobles.

כָּל־גּוֹיִם סְבָבוּנִי בְּשֵׁם יְהֹוָה
כִּי אֲמִילַם:

10 All the nations surrounded me; it is in the name of the Lord that I cut them down.

סַבּוּנִי גַם־סְבָבוּנִי בְּשֵׁם יְהֹוָה
כִּי אֲמִילַם:

11 They swarmed around me, indeed they surrounded me; it is in the name of the Lord that I cut them down.

---

6 **The Lord is with me; I shall not fear. What can man do to me** if God is with me?

7 **The Lord is with me, with those who help me; I will gaze upon** the downfall of **my enemies.**

8 **It is better to take refuge in the Lord than to trust in man,** both because of His superior power and, as is pointed out so frequently in Psalms, His unsurpassed trustworthiness.

9 **It is better to take refuge in the Lord than to trust in nobles.**

10 **All the nations surrounded me.** The psalmist depicts his desperation in the face of a military attack by his enemies, who were closing in from all directions. But, he declares: **It is in the name of the Lord** that I put my trust, and it is because of this **that I** am able to **cut them down.**

11 **They,** those enemies, **swarmed around me, indeed they surrounded me; it is in the name of the Lord that I cut them down.**

סַבּוּנִי כִדְבֹרִים דֹּעֲכוּ כְּאֵשׁ קוֹצִים בְּשֵׁם יהוה כִּי אֲמִילַם: יב

דָּחֹה דְחִיתַנִי לִנְפֹּל וַיהוה עֲזָרָנִי: יג

עָזִּי וְזִמְרָת יָהּ וַיְהִי־לִי לִישׁוּעָה: יד

קוֹל ׀ רִנָּה וִישׁוּעָה בְּאָהֳלֵי צַדִּיקִים יְמִין יהוה עֹשָׂה חָיִל: טו

יְמִין יהוה רוֹמֵמָה יְמִין יהוה עֹשָׂה חָיִל: טז

12 They swarmed around me like bees; they flickered and faded like fire amid thorns. It is in the name of the Lord that I cut them down.

13 You pushed me hard to make me fall, but the Lord helped me.

14 The Lord is my strength and song, and He has become my salvation.

15 A voice of song and deliverance is among the tents of the righteous: The right hand of the Lord brings success.

16 The right hand of the Lord is exalted; the right hand of the Lord brings success.

---

12 **They swarmed around me like bees** that attack one who approaches their hive, swarming around him, seeking to sting him and drive him away. **They flickered and faded like fire amid thorns.** The psalmist now depicts his enemies as a raging fire; but their conflagration is in fact nothing but a fire among thorns, which begins with a huge flame but very quickly dissipates. **It is in the name of the Lord that I cut them down.**

13 The psalmist now addresses his enemies: **You pushed me hard to make me fall, but the Lord helped me** to prevent this from happening.

14 **The Lord is my strength and song, and He has become my salvation.** This phrase is borrowed from the Song at the Sea.[7] All my strength is derived from God, and therefore God is the object of all my songs of praise.

15 After God delivers me from my enemies, **a voice of song and deliverance is** heard **among the tents of the righteous** who praise Him for His salvation, saying: **The right hand of the Lord brings success.** The "right hand" of God is a poetic symbol of power, as the right hand is generally the stronger one.

16 **The right hand of the Lord is exalted; the right hand of the Lord brings success.**

לֹא־אָמוּת כִּי־אֶחְיֶה וַאֲסַפֵּר
מַעֲשֵׂי יָהּ:

יַסֹּר יִסְּרַנִּי יָּהּ וְלַמָּוֶת לֹא
נְתָנָנִי:

פִּתְחוּ־לִי שַׁעֲרֵי־צֶדֶק אָבֹא־
בָם אוֹדֶה יָהּ:

זֶה־הַשַּׁעַר לַיהוָה צַדִּיקִים
יָבֹאוּ בוֹ:

אוֹדְךָ כִּי עֲנִיתָנִי וַתְּהִי־לִי
לִישׁוּעָה:

אֶבֶן מָאֲסוּ הַבּוֹנִים הָיְתָה
לְרֹאשׁ פִּנָּה:

יז 17 May I not die but live, so I may tell the deeds of the Lord.

יח 18 The Lord chastised me severely, but He did not deliver me to death.

יט 19 Open for me the gates of righteousness. I will enter through them; I will give thanks to the Lord.

כ 20 This is the gate to the Lord; the vindicated will enter through it.

כא 21 I will give thanks to You, for You answered me; You have been my salvation.

כב 22 The stone that the builders rejected became the cornerstone.

---

17 The psalmist now offers words of prayer: **May I not die but live, so I may tell the deeds of the Lord.** This is one of many verses in the Bible that reflect the idea that if a person survives mortal danger, it is incumbent on him to make his story known to others and acknowledge God's hand in his survival, thanking God publicly.

18 **The Lord chastised me severely** during those periods of peril and distress, **but He did not deliver me to death.**

19 Because of God's salvation in protecting me from death, I must recount His deeds and thank Him, and so I declare: **Open for me the gates of righteousness,** apparently a reference to the gates of the Temple, where the psalmist goes to offer his thanks in public. **I will enter through them; I will give thanks to the Lord.**

20 **This is the gate to the Lord; the vindicated,** those who were found by God to be deserving, and were granted victory by Him, **will enter through it** to praise God.

21 **I will give thanks to You, for You answered me** in my prayers; **You have been my salvation.**

22 **The stone that the builders rejected,** considering it of inferior quality or appearance, subsequently **became the cornerstone,** the most structurally essential and most visible part of

^{כג} מֵאֵת יְהוָה הָיְתָה זֹּאת הִיא
נִפְלָאת בְּעֵינֵינוּ:

^{כד} זֶה־הַיּוֹם עָשָׂה יְהוָה נָגִילָה
וְנִשְׂמְחָה בוֹ:

^{כה} אָנָּא יְהוָה הוֹשִׁיעָה נָּא אָנָּא
יְהוָה הַצְלִיחָה נָּא:

^{כו} בָּרוּךְ הַבָּא בְּשֵׁם יְהוָה
בֵּרַכְנוּכֶם מִבֵּית יְהוָה:

^{כז} אֵל ׀ יְהוָה וַיָּאֶר לָנוּ אִסְרוּ־
חַג בַּעֲבֹתִים עַד־קַרְנוֹת
הַמִּזְבֵּחַ:

²³ This was from the Lord; it is wondrous in our eyes.

²⁴ This is the day of the Lord's doing; we rejoice and exult in Him.

²⁵ Lord, save us, we beseech You! Lord, grant us success, we beseech You!

²⁶ Blessed be the one who comes in the name of the Lord; we bless you from the House of the Lord.

²⁷ The Lord is God; He has given us light. Bind the festival offering with cords, and from there to the horns of the altar.

---

the building. This metaphor is intended to express the idea that sometimes a person's perspective can change, in retrospect, upon pondering events that have occurred. Things or people that may have at first seemed insignificant may turn out to be the key to one's deliverance.

²³ Concerning such reversals of import and significance, it may be said: **This was from the Lord.** When seemingly decisive or critical events turn out to be inconsequential, or vice versa, it is God's doing. **It is wondrous,** remarkable and surprising, **in our eyes.**

²⁴ **This** day of deliverance **is the day of the Lord's doing; we rejoice and exult in Him.**

²⁵ The first part of this verse is a prayer offered during a time of distress: **Lord, save us, we beseech You!** It is followed by words that are said after the danger has passed: **Lord, grant us success, we beseech You!**

²⁶ The preceding verse marks the end of the prayer of the person who, having been saved from peril, comes to the Temple to offer his thanks. At this point, the priests or others within the Temple offer their response: **Blessed be the one who comes in the name of the Lord; we bless you from the House of the Lord.**

²⁷ Both parties continue: **The Lord is God; He has given us light** by delivering us from distress and darkness into bright salvation. **Bind the festival offering with cords,** in order to prevent it from running free and creating havoc, **and from there to the horns of the altar.**

כח אֵלִי אַתָּה וְאוֹדֶךָּ אֱלֹהַי
אֲרוֹמְמֶךָּ:

²⁸ You are my Almighty, and I give thanks to You. My God, I will exalt You.

כט הוֹדוּ לַיהוָה כִּי־טוֹב
כִּי לְעוֹלָם חַסְדּוֹ:

²⁹ Give thanks to the Lord, for He is good, for His kindness is forever.

PSALM 119

A distinctly didactic psalm comprising short verses, often not linked to one another in terms of their content, arranged in an alphabetical structure, with eight verses allotted to each of the twenty-two letters of the Hebrew alphabet. Although each verse is an independent unit, two features unify the psalm into a coherent whole. First, nearly all the verses are written in the first-person singular voice, reflecting an individual turning to the Almighty both to express his prayers and wishes and to recount His deeds. The second theme repeated throughout the psalm is that of praise for God's Torah and commandments. The unifying motif of the psalm is the psalmist's devotion to God and his moving ever closer to Him by perceiving His revelation in the Torah.

A great deal has been written about the precision of phrasing and the recurring patterns in this psalm. Some commentators suggest that it is a collection of one-line sayings meant to be recited sequentially, one verse per day, meaning that two full cycles would be completed in a lunar year.

א ‏א אַשְׁרֵי תְמִימֵי־דָרֶךְ הַהֹלְכִים
בְּתוֹרַת יְהוָה:

¹ Happy are those whose path is blameless, who follow the teaching of the Lord.

כה לחודש
25th day
of month

---

28 The psalmist restates his gratitude to God: **You are my Almighty, and I give thanks to You. My God, I will exalt You.**

29 The psalm ends with a repetition of the praise of the first verse: **Give thanks to the Lord, for He is good, for His kindness is forever.**

PSALM 119

1 **Happy are those whose path is blameless,** those who follow the proper path, those **who follow the teaching of the Lord**. Note that here and elsewhere in this psalm the word Torah is translated as "teaching."

אַשְׁרֵי נֹצְרֵי עֵדֹתָיו בְּכָל־לֵב
יִדְרְשֽׁוּהוּ׃

אַף לֹא־פָעֲלוּ עַוְלָה בִּדְרָכָיו
הָלָֽכוּ׃

אַתָּה צִוִּיתָה פִקֻּדֶיךָ לִשְׁמֹר
מְאֹד׃

אַחֲלַי יִכֹּנוּ דְרָכָי לִשְׁמֹר
חֻקֶּֽיךָ׃

אָז לֹא־אֵבוֹשׁ בְּהַבִּיטִי אֶל־
כָּל־מִצְוֹתֶֽיךָ׃

אוֹדְךָ בְּיֹשֶׁר לֵבָב בְּלָמְדִי
מִשְׁפְּטֵי צִדְקֶֽךָ׃

אֶת־חֻקֶּיךָ אֶשְׁמֹר אַל־
תַּעַזְבֵנִי עַד־מְאֹד׃

2 Happy are those who uphold His precepts and seek Him wholeheartedly.

3 They do not engage in wrongdoing, but rather walk in His ways.

4 You commanded Your edicts to be diligently observed.

5 It is my wish that my ways be firmly set to observe Your statutes,

6 for then I would not be ashamed when looking upon all Your commandments.

7 I give thanks to You with a sincere heart as I study Your righteous laws.

8 I follow Your statutes; do not utterly forsake me.

---

2 **Happy are those who uphold His precepts and seek Him wholeheartedly** through observance of those commandments.

3 **They do not engage in wrongdoing, but rather walk in His ways** that He has set forth in His Torah.

4 The psalmist speaks to God: **You commanded Your edicts to be diligently observed.**

5 **It is my wish that my ways be firmly set to observe Your statutes,**

6 **for then I would not be ashamed when looking upon all Your commandments,** for I could honestly say that I had done my best to observe them.

7 **I give thanks to You with a sincere heart as I study Your righteous laws.** This verse can be understood in two ways: The very act of studying God's laws is a form of giving thanks. Alternatively, after having studied the laws, I give thanks to God for having shown me, in the Torah, the true and proper path.

8 **I follow Your statutes,** I strive to observe Your commandments, and therefore I pray: **Do not utterly forsake me** so that I can continue following this path.

ב

בַּמֶּה יְזַכֶּה־נַּעַר אֶת־אָרְחוֹ
לִשְׁמֹר כִּדְבָרֶךָ׃

בְּכָל־לִבִּי דְרַשְׁתִּיךָ אַל־
תַּשְׁגֵּנִי מִמִּצְוֹתֶיךָ׃

בְּלִבִּי צָפַנְתִּי אִמְרָתֶךָ לְמַעַן
לֹא אֶחֱטָא־לָךְ׃

בָּרוּךְ אַתָּה יהוה לַמְּדֵנִי
חֻקֶּיךָ׃

בִּשְׂפָתַי סִפַּרְתִּי כֹּל מִשְׁפְּטֵי־
פִיךָ׃

בְּדֶרֶךְ עֵדְוֹתֶיךָ שַׂשְׂתִּי כְּעַל
כָּל־הוֹן׃

בְּפִקּוּדֶיךָ אָשִׂיחָה וְאַבִּיטָה
אֹרְחֹתֶיךָ׃

9 How can a young man bring merit to his path? By following it as befits Your word.

10 I seek You with all my heart; let me not stray from Your commandments.

11 I store Your saying in my heart, so as not to sin against You.

12 Blessed are You, Lord; teach me Your statutes.

13 With my lips I recount all the laws of Your mouth.

14 I rejoice in the path of Your precepts as over all riches.

15 I speak about Your edicts and look upon Your ways.

---

9 **How can a young man bring merit to his path?** How can a young person choose the right path? **By following it as befits Your word,** by following everything You have commanded.

10 **I seek You with all my heart,** I desire to become close to You, and I pray to you: **Let me not stray from Your commandments.** Grant me the strength to continue in my observance of Your commandments.

11 **I store Your saying in my heart, so as not to sin against You.** I keep Your teachings in my heart; this helps me to avoid sinning, or at least guards me from sinning out of ignorance.

12 A short prayer: **Blessed are You, Lord; teach me Your statutes.**

13 **With my lips I recount all the laws of Your mouth.** I speak words of Torah aloud, and impart them to others as well.

14 **I rejoice in** following **the path of Your precepts as** a person would rejoice **over all riches,** over suddenly receiving a great fortune.

15 **I speak about Your edicts and** I also **look upon Your ways,** pondering their meaning.

טז בְּחֻקֹּתֶיךָ אֶשְׁתַּעֲשָׁע לֹא
אֶשְׁכַּח דְּבָרֶךָ:

ג

יז גְּמֹל עַל־עַבְדְּךָ אֶחְיֶה
וְאֶשְׁמְרָה דְבָרֶךָ:

יח גַּל־עֵינַי וְאַבִּיטָה נִפְלָאוֹת
מִתּוֹרָתֶךָ:

יט גֵּר אָנֹכִי בָאָרֶץ אַל־תַּסְתֵּר
מִמֶּנִּי מִצְוֹתֶיךָ:

כ גָּרְסָה נַפְשִׁי לְתַאֲבָה אֶל־
מִשְׁפָּטֶיךָ בְכָל־עֵת:

כא גָּעַרְתָּ זֵדִים אֲרוּרִים הַשֹּׁגִים
מִמִּצְוֹתֶיךָ:

16 I delight in Your statutes; I do not forget Your word.

17 Grant kindness to Your servant, that I might live and keep Your word.

18 Uncover my eyes so I might perceive the wonders of Your teaching.

19 I am but a sojourner on earth; do not hide Your commandments from me.

20 My soul longingly partakes of Your laws at all times.

21 You rebuke the accursed, insolent ones who stray from Your commandments.

---

16 **I delight in Your statutes.** Your commandments and Your Torah are not a burden for me. In fact, I actually delight in them, as I find them engaging and interesting. As a result, **I do not forget Your word** or your teaching.

17 **Grant kindness to** me, **Your servant, that I might live and keep Your word.**

18 **Uncover my eyes,** grant me understanding and insight, **so I might perceive the wonders of Your teaching.** To fully appreciate the greatness of the Torah, it is not sufficient merely to speak about it or to observe its commandments; therefore, the psalmist implores God for enlightenment.

19 **I am but a sojourner on earth.** I am here on earth for a limited time, like a traveler on the road, so **do not hide Your commandments from me.** Allow me to use the limited time that I have to learn Your commandments. This can be seen as a continuation of the previous verses, in which the psalmist prayed for life and enlightenment. Alternatively, the verse can be read as a plea for guidance: During my days on earth, I am like a stranger in a foreign land, requiring instruction in the laws and customs of the land, that is, the law of Your Torah.

20 **My soul longingly partakes of Your laws at all times.** The word *garsa*, translated as "partakes," conjures up the image of someone eating a delicacy with great enthusiasm.

21 **You rebuke the accursed, insolent ones who stray from Your commandments.**

כב גַּל מֵעָלַי חֶרְפָּה וָבוּז כִּי
עֵדֹתֶיךָ נָצָרְתִּי:

22 Remove disgrace and abuse from me, for I have upheld Your precepts.

כג גַּם יָשְׁבוּ שָׂרִים בִּי נִדְבָּרוּ
עַבְדְּךָ יָשִׂיחַ בְּחֻקֶּיךָ:

23 Even when princes sit and talk about me, Your servant reflects on Your statutes.

כד גַּם־עֵדֹתֶיךָ שַׁעֲשֻׁעָי אַנְשֵׁי
עֲצָתִי:

24 Also Your precepts are my delight, my counselors.

ד

כה דָּבְקָה לֶעָפָר נַפְשִׁי חַיֵּנִי
כִּדְבָרֶךָ:

25 My soul cleaves to the dust; revive me as Your word.

כו דְּרָכַי סִפַּרְתִּי וַתַּעֲנֵנִי לַמְּדֵנִי
חֻקֶּיךָ:

26 I told of my ways, and You answered me. Teach me Your statutes.

כז דֶּרֶךְ־פִּקּוּדֶיךָ הֲבִינֵנִי
וְאָשִׂיחָה בְּנִפְלְאוֹתֶיךָ:

27 Make me understand the way of Your edicts, and I will speak about Your wonders.

---

22 **Remove disgrace and abuse from me, for I have upheld Your precepts** and can therefore ask You to protect me from the shame and humiliation that is heaped upon me.

23 **Even when princes sit and talk about me,** engaging in a discussion that should interest me and elicit my participation, **Your servant** instead **reflects on Your statutes**; I as Your servant avoid joining the conversation.

24 **Also Your precepts are my delight.** Even my entertainment consists of studying Your Torah. Moreover, those precepts function as **my counselors,** in the sense that they provide me with guidance as to how best to conduct my life.

25 **My soul cleaves to the dust.** I am completely depressed and disheartened. In this difficult situation, all I can do is pray: **Revive me as Your word.** Grant me life just as there is life in the words of Your Torah.

26 **I told of my ways,** I recounted to You the various matters and troubles in my life, **and You answered me.** You responded to my prayers. Now that You have granted me relief, I have one primary request: **Teach me Your statutes**.

27 **Make me understand the way of Your edicts, and** then **I will** be able to **speak about Your wonders.**

כח דָּלְפָה נַפְשִׁי מִתּוּגָה קַיְּמֵנִי
כִּדְבָרֶךָ:

כט דֶּרֶךְ־שֶׁקֶר הָסֵר מִמֶּנִּי
וְתוֹרָתְךָ חָנֵּנִי:

ל דֶּרֶךְ־אֱמוּנָה בָחָרְתִּי
מִשְׁפָּטֶיךָ שִׁוִּיתִי:

לא דָּבַקְתִּי בְעֵדְוֹתֶיךָ יהוה אַל־
תְּבִישֵׁנִי:

לב דֶּרֶךְ־מִצְוֹתֶיךָ אָרוּץ כִּי
תַרְחִיב לִבִּי:

ה   לג הוֹרֵנִי יהוה דֶּרֶךְ חֻקֶּיךָ
וְאֶצְּרֶנָּה עֵקֶב:

28 My soul is dripping with anguish; sustain me, as befits Your word.

29 Remove the path of falsehood from me; grant me Your teaching.

30 I have chosen the path of faith; I have placed Your laws.

31 I cleave to Your precepts; Lord, do not shame me.

32 I run in the path of Your commandments, for You widen my heart.

33 Teach me, Lord, the way of Your statutes, and I will uphold it to the end.

---

28 **My soul is dripping with anguish.** The image here is of a soul crying incessantly, to the extent that it becomes wrung out and desiccated. Therefore, the psalmist pleads: **Sustain me, as befits Your word.**

29 **Remove the path of falsehood from me.** Allow me to learn only about the true path. This may also be seen as a request that God grant the wisdom to avoid living one's life in accordance with false beliefs. **Grant me** knowledge of **Your teaching.**

30 **I have chosen the path of faith; I have placed Your laws** before me.

31 Moreover, **I cleave to Your precepts; Lord, do not shame me.** Keep me from experiencing shame, since I am doing my utmost to follow Your laws.

32 **I run in the path of Your commandments, for You widen my heart.** If You grant me breadth of heart, that is, adequate temperament and ability, I will fulfill Your commandments with alacrity, as one might run down a path.

33 **Teach me, Lord, the way of Your statutes, and I will** then be able to **uphold it to the end.**

הֲבִינֵנִי וְאֶצְּרָה תוֹרָתֶךָ
וְאֶשְׁמְרֶנָּה בְכָל־לֵב:

הַדְרִיכֵנִי בִּנְתִיב מִצְוֹתֶיךָ כִּי־
בוֹ חָפָצְתִּי:

הַט־לִבִּי אֶל־עֵדְוֹתֶיךָ וְאַל
אֶל־בָּצַע:

הַעֲבֵר עֵינַי מֵרְאוֹת שָׁוְא
בִּדְרָכֶךָ חַיֵּנִי:

הָקֵם לְעַבְדְּךָ אִמְרָתֶךָ אֲשֶׁר
לְיִרְאָתֶךָ:

הַעֲבֵר חֶרְפָּתִי אֲשֶׁר יָגֹרְתִּי
כִּי מִשְׁפָּטֶיךָ טוֹבִים:

הִנֵּה תָּאַבְתִּי לְפִקֻּדֶיךָ
בְּצִדְקָתְךָ חַיֵּנִי:

³⁴ Give me understanding, so I might uphold Your teaching and follow it wholeheartedly.

³⁵ Guide me in the path of Your commandments, for in it is my desire.

³⁶ Incline my heart toward Your precepts and not toward material gain.

³⁷ Avert my eyes from seeing falsehood; through Your ways give me life.

³⁸ Fulfill the promise You made to Your servant, which is for those who fear You.

³⁹ Remove my disgrace, which I dread, for Your laws are good.

⁴⁰ How I long for Your edicts! In Your righteousness give me life.

---

34 **Give me understanding, so I might** then **uphold Your teaching and follow it wholeheartedly.**

35 **Guide me in the path of Your commandments, for in it is my desire.** Although I freely desire and choose this path, I need guidance in following it.

36 **Incline my heart toward Your precepts** so that they become my chief interest and delight, **and** do **not** direct it **toward** seeking **material gain.**

37 Similarly, **avert my eyes from seeing falsehood; through Your ways** rather than through false ideas and visions, **give me life.**

38 **Fulfill the promise You made to Your servant, which is for those who fear You,** for You have given Your word that those who serve and fear You are worthy of Your protection.

39 **Remove my disgrace** that others have heaped upon me, **which I dread, for Your laws,** which I follow faithfully, **are good,** and it would be inappropriate to allow me to suffer such disgrace.

40 **How I long for Your edicts!** And for this reason, I pray to You: **In Your righteousness give me life.**

ו

מא וִיבֹאֻנִי חֲסָדֶךָ יהוה
תְּשׁוּעָתְךָ כְּאִמְרָתֶךָ:

מב וְאֶעֱנֶה חֹרְפִי דָבָר כִּי־
בָטַחְתִּי בִּדְבָרֶךָ:

מג וְאַל־תַּצֵּל מִפִּי דְבַר־אֱמֶת
עַד־מְאֹד כִּי לְמִשְׁפָּטֶךָ
יִחָלְתִּי:

מד וְאֶשְׁמְרָה תוֹרָתְךָ תָמִיד
לְעוֹלָם וָעֶד:

מה וְאֶתְהַלְּכָה בָרְחָבָה כִּי
פִקֻּדֶיךָ דָרָשְׁתִּי:

מו וַאֲדַבְּרָה בְעֵדֹתֶיךָ נֶגֶד
מְלָכִים וְלֹא אֵבוֹשׁ:

41 Let Your kindness reach me, Lord, as well as Your deliverance, as befits Your promise.

42 And I will answer those who revile me, for I trust in Your word.

43 Do not withhold the word of truth altogether from my mouth, for I trust in Your laws.

44 May I follow Your teaching always and forever.

45 Let me walk in a wide, expansive place, for I have sought Your edicts.

46 I will recount Your precepts before kings and not be ashamed.

---

41 **Let Your kindness reach me, Lord, as well as Your deliverance, as befits Your promise.**

42 **And I will** have the strength and confidence to **answer** and stand firm against **those who revile me, for I trust in Your word,** which gives me the courage of conviction.

43 **Do not withhold the word of truth altogether from my mouth.** Do not hold back my ability to speak truth and avoid falsehood. **For I trust in Your laws** and therefore hope that You will help me in this matter. The word *yiḥalti,* translated here as "I trust," can be understood as both anticipation and hope.

44 **May I follow Your teaching always and forever.**

45 **Let me walk in a wide, expansive place,** free from the confinement of distress, **for I have sought Your edicts** and am therefore deserving of Your aid in this respect.

46 **I will recount Your precepts,** discussing the Torah and its commandments, **before kings,** perhaps referring even to foreign kings who have never heard of the Torah or its laws, **and not be ashamed** to do so, because I take such pride in Your Torah.

וְאֶשְׁתַּעֲשַׁע בְּמִצְוֹתֶיךָ אֲשֶׁר
אָהָבְתִּי:

מה

⁴⁷ I will delight in Your commandments, which I love.

וְאֶשָּׂא־כַפַּי אֶל־מִצְוֹתֶיךָ
אֲשֶׁר אָהָבְתִּי וְאָשִׂיחָה
בְחֻקֶּיךָ:

מח

⁴⁸ I will lift my hands to Your commandments, which I love, and I will reflect on Your statutes.

זְכֹר־דָּבָר לְעַבְדֶּךָ עַל אֲשֶׁר
יִחַלְתָּנִי:

מט

ז

⁴⁹ Remember the word to Your servant, with which You gave me hope.

זֹאת נֶחָמָתִי בְעָנְיִי כִּי
אִמְרָתְךָ חִיָּתְנִי:

נ

⁵⁰ This is my comfort in my affliction: That Your saying revives me.

זֵדִים הֱלִיצֻנִי עַד־מְאֹד
מִתּוֹרָתְךָ לֹא נָטִיתִי:

נא

⁵¹ Evildoers mock me greatly, but I do not veer from Your teaching.

זָכַרְתִּי מִשְׁפָּטֶיךָ מֵעוֹלָם ׀
יְהוָה וָאֶתְנֶחָם:

נב

⁵² I have always remembered Your laws, Lord, and I am comforted.

---

⁴⁷ **I will delight in Your commandments, which I love.** Because I love the commandments, I enjoy occupying myself with them.

⁴⁸ **I will lift my hands** in prayer **to** be able to delve more and more into **Your commandments, which I love, and I will reflect on Your statutes.**

⁴⁹ **Remember the word to Your servant, with which You gave me hope.** This interpretation renders *yihaltani* as "You gave me hope." The word can also be translated as "You put Your trust in me," in which case the verse would mean: I ask You to remember the promises You made to me because You put Your trust in me; that is, You found favor in me and brought me close to You.

⁵⁰ **This is my comfort in my affliction:** My one consolation during times of distress is **that Your saying revives me** and gives me relief.

⁵¹ **Evildoers mock me** and my way of life **greatly, but I do not veer from Your teaching.**

⁵² **I have always remembered Your laws, Lord, and I am** thereby **comforted.**

נג וַלְעָפָה אֲחָזַתְנִי מֵרְשָׁעִים
עֹזְבֵי תּוֹרָתֶךָ:

נד זְמִרוֹת הָיוּ־לִי חֻקֶּיךָ בְּבֵית
מְגוּרָי:

נה זָכַרְתִּי בַלַּיְלָה שִׁמְךָ יהוה
וָאֶשְׁמְרָה תּוֹרָתֶךָ:

נו זֹאת הָיְתָה־לִּי כִּי פִקֻּדֶיךָ
נָצָרְתִּי:

ח חֶלְקִי יהוה אָמַרְתִּי לִשְׁמֹר
דְּבָרֶיךָ:

נח חִלִּיתִי פָנֶיךָ בְכָל־לֵב חָנֵּנִי
כְּאִמְרָתֶךָ:

53 Great distress has seized me
because of the wicked who
have forsaken Your teaching.

54 Your statutes were songs to me
in the house of my sojourning.

55 Lord, I remember Your name
in the night, and I follow Your
teaching.

56 This became mine, because I
upheld Your precepts.

57 I have declared that the Lord
is my portion, to follow
Your words.

58 I plead for Your countenance
with a whole heart; be gracious
to me, as befits Your promise.

---

53 **Great distress has seized me because of the wicked who have forsaken Your teaching.** I cannot be indifferent about people who abandon Your Torah; their very existence weighs heavily on me and causes me pain.

54 **Your statutes were** as pleasant as **songs to me.** *Hukekha*, "Your statutes," usually refers to those commandments whose rationale is not known. These bring me great joy **in the house of my sojourning,** even when I am a sojourner in a strange place, not in a comfortable or tranquil setting.

55 **Lord, I remember Your name** even **in the night,** when I am alone, **and I follow Your teaching.**

56 **This,** an apparent reference to the comfort and success mentioned in the previous verses, **became mine, because I upheld Your precepts.**

57 **I have declared** my decision **that the Lord is my portion,** and therefore it is my desire **to follow Your words.**

58 **I plead for Your countenance with a whole heart; be gracious to me, as befits Your promise** to grant reward to those who follow Your ways.

חִשַּׁבְתִּי דְרָכָי וָאָשִׁיבָה רַגְלַי
אֶל־עֵדֹתֶיךָ: נט

⁵⁹ I consider my ways, and I turn my feet toward Your precepts.

חַשְׁתִּי וְלֹא הִתְמַהְמָהְתִּי
לִשְׁמֹר מִצְוֹתֶיךָ: ס

⁶⁰ I hasten, I do not delay, in following Your commandments.

חֶבְלֵי רְשָׁעִים עִוְּדֻנִי תּוֹרָתְךָ
לֹא שָׁכָחְתִּי: סא

⁶¹ The pains of the wicked contorted me, but I did not forget Your teaching.

חֲצוֹת־לַיְלָה אָקוּם לְהוֹדוֹת
לָךְ עַל מִשְׁפְּטֵי צִדְקֶךָ: סב

⁶² At midnight, I rise to give thanks to You for Your righteous laws.

חָבֵר אָנִי לְכָל־אֲשֶׁר יְרֵאוּךָ
וּלְשֹׁמְרֵי פִּקּוּדֶיךָ: סג

⁶³ I am a friend to all who fear You, to those who follow Your edicts.

חַסְדְּךָ יְהוָה מָלְאָה הָאָרֶץ
חֻקֶּיךָ לַמְּדֵנִי: סד

⁶⁴ The earth is full of Your kindness, Lord; teach me Your statutes.

---

⁵⁹ I periodically **consider** and evaluate **my ways, and** when I find that improvement is needed, **I turn my feet toward Your precepts.**

⁶⁰ **I hasten, I do not delay, in following Your commandments**.

⁶¹ **The pains of the wicked** that they inflicted upon me **contorted me, but** nevertheless, **I did not forget Your teaching**.

⁶² **At midnight,** a time when most people are asleep, **I rise to give thanks to You for Your righteous laws.**

⁶³ **I am a friend to all who fear You.** I attempt to be close to such people, **to those who follow your edicts.**

⁶⁴ **The earth is full of Your kindness, Lord,** and I pray: **Teach me Your statutes.** I wish not only to benefit from Your beneficence, but also to understand Your ways.

ט   טֽוֹב עָשִׂ֣יתָ עִֽם־עַבְדְּךָ֑ יְ֝הֹוָ֗ה
כִּדְבָרֶֽךָ׃

טֽוּב טַ֣עַם וָדַ֣עַת לַמְּדֵ֑נִי כִּ֖י
בְמִצְוֺתֶ֣יךָ הֶאֱמָֽנְתִּי׃

טֶ֣רֶם אֶ֭עֱנֶה אֲנִ֣י שֹׁגֵ֑ג וְ֝עַתָּ֗ה
אִמְרָתְךָ֥ שָׁמָֽרְתִּי׃

טֽוֹב־אַתָּ֥ה וּמֵטִ֗יב לַמְּדֵ֥נִי
חֻקֶּֽיךָ׃

טָפְל֬וּ עָלַ֣י שֶׁ֣קֶר זֵדִ֑ים אֲ֝נִ֗י
בְּכׇל־לֵ֤ב ׀ אֱצֹּ֬ר פִּקּוּדֶֽיךָ׃

טָפַ֣שׁ כַּחֵ֣לֶב לִבָּ֑ם אֲ֝נִ֗י
תוֹרָתְךָ֥ שִׁעֲשָֽׁעְתִּי׃

⁶⁵ You dealt well with Your servant, Lord, as befits Your word.

⁶⁶ Teach me good discernment and understanding, for I believe in Your commandments.

⁶⁷ Before I discussed it, I would go astray, but now I follow Your saying.

⁶⁸ You are good, and do good; teach me Your statutes.

⁶⁹ Evildoers pin falsehoods on me; I uphold Your edicts with a whole heart.

⁷⁰ Their hearts are dulled, as if covered with fat; I delight in Your teaching.

---

⁶⁵ **You dealt well with Your servant, Lord, as befits Your word** that You promised, to do good to the righteous.

⁶⁶ **Teach me good discernment,** literally "a good taste," **and understanding.** Show me both the pleasure and the wisdom that are gained from Your Torah. **For I believe in Your commandments,** and therefore I beseech You to deepen my understanding so that I can delight even more in Your commandments.

⁶⁷ **Before I discussed it,** before I immersed myself in the ways of the Torah, **I would go astray** because I did not have sufficient knowledge to know what needed to be done; **but now** that I have studied the Torah, **I** faithfully **follow Your saying.**

⁶⁸ **You are good, and do good** for the entire world. **Teach me Your statutes.** My personal request is for Your goodness toward me to be reflected in Your teaching me Your laws.

⁶⁹ **Evildoers pin falsehoods on me.** But I pay no heed to them and their slander, and **I uphold Your edicts with a whole heart.**

⁷⁰ **Their hearts are dulled, as if covered with fat,** without feeling or understanding. But **I delight in Your teaching** and have no share in their illusory pleasures.

עא טֽוֹב־לִ֥י כִֽי־עֻנֵּ֑יתִי לְמַ֖עַן אֶלְמַ֣ד חֻקֶּֽיךָ׃

71 It is good for me that I was afflicted, so I might learn Your statutes.

עב טֽוֹב־לִ֥י תוֹרַת־פִּ֑יךָ מֵֽ֝אַלְפֵ֗י זָהָ֥ב וָכָֽסֶף׃

72 The teaching of Your mouth is better for me than thousands of gold and silver pieces.

עג יָדֶ֣יךָ עָ֭שׂוּנִי וַֽיְכוֹנְנ֑וּנִי הֲ֝בִינֵ֗נִי וְאֶלְמְדָ֥ה מִצְוֺתֶֽיךָ׃

73 Your hands made me and set me in place. Give me understanding, so I might learn Your commandments.

עד יְ֭רֵאֶיךָ יִרְא֣וּנִי וְיִשְׂמָ֑חוּ כִּ֖י לִדְבָֽרְךָ֣ יִחָֽלְתִּי׃

74 May those who fear You see me and be glad, because I hope for Your word.

עה יָדַ֣עְתִּי יְ֭הֹוָה כִּי־צֶ֣דֶק מִשְׁפָּטֶ֑יךָ וֶ֝אֱמוּנָ֗ה עִנִּיתָֽנִי׃

75 I know, Lord, that Your rulings are just, and that You afflicted me in faithfulness.

עו יְהִי־נָ֣א חַסְדְּךָ֣ לְנַֽחֲמֵ֑נִי כְּאִמְרָֽתְךָ֥ לְעַבְדֶּֽךָ׃

76 May Your kindness comfort me, as You promised Your servant.

---

71 **It is good for me that I was afflicted** whenever I strayed from the proper path, for Your chastisement caused me to correct my conduct, **so I might learn Your statutes.**

72 **The teaching of Your mouth is better for me than thousands of gold and silver pieces.**

73 **Your hands made me and set me in place.** Now my request is: **Give me understanding, so I might learn Your commandments.**

74 **May those** other people **who fear You see me and be glad, because I hope for Your word.** These God-fearing people are happy to see that I share their desire for the word of God.

75 **I know, Lord, that Your rulings are just.** I acknowledge Your justice even when things do not go my way, **and that** when **You afflicted me,** You did so **in faithfulness,** with good reason.

76 **May Your kindness comfort me** in my times of distress, **as You promised Your servant** that You would come to his assistance.

עו יְבֹאֻנִי רַחֲמֶיךָ וְאֶחְיֶה כִּי־
תוֹרָתְךָ שַׁעֲשֻׁעָי:

עז יֵבֹשׁוּ זֵדִים כִּי־שֶׁקֶר עִוְּתוּנִי
אֲנִי אָשִׂיחַ בְּפִקּוּדֶיךָ:

עח יָשׁוּבוּ לִי יְרֵאֶיךָ וְיֹדְעֵי
עֵדֹתֶיךָ:

וְיֹדְעֵי

פ יְהִי־לִבִּי תָמִים בְּחֻקֶּיךָ לְמַעַן
לֹא אֵבוֹשׁ:

כ

פא כָּלְתָה לִתְשׁוּעָתְךָ נַפְשִׁי
לִדְבָרְךָ יִחָלְתִּי:

פב כָּלוּ עֵינַי לְאִמְרָתֶךָ לֵאמֹר
מָתַי תְּנַחֲמֵנִי:

77 May Your mercy come to me, so I might live; Your teaching is my delight.

78 May the evildoers be shamed for contorting me with lies; I will reflect on Your edicts.

79 May those who fear You and who know Your precepts turn to me.

80 May my heart be blameless in Your statutes, lest I be ashamed.

81 My soul goes out in yearning for Your salvation; I await Your word.

82 My eyes pine for Your promise, saying: When will You comfort me?

---

77 **May Your mercy come to me, so I might live; Your teaching is my delight,** and I am therefore deserving of Your mercy.

78 **May the evildoers be shamed for contorting me with lies.** They defame me and my path of righteousness. But despite their falsehoods, **I will reflect on Your edicts.**

79 Even when I have sinned and caused the God-fearing people to shun me, **may those who fear You and who know Your precepts,** the people whom I respect and whose company I desire, **turn to me** and again draw near to me.

80 **May my heart be blameless in Your statutes,** may I conduct myself with complete integrity and virtue and not stray from the true path, **lest I be ashamed** of myself.

81 **My soul goes out in yearning for Your salvation; I await** the fulfillment of **Your word.**

82 **My eyes pine for** the fulfillment of **Your promise, saying: When will You comfort me?**

כִּי־הָיִיתִי כְּנֹאד בְּקִיטוֹר 83
חֻקֶּיךָ לֹא שָׁכָחְתִּי:

כַּמָּה יְמֵי־עַבְדֶּךָ מָתַי תַּעֲשֶׂה 84
בְרֹדְפַי מִשְׁפָּט:

כָּרוּ־לִי זֵדִים שִׁיחוֹת אֲשֶׁר 85
לֹא כְתוֹרָתֶךָ:

כָּל־מִצְוֺתֶיךָ אֱמוּנָה שֶׁקֶר 86
רְדָפוּנִי עָזְרֵנִי:

כִּמְעַט כִּלּוּנִי בָאָרֶץ וַאֲנִי 87
לֹא־עָזַבְתִּי פִקֻּדֶיךָ:

כְּחַסְדְּךָ חַיֵּנִי וְאֶשְׁמְרָה 88
עֵדוּת פִּיךָ:

83 Even when I am like a wineskin in steam, I do not forget Your statutes.

84 How many are the days of Your servant? When will You pass judgment on my pursuers?

85 Evildoers dig pits that are meant for me; they do not act as befits Your teaching.

86 All Your commandments are truth, yet they pursue me with lies; help me.

87 They nearly rid the earth of me; I do not forsake Your edicts.

88 Give me life, as befits Your kindness, so I might follow the precept of Your mouth.

---

83 **Even when I am** in distress **like a wineskin in steam,** which shrivels and shrinks, **I do not forget Your statutes.**

84 **How many are the days of Your servant?** The days of my life are numbered. Therefore, I ask: **When will You pass judgment on my pursuers?** This is not an expression of lack of faith in God, but rather a request: Since my days are short, please allow me to see in my lifetime that my enemies receive the punishment they deserve.

85 **Evildoers dig pits,** traps, **that are meant for me; they do not act as befits Your teaching,** for they are not concerned about transgressing the Torah.

86 **All Your commandments are truth,** I believe in them faithfully, **yet they pursue me with lies,** the opposite of truth; **help me** to evade their pursuit.

87 **They nearly rid the earth of me,** yet despite my anguish, **I do not forsake Your edicts.**

88 **Give me life, as befits Your kindness, so I might** have the ability to **follow the precept of Your mouth.**

ל

פט לְעוֹלָם יהוה דְּבָרְךָ נִצָּב
בַּשָּׁמָיִם:

89 Forever, Lord, does Your word stand in the heavens.

צ לְדֹר וָדֹר אֱמוּנָתֶךָ כּוֹנַנְתָּ
אֶרֶץ וַתַּעֲמֹד:

90 Your faithfulness is for all generations; You established the earth, and it stands.

צא לְמִשְׁפָּטֶיךָ עָמְדוּ הַיּוֹם כִּי
הַכֹּל עֲבָדֶיךָ:

91 They stand today for Your judgment, for all are Your servants.

צב לוּלֵי תוֹרָתְךָ שַׁעֲשֻׁעָי אָז
אָבַדְתִּי בְעָנְיִי:

92 Had Your teaching not been my delight, I would have perished in my affliction.

צג לְעוֹלָם לֹא־אֶשְׁכַּח פִּקּוּדֶיךָ
כִּי־בָם חִיִּיתָנִי:

93 I will never forget Your edicts, for through them You gave me life.

צד לְךָ־אֲנִי הוֹשִׁיעֵנִי כִּי פִקּוּדֶיךָ
דָרָשְׁתִּי:

94 I am Yours; save me, for I have sought Your edicts.

---

89 **Forever, Lord, does Your word stand in the heavens.** This verse has traditionally been interpreted to mean that the word of God, that which created the world, is what continues today to sustain the heavens.

90 **Your faithfulness is for all generations; You established the earth, and it stands.** The earth, like the heavens mentioned in the previous verse, is upheld by God's word.

91 **They,** all the people of the world, **stand today for Your judgment, for all are Your servants,** under Your jurisdiction, even if they do not acknowledge this. From the context, it would appear that the word "today" refers to any and every day.

92 **Had Your teaching not been my delight,** expanding my heart, filling me with joy, and acting as a constant source of comfort, **I would have perished in my affliction**.

93 **I will never forget Your edicts,** not only out of dedication to them, but for my very survival, **for through them You gave me life.**

94 **I am Yours; save me, for I have sought Your edicts.** The second half of the verse explains the first half: "I am Yours," in that I am always seeking out Your commandments.

צה 95 לִי קִוּוּ רְשָׁעִים לְאַבְּדֵנִי
עֵדֹתֶיךָ אֶתְבּוֹנָן:

95 The wicked wish to destroy
me; I ponder your precepts.

צו 96 לְכָל־תִּכְלָה רָאִיתִי קֵץ
רְחָבָה מִצְוָתְךָ מְאֹד:

96 I see an end to all great things,
but Your commandments are
exceedingly wide.

מ

צז 97 מָה־אָהַבְתִּי תוֹרָתֶךָ כָּל־
הַיּוֹם הִיא שִׂיחָתִי:

97 How I love Your teaching! It is
what I speak of all day.

כו לחודש
26th day
of month

צח 98 מֵאֹיְבַי תְּחַכְּמֵנִי מִצְוֹתֶךָ כִּי
לְעוֹלָם הִיא־לִי:

98 Your commandments make
me wiser than my enemies, for
they are always mine.

צט 99 מִכָּל־מְלַמְּדַי הִשְׂכַּלְתִּי כִּי
עֵדְוֹתֶיךָ שִׂיחָה לִי:

99 I have gained discernment
beyond that of all my teachers,
for Your precepts are my
conversation.

ק 100 מִזְּקֵנִים אֶתְבּוֹנָן כִּי פִקּוּדֶיךָ
נָצָרְתִּי:

100 I gain insight from the elders,
for I uphold Your edicts.

---

95 **The wicked wish to destroy me,** and **I ponder Your precepts** because they are a source of
strength for me in the face of adversity. Moreover, "I ponder Your precepts" because they heighten
my awareness of the fact that You oversee the world, and my enemies can do nothing to me against
Your will.

96 **I see** that there is **an end to all** things, even to **great** and complex **things, but Your
commandments are exceedingly wide** and boundless; they have no end.

97 **How I love Your teaching! It is what I speak of all day.** I love the Torah to such an extent
that it is the main subject of my conversation.

98 **Your commandments make me wiser than my enemies,** affording me protection from
them; **for they are always mine** as I am constantly involved in their study and observance. The
Torah is not only a spiritual guide but a fount of practical knowledge, which enables me to triumph
over my foes.

99 **I have gained discernment beyond that of all my teachers, for Your precepts are my
conversation.** In addition to all the wisdom I received from my teachers, the fact that I constantly
speak about the commandments has given me the ability to surpass them in knowledge.

100 **I gain insight from the elders, for I uphold Your edicts** and am thereby better able to hear
and absorb the wisdom they impart.

קא מִכָּל־אֹרַח רָע כָּלִאתִי רַגְלָי
לְמַעַן אֶשְׁמֹר דְּבָרֶךָ:

קב מִמִּשְׁפָּטֶיךָ לֹא־סָרְתִּי כִּי־
אַתָּה הוֹרֵתָנִי:

קג מַה־נִּמְלְצוּ לְחִכִּי אִמְרָתֶךָ
מִדְּבַשׁ לְפִי:

קד מִפִּקּוּדֶיךָ אֶתְבּוֹנָן עַל־כֵּן
שָׂנֵאתִי ׀ כָּל־אֹרַח שָׁקֶר:

נ קה נֵר־לְרַגְלִי דְבָרֶךָ וְאוֹר
לִנְתִיבָתִי:

קו נִשְׁבַּעְתִּי וָאֲקַיֵּמָה לִשְׁמֹר
מִשְׁפְּטֵי צִדְקֶךָ:

קז נַעֲנֵיתִי עַד־מְאֹד יהוה חַיֵּנִי
כִדְבָרֶךָ:

¹⁰¹From all evil paths I bar my feet, so I might follow Your word.

¹⁰²I have not turned away from Your laws, for You Yourself have taught me.

¹⁰³How sweet is Your saying to my palate, more than honey to my mouth.

¹⁰⁴I gain insights from Your edicts; therefore, I hate every path of falsehood.

¹⁰⁵A lamp to my feet is Your word, and a light for my path.

¹⁰⁶I have sworn and will fulfill my oath, to follow Your righteous laws.

¹⁰⁷I am exceedingly afflicted; give me life, Lord, as befits Your word.

---

101 **From all evil paths I bar my feet.** I fetter my feet, as it were, in order to prevent myself from going to inappropriate places, **so I might follow Your word.**

102 **I have not turned away from Your laws, for You Yourself have taught me** the proper, true path.

103 **How sweet is Your saying to my palate, more than honey to my mouth.**

104 **I gain insight from Your edicts; therefore, I hate every path of falsehood.** Your laws teach me not only how to conduct myself but also how to discern the true value of things.

105 **A lamp to my feet is Your word,** because it guides me and shows me where to go, like a light in the dark **and a light for my path.**

106 **I have sworn and will fulfill my oath, to follow Your righteous laws.** Although Jewish law generally discourages taking vows and oaths, an exception is made for vows pertaining to the observance of commandments, as these provide impetus to act in cases where a person needs additional motivation to fulfill his obligations.

107 **I am exceedingly afflicted; give me life, Lord, as befits Your word.**

נְדְבוֹת פִּי רְצֵה־נָא יהוה
וּמִשְׁפָּטֶיךָ לַמְּדֵנִי:

נַפְשִׁי בְכַפִּי תָמִיד וְתוֹרָתְךָ
לֹא שָׁכָחְתִּי:

נָתְנוּ רְשָׁעִים פַּח לִי
וּמִפִּקּוּדֶיךָ לֹא תָעִיתִי:

נָחַלְתִּי עֵדְוֺתֶיךָ לְעוֹלָם כִּי־
שְׂשׂוֹן לִבִּי הֵמָּה:

נָטִיתִי לִבִּי לַעֲשׂוֹת חֻקֶּיךָ
לְעוֹלָם עֵקֶב:

סֵעֲפִים שָׂנֵאתִי וְתוֹרָתְךָ
אָהָבְתִּי:

סִתְרִי וּמָגִנִּי אָתָּה לִדְבָרְךָ
יִחָלְתִּי:

108 Please, Lord, accept the offerings of my mouth, and teach me Your laws.

109 My life is always in my hand, but I do not forget Your teaching.

110 The wicked set a snare for me, but I do not veer from Your edicts.

111 Your precepts are my possession forever, for they are the joy of my heart.

112 I incline my heart to carry out Your statutes forever, to the end.

113 I hate what is twisted, but I love Your teaching.

114 You are my shelter and shield; I hope for Your word.

---

108 **Please, Lord, accept** favorably **the offerings of my mouth,** such as my words, my prayers, and my songs, **and** continue to **teach me Your laws.**

109 **My life is always in my hand.** I am in such great and constant danger that it is as though I have to hold my life in my hand in order to protect it. **But** despite this, **I do not forget Your teaching.**

110 In a similar vein: **The wicked set a snare for me,** forcing me to alter my route to avoid them, **but** despite this, **I do not veer from Your edicts.**

111 **Your precepts are my possession forever,** my portion and inheritance in life. **For they are the joy of my heart,** not out of any special privilege, but simply because I love them so deeply.

112 **I incline my heart to carry out Your statutes forever, to the end,** to the last detail.

113 **I hate what is twisted.** The word *se'afim* is related to *se'ifim*, the branches of a tree, which extend outward in haphazard directions. Here it refers to people or ideas that are "twisted," not upright and truthful. **But I love Your teaching.**

114 **You are my shelter and** my **shield; I hope** in anxious anticipation **for Your word.**

קטו סוּרוּ מִמֶּנִּי מְרֵעִים וְאֶצְּרָה
מִצְוֺת אֱלֹהָי:

קטו סָמְכֵנִי כְאִמְרָתְךָ וְאֶחְיֶה
וְאַל־תְּבִישֵׁנִי מִשִּׂבְרִי:

קיז סְעָדֵנִי וְאִוָּשֵׁעָה וְאֶשְׁעָה
בְחֻקֶּיךָ תָמִיד:

קיח סָלִיתָ כָּל־שׁוֹגִים מֵחֻקֶּיךָ כִּי־
שֶׁקֶר תַּרְמִיתָם:

קיט סִגִים הִשְׁבַּתָּ כָל־רִשְׁעֵי־אָרֶץ
לָכֵן אָהַבְתִּי עֵדֹתֶיךָ:

[115] Depart from me, evildoers,
so I might uphold the
commandments of my God.

[116] Sustain me, as befits Your word,
so I might live. Let me not be
ashamed of my hope.

[117] Support me and I will be saved,
and I will always turn my
attention to Your statutes.

[118] You turn aside all those who
stray from Your statutes, for
their deception is a lie.

[119] Like dross, You destroy the
wicked of the earth; therefore I
love Your precepts.

---

[115] The psalmist prays, addressing himself to the sinners who torment him: **Depart from me,
evildoers, so I might uphold the commandments of my God** without hindrance.

[116] **Sustain me, as befits Your word, so I might live,** so I might survive the attacks of the
evildoers, alternatively, so I might live a good life. **Let me not be ashamed of my hope,** shame
that would come about by Your not granting me the ability to realize my aspirations.

[117] **Support me and I will** thereby **be saved. And** then, when I can be relieved of the need to
battle evil, **I will** be free to **always turn my attention to Your statutes.**

[118] **You turn aside all those who stray from Your statutes, for their deception is a lie.**
Evildoers attempt to justify their actions by means of deceptions and excuses. These justifications,
however, are nothing but lies.

[119] **Like dross, You destroy the wicked of the earth.** The wicked are likened to dross, waste that
is separated from precious metal and discarded. **Therefore I love Your precepts,** so I should
not be treated in this fashion.

קכ סָמַר מִפַּחְדְּךָ בְשָׂרִי
וּמִמִּשְׁפָּטֶיךָ יָרֵאתִי:

ע קכא עָשִׂיתִי מִשְׁפָּט וָצֶדֶק בַּל־
תַּנִּיחֵנִי לְעֹשְׁקָי:

קכב עֲרֹב עַבְדְּךָ לְטוֹב אַל־
יַעַשְׁקֻנִי זֵדִים:

קכג עֵינַי כָּלוּ לִישׁוּעָתֶךָ וּלְאִמְרַת
צִדְקֶךָ:

קכד עֲשֵׂה עִם־עַבְדְּךָ כְחַסְדֶּךָ
וְחֻקֶּיךָ לַמְּדֵנִי:

קכה עַבְדְּךָ־אָנִי הֲבִינֵנִי וְאֵדְעָה
עֵדֹתֶיךָ:

120 My flesh prickles in fright because of You, for I fear Your judgments.

121 I have practiced justice and righteousness; do not leave me to my oppressors.

122 Vouch for Your servant, for good. Keep evildoers from oppressing me.

123 My eyes pine for Your salvation and Your righteous word.

124 Deal with Your servant as befits Your kindness, and teach me Your statutes.

125 I am Your servant; give me understanding, so I might know Your precepts.

---

120 **My flesh prickles in fright,** or the hair of my body stands on end, **because of You, for I fear Your judgments.** Although this psalm is full of expressions of love and devotion, there are also many verses like this one that convey fear and awe of God.

121 **I have practiced justice and righteousness,** so **do not leave me to my oppressors.**

122 **Vouch for Your servant, for good.** Grant me protection. The word *arov*, translated here as "vouch for," literally refers to one who undertakes to be the guarantor of a loan. **Keep evildoers from oppressing me.**

123 **My eyes pine for Your salvation,** Your assistance in times of trouble, **and** I also long for **Your righteous word,** by which You will grant me instruction for my future conduct.

124 **Deal with Your servant** beneficently, **as befits Your kindness.** Consider me with Your attribute of mercy; do not judge me harshly for my sins. **And teach me Your statutes.**

125 **I am Your servant; give me understanding, so I might know Your precepts.**

עֵת לַעֲשׂוֹת לַיהוָה הֵפֵרוּ תּוֹרָתֶךָ:

קכו

עַל־כֵּן אָהַבְתִּי מִצְוֹתֶיךָ מִזָּהָב וּמִפָּז:

קכז

עַל־כֵּן ׀ כָּל־פִּקּוּדֵי כֹל יִשָּׁרְתִּי כָּל־אֹרַח שֶׁקֶר שָׂנֵאתִי:

קכח

פְּלָאוֹת עֵדְוֹתֶיךָ עַל־כֵּן נְצָרָתַם נַפְשִׁי:

קכט

פ

פֵּתַח־דְּבָרֶיךָ יָאִיר מֵבִין פְּתָיִים:

קל

פִּי־פָעַרְתִּי וָאֶשְׁאָפָה כִּי לְמִצְוֹתֶיךָ יָאָבְתִּי:

קלא

126 It is time to act for the Lord, for they have violated Your teaching.

127 Indeed, I love Your commandments more than gold, more than fine gold.

128 Indeed, I have dealt straightly with all Your edicts; I hate every false path.

129 Your precepts are wondrous, therefore my soul upholds them.

130 Your opening words enlighten; they bring understanding to the simple.

131 I open my mouth wide and breathe in deep, longing for Your commandments.

---

126 **It is time to act for the Lord, for they have violated Your teaching.** When a time arrives that the Torah has been widely abandoned, we are obligated to act with renewed effort and urgency.

127 **Indeed, I love Your commandments more than gold, more than fine gold.**

128 **Indeed, I have dealt straightly with all Your edicts.** I try to stay on the straight path of Your commandments. **I hate every false path,** shunning everything that deviates from the straight path.

129 **Your precepts are wondrous, therefore my soul upholds them.**

130 **Your opening words enlighten.** From the very start, Your words bring enlightenment. **They bring understanding** even **to the simple.** Even those who are totally ignorant are granted a glimmer of understanding, already at the very beginning of their study.

131 **I open my mouth wide and breathe in deep, longing for Your commandments.** I open my mouth as if to inhale whatever I can from the commandments, so great is my desire for them.

פְּנֵה־אֵלַי וְחָנֵּנִי כְּמִשְׁפָּט
לְאֹהֲבֵי שְׁמֶךָ:

פְּעָמַי הָכֵן בְּאִמְרָתֶךָ וְאַל־
תַּשְׁלֶט־בִּי כָל־אָוֶן:

פְּדֵנִי מֵעֹשֶׁק אָדָם וְאֶשְׁמְרָה
פִּקּוּדֶיךָ:

פָּנֶיךָ הָאֵר בְּעַבְדֶּךָ וְלַמְּדֵנִי
אֶת־חֻקֶּיךָ:

פַּלְגֵי־מַיִם יָרְדוּ עֵינָי עַל לֹא־
שָׁמְרוּ תוֹרָתֶךָ:

צַדִּיק אַתָּה יהוה וְיָשָׁר
מִשְׁפָּטֶיךָ:

צִוִּיתָ צֶדֶק עֵדֹתֶיךָ וֶאֱמוּנָה
מְאֹד:

קלב Turn to me and treat me graciously, as befits those who love Your name.

קלג Make my footsteps firm with Your saying; let no wrongdoing rule over me.

קלד Redeem me from the oppression of man, so I might follow Your edicts.

קלה Shine Your face on Your servant, and teach me Your statutes.

קלו Streams of water flow from my eyes, for those who do not follow Your teaching.

קלז Righteous are You, Lord, and upright are Your judgments.

קלח With Your precepts, You greatly ordain righteousness and faith.

צ

---

132 **Turn to me and treat me graciously, as befits those who love Your name.**

133 **Make my footsteps firm with Your saying** so that You **let no wrongdoing rule over me.**

134 **Redeem me from the oppression of man, so I might follow Your edicts,** for my enemies' constant oppression prevents me from devoting myself fully to following Your commandments.

135 **Shine Your face on Your servant,** show me Your favor, **and teach me Your statutes**.

136 **Streams of water flow from my eyes,** so profusely do I weep **for those who do not follow Your teaching.**

137 **Righteous are You** at all times, **Lord, and upright are Your judgments,** even if we are not always able to understand how they are fair.

138 **With Your precepts, You greatly ordain righteousness and faith.** With Your commandments, You show the path to righteousness and faith, for these two qualities are embedded in all the precepts of the Torah.

צַמְּתַ֫תְנִי קִנְאָתִ֑י כִּי־שָׁכְח֖וּ
דְבָרֶ֣יךָ צָרָֽי׃

צְרוּפָ֖ה אִמְרָתְךָ֣ מְאֹ֑ד
וְֽעַבְדְּךָ֥ אֲהֵבָֽהּ׃

צָעִ֣יר אָנֹכִ֣י וְנִבְזֶ֑ה פִּ֝קֻּדֶ֗יךָ
לֹ֣א שָׁכָֽחְתִּי׃

צִדְקָֽתְךָ֣ צֶ֣דֶק לְעוֹלָ֑ם
וְֽתוֹרָתְךָ֥ אֱמֶֽת׃

צַר־וּמָצ֥וֹק מְצָא֑וּנִי מִ֝צְוֺתֶ֗יךָ
שַׁעֲשֻׁעָֽי׃

צֶ֖דֶק עֵֽדְוֺתֶ֣יךָ לְעוֹלָ֑ם הֲבִינֵ֥נִי
וְאֶחְיֶֽה׃

קָרָ֣אתִי בְכָל־לֵ֭ב עֲנֵ֣נִי יְהֹוָ֑ה   ק
חֻקֶּ֥יךָ אֶצֹּֽרָה׃

139My zealotry consumes me,
   for my foes have forgotten
   Your words.

140Your saying is exceedingly pure,
   and Your servant loves it.

141Young am I, and disdained. Yet
   I do not forget Your edicts.

142Your righteousness is eternal.
   Your teaching is truth.

143Trouble and distress
   have found me; Your
   commandments are my delight.

144Your precepts are forever
   righteous. Give me
   understanding, so I might live.

145I call out wholeheartedly;
   answer me, Lord. I will uphold
   Your statutes.

---

139 **My zealotry consumes me, for my foes have forgotten Your words.** I am consumed by anger against those who ignore Your words.

140 **Your saying is exceedingly pure, and Your servant loves it.**

141 **Young** and inexperienced **am I,** with limited knowledge, **and** I am therefore **disdained,** regarded as unworthy, both in my own eyes and in those of others. **Yet** despite this, **I do not forget Your edicts.**

142 **Your righteousness is eternal. Your teaching is truth.**

143 **Trouble and distress have found me** often during my life, but offsetting my suffering is the fact that **Your commandments are my delight.**

144 **Your precepts are forever righteous. Give me understanding, so I might live,** by understanding and cleaving to Your laws.

145 **I call out wholeheartedly** to You; **answer me, Lord,** and as a result of Your assistance, **I will** be better able to **uphold Your statutes.**

קָרָאתִ֣יךָ הוֹשִׁיעֵ֑נִי וְ֝אֶשְׁמְרָ֗ה עֵדֹתֶֽיךָ׃

¹⁴⁶I call out to You; save me, and I will follow Your precepts.

קִדַּ֣מְתִּי בַ֭נֶּשֶׁף וָאֲשַׁוֵּ֑עָה לִדְבָרְךָ֥ יִחָֽלְתִּי׃

¹⁴⁷I rise before dawn and cry for help; for Your word I do wait.

קִדְּמ֣וּ עֵ֭ינַי אַשְׁמֻר֑וֹת לָ֝שִׂ֗יחַ בְּאִמְרָתֶֽךָ׃

¹⁴⁸My eyes precede the night watches to reflect on Your word.

קוֹלִ֣י שִׁמְעָ֣ה כְחַסְדֶּ֑ךָ יְהֹוָ֗ה כְּֽמִשְׁפָּטֶ֥ךָ חַיֵּֽנִי׃

¹⁴⁹Hear my voice, as befits Your kindness; Lord, give me life when You judge me.

קָ֭רְבוּ רֹדְפֵ֣י זִמָּ֑ה מִתּוֹרָתְךָ֥ רָחָֽקוּ׃

¹⁵⁰Pursuers of loathsomeness draw near; they distance themselves from Your teaching.

קָר֣וֹב אַתָּ֣ה יְהֹוָ֑ה וְֽכָל־מִצְוֺתֶ֥יךָ אֱמֶֽת׃

¹⁵¹You are near, Lord, and all Your commandments are truth.

קֶ֣דֶם יָ֭דַעְתִּי מֵעֵדֹתֶ֑יךָ כִּ֖י לְעוֹלָ֣ם יְסַדְתָּֽם׃

¹⁵²Your precepts, I know, are of old; You established them for eternity.

---

¹⁴⁶ **I call out to You; save me, and I will follow Your precepts.**

¹⁴⁷ **I rise before dawn and cry for help; for Your word I do wait.**

¹⁴⁸ **My eyes precede the** late **night watches,** I wake up while it is still nighttime, **to reflect on Your word.**

¹⁴⁹ **Hear my voice, as befits Your kindness; Lord, give me life when You judge me** mercifully.

¹⁵⁰ **Pursuers of loathsomeness draw near** to their sinful ambitions. The word *zima*, translated here as "loathsomeness," refers to wickedness in general and debauchery in particular. **They distance themselves from Your teaching.** They do not realize that the path they have chosen leads them farther and farther away from Your Torah.

¹⁵¹ **You are near** to me, **Lord, and all Your commandments are truth.**

¹⁵² **Your precepts, I know, are of old,** from the very beginning of time; **You established them for eternity.** And since they are eternal, I can always cleave to them.

ר

^{קנג}רְאֵה־עָנְיִי וְחַלְּצֵנִי כִּי־
תוֹרָתְךָ לֹא שָׁכָחְתִּי:

^{קנד}רִיבָה רִיבִי וּגְאָלֵנִי לְאִמְרָתְךָ
חַיֵּנִי:

^{קנה}רָחוֹק מֵרְשָׁעִים יְשׁוּעָה כִּי־
חֻקֶּיךָ לֹא דָרָשׁוּ:

^{קנו}רַחֲמֶיךָ רַבִּים ׀ יהוה
כְּמִשְׁפָּטֶיךָ חַיֵּנִי:

^{קנז}רַבִּים רֹדְפַי וְצָרָי מֵעֵדְוֹתֶיךָ
לֹא נָטִיתִי:

^{קנח}רָאִיתִי בֹגְדִים וָאֶתְקוֹטָטָה
אֲשֶׁר אִמְרָתְךָ לֹא שָׁמָרוּ:

¹⁵³See my affliction and rescue me, for I have not forgotten Your teaching.

¹⁵⁴Plead my cause and redeem me; give me life, as befits Your promise.

¹⁵⁵Salvation is far from the wicked, for they do not seek Your statutes.

¹⁵⁶Great are Your mercies, Lord; give me life when You judge me.

¹⁵⁷Many are my pursuers and my foes, yet I do not veer from Your precepts.

¹⁵⁸I see traitors and contend with them, for they do not follow Your word.

---

153 **See my affliction and rescue me, for I have not forgotten Your teaching.**

154 **Plead my cause and redeem me; give me life, as befits Your promise.**

155 **Salvation is far from the wicked, for they do not seek Your statutes** and do not merit Your intervention on their behalf.

156 **Great are Your mercies, Lord; give me life when You judge me** in accordance with those mercies.

157 **Many are my pursuers and my foes,** and I am forced to take action to protect myself from my enemies, **yet I do not veer from Your precepts.**

158 **I see traitors and contend with them,** but not **for** my own sake; rather, it is because **they do not follow Your word.**

קנט רְאֵה כִּי־פִקּוּדֶיךָ אָהָבְתִּי
יהוה כְּחַסְדְּךָ חַיֵּנִי:

קס רֹאשׁ־דְּבָרְךָ אֱמֶת וּלְעוֹלָם
כָּל־מִשְׁפַּט צִדְקֶךָ:

קסא שָׂרִים רְדָפוּנִי חִנָּם וּמִדְּבָרֶיךָ ש
וּמִדְּבָ פָּחַד לִבִּי:

קסב שָׂשׂ אָנֹכִי עַל־אִמְרָתֶךָ
כְּמוֹצֵא שָׁלָל רָב:

קסג שֶׁקֶר שָׂנֵאתִי וַאֲתַעֵבָה
תּוֹרָתְךָ אָהָבְתִּי:

קסד שֶׁבַע בַּיּוֹם הִלַּלְתִּיךָ עַל
מִשְׁפְּטֵי צִדְקֶךָ:

159 See how I love Your edicts; Lord, give me life, as befits Your kindness.

160 Your word begins in truth; eternal are all Your righteous laws.

161 Princes pursue me without cause, yet my heart fears Your words.

162 I rejoice at Your sayings, as one who finds great spoils.

163 I hate and abhor falsehood; I love Your teaching.

164 Seven times a day do I praise You for Your righteous laws.

---

159 **See how I love Your edicts; Lord, give me life, as befits Your kindness.**

160 **Your word begins in truth; eternal are all Your righteous laws.** Introductory words of some written works are of minor importance, but regarding Your Torah, everything You have said and ordained, from the very first word, is true and eternal.

161 **Princes,** that is, people in powerful positions, **pursue me without cause, yet my heart fears** only **Your words,** not their threats.

162 **I rejoice at Your sayings, as one who finds great spoils.**

163 **I hate and abhor falsehood,** but **I love Your teaching.**

164 **Seven times a day do I praise You for Your righteous laws.** It would appear that the number seven here is not an exact number, but as elsewhere in the Torah, it means many times. However, there are those who maintain that there are indeed seven daily prayers: the morning, afternoon, and evening prayers, plus the blessings after meals three times a day and the *Shema* prayer recited at bedtime.

קסה שָׁלוֹם רָב לְאֹהֲבֵי תוֹרָתֶךָ
וְאֵין־לָמוֹ מִכְשׁוֹל:

קסו שִׂבַּרְתִּי לִישׁוּעָתְךָ יהוה
וּמִצְוֹתֶיךָ עָשִׂיתִי:

קסז שָׁמְרָה נַפְשִׁי עֵדֹתֶיךָ וָאֹהֲבֵם
מְאֹד:

קסח שָׁמַרְתִּי פִקּוּדֶיךָ וְעֵדֹתֶיךָ כִּי
כָל־דְּרָכַי נֶגְדֶּךָ:

ת קסט תִּקְרַב רִנָּתִי לְפָנֶיךָ יהוה
כִּדְבָרְךָ הֲבִינֵנִי:

ק תָּבוֹא תְחִנָּתִי לְפָנֶיךָ
כְּאִמְרָתְךָ הַצִּילֵנִי:

165 Those who love Your teaching know great peace; for them there is no obstacle.

166 I await Your salvation, Lord, and I have fulfilled Your commandments.

167 My soul follows Your precepts, and I love them exceedingly.

168 I follow Your edicts and Your precepts, for all my ways are before You.

169 Let my song draw near You, Lord; give me understanding, as befits Your word.

170 Let my plea come before You; rescue me, as befits Your promise.

---

165 **Those who love Your teaching know great peace; for them there is no obstacle,** because this great peace, granted by God, protects them.

166 **I await Your salvation, Lord, and I have fulfilled Your commandments,** even now, when Your salvation has not yet come.

167 **My soul follows your precepts, and I love them exceedingly.** I keep Your commandments not only out of a sense of obligation but because I have an emotional connection to them.

168 **I follow Your edicts and Your precepts.** Indeed, I am obliged to do so, and I in fact have no alternative, **for all my ways are before You,** and You are aware of everything I do.

169 **Let my song draw near You, Lord.** That is, accept my prayer favorably. **Give me understanding, as befits Your word.**

170 **Let my plea come before You; rescue me, as befits Your promise.**

קעא תַּבַּעְנָה שְׂפָתַי תְּהִלָּה כִּי
תְלַמְּדֵנִי חֻקֶּיךָ:

171 Let my lips utter praise, for You teach me Your statutes.

קעב תַּעַן לְשׁוֹנִי אִמְרָתֶךָ כִּי כָל־
מִצְוֹתֶיךָ צֶּדֶק:

172 Let my tongue declare Your saying, for all Your commandments are just.

קעג תְּהִי־יָדְךָ לְעָזְרֵנִי כִּי פִקּוּדֶיךָ
בָחָרְתִּי:

173 Let Your hand be ready to help me, for I have chosen Your edicts.

קעד תָּאַבְתִּי לִישׁוּעָתְךָ יְהוָה
וְתוֹרָתְךָ שַׁעֲשֻׁעָי:

174 I long for Your salvation, Lord, and Your teaching is my delight.

קעה תְּחִי־נַפְשִׁי וּתְהַלְלֶךָּ
וּמִשְׁפָּטֶךָ יַעְזְרֻנִי:

175 May my soul live, so I might praise You; may Your laws come to my aid.

קעו תָּעִיתִי כְּשֶׂה אֹבֵד בַּקֵּשׁ
עַבְדֶּךָ כִּי מִצְוֹתֶיךָ לֹא
שָׁכָחְתִּי:

176 I have gone astray like a lost sheep. Seek Your servant, for I do not forget Your commandments.

---

171 **Let my lips utter praise, for You teach me Your statutes.** If You teach me Your laws, that will enable me both to speak about them and to offer words of praise for Your guidance.

172 **Let my tongue declare Your saying** aloud, **for all Your commandments are just.**

173 **Let Your hand be ready to help me, for I have chosen Your edicts.**

174 **I long for Your salvation, Lord, and Your teaching is my delight** at all times.

175 **May my soul live, so I might praise You; may Your laws come to my aid.**

176 **I have gone astray,** both physically and spiritually, **like a lost sheep. Seek Your servant,** as a shepherd searches for his lost sheep, **for** even when I am lost and cannot discern a straight path before me, **I do not forget Your commandments.**

SHABBAT

THE SONGS OF ASCENTS

Many explanations have been offered for the term "song of ascents," which introduces the next
fifteen psalms. According to one interpretation, "ascents" refers to journeys to the Temple in
Jerusalem for the three yearly pilgrimage festivals, and these fifteen songs were composed to be
sung by the pilgrims on those occasions. Another opinion is that "ascents" refers to the fifteen stairs
by which one ascended from the outer courtyard to the inner, sacred courtyard of the Temple area,
upon which the Levites would stand with their instruments and sing these psalms. Yet another
opinion is that the term refers to a particular kind of musical style, like many
similarly unfamiliar terms found in the introductory verses of other psalms.

PSALM 120

The first of the Songs of Ascents, a supplication for relief from the distress
stemming from hostility on the part of internal and external enemies. The psalmist
also expresses his gratitude to God for answering his prayers.

כו לחודש
27th day
of month

שִׁיר הַמַּעֲלוֹת אֶל־יהוה
בַּצָּרָתָה לִּי קָרָאתִי וַיַּעֲנֵנִי׃

יהוה הַצִּילָה נַפְשִׁי מִשְּׂפַת־
שֶׁקֶר מִלָּשׁוֹן רְמִיָּה׃

מַה־יִּתֵּן לְךָ וּמַה־יֹּסִיף לָךְ
לָשׁוֹן רְמִיָּה׃

1 A song of ascents. I called out
to the Lord in my distress, and
He answered me.

2 Lord, save me from lying lips,
from a deceitful tongue.

3 What gain will it give you,
deceitful tongue? What will
it avail?

PSALM 120

1 **A song of ascents. I called out to the Lord in my distress, and He answered me.**

2 **Lord, save me from lying lips,** save me from the lies that people are spreading about me, **from a deceitful tongue.**

3 To this, the psalmist adds words of reproof: Lies, deceit, and slander offer nothing but twisted satisfaction to those who wish to harm others. **What gain will it give you, deceitful tongue? What will it avail?** While slander often spreads quickly and reaches a large number of people, causing great harm, it rarely benefits the slanderer.

חִצֵּי גִבּוֹר שְׁנוּנִים עָם גַּחֲלֵי
רְתָמִים:

Sharp arrows of the warrior, burning coals of the broom bush.

אוֹיָה־לִי כִּי־גַרְתִּי מֶשֶׁךְ
שָׁכַנְתִּי עִם־אָהֳלֵי קֵדָר:

Woe is me, that I sojourn in Meshekh, that I dwell among the tents of Kedar.

רַבַּת שָׁכְנָה־לָּהּ נַפְשִׁי עִם
שׂוֹנֵא שָׁלוֹם:

My soul has long dwelt with those who hate peace.

אֲנִי־שָׁלוֹם וְכִי אֲדַבֵּר הֵמָּה
לַמִּלְחָמָה:

I am all peace; yet when I speak, they are for war.

PSALM 121

A song of trust in God that is intended for all, even those who might seem to be utterly defenseless. It contains words of reassurance and encouragement rather than prayer.

שִׁיר לַמַּעֲלוֹת אֶשָּׂא עֵינַי
אֶל־הֶהָרִים מֵאַיִן יָבֹא עֶזְרִי:

A song of ascents. I lift my eyes to the mountains; from where will my help come?

---

4 Indeed, in some instances, the slanderer not only receives no benefit from his malicious speech but is actually punished, whether directly or indirectly, and all he receives as a consequence of his malicious speech are the **sharp arrows of the warrior** that are aimed at him, and **burning coals of the broom bush,** which burn for a considerable amount of time. Far from being rewarded, the slanderer will be punished with prolonged suffering.

5 The psalmist shifts to the suffering that is experienced by a person who is being maligned. Such a person feels akin to one facing hostile forces on all sides. **Woe is me, that I sojourn in Meshekh,** a nation residing outside of the borders of the Land of Israel, **that I dwell among the tents of Kedar,** that is, Ishmaelites or Arabs. Both groups displayed longstanding hostility toward Israel and posed a continual threat of war.

6 **My soul has long dwelt,** that is, I find myself dwelling, **with those who hate peace.**

7 **I am all peace,** I desire peace; **yet when I speak** to them, **they are for war.**

PSALM 121

1 **A song of ascents. I lift my eyes to the mountains; from where will my help come?**

עֶזְרִי מֵעִם יהוה עֹשֵׂה שָׁמַיִם
וָאָרֶץ:

2 My help is from the Lord,
Maker of heaven and earth.

אַל־יִתֵּן לַמּוֹט רַגְלֶךָ אַל־
יָנוּם שֹׁמְרֶךָ:

3 He will not let your foot give
way. He who watches over you
will not slumber.

הִנֵּה לֹא־יָנוּם וְלֹא יִישָׁן
שׁוֹמֵר יִשְׂרָאֵל:

4 Behold, the Guardian of Israel
neither slumbers nor sleeps.

יהוה שֹׁמְרֶךָ יהוה צִלְּךָ עַל־
יַד יְמִינֶךָ:

5 The Lord is your guardian; the
Lord is your shade by your
right hand.

יוֹמָם הַשֶּׁמֶשׁ לֹא־יַכֶּכָּה וְיָרֵחַ
בַּלָּיְלָה:

6 By day, the sun will not strike
you, nor the moon at night.

The opening verse depicts an individual, possibly someone who is under siege or who belongs to an armed force facing imminent attack, who looks to the mountains, hoping to see signs of help on the way.

2 The psalmist answers his own question. There may in fact not be any help coming in the form of soldiers from the mountains. But that does not matter, for **my help is from the Lord, Maker of heaven and earth.** It is God who rules over the entire world, with all power in His hands.

3 The petitioner of the previous verses is now told: **He,** God, **will not let your foot give way. He who watches over you will not slumber.**

4 **Behold, the Guardian of Israel neither slumbers nor sleeps.** For the "Guardian of Israel," identified in the following verse as God, the concept of sleep does not apply.

5 **The Lord is your guardian.** As a guardian, God is so close to you that it is as if **the Lord is your shade,** your shadow, **by your right hand.** In this context, "right hand" conveys the notion of assistance and rescue.

6 God provides protection not only against human foes but also against perils of any other sort. **By day, the sun will not strike you,** afflicting you with its heat, **nor the moon at night.** At night, when the moon shines, no harm will befall you either.

יְהֹוָה יִשְׁמָרְךָ מִכָּל־רָע
יִשְׁמֹר אֶת־נַפְשֶׁךָ:

> 7 The Lord will guard you from all evil; He will guard your life.

יְהֹוָה יִשְׁמָר־צֵאתְךָ וּבוֹאֶךָ
מֵעַתָּה וְעַד־עוֹלָם:

> 8 The Lord will guard your going and your coming, from now until eternity.

PSALM 122

A psalm of joy and praise to Jerusalem, sung by pilgrims making their ascent to the city during the three pilgrimage festivals. The psalm describes the city in its glory at the time of the Temple, when all the tribes would get together, and when the city served as the center of sovereignty of the Jewish nation.

שִׁיר הַמַּעֲלוֹת לְדָוִד שָׂמַחְתִּי
בְּאֹמְרִים לִי בֵּית יְהֹוָה נֵלֵךְ:

> 1 A song of ascents, of David. I rejoiced when they said to me: Let us go to the House of the Lord.

עֹמְדוֹת הָיוּ רַגְלֵינוּ בִּשְׁעָרַיִךְ
יְרוּשָׁלָ͏ִם:

> 2 Our feet are standing at your gates, Jerusalem.

---

7 **The Lord will guard you from all evil; He will guard your life.**
8 **The Lord will guard your going and your coming.** God will watch over you whenever you leave your home, wherever your travels take you, both there and back, **from now until eternity.**

PSALM 122
1 **A song of ascents, of David.** "Of David" could indicate David's authorship of this psalm, but it can also mean that it was written by someone else in his honor. **I rejoiced when they said to me: Let us go to the House of the Lord.** The ascent to Jerusalem is a joyous experience in its own right.
2 As the pilgrims approach the entrance to Jerusalem, they say: **Our feet are standing at your gates, Jerusalem.**

ָיְרוּשָׁלַ֖͏ִם הַבְּנוּיָ֑ה כְּעִ֕יר
שֶׁחֻבְּרָה־לָּ֥הּ יַחְדָּֽו׃

שֶׁשָּׁ֨ם עָל֪וּ שְׁבָטִ֡ים שִׁבְטֵי־
יָ֭הּ עֵד֣וּת לְיִשְׂרָאֵ֑ל לְ֝הֹד֗וֹת
לְשֵׁ֣ם יְהוָֽה׃

כִּ֤י שָׁ֨מָּה ׀ יָשְׁב֣וּ כִסְא֣וֹת
לְמִשְׁפָּ֑ט כִּ֝סְא֗וֹת לְבֵ֣ית דָּוִֽד׃

שַׁאֲל֗וּ שְׁל֥וֹם יְרוּשָׁלָ֑͏ִם
יִ֝שְׁלָ֗יוּ אֹהֲבָֽיִךְ׃

יְהִי־שָׁל֥וֹם בְּחֵילֵ֑ךְ שַׁ֝לְוָ֗ה
בְּאַרְמְנוֹתָֽיִךְ׃

3 The built-up Jerusalem is like a
city joined together.

4 There the tribes went up, the
tribes of the Lord, a testimony
for Israel, to give thanks to the
name of the Lord.

5 For there stood the thrones of
judgment, thrones of the house
of David.

6 Pray for the peace of Jerusalem;
may those who love you be
tranquil.

7 May peace be within your walls,
tranquility within your towers.

---

3 From our vantage point at the city's gates, we can see how **the built-up Jerusalem is like a
city** that has been **joined together,** in a literal sense. The city was built on a cluster of adjacent
hills that, before the time of David, may have been separate civic, and perhaps also military, units.
It was David who unified the city, though it was only during the reign of Solomon that the wall
encompassing it was built.

4 **There,** to Jerusalem, **the tribes went up, the tribes of the Lord, a testimony for Israel,**
who made the pilgrimage there **to give thanks to the name of the Lord.**

5 The psalmist now sings the praise of Jerusalem, which is not only the Holy City but also the capital:
For there stood the thrones of judgment, as it was the seat of the supreme court of justice,
which convened near the Temple and the king's palace, and it was there that were situated the
thrones of the house of David. David and his descendants who reigned after him acted as
both rulers and judges in all civil matters.

6 The psalmist offers his blessing to Jerusalem: **Pray for the peace of Jerusalem; may those
who love you be tranquil.** The psalmist asks that those who love Jerusalem, the ones who
pray for its peace, themselves be rewarded with peace and tranquility. The unusual word *yishlayu,*
"be tranquil," might be used here because of its consonance with the word *sha'alu,* "pray."

7 A further prayer for Jerusalem: **May peace be within your walls,** *heilekh* referring to a
secondary, lower wall that surrounds parts of the main, fully fortified city wall, **tranquility
within your towers.** *Armonot,* translated here as "towers," usually refers to large palaces, but it
can also connote fortresses.

לְמַעַן אַחַי וְרֵעָי אֲדַבְּרָה־נָּא
שָׁלוֹם בָּךְ:

8 For the sake of my brothers and companions, I now say: Peace be with you.

לְמַעַן בֵּית־יהוה אֱלֹהֵינוּ
אֲבַקְשָׁה טוֹב לָךְ:

9 For the sake of the House of the Lord our God, I seek your good.

PSALM 123

A song of entreaty and plea for assistance, written from the perspective
of one who is downtrodden and held in contempt.

שִׁיר הַמַּעֲלוֹת אֵלֶיךָ נָשָׂאתִי
אֶת־עֵינַי הַיֹּשְׁבִי בַּשָּׁמָיִם:

1 A song of ascents. I lift my eyes to You, who dwell in heaven.

הִנֵּה כְעֵינֵי עֲבָדִים אֶל־יַד
אֲדוֹנֵיהֶם כְּעֵינֵי שִׁפְחָה אֶל־
יַד גְּבִרְתָּהּ כֵּן עֵינֵינוּ אֶל־
יהוה אֱלֹהֵינוּ עַד שֶׁיְּחָנֵּנוּ:

2 Behold, as the eyes of servants to their master's hand, as the eyes of a maid to the hand of her mistress, so our eyes are to the Lord our God until He is gracious to us.

---

8 **For the sake of my brothers and companions,** my prayer for Jerusalem is on behalf of all those in the city, whether residents or visitors, **I now say: Peace be with you.**

9 **For the sake of the House of the Lord our God,** itself located here in Jerusalem, **I seek your good.**

PSALM 123

1 **A song of ascents.** I who am so distant from heaven, having reached the lowest point, **I lift my eyes to You;** I raise my eyes in prayer and supplication to You, **who dwell in heaven.**

2 **Behold, as the eyes of servants to their master's hand,** and even **as the eyes of a maid to the hand of her mistress,** for if male servants are dependent and submissive, even more so

חָנֵּנוּ יהוה חָנֵּנוּ כִּי־רַב
שָׂבַעְנוּ בוּז:

³ Be gracious to us, Lord; be gracious to us, for we are sated with scorn.

רַבַּת שָׂבְעָה־לָּהּ נַפְשֵׁנוּ
הַלַּעַג הַשַּׁאֲנַנִּים הַבּוּז
לְגַאֲיוֹנִים:

לִגְאֵי יוֹנִים

⁴ We are sated with the mockery of the complacent, the abuse of the arrogant.

PSALM 124

A psalm of thanksgiving to God for rescuing His servants
at a time when their situation appeared to be hopeless.

שִׁיר הַמַּעֲלוֹת לְדָוִד לוּלֵי
יהוה שֶׁהָיָה לָנוּ יֹאמַר־נָא
יִשְׂרָאֵל:

א A song of ascents, by David. Let Israel now say: Had it not been for the Lord, who was with us,

---

are maidservants, who are weaker, **so our eyes are to the Lord our God until He is gracious to us.** A "master's hand" is the source of giving and succor as well as punishment, and the slave has no recourse other than his master's goodwill. Similarly, our position vis-à-vis God is that of utter dependency and submission, and we are thus wholeheartedly beseeching His aid, in the knowledge that only He can help us.

3 And this is our prayer: **Be gracious to us, Lord; be gracious to us, for we are sated with scorn.** Beyond our other suffering, we have been subjected to a full measure of degradation.

4 **We are sated with the mockery of the complacent, the abuse of the arrogant.** The translation "of the arrogant" accords with the word as it is written in the text, as one word, *ligeyonim*. However, it is pronounced as two separate words, *ligei yonim*. Some explain the pronounced version as follows: *Ligei* refers to arrogant people, and *yonim* refers to those who cause harassment and distress by means of contemptuous words or deeds.

PSALM 124

1 **A song of ascents, by David.** In a certain sense, this psalm of thanksgiving comes as a response to the previous psalm of supplication, as it mentions not only a prayer to God but also His resulting salvation. It is not a description of complete salvation, but it nevertheless depicts extrication from

לוּלֵי יהוה שֶׁהָיָה לָנוּ בְּקוּם עָלֵינוּ אָדָם:

אֲזַי חַיִּים בְּלָעוּנוּ בַּחֲרוֹת אַפָּם בָּנוּ:

אֲזַי הַמַּיִם שְׁטָפוּנוּ נַחְלָה עָבַר עַל־נַפְשֵׁנוּ:

אֲזַי עָבַר עַל־נַפְשֵׁנוּ הַמַּיִם הַזֵּידוֹנִים:

בָּרוּךְ יהוה שֶׁלֹּא נְתָנָנוּ טֶרֶף לְשִׁנֵּיהֶם:

נַפְשֵׁנוּ כְּצִפּוֹר נִמְלְטָה מִפַּח יוֹקְשִׁים הַפַּח נִשְׁבָּר וַאֲנַחְנוּ נִמְלָטְנוּ:

2 had it not been for the Lord, who was with us when men rose against us,

3 they would have swallowed us alive when their anger was kindled against us.

4 Then the waters would have engulfed us; the torrent would have swept over us,

5 the wicked waters would have swept over us.

6 Blessed be the Lord, who did not give us over as prey to their teeth.

7 We were like a bird escaping from a trapper's snare. The snare broke, and we escaped.

---

a dire predicament. **Let Israel now say: Had it not been for the Lord, who was with us.** This is a song of gratitude on the part of the entire nation, as indicated by the phrase "Let Israel now say."

2 **Had it not been for the Lord,** had God not supported our cause, God **who was with us when men rose against us,** to fight against us and disparage us,

3 **they would have swallowed us alive when their anger was kindled against us.**

4 **Then,** if God had not come to our aid, **the waters would have engulfed us.** We would have been washed away by the "waters" of hordes of many nations;[8] **the torrent would have swept over us,**

5 **the wicked waters would have swept over us.** Since the waters mentioned in these verses is a metaphor for an outpouring of malice and evil, the word "wicked" is appropriate here.

6 Now follows a more explicit expression of thanks to God: **Blessed be the Lord, who did not give us over as prey to their teeth.** Although our enemies are continually lying in wait, God does not allow them to trap us.

7 **We were like a bird escaping from a trapper's snare.** It sometimes happens that a bird

עֶזְרֵנוּ בְּשֵׁם יהוֹה עֹשֵׂה ח 8 Our help is in the name of
שָׁמַיִם וָאָרֶץ: the Lord, Maker of heaven
                                                 and earth.

PSALM 125

A song of prayer and thanksgiving whose main theme is trust in God.

שִׁיר הַמַּעֲלוֹת הַבֹּטְחִים א 1 A song of ascents. Those
בַּיהוֹה כְּהַר־צִיּוֹן לֹא־יִמּוֹט   who trust in the Lord are like
לְעוֹלָם יֵשֵׁב: Mount Zion, which will never
                                                      topple and will forever endure.

יְרוּשָׁלַ͏ִם הָרִים סָבִיב לָהּ ב 2 Jerusalem, mountains
וַיהוֹה סָבִיב לְעַמּוֹ מֵעַתָּה   surround it, and the Lord
וְעַד־עוֹלָם: surrounds His people, from
                                                      now until eternity.

---

caught in a snare manages to break free of it. In our case as well, **the snare broke, and we escaped.**

8 This miraculous rescue occurred to us because **our help is in the name of the Lord, Maker of heaven and earth.**

PSALM 125

1 **A song of ascents. Those who trust in the Lord are like Mount Zion, which will never topple and will forever endure.**

2 This comparison elicits another: **Jerusalem, mountains surround it.** Jerusalem is not situated on the highest hill in the area but rather is surrounded by a number of hills of the same approximate height, which can serve to fortify the city from every direction. **And the Lord surrounds His people.** Just as Jerusalem is surrounded by mountains, so too God surrounds and protects His people from all evil, **from now until eternity.**

כִּי לֹ֤א יָנ֨וּחַ שֵׁ֥בֶט הָרֶ֗שַׁע עַל֮
גּוֹרַ֪ל הַֽצַּדִּ֫יקִ֥ים לְמַ֡עַן לֹא־
יִשְׁלְח֖וּ הַצַּדִּיקִ֥ים ׀ בְּעַוְלָ֗תָה
יְדֵיהֶֽם׃

הֵיטִ֣יבָה יְ֭הוָה לַטּוֹבִ֑ים
וְ֝לִֽישָׁרִ֗ים בְּלִבּוֹתָֽם׃

וְהַמַּטִּ֤ים עֲֽקַלְקַלּוֹתָ֗ם יוֹלִיכֵ֣ם
יְ֭הוָה אֶת־פֹּעֲלֵ֣י הָאָ֑וֶן שָׁל֗וֹם
עַל־יִשְׂרָאֵֽל׃

3 Indeed, the rod of wickedness will not rest upon the lot of the righteous, lest the righteous set their hands to wrongdoing.

4 Be good, Lord, to those who are good, and to the upright of heart.

5 As for those who twist their crooked ways, may the Lord lead them away with the evildoers. Peace be to Israel.

---

3 **Indeed, the rod of wickedness will not rest upon the lot of the righteous.** *Shevet*, translated here as "rod," also refers to the scepter of a ruler. God will not allow the righteous to fall under the rule of evil sovereigns, **lest the righteous set their hands to wrongdoing,** for when evil men rule, even righteous people, in order to survive, have no choice but to be compliant to a greater or lesser extent, and then it is as if they themselves participate in wrongdoing.

4 **Be good, Lord, to those who are good, and to the upright of heart,** that is, all those who always refrain from entering a world of evil and wrongdoing.

5 **As for those who twist their crooked ways,** as opposed to the righteous people mentioned in the previous verse, they believe they are permitted to act in devious ways in order to gain something or to extricate themselves from evil. Even though they are not really wicked, they "twist their crooked ways," that is, they will not only follow crooked routes but will also make such paths even more twisted than they are. **May the Lord lead them away with the evildoers.** Because they are not honest and upright, God will carry them off with the outright evildoers. **Peace be to Israel.** In contrast, when people follow a path of righteousness and integrity, there will be peace upon Israel.

PSALM 126

A song of praise about the time of the final redemption, which, when it arrives,
will make the previous experiences of suffering seem like a mere dream. The past will then
be read differently, revealed as a period of toil and preparation for the ultimate reward.

שִׁיר הַמַּעֲלוֹת בְּשׁוּב יהוה
אֶת־שִׁיבַת צִיּוֹן הָיִינוּ
כְּחֹלְמִים:

אָז יִמָּלֵא שְׂחוֹק פִּינוּ
וּלְשׁוֹנֵנוּ רִנָּה אָז יֹאמְרוּ
בַגּוֹיִם הִגְדִּיל יהוה לַעֲשׂוֹת
עִם־אֵלֶּה:

1 A song of ascents. When the
Lord brings about the return to
Zion, we are like dreamers.

2 Then our mouths are filled
with laughter, and our tongues
with song. Then the nations
say: The Lord has done great
things for them.

PSALM 126

1 **A song of ascents. When the Lord brings about the return to Zion, we are like dreamers.** All the commentaries, from the time of the Talmud onward, interpret the phrase "we are like dreamers" as describing not the time of redemption, which will seem to be the fulfillment of a dream, but rather the time of exile, which is dreamlike in the sense that it is abnormal, even nightmarish. When we dream, we perceive the dream to be actual reality that is coherent and meaningful, despite its many distortions, such as those regarding the relationship between ruler and ruled, or between truth and lies. Similarly, it is only with redemption, when we are restored to a true, nondistorted state of being, that we come to an awareness of how dreamlike our entire exilic existence actually was.

2 **Then our mouths are filled with laughter, and our tongues with song.** The emphasis here is on "filled." While we certainly do laugh even when in exile, our laughter is always tempered by the knowledge that there are many things wrong with the world, and we are in a situation that constrains joy. Only with redemption will we be able to laugh wholeheartedly, without a trace of sadness. In addition, **then the nations say: The Lord has done great things for them.** Even people from foreign and distant lands will speak about our redemption as a remarkable and unprecedented event.

הִגְדִּיל יְהוָה לַעֲשׂוֹת עִמָּנוּ
הָיִינוּ שְׂמֵחִים:

שׁוּבָה יְהוָה אֶת־שְׁבוּתֵנוּ
כַּאֲפִיקִים בַּנֶּגֶב:

הַזֹּרְעִים בְּדִמְעָה בְּרִנָּה
יִקְצֹרוּ:

הָלוֹךְ יֵלֵךְ ׀ וּבָכֹה נֹשֵׂא
מֶשֶׁךְ־הַזָּרַע בֹּא־יָבֹא בְרִנָּה
נֹשֵׂא אֲלֻמֹּתָיו:

שְׁבִיעִי

³ The Lord has done great things for us; we are joyful.

⁴ Lord, bring about our return, like riverbeds in the Negev.

⁵ Those who sow in tears, with joyous song they reap.

⁶ He who weeps as he walks to and fro, bearing his sack of seed, indeed returns in joyous song, bearing his sheaves.

---

3 And at that time, we too will be able to say that **the Lord has done great things for us.** He has done more for us than we deserve; His deliverance has exceeded our wildest expectations. Then we will be able to exclaim that **we are joyful** in the fullest sense.

4 **Lord, bring about our return, like riverbeds in the Negev.** Riverbeds of the Negev, the Land of Israel's southern desert, are almost always dry. The waters that do flow in them are the outcome of a distant rainfall, and they arrive without any advance warning in the form of clouds or wind; at once the riverbeds are filled with a torrent of water. This description is not only a plea for the coming of the redemption, for which we wait all the time, but also a prayer that it will come even if the existing reality makes it seem impossible. While redemption and exile are described here as two entirely different states of being, in truth they are linked. Exile, with all its concomitant suffering, serves as a kind of preparation for redemption; and although in exile we have no respite, and the manifest reality is one of exile, and exile only, still there is hope for redemption. This situation is likened to that of a farmer sowing his seeds:

5 **Those who sow** toil **in tears.** Sowing seeds is hard work that requires tremendous effort and it is invariably accompanied by anxiety: Will the seeds bear fruit? But when harvest time comes, **with joyous song they reap.**

6 The psalm concludes with a broader description of the process of the toil of sowing and the joy of reaping: **He who weeps as he walks to and fro,** and as he is **bearing his sack of seed,** the farmer scatters it with a certain amount of trepidation, as the seeds could have been, and perhaps should have been, used for food rather than having them decompose in the ground. In the end, however, he **indeed returns in joyous song,** this time too **bearing** a burden, but now it is **his sheaves** of bounteous harvest that he carries in his arms.

PSALM 127

A psalm of moral instruction attributed to Solomon, or perhaps written by King David for his son Solomon. Its main message is that man's actions, in and of themselves, can never guarantee success. It is only God's graciousness that helps us, even in the things that we ourselves do.

שִׁיר הַמַּעֲלוֹת לִשְׁלֹמֹה אִם־ א
יהוה ׀ לֹא־יִבְנֶה בַיִת שָׁוְא
עָמְלוּ בוֹנָיו בּוֹ אִם־יהוה
לֹא־יִשְׁמָר־עִיר שָׁוְא ׀ שָׁקַד
שׁוֹמֵר:

שָׁוְא לָכֶם ׀ מַשְׁכִּימֵי קוּם ב
מְאַחֲרֵי־שֶׁבֶת אֹכְלֵי לֶחֶם
הָעֲצָבִים כֵּן יִתֵּן לִידִידוֹ
שֵׁנָא:

הִנֵּה נַחֲלַת יהוה בָּנִים שָׂכָר ג
פְּרִי הַבָּטֶן:

A song of ascents, by Solomon. If the Lord does not build a house, those who build it labor in vain. If the Lord does not guard a city, in vain does the watchman keep vigil.

It is futile, you early risers and you who linger, you who eat the bread of sorrow. For surely He grants sleep to His beloved.

Truly, children are a portion of the Lord; reward is the fruit of one's womb.

PSALM 127

1 **A song of ascents, by Solomon.** Alternatively, for Solomon. **If the Lord does not build a house,** the house will collapse and **those who build it labor in vain. If the Lord does not guard a city, in vain does the watchman keep vigil.** The city's defenses will be breached if God does not provide His protection.

2 God also determines success or failure in matters involving day-to-day sustenance. This verse describes those who believe that success is a matter of diligence: **It is futile, you early risers,** getting to work early, **and you who linger,** staying on and on, working long after everyone else is gone, **you who eat the bread of sorrow.** They are consumed with planning and worrying, too distracted even to enjoy their food. **For surely He grants sleep to His beloved.** Those whom God assists are granted a good night's sleep and still succeed in their everyday affairs, whereas those who are continually obsessed with thoughts and plans may find that those plans all come to naught.

3 This holds true for other things in life that are essentially gifts from God. **Truly, children are a portion of the Lord.** Children are God's greatest gift to man, the gift that is most readily

כְּחִצִּים בְּיַד־גִּבּוֹר כֵּן בְּנֵי
הַנְּעוּרִים:

Like arrows in the hand of a
warrior, so are the children
of youth.

אַשְׁרֵי הַגֶּבֶר אֲשֶׁר מִלֵּא
אֶת־אַשְׁפָּתוֹ מֵהֶם לֹא־
יֵבֹשׁוּ כִּי־יְדַבְּרוּ אֶת־אוֹיְבִים
בַּשָּׁעַר:

Happy is the man who fills his
quiver with them; they will
not be put to shame when they
confront enemies at the gate.

PSALM 128

A hymn that depicts blessing in the form of tranquility, while offering praise for those who fear God.

שִׁיר הַמַּעֲלוֹת אַשְׁרֵי כָּל־
יְרֵא יהוה הַהֹלֵךְ בִּדְרָכָיו:

A song of ascents. Blessed are
all who fear the Lord, who
walk in His ways.

---

recognized as having been bestowed by God. **Reward is the fruit of one's womb.** They are the greatest reward, the most valuable assets one can obtain in this world.

4 **Like arrows in the hand of a warrior, so are the children of youth.** The children born to us in our youth are those who shape the future.

5 The arrow imagery is further developed in the concluding verse: **Happy is the man who fills his quiver with them.** A man with many children is like a well-armed warrior. **They will not be put to shame when they confront enemies at the gate.** In confronting enemies, his children will not be put to shame both because of their physical numbers, which enable them to withstand attack, and because they have the requisite wisdom to take part in public meetings held at the city gate, in which internal affairs and the best means of combating foes are discussed. The phrase *ki yedabru*, translated here as "when they confront," can also mean "when they speak to."

PSALM 128
1 **A song of ascents. Blessed are all who fear the Lord, who walk in His ways.**

יְגִיעַ כַּפֶּיךָ כִּי תֹאכֵל אַשְׁרֶיךָ
וְטוֹב לָךְ:

² When you eat of the labor of
your hands, you are happy, and
it is good for you.

אֶשְׁתְּךָ ׀ כְּגֶפֶן פֹּרִיָּה בְּיַרְכְּתֵי
בֵיתֶךָ בָּנֶיךָ כִּשְׁתִלֵי זֵיתִים
סָבִיב לְשֻׁלְחָנֶךָ:

³ Your wife is like a fruitful vine
by the side of your house; your
children, like young olive trees
surrounding your table.

הִנֵּה כִי־כֵן יְבֹרַךְ גָּבֶר יְרֵא
יְהֹוָה:

⁴ Indeed, so shall a man who
fears the Lord be blessed.

יְבָרֶכְךָ יְהֹוָה מִצִּיּוֹן וּרְאֵה
בְּטוֹב יְרוּשָׁלָ͏ִם כֹּל יְמֵי חַיֶּיךָ:

⁵ May the Lord bless you
from Zion; may you see the
prosperity of Jerusalem all the
days of your life.

וּרְאֵה־בָנִים לְבָנֶיךָ שָׁלוֹם
עַל־יִשְׂרָאֵל:

⁶ And may you see the children
of your children. Peace to Israel.

---

² Such people are not necessarily occupied with great, grandiose matters. Rather, **when You eat of
the labor of your hands, you are happy.** Happiness is the lot of a simple, ordinary person who
enjoys the fruits of his labor. **And it is good for you,** for honest physical labor provides spiritual
tranquility as well as the basic necessities.

³ In this pastoral image, a large and flourishing vine is growing on the side of the house and is
leaning against it, with the whole family nourished by it. **Your wife is like a fruitful vine by
the side of your house.** The wife is likened to this nourishing vine. **Your children, like young
olive trees surrounding your table.** The children are depicted as young olive shoots sitting
serenely around their father's table. This latter image is true to nature: When left undisturbed, an
olive tree often sprouts sprigs from its roots that encircle its trunk.

⁴ **Indeed, so shall a man who fears the Lord be blessed.** The blessing is that of a serene and
happy domestic life.

⁵ **May the Lord bless you from Zion; may you see the prosperity of Jerusalem all the
days of your life.** This is an additional blessing addressed to the God-fearing man mentioned in
the previous verse.

⁶ To this are added other blessings: **And may you see the children of your children.** This
God-fearing man will also merit seeing the continuity of generations, not only children but also
grandchildren. And finally, **peace to Israel,** a concluding blessing that encompasses everything.

PSALM 129

A psalm combining gratitude and rebuke: Gratitude to God for His salvation,
and rebuke to those who plot against the righteous.

שִׁיר הַמַּעֲלוֹת רַבַּת צְרָרוּנִי
מִנְּעוּרַי יֹאמַר־נָא יִשְׂרָאֵל:

רַבַּת צְרָרוּנִי מִנְּעוּרָי גַּם לֹא־
יָכְלוּ לִי:

עַל־גַּבִּי חָרְשׁוּ חֹרְשִׁים
הֶאֱרִיכוּ לְמַעֲנִיתָם: לְמַעֲנִיתָם

יְהוָה צַדִּיק קִצֵּץ עֲבוֹת
רְשָׁעִים:

יֵבֹשׁוּ וְיִסֹּגוּ אָחוֹר כֹּל שֹׂנְאֵי
צִיּוֹן:

1 A song of ascents. Let Israel now say: They have greatly beleaguered me from the time of my youth.

2 They have greatly beleaguered me from the time of my youth, yet they did not prevail against me.

3 Across my back the plowers plowed. They extended their furrows.

4 The Lord is righteous; He cuts the cords of the wicked.

5 All those who hate Zion will be put to shame and made to retreat.

PSALM 129

1 **A song of ascents. Let Israel now say: They have greatly beleaguered me from the time of my youth.** The nation of Israel can truthfully claim that it has been surrounded by enemies from the very dawn of its history.

2 **They have greatly beleaguered me from the time of my youth, yet they did not prevail against me.** Even though I have been plagued relentlessly by foes, they have been unsuccessful in fulfilling their desire to destroy me.

3 **Across my back the plowers plowed.** It is as if they slashed at my flesh. **They extended their furrows,** creating a seemingly endless furrow.

4 But **the Lord is righteous; He cuts the cords of the wicked,** those thick cords by which they try to bind the righteous.

5 And eventually, **all those who hate Zion will be put to shame and made to retreat.**

ישׁ They will be like grass on a roof,
יֶהְיוּ כֶּחֲצִיר גַּגּוֹת שֶׁקַּדְמַת which withers before it flowers,
שָׁלַף יָבֵשׁ:

שׁ which does not fill the palm of
שֶׁלֹּא מִלֵּא כַפּוֹ קוֹצֵר וְחִצְנוֹ the reaper, nor the bosom of
מְעַמֵּר: the sheaf binder.

ח And those who pass by will not
וְלֹא אָמְרוּ ׀ הָעֹבְרִים בִּרְכַּת־ say: The blessing of the Lord
יהוה אֲלֵיכֶם בֵּרַכְנוּ אֶתְכֶם be upon you; we bless you in
בְּשֵׁם יהוה: the name of the Lord.

PSALM 130

A psalm of supplication and a plea for forgiveness that is recited on special days of prayer,
including the Ten Days of Repentance between Rosh HaShana and Yom Kippur.

א A song of ascents. Out of the
שִׁיר הַמַּעֲלוֹת מִמַּעֲמַקִּים depths I call to You, Lord.
קְרָאתִיךָ יהוה:

---

6 The psalmist now presents a graphic image of what will eventually befall these enemies. Houses
in those days had flat roofs, some of which were made of a mixture of mud and clay. Therefore, at
times, seeds of grain would take root, though these never got beyond the initial stage of sprouting,
as there was not enough soil to sustain their growth. The psalmist expresses his wish that the
enemies be like this roof grass: **They will be like grass on a roof, which withers before it
flowers,** which dries up before it can produce a flower or an ear of corn,

7 **which does not fill the palm of the reaper, nor the bosom of the sheaf binder,** as there
are no stalks to harvest.

8 **And those who pass by will not say: The blessing of the Lord be upon you; we bless
you in the name of the Lord.** The custom was for passersby to offer a blessing to those engaged
in harvesting. No such blessing is issued in this case, for there is nothing to harvest.

PSALM 130

1 **A song of ascents. Out of the depths I call to You, Lord.** The word *mima'amakim*, "out of
the depths," has a twofold meaning: I feel like someone thrust into a deep pit, and I am calling
from the innermost depths of my heart.

אֲדֹנָ֥י שִׁמְעָ֗ה בְק֫וֹלִ֥י תִּהְיֶ֣ינָה אָזְנֶ֥יךָ קַשֻּׁב֑וֹת לְק֝֗וֹל תַּחֲנוּנָֽי׃

אִם־עֲוֺנ֥וֹת תִּשְׁמׇר־יָ֑הּ אֲ֝דֹנָ֗י מִ֣י יַעֲמֹֽד׃

כִּֽי־עִמְּךָ֥ הַסְּלִיחָ֑ה לְ֝מַ֗עַן תִּוָּרֵֽא׃

קִוִּ֣יתִי יְ֭הֹוָה קִוְּתָ֣ה נַפְשִׁ֑י וְֽלִדְבָר֥וֹ הוֹחָֽלְתִּי׃

נַפְשִׁ֥י לַֽאדֹנָ֑י מִשֹּׁמְרִ֥ים לַבֹּ֝֗קֶר שֹׁמְרִ֥ים לַבֹּֽקֶר׃

יַחֵ֥ל יִשְׂרָאֵ֗ל אֶל־יְ֫הֹוָ֥ה כִּֽי־עִם־יְהֹוָ֥ה הַחֶ֑סֶד וְהַרְבֵּ֖ה עִמּ֣וֹ פְדֽוּת׃

2 Lord, hear my voice; let Your ears be attentive to the sound of my pleas.

3 If You hold fast, Lord, to iniquities, my Lord, who can stand?

4 Yet forgiveness is with You, that You might be feared.

5 I hope, Lord, my soul hopes; I long for His word.

6 My soul awaits the Lord, more than watchers for the morning, watchers for the morning.

7 Await the Lord, Israel, for kindness is with the Lord, and abundant redemption is with Him.

---

2 And this is what I call out to Him: **Lord, hear my voice; let Your ears be attentive to the sound of my pleas.**

3 **If You hold fast, Lord, to iniquities,** if You remember and keep a record of all our sins, **my Lord, who can stand?** We cannot survive. Our sins are many, and without Your forgiveness, we will not be able to bear their accumulated weight.

4 **Yet forgiveness is with You, that You might be feared.** God's forgiveness instills in man a desire to remain in His good graces and to avoid future sin. By contrast, in a world without forgiveness, there would also be no fear of God. If man knew there was no remedy for him, he would, in his hopelessness, simply do as he pleased.

5 **I hope, Lord, my soul hopes; I long for His word.**

6 **My soul awaits the Lord,** I anticipate and await God, **more than watchers for the morning, watchers for the morning,** even more than those who awaken at dawn in anticipation of redemption and relief.

7 **Await the Lord, Israel, for kindness is with the Lord, and abundant redemption is with Him.** God has the power to redeem and save whomever and whatever He wants.

וְהוּא יִפְדֶּה אֶת־יִשְׂרָאֵל
מִכֹּל עֲוֺנוֹתָיו:

ח 8 And He will redeem Israel
from all its iniquities.

PSALM 131

A song of devotion to God, characterized not by ecstasy or passion but rather by a sense of inner peace that comes from accepting a loving self-abandonment for the sake of God.

שִׁיר הַמַּעֲלוֹת לְדָוִד יהוה
וְ לֹא־גָבַהּ לִבִּי וְלֹא־רָמוּ
עֵינַי וְלֹא־הִלַּכְתִּי ׀ בִּגְדֹלוֹת
וּבְנִפְלָאוֹת מִמֶּנִּי:

א 1 A song of ascents, by David.
Lord, my heart is not haughty,
nor my eyes lofty, and I do not
aspire to something too great
or too wonderful for me.

אִם־לֹא שִׁוִּיתִי ׀ וְדוֹמַמְתִּי
נַפְשִׁי כְּגָמֻל עֲלֵי אִמּוֹ כַּגָּמֻל
עָלַי נַפְשִׁי:

ב 2 Instead I have composed and
quieted my soul, like a weaned
child on its mother. Like a
weaned child is my soul.

---

8 **And** consequently, **He will redeem Israel from all its iniquities.**

PSALM 131

1 **A song of ascents, by David.** In common with several other psalms among the Songs of Ascents, this one develops a single idea, or essentially a single image. **Lord, my heart is not haughty, nor my eyes lofty.** A haughty heart and lofty eyes are expressions not only of arrogance but also of desire for fortune. **And I do not aspire to something too great or too wonderful for me.** I have no such aspirations. I remain where I am, and as I am, without trying to go farther or to reach higher.

2 **Instead I have composed and quieted my soul.** *Shiviti*, translated here as "composed," literally means "equal to." It describes the absence of any ambition, the sense of being completely at peace with the status quo. The soul is in a state of silence and quiet acceptance. It is **like a weaned child on its mother.** The central image is that of a weaned young child held in its mother's bosom. This image conveys both intimacy and great serenity. Unlike a nursing baby who cuddles in his mother's lap because he both wants and needs to nurse, the weaned child nestling in his mother's arms is seeking and receiving only one thing, an intimacy devoid of any material

יַחֵל יִשְׂרָאֵל אֶל־יהוה
מֵעַתָּה וְעַד־עוֹלָם:

³ Await the Lord, Israel, from now until eternity.

PSALM 132

A song in honor of King David, describing his efforts and the preparations he made
to build the Temple in Jerusalem. This psalm also contains God's promise
to David and his descendants throughout the generations.

שִׁיר הַמַּעֲלוֹת זְכוֹר־יהוה
לְדָוִד אֵת כָּל־עֻנּוֹתוֹ:

¹ A song of ascents. Remember, Lord, all of David's afflictions.

אֲשֶׁר נִשְׁבַּע לַיהוה נָדַר
לַאֲבִיר יַעֲקֹב:

² How he swore to the Lord and vowed to the Champion of Jacob:

אִם־אָבֹא בְּאֹהֶל בֵּיתִי אִם־
אֶעֱלֶה עַל־עֶרֶשׂ יְצוּעָי:

³ I will not enter the roof of my house nor lie on my bed,

---

desire. **Like a weaned child is my soul.** By way of analogy, the psalmist's soul experiences a
state of intimacy and devotion that is characterized by an all-encompassing inner peace and quiet.
3   The psalmist concludes with what may be seen as overall advice to Israel: **Await the Lord, Israel,
from now until eternity.** Try to achieve intimacy with God that is free of any request or desire,
other than that of being close to Him.

PSALM 132
1   **A song of ascents. Remember, Lord, all of David's afflictions.** After this brief reminder of
David's many trials and tribulations, the psalm goes on to praise him:
2   **How he swore to the Lord and vowed to the Champion of Jacob,** an unusual expression
referring to the Almighty.
3   And this is the vow that David undertook: **I will not enter the roof of my house nor lie on
my bed,**

⁴ I will not give sleep to my eyes nor slumber to my eyelids,

אִם־אֶתֵּן שְׁנַת לְעֵינָי
לְעַפְעַפַּי תְּנוּמָה:

⁵ until I find a place for the Lord, a dwelling place for the Champion of Jacob.

עַד־אֶמְצָא מָקוֹם לַיהֹוָה
מִשְׁכָּנוֹת לַאֲבִיר יַעֲקֹב:

⁶ Indeed, we heard it in Efrat; we found it in the fields of the forest.

הִנֵּה־שְׁמַעֲנוּהָ בְאֶפְרָתָה
מְצָאנוּהָ בִּשְׂדֵי־יָעַר:

⁷ Let us go to His dwelling place; let us bow down to His footstool.

נָבוֹאָה לְמִשְׁכְּנוֹתָיו
נִשְׁתַּחֲוֶה לַהֲדֹם רַגְלָיו:

⁸ Arise, Lord, to Your resting place, You and the ark of Your strength.

קוּמָה יְהֹוָה לִמְנוּחָתֶךָ אַתָּה
וַאֲרוֹן עֻזֶּךָ:

⁹ Your priests will be clothed in righteousness; Your devoted ones will sing for joy.

כֹּהֲנֶיךָ יִלְבְּשׁוּ־צֶדֶק וַחֲסִידֶיךָ
יְרַנֵּנוּ:

---

⁴ **I will not give sleep to my eyes nor slumber to my eyelids,**

⁵ **until I find a place for the Lord, a dwelling place for the Champion of Jacob.** In David's time, the Ark of the Covenant had no permanent abode but was transferred from place to place. David's great dream was to build the Temple, which would house the ark.

⁶ The people of Israel speak next: **Indeed, we heard it,** the good tidings that the Temple would be built, while David was still **in Efrat,** or Bethlehem. **We found it,** the actualization of this plan, **in the fields of the forest,** referring to the granary of Aravna the Yevusite, the site upon which the Temple was built.⁹

⁷ The psalmist continues, full of passion: **Let us go to His dwelling place; let us bow down to His footstool,** the Temple.

⁸ **Arise, Lord, to Your resting place.** This verse is similar to the words that were recited when the Ark of the Covenant was moved from one place to another in the wilderness.¹⁰ **You and the ark of Your strength,** the symbol of the revelation of the Divine Presence.

⁹ In the Temple, the service of God will return to its rightful place: **Your priests will be clothed in righteousness; Your devoted ones will sing for joy.**

בַּעֲבוּר דָּוִד עַבְדֶּךָ אַל־תָּשֵׁב
פְּנֵי מְשִׁיחֶךָ:

נִשְׁבַּע־יְהֹוָה ׀ לְדָוִד אֱמֶת
לֹא־יָשׁוּב מִמֶּנָּה מִפְּרִי בִטְנְךָ
אָשִׁית לְכִסֵּא־לָךְ:

אִם־יִשְׁמְרוּ בָנֶיךָ ׀ בְּרִיתִי
וְעֵדֹתִי זוֹ אֲלַמְּדֵם גַּם־בְּנֵיהֶם
עֲדֵי־עַד יֵשְׁבוּ לְכִסֵּא־לָךְ:

כִּי־בָחַר יְהֹוָה בְּצִיּוֹן אִוָּהּ
לְמוֹשָׁב לוֹ:

זֹאת־מְנוּחָתִי עֲדֵי־עַד פֹּה
אֵשֵׁב כִּי אִוִּתִיהָ:

צֵידָהּ בָּרֵךְ אֲבָרֵךְ אֶבְיוֹנֶיהָ
אַשְׂבִּיעַ לָחֶם:

¹⁰ For the sake of David Your servant, do not turn away the face of Your anointed one.

¹¹ The Lord has sworn a true oath to David and will not recant: From the fruit of your loins I will establish a throne for you.

¹² If your sons follow My covenant and My precept, which I will teach them, their sons too shall sit upon your throne forever.

¹³ For the Lord has chosen Zion; He desired it for His dwelling.

¹⁴ This is My resting place forever; here I will settle, for I desired it.

¹⁵ I will bless its provisions abundantly; I will satisfy its needy ones with bread.

---

10 All this will come to pass **for the sake of David, Your servant,** because of his great efforts to bring the ark to a permanent place and to build the Temple. For his sake, **do not turn away the face of Your anointed one.**

11 And David is indeed rewarded. **The Lord has sworn a true oath to David and will not recant** for all time: **From the fruit of your loins I will establish a throne for you.** God promised David that the monarchy would be passed on to his descendants for all generations to come.

12 However, this promise carries a proviso: **If your sons follow My covenant and My precept, which I will teach them,** only then **their sons too shall sit upon your throne forever.**

13 **For the Lord has chosen Zion; He desired it for His dwelling.**

14 Here the psalmist speaks in the name of God: **This is My resting place forever.** I have chosen Jerusalem as My eternal dwelling place. **Here I will settle, for I desired it.**

15 **I will bless its provisions abundantly; I will satisfy its needy ones with bread.**

טז וְכֹהֲנֶיהָ אַלְבִּישׁ יֶשַׁע
וַחֲסִידֶיהָ רַנֵּן יְרַנֵּנוּ:

יז שָׁם אַצְמִיחַ קֶרֶן לְדָוִד
עָרַכְתִּי נֵר לִמְשִׁיחִי:

יח אוֹיְבָיו אַלְבִּישׁ בֹּשֶׁת וְעָלָיו
יָצִיץ נִזְרוֹ:

16 And I will clothe its priests with salvation; its devoted ones will truly sing for joy.

17 There I will make the horn of David spring forth; I have prepared a lamp for My anointed one.

18 I will clothe his enemies in humiliation; on him a crown will glitter.

PSALM 133

A psalm of praise and glory about Jerusalem and the Temple during an era of tranquility.

א שִׁיר הַמַּעֲלוֹת לְדָוִד הִנֵּה
מַה־טּוֹב וּמַה־נָּעִים שֶׁבֶת
אַחִים גַּם־יָחַד:

1 A song of ascents, by David. Indeed, how good and how pleasant it is for brothers to dwell together in unity.

---

16 **And I will clothe its priests with salvation.** The priests will be clothed in the priestly garments. God will also ensure that they enjoy respect and stature in the Temple: **Its devoted ones will truly sing for joy.**

17 **There I will make the horn of David spring forth.** This image is a figurative way of describing greatness that is perceived by all. God promises to grant David extraordinary strength and power. **I have prepared a lamp for My anointed one.** From here we learn that it was customary to light a lantern in honor of kings and other important individuals.

18 **I will clothe his enemies in humiliation; on him a crown will glitter.** God will humiliate David's enemies while bringing glory to his monarchy.

PSALM 133

1 **A song of ascents, by David. Indeed, how good and how pleasant it is for brothers to dwell together in unity.** How good it is when all of the people of Israel, and the people of Jerusalem in particular, are in the place where they belong and enjoy one another's company.

כְּשֶׁמֶן הַטּוֹב ׀ עַל־הָרֹאשׁ
יֹרֵד עַל־הַזָּקָן זְקַן־אַהֲרֹן
שֶׁיֹּרֵד עַל־פִּי מִדּוֹתָיו:

2 It is like fine oil on the head,
running down the beard, the
beard of Aaron, coming down
onto his robes,

כְּטַל־חֶרְמוֹן שֶׁיֹּרֵד עַל־הַרְרֵי
צִיּוֹן כִּי שָׁם ׀ צִוָּה יהוה אֶת־
הַבְּרָכָה חַיִּים עַד־הָעוֹלָם:

3 like the dew of Hermon
descending upon the
mountains of Zion, for there
the Lord commanded the
blessing of life, for eternity.

2 These people, sitting at ease and in good fellowship, behold the priests in their glory as they anoint
their heads with fragrant oil; this is a description of both dignity and ease. **It is like fine oil** applied
on the head, which subsequently drips and goes **running down the beard,** in this case **the
beard of Aaron** as well as those of his descendants the priests, **coming down onto his robes.**
The image of precious scented oil, glistening from the top of the head to the bottom of the beard,
is a symbol of greatness and contentment. In the case of Aaron and his sons, their beards reached
their priestly garments. This, too, is a depiction of abundance and tranquility.

3 The concluding verse makes use of opposing images to depict a life of great wealth. It is **like the
dew of Hermon descending upon the mountains of Zion.** Because of its altitude and its
location in the north of Israel, Mount Hermon benefits from abundant rainfall and dew, in contrast
to the relatively arid hills of Zion. In a perfect world, Mount Hermon's dew would be falling on the
hills of Zion, **for** it is **there** that **the Lord commanded the blessing of life, for eternity,**
that is, life in all its fullness.

PSALM 134

The last of the fifteen Songs of Ascents, another psalm of praise and glory that relates to the Temple.

שִׁיר הַמַּעֲלוֹת הִנֵּה ׀ בָּרְכוּ
אֶת־יהוה כָּל־עַבְדֵי יהוה
הָעֹמְדִים בְּבֵית־יהוה
בַּלֵּילוֹת:

שְׂאוּ־יְדֵכֶם קֹדֶשׁ וּבָרְכוּ אֶת־
יהוה:

יְבָרֶכְךָ יהוה מִצִּיּוֹן עֹשֵׂה
שָׁמַיִם וָאָרֶץ:

A song of ascents. Indeed, bless the Lord, all you servants of the Lord who stand by night in the House of the Lord.

Lift up your hands toward the Sanctuary and bless the Lord.

The Lord who made heaven and earth will bless you from Zion.

PSALM 135

A Halleluya psalm, that is, a psalm in praise of God. Its main theme is God's greatness in the world and how this is revealed through the history of the people of Israel.

הַלְלוּיָהּ ׀ הַלְלוּ אֶת־שֵׁם
יהוה הַלְלוּ עַבְדֵי יהוה:

Halleluya. Praise the name of the Lord. Praise Him, servants of the Lord,

---

PSALM 134

1 **A song of ascents. Indeed, bless the Lord, all you servants of the Lord who stand** and serve **by night in the House of the Lord.** Since sacrifices were not brought at night, this verse may be referring to individuals who would come regularly to the Temple at night to stand before God in devotion or to pray.

2 **Lift up your hands toward the Sanctuary and bless the Lord.**

3 The concluding verse offers a blessing for all of Israel: **The Lord who made heaven and earth will bless you from Zion.**

PSALM 135

1 **Halleluya. Praise the name of the Lord. Praise Him, servants of the Lord,**

שֶׁעֹמְדִים בְּבֵית יְהוָה
בְּחַצְרוֹת בֵּית אֱלֹהֵינוּ׃

הַלְלוּיָהּ כִּי־טוֹב יְהוָה זַמְּרוּ
לִשְׁמוֹ כִּי נָעִים׃

כִּי־יַעֲקֹב בָּחַר לוֹ יָהּ יִשְׂרָאֵל
לִסְגֻלָּתוֹ׃

כִּי אֲנִי יָדַעְתִּי כִּי־גָדוֹל יְהוָה
וַאֲדֹנֵינוּ מִכָּל־אֱלֹהִים׃

כֹּל אֲשֶׁר־חָפֵץ יְהוָה עָשָׂה
בַּשָּׁמַיִם וּבָאָרֶץ בַּיַּמִּים וְכָל־
תְּהֹמוֹת׃

מַעֲלֶה נְשִׂאִים מִקְצֵה הָאָרֶץ
בְּרָקִים לַמָּטָר עָשָׂה מוֹצֵא־
רוּחַ מֵאוֹצְרוֹתָיו׃

2 who stand in the House of the Lord, in the courts of the House of our God.

3 Praise the Lord, for the Lord is good. Sing praises to His name, for He is pleasant.

4 For the Lord has chosen Jacob for Himself, Israel as His treasured possession.

5 For I know the Lord is great, and that our Master is above all gods.

6 Whatever the Lord desires to do, He does, in the heavens and on the earth, in the seas and all the depths.

7 He makes clouds ascend from the ends of the earth; He makes lightning for the rain, brings out winds from His vaults.

---

2 **who stand in the House of the Lord, in the courts of the House of our God.** This verse might refer to the Levites who, as choristers in the Temple, sang these psalms. It is also possible that the reference is both to the Levites and to other God-fearing people who join in their singing.

3 **Praise the Lord, for the Lord is good. Sing praises to His name, for He is pleasant.**

4 **For the Lord has chosen Jacob for Himself, Israel as His treasured possession,** His chosen people.

5 **For I know the Lord is great, and that our Master is above all gods.**

6 **Whatever the Lord desires to do, He does,** for He rules over all aspects of creation: **In the heavens and on the earth, in the seas and all the depths.**

7 **He makes clouds ascend from the ends of the earth; He makes lightning for the rain.** Lightning and thunder often herald rain. He **brings out winds from His vaults.** In the imagery

ח שֶׁהִכָּה בְּכוֹרֵי מִצְרָיִם מֵאָדָם
עַד־בְּהֵמָה:

ט שָׁלַח ׀ אֹתֹת וּמֹפְתִים
בְּתוֹכֵכִי מִצְרָיִם בְּפַרְעֹה
וּבְכָל־עֲבָדָיו:

י שֶׁהִכָּה גּוֹיִם רַבִּים וְהָרַג
מְלָכִים עֲצוּמִים:

יא לְסִיחוֹן ׀ מֶלֶךְ הָאֱמֹרִי וּלְעוֹג
מֶלֶךְ הַבָּשָׁן וּלְכֹל מַמְלְכוֹת
כְּנָעַן:

יב וְנָתַן אַרְצָם נַחֲלָה נַחֲלָה
לְיִשְׂרָאֵל עַמּוֹ:

8 He smote the firstborn of Egypt, from man to beast.

9 He sent signs and wonders into the midst of Egypt, to Pharaoh and all his servants.

10 He struck down many nations and slew mighty kings.

11 Sihon king of the Emorites, and Og king of Bashan, and all the kingdoms of Canaan,

12 and He gave their lands as a portion, a portion to Israel, His people.

---

of this verse, the winds of the world are stored in a special repository and are taken out and released by God.

8 From here, the psalmist turns from God's greatness in the world to His greatness in history: **He smote the firstborn of Egypt, from man to beast,** during the last and most severe of the ten plagues brought upon Egypt, as related in the book of Exodus.

9 The smiting of the firstborn marked the end and summation of the period when **He sent signs and wonders into the midst of Egypt, to Pharaoh and all his servants**.

10 **He struck down many nations and slew mighty kings.** This verse refers to the wars waged by the children of Israel when they came to the Land of Israel.

11 The psalmist cites some illustrious examples of these "mighty kings": **Sihon king of the Emorites, and Og king of Bashan, and all the kingdoms of Canaan.** A host of Canaanite kings were defeated over the course of several years of conquest. The two kings specifically mentioned here, Sihon and Og, controlled more extensive territories than did the other Canaanite kings.

12 **And He gave their lands as a portion, a portion to Israel, His people.**

יְהוָה שִׁמְךָ לְעוֹלָם יְהֹוָה
זִכְרְךָ לְדֹר־וָדֹר:

כִּי־יָדִין יְהוָה עַמּוֹ וְעַל־
עֲבָדָיו יִתְנֶחָם:

עֲצַבֵּי הַגּוֹיִם כֶּסֶף וְזָהָב
מַעֲשֵׂה יְדֵי אָדָם:

פֶּה־לָהֶם וְלֹא יְדַבֵּרוּ עֵינַיִם
לָהֶם וְלֹא יִרְאוּ:

אָזְנַיִם לָהֶם וְלֹא יַאֲזִינוּ אַף
אֵין־יֶשׁ־רוּחַ בְּפִיהֶם:

כְּמוֹהֶם יִהְיוּ עֹשֵׂיהֶם כֹּל
אֲשֶׁר־בֹּטֵחַ בָּהֶם:

13 Lord, Your name is eternal; Your remembrance, Lord, for all generations.

14 For the Lord will judge His people and will take pity on His servants.

15 The idols of the nations are silver and gold, the work of man's hands.

16 Mouths they have but cannot speak. Eyes they have but cannot see.

17 Ears they have, yet they do not hear, nor is there any breath in their mouths.

18 May their makers become like them; so too all who trust in them.

---

13 The following verses offer words of praise and gratitude to God: **Lord, Your name is eternal; Your remembrance, Lord, for all generations.** This verse uses language that echoes Exodus 3:15: "This is My name forever, and this is My appellation for all generations."

14 **For the Lord will judge His people and will take pity on His servants.** When God juxtaposes the people of Israel, His servants, to other nations of the world, what is most apparent, and what stands in their favor, is their closeness to Him.

15 **The idols of the nations are silver and gold, the work of man's hands.** As the next verses demonstrate, these idols are devoid of life.

16 **Mouths they have but cannot speak. Eyes they have but cannot see.**

17 **Ears they have, yet they do not hear, nor is there any breath in their mouths.** They are nothing but lifeless dolls.

18 The psalmist's reaction to these facts combines mockery with imprecation: **May their makers become like them,** may they become as lifeless as the idols themselves. **So too all who trust in them.**

יט בֵּית יִשְׂרָאֵל בָּרְכוּ אֶת־יהוה
בֵּית אַהֲרֹן בָּרְכוּ אֶת־יהוה:

19 House of Israel, bless the Lord;
house of Aaron, bless the Lord.

כ בֵּית הַלֵּוִי בָּרְכוּ אֶת־יהוה
יִרְאֵי יהוה בָּרְכוּ אֶת־יהוה:

20 House of Levi, bless the Lord;
you who fear the Lord, bless
the Lord.

כא בָּרוּךְ יהוה ׀ מִצִּיּוֹן שֹׁכֵן
יְרוּשָׁלָ͏ִם הַלְלוּיָהּ:

21 Blessed be the Lord from Zion,
He who dwells in Jerusalem.
Halleluya.

PSALM 136

Another psalm in praise of God, very similar to the preceding psalm in content and wording.
The main difference between them is that this psalm is clearly meant to be recited responsively.
Each of its verses begins with a specific praise of God, which is answered by the repeated refrain:
"For His kindness is forever."

א הוֹדוּ לַיהוה כִּי־טוֹב
כִּי לְעוֹלָם חַסְדּוֹ:

1 Give thanks to the Lord, for He
is good,
for His kindness is forever.

---

19 In contrast to the other nations and their idols, **house of Israel, bless the Lord; house of
Aaron,** the priests, **bless the Lord.**

20 **House of Levi, bless the Lord; you who fear the Lord,** probably referring to those who
worship God and who, unlike the priests and Levites, have no specific or designated role in the
Temple service, **bless the Lord.**

21 All say, in unison: **Blessed be the Lord from Zion, He who dwells in Jerusalem. Halleluya.**

PSALM 136

1 The leader exclaims: **Give thanks to the Lord, for He is good!** And the chorus or congregation
responds: **For His kindness is forever.** And so on throughout the psalm.

הוֹדוּ לֵאלֹהֵי הָאֱלֹהִים
כִּי לְעוֹלָם חַסְדּוֹ:

2 Give thanks to the God of heavenly powers,
for His kindness is forever.

הוֹדוּ לַאֲדֹנֵי הָאֲדֹנִים
כִּי לְעוֹלָם חַסְדּוֹ:

3 Give thanks to the Master of masters,
for His kindness is forever.

לְעֹשֵׂה נִפְלָאוֹת גְּדֹלוֹת לְבַדּוֹ
כִּי לְעוֹלָם חַסְדּוֹ:

4 To Him who alone does great wonders,
for His kindness is forever.

לְעֹשֵׂה הַשָּׁמַיִם בִּתְבוּנָה
כִּי לְעוֹלָם חַסְדּוֹ:

5 To Him who made the heavens with wisdom,
for His kindness is forever.

לְרֹקַע הָאָרֶץ עַל־הַמָּיִם
כִּי לְעוֹלָם חַסְדּוֹ:

6 To Him who spreads out the earth above the waters,
for His kindness is forever.

לְעֹשֵׂה אוֹרִים גְּדֹלִים
כִּי לְעוֹלָם חַסְדּוֹ:

7 He, who made the great lights,
for His kindness is forever,

אֶת־הַשֶּׁמֶשׁ לְמֶמְשֶׁלֶת בַּיּוֹם
כִּי לְעוֹלָם חַסְדּוֹ:

8 the sun to rule by day,
for His kindness is forever,

---

2 **Give thanks to the God of heavenly powers, for His kindness is forever.**

3 **Give thanks to the Master of masters, for His kindness is forever.**

4 **To Him who alone does great wonders, for His kindness is forever.** God alone is capable of performing great miracles.

5 A description of some of these miracles follows: **To Him who made the heavens with wisdom, for His kindness is forever.**

6 **To Him who spreads out the earth above the waters, for His kindness is forever.** The earth is depicted here as covering all the deep waters of the world.

7 **He, who made the great lights, for His kindness is forever,**

8 **the sun to rule by day, for His kindness is forever,**

ט אֶת־הַיָּרֵחַ וְכוֹכָבִים
לְמֶמְשְׁלוֹת בַּלָּֽיְלָה
כִּי לְעוֹלָם חַסְדּוֹ:

לְמַכֵּה מִצְרַיִם בִּבְכוֹרֵיהֶם
כִּי לְעוֹלָם חַסְדּוֹ:

יא וַיּוֹצֵא יִשְׂרָאֵל מִתּוֹכָם
כִּי לְעוֹלָם חַסְדּוֹ:

בְּיָד חֲזָקָה וּבִזְרוֹעַ נְטוּיָה
כִּי לְעוֹלָם חַסְדּוֹ:

לְגֹזֵר יַם־סוּף לִגְזָרִים
כִּי לְעוֹלָם חַסְדּוֹ:

יד וְהֶעֱבִיר יִשְׂרָאֵל בְּתוֹכוֹ
כִּי לְעוֹלָם חַסְדּוֹ:

[9] the moon and stars to rule by night,
for His kindness is forever.

[10] He, who smote Egypt through their firstborn,
for His kindness is forever,

[11] and who brought Israel out from their midst,
for His kindness is forever,

[12] with a strong hand and an outstretched arm,
for His kindness is forever.

[13] He, who split the Red Sea asunder,
for His kindness is forever,

[14] and led Israel through the midst of it,
for His kindness is forever,

---

[9] **the moon and stars to rule by night, for His kindness is forever.**

[10] As in the preceding psalm, the psalmist proceeds from a general description of God's greatness in the world to examples of His greatness as manifest in historical events: **He, who smote Egypt through their firstborn, for His kindness is forever,**

[11] **and who brought Israel out from their midst,** from the midst of the Egyptians, **for His kindness is forever,**

[12] **with a strong hand and an outstretched arm, for His kindness is forever.**

[13] **He, who split the Red Sea asunder, for His kindness is forever.** The splitting of the Red Sea was a three-part miracle; this is the first part.

[14] **And led Israel through the midst of it,** the midst of the sea, the second part of the miracle, **for His kindness is forever,**

טו וְנִעֵר פַּרְעֹה וְחֵילוֹ בְיַם־סוּף
כִּי לְעוֹלָם חַסְדּוֹ:

טז לְמוֹלִיךְ עַמּוֹ בַּמִּדְבָּר
כִּי לְעוֹלָם חַסְדּוֹ:

יז לְמַכֵּה מְלָכִים גְּדֹלִים
כִּי לְעוֹלָם חַסְדּוֹ:

יח וַיַּהֲרֹג מְלָכִים אַדִּירִים
כִּי לְעוֹלָם חַסְדּוֹ:

יט לְסִיחוֹן מֶלֶךְ הָאֱמֹרִי
כִּי לְעוֹלָם חַסְדּוֹ:

כ וּלְעוֹג מֶלֶךְ הַבָּשָׁן
כִּי לְעוֹלָם חַסְדּוֹ:

כא וְנָתַן אַרְצָם לְנַחֲלָה
כִּי לְעוֹלָם חַסְדּוֹ:

כב נַחֲלָה לְיִשְׂרָאֵל עַבְדּוֹ כִּי
לְעוֹלָם חַסְדּוֹ:

15 while He hurled Pharaoh and his army into the Red Sea, for His kindness is forever.

16 He, who led His people through the wilderness, for His kindness is forever.

17 He, who smote great kings, for His kindness is forever,

18 and slew mighty kings, for His kindness is forever,

19 Sihon king of the Emorites, for His kindness is forever,

20 and Og king of Bashan, for His kindness is forever.

21 He gave their land as a portion, for His kindness is forever,

22 a portion to Israel His servant, for His kindness is forever.

---

15 **while He hurled Pharaoh and his army into the Red Sea,** the third part of the miracle, **for His kindness is forever.**

16 **He, who led His people through the wilderness, for His kindness is forever.** Throughout their wanderings, God always supplied the people with all their needs.

17 **He, who smote great kings** in the course of the conquest of the Canaanites, **for His kindness is forever,**

18 **and slew mighty kings, for His kindness is forever.**

19 Two of those kings are now mentioned: **Sihon king of the Emorites, for His kindness is forever,**

20 **and Og king of Bashan, for His kindness is forever.**

21 **He gave their land as a portion, for His kindness is forever,**

22 **a portion to Israel His servant, for His kindness is forever.**

כג ‏שֶׁבְּשִׁפְלֵנוּ זָכַר לָנוּ
כִּי לְעוֹלָם חַסְדּוֹ:

23 Who, in our lowliness,
   remembered us,
   for His kindness is forever,

כד ‏וַיִּפְרְקֵנוּ מִצָּרֵינוּ
כִּי לְעוֹלָם חַסְדּוֹ:

24 and He freed us from our foes,
   for His kindness is forever.

כה ‏נֹתֵן לֶחֶם לְכָל־בָּשָׂר
כִּי לְעוֹלָם חַסְדּוֹ:

25 He gives food to all flesh,
   for His kindness is forever.

כו ‏הוֹדוּ לְאֵל הַשָּׁמָיִם
כִּי לְעוֹלָם חַסְדּוֹ:

26 Give thanks to the Almighty of
   heaven,
   for His kindness is forever.

PSALM 137

An elegy of people in exile who are in a state of utmost decline and humiliation. It contains both
reminiscences of the destruction and a prayer for punishment to be meted out on the enemy.

א ‏עַל־נַהֲרוֹת ׀ בָּבֶל שָׁם יָשַׁבְנוּ
גַּם־בָּכִינוּ בְּזָכְרֵנוּ אֶת־צִיּוֹן:

By the rivers of Babylon, there
we sat, and also wept, when we
remembered Zion.

---

23 Here the psalmist offers two general examples of God's kindness that do not pertain to any specific
   historical event: **Who, in our lowliness, remembered us** and rescued us at times of decline
   and degradation, **for His kindness is forever,**
24 **and He freed us from our foes, for His kindness is forever.**
25 Finally, each and every day: **He gives food to all flesh.** God sustains all the creatures of the world,
   for His kindness is forever.
26 The psalmist concludes on a joyous note: **Give thanks to the Almighty of heaven, for His
   kindness is forever.**

PSALM 137

1 The speakers are the exiles who arrived in Babylon. They say: **By the rivers of Babylon,
   there we sat, and also wept, when we remembered Zion** and our exile from there to a
   foreign land.

עַל־עֲרָבִים בְּתוֹכָהּ תָּלִינוּ
כִּנֹּרוֹתֵֽינוּ:

2 On the willows in its midst, we hung our lyres.

כִּי שָׁם ׀ שְׁאֵלֽוּנוּ שׁוֹבֵינוּ
דִּבְרֵי־שִׁיר וְתוֹלָלֵֽינוּ שִׂמְחָה
שִׁירוּ לָֽנוּ מִשִּׁיר צִיּֽוֹן:

3 For there our captors asked us for songs, and our tormentors, mirth: Sing to us of the songs of Zion.

אֵיךְ נָשִׁיר אֶת־שִׁיר־יְהֹוָה
עַל אַדְמַת נֵכָֽר:

4 How can we sing the song of the Lord on foreign soil?

אִם־אֶשְׁכָּחֵךְ יְֽרוּשָׁלָ͏ִם
תִּשְׁכַּח יְמִינִֽי:

5 If I forget you, Jerusalem, let my right hand lose its power.

תִּדְבַּק־לְשׁוֹנִי ׀ לְחִכִּי אִם־לֹא
אֶזְכְּרֵכִי אִם־לֹא אַעֲלֶה אֶת־
יְרוּשָׁלַ͏ִם עַל רֹאשׁ שִׂמְחָתִֽי:

6 Let my tongue cleave to my palate if I do not recall you, if I do not set Jerusalem above my foremost joy.

---

2 **On the willows in its midst,** in Babylon's midst, **we hung our lyres.** The people lamenting were sitting by rivers, where willows often grow. Hanging the lyres on the willows is a way of saying that the exiles do not want to use them, because they are no longer willing, or able, to sing.

3 **For there our captors asked us for songs, and our tormentors, mirth.** The captors asked their captives to play for them, in some instances because of their curiosity to hear different types of melodies and, in other cases, as a way of tormenting them. They said: **Sing to us of the songs of Zion.** There were many kinds of songs sung in Jerusalem, but the term "Zion" refers specifically to the Temple Mount; the captors were asking the captives to sing the songs that had been sung in the Temple.

4 The captives respond: **How can we sing the song of the Lord,** which is the song of Zion, the Temple, **on foreign soil?**

5 The exiles then speak about the memory of Jerusalem: **If I forget you, Jerusalem, let my right hand,** my stronger hand, **lose its power.**

6 **Let my tongue cleave to my palate,** so that I will be unable to speak, **if I do not recall you,** if I do not recall the memory of Jerusalem. It would be best for me not to speak at all **if I do not set Jerusalem above my foremost joy.** Even at the height of personal joy I will never forget Jerusalem and the humiliation it suffered.

זְכֹ֤ר יְהוָ֨ה ׀ לִבְנֵ֬י אֱד֗וֹם אֵת֮ י֤וֹם יְֽרוּשָׁ֫לִָ֥ם הָ֭אֹמְרִים עָ֤רוּ ׀ עָ֑רוּ עַ֝֗ד הַיְס֥וֹד בָּֽהּ׃

בַּת־בָּבֶ֗ל הַשְּׁד֫וּדָ֥ה אַ֭שְׁרֵי שֶׁיְשַׁלֶּם־לָ֑ךְ אֶת־גְּ֝מוּלֵ֗ךְ שֶׁגָּמַ֥לְתְּ לָֽנוּ׃

אַשְׁרֵ֤י ׀ שֶׁיֹּאחֵ֓ז וְנִפֵּ֬ץ אֶֽת־עֹלָלַ֗יִךְ אֶל־הַסָּֽלַע׃

7 Remember, Lord, for the sons of Edom the day of Jerusalem, who said: Tear it down, tear it down, to its very foundation.

8 Thieving daughter of Babylon, happy is he who pays you back for what you did to us.

9 Happy is he who will seize and dash your infants against the rock.

PSALM 138

A psalm of thanksgiving for God's help to individuals and to the nation as a whole.

לְדָוִ֨ד ׀ אוֹדְךָ֥ בְכָל־לִבִּ֑י נֶ֖גֶד אֱלֹהִ֣ים אֲזַמְּרֶֽךָּ׃

1 By David. I praise You with all my heart; before divine beings, I sing praises to You.

---

7 Besides remembering the destruction of Jerusalem, we will also never forget the war and our enemies. **Remember, Lord, for the sons of Edom,** who joined forces with the other enemies of Israel, **the day of** the destruction and downfall of **Jerusalem,** and those **who said: Tear it down, tear it down, to its very foundation.** They called not only for the conquest of Jerusalem, but also for its total destruction.

8 **Thieving daughter of Babylon, happy is he who pays you back for what you did to us,** and does to you what you have done to us.

9 **Happy is he who will seize and dash your infants against the rock.** The psalmist does not say that he, personally, would be happy to carry out this act of vengeance, but rather wishes that someone else would do so.

PSALM 138

1 **By David. I praise You with all my heart; before divine beings, I sing praises to You.** This verse refers to "divine beings," or angels. The psalmist, as it were, is singing not only among men but also before angels, who cannot themselves give thanks to God in the same way as people.

אֶשְׁתַּחֲוֶה אֶל־הֵיכַל קָדְשְׁךָ
וְאוֹדֶה אֶת־שְׁמֶךָ עַל־חַסְדְּךָ
וְעַל־אֲמִתֶּךָ כִּי־הִגְדַּלְתָּ עַל־
כָּל־שִׁמְךָ אִמְרָתֶךָ:

בְּיוֹם קָרָאתִי וַתַּעֲנֵנִי
תַּרְהִבֵנִי בְנַפְשִׁי עֹז:

יוֹדוּךָ יְהוָה כָּל־מַלְכֵי־אָרֶץ
כִּי שָׁמְעוּ אִמְרֵי־פִיךָ:

וְיָשִׁירוּ בְּדַרְכֵי יְהוָה כִּי־גָדוֹל
כְּבוֹד יְהוָה:

כִּי־רָם יְהוָה וְשָׁפָל יִרְאֶה
וְגָבֹהַּ מִמֶּרְחָק יְיֵדָע:

2 I bow down toward Your holy Sanctuary, and I acclaim Your name for Your kindness and Your truth; for You have made Your word greater than Your entire name.

3 On the day that I called, You answered me; You gave my soul strength and made it exalted.

4 All kings of the earth will give thanks to You, Lord, when they hear the words of Your mouth.

5 They will sing of the ways of the Lord, for great is the Lord's honor.

6 Though the Lord is exalted, He sees the lowly; the haughty He knows from afar.

---

2 **I bow down toward Your holy Sanctuary, and I acclaim Your name for Your kindness and Your truth.** "Truth" refers to God's faithful fulfillment of His promises to David. **For You have made Your word greater than Your entire name.** Your kindness and Your fulfillment of Your word exceed everything I previously knew about Your name.

3 **On the day that I called, You answered me; You gave my soul strength and made it exalted.** You emboldened my soul to such an extent that it reached an elevated, exalted state.

4 **All kings of the earth will give thanks to You, Lord, when they hear the words of Your mouth.** Those among the kings and rulers who have heard the word of God will thank Him.

5 **They will sing** praises **of the ways of the Lord, for great is the Lord's honor** throughout the world.

6 **Though the Lord is exalted,** though God is in the highest heavens, **He sees the lowly,** He pays heed to the lowest of the low. **The haughty He knows from afar.** He is also cognizant of those who are full of arrogance, and can punish them accordingly.

אִם־אֵלֵךְ ׀ בְּקֶרֶב צָרָה
תְּחַיֵּנִי עַל אַף אֹֽיְבַי תִּשְׁלַח
יָדֶךָ וְתוֹשִׁיעֵנִי יְמִינֶךָ:

יְהֹוָה יִגְמֹר בַּעֲדִי יְהֹוָה
חַסְדְּךָ לְעוֹלָם מַעֲשֵׂי יָדֶיךָ
אַל־תֶּרֶף:

Though I walk in the midst of distress, You keep me alive. In spite of my enemies, You send forth Your hand; Your right hand saves me.

8 The Lord will complete this for me. Your kindness, Lord, is forever; do not forsake the work of Your hands.

PSALM 139

A psalm of introspection and devotion; in essence, it is praise of God's closeness.

לַמְנַצֵּחַ לְדָוִד מִזְמוֹר יְהֹוָה
חֲקַרְתַּנִי וַתֵּדָע:

For the chief musician, a psalm by David. Lord, You have searched me, and You know me.

---

7 **Though I walk in the midst of distress,** when I am surrounded by adversity on all sides, **You keep me alive. In spite of my enemies, You send forth Your hand; Your right hand saves me.**

8 **The Lord will complete this for me.** Some commentators understand the word *yigmor* in the sense of *gemul*, or recompense, so that the verse is saying: God will repay me for my good deeds. However, it can also be interpreted literally, in the sense of finishing or completing for me the things that I want to do. **Your kindness, Lord, is forever; do not forsake the work of Your hands,** but rather help them to accomplish their goals to completion.

PSALM 139

1 **For the chief musician, a psalm by David. Lord, You have searched me, and You know me.**

אַתָּה יָדַעְתָּ שִׁבְתִּי וְקוּמִי בַּנְתָּה לְרֵעִי מֵרָחוֹק: ²

² You know when I sit and when I rise; You understand my thoughts from afar.

אָרְחִי וְרִבְעִי זֵרִיתָ וְכָל־דְּרָכַי הִסְכַּנְתָּה: ³

³ You discern my path and my resting place; You are familiar with all my ways.

כִּי אֵין מִלָּה בִּלְשׁוֹנִי הֵן יהוה יָדַעְתָּ כֻלָּהּ: ⁴

⁴ Even when there is no word on my tongue, truly, Lord, You know it all.

אָחוֹר וָקֶדֶם צַרְתָּנִי וַתָּשֶׁת עָלַי כַּפֶּכָה: ⁵

⁵ From back and front, You shaped me; You placed Your palm on me.

פְּלִיאָ פְּלִאיָה דַעַת מִמֶּנִּי נִשְׂגְּבָה לֹא־אוּכַל לָהּ: ⁶

⁶ This knowledge is too wonderful for me. It is sublime; I cannot reach it.

אָנָה אֵלֵךְ מֵרוּחֶךָ וְאָנָה מִפָּנֶיךָ אֶבְרָח: ⁷

⁷ Where can I go from Your spirit? And where can I flee from Your presence?

---

² **You know when I sit and when I rise.** Every move I make is known to You. **You understand my thoughts from afar.** You know me inside and out.

³ **You discern my path and my resting place.** You know my actions both when I am traveling on the path and when I am resting in one place. **You are familiar with all my ways.**

⁴ **Even when there is no word on my tongue,** that is, nothing that I say is new to You, **truly, Lord, You know it all,** even words that I wish to say but have not yet uttered.

⁵ **From back and front, You shaped me.** From the outset, You have been as close to me as can possibly be, for You created and shaped me. Moreover, from the beginning, **You placed Your palm on me,** I have been under Your protection. In this sense of divine intimacy, God always knows and cares for man and, despite His unfathomable greatness, is always close at hand.

⁶ **This knowledge is too wonderful for me.** It is like a wonder, beyond my comprehension. **It is sublime; I cannot reach it.** I cannot fathom the fact that You are always with me and that no side of me is unexposed, unexamined, or unrevealed to You.

⁷ **Where can I go from Your spirit?** Even if I wanted to escape from You, to go away and vanish,

אִם־אֶסַּק שָׁמַיִם שָׁם אָתָּה
וְאַצִּיעָה שְּׁאוֹל הִנֶּךָ:

אֶשָּׂא כַנְפֵי־שָׁחַר אֶשְׁכְּנָה
בְּאַחֲרִית יָם:

גַּם־שָׁם יָדְךָ תַנְחֵנִי וְתֹאחֲזֵנִי
יְמִינֶךָ:

וָאֹמַר אַךְ־חֹשֶׁךְ יְשׁוּפֵנִי
וְלַיְלָה אוֹר בַּעֲדֵנִי:

גַּם־חֹשֶׁךְ לֹא־יַחְשִׁיךְ מִמֶּךָ
וְלַיְלָה כַּיּוֹם יָאִיר כַּחֲשֵׁיכָה
כָּאוֹרָה:

כִּי־אַתָּה קָנִיתָ כִלְיֹתָי תְּסֻכֵּנִי
בְּבֶטֶן אִמִּי:

8 If I ascend to heaven, You are there; if I lie down in the netherworld, You are there.

9 Were I to travel on the wings of dawn, were I to dwell at the end of the sea,

10 even there Your hand would guide me; Your right hand would hold me fast.

11 Even if I say that darkness will conceal me, that night, for me, is light,

12 even darkness does not darken for You. The night, as if day, gives forth light. Darkness and light are the same.

13 For You formed my innermost parts; You sheltered me in my mother's womb.

---

there is no way I could. **And where can I flee from Your presence,** since You are everywhere, and in everything?

8 **If I ascend to heaven, You are there; if I lie down in the netherworld, You are there.**

9 **Were I to travel on the wings of dawn,** to the easternmost point, **were I to dwell at the end of the sea,** to the west,

10 **even there Your hand would guide me.** You are there, no matter how far away I may go. **Your right hand would hold me fast.**

11 In this verse, the word "light" is used euphemistically to mean just the opposite, darkness: **Even if I say that darkness will conceal me, that night, for me, is light,**

12 **even darkness does not darken for You.** No matter how dark the night becomes, it cannot hide me from You. **The night, as if day, gives forth light.** For You, darkness does not conceal; it is as if night is as bright as day. **Darkness and light are the same.** Although for us light and darkness are opposites, from God's perspective, there is no difference between them.

13 The psalmist goes on to express the sentiment that everything he has done is actually a result of

אֽוֹדְךָ עַל כִּי נוֹרָאוֹת נִפְלֵיתִי

נִפְלָאִים מַעֲשֶׂיךָ וְנַפְשִׁי

יֹדַעַת מְאֹד:

לֹא־נִכְחַד עָצְמִי מִמֶּךָּ

אֲשֶׁר־עֻשֵּׂיתִי בַסֵּתֶר רֻקַּמְתִּי

בְּתַחְתִּיּוֹת אָרֶץ:

גָּלְמִי ׀ רָאוּ עֵינֶיךָ וְעַל־סִפְרְךָ

כֻּלָּם יִכָּתֵבוּ יָמִים יֻצָּרוּ וְלֹא   וְלוֹ

אֶחָד בָּהֶם:

וְלִי מַה־יָּקְרוּ רֵעֶיךָ אֵל מֶה

עָצְמוּ רָאשֵׁיהֶם:

14 I will give thanks to You, for I was made in a wondrous manner. Wonderful are Your works; I know this well.

15 My essence was not hidden from You when I was wrought in a secret place, knitted in the depths of the earth.

16 Your eyes saw my unformed parts; in Your book, they are all recorded. Of the days that were created, each one is His.

17 How precious to me are thoughts of You, God; how vast is their beginning.

God's creation of him. **For You formed my innermost parts.** From the very beginning, my being has been Your handiwork. Everything in my life stems from Your creation of me, even my innermost, hidden parts. **You sheltered me in my mother's womb.**

14 **I will give thanks to You, for I was made in a wondrous manner.** My complex, unique existence is the work of Your hands. **Wonderful are Your works.** Your deeds are miraculous both in their entirety and in their smallest details. **I know this well.**

15 **My essence was not hidden from You when I was wrought in a secret place,** in my mother's womb, **knitted,** formed, in a place hidden from sight as if it were **in the depths of the earth.**

16 You recognized and shaped the template of my being, both physical and spiritual. **Your eyes saw my unformed parts.** You know me not only as I am now, fully formed and distinct, but also as nothing more than a shapeless mass. **In Your book, they are all recorded.** Every individual is counted and recorded before You. Moreover, God regards each and every day and its events not only in the general sense of a unit of time, but also as a unique entity: **Of the days that were created, each one is His.**

17 **How precious to me,** when I ponder my reality, my existence as an individual, **are thoughts of You, God.** I realize how important to me are my thoughts and ideas about You. **How vast is their beginning.** How great and manifold are the essentials, the foundations of my thoughts, concerning God!

יח אֶסְפְּרֵם מֵחוֹל יִרְבּוּן
הֱקִיצֹתִי וְעוֹדִי עִמָּךְ:

יט אִם־תִּקְטֹל אֱלֹוהַּ ׀ רָשָׁע
וְאַנְשֵׁי דָמִים סוּרוּ מֶנִּי:

כ אֲשֶׁר יֹמְרוּךָ לִמְזִמָּה נָשׂוּא
לַשָּׁוְא עָרֶיךָ:

כא הֲלוֹא־מְשַׂנְאֶיךָ יהוה ׀
אֶשְׂנָא וּבִתְקוֹמְמֶיךָ
אֶתְקוֹטָט:

18 When I count them, they outnumber the sand; when I awake, I am still with You.

19 If only You, my God, would slay the wicked, and men of bloodshed would turn away from me,

20 Your enemies, who defy You for the sake of intrigue, exalting themselves in vain.

21 For surely Your enemies, Lord, I hate, and I contend with those who rise against You.

---

18 **When I count them,** my thoughts about You, Your being, and Your greatness, **they outnumber the sand,** they are more numerous than grains of sand. **When I awake, I am still with You.** These thoughts are with me at all times, whether it is evident to others or not. Of course, I do not think about You when I sleep, but as soon as I awake, I once again find myself close to You.

19 As in other psalms contemplating the unity and harmony of God vis-à-vis His world and creations, this psalm also addresses darker matters, namely, flaws and imperfections in the world. These flaws are not intrinsic to creation but rather are the outcome of human behavior. Only humans, who have been given free will, are capable of consciously doing evil; only they can create the deformities and voids that mar the world's harmony. The psalmist thus beseeches God: **If only You, my God, would slay the wicked, and men of bloodshed would turn away from me;** if You, God, were to kill the wicked and banish men of violence from my presence, the world would be a brighter place.

20 If only You would slay **Your enemies, who defy You for the sake of intrigue, exalting themselves in vain.** Whenever people aspire to greatness and scheme to promote themselves, their efforts are for naught. The phrase "exalting themselves in vain" refers not only to the outcome of their behavior but also to their very aspirations, which are devoid of any value or substance.

21 Although these enemies are not the psalmist's personal foes, he cannot remain on the sidelines in this war between good and evil. **For surely Your enemies, Lord, I hate, and I contend with those who rise against You.**

תַּכְלִית שִׂנְאָה שְׂנֵאתִים ²²
לְאוֹיְבִים הָיוּ לִי:

²² I hate them with utter hatred;
they have become my enemies.

חָקְרֵנִי אֵל וְדַע לְבָבִי בְּחָנֵנִי ²³
וְדַע שַׂרְעַפָּי:

²³ Search me, God, and know my
heart; test me and know my
thoughts,

וּרְאֵה אִם־דֶּרֶךְ־עֹצֶב בִּי ²⁴
וּנְחֵנִי בְּדֶרֶךְ עוֹלָם:

²⁴ and see if there is any grievous
way in me. Lead me on the
path to eternity.

PSALM 140

A psalm of supplication and entreaty, written by David at a time when he was pursued
by King Saul's men while being slandered and falsely accused.

לַמְנַצֵּחַ מִזְמוֹר לְדָוִד: א

¹ For the chief musician, a psalm
by David.

חַלְּצֵנִי יהוה מֵאָדָם רָע ב
מֵאִישׁ חֲמָסִים תִּנְצְרֵנִי:

² Rescue me, Lord, from
evil men; protect me from
unjust men,

כט לחודש
29th day
of month

---

²² **I hate them with utter hatred; they have become my enemies.** I hate them not because
they have at any time harmed me or hurt my feelings, but because I am obliged to take part in
a war that is essentially directed against You. At the very least, I am obliged to state which side I
support and which side I oppose.

²³ **Search me, God,** concerning these and other matters, **and know my heart.** Know that my
most profound intentions are directed solely toward You. **Test me and know my thoughts,**

²⁴ **and see if there is any grievous way in me.** If You find that my heart's inclination has in any
way led me astray, **lead me on the path to eternity,** guide me to the right path, that which
leads to eternity.

PSALM 140
¹ For the chief musician, a psalm by David.
² Rescue me, Lord, from evil men; protect me from unjust men,

אֲשֶׁר חָשְׁבוּ רָעוֹת בְּלֵב כָּל־
יוֹם יָגוּרוּ מִלְחָמוֹת:

³ those who devise wicked plans in their hearts, each day provoking wars.

שָׁנְנוּ לְשׁוֹנָם כְּמוֹ־נָחָשׁ
חֲמַת עַכְשׁוּב תַּחַת שְׂפָתֵימוֹ
סֶלָה:

⁴ They sharpen their tongues like a serpent, the venom of spiders is under their lips, Selah.

שָׁמְרֵנִי יהוה ׀ מִידֵי רָשָׁע
מֵאִישׁ חֲמָסִים תִּנְצְרֵנִי אֲשֶׁר
חָשְׁבוּ לִדְחוֹת פְּעָמָי:

⁵ Guard me, Lord, from the hands of the wicked; protect me from unjust men who seek to trip my feet.

טָמְנוּ־גֵאִים ׀ פַּח לִי וַחֲבָלִים
פָּרְשׂוּ רֶשֶׁת לְיַד־מַעְגָּל
מֹקְשִׁים שָׁתוּ־לִי סֶלָה:

⁶ The arrogant laid a trap for me; they spread a net with cords by the wayside and set snares for me, Selah.

אָמַרְתִּי לַיהוה אֵלִי אָתָּה
הַאֲזִינָה יהוה קוֹל תַּחֲנוּנָי:

⁷ I said to the Lord: You are my God; listen, Lord, to the sound of my pleas.

---

³ **those who devise wicked plans in their hearts, each day provoking wars.** It is as if they live their lives in continual warfare.

⁴ **They sharpen their tongues like a serpent.** In the book of Psalms and elsewhere in the Bible, the serpent's tongue symbolizes slander. **The venom of spiders is under their lips, Selah.** According to some, the word *akhshuv* refers to a spider, as translated here. Others believe it is a different kind of venomous creature that is similar to a spider.

⁵ **Guard me, Lord, from the hands of the wicked; protect me from unjust men who seek to trip my feet.**

⁶ Such men attempt to bring about my downfall, and for this purpose they use all kinds of cunning tricks. **The arrogant laid a trap for me; they spread a net with cords by the wayside and set snares for me, Selah.** Animals are often trapped in this fashion; their feet get entangled in netting that is spread near the places that they frequent. The psalmist is referring to various traps that his enemies set for him.

⁷ At such times, the psalmist has no recourse other than prayer. **I said to the Lord: You are my God; listen, Lord, to the sound of my pleas.**

יְהֹוִה אֲדֹנָי עֹז יְשׁוּעָתֵי ח
סַכֹּתָה לְרֹאשִׁי בְּיוֹם נָשֶׁק:

אַל־תִּתֵּן יְהוָה מַאֲוַיֵּי רָשָׁע ט
זְמָמוֹ אַל־תָּפֵק יָרוּמוּ סֶלָה:

רֹאשׁ מְסִבָּי עֲמַל שְׂפָתֵימוֹ י
יכַסֵּ֫מוֹ

יַכַסֵּמוֹ

יָמִיטוּ עֲלֵיהֶם גֶּחָלִים בָּאֵשׁ יא
יַפִּלֵם בְּמַהֲמֹרוֹת בַּל־יָקוּמוּ:

יָמוֹט

אִישׁ לָשׁוֹן בַּל־יִכּוֹן בָּאָרֶץ יב
אִישׁ־חָמָס רָע יְצוּדֶנּוּ
לְמַדְחֵפֹת:

8 Lord, my Lord, strength of my deliverance, You shielded my head on the day of battle.

9 Lord, do not grant the desires of the wicked. Do not bring their scheme to fruition; may they depart, Selah.

10 May the mischief of their lips cover the heads of those who surround me.

11 May burning coals fall on them; may they be cast into the fire, into deep pits, never to rise.

12 May slanderers have no place in the land; may evil trap unjust men and thrust them into the depths.

---

8 **Lord, my Lord, strength of my deliverance, You shielded my head on the day of battle.**

9 **Lord, do not grant the desires of the wicked. Do not bring their scheme to fruition.** Do not allow the wicked to succeed in carrying out their evil plans. **May they depart** from me, **Selah.**

10 **May the mischief of their lips cover the heads of those who surround me.** The essence of David's request is that the evildoers be brought down by their own evil.

11 **May burning coals fall on them; may they be cast into the fire, into deep pits**, another means of trapping animals, **never to rise**.

12 **May slanderers have no place in the land; may evil trap unjust men and thrust them into the depths.**

יָדַ֗עְתִּי כִּֽי־יַעֲשֶׂ֣ה יהו֣ה דִּ֑ין
עֲנִ֖י מִשְׁפַּ֣ט אֶבְיֹנִֽים:

אַ֣ךְ צַ֭דִּיקִים יוֹד֣וּ לִשְׁמֶ֑ךָ
יֵשְׁב֥וּ יְ֝שָׁרִ֗ים אֶת־פָּנֶֽיךָ:

13 I know the Lord will minister justice to the poor, fair judgment to the needy.

14 The righteous will surely give thanks to Your name; the upright will dwell in Your presence.

PSALM 141

Another psalm depicting an individual pursued by enemies, whose wickedness he decries. In addition, the psalmist prays to be spared from becoming like his foes; he wants no part of their modes of behavior.

מִזְמ֗וֹר לְדָ֫וִ֥ד יהו֣ה קְ֭רָאתִיךָ
ח֣וּשָׁה לִּ֑י הַאֲזִ֥ינָה ק֝וֹלִ֗י
בְּקָרְאִי־לָֽךְ:

תִּכּ֤וֹן תְּפִלָּתִ֣י קְטֹ֣רֶת לְפָנֶ֑יךָ
מַשְׂאַ֥ת כַּ֝פַּ֗י מִנְחַת־עָֽרֶב:

1 A psalm by David. Lord, I have called out to You; make haste to help me. Listen to my voice as I call out to You.

2 Let my prayer stand as an offering of incense before You; the lifting of my hands, an evening offering.

---

13 In contrast to the fate of the wicked, who are brought down by their own evil deeds, the righteous will eventually be aided and rescued. **I know the Lord will minister justice to the poor, fair judgment to the needy.**

14 And after the enemy has collapsed, **the righteous will surely give thanks to Your name; the upright will dwell** in peace **in Your presence.**

PSALM 141

1 **A psalm by David. Lord, I have called out to You; make haste to help me.** I am in need of immediate rescue. **Listen to my voice as I call out to You.**

2 **Let my prayer stand as an offering of incense before You.** Let my prayer, although it consists only of words, be considered as pleasing before You as an incense offering. **The lifting of my hands, an evening offering.** Let my hands lifted in prayer be deemed a sacrificial offering.

שִׁיתָה יהוה שָׁמְרָה לְפִי
נִצְּרָה עַל־דַּל שְׂפָתָי:

אַל־תַּט־לִבִּי לְדָבָר רָע
לְהִתְעוֹלֵל עֲלִלוֹת בְּרֶשַׁע
אֶת־אִישִׁים פֹּעֲלֵי־אָוֶן וּבַל־
אֶלְחַם בְּמַנְעַמֵּיהֶם:

יֶהֶלְמֵנִי צַדִּיק חֶסֶד וְיוֹכִיחֵנִי
שֶׁמֶן רֹאשׁ אַל־יָנִי רֹאשִׁי כִּי־
עוֹד וּתְפִלָּתִי בְּרָעוֹתֵיהֶם:

נִשְׁמְטוּ בִידֵי־סֶלַע שֹׁפְטֵיהֶם
וְשָׁמְעוּ אֲמָרַי כִּי נָעֵמוּ:

³ Place a sentinel, Lord, at my mouth; guard the door to my lips.

⁴ Do not incline my heart to anything evil, to carry out deeds of wickedness with men who are evildoers. And let me not eat of their delicacies.

⁵ May the Righteous One strike me, for it is a kindness. May He rebuke me; it is like fragrant oil. Let it not be removed from my head; my prayer is still against their evil doings.

⁶ Their judges will slip down from the rocks; they will hear my words, for they are pleasing.

---

3 And this is the prayer I offer up to You: **Place a sentinel, Lord, at my mouth,** guard my tongue so that I do not engage in evil speech as do my enemies. **Guard the door to my lips,** enable me to remain silent, to keep my mouth closed.

4 **Do not incline my heart to anything evil, to carry out deeds of wickedness with men who are evildoers.** Although I am in a difficult situation that may stem in part from my refusal to collaborate with evildoers, I pray for the strength to remain steadfast. **And let me not eat of their delicacies.** I do not wish to break bread with them or to enjoy any of the delicacies they may offer.

5 **May the Righteous One strike me, for it is a kindness.** Even if You hit me, You are righteous, and You do me a kindness. **May He rebuke me; it is like fragrant oil.** Your rebuke is like fragrant oil anointing my head, and I pray: **Let it,** this oil, **not be removed from my head; my prayer is still against their evil doings.** As I continue my way, I pray to be rescued from my enemies.

6 **Their judges will slip down from the rocks.** "Their judges" refers to their leaders. Ultimately, they will collapse, as if tumbling off a boulder, and **they will hear my words, for they are pleasing.** At that point, my enemies may be ready to understand that I am not at the root of the

כְּמוֹ פֹלֵחַ וּבֹקֵעַ בָּאָרֶץ נִפְזְרוּ
עֲצָמֵינוּ לְפִי שְׁאוֹל:

כִּי אֵלֶיךָ ׀ יֱהֹוִה אֲדֹנָי עֵינָי
בְּכָה חָסִיתִי אַל־תְּעַר נַפְשִׁי:

שָׁמְרֵנִי מִידֵי פַח יָקְשׁוּ לִי
וּמֹקְשׁוֹת פֹּעֲלֵי אָוֶן:

יִפְּלוּ בְמַכְמֹרָיו רְשָׁעִים יַחַד
אָנֹכִי עַד־אֶעֱבוֹר:

7 As if chopping and breaking
the earth, our bones are
scattered at the mouth of
the grave.

8 Yet my eyes are toward You,
Lord my God. In You I take
refuge; do not discard me.

9 Guard me from the trap they
laid for me, from the snares of
evildoers.

10 Let the wicked fall together
into their own nets, until
I escape.

---

animosity between us. On the contrary, I am trying to conduct myself in the best possible way, for their sake as well as my own.

7 In the meantime, however, **as if** a woodcutter is **chopping and breaking the earth,** where in the course of chopping and splitting wood he makes holes in the ground underneath, I am receiving blows from all sides. Moreover, I feel as if **our bones are scattered at the mouth of the grave,** as if we are being torn apart, leading to our death.

8 **Yet my eyes are toward You, Lord my God. In You I take refuge; do not discard me.**

9 **Guard me from the trap they laid for me, from the snares of evildoers.**

10 **Let the wicked fall together into their own nets.** May they all be snared by their own devices, **until I escape,** so that I may escape to safety.

PSALM 142

A psalm of entreaty by one who is isolated. Surrounded by hatred
and by enemies pursuing him, he prays to be rescued.

מַשְׂכִּיל לְדָוִד בִּהְיוֹתוֹ
בַמְּעָרָה תְפִלָּה:

קוֹלִי אֶל־יהוה אֶזְעָק קוֹלִי
אֶל־יהוה אֶתְחַנָּן:

אֶשְׁפֹּךְ לְפָנָיו שִׂיחִי צָרָתִי
לְפָנָיו אַגִּיד:

בְּהִתְעַטֵּף עָלַי ׀ רוּחִי וְאַתָּה
יָדַעְתָּ נְתִיבָתִי בְּאֹרַח־זוּ
אֲהַלֵּךְ טָמְנוּ פַח לִי:

הַבֵּיט יָמִין ׀ וּרְאֵה וְאֵין־לִי
מַכִּיר אָבַד מָנוֹס מִמֶּנִּי אֵין
דּוֹרֵשׁ לְנַפְשִׁי:

1 A contemplation by David when he was in the cave, a prayer.

2 My voice is to the Lord when I cry out; my voice is to the Lord when I plead.

3 I pour out my woe before Him; before Him, I speak of my trouble.

4 When my spirit grows faint, You know my way; on the road where I go, they have laid a trap for me.

5 Look on the right and see; I have no one who knows me, there is nowhere to flee. No one seeks my well-being.

PSALM 142

1 **A contemplation by David when he was in the cave,** hiding from Saul's henchmen;[11] it is also **a** song of **prayer.**

2 **My voice is to the Lord when I cry out; my voice is to the Lord when I plead.**

3 **I pour out my woe before Him.** The word *siḥi*, translated here as "my woe," connotes both prayer and sorrow. **Before Him, I speak of my trouble.**

4 **When my spirit grows faint, You know my way.** You know that the path I follow is not one of evil. Nonetheless, **on the road where I go, they have laid a trap for me.**

5 **Look on the right and see.** One's right side represents his strength, or this may refer to the place where one's friends stand by him. **I have no one who knows me,** I am completely alone; **there is nowhere to flee. No one seeks my well-being.** No one is looking after me or seeking ways to help me.

זָעַקְתִּי אֵלֶיךָ יהוה אָמַרְתִּי
אַתָּה מַחְסִי חֶלְקִי בְּאֶרֶץ
הַחַיִּים:

הַקְשִׁיבָה ׀ אֶל־רִנָּתִי כִּי־
דַלּוֹתִי מְאֹד הַצִּילֵנִי מֵרֹדְפַי
כִּי אָמְצוּ מִמֶּנִּי:

הוֹצִיאָה מִמַּסְגֵּר ׀ נַפְשִׁי
לְהוֹדוֹת אֶת־שְׁמֶךָ בִּי יַכְתִּרוּ
צַדִּיקִים כִּי תִגְמֹל עָלָי:

⁶ I cried out to You, Lord, and said: You are my refuge, my portion in the land of the living.

⁷ Listen to my cry, for I am greatly weakened. Rescue me from my pursuers, for they are too strong for me.

⁸ Release me from confinement, so I may give thanks to Your name. The righteous, through me, will be glorified when You deal kindly with me.

PSALM 143

A song of prayer and entreaty at a time of distress, mainly caused by outside enemies.

מִזְמוֹר לְדָוִד ׀ יהוה ׀ שְׁמַע
תְּפִלָּתִי הַאֲזִינָה אֶל־תַּחֲנוּנַי
בֶּאֱמֻנָתְךָ עֲנֵנִי בְּצִדְקָתֶךָ:

¹ A psalm by David. Lord, hear my prayer, listen to my pleas. In Your faithfulness, in Your righteousness, answer me.

---

⁶ **I cried out to You, Lord, and said: You are my refuge,** my only refuge, **my portion in the land of the living,** my only source of help in this world.

⁷ **Listen to my cry, for I am greatly weakened. Rescue me from my pursuers, for they are too strong for me.** I have become so weakened that I cannot hold my own against my enemies.

⁸ **Release me from confinement, so I may give thanks to Your name. The righteous, through me, will be glorified when You deal kindly with me.**

PSALM 143

¹ **A psalm by David. Lord, hear my prayer, listen to my pleas.** David's plea for help and protection is grounded on God's mercy: **In Your faithfulness, in Your righteousness, answer**

וְאַל־תָּבוֹא בְמִשְׁפָּט אֶת־ נ
עַבְדֶּךָ כִּי לֹא־יִצְדַּק לְפָנֶיךָ
כָל־חָי:

כִּי רָדַף אוֹיֵב ׀ נַפְשִׁי דִּכָּא ג
לָאָרֶץ חַיָּתִי הוֹשִׁבַנִי
בְמַחֲשַׁכִּים כְּמֵתֵי עוֹלָם:

וַתִּתְעַטֵּף עָלַי רוּחִי בְּתוֹכִי ד
יִשְׁתּוֹמֵם לִבִּי:

זָכַרְתִּי יָמִים ׀ מִקֶּדֶם הָגִיתִי ה
בְכָל־פָּעֳלֶךָ בְּמַעֲשֵׂה יָדֶיךָ
אֲשׂוֹחֵחַ:

פֵּרַשְׂתִּי יָדַי אֵלֶיךָ נַפְשִׁי ׀ ו
כְּאֶרֶץ־עֲיֵפָה לְךָ סֶלָה:

2 And do not put Your servant to judgment, for no living thing can be justified before You.

3 Indeed, the enemy has pursued me, crushed my life to the ground, made me dwell in dark places, like those forever dead.

4 My spirit grows faint; my heart is stunned within me.

5 I remember days of old when I meditated on all Your doings and spoke of the work of Your hands.

6 I stretch out my hands to You; my soul, like a parched land, to You, Selah.

---

me. Despite his admitted imperfections, David emphasizes that he has always striven to be close to God and to serve Him. Thus, he entreats God to heed his prayer out of His mercy and righteousness.

2 **And do not put Your servant to judgment.** I am not requesting justice but rather mercy. And it is not only for myself that I say this, **for no living thing can be justified before You.** Thus, were I to be judged, I would certainly be found guilty.

3 In the meantime, however, I am suffering. **Indeed, the enemy has pursued me, crushed my life to the ground;** my foes are crushing the life out of me. They **made me dwell in dark places, like those forever dead.**

4 **My spirit grows faint.** The phrase *vatitatef alai ruḥi*, "my spirit grows faint," literally, "my soul is wrapped up within me," is an expression of pain and distress. It also conveys the soul's becoming constricted, shrinking, almost as if enveloping itself in sorrow. **My heart is stunned within me.**

5 **I remember days of old,** when I was at ease, **when I meditated on all Your doings and spoke of the work of Your hands.**

6 **I stretch out my hands to You** in prayer; **my soul, like a parched land, to You, Selah.** I turn to you as desperately as parched earth needs rain.

מַהֵר עֲנֵנִי ׀ יהוה כָּלְתָה
רוּחִי אַל־תַּסְתֵּר פָּנֶיךָ מִמֶּנִּי
וְנִמְשַׁלְתִּי עִם־יָֽרְדֵי בֽוֹר׃

הַשְׁמִיעֵנִי בַבֹּקֶר ׀ חַסְדֶּךָ כִּי־
בְךָ בָטָחְתִּי הוֹדִיעֵנִי דֶּֽרֶךְ־זוּ
אֵלֵךְ כִּי־אֵלֶיךָ נָשָׂאתִי נַפְשִֽׁי׃

הַצִּילֵנִי מֵאֹיְבַי ׀ יהוה אֵלֶיךָ
כִסִּֽתִי׃

לַמְּדֵנִי ׀ לַעֲשׂוֹת רְצוֹנֶךָ כִּי־
אַתָּה אֱלוֹהָי רֽוּחֲךָ טוֹבָה
תַּנְחֵנִי בְּאֶרֶץ מִישֽׁוֹר׃

לְמַֽעַן־שִׁמְךָ יהוה תְּחַיֵּנִי
בְּצִדְקָתְךָ ׀ תּוֹצִיא מִצָּרָה
נַפְשִֽׁי׃

7 Answer me quickly, Lord; my spirit fails. Do not hide Your face from me, lest I be like those who descend to the pit.

8 Let me hear Your kindness in the morning, for in You I have trusted. Show me the way in which I should walk, for I lift up my soul to You.

9 Rescue me from my enemies, Lord, for in You I take cover.

10 Teach me to do Your will, for You are my God. Your spirit is good; lead me to a level land.

11 For the sake of Your name, Lord, save my life. In Your righteousness, free me from distress.

---

7 **Answer me quickly, Lord; my spirit fails.** I feel as though I am getting less and less air to breathe. **Do not hide Your face from me, lest I be like those who descend to the pit.** If You do not turn to me, I will be like someone who is already dead.

8 **Let me hear Your kindness in the morning, for in You I have trusted.** I have always been bound and connected to You, and You are my main support. **Show me the way in which I should walk, for I lift up my soul to You** now, as I have always done in the past.

9 **Rescue me from my enemies, Lord, for in You I take cover.** I take cover and protection in Your shadow; You are my shelter and my armor.

10 **Teach me to do Your will,** as perhaps I am inadvertently erring in my ways, **for You are my God. Your spirit is good,** and You can lead me on the correct path. **Lead me to a level land.** Mountain paths are tortuous and dangerous, whereas on a level path, one can move more freely and see both far and near.

11 **For the sake of Your name, Lord, save my life. In Your righteousness, free me from distress.**

וּבְחַסְדְּךָ תַּצְמִית אֹיְבָי
וְהַאֲבַדְתָּ כָּל־צֹרְרֵי נַפְשִׁי כִּי
אֲנִי עַבְדֶּךָ:

And in Your kindness, destroy my enemies; lay waste to all my foes, for I am Your servant.

PSALM 144

A psalm depicting a time of war, a prayer for God's help and an expression of gratitude for the victory that was wrought. It concludes with a description of ensuing peace and tranquility in the land once there are no longer any enemies to threaten it.

לְדָוִד ׀ בָּרוּךְ יהוה ׀ צוּרִי
הַמְלַמֵּד יָדַי לַקְרָב אֶצְבְּעוֹתַי
לַמִּלְחָמָה:

By David. Blessed is the Lord, my rock, who trains my hands for battle and my fingers for warfare.

חַסְדִּי וּמְצוּדָתִי מִשְׂגַּבִּי
וּמְפַלְטִי לִי מָגִנִּי וּבוֹ חָסִיתִי
הָרוֹדֵד עַמִּי תַחְתָּי:

My kindness and my fortress, my stronghold and my rescuer, my shield in whom I shelter, who subdues my people under me.

יהוה מָה־אָדָם וַתֵּדָעֵהוּ בֶּן־
אֱנוֹשׁ וַתְּחַשְּׁבֵהוּ:

Lord, what is man that You should know him, a mortal whom You should consider?

---

12 **And in Your kindness** toward me, **destroy my enemies; lay waste to all my foes, for I am Your servant,** and as one under Your protection, I ask for Your help.

PSALM 144
1 **By David. Blessed is the Lord, my rock, who trains my hands for battle and my fingers for warfare,** thereby enabling me to be victorious in battle.
2 **My kindness,** the one who bestows kindness upon me, **and my fortress,** who protects me, **my stronghold and my rescuer, my shield in whom I shelter, who subdues my people under me,** enabling me to be a king and leader of my people.
3 This is a song of gratitude, not glorification. For even the victorious king knows well that God's beneficence is responsible for his victory, and this leads him to reflect: **Lord, what is man that**

אָדָם לַהֶבֶל דָּמָה יָמָיו כְּצֵל
עוֹבֵר:

יהוה הַט־שָׁמֶיךָ וְתֵרֵד גַּע
בֶּהָרִים וְיֶעֱשָׁנוּ:

בְּרוֹק בָּרָק וּתְפִיצֵם שְׁלַח
חִצֶּיךָ וּתְהֻמֵּם:

שְׁלַח יָדֶיךָ מִמָּרוֹם פְּצֵנִי
וְהַצִּילֵנִי מִמַּיִם רַבִּים מִיַּד בְּנֵי
נֵכָר:

4 Man is like vapor, his days like a passing shadow.

5 Lord, tilt Your heavens and descend; touch the mountains and they will smolder.

6 Send forth lightning and scatter them; let fly Your arrows and confound them.

7 Stretch out Your hand from above; deliver and rescue me from surging waters, from the hands of foreigners,

---

You should know him? Why should humans merit Your love and attention? **A mortal whom You should consider?** What is their worth that You think about them and accord them status?

4 After all, **man is like vapor.** Human life is ephemeral, like a whiff of vapor or a blowing wind. **His days** are **like a passing shadow.** Man's life has even less substance than a fixed shadow; it is like a "passing shadow," such as that of a moving cloud or bird. The psalmist realizes this, and therefore prays for God's continued beneficence rather than arguing that man has any special merit.

5 The following is the psalmist's prayer for victory in the wars he is waging: **Lord, tilt Your heavens,** bring the heavens closer to earth, so to speak, **and descend** so that You can intervene in what is happening. **Touch the mountains and they will smolder.** When You merely touch the mountains, they begin to burn.

6 **Send forth lightning and scatter them,** my enemies; **let fly Your arrows and confound them.**

7 **Stretch out Your hand from above** to aid me; **deliver and rescue me from surging waters,** a metaphor that the psalmist goes on to clarify: **From the hands of foreigners** who are waging war against me.

אֲשֶׁר פִּיהֶם דִּבֶּר־שָׁוְא
וִימִינָם יְמִין שָׁקֶר:

אֱלֹהִים שִׁיר חָדָשׁ אָשִׁירָה
לָּךְ בְּנֵבֶל עָשׂוֹר אֲזַמְּרָה־לָּךְ:

הַנּוֹתֵן תְּשׁוּעָה לַמְּלָכִים
הַפּוֹצֶה אֶת־דָּוִד עַבְדּוֹ
מֵחֶרֶב רָעָה:

פְּצֵנִי וְהַצִּילֵנִי מִיַּד בְּנֵי־נֵכָר
אֲשֶׁר פִּיהֶם דִּבֶּר־שָׁוְא
וִימִינָם יְמִין שָׁקֶר:

8 whose mouths speak deceit, whose right hand is a right hand of lies.

9 God, I will sing a new song to You, on a harp of ten strings I will sing praises to You,

10 who gives salvation to kings, who delivers David His servant from the sword of evil.

11 Deliver and rescue me from the hands of foreigners whose mouths speak deceit, whose right hand is a right hand of lies,

---

8 Those enemies are dangerous not only as foes but also as allies, because their loyalty cannot be trusted: They are those **whose mouths speak deceit, whose right hand,** the hand generally extended in assistance or in the forging of a covenant, **is a right hand of lies.**

9 **God, I will sing a new song to You, on a harp of ten strings.** A ten-stringed harp is unusual; harps of that time generally had no more than seven or eight strings. **I will sing praises to You,**

10 and this is my song of praise: It is He **who gives salvation to kings, who delivers David His servant from the sword of evil.** He saves me in times of battle and also from any form of evil.

11 Here the psalmist repeats his plea: **Deliver and rescue me from the hands of foreigners whose mouths speak deceit, whose right hand is a right hand of lies,**

יב אֲשֶׁ֤ר בָּנֵ֨ינוּ ׀ כִּנְטִעִים֮
מְגֻדָּלִ֪ים בִּנְעֽוּרֵ֫יהֶ֥ם בְּנוֹתֵ֥ינוּ
כְזָוִיֹּ֑ת מְ֝חֻטָּב֗וֹת תַּבְנִ֥ית
הֵיכָֽל׃

יג מְזָוֵ֣ינוּ מְלֵאִים֮ מְפִיקִ֪ים מִזַּ֫ן
אֶל־זַ֥ן צֹאונֵ֥נוּ מַאֲלִיפ֑וֹת
מְ֝רֻבָּב֗וֹת בְּחֽוּצוֹתֵֽינוּ׃

יד אַלּוּפֵ֗ינוּ מְֽסֻבָּ֫לִ֥ים אֵֽין־פֶּ֭רֶץ
וְאֵ֣ין יוֹצֵ֑את וְאֵ֥ין צְ֝וָחָ֗ה
בִּרְחֹבֹתֵֽינוּ׃

טו אַשְׁרֵ֣י הָ֭עָם שֶׁכָּ֣כָה לּ֑וֹ אַֽשְׁרֵ֥י
הָ֝עָ֗ם שֶׁיֳהֹוָ֥ה אֱלֹהָֽיו׃

12 so that our sons will be like saplings tended in their youth, our daughters like shapely corner pillars, like the form of a palace.

13 Our storehouses are full, supplying all manner of goods; our flocks multiplying to thousands and tens of thousands in our marketplaces.

14 Our oxen are laden. There is no breach and no going forth; there is no shrieking in our streets.

15 Happy the nation for whom this is so; happy the nation whose God is the Lord.

---

12 **so that our sons will be like saplings tended in their youth.** After the descriptions of war, this verse and the ones that follow depict the nation during an era of tranquility and prosperity following their victory. The people's sons are likened to saplings that grow without impediments. **Our daughters** will be **like shapely corner pillars, like the form of a palace.** The daughters are described as decorated pillars in a palace. *Heikhal* is a word that can also refer to the Temple. This description evokes not only beauty but holiness and perfection.

13 **Our storehouses are full, supplying all manner of goods; our flocks multiplying to thousands and tens of thousands in our marketplaces.**

14 **Our oxen are laden** with goods. **There is no breach and no going forth.** This sentence refers both to the cattle, which remain safely confined, and to life in general, which is tranquil and secure. **There is no shrieking** out of anger or fighting **in our streets.**

15 **Happy** is **the nation for whom this is so,** who is blessed by God with a good life of peace and prosperity; **happy** is **the nation whose God is the Lord.**

PSALM 145

The most well-known chapter of the book of Psalms, since the Sages included it in the
daily prayer book and it is recited at least three times a day. Essentially, this psalm is one of
praise and thanks for God's eternal kindness; it contains no entreaties or requests. It is structured
alphabetically, and while there is no continuous line of thought from one verse to the next,
all the verses taken together form a portrait of God's beneficence in the world. In the prayer book,
the psalm is bracketed by two verses at the beginning and one at the end, Psalms 84:5 and 144:15
at the beginning and Psalms 115:18 at the end. These verses were added in order to complete
certain aspects of the psalm that had not been emphasized in the words of this chapter.

תְּהִלָּה לְדָוִד אֲרוֹמִמְךָ
אֱלוֹהַי הַמֶּלֶךְ וַאֲבָרְכָה שִׁמְךָ
לְעוֹלָם וָעֶד:

בְּכָל־יוֹם אֲבָרְכֶךָּ וַאֲהַלְלָה
שִׁמְךָ לְעוֹלָם וָעֶד:

גָּדוֹל יהוה וּמְהֻלָּל מְאֹד
וְלִגְדֻלָּתוֹ אֵין חֵקֶר:

א 1 A psalm of praise, by David. I
extol You, my God, the King,
and I bless Your name forever
and ever.

ב 2 Every day I bless You, and
I praise Your name forever
and ever.

ג 3 The Lord is great and highly
extolled, and His greatness is
unfathomable.

לחודש
30th day
of month

PSALM 145

1 **A psalm of praise, by David.** The heading, "a psalm of praise," is a fitting characterization
of this psalm. Two main themes are presented in the verses that follow. The first pertains to the
the Holy One as a gracious God who sustains His world. The second describes God's majesty and
might, which are referred to repeatedly, explicitly and implicitly. Thus, **I extol You, my God, the
King.** I give You honor, and in this way Your greatness in the world is magnified. The second half
of the verse, **and I bless Your name forever and ever,** reiterates and emphasizes this point.
"Forever" means that God is blessed at all times, continually; "and ever" indicates that He is blessed
for eternity.

2 **Every day I bless You.** This phrase, among other things, accounts for the Sages' decision to
include this psalm in the daily prayer service. However, the concluding phrase, **and I praise Your
name forever and ever,** introduces a certain tension or contrast between the daily obligation
to bless God and His eternal praise. It should be noted that, with one significant exception in verse
18, all verses in this psalm have a two-part structure, whereby the theme of the first half is either
reiterated or complemented from a different perspective in the second half.

3 **The Lord is great and highly extolled, and His greatness is unfathomable.** The manifold

דּוֹר לְדוֹר יְשַׁבַּח מַעֲשֶׂיךָ
וּגְבוּרֹתֶיךָ יַגִּידוּ:

ד

From generation to generation
Your works are praised, and
they tell of Your mighty acts.

4

הֲדַר כְּבוֹד הוֹדֶךָ וְדִבְרֵי
נִפְלְאֹתֶיךָ אָשִׂיחָה:

ה

I speak about the glorious
honor of Your majesty, and of
Your wondrous deeds.

5

וֶעֱזוּז נוֹרְאֹתֶיךָ יֹאמֵרוּ
וּגְדוּלָּתֶךָ אֲסַפְּרֶנָּה:

ו

וגדלתך

They speak of the power of
Your awesome acts, and I tell of
Your greatness.

6

זֵכֶר רַב־טוּבְךָ יַבִּיעוּ
וְצִדְקָתְךָ יְרַנֵּנוּ:

ז

They give voice to the
recollection of Your
great goodness, and of
Your righteousness they
joyously sing.

7

חַנּוּן וְרַחוּם יְהוָה אֶרֶךְ אַפַּיִם
וּגְדָל־חָסֶד:

ח

Gracious and merciful is the
Lord, slow to anger, and great
in kindness.

8

---

forms of praise offered to God cannot convey the full extent of His greatness; it is beyond human comprehension.

4 **From generation to generation Your works are praised.** Every generation transmits its praises of God to the generation that follows; in this way, praise of God is continually being created, added to, and renewed. **And they tell of Your mighty acts.** Although this is a hymn of praise for God's kindness, His attribute of might, while not expounded on here, is always in the background.

5 **I speak about the glorious honor of Your majesty,** I will say everything that can possibly be said to honor and glorify God, **and of Your wondrous deeds**.

6 **They speak of the power of Your awesome acts.** God's attributes of power and awesomeness appear elsewhere in Psalms and throughout the Bible. **And I tell of Your greatness;** "greatness" refers to a softer, more merciful aspect of God's power.

7 **They,** those who worship You, **give voice to the recollection of Your great goodness, and of Your righteousness,** Your beneficence and generosity on their behalf and on behalf of the entire world, **they joyously sing.**

8 And this is their praise that they sing: **Gracious and merciful is the Lord, slow to anger, and great in kindness.**

ט טוֹב־יְהוָה לַכֹּל וְרַחֲמָיו עַל־
כָּל־מַעֲשָׂיו:

יוֹדוּךָ יְהוָה כָּל־מַעֲשֶׂיךָ
וַחֲסִידֶיךָ יְבָרְכוּכָה:

יא כְּבוֹד מַלְכוּתְךָ יֹאמֵרוּ
וּגְבוּרָתְךָ יְדַבֵּרוּ:

יב לְהוֹדִיעַ ׀ לִבְנֵי הָאָדָם
גְּבוּרֹתָיו וּכְבוֹד הֲדַר
מַלְכוּתוֹ:

יג מַלְכוּתְךָ מַלְכוּת כָּל־עֹלָמִים
וּמֶמְשַׁלְתְּךָ בְּכָל־דּוֹר וָדֹר:

⁹ The Lord is good to all, and His mercy extends to all of His creations.

¹⁰ All Your creations thank You, Lord, and Your devoted ones bless You.

¹¹ They speak of the honor of Your kingdom, and they tell of Your might,

¹² to make known to people His mighty acts, and the honored splendor of His kingdom.

¹³ Your kingship is an eternal kingship, and Your reign is in every generation.

---

⁹ **The Lord is good to all, and His mercy extends to all of His creations.** A new idea is introduced here: God's beneficence is not limited to a specific category of creation. It is all-inclusive and therefore also balanced. It follows that if God is good "to all," He is good to celestial as well as earthly beings, merciful to predators as well as to their prey.

¹⁰ **All Your creations thank You, Lord.** Everything You have created is grateful to You. **And Your devoted ones,** those who are closest to You, **bless You.**

¹¹ After mentioning giving thanks in general, more specific praise is articulated: **They speak of the honor of Your kingdom, and they tell of Your might.**

¹² It is important to speak about these matters and explain them to others, as it enables God's greatness to be acknowledged by all, and **to make known to people His mighty acts, and the honored splendor of His kingdom.** It is the obligation of those who know this, and who can tell about it, to do so.

¹³ A partial list of praise follows: **Your kingship is an eternal kingship, and Your reign is in every generation.** God's sovereignty is eternal. There is a difference in nuance between the two terms used in this verse. *Malkhut*, "kingship," conveys a knowing and willing acceptance of God's sovereignty, whereas *memshala*, "reign," refers to God's controlling rule, which exists independent of man's awareness and acknowledgment.

יד סוֹמֵךְ יְהוָה לְכָל־הַנֹּפְלִים
וְזוֹקֵף לְכָל־הַכְּפוּפִים:

טו עֵינֵי־כֹל אֵלֶיךָ יְשַׂבֵּרוּ וְאַתָּה
נוֹתֵן־לָהֶם אֶת־אָכְלָם
בְּעִתּוֹ:

טז פּוֹתֵחַ אֶת־יָדֶךָ וּמַשְׂבִּיעַ
לְכָל־חַי רָצוֹן:

יז צַדִּיק יְהוָה בְּכָל־דְּרָכָיו
וְחָסִיד בְּכָל־מַעֲשָׂיו:

יח קָרוֹב יְהוָה לְכָל־קֹרְאָיו לְכֹל
אֲשֶׁר יִקְרָאֻהוּ בֶאֱמֶת:

14 The Lord supports all those who fall, and He straightens all who are bent over.

15 The eyes of all look to You in hope, and You give them their food in its proper time.

16 You open Your hand, and satisfy the desire of every living thing.

17 Just is the Lord in all His ways, and kind in all His deeds.

18 The Lord is close to all who call Him, to all who call Him in truth.

---

14 In accordance with the alphabetical structure of the psalm, this verse should begin with the letter *nun*. However, this letter is skipped,[12] and the psalm continues with a verse beginning with the following letter, *samekh*: **The Lord supports all those who fall.** The word *hanofelim*, translated here as "those who fall," refers to people who are unstable and thus liable to fall unless they are somehow supported. **And He straightens all who are bent over.**

15 **The eyes of all** mankind, and all of creation, **look to You in hope.** You are the source of all hope. **And You** indeed **give them,** all the world's creatures, **their food in its proper time.**

16 **You open Your hand, and satisfy the desire of every living thing.** You see to it that the needs and desires of every living thing are met.

17 **Just is the Lord in all His ways.** As has been noted in many places, our comprehension is exceedingly limited, and because of this we sometimes perceive the ways in which the world works as being unjust. It is precisely for this reason that we are called upon to offer these words of praise. **And kind in all His deeds.** Beyond being just, God extends kindness that greatly exceeds the criteria of justice.

18 **The Lord is close to all who call Him, to all who call Him in truth.** When people turn to God in prayer, He is always near. Or, more precisely, He is always accessible to those who reach out to Him in a sincere manner, calling to Him "in truth." This explanation is indicated by the structure of the verse, the only one in this psalm that does not consist of two clauses linked by the word "and." As previously noted, in all the other verses, the second clause expands upon the first, whereas here the second clause, "to all who call Him in truth," serves to define and qualify the meaning of

רְצוֹן־יְרֵאָיו יַעֲשֶׂה וְאֶת־
שַׁוְעָתָם יִשְׁמַע וְיוֹשִׁיעֵם:

רְצוֹן
יט

19 He grants the wishes of those
who fear Him, and He hears
their cry and saves them.

שׁוֹמֵר יְהוָה אֶת־כָּל־אֹהֲבָיו
וְאֵת כָּל־הָרְשָׁעִים יַשְׁמִיד:

כ

20 The Lord watches over all who
love Him, and He will destroy
all the wicked.

תְּהִלַּת יְהוָה יְדַבֶּר־פִּי
וִיבָרֵךְ כָּל־בָּשָׂר שֵׁם קָדְשׁוֹ
לְעוֹלָם וָעֶד:

כא

21 My mouth speaks praise of the
Lord, and all flesh blesses His
holy name forever and ever.

PSALM 146

A psalm glorifying God's kindness and beneficence,
and avowing that He alone is the source of all good.

הַלְלוּיָהּ הַלְלִי נַפְשִׁי אֶת־
יְהוָה:

א

1 Halleluya. Praise the Lord,
my soul.

אֲהַלְלָה יְהוָה בְּחַיָּי אֲזַמְּרָה
לֵאלֹהַי בְּעוֹדִי:

ב

2 I will praise the Lord as long as
I live; I will sing praises to my
God as long as I am.

---

the first clause, namely, those who do not call to God with sincerity do not achieve closeness to
Him, nor are they answered.

19 When the righteous call out to Him, as mentioned in the previous verse, **He grants the wishes
of those who fear Him, and He hears their cry** when they call out to Him in time of need,
and saves them.

20 **The Lord watches over all who love Him, and He will destroy all the wicked.**

21 In conclusion: **My mouth speaks praise of the Lord.** With this psalm, I, the psalmist, express
the glory of God. **And** in turn it is my hope that **all flesh,** that is, all people, and perhaps all beings
in creation, **blesses His holy name forever and ever.**

PSALM 146

1 **Halleluya. Praise the Lord, my soul.**

2 **I will praise the Lord as long as I live; I will sing praises to my God as long as I am.**

אַל־תִּבְטְח֥וּ בִנְדִיבִ֑ים בְּבֶן־
אָדָ֓ם ׀ שֶׁאֵ֖ין ל֣וֹ תְשׁוּעָֽה:

תֵּצֵ֣א ר֭וּחוֹ יָשֻׁ֣ב לְאַדְמָת֑וֹ
בַּיּ֥וֹם הַ֝ה֗וּא אָבְד֥וּ
עֶשְׁתֹּנֹתָֽיו:

אַשְׁרֵ֗י שֶׁ֤אֵ֣ל יַעֲקֹ֣ב בְּעֶזְר֑וֹ
שִׂ֝בְר֗וֹ עַל־יְהֹוָ֥ה אֱלֹהָֽיו:

עֹשֶׂ֤ה ׀ שָׁמַ֣יִם וָ֭אָרֶץ אֶת־הַיָּ֣ם
וְאֶת־כׇּל־אֲשֶׁר־בָּ֑ם הַשֹּׁמֵ֖ר
אֱמֶ֣ת לְעוֹלָֽם:

עֹשֶׂ֤ה מִשְׁפָּ֨ט ׀ לָעֲשׁוּקִ֗ים
נֹתֵ֣ן לֶ֭חֶם לָרְעֵבִ֑ים יְהֹוָ֗ה
מַתִּ֥יר אֲסוּרִֽים:

³ Do not trust in princes, in man in whom there is no salvation.

⁴ His spirit departs, he returns to the earth; on that day, his plans cease to be.

⁵ Happy is he whose help is from the God of Jacob, whose hope is in the Lord his God,

⁶ who made heaven and earth, the sea and all that is in them, who guards truth forever,

⁷ performing justice for the oppressed, giving bread to the hungry. The Lord releases the imprisoned.

---

³ **Do not trust in princes.** It is important to keep in mind that no one, no matter how rich, powerful, generous, or kind, is entirely a free agent. Individuals invariably depend on others, and many factors are beyond human control. Even if the person has the best of intentions, he is not completely reliable, for one can never truly trust **in man in whom there is no salvation.** Humans can never be a stable, permanent source of security.

⁴ When a person dies, **his spirit departs, he returns to the earth; on that day, his plans cease to be.** His thoughts and plans for the future are buried with him. This holds true for everyone, even for those who, while still alive, are true to their word.

⁵ In contrast: **Happy is he whose help is from the God of Jacob, whose hope is in the Lord his God,** who is both everlasting and omnipotent, as the following verse elaborates:

⁶ **Who made heaven and earth, the sea and all that is in them, Who guards truth forever.** God's truth, and His promises, are unassailable.

⁷ Moreover, God not only created the world, but also continues to watch over it, **performing justice for the** ones who are **oppressed** and abused, who have no one else to rely on, **giving bread to the hungry. The Lord releases the imprisoned.**

יְהוָה ׀ פֹּקֵחַ עִוְרִים יְהוָה זֹקֵף   ח   8   The Lord opens the eyes of
כְּפוּפִים 'יְהוָה אֹהֵב צַדִּיקִים: the blind; the Lord straightens
                                            those bowed down; the Lord
יְהוָה ׀ שֹׁמֵר אֶת־גֵּרִים   ט   loves the righteous.
יָתוֹם וְאַלְמָנָה יְעוֹדֵד וְדֶרֶךְ   9   The Lord protects proselytes;
רְשָׁעִים יְעַוֵּת: He heartens the orphan and
                                            the widow and twists the path
יִמְלֹךְ יְהוָה ׀ לְעוֹלָם אֱלֹהַיִךְ   of the wicked.
צִיּוֹן לְדֹר וָדֹר הַלְלוּיָהּ:   10   May the Lord reign forever,
                                            your God, Zion, for all
                                            generations. Halleluya.

PSALM 147

A song of praise whose distinctive beauty lies in its continual movement from one theme
to another, oscillating between the personal and the more general, the national and the cosmic,
man's problems and the magnitude of the universe. It is akin to an orchestral piece
in which a variety of instruments have been given solo parts.

הַלְלוּיָהּ ׀ כִּי־טוֹב זַמְּרָה   א   1   Halleluya, for it is good to sing
אֱלֹהֵינוּ כִּי־נָעִים נָאוָה   to our God, for it is pleasant;
תְּהִלָּה: praise is lovely.

---

8   **The Lord opens the eyes of the blind; the Lord straightens those** who are **bowed down;
the Lord loves the righteous** and protects them even when they have no human protector.

9   **The Lord protects proselytes,** who have no family or tribe to lean on for support. **He heartens
the orphan and the widow,** who are similarly helpless, **and** by contrast, He **twists the path
of the wicked,** thwarting them in their ways.

10   In light of all the above, it is proper to praise God and pray: **May the Lord reign forever;** may
your God, Zion, rule **for all generations. Halleluya.**

PSALM 147
1   **Halleluya, for it is good to sing to our God.** Praising God is good not only in a moral sense;

בּוֹנֵה יְרוּשָׁלַם יְהֹוָה נִדְחֵי
יִשְׂרָאֵל יְכַנֵּס:

² The Lord is the builder of Jerusalem; He gathers in the dispersed of Israel.

הָרוֹפֵא לִשְׁבוּרֵי לֵב וּמְחַבֵּשׁ
לְעַצְּבוֹתָם:

³ He heals the brokenhearted and binds their wounds.

מוֹנֶה מִסְפָּר לַכּוֹכָבִים לְכֻלָּם
שֵׁמוֹת יִקְרָא:

⁴ He sets a number for the stars, and calls them all by name.

גָּדוֹל אֲדוֹנֵינוּ וְרַב־כֹּחַ
לִתְבוּנָתוֹ אֵין מִסְפָּר:

⁵ Our Lord is great and abundant in strength, His understanding beyond measure.

מְעוֹדֵד עֲנָוִים יְהֹוָה מַשְׁפִּיל
רְשָׁעִים עֲדֵי־אָרֶץ:

⁶ The Lord heartens the humble and casts the wicked to the ground.

---

it also brings happiness to the person praising Him. **For it is pleasant** to sing to Him. **Praise is lovely.**

2 The psalmist now begins with praise of God's greatness and emphasizes the way in which His power is manifest in the cosmos as a whole. God also provides assistance to all men and other beings in distress. **The Lord is the builder of Jerusalem; He gathers in the dispersed of Israel.** God will bring back those who have fled or who have been exiled to different places.

3 **He heals the brokenhearted and binds their wounds.** The word *atzvotam*, translated here as "wounds," more literally means "sorrows." God "binds their wounds" spiritually as well as physically, providing solace for those in sorrow.

4 While God attends to even the smallest of matters, He is, at the same time, sovereign over all that exists: **He sets a number for the stars.** The stars belong to Him; they are all numbered by Him. **And He calls them all by name,** because they all belong to Him.

5 **Our Lord is great and abundant in strength, His understanding** is **beyond measure.**

6 Here the psalmist stops discussing the cosmos and returns to the world of man: **The Lord heartens the humble and casts the wicked to the ground.**

עֱנוּ לַיהוָה בְּתוֹדֶה זַמְּרוּ
לֵאלֹהֵינוּ בְכִנּֽוֹר:

הַמְכַסֶּה שָׁמַֽיִם ׀ בְּעָבִים
הַמֵּכִין לָאָֽרֶץ מָטָר הַמַּצְמִיחַ
הָרִים חָצִיר:

נוֹתֵן לִבְהֵמָה לַחְמָהּ לִבְנֵי
עֹרֵב אֲשֶׁר יִקְרָֽאוּ:

לֹא בִגְבוּרַת הַסּוּס יֶחְפָּץ
לֹא־בְשׁוֹקֵי הָאִישׁ יִרְצֶה:

רוֹצֶה יְהוָה אֶת־יְרֵאָיו אֶת־
הַמְיַחֲלִים לְחַסְדּֽוֹ:

שַׁבְּחִי יְרוּשָׁלַֽםִ אֶת־יְהוָה
הַלְלִי אֱלֹהַֽיִךְ צִיּֽוֹן:

⁷ Sing to the Lord with songs of thanksgiving; sing praises to our God with the lyre,

⁸ who covers the heavens with clouds, provides the earth with rain, makes grass grow on the mountains.

⁹ He gives food to the beasts and to the fledgling ravens when they call.

¹⁰ It is not the might of horses that He desires; nor does He want the legs of a man.

¹¹ The Lord wants those who fear Him, those who long for His kindness.

¹² Extol the Lord, Jerusalem; praise your God, Zion,

---

⁷ **Sing to the Lord with songs of thanksgiving; sing praises to our God with the lyre,** lauding His providence and greatness always and everywhere.

⁸ It is He **who covers the heavens with clouds, provides the earth with rain, makes grass grow on the mountains.**

⁹ **He gives food to the beasts.** God cares for all His creatures, **and** He even attends **to the fledging ravens,** among the most pitiful and unsightly creatures, **when they call.**

¹⁰ Such care is solely an expression of God's kindness; it is in no way indicative of a reciprocal relationship between God and His creatures: **It is not the might of horses that He desires; nor does He want the legs of a man,** the legs representing a person's main source of stability and strength.

¹¹ **The Lord wants those who fear Him,** regardless of whether they are powerful or brave, **those who long for His kindness.**

¹² From here, the psalmist shifts focus: **Extol the Lord, Jerusalem; praise your God, Zion.** God has a special relationship with Jerusalem, His city, and with His Temple.

כִּי־חִזַּק בְּרִיחֵי שְׁעָרֶיךְ בֵּרַךְ
בָּנַיִךְ בְּקִרְבֵּךְ:

הַשָּׂם־גְּבוּלֵךְ שָׁלוֹם חֵלֶב
חִטִּים יַשְׂבִּיעֵךְ:

הַשֹּׁלֵחַ אִמְרָתוֹ אָרֶץ עַד־
מְהֵרָה יָרוּץ דְּבָרוֹ:

הַנֹּתֵן שֶׁלֶג כַּצָּמֶר כְּפוֹר
כָּאֵפֶר יְפַזֵּר:

מַשְׁלִיךְ קַרְחוֹ כְפִתִּים לִפְנֵי
קָרָתוֹ מִי יַעֲמֹד:

יִשְׁלַח דְּבָרוֹ וְיַמְסֵם יַשֵּׁב
רוּחוֹ יִזְּלוּ־מָיִם:

13 for He has strengthened the bars of your gates; He has blessed your sons within.

14 Who sets your borders at peace, sates you with the fat of wheat.

15 Who sends His commands to earth, His word swiftly running.

16 Who bestows snow like fleece, scatters frost like ashes,

17 flinging His ice like crumbs; who can withstand His cold?

18 He sends His word and melts them; He makes His wind blow, and they flow like water.

---

13 **For He has strengthened the bars of your gates.** With His divine protection, He bolsters, as it were, the bars of the city's gates against enemy forces trying to gain entrance. **He has blessed your sons within.**

14 **Who sets your borders,** referring both to the borders of the Land of Israel and to those of Jerusalem, **at peace, sates you with the fat of wheat,** the most desired and nutritious part of the wheat kernel.

15 Here the psalmist returns to the world as a whole: **Who sends His commands to earth, His word swiftly running.** God's commandments have an immediate impact on earth.

16 **Who bestows snow** that is **like fleece** in its pure whiteness, and **scatters frost like ashes,** for a layer of frost on the ground is as fine and smooth as a layer of ash,

17 **flinging His ice,** in the form of hail and snowflakes, **like crumbs; who can withstand His cold?**

18 But then, in time **He sends His word and melts them.** At God's word, all the ice and snow melt. **He makes His wind blow.** His warm breeze, God's breath, as it were, melts them **and they flow like water.**

יט ‏מַגִּיד דְּבָרָו לְיַעֲקֹב חֻקָּיו‏
‏וּמִשְׁפָּטָיו לְיִשְׂרָאֵל:‏

כ ‏לֹא עָשָׂה כֵן ׀ לְכָל־גּוֹי‏
‏וּמִשְׁפָּטִים בַּל־יְדָעוּם‏
‏הַלְלוּיָהּ:‏

19 He declares His words to Jacob,
His statutes and laws to Israel.

20 He did not do so with any
other nation; they do not know
the laws. Halleluya.

PSALM 148

A hymn of praise calling on all of creation to sing God's praises. The first part of the psalm addresses heavenly bodies and creatures; the second is a similar appeal to earthly beings.

א ‏הַלְלוּיָהּ ׀ הַלְלוּ אֶת־יהוה‏
‏מִן־הַשָּׁמַיִם‏
‏הַלְלוּהוּ בַּמְּרוֹמִים:‏

ב ‏הַלְלוּהוּ כָל־מַלְאָכָיו‏
‏הַלְלוּהוּ כָּל־צְבָאָו:‏

1 Halleluya. Praise the Lord from
the heavens;
praise Him in the heights.

2 Praise Him, all His angels;
praise Him, all His hosts.

---

19 In addition to all this, we should be grateful for something else: **He declares His words,** the words of the Torah, **to Jacob, His statutes and laws to Israel.**

20 **He did not do so with any other nation; they do not know the laws** of God. The Torah and its commandments are God's exclusive gift to the people of Israel. **Halleluya.**

PSALM 148

1 **Halleluya. Praise the Lord from the heavens; praise Him in the heights.** The psalmist specifies which heavenly bodies and creatures are being called upon to praise God:

2 **Praise Him, all His angels; praise Him, all His hosts.** "His angels" are spiritual beings created to fulfill specific missions for God, whether by way of verbal pronouncement or by more direct intervention in the affairs of lower worlds. "His hosts" include celestial beings, such as those described in chapter 1 of the book of Ezekiel.

הַלְלוּהוּ שֶׁמֶשׁ וְיָרֵחַ
הַלְלוּהוּ כָּל־כּוֹכְבֵי אוֹר:

הַלְלוּהוּ שְׁמֵי הַשָּׁמָיִם וְהַמַּיִם
אֲשֶׁר ׀ מֵעַל הַשָּׁמָיִם:

יְהַלְלוּ אֶת־שֵׁם יהוה כִּי הוּא
צִוָּה וְנִבְרָאוּ:

וַיַּעֲמִידֵם לָעַד לְעוֹלָם חָק־
נָתַן וְלֹא יַעֲבוֹר:

הַלְלוּ אֶת־יהוה מִן־הָאָרֶץ
תַּנִּינִים וְכָל־תְּהֹמוֹת:

אֵשׁ וּבָרָד שֶׁלֶג וְקִיטוֹר רוּחַ
סְעָרָה עֹשָׂה דְבָרוֹ:

3 Praise Him, sun and moon;
praise Him, all stars giving light.

4 Praise Him, heavens on
heavens, and the waters above
the heavens.

5 Let them praise the name of
the Lord, for He commanded
and they were created.

6 He established them forever,
for all time; He gave a statute
that will not be revoked.

7 Praise the Lord from the earth,
sea creatures and all depths,

8 Fire and hail, snow and vapor,
storm wind that carries out
His word,

---

3 **Praise Him, sun and moon.** These, too, are located on high, though they are not in heaven in the same sense as the celestial beings. **Praise Him, all stars giving light.**

4 **Praise Him, heavens on heavens, and the waters above the heavens.** The heavens are perceived as multilayered, one layer above the other; our Sages speak of seven heavens. The waters that are "above the heavens" are the heavenly reservoirs of water and rain from which bounty flows down to our world.

5 **Let them praise the name of the Lord.** They praise Him for their very existence, as they have no material needs; they thank Him **for** the fact that **He commanded and they were created.**

6 **He established them,** the heavens and all they contain, **forever, for all time; He gave a statute,** the laws of nature and physics, **that will not be revoked.** From our perspective, all of these heavenly phenomena are constant and eternal.

7 In the second part of the psalm, God's legions on earth are addressed: **Praise the Lord from the earth, sea creatures and all depths.** "Depths" in this verse complements "the waters above the heavens" in verse 4.

8 Joining in the praise of God are **fire and hail, snow and vapor, storm wind that carries out His word,**

הֶהָרִים וְכָל־גְּבָעוֹת עֵץ פְּרִי וְכָל־אֲרָזִים:

הַחַיָּה וְכָל־בְּהֵמָה רֶמֶשׂ וְצִפּוֹר כָּנָף:

מַלְכֵי־אֶרֶץ וְכָל־לְאֻמִּים שָׂרִים וְכָל־שֹׁפְטֵי אָרֶץ:

בַּחוּרִים וְגַם־בְּתוּלוֹת זְקֵנִים עִם־נְעָרִים:

יְהַלְלוּ ׀ אֶת־שֵׁם יהוה כִּי־נִשְׂגָּב שְׁמוֹ לְבַדּוֹ הוֹדוֹ עַל־אֶרֶץ וְשָׁמָיִם:

וַיָּרֶם קֶרֶן ׀ לְעַמּוֹ תְּהִלָּה לְכָל־חֲסִידָיו לִבְנֵי יִשְׂרָאֵל עַם קְרֹבוֹ הַלְלוּיָהּ:

⁹ the mountains and all the hills, fruit trees and all the cedars,

¹⁰ beasts and all cattle, creeping things, and winged fowl,

¹¹ kings of the earth and all nations, princes and all judges on earth,

¹² young men and maidens, old men with youths.

¹³ Let them praise the name of the Lord, for His name alone is exalted, His glory across earth and heaven.

¹⁴ He raises a horn for His people, glory for all His devoted ones, for the children of Israel, the people who are near to Him. Halleluya.

---

9 **the mountains and all the hills, fruit trees and** also **all the cedars,** the non-fruit-bearing trees, which also participate in singing God's praises,

10 **beasts and all cattle, creeping things, and winged fowl,**

11 **kings of the earth and all nations, princes and all judges on earth,**

12 **young men and maidens, old men with youths.** Not only the great, but also the common folk, one and all, are called upon to sing God's praises.

13 The psalmist concludes: **Let them** all **praise the name of the Lord, for His name alone is exalted, His glory across earth and heaven.** God's glory illuminates earth and the heavens, and therefore they must both praise Him.

14 **He raises a horn,** denoting uplifting of glory, **for His people, glory for all His devoted ones,** those who are close to God are uplifted by Him, **for the children of Israel, the people who are near to Him. Halleluya.**

PSALM 149

A psalm of praise that becomes ever more vigorous in tone,
as if to reflect the psalmist's hope that the scenes he depicts will one day be realized.

הַלְלוּיָֽהּ ׀ שִׁירוּ לַיהוָה
שִׁיר חָדָשׁ תְּהִלָּתוֹ בִּקְהַל
חֲסִידִֽים:

יִשְׂמַח יִשְׂרָאֵל בְּעֹשָׂיו בְּנֵי־
צִיּוֹן יָגִילוּ בְמַלְכָּֽם:

יְהַלְלוּ שְׁמוֹ בְמָחוֹל בְּתֹף
וְכִנּוֹר יְזַמְּרוּ־לֽוֹ:

כִּי־רוֹצֶה יְהוָה בְּעַמּוֹ יְפָאֵר
עֲנָוִים בִּישׁוּעָֽה:

יַעְלְזוּ חֲסִידִים בְּכָבוֹד יְרַנְּנוּ
עַל־מִשְׁכְּבוֹתָֽם:

Halleluya. Sing to the Lord a new song, His praise in the assembly of the devoted.

² Let Israel rejoice in its Maker; let the sons of Zion delight in their King.

³ Let them praise His name with dance; with timbrel and lyre let them sing to Him.

⁴ For the Lord desires His people; He glorifies the humble with salvation.

⁵ Let the devoted ones exult in honor; let them sing for joy in their beds.

PSALM 149

1 **Halleluya. Sing to the Lord a new song, His praise in the assembly of the devoted.** "A new song" usually refers to one that offers new insight on a well-known topic. Part of this psalm is addressed specifically to "the assembly of the devoted," those who regard themselves as being most loyal to God and most profoundly connected to Him.

2 **Let Israel rejoice in its Maker; let the sons of Zion delight in their King.**

3 **Let them praise His name with dance.** *Maḥol*, translated here as "dance," may also refer to a musical instrument. **With timbrel and lyre let them sing to Him.**

4 This is the main focus of gratitude: **For the Lord desires His people; He glorifies the humble with salvation.** When salvation arrives, all who had been oppressed and humbled will be raised to positions of honor.

5 **Let the devoted ones exult in honor** when that salvation occurs; **let them sing for joy** even when **in their beds,** when they retire for the night.

רוֹמְמוֹת אֵל בִּגְרוֹנָם וְחֶרֶב

פִּיפִיּוֹת בְּיָדָם:

לַעֲשׂוֹת נְקָמָה בַּגּוֹיִם

תּוֹכֵחוֹת בַּלְאֻמִּים:

לֶאְסֹר מַלְכֵיהֶם בְּזִקִּים

וְנִכְבְּדֵיהֶם בְּכַבְלֵי בַרְזֶל:

לַעֲשׂוֹת בָּהֶם ׀ מִשְׁפָּט כָּתוּב

הָדָר הוּא לְכָל־חֲסִידָיו

הַלְלוּיָהּ:

6 Exaltation of the Almighty is in their throats and a double-edged sword is in their hand,

7 to wreak vengeance on the nations, rebuke among the peoples,

8 to bind their kings with fetters and their nobles with iron chains,

9 to execute judgment as it is written; this is glory for all His devoted ones. Halleluya.

---

6 The devoted ones do not merely benefit from God's salvation; they are also expected to exert themselves in order to change and improve the world. Although the psalm speaks of God's salvation, man's efforts also facilitate its arrival: **Exaltation of the Almighty is in their throats and** at the same time **a double-edged sword** with which to wage war **is in their hand,**

7 **to wreak vengeance on the nations, rebuke among the peoples,**

8 **to bind their kings with fetters and their nobles with iron chains,** an act carried out in the wake of a final and total victory,

9 **to execute judgment as it is written.** Judgment will be carried out "as it is written" in the book of justice, with each individual receiving his just punishment. Although the act of bringing enemies to justice does not fall within the category of singing songs of praises in holy places, being instead a matter of taking vigorous action in this world, **this is** nonetheless **glory for all His devoted ones. Halleluya.**

PSALM 150

A psalm that calls on everyone to praise God in all ways,
both in terms of ideas and with a variety of sounds.

הַלְלוּיָהּ ׀ הַלְלוּ־אֵל בְּקָדְשׁוֹ
הַלְלוּהוּ בִּרְקִיעַ עֻזּוֹ:

הַלְלוּהוּ בִּגְבוּרֹתָיו
הַלְלוּהוּ כְּרֹב גֻּדְלוֹ:

הַלְלוּהוּ בְּתֵקַע שׁוֹפָר
הַלְלוּהוּ בְּנֵבֶל וְכִנּוֹר:

הַלְלוּהוּ בְּתֹף וּמָחוֹל
הַלְלוּהוּ בְּמִנִּים וְעֻגָב:

1 Halleluya. Praise the Almighty in His holy place;
praise Him in His heavenly stronghold.

2 Praise Him for His mighty deeds;
praise Him as befits His abundant might.

3 Praise Him with the blowing of the shofar;
praise Him with harp and lyre.

4 Praise Him with timbrel and tambourine;
praise Him with stringed instruments.

PSALM 150

1 **Halleluya. Praise the Almighty in His holy place,** in His holy precincts here on earth, when His presence is revealed to us there; and **praise Him in His heavenly stronghold,** when He is exalted in the worlds beyond.

2 **Praise Him for His mighty deeds,** His deeds of strength; and also **praise Him as befits His abundant might,** His power as expressed in splendor and kindness.

3 Such praise is carried out in various ways, each one expressing a different facet of tribute: **Praise Him with the blowing of the shofar,** which is expressive of glory and majesty. And **praise Him** as well **with harp and lyre,** such stringed instruments producing a gentler, more lyrical sound.

4 **Praise Him with timbrel and tambourine,** which produce sound through percussion. The word *maḥol* is often translated as "dance" (see 149:3), but here it refers to a musical instrument similar to a timbrel or perhaps a drum frame surrounded by bells. **Praise Him with stringed instruments,** which, in contrast to the percussion instruments, produce gentler sounds.

הַלְלוּהוּ בְּצִלְצְלֵי־שָׁמַע
הַלְלוּהוּ בְּצִלְצְלֵי תְרוּעָה:

כֹּל הַנְּשָׁמָה תְּהַלֵּל יָהּ
הַלְלוּיָהּ:

5 Praise Him with the sound of cymbals;
   praise Him with crashing cymbals.

6 Let all who breathe praise the Lord. Halleluya.

---

5 **Praise Him with the sound of cymbals; praise Him with crashing cymbals.** Two types of cymbals are mentioned here. One was apparently a small cymbal that was used to accompany another instrument, whereas the "crashing cymbals" was a larger instrument that produced loud clanging sounds. Here, too, different aspects of song and praise are expressed by the combination of stronger and more delicate sounds.

6 **Let all who breathe praise the Lord.** The expression "let all who breathe" or, more literally, "all breaths," relates both to every individual and to all forms of praise. It follows that praise of God can be expressed in all types of sound, as well as in every nuance and facet of a person's soul. The additional meaning of "all who breathe" is that the totality of voices, in all their distinct varieties of tone, join in a single chorus of praise: **Halleluya.**

Prayer after the Reading of Psalms

After reading Psalms it is customary to say the following:

מִי May the salvation of Israel emerge from Zion! When the Lord returns the captives of His people, Jacob will rejoice and Israel will exult. *Ps. 14*

The salvation of the righteous is from the Lord; He is their strength in times of trouble. The Lord helps them and rescues them; He will rescue and deliver them from the wicked, because they took refuge in Him. *Ps. 37*

On weekdays say:

יְהִי רָצוֹן May it be Your will, Lord our God, God of our ancestors, that by the merit of the first / second / third / fourth / fifth book of Psalms that we have read before You, corresponding to the book of Genesis / Exodus / Leviticus / Numbers / Deuteronomy, by the merit of its songs, by the merit of its verses and its words, by the merit of Your holy and pure names found therein, that You grant us atonement for all our sins, and forgive us all the transgressions by which we have sinned, we have done wrong, we have rebelled before You. And bring us back in perfect repentance before You, and guide us in the service of You, and open our hearts in the study of Your Torah, and send a complete recovery to all the afflicted of Your people [and among them the patient (*name*) son/daughter of (*mother's name*)], and proclaim liberty for captives and release for the imprisoned. Save all the travelers among Your people Israel, *Is. 61* and all those journeying by sea, from any distress or harm; and bring them to their desired destinations in life and in peace. And remember all those deprived of sons and daughters, bringing them healthy children who will serve You and hold You in awe. And protect the pregnant women among Your people Israel, that none of them miscarry. And as for those who are now in labor, in Your great compassion save them from all evil; and give of Your own plenty to the nursing mothers, that their breasts may never lack milk. And never let the plague or demons, spirits or liliths, injuries or illness exert power on any of the children of Your people; raise them by Your Torah, to study Torah for its own sake, and save them from the evil eye, and from pestilence and plague and adversary and the evil instinct. Nullify all harsh and evil decrees, for us and for all Your people Israel, wherever they may be. And incline the heart of the government to favor

תפילה לאחר אמירת תהלים

After reading Psalms it is customary to say the following:

תהלים יד

מִי יִתֵּן מִצִּיּוֹן יְשׁוּעַת יִשְׂרָאֵל

בְּשׁוּב יהוה שְׁבוּת עַמּוֹ, יָגֵל יַעֲקֹב, יִשְׂמַח יִשְׂרָאֵל:

תהלים לו

וּתְשׁוּעַת צַדִּיקִים מֵיהוה, מָעוּזָּם בְּעֵת צָרָה:

וַיַּעְזְרֵם יהוה וַיְפַלְּטֵם, יְפַלְּטֵם מֵרְשָׁעִים וְיוֹשִׁיעֵם, כִּי־חָסוּ בוֹ:

On weekdays say:

יְהִי רָצוֹן מִלְּפָנֶיךָ יהוה אֱלֹהֵינוּ וֵאלֹהֵי אֲבוֹתֵינוּ, בִּזְכוּת שֶׁבִּזְכוּת מִזְמוֹרֵי הַתְּהִלִּים שֶׁקָּרָאנוּ לְפָנֶיךָ, וּבִזְכוּת פְּסוּקֵיהֶם וְתֵבוֹתֵיהֶם, וְאוֹתִיּוֹתֵיהֶם וּנְקֻדּוֹתֵיהֶם, וְטַעֲמֵיהֶם, וּבִזְכוּת שְׁמוֹתֶיךָ הַקְּדוֹשִׁים וְהַטְּהוֹרִים הַיּוֹצְאִים מֵהֶם סֵפֶר רִאשׁוֹן / שֵׁנִי / שְׁלִישִׁי / רְבִיעִי / חֲמִישִׁי שֶׁבַּתְּהִלִּים שֶׁקָּרָאנוּ לְפָנֶיךָ שֶׁהוּא כְּנֶגֶד סֵפֶר בְּרֵאשִׁית / שְׁמוֹת / וַיִּקְרָא / בְּמִדְבַּר / דְּבָרִים בִּזְכוּת מִזְמוֹרָיו וּבִזְכוּת פְּסוּקָיו וּבִזְכוּת תֵּבוֹתָיו וּבִזְכוּת שְׁמוֹתֶיךָ הַקְּדוֹשִׁים וְהַטְּהוֹרִים הַיּוֹצְאִים מִמֶּנּוּ, שֶׁתְּכַפֶּר לָנוּ עַל כָּל חַטֹּאתֵינוּ, וְתִסְלַח לָנוּ עַל כָּל עֲווֹנוֹתֵינוּ, וְתִמְחַל לָנוּ עַל כָּל פְּשָׁעֵינוּ, שֶׁחָטָאנוּ וְשֶׁעָוִינוּ וְשֶׁפָּשַׁעְנוּ לְפָנֶיךָ, וְהַחֲזִירֵנוּ בִּתְשׁוּבָה שְׁלֵמָה לְפָנֶיךָ, וְהַדְרִיכֵנוּ לַעֲבוֹדָתֶךָ, וְתִפְתַּח לִבֵּנוּ בְּתַלְמוּד תּוֹרָתֶךָ, וְתִשְׁלַח רְפוּאָה שְׁלֵמָה לְחוֹלֵי עַמֶּךָ (לַחוֹלֶה/

ישעיה סא

לַחוֹלָה פְּלוֹנִי/ת בֶּן/בַּת פְּלוֹנִית), וְתִקְרָא לִשְׁבוּיִם דְּרוֹר, וְלַאֲסוּרִים פְּקַח־קוֹחַ: וּלְכָל הוֹלְכֵי דְרָכִים וְעוֹבְרֵי יַמִּים וּנְהָרוֹת מֵעַמְּךָ יִשְׂרָאֵל תַּצִּילֵם מִכָּל צַעַר וָנֶזֶק, וְתַגִּיעֵם לִמְחוֹז חֶפְצָם לְחַיִּים וּלְשָׁלוֹם. וְתִפְקֹד לְכָל חֲשׂוּכֵי בָנִים בְּזֶרַע שֶׁל קַיָּמָא לַעֲבוֹדָתֶךָ וּלְיִרְאָתֶךָ, וְעֻבָּרוֹת שֶׁל עַמְּךָ בֵּית יִשְׂרָאֵל תַּצִּילֵן שֶׁלֹּא תַפֵּלְנָה וַלְדוֹתֵיהֶן, וְהַיּוֹשְׁבוֹת עַל הַמַּשְׁבֵּר בְּרַחֲמֶיךָ הָרַבִּים תַּצִּילֵן מִכָּל רָע, וְאֶל הַמֵּינִיקוֹת תַּשְׁפִּיעַ שֶׁלֹּא יֶחְסַר חָלָב מִדַּדֵּיהֶן. וְאַל יִמְשֹׁל אַסְכְּרָה וְשֵׁדִין וְרוּחִין וְלִילִין וְכָל פְּגָעִים וּמַרְעִין בִּישִׁין בְּכָל יַלְדֵי עַמְּךָ בֵּית יִשְׂרָאֵל, וּתְגַדְּלֵם לְתוֹרָתֶךָ לִלְמֹד תּוֹרָה לִשְׁמָהּ, וְתַצִּילֵם מֵעַיִן הָרָע וּמִדֶּבֶר וּמִמַּגֵּפָה וּמִשָּׂטָן וּמִיֵּצֶר הָרָע. וּתְבַטֵּל מֵעָלֵינוּ וּמִכָּל עַמְּךָ בֵּית

us, decree good decrees regarding us, and send blessing and success to all that we do. Prepare our sustenance, coming from Your own broad, full hand, and let Your people Israel never be dependent on the charity of one another or of any other people. Grant every single person what he needs, and every single body what it lacks, and hurry and make haste to redeem us, and build the house of our sanctuary, our glory.

This passage, from *uvizkhut* until *milfanekha* may be recited only in a minyan:

All this by the merit of Your thirteen attributes of compassion, as they are written in Your Torah: "The Lord, the Lord, God, merciful and gra- Ex. 34:6–7 cious, slow to anger, and abounding in kindness and truth. He maintains kindness to the thousands bearing iniquity and transgression and sin," for never do they come empty-handed away from Your presence. Help us, Ps. 79 God of our salvation, for the glory of Your name; deliver us and forgive us our sins for the sake of Your name. Blessed be the Lord forever, amen Ps. 89 and amen.

On Shabbat and festivals say:

May it be Your will, Lord our God, God of our ancestors, that by the merit of the first / second / third / fourth / fifth book of Psalms that we have read before You, corresponding to the book of Genesis / Exodus / Leviticus / Numbers / Deuteronomy, by the merit of its songs, by the merit of its verses and its words, by the merit of Your holy and pure names found therein, that these psalms we have spoken may be considered as if it were David, king of Israel himself who had spoken them, may his merit protect us. And may he stand up for us, to join the Bride of His youth with the Beloved, in friendship and in brotherhood and love – and from that place may plenty be drawn down to us, to soul and spirit and higher soul. And just as we sing songs in this world, so may we have the merit to sing before You, Lord our God, God of our ancestors, song and praise in the World to Come. And through our speaking these Psalms, may the Rose of Sharon be awakened to sing with a lovely voice, rejoicing, and song, for the glory of Lebanon is given to her. Glory and splendor in the House of Is. 35:2 our God, speedily in our days. Amen, Selah.

יִשְׂרָאֵל בְּכָל מָקוֹם שֶׁהֵם כָּל גְּזֵרוֹת קָשׁוֹת וְרָעוֹת. וְתַטֶּה לֵב הַמַּלְכוּת
עָלֵינוּ לְטוֹבָה, וְתִגְזוֹר עָלֵינוּ גְּזֵרוֹת טוֹבוֹת, וְתִשְׁלַח בְּרָכָה וְהַצְלָחָה בְּכָל
מַעֲשֵׂה יָדֵינוּ. וְהָכֵן פַּרְנָסָתֵנוּ מִיָּדְךָ הָרְחָבָה וְהַמְּלֵאָה, וְלֹא יִצְטָרְכוּ עַמְּךָ
בֵּית יִשְׂרָאֵל זֶה לָזֶה וְלֹא לְעַם אַחֵר, וְתֵן לְכָל אִישׁ וָאִישׁ דֵּי פַּרְנָסָתוֹ וּלְכָל
גְּוִיָּה וּגְוִיָּה דֵּי מַחֲסוֹרָהּ וּתְמַהֵר וְתָחִישׁ לְגָאֳלֵנוּ, וְתִבְנֶה בֵּית מִקְדָּשֵׁנוּ
וְתִפְאַרְתֵּנוּ.

This passage, from וּבִזְכוּת until מִלְפָנֶיךָ, may be recited only in a minyan:

וּבִזְכוּת שְׁלֹשׁ עֶשְׂרֵה מִדּוֹתֶיךָ שֶׁל רַחֲמִים הַכְּתוּבִים בְּתוֹרָתֶךָ, כְּמוֹ
שֶׁנֶּאֱמַר: יהוה, יהוה, אֵל רַחוּם וְחַנּוּן, אֶרֶךְ אַפַּיִם וְרַב־חֶסֶד וֶאֱמֶת: *שמות לד:ו-ז*
נוֹצֵר חֶסֶד לָאֲלָפִים, נֹשֵׂא עָוֹן וָפֶשַׁע וְחַטָּאָה, וְנַקֵּה: שֶׁאֵינָן חוֹזְרוֹת רֵיקָם
מִלְּפָנֶיךָ. עָזְרֵנוּ אֱלֹהֵי יִשְׁעֵנוּ עַל־דְּבַר כְּבוֹד־שְׁמֶךָ, וְהַצִּילֵנוּ וְכַפֵּר עַל־ *תהלים עט*
חַטֹּאתֵינוּ לְמַעַן שְׁמֶךָ: בָּרוּךְ יהוה לְעוֹלָם אָמֵן וְאָמֵן: *תהלים פט*

On שבת and יום טוב say:

יְהִי רָצוֹן מִלְּפָנֶיךָ יהוה אֱלֹהֵינוּ וֵאלֹהֵי אֲבוֹתֵינוּ, בִּזְכוּת סֵפֶר רִאשׁוֹן /
שֵׁנִי / שְׁלִישִׁי / רְבִיעִי / חֲמִישִׁי שֶׁבַּתְּהִלִּים שֶׁקְּרָאנוּ לְפָנֶיךָ שֶׁהוּא כְּנֶגֶד
סֵפֶר בְּרֵאשִׁית / שְׁמוֹת / וַיִּקְרָא / בְּמִדְבַּר / דְּבָרִים בִּזְכוּת מִזְמוֹרָיו וּבִזְכוּת
פְּסוּקָיו וּבִזְכוּת תֵּבוֹתָיו וּבִזְכוּת שְׁמוֹתֶיךָ הַקְּדוֹשִׁים וְהַטְּהוֹרִים הַיּוֹצְאִים
מִמֶּנּוּ שֶׁתְּהֵא נֶחְשֶׁבֶת לָנוּ אֲמִירַת מִזְמוֹרֵי תְהִלִּים אֵלּוּ כְּאִלּוּ אֲמָרָם דָּוִד
מֶלֶךְ יִשְׂרָאֵל בְּעַצְמוֹ, זְכוּתוֹ תָגֵן עָלֵינוּ, וְיַעֲמָד לָנוּ לְחַבֵּר אֵשֶׁת נְעוּרִים עִם
דּוֹדָהּ בְּאַהֲבָה וְאַחֲוָה וְרֵעוּת, וּמִשָּׁם יִמָּשֵׁךְ לָנוּ שֶׁפַע לְנֶפֶשׁ רוּחַ וּנְשָׁמָה.
וּכְשֵׁם שֶׁאֲנַחְנוּ אוֹמְרִים שִׁירִים בָּעוֹלָם הַזֶּה, כָּךְ נִזְכֶּה לוֹמַר לְפָנֶיךָ יהוה
אֱלֹהֵינוּ וֵאלֹהֵי אֲבוֹתֵינוּ, שִׁיר וּשְׁבָחָה לָעוֹלָם הַבָּא. וְעַל יְדֵי אֲמִירַת
תְּהִלִּים תִּתְעוֹרֵר חֲבַצֶּלֶת הַשָּׁרוֹן לָשִׁיר בְּקוֹל נָעִים גִּילַת וְרַנֵּן, כְּבוֹד הַלְּבָנוֹן *ישעיה לה:ב*
נִתַּן־לָהּ: הוֹד וְהָדָר בְּבֵית אֱלֹהֵינוּ בִּמְהֵרָה בְיָמֵינוּ, אָמֵן סֶלָה.

תפילות מיוחדות

•

SPECIAL PRAYERS

The Traveler's Prayer

If one intends to return home on the same day, add the words in parentheses:

יְהִי רָצוֹן May it be Your will,
Lord our God and God of our fathers,
to lead us to peace, direct our steps to peace,
guide us to peace, and bring us to our desired destination in life,
joy and peace
(and bring us back to our home in peace).
Rescue us from any enemy or ambush on the way,
and from all afflictions that trouble the world.
Send blessing to the work of our hands,
and let us find grace, kindness and compassion
from You and from all who see us.
Hear our pleas,
for You are a God who hears prayer and pleas.
Blessed are You, Lord, who listens to prayer.

The Lord will guard your going and your coming,   *Ps. 121:8*
from now until eternity.

Repeat three times:

וַיַּעֲקֹב And Jacob went on his way   *Gen. 32:1–2*
and angels of God encountered him.
Jacob said when he saw them: This is the camp [*maḥaneh*] of God.
He called the name of that place Mahanayim.

Repeat three times:

יְבָרֶכְךָ The Lord shall bless you, and keep you.   *Num. 6:24–26*
The Lord shall shine His countenance to you, and be gracious to you.
The Lord shall lift his countenance to you, and grant you peace.

שִׁיר לַמַּעֲלוֹת A song of ascents. I lift my eyes to the mountains; from where   *Ps. 121*
will my help come? My help is from the Lord, Maker of heaven and earth.
He will not let your foot give way. He who watches over you will not slumber.
Behold, the Guardian of Israel neither slumbers nor sleeps. The Lord is your
guardian; the Lord is your shade by your right hand. By day, the sun will not
strike you, nor the moon at night. The Lord will guard you from all evil; He
will guard your life. The Lord will guard your going and your coming, from
now until eternity.

תפילת הדרך

If one intends to return home on the same day, add the words in parentheses:

יְהִי רָצוֹן מִלְּפָנֶיךָ, יהוה אֱלֹהֵינוּ וֵאלֹהֵי אֲבוֹתֵינוּ
שֶׁתּוֹלִיכֵנוּ לְשָׁלוֹם, וְתַצְעִידֵנוּ לְשָׁלוֹם, וְתַדְרִיכֵנוּ לְשָׁלוֹם
וְתַגִּיעֵנוּ לִמְחוֹז חֶפְצֵנוּ לְחַיִּים וּלְשִׂמְחָה וּלְשָׁלוֹם
(וְתַחֲזִירֵנוּ לְבֵיתֵנוּ לְשָׁלוֹם)
וְתַצִּילֵנוּ מִכַּף כָּל אוֹיֵב וְאוֹרֵב בַּדֶּרֶךְ
וּמִכָּל מִינֵי פֻּרְעָנִיּוֹת הַמִּתְרַגְּשׁוֹת לָבוֹא לָעוֹלָם
וְתִשְׁלַח בְּרָכָה בְּמַעֲשֵׂה יָדֵינוּ
וְתִתְּנֵנוּ לְחֵן וּלְחֶסֶד וּלְרַחֲמִים בְּעֵינֶיךָ וּבְעֵינֵי כָל רוֹאֵינוּ
וְתִשְׁמַע קוֹל תַּחֲנוּנֵינוּ
כִּי אֵל שׁוֹמֵעַ תְּפִלָּה וְתַחֲנוּן אָתָּה.
בָּרוּךְ אַתָּה יהוה, שׁוֹמֵעַ תְּפִלָּה.

תהלים קכא:ח

יהוה יִשְׁמָר־צֵאתְךָ וּבוֹאֶךָ, מֵעַתָּה וְעַד־עוֹלָם:

Repeat three times:

בראשית לב:א-ב

וְיַעֲקֹב הָלַךְ לְדַרְכּוֹ, וַיִּפְגְּעוּ־בוֹ מַלְאֲכֵי אֱלֹהִים:
וַיֹּאמֶר יַעֲקֹב כַּאֲשֶׁר רָאָם, מַחֲנֵה אֱלֹהִים זֶה
וַיִּקְרָא שֵׁם־הַמָּקוֹם הַהוּא מַחֲנָיִם:

Repeat three times:

במדבר ו:כד-כו

יְבָרֶכְךָ יהוה וְיִשְׁמְרֶךָ:
יָאֵר יהוה פָּנָיו אֵלֶיךָ וִיחֻנֶּךָּ:
יִשָּׂא יהוה פָּנָיו אֵלֶיךָ וְיָשֵׂם לְךָ שָׁלוֹם:

תהלים קכא

שִׁיר לַמַּעֲלוֹת, אֶשָּׂא עֵינַי אֶל־הֶהָרִים, מֵאַיִן יָבֹא עֶזְרִי: עֶזְרִי מֵעִם יהוה,
עֹשֵׂה שָׁמַיִם וָאָרֶץ: אַל־יִתֵּן לַמּוֹט רַגְלֶךָ, אַל־יָנוּם שֹׁמְרֶךָ: הִנֵּה לֹא־יָנוּם
וְלֹא יִישָׁן, שׁוֹמֵר יִשְׂרָאֵל: יהוה שֹׁמְרֶךָ, יהוה צִלְּךָ עַל־יַד יְמִינֶךָ: יוֹמָם
הַשֶּׁמֶשׁ לֹא־יַכֶּכָּה, וְיָרֵחַ בַּלָּיְלָה: יהוה יִשְׁמָרְךָ מִכָּל־רָע, יִשְׁמֹר אֶת־נַפְשֶׁךָ:
יהוה יִשְׁמָר־צֵאתְךָ וּבוֹאֶךָ, מֵעַתָּה וְעַד־עוֹלָם:

Shema Recited at Bedtime

הֲרֵינִי I hereby forgive anyone who has angered or provoked me or sinned against me, physically or financially or by failing to give me due respect, or in any other matter relating to me, involuntarily or willingly, inadvertently or deliberately, whether in word or deed: let no one incur punishment because of me.

בָּרוּךְ Blessed are You, Lord our God, King of the Universe, who makes the bonds of sleep fall on my eyes, and slumber on my eyelids. May it be Your will, Lord my God and God of my fathers, that You make me lie down in peace and arise in peace. Let not my imagination, bad dreams or troubling thoughts disturb me. May my bed be flawless before You. Enlighten my eyes lest I sleep the sleep of death, for it is You who illuminates the pupil of the eye. Blessed are You, Lord, who gives light to the whole world in His glory.

When saying all three paragraphs of *Shema*, say:

God, faithful King!

The following verse should be said aloud, while covering the eyes with the right hand:

Hear, Israel: the Lord is our God, the Lord is one.

Deut. 6:4

Quietly: Blessed be the name of His glorious kingdom for ever and all time.

וְאָהַבְתָּ You shall love the Lord with all your heart, and with all your soul, and with all your might. These matters that I command you today shall be upon your heart. You shall inculcate them in your children, and you shall speak of them while you are sitting in your house, and while you are walking on the way, and while you are lying down, and while you are rising. You shall bind them as a sign on your arm. And they shall be for ornaments, between your eyes. You shall write them on the doorposts of your house, and on your gates.

Deut. 6:5–9

וִיהִי May the graciousness of the Lord our God be upon us, establishing the work of our hands for us; indeed, establishing the work of our hands.

Ps. 90:17

יֹשֵׁב He who dwells in the shelter of the Most High, who abides in the shadow of the Almighty. I will say of the Lord: He is my shelter and my fortress, my God in whom I trust. For He will rescue you from the ensnaring trap, from devastating pestilence. He will cover You with His pinion; you will find refuge under His wings. His truth is a shield and armor. You will not fear the terror of

Ps. 91

קריאת שמע על המיטה

הֲרֵינִי מוֹחֵל לְכָל מִי שֶׁהִכְעִיס וְהִקְנִיט אוֹתִי אוֹ שֶׁחָטָא כְּנֶגְדִּי, בֵּין בְּגוּפִי בֵּין בְּמָמוֹנִי בֵּין בִּכְבוֹדִי בֵּין בְּכָל אֲשֶׁר לִי, בֵּין בְּאֹנֶס בֵּין בְּרָצוֹן, בֵּין בְּשׁוֹגֵג בֵּין בְּמֵזִיד, בֵּין בְּדִבּוּר בֵּין בְּמַעֲשֶׂה, וְלֹא יֵעָנֵשׁ שׁוּם אָדָם בְּסִבָּתִי.

בָּרוּךְ אַתָּה יהוה אֱלֹהֵינוּ מֶלֶךְ הָעוֹלָם, הַמַּפִּיל חֶבְלֵי שֵׁנָה עַל עֵינַי וּתְנוּמָה עַל עַפְעַפָּי. וִיהִי רָצוֹן מִלְּפָנֶיךָ, יהוה אֱלֹהַי וֵאלֹהֵי אֲבוֹתַי, שֶׁתַּשְׁכִּיבֵנִי לְשָׁלוֹם וְתַעֲמִידֵנִי לְשָׁלוֹם, וְאַל יְבַהֲלוּנִי רַעְיוֹנַי וַחֲלוֹמוֹת רָעִים וְהִרְהוּרִים רָעִים, וּתְהֵא מִטָּתִי שְׁלֵמָה לְפָנֶיךָ, וְהָאֵר עֵינַי פֶּן אִישַׁן הַמָּוֶת, כִּי אַתָּה הַמֵּאִיר לְאִישׁוֹן בַּת עָיִן. בָּרוּךְ אַתָּה יהוה, הַמֵּאִיר לָעוֹלָם כֻּלּוֹ בִּכְבוֹדוֹ.

When saying all three paragraphs of שמע, say:

אֵל מֶלֶךְ נֶאֱמָן

The following verse should be said aloud, while covering the eyes with the right hand:

דברים ו:ד

שְׁמַע יִשְׂרָאֵל, יהוה אֱלֹהֵינוּ, יהוה ׀ אֶחָד:

Quietly
בָּרוּךְ שֵׁם כְּבוֹד מַלְכוּתוֹ לְעוֹלָם וָעֶד.

דברים ו:ה-ט

וְאָהַבְתָּ אֵת יהוה אֱלֹהֶיךָ, בְּכָל-לְבָבְךָ, וּבְכָל-נַפְשְׁךָ וּבְכָל-מְאֹדֶךָ: וְהָיוּ הַדְּבָרִים הָאֵלֶּה, אֲשֶׁר אָנֹכִי מְצַוְּךָ הַיּוֹם, עַל-לְבָבֶךָ: וְשִׁנַּנְתָּם לְבָנֶיךָ וְדִבַּרְתָּ בָּם, בְּשִׁבְתְּךָ בְּבֵיתֶךָ וּבְלֶכְתְּךָ בַדֶּרֶךְ, וּבְשָׁכְבְּךָ וּבְקוּמֶךָ: וּקְשַׁרְתָּם לְאוֹת עַל-יָדֶךָ וְהָיוּ לְטֹטָפֹת בֵּין עֵינֶיךָ: וּכְתַבְתָּם עַל-מְזֻזוֹת בֵּיתֶךָ וּבִשְׁעָרֶיךָ:

תהלים צ:יז

וִיהִי נֹעַם אֲדֹנָי אֱלֹהֵינוּ עָלֵינוּ וּמַעֲשֵׂה יָדֵינוּ כּוֹנְנָה עָלֵינוּ וּמַעֲשֵׂה יָדֵינוּ כּוֹנְנֵהוּ:

תהלים צא

יֹשֵׁב בְּסֵתֶר עֶלְיוֹן, בְּצֵל שַׁדַּי יִתְלוֹנָן: אֹמַר לַיהוה מַחְסִי וּמְצוּדָתִי, אֱלֹהַי אֶבְטַח-בּוֹ: כִּי הוּא יַצִּילְךָ מִפַּח יָקוּשׁ, מִדֶּבֶר הַוּוֹת: בְּאֶבְרָתוֹ יָסֶךְ לָךְ, וְתַחַת-כְּנָפָיו תֶּחְסֶה, צִנָּה וְסֹחֵרָה אֲמִתּוֹ: לֹא-תִירָא מִפַּחַד לָיְלָה, מֵחֵץ יָעוּף יוֹמָם: מִדֶּבֶר בָּאֹפֶל יַהֲלֹךְ, מִקֶּטֶב יָשׁוּד צָהֳרָיִם: יִפֹּל מִצִּדְּךָ אֶלֶף,

night, nor the arrow that flies by day, nor the pestilence that stalks in darkness, nor the destruction that lays waste at noon. A thousand may fall at your side, and ten thousand at your right hand, but it will not reach you. You will just look with your eyes and see the punishment of the wicked. For you, Lord, are my shelter. You have made the Most High your dwelling place. No evil will befall you and no plague will come near your tent, for He will charge His angels on your behalf, to guard you in all your ways. They will carry you on their palms, lest your foot be struck by a stone. You will tread upon lions and vipers; you will trample young lions and serpents. Because he desired Me greatly, I will rescue him; I will be his fortress, for he has known My name. When he calls upon Me, I will answer him. I will be with him in times of trouble; I will deliver him and honor him. I will sate him with length of days, and I will show him My salvation. I will sate him with length of days, and I will show him My salvation.

יהוה Lord, how numerous are my tormentors; many rise up against me. Many *Ps. 3* say of me: There is no salvation for him in God, Selah. But You, Lord, protect me. You are my glory; You lift my head. I cried aloud to the Lord and He answered me from His holy mount, Selah. I lay down and slept; I awoke because the Lord sustains me. I shall have no fear of the myriads that surround me and oppose me. Arise, Lord; save me, my God. For You have smitten my enemies on the cheek; you have broken the teeth of the wicked. Salvation belongs to the Lord. Your blessing is on Your people, Selah.

הַשְׁכִּיבֵנוּ Help us lie down, Lord our God, in peace, and rise up, our King, to life. Spread over us Your canopy of peace. Direct us with Your good counsel, and save us for the sake of Your name. Shield us and remove from us every enemy, plague, sword, famine, and sorrow. Remove the adversary from before and behind us. Shelter us in the shadow of Your wings, for You, God, are our Guardian and Deliverer; You, God, are a gracious and compassionate King. Guard our going out and our coming in, for life and peace, from now and forever.

בָּרוּךְ Blessed is the Lord by day, blessed is the Lord by night. Blessed is the Lord when we lie down; blessed is the Lord when we rise. For in Your hand are the souls of the living and the dead, [as it is written:] In whose hand is *Job 12:10* the life of every living thing and the spirit of all flesh of man. Into Your hand *Ps. 31:6* I commit my spirit; You redeem me, Lord, Almighty God of truth. Our God in heaven, bring unity to Your name, establish Your kingdom constantly and reign over us for ever and all time.

וְּרְבָבָה מִימִינֶךָ, אֵלֶיךָ לֹא יִגָּשׁ: רַק בְּעֵינֶיךָ תַבִּיט, וְשִׁלֻּמַת רְשָׁעִים תִּרְאֶה: כִּי־אַתָּה יְהוָה מַחְסִי, עֶלְיוֹן שַׂמְתָּ מְעוֹנֶךָ: לֹא־תְאֻנֶּה אֵלֶיךָ רָעָה, וְנֶגַע לֹא־יִקְרַב בְּאָהֳלֶךָ: כִּי מַלְאָכָיו יְצַוֶּה־לָּךְ, לִשְׁמָרְךָ בְּכָל־דְּרָכֶיךָ: עַל־כַּפַּיִם יִשָּׂאוּנְךָ, פֶּן־תִּגֹּף בָּאֶבֶן רַגְלֶךָ: עַל־שַׁחַל וָפֶתֶן תִּדְרֹךְ, תִּרְמֹס כְּפִיר וְתַנִּין: כִּי בִי חָשַׁק וַאֲפַלְּטֵהוּ, אֲשַׂגְּבֵהוּ כִּי־יָדַע שְׁמִי: יִקְרָאֵנִי וְאֶעֱנֵהוּ, עִמּוֹ־אָנֹכִי בְצָרָה, אֲחַלְּצֵהוּ וַאֲכַבְּדֵהוּ: אֹרֶךְ יָמִים אַשְׂבִּיעֵהוּ, וְאַרְאֵהוּ בִּישׁוּעָתִי: אֹרֶךְ יָמִים אַשְׂבִּיעֵהוּ, וְאַרְאֵהוּ בִּישׁוּעָתִי:

תהלים ג

יְהוָה מָה־רַבּוּ צָרָי, רַבִּים קָמִים עָלָי: רַבִּים אֹמְרִים לְנַפְשִׁי, אֵין יְשׁוּעָתָה לּוֹ בֵאלֹהִים, סֶלָה: וְאַתָּה יְהוָה מָגֵן בַּעֲדִי, כְּבוֹדִי וּמֵרִים רֹאשִׁי: קוֹלִי אֶל־יְהוָה אֶקְרָא, וַיַּעֲנֵנִי מֵהַר קָדְשׁוֹ, סֶלָה: אֲנִי שָׁכַבְתִּי וָאִישָׁנָה, הֱקִיצוֹתִי כִּי יְהוָה יִסְמְכֵנִי: לֹא־אִירָא מֵרִבְבוֹת עָם, אֲשֶׁר סָבִיב שָׁתוּ עָלָי: קוּמָה יְהוָה, הוֹשִׁיעֵנִי אֱלֹהַי, כִּי־הִכִּיתָ אֶת־כָּל־אֹיְבַי לֶחִי, שִׁנֵּי רְשָׁעִים שִׁבַּרְתָּ: לַיהוָה הַיְשׁוּעָה, עַל־עַמְּךָ בִרְכָתֶךָ סֶּלָה:

הַשְׁכִּיבֵנוּ, יְהוָה אֱלֹהֵינוּ, לְשָׁלוֹם. וְהַעֲמִידֵנוּ, מַלְכֵּנוּ, לְחַיִּים. וּפְרֹשׂ עָלֵינוּ סֻכַּת שְׁלוֹמֶךָ, וְתַקְּנֵנוּ בְּעֵצָה טוֹבָה מִלְּפָנֶיךָ, וְהוֹשִׁיעֵנוּ לְמַעַן שְׁמֶךָ. וְהָגֵן בַּעֲדֵנוּ, וְהָסֵר מֵעָלֵינוּ אוֹיֵב, דֶּבֶר וְחֶרֶב וְרָעָב וְיָגוֹן. וְהָסֵר שָׂטָן מִלְּפָנֵינוּ וּמֵאַחֲרֵינוּ, וּבְצֵל כְּנָפֶיךָ תַּסְתִּירֵנוּ, כִּי אֵל שׁוֹמְרֵנוּ וּמַצִּילֵנוּ אָתָּה, כִּי אֵל מֶלֶךְ חַנּוּן וְרַחוּם אָתָּה. וּשְׁמֹר צֵאתֵנוּ וּבוֹאֵנוּ לְחַיִּים וּלְשָׁלוֹם מֵעַתָּה וְעַד עוֹלָם.

בָּרוּךְ יְהוָה בַּיּוֹם, בָּרוּךְ יְהוָה בַּלָּיְלָה, בָּרוּךְ יְהוָה בְּשָׁכְבֵנוּ, בָּרוּךְ יְהוָה בְּקוּמֵנוּ. כִּי בְיָדְךָ נַפְשׁוֹת הַחַיִּים וְהַמֵּתִים. אֲשֶׁר בְּיָדוֹ נֶפֶשׁ כָּל־חָי,

איוב יב:

וְרוּחַ כָּל־בְּשַׂר־אִישׁ: בְּיָדְךָ אַפְקִיד רוּחִי, פָּדִיתָה אוֹתִי יְהוָה אֵל אֱמֶת:

תהלים לא:

אֱלֹהֵינוּ שֶׁבַּשָּׁמַיִם, יַחֵד שִׁמְךָ וְקַיֵּם מַלְכוּתְךָ תָּמִיד, וּמְלֹךְ עָלֵינוּ לְעוֹלָם וָעֶד.

יִרְאוּ May our eyes see, our hearts rejoice, and our souls be glad in Your true salvation, when Zion is told, "Your God reigns." The Lord is King, the Lord was King, and the Lord will be King for ever and all time. For sovereignty is Yours, and to all eternity You will reign in glory, for we have no king but You.

הַמַּלְאָךְ May the angel who delivers me from all evil, bless the lads. And let *Gen. 48:16* my name and the name of my fathers, Abraham and Isaac, be called upon them. May they proliferate like fish in the midst of the earth.

וַיֹּאמֶר He said: If you heed the voice of the Lord your God and will perform *Ex. 15:26* what is right in His eyes and listen to His commandments and observe all His statutes, all of the diseases that I placed on Egypt I will not place upon you, as I am the Lord your healer. The Lord said to the accuser: May the *Zech. 3:2* Lord rebuke you, the accuser, and may the Lord who has chosen Jerusalem rebuke you. Is this not a firebrand salvaged from the fire? Behold the bed of *Songs 3:7–8* Solomon: There are sixty valiant men around it, from the valiant of Israel, all armed with a sword, trained in war; each man, a sword on his thigh, from fear in the nights.

Say three times:

יְבָרֶכְךָ The Lord shall bless you, and keep you. *Num. 6:24–26*
The Lord shall shine His countenance to you, and be gracious to you.
The Lord shall lift his countenance to you, and grant you peace.

Say three times:

הִנֵּה Behold, the Guardian of Israel neither slumbers nor sleeps. *Ps. 121:4*

Say three times:

לִישׁוּעָתְךָ For Your salvation I await, Lord. *Gen. 49:18*
I await, Lord, for Your salvation.
Lord, for Your salvation I await.

Say three times:

בְּשֵׁם In the name of the Lord, God of Israel:
may Michael be at my right hand,
Gabriel, at my left;
in front of me, Uriel,
behind me, Raphael;
and above my head the Presence of God.

יִרְאוּ עֵינֵינוּ וְיִשְׂמַח לִבֵּנוּ, וְתָגֵל נַפְשֵׁנוּ בִּישׁוּעָתְךָ בֶּאֱמֶת, בֶּאֱמֹר לְצִיּוֹן מָלַךְ אֱלֹהָיִךְ. יהוה מֶלֶךְ, יהוה מָלָךְ, יהוה יִמְלֹךְ לְעוֹלָם וָעֶד. כִּי הַמַּלְכוּת שֶׁלְּךָ הִיא, וּלְעוֹלְמֵי עַד תִּמְלֹךְ בְּכָבוֹד, כִּי אֵין לָנוּ מֶלֶךְ אֶלָּא אָתָּה.

בראשית מח:טז הַמַּלְאָךְ הַגֹּאֵל אֹתִי מִכָּל־רָע יְבָרֵךְ אֶת־הַנְּעָרִים, וְיִקָּרֵא בָהֶם שְׁמִי וְשֵׁם אֲבֹתַי אַבְרָהָם וְיִצְחָק, וְיִדְגּוּ לָרֹב בְּקֶרֶב הָאָרֶץ:

שמות טו:כו וַיֹּאמֶר אִם־שָׁמוֹעַ תִּשְׁמַע לְקוֹל יהוה אֱלֹהֶיךָ, וְהַיָּשָׁר בְּעֵינָיו תַּעֲשֶׂה, וְהַאֲזַנְתָּ לְמִצְוֹתָיו וְשָׁמַרְתָּ כָּל־חֻקָּיו, כָּל־הַמַּחֲלָה אֲשֶׁר־שַׂמְתִּי בְמִצְרַיִם לֹא־אָשִׂים עָלֶיךָ, כִּי אֲנִי יהוה רֹפְאֶךָ: וַיֹּאמֶר יהוה אֶל־הַשָּׂטָן, יִגְעַר זכריה ג:ב יהוה בְּךָ הַשָּׂטָן, וְיִגְעַר יהוה בְּךָ הַבֹּחֵר בִּירוּשָׁלָיִם, הֲלוֹא זֶה אוּד מֻצָּל מֵאֵשׁ: הִנֵּה מִטָּתוֹ שֶׁלִּשְׁלֹמֹה, שִׁשִּׁים גִּבֹּרִים סָבִיב לָהּ, מִגִּבֹּרֵי יִשְׂרָאֵל: שיר השירים ג:ז-ח כֻּלָּם אֲחֻזֵי חֶרֶב, מְלֻמְּדֵי מִלְחָמָה, אִישׁ חַרְבּוֹ עַל־יְרֵכוֹ מִפַּחַד בַּלֵּילוֹת:

Say three times:

במדבר ו:כד-כו יְבָרֶכְךָ יהוה וְיִשְׁמְרֶךָ:
יָאֵר יהוה פָּנָיו אֵלֶיךָ וִיחֻנֶּךָּ:
יִשָּׂא יהוה פָּנָיו אֵלֶיךָ וְיָשֵׂם לְךָ שָׁלוֹם:

Say three times:

תהלים קכא:ד הִנֵּה לֹא־יָנוּם וְלֹא יִישָׁן שׁוֹמֵר יִשְׂרָאֵל:

Say three times:

בראשית מט:יח לִישׁוּעָתְךָ קִוִּיתִי יהוה:
קִוִּיתִי יהוה לִישׁוּעָתְךָ
יהוה לִישׁוּעָתְךָ קִוִּיתִי

Say three times:

בְּשֵׁם יהוה אֱלֹהֵי יִשְׂרָאֵל
מִימִינִי מִיכָאֵל, וּמִשְּׂמֹאלִי גַּבְרִיאֵל
וּמִלְּפָנַי אוּרִיאֵל, וּמֵאֲחוֹרַי רְפָאֵל
וְעַל רֹאשִׁי שְׁכִינַת אֵל.

שִׁיר הַמַּעֲלוֹת A song of ascents.   *Ps. 128*
Blessed are all who fear the Lord, who walk in His ways.
When you eat of the labor of your hands, you are happy, and it is good for you.
Your wife is like a fruitful vine by the side of your house;
your children, like young olive trees surrounding your table.
Indeed, so shall a man who fears the Lord be blessed.
May the Lord bless you from Zion;
may you see the prosperity of Jerusalem all the days of your life.
And may you see the children of your children. Peace to Israel.

Say three times:

רִגְזוּ Tremble, and do not sin;   *Ps. 4:5*
say in your heart, upon your bed, and be still, Selah

אֲדוֹן עוֹלָם Lord of the Universe,
who reigned before the birth of any thing;
when by His will all things were made,
then was His name proclaimed King.
And when all things shall cease to be,
He alone will reign in awe.
He was, He is, and He shall be glorious for evermore.
He is One, there is none else, alone, unique, beyond compare;
without beginning, without end, His might, His rule are everywhere.
He is my God; my Redeemer lives.
He is the Rock on whom I rely –
my banner and my safe retreat, my cup, my portion when I cry.
Into His hand my soul I place, when I awake and when I sleep.
The Lord is with me, I shall not fear;
body and soul from harm will He keep.

שִׁיר הַמַּעֲלוֹת, אַשְׁרֵי כָּל־יְרֵא יהוה, הַהֹלֵךְ בִּדְרָכָיו:

יְגִיעַ כַּפֶּיךָ כִּי תֹאכֵל, אַשְׁרֶיךָ וְטוֹב לָךְ:

אֶשְׁתְּךָ כְּגֶפֶן פֹּרִיָּה בְּיַרְכְּתֵי בֵיתֶךָ

בָּנֶיךָ כִּשְׁתִלֵי זֵיתִים, סָבִיב לְשֻׁלְחָנֶךָ:

הִנֵּה כִי־כֵן יְבֹרַךְ גָּבֶר יְרֵא יהוה:

יְבָרֶכְךָ יהוה מִצִּיּוֹן, וּרְאֵה בְּטוּב יְרוּשָׁלָ͏ִם, כֹּל יְמֵי חַיֶּיךָ:

וּרְאֵה־בָנִים לְבָנֶיךָ, שָׁלוֹם עַל־יִשְׂרָאֵל:

Say three times:

רִגְזוּ וְאַל־תֶּחֱטָאוּ

אִמְרוּ בִלְבַבְכֶם עַל־מִשְׁכַּבְכֶם, וְדֹמּוּ סֶלָה:

אֲדוֹן עוֹלָם אֲשֶׁר מָלַךְ בְּטֶרֶם כָּל־יְצִיר נִבְרָא.

לְעֵת נַעֲשָׂה בְחֶפְצוֹ כֹּל אֲזַי מֶלֶךְ שְׁמוֹ נִקְרָא.

וְאַחֲרֵי כִּכְלוֹת הַכֹּל לְבַדּוֹ יִמְלֹךְ נוֹרָא.

וְהוּא הָיָה וְהוּא הֹוֶה וְהוּא יִהְיֶה בְּתִפְאָרָה.

וְהוּא אֶחָד וְאֵין שֵׁנִי לְהַמְשִׁיל לוֹ לְהַחְבִּירָה.

בְּלִי רֵאשִׁית בְּלִי תַכְלִית וְלוֹ הָעֹז וְהַמִּשְׂרָה.

וְהוּא אֵלִי וְחַי גוֹאֲלִי וְצוּר חֶבְלִי בְּעֵת צָרָה.

וְהוּא נִסִּי וּמָנוֹס לִי מְנָת כּוֹסִי בְּיוֹם אֶקְרָא.

בְּיָדוֹ אַפְקִיד רוּחִי בְּעֵת אִישַׁן וְאָעִירָה.

וְעִם רוּחִי גְּוִיָּתִי יהוה לִי וְלֹא אִירָא.

Prayer for Recovery from Illness

מִזְמוֹר לְדָוִד A psalm of David. The Lord is my shepherd; I lack nothing. He has *Ps. 23*
me lie down in green pastures; He leads me beside still waters. He restores my
soul; He leads me in paths of righteousness for His name's sake. Even when I
walk through the valley of the shadow of death, I fear no evil, for You are with
me; Your rod and Your staff, they comfort me. You prepare a table before me in
the presence of my enemies. You anoint my head with oil; my cup is full. May
only goodness and kindness pursue me all the days of my life, and I will dwell
in the House of the Lord forever.

לְדָוִד By David. Bless the Lord, my soul, and all that is within me bless His holy *Ps. 103*
name. Bless the Lord, my soul, and do not forget all His acts of kindness. It is
He who forgives all your iniquities, who heals all your diseases, who redeems
your life from the pit, who crowns you with kindness and mercy, who sates
your spirit with good; your youth renewed like an eagle. The Lord performs
righteous deeds and metes out justice to all the oppressed. He made His ways
known to Moses, His deeds to the children of Israel. Merciful and gracious is
the Lord, slow to anger and abounding in kindness. He will not contend to
eternity or forever keep His anger. He has not dealt with us as befits our sins;
He has not requited our iniquities in kind. Rather, as high as the heavens above
the earth, so is His kindness great for those who fear Him. As far as east from
west, so has He distanced our transgressions from us. Just as a father has mercy
on his children, so the Lord has mercy on those who fear Him. For He knows
our impulses; He is mindful that we are but dust. As for man, his days are like
grass; he springs up like a bud in the field, which, when a wind passes over it,
it ceases to be; its own place knows it no more. But the kindness of the Lord is
forever, to those who fear Him; His righteousness for the children's progeny,
for those who keep His covenant and remember His precepts, to observe them.
The Lord has established His throne in the heavens; His kingship rules over all.
Bless the Lord, His angels, mighty in strength, who do His bidding, heeding
His word. Bless the Lord, all His hosts, His servants who do His will. Bless the
Lord, all of His works, in all places of His dominion. Bless the Lord, my soul.

לַמְנַצֵּחַ For the chief musician, a psalm by David. Lord, You have searched me, *Ps. 139*
and You know me. You know when I sit and when I rise; You understand my
thoughts from afar. You discern my path and my resting place; You are familiar
with all my ways. Even when there is no word on my tongue, truly, Lord, You
know it all. From back and front, You shaped me; You placed Your palm on me.

תפילה לחולה

מִזְמוֹר לְדָוִד, יהוה רֹעִי לֹא אֶחְסָר: בִּנְאוֹת דֶּשֶׁא יַרְבִּיצֵנִי, עַל־מֵי מְנֻחוֹת יְנַהֲלֵנִי: נַפְשִׁי יְשׁוֹבֵב, יַנְחֵנִי בְמַעְגְּלֵי־צֶדֶק לְמַעַן שְׁמוֹ: גַּם כִּי־אֵלֵךְ בְּגֵיא צַלְמָוֶת לֹא־אִירָא רָע, כִּי־אַתָּה עִמָּדִי, שִׁבְטְךָ וּמִשְׁעַנְתֶּךָ הֵמָּה יְנַחֲמֻנִי: תַּעֲרֹךְ לְפָנַי שֻׁלְחָן נֶגֶד צֹרְרָי, דִּשַּׁנְתָּ בַשֶּׁמֶן רֹאשִׁי, כּוֹסִי רְוָיָה: אַךְ טוֹב וָחֶסֶד יִרְדְּפוּנִי כָּל־יְמֵי חַיָּי, וְשַׁבְתִּי בְּבֵית־יהוה לְאֹרֶךְ יָמִים:

לְדָוִד, בָּרְכִי נַפְשִׁי אֶת־יהוה, וְכָל־קְרָבַי אֶת־שֵׁם קָדְשׁוֹ: בָּרְכִי נַפְשִׁי אֶת־יהוה, וְאַל־תִּשְׁכְּחִי כָּל־גְּמוּלָיו: הַסֹּלֵחַ לְכָל־עֲוֹנֵכִי, הָרֹפֵא לְכָל־ תַּחֲלֻאָיְכִי: הַגּוֹאֵל מִשַּׁחַת חַיָּיְכִי, הַמְעַטְּרֵכִי חֶסֶד וְרַחֲמִים: הַמַּשְׂבִּיעַ בַּטּוֹב עֶדְיֵךְ, תִּתְחַדֵּשׁ כַּנֶּשֶׁר נְעוּרָיְכִי: עֹשֵׂה צְדָקוֹת יהוה, וּמִשְׁפָּטִים לְכָל־עֲשׁוּקִים: יוֹדִיעַ דְּרָכָיו לְמֹשֶׁה, לִבְנֵי יִשְׂרָאֵל עֲלִילוֹתָיו: רַחוּם וְחַנּוּן יהוה, אֶרֶךְ אַפַּיִם וְרַב־חָסֶד: לֹא־לָנֶצַח יָרִיב, וְלֹא לְעוֹלָם יִטּוֹר: לֹא כַחֲטָאֵינוּ עָשָׂה לָנוּ, וְלֹא כַעֲוֹנֹתֵינוּ גָּמַל עָלֵינוּ: כִּי כִגְבֹהַּ שָׁמַיִם עַל־הָאָרֶץ, גָּבַר חַסְדּוֹ עַל־יְרֵאָיו: כִּרְחֹק מִזְרָח מִמַּעֲרָב, הִרְחִיק מִמֶּנּוּ אֶת־פְּשָׁעֵינוּ: כְּרַחֵם אָב עַל־בָּנִים, רִחַם יהוה עַל־יְרֵאָיו: כִּי־הוּא יָדַע יִצְרֵנוּ, זָכוּר כִּי־עָפָר אֲנָחְנוּ: אֱנוֹשׁ כֶּחָצִיר יָמָיו, כְּצִיץ הַשָּׂדֶה כֵּן יָצִיץ: כִּי רוּחַ עָבְרָה־בּוֹ וְאֵינֶנּוּ, וְלֹא־יַכִּירֶנּוּ עוֹד מְקוֹמוֹ: וְחֶסֶד יהוה מֵעוֹלָם וְעַד־עוֹלָם עַל־יְרֵאָיו, וְצִדְקָתוֹ לִבְנֵי בָנִים: לְשֹׁמְרֵי בְרִיתוֹ, וּלְזֹכְרֵי פִקֻּדָיו לַעֲשׂוֹתָם: יהוה בַּשָּׁמַיִם הֵכִין כִּסְאוֹ, וּמַלְכוּתוֹ בַּכֹּל מָשָׁלָה: בָּרְכוּ יהוה מַלְאָכָיו, גִּבֹּרֵי כֹחַ עֹשֵׂי דְבָרוֹ, לִשְׁמֹעַ בְּקוֹל דְּבָרוֹ: בָּרְכוּ יהוה כָּל־צְבָאָיו, מְשָׁרְתָיו עֹשֵׂי רְצוֹנוֹ: בָּרְכוּ יהוה כָּל־מַעֲשָׂיו, בְּכָל־מְקֹמוֹת מֶמְשַׁלְתּוֹ, בָּרְכִי נַפְשִׁי אֶת־יהוה:

לַמְנַצֵּחַ לְדָוִד מִזְמוֹר, יהוה חֲקַרְתַּנִי וַתֵּדָע: אַתָּה יָדַעְתָּ שִׁבְתִּי וְקוּמִי, בַּנְתָּה לְרֵעִי מֵרָחוֹק: אָרְחִי וְרִבְעִי זֵרִיתָ, וְכָל־דְּרָכַי הִסְכַּנְתָּה: כִּי אֵין מִלָּה בִּלְשׁוֹנִי, הֵן יהוה יָדַעְתָּ כֻלָּהּ: אָחוֹר וָקֶדֶם צַרְתָּנִי, וַתָּשֶׁת עָלַי כַּפֶּכָה: פְּלִיאָה דַעַת מִמֶּנִּי, נִשְׂגְּבָה לֹא־אוּכַל לָהּ: אָנָה אֵלֵךְ מֵרוּחֶךָ,

This knowledge is too wonderful for me. It is sublime; I cannot reach it. Where can I go from Your spirit? And where can I flee from Your presence? If I ascend to heaven, You are there; if I lie down in the netherworld, You are there. Were I to travel on the wings of dawn, were I to dwell at the end of the sea, even there Your hand would guide me; Your right hand would hold me fast. Even if I say that darkness will conceal me, that night, for me, is light, even darkness does not darken for You. The night, as if day, gives forth light. Darkness and light are the same. For You formed my innermost parts; You sheltered me in my mother's womb. I will give thanks to You, for I was made in a wondrous manner. Wonderful are Your works; I know this well. My essence was not hidden from You when I was wrought in a secret place, knitted in the depths of the earth. Your eyes saw my unformed parts; in Your book, they are all recorded. Of the days that were created, each one is His. How precious to me are thoughts of You, God; how vast is their beginning. When I count them, they outnumber the sand; when I awake, I am still with You. If You, my God, would slay the wicked, and men of bloodshed would turn away from me, Your enemies, who defy You for the sake of intrigue, exalting themselves in vain. For surely Your enemies, Lord, I hate, and I contend with those who rise against You. I hate them with utter hatred; they have become my enemies. Search me, God, and know my heart; test me and know my thoughts, and see if there is any grievous way in me. Lead me on the path to eternity.

תְּפִלָּה לְעָנִי The prayer of a poor man, when he feels overwhelmed and pours *Ps. 102:1–3* out his woes before the Lord. Lord, hear my prayer; let my cry for help reach You. Do not hide Your face from me at the time of my distress. Incline Your ear to me on the day that I call; answer me quickly.

אָנָּא Please, Lord, Healer of all flesh, have pity on me, and support me on my sick bed, in Your great love, for I am weak. Send relief and healing to me and to the others of Your children who are sick. Heal my pain and renew my youth as the eagle's. Grant wisdom to the physician that he may cure my illness, so that my healing may spring up swiftly. Hear my prayer, prolong my life, and let me complete my years in happiness, so that I may be able to serve You and keep Your precepts with a perfect heart. Grant me the understanding to know that this bitter trial has come upon me for my welfare. Let me not reject Your discipline or spurn Your rebuke.

אֱלוֹהַּ סְלִיחוֹת God of forgiveness, gracious and compassionate, slow to anger, abounding in love, I acknowledge before You with a broken and contrite heart that I have sinned and done evil in Your sight. I hereby repent of my evil and

וְאָנָה מִפָּנֶיךָ אֶבְרָח: אִם־אֶסַּק שָׁמַיִם שָׁם אָתָּה, וְאַצִּיעָה שְּׁאוֹל הִנֶּךָּ: אֶשָּׂא כַנְפֵי־שָׁחַר, אֶשְׁכְּנָה בְּאַחֲרִית יָם: גַּם־שָׁם יָדְךָ תַנְחֵנִי, וְתֹאחֲזֵנִי יְמִינֶךָ: וָאֹמַר אַךְ־חֹשֶׁךְ יְשׁוּפֵנִי, וְלַיְלָה אוֹר בַּעֲדֵנִי: גַּם־חֹשֶׁךְ לֹא־יַחְשִׁיךְ מִמֶּךָּ, וְלַיְלָה כַּיּוֹם יָאִיר, כַּחֲשֵׁיכָה כָּאוֹרָה: כִּי־אַתָּה קָנִיתָ כִלְיֹתָי, תְּסֻכֵּנִי בְּבֶטֶן אִמִּי: אוֹדְךָ עַל כִּי נוֹרָאוֹת נִפְלֵיתִי, נִפְלָאִים מַעֲשֶׂיךָ, וְנַפְשִׁי יֹדַעַת מְאֹד: לֹא־נִכְחַד עָצְמִי מִמֶּךָּ, אֲשֶׁר־עֻשֵּׂיתִי בַסֵּתֶר, רֻקַּמְתִּי בְּתַחְתִּיּוֹת אָרֶץ: גָּלְמִי רָאוּ עֵינֶיךָ, וְעַל־סִפְרְךָ כֻּלָּם יִכָּתֵבוּ, יָמִים יֻצָּרוּ, וְלוֹ אֶחָד בָּהֶם: וְלִי מַה־יָּקְרוּ רֵעֶיךָ אֵל, מֶה עָצְמוּ רָאשֵׁיהֶם: אֶסְפְּרֵם מֵחוֹל יִרְבּוּן, הֱקִיצֹתִי וְעוֹדִי עִמָּךְ: אִם־תִּקְטֹל אֱלוֹהַּ רָשָׁע, וְאַנְשֵׁי דָמִים סוּרוּ מֶנִּי: אֲשֶׁר יֹמְרוּךָ לִמְזִמָּה, נָשׂוּא לַשָּׁוְא עָרֶיךָ: הֲלוֹא־מְשַׂנְאֶיךָ יהוה אֶשְׂנָא, וּבִתְקוֹמְמֶיךָ אֶתְקוֹטָט: תַּכְלִית שִׂנְאָה שְׂנֵאתִים, לְאוֹיְבִים הָיוּ לִי: חָקְרֵנִי אֵל וְדַע לְבָבִי, בְּחָנֵנִי וְדַע שַׂרְעַפָּי: וּרְאֵה אִם־דֶּרֶךְ־עֹצֶב בִּי, וּנְחֵנִי בְּדֶרֶךְ עוֹלָם:

תהלים קב: א–ג

תְּפִלָּה לְעָנִי כִי־יַעֲטֹף, וְלִפְנֵי יהוה יִשְׁפֹּךְ שִׂיחוֹ: יהוה שִׁמְעָה תְפִלָּתִי, וְשַׁוְעָתִי אֵלֶיךָ תָבוֹא: אַל־תַּסְתֵּר פָּנֶיךָ מִמֶּנִּי בְּיוֹם צַר לִי, הַטֵּה־אֵלַי אָזְנֶךָ, בְּיוֹם אֶקְרָא מַהֵר עֲנֵנִי:

אָנָּא יהוה רוֹפֵא כָל בָּשָׂר, רַחֵם עָלַי, וּסְעָדֵנִי בְּחַסְדְּךָ הַגָּדוֹל עַל עֶרֶשׂ דְּוָי, כִּי אֻמְלַל אָנִי. שְׁלַח לִי תְרוּפָה וּתְעָלָה, בְּתוֹךְ שְׁאָר חוֹלֵי יִשְׂרָאֵל. רְפָא אֶת מַכְאוֹבִי, וְחַדֵּשׁ כַּנֶּשֶׁר נְעוּרָי. תֵּן בִּינָה לָרוֹפְאָא, וְיִגְהֶה מִמֶּנִּי מְזוֹרִי, וַאֲרוּכָתִי מְהֵרָה תִצְמָח. שְׁמַע תְּפִלָּתִי, וְהוֹסֵף יָמִים עַל יָמָי, וַאֲכַלֶּה שְׁנוֹתַי בַּנְּעִימִים, לְמַעַן אוּכַל לַעֲבֹד אוֹתָךְ, וְלִשְׁמֹר פִּקּוּדֶיךָ בְּלֵב שָׁלֵם. הֲבִינֵנִי וְאֵדְעָה, כִּי לִשְׁלוֹמִי מַר לִי מָר. וְאַל אֶמְאַס אֶת מוּסָרְךָ, וּבְתוֹכַחְתְּךָ אַל אָקוּץ.

אֱלוֹהַּ סְלִיחוֹת, חַנּוּן וְרַחוּם אֶרֶךְ אַפַּיִם וְרַב חָסֶד, מוֹדֶה אֲנִי לְפָנֶיךָ בְּלֵב נִשְׁבָּר וְנִדְכֶּה כִּי חָטָאתִי, וְהָרַע בְּעֵינֶיךָ עָשִׂיתִי. הִנֵּה נִחַמְתִּי עַל רָעָתִי, וְאָשׁוּב בִּתְשׁוּבָה שְׁלֵמָה לְפָנֶיךָ. עָזְרֵנִי אֱלֹהֵי יִשְׁעִי, וְלֹא אָשׁוּב

turn to You in complete repentance. Help me, God of my salvation, that I may not turn to folly again, but instead walk before You in truth and integrity. Gladden the soul of Your servant, for to You, Lord, I lift up my soul. Heal me, *Ps. 86:4* Lord, and I will be healed; save me, and I will be saved, for You are my praise. *Jer. 17:14* Amen and Amen!

Thanksgiving Prayer after Recovery from Illness

Say Psalms 23 and 103. Then continue with:

אָנָּא Great, mighty, and awesome God: By Your great love I come before You to offer thanks for all the good You have bestowed on me. In my distress I called to You and You answered me; from my sick bed I cried to You, and You heard my voice and my pleas. You chastened me severely, Lord, but You did not hand me over to death. In Your love and compassion You lifted my soul from the grave. For Your anger is for a moment, Your favor for a lifetime. At night there may be weeping, but in the morning there is joy. The living, the *Is. 38:19* living, he will thank You; like me, today. My soul which You have redeemed shall tell of Your wonders to the children of men. Blessed are You, the faithful Healer of all flesh.

אֵל רַחוּם God, compassionate and gracious, who grants favors to the undeserving: I am not worthy of all the kindness You have shown to me until now. Purify, please, my heart that I may be worthy to walk before You in the way of the upright. Extend Your help to Your servant. Grant me the strength and resolution to overcome my weakness, and bless me with physical health. Keep sorrow and grief far from me; protect me from all harm, and guide me with Your counsel. May the sun of righteousness shine for me, bringing healing in its wings. Let the words of my mouth and the meditation of my heart be ac- *Ps. 19:15* ceptable before you, Lord, my rock and my redeemer.

תהלים פז:ד לְכְסְלָה, וְאֶתְהַלֵּךְ לְפָנֶיךָ בֶּאֱמֶת וּבְתָמִים. שַׂמֵּחַ נֶפֶשׁ עַבְדֶּךָ, כִּי־אֵלֶיךָ

ירמיה יז:יד אֲדֹנָי, נַפְשִׁי אֶשָּׂא: רְפָאֵנִי יהוה וְאֵרָפֵא, הוֹשִׁיעֵנִי וְאִוָּשֵׁעָה, כִּי תְהִלָּתִי אֶתָּה: אָמֵן וְאָמֵן.

תפילה לעומד מחליו

Say תהלים כג and קג. Then continue with:

אָנָּא הָאֵל הַגָּדוֹל הַגִּבּוֹר וְהַנּוֹרָא, בְּרֹב חַסְדְּךָ אָבוֹא לְפָנֶיךָ לְהוֹדוֹת
לְךָ עַל כָּל הַטּוֹבוֹת אֲשֶׁר גָּמַלְתָּ עָלִי. מִן הַמֵּצַר קְרָאתִיךָ וַתַּעֲנֵנִי, מֵעֶרֶשׂ
דְּוַי שִׁוַּעְתִּי אֵלֶיךָ, וַתִּשְׁמַע אֶת קוֹלִי תַּחֲנוּנָי. יַסֹּר יִסַּרְתַּנִי יָהּ, וְלַמָּוֶת לֹא
נְתַתָּנִי. בְּאַהֲבָתְךָ וּבְחֶמְלָתְךָ הֶעֱלִיתָ מִן שְׁאוֹל נַפְשִׁי. כִּי רֶגַע בְּאַפּוֹ,
חַיִּים בִּרְצוֹנוֹ, בָּעֶרֶב יָלִין בֶּכִי וְלַבֹּקֶר רִנָּה. חַי חַי הוּא יוֹדֶךָ, כָּמוֹנִי
ישעיה לח:יט הַיּוֹם: וְנַפְשִׁי אֲשֶׁר פָּדִיתָ, תְּסַפֵּר נִפְלְאוֹתֶיךָ לִבְנֵי אָדָם. בָּרוּךְ אַתָּה,
רוֹפֵא נֶאֱמָן לְכָל בָּשָׂר.

אֵל רַחוּם וְחַנּוּן, הַגּוֹמֵל לְחַיָּבִים טוֹבוֹת, קָטֹנְתִּי מִכֹּל הַחֲסָדִים אֲשֶׁר
עָשִׂיתָ עִמָּדִי עַד הֵנָּה. אָנָּא טַהֵר לִבָּבִי, וְזַכֵּנִי לָלֶכֶת בְּדֶרֶךְ יְשָׁרִים לְפָנֶיךָ,
וּמֶשֹׁךְ עֶזְרְךָ לְעַבְדֶּךָ. חַזְּקֵנִי וְאַמְּצֵנִי מֵרִפְיוֹן, וּבְחִלּוּץ עֲצָמוֹת תְּבָרְכֵנִי.
הַרְחֵק מֵעָלַי כָּל צָרָה וְתוּגָה, שָׁמְרֵנִי מִכָּל רָע, וּבְעֶצָתְךָ תַנְחֵנִי. וְזָרְחָה לִי
תהלים יט:טו שֶׁמֶשׁ צְדָקָה, וּמַרְפֵּא בִּכְנָפֶיהָ. יִהְיוּ לְרָצוֹן אִמְרֵי־פִי וְהֶגְיוֹן לִבִּי לְפָנֶיךָ,
יהוה צוּרִי וְגֹאֲלִי: אָמֵן.

Prayers at the Cemetery

On visiting a cemetery for the first time in thirty days, it is customary to say the following:

בָּרוּךְ Blessed are You, Lord our God, King of the Universe,
who justly formed you,
and justly nourished and sustained you,
and justly brought death to you,
and justly knows you, one by one,
and is one day justly to bring you back and revive you;
blessed are You, Lord,
who revives the dead.

אַתָּה You are eternally mighty, Lord.
You give life to the dead and have great power to save.
He sustains the living with loving-kindness,
and with great compassion revives the dead.
He supports the fallen, heals the sick, sets captives free,
and keeps His faith with those who sleep in the dust.
Who is like You, Master of might,
and to whom can You be compared,
King who brings death and gives life,
and makes salvation grow?
Faithful are You to revive the dead.

When visiting a cemetery, especially for a memorial service or on the anniversary of a death,
it is customary to say the following seven psalms by the graveside. These are followed
by the verses of Psalm 119 (which is arranged alphabetically in groups of eight verses
for each letter) that spell out the deceased person's name, and then the groups of verses
that spell out the word נשמה, "soul."

33   Rejoice in the Lord, righteous ones; it is comely for the upright to offer praise.
Give thanks to the Lord with the lyre; sing praises to Him with a ten-
stringed harp.
Sing Him a new song; play beautifully with loud sound.
For the word of the Lord is upright, all His deeds faithfully wrought.
He loves righteousness and justice; the Lord's kindness fills the world.
By the word of the Lord were the heavens made; by the breath of His
mouth, all their hosts.
He heaps together the waters of the sea, storing in vaults the waters of
the deep.

תפילות לבית הקברות

On visiting a cemetery for the first time in thirty days, it is customary to say the following:

בָּרוּךְ אַתָּה יהוה, אֱלֹהֵינוּ מֶלֶךְ הָעוֹלָם

אֲשֶׁר יָצַר אֶתְכֶם בַּדִּין

וְזָן וְכִלְכֵּל אֶתְכֶם בַּדִּין

וְהֵמִית אֶתְכֶם בַּדִּין

וְיוֹדֵעַ מִסְפַּר כֻּלְּכֶם בַּדִּין

וְעָתִיד לְהַחֲזִיר וּלְהַחֲיוֹתְכֶם בַּדִּין.

בָּרוּךְ אַתָּה יהוה, מְחַיֵּה הַמֵּתִים.

אַתָּה גִּבּוֹר לְעוֹלָם, אֲדֹנָי

מְחַיֵּה מֵתִים אַתָּה, רַב לְהוֹשִׁיעַ

מְכַלְכֵּל חַיִּים בְּחֶסֶד, מְחַיֵּה מֵתִים בְּרַחֲמִים רַבִּים

סוֹמֵךְ נוֹפְלִים, וְרוֹפֵא חוֹלִים, וּמַתִּיר אֲסוּרִים

וּמְקַיֵּם אֱמוּנָתוֹ לִישֵׁנֵי עָפָר.

מִי כָמוֹךָ, בַּעַל גְּבוּרוֹת וּמִי דּוֹמֶה לָּךְ

מֶלֶךְ, מֵמִית וּמְחַיֶּה וּמַצְמִיחַ יְשׁוּעָה.

וְנֶאֱמָן אַתָּה לְהַחֲיוֹת מֵתִים.

When visiting a cemetery, especially for a memorial service or on the anniversary of a death, it is customary to say the following seven תהלים by the graveside. These are followed by the verses of תהלים קיט (which is arranged alphabetically in groups of eight verses for each letter) that spell out the deceased person's name, and then the groups of verses that spell out the word נשמה, "soul."

לג רַנְּנוּ צַדִּיקִים בַּיהוה לַיְשָׁרִים נָאוָה תְהִלָּה:
הוֹדוּ לַיהוה בְּכִנּוֹר בְּנֵבֶל עָשׂוֹר זַמְּרוּ־לוֹ:
שִׁירוּ־לוֹ שִׁיר חָדָשׁ הֵיטִיבוּ נַגֵּן בִּתְרוּעָה:
כִּי־יָשָׁר דְּבַר־יהוה וְכָל־מַעֲשֵׂהוּ בֶּאֱמוּנָה:
אֹהֵב צְדָקָה וּמִשְׁפָּט חֶסֶד יהוה מָלְאָה הָאָרֶץ:
בִּדְבַר יהוה שָׁמַיִם נַעֲשׂוּ וּבְרוּחַ פִּיו כָּל־צְבָאָם:

Let the entire world be in awe of the Lord; let all earth's inhabitants fear Him.

For He spoke, and it was done; He commanded, and it took form.

The Lord overturns the counsel of nations, annuls the schemes of peoples.

The Lord's counsel endures forever, the plans of His heart for all generations.

Happy is the nation whose God is the Lord, the people whom He chose as His possession.

The Lord looks from heaven; He sees all mankind.

From His dwelling place He observes all the inhabitants of the earth.

He who fashions all their hearts, who understands all their deeds.

The king is not saved by a mighty army, the warrior not rescued by great strength.

A horse is false hope for victory; even in its great power, it cannot offer escape.

Truly, the eye of the Lord is on those who fear Him, on those who await His kindness

to deliver them from death, to sustain them in famine.

Our soul longs for the Lord; He is our help and our shield.

For our heart rejoices in Him, for we trust in His holy name.

Let Your kindness, Lord, be upon us, as we have put our hope in You.

16   An instruction by David. Almighty, protect me, for I take refuge in You.

You said to the Lord: You are my Lord. I have no goodness but from You.

With the holy of the earth and the majestic ones, all my wishes are with them.

They are engaged in many matters, they who have dealings with strange things. I will not pour their libations of blood or carry their names on my lips.

The Lord is my lot and my portion; You sustain my fate.

The lots that have fallen to me are pleasant; my estate is lovely.

I bless the Lord who counsels me, even on nights when my thoughts are anguished.

I set the Lord before me always. He is on my right; I will not stumble.

Because of this my heart is glad. My being is joyous; my body rests securely.

For You will not abandon me to the netherworld; You will not allow Your devoted one to see the grave.

May You show me the path of life, abundance and joy in Your presence.

Eternal pleasure is by Your right hand.

כְּנֵס כַּנֵּד מֵי הַיָּם נֹתֵן בְּאוֹצָרוֹת תְּהוֹמוֹת:

יִירְאוּ מֵיהוה כָּל־הָאָרֶץ מִמֶּנּוּ יָגוּרוּ כָּל־יֹשְׁבֵי תֵבֵל:

כִּי הוּא אָמַר וַיֶּהִי הוּא־צִוָּה וַיַּעֲמֹד:

יהוה הֵפִיר עֲצַת־גּוֹיִם הֵנִיא מַחְשְׁבוֹת עַמִּים:

עֲצַת יהוה לְעוֹלָם תַּעֲמֹד מַחְשְׁבוֹת לִבּוֹ לְדֹר וָדֹר:

אַשְׁרֵי הַגּוֹי אֲשֶׁר־יהוה אֱלֹהָיו הָעָם ׀ בָּחַר לְנַחֲלָה לוֹ:

מִשָּׁמַיִם הִבִּיט יהוה רָאָה אֶת־כָּל־בְּנֵי הָאָדָם:

מִמְּכוֹן־שִׁבְתּוֹ הִשְׁגִּיחַ אֶל כָּל־יֹשְׁבֵי הָאָרֶץ:

הַיֹּצֵר יַחַד לִבָּם הַמֵּבִין אֶל־כָּל־מַעֲשֵׂיהֶם:

אֵין־הַמֶּלֶךְ נוֹשָׁע בְּרָב־חָיִל גִּבּוֹר לֹא־יִנָּצֵל בְּרָב־כֹּחַ:

שֶׁקֶר הַסּוּס לִתְשׁוּעָה וּבְרֹב חֵילוֹ לֹא יְמַלֵּט:

הִנֵּה עֵין יהוה אֶל־יְרֵאָיו לַמְיַחֲלִים לְחַסְדּוֹ:

לְהַצִּיל מִמָּוֶת נַפְשָׁם וּלְחַיּוֹתָם בָּרָעָב:

נַפְשֵׁנוּ חִכְּתָה לַיהוה עֶזְרֵנוּ וּמָגִנֵּנוּ הוּא:

כִּי־בוֹ יִשְׂמַח לִבֵּנוּ כִּי בְשֵׁם קָדְשׁוֹ בָטָחְנוּ:

יְהִי־חַסְדְּךָ יהוה עָלֵינוּ כַּאֲשֶׁר יִחַלְנוּ לָךְ:

טז מִכְתָּם לְדָוִד שָׁמְרֵנִי אֵל כִּי־חָסִיתִי בָךְ:

אָמַרְתְּ לַיהוה אֲדֹנָי אָתָּה טוֹבָתִי בַּל־עָלֶיךָ:

לִקְדוֹשִׁים אֲשֶׁר־בָּאָרֶץ הֵמָּה וְאַדִּירֵי כָּל־חֶפְצִי־בָם:

יִרְבּוּ עַצְּבוֹתָם אַחֵר מָהָרוּ

בַּל־אַסִּיךְ נִסְכֵּיהֶם מִדָּם וּבַל־אֶשָּׂא אֶת־שְׁמוֹתָם עַל־שְׂפָתָי:

יהוה מְנָת־חֶלְקִי וְכוֹסִי אַתָּה תּוֹמִיךְ גּוֹרָלִי:

חֲבָלִים נָפְלוּ־לִי בַּנְּעִמִים אַף־נַחֲלָת שָׁפְרָה עָלָי:

אֲבָרֵךְ אֶת־יהוה אֲשֶׁר יְעָצָנִי אַף־לֵילוֹת יִסְּרוּנִי כִלְיוֹתָי:

שִׁוִּיתִי יהוה לְנֶגְדִּי תָמִיד כִּי מִימִינִי בַּל־אֶמּוֹט:

לָכֵן ׀ שָׂמַח לִבִּי וַיָּגֶל כְּבוֹדִי אַף־בְּשָׂרִי יִשְׁכֹּן לָבֶטַח:

כִּי ׀ לֹא־תַעֲזֹב נַפְשִׁי לִשְׁאוֹל לֹא־תִתֵּן חֲסִידְךָ לִרְאוֹת שָׁחַת:

תּוֹדִיעֵנִי אֹרַח חַיִּים שֹׂבַע שְׂמָחוֹת אֶת־פָּנֶיךָ נְעִמוֹת בִּימִינְךָ נֶצַח:

17   A prayer by David. Hear, Lord, what is just; heed my cry. Give ear to my prayer, which does not come from deceitful lips.

Let my judgment come forth from Your presence; let Your eyes see what is right.

You have examined my heart, taken an account at night. You inspected me and found nothing; I pondered and nothing passed my lips.

In the doings of men, I follow Your instruction; I have avoided the ways of trespassers.

Secure my steps on Your paths, so my feet will not stumble.

I call upon You that You answer me, Almighty. Incline Your ear to me; hear my speech.

Reveal Your kindness, Redeemer of those who take refuge from the enemies who rise up, sheltering in Your right hand.

Guard me like the pupil of an eye, hide me in the shadow of Your wings, from the wicked who rob me, my mortal enemies who encircle me.

They are encased in their fat; their mouths speak with haughtiness.

I see them now surrounding us. They cast their eyes, spreading them over the land.

He is akin to a lion yearning to tear at his prey, like a lion cub lurking in hidden lairs.

Arise, Lord, confront him and subdue him. Rescue me from the wicked with Your sword.

Among those people under Your hand, Lord, those people in the land whose portion is life. Fill their bellies with Your hidden treasures; sate their sons, too, and let them leave what is left to their offspring.

Truly, I shall see Your face; Your image will fill my waking vision.

72   For Solomon. Endow the king with Your justice, God, and the king's son with Your righteousness.

May he judge Your people with righteousness, and Your poor with justice.

The mountains will bear peace for the people, and the hills, righteousness.

He will bring justice to the afflicted of the people, save the destitute, and crush the oppressor.

They will fear You as long as the sun and moon endure, throughout the generations.

It will descend like rain on fleece, like light showers that water the earth.

יז תְּפִלָּה לְדָוִד

שִׁמְעָה יְהֹוָה ׀ צֶדֶק הַקְשִׁיבָה רִנָּתִי הַאֲזִינָה תְפִלָּתִי
בְּלֹא שִׂפְתֵי מִרְמָה:

מִלְּפָנֶיךָ מִשְׁפָּטִי יֵצֵא עֵינֶיךָ תֶּחֱזֶינָה מֵישָׁרִים:

בָּחַנְתָּ לִבִּי ׀ פָּקַדְתָּ לַּיְלָה צְרַפְתַּנִי בַל־תִּמְצָא
זַמֹּתִי בַּל־יַעֲבָר־פִּי:

לִפְעֻלּוֹת אָדָם בִּדְבַר שְׂפָתֶיךָ אֲנִי שָׁמַרְתִּי אָרְחוֹת פָּרִיץ:

תָּמֹךְ אֲשֻׁרַי בְּמַעְגְּלוֹתֶיךָ בַּל־נָמוֹטּוּ פְעָמָי:

אֲנִי־קְרָאתִיךָ כִי־תַעֲנֵנִי אֵל הַט־אָזְנְךָ לִּי שְׁמַע אִמְרָתִי:

הַפְלֵה חֲסָדֶיךָ מוֹשִׁיעַ חוֹסִים מִמִּתְקוֹמְמִים בִּימִינֶךָ:

שָׁמְרֵנִי כְּאִישׁוֹן בַּת־עָיִן בְּצֵל כְּנָפֶיךָ תַּסְתִּירֵנִי:

מִפְּנֵי רְשָׁעִים זוּ שַׁדּוּנִי אֹיְבַי בְּנֶפֶשׁ יַקִּיפוּ עָלָי:

חֶלְבָּמוֹ סָגְרוּ פִּימוֹ דִּבְּרוּ בְגֵאוּת:

אַשֻּׁרֵינוּ עַתָּה סבבוני עֵינֵיהֶם יָשִׁיתוּ לִנְטוֹת בָּאָרֶץ:

דִּמְיֹנוֹ כְּאַרְיֵה יִכְסוֹף לִטְרֹף וְכִכְפִיר יֹשֵׁב בְּמִסְתָּרִים:

קוּמָה יְהֹוָה קַדְּמָה פָנָיו הַכְרִיעֵהוּ
פַּלְּטָה נַפְשִׁי מֵרָשָׁע חַרְבֶּךָ:

מִמְתִים יָדְךָ ׀ יְהֹוָה מִמְתִים מֵחֶלֶד חֶלְקָם בַּחַיִּים
וּצְפוּנְךָ תְּמַלֵּא בִטְנָם יִשְׂבְּעוּ בָנִים
וְהִנִּיחוּ יִתְרָם לְעוֹלְלֵיהֶם:

אֲנִי בְּצֶדֶק אֶחֱזֶה פָנֶיךָ אֶשְׂבְּעָה בְהָקִיץ תְּמוּנָתֶךָ:

עב לִשְׁלֹמֹה ׀ אֱלֹהִים מִשְׁפָּטֶיךָ לְמֶלֶךְ תֵּן וְצִדְקָתְךָ לְבֶן־מֶלֶךְ:

יָדִין עַמְּךָ בְצֶדֶק וַעֲנִיֶּיךָ בְמִשְׁפָּט:

יִשְׂאוּ הָרִים שָׁלוֹם לָעָם וּגְבָעוֹת בִּצְדָקָה:

יִשְׁפֹּט ׀ עֲנִיֵּי־עָם יוֹשִׁיעַ לִבְנֵי אֶבְיוֹן וִידַכֵּא עוֹשֵׁק:

יִירָאוּךָ עִם־שָׁמֶשׁ וְלִפְנֵי יָרֵחַ דּוֹר דּוֹרִים:

יֵרֵד כְּמָטָר עַל־גֵּז כִּרְבִיבִים זַרְזִיף אָרֶץ:

יִפְרַח־בְּיָמָיו צַדִּיק וְרֹב שָׁלוֹם עַד־בְּלִי יָרֵחַ:

The righteous will flourish in his days; abundant peace until the moon is no more.

He will rule from sea to sea, from river to the ends of the land.

Seafarers will kneel before him, and his enemies will lick the dust.

The kings of Tarshish and of the islands will bring tribute; the kings of Sheba and Seva will offer gifts.

And all kings will bow down before him, all nations will serve him.

For he will rescue the needy who cry out, and the poor man with no one to help him.

He will have compassion on the poor and needy, and the lives of the needy he will save.

He will redeem them from deceit and violence, and their blood will be precious in his sight.

So will he live, and He will give him the gold of Sheba. People will pray for him always; they will bless him all day long.

There will be abundance of grain in the land, on the mountain tops. Its fruit will rustle as the Lebanon; there will be sprouting in the city like grass of the earth.

May his name endure forever. May his name be praised as long as the sun shines, and may all people bless themselves by him; may all the nations acclaim him.

Blessed be the Lord God, the God of Israel, who alone works wonders.

And blessed be His glorious name forever; may the whole earth be filled with His glory, Amen and Amen.

Here end the prayers of David son of Yishai.

91   He who dwells in the shelter of the Most High, who abides in the shadow of the Almighty.

I will say of the Lord: He is my shelter and my fortress, my God in whom I trust.

For He will rescue you from the ensnaring trap, from devastating pestilence.

He will cover You with His pinion; you will find refuge under His wings. His truth is a shield and armor.

You will not fear the terror of night, nor the arrow that flies by day, nor the pestilence that stalks in darkness, nor the destruction that lays waste at noon.

וְיֵרְדְּ מִיָּם עַד־יָם וּמִנָּהָר עַד־אַפְסֵי־אָרֶץ:

לְפָנָיו יִכְרְעוּ צִיִּים וְאֹיְבָיו עָפָר יְלַחֵכוּ:

מַלְכֵי תַרְשִׁישׁ וְאִיִּים מִנְחָה יָשִׁיבוּ

מַלְכֵי שְׁבָא וּסְבָא אֶשְׁכָּר יַקְרִיבוּ:

וְיִשְׁתַּחֲווּ־לוֹ כָל־מְלָכִים כָּל־גּוֹיִם יַעַבְדוּהוּ:

כִּי־יַצִּיל אֶבְיוֹן מְשַׁוֵּעַ וְעָנִי וְאֵין עֹזֵר לוֹ:

יָחֹס עַל־דַּל וְאֶבְיוֹן וְנַפְשׁוֹת אֶבְיוֹנִים יוֹשִׁיעַ:

מִתּוֹךְ וּמֵחָמָס יִגְאַל נַפְשָׁם וְיֵיקַר דָּמָם בְּעֵינָיו:

וִיחִי וְיִתֶּן־לוֹ מִזְּהַב שְׁבָא

וְיִתְפַּלֵּל בַּעֲדוֹ תָמִיד כָּל־הַיּוֹם יְבָרֲכֶנְהוּ:

יְהִי פִסַּת־בַּר ׀ בָּאָרֶץ בְּרֹאשׁ הָרִים

יִרְעַשׁ כַּלְּבָנוֹן פִּרְיוֹ וְיָצִיצוּ מֵעִיר כְּעֵשֶׂב הָאָרֶץ:

יְהִי שְׁמוֹ ׀ לְעוֹלָם לִפְנֵי־שֶׁמֶשׁ יִנּוֹן שְׁמוֹ

וְיִתְבָּרְכוּ בוֹ כָּל־גּוֹיִם יְאַשְּׁרוּהוּ:

בָּרוּךְ ׀ יְהוָה אֱלֹהִים אֱלֹהֵי יִשְׂרָאֵל

עֹשֵׂה נִפְלָאוֹת לְבַדּוֹ:

וּבָרוּךְ ׀ שֵׁם כְּבוֹדוֹ לְעוֹלָם

וְיִמָּלֵא כְבוֹדוֹ אֶת־כֹּל הָאָרֶץ אָמֵן ׀ וְאָמֵן:

כָּלּוּ תְפִלּוֹת דָּוִד בֶּן־יִשָׁי:

צא יֹשֵׁב בְּסֵתֶר עֶלְיוֹן בְּצֵל שַׁדַּי יִתְלוֹנָן:

אֹמַר לַיהוָה מַחְסִי וּמְצוּדָתִי אֱלֹהַי אֶבְטַח־בּוֹ:

כִּי הוּא יַצִּילְךָ מִפַּח יָקוּשׁ מִדֶּבֶר הַוּוֹת:

בְּאֶבְרָתוֹ ׀ יָסֶךְ לָךְ וְתַחַת־כְּנָפָיו תֶּחְסֶה

צִנָּה וְסֹחֵרָה אֲמִתּוֹ:

לֹא־תִירָא מִפַּחַד לָיְלָה מֵחֵץ יָעוּף יוֹמָם:

מִדֶּבֶר בָּאֹפֶל יַהֲלֹךְ מִקֶּטֶב יָשׁוּד צָהֳרָיִם:

יִפֹּל מִצִּדְּךָ ׀ אֶלֶף וּרְבָבָה מִימִינֶךָ אֵלֶיךָ לֹא יִגָּשׁ:

רַק בְּעֵינֶיךָ תַבִּיט וְשִׁלֻּמַת רְשָׁעִים תִּרְאֶה:

A thousand may fall at your side, and ten thousand at your right hand, but you it will not reach.

You will just look with your eyes and see the punishment of the wicked.

For you, Lord, are my shelter. You have made the Most High your dwelling place.

No evil will befall you and no plague will come near your tent,

for He will charge His angels on your behalf, to guard you in all your ways.

They will carry you on their palms, lest your foot be struck by a stone.

You will tread upon lions and vipers; you will trample young lions and serpents.

Because he desired Me greatly, I will rescue him; I will be his fortress, for he has known My name.

When he calls upon Me, I will answer him. I will be with him in times of trouble; I will deliver him and honor him.

I will sate him with length of days, and I will show him My salvation.

04   Bless the Lord, my soul. Lord my God, You are greatly exalted, You are clothed in splendor and glory.

Enveloping with light as if with a cloak, He spreads out the heavens like a tent cloth.

He covers His upper chambers with water, He makes clouds His chariot, He moves on wings of wind.

He makes the winds His messengers, the flaming fires His servants.

He established the earth on its foundations, never to be shaken.

He covered the depths as with a garment; waters stood above the mountains.

At Your rebuke they fled; at the sound of Your thunder they hastened away.

They rose to the mountains, descended in the valleys to the place You established for them.

You set a boundary they could not cross, so they would not come back to cover the earth.

He sends forth springs through the valleys; between the mountains they flow.

They give drink to all beasts of the field; wild asses quench their thirst.

Birds of the sky dwell alongside them, giving voice among the branches.

He waters the mountains from His upper chambers; the earth is sated with the product of Your works.

כִּי־אַתָּה יְהֹוָה מַחְסִי עֶלְיוֹן שַׂמְתָּ מְעוֹנֶךָ:
לֹא־תְאֻנֶּה אֵלֶיךָ רָעָה וְנֶגַע לֹא־יִקְרַב בְּאׇהֳלֶךָ:
כִּי מַלְאָכָיו יְצַוֶּה־לָּךְ לִשְׁמׇרְךָ בְּכׇל־דְּרָכֶיךָ:
עַל־כַּפַּיִם יִשָּׂאוּנְךָ פֶּן־תִּגֹּף בָּאֶבֶן רַגְלֶךָ:
עַל־שַׁחַל וָפֶתֶן תִּדְרֹךְ תִּרְמֹס כְּפִיר וְתַנִּין:
כִּי בִי חָשַׁק וַאֲפַלְּטֵהוּ אֲשַׂגְּבֵהוּ כִּי־יָדַע שְׁמִי:
יִקְרָאֵנִי ׀ וְאֶעֱנֵהוּ עִמּוֹ־אָנֹכִי בְצָרָה אֲחַלְּצֵהוּ וַאֲכַבְּדֵהוּ:
אֹרֶךְ יָמִים אַשְׂבִּיעֵהוּ וְאַרְאֵהוּ בִּישׁוּעָתִי:

קד בָּרְכִי נַפְשִׁי אֶת־יְהֹוָה יְהֹוָה אֱלֹהַי גָּדַלְתָּ מְּאֹד
הוֹד וְהָדָר לָבָשְׁתָּ:
עֹטֶה־אוֹר כַּשַּׂלְמָה נוֹטֶה שָׁמַיִם כַּיְרִיעָה:
הַמְקָרֶה בַמַּיִם עֲלִיּוֹתָיו
הַשָּׂם־עָבִים רְכוּבוֹ הַמְהַלֵּךְ עַל־כַּנְפֵי־רוּחַ:
עֹשֶׂה מַלְאָכָיו רוּחוֹת מְשָׁרְתָיו אֵשׁ לֹהֵט:
יָסַד־אֶרֶץ עַל־מְכוֹנֶיהָ בַּל־תִּמּוֹט עוֹלָם וָעֶד:
תְּהוֹם כַּלְּבוּשׁ כִּסִּיתוֹ עַל־הָרִים יַעַמְדוּ־מָיִם:
מִן־גַּעֲרָתְךָ יְנוּסוּן מִן־קוֹל רַעַמְךָ יֵחָפֵזוּן:
יַעֲלוּ הָרִים יֵרְדוּ בְקָעוֹת אֶל־מְקוֹם זֶה ׀ יָסַדְתָּ לָהֶם:
גְּבוּל־שַׂמְתָּ בַּל־יַעֲבֹרוּן בַּל־יְשׁוּבוּן לְכַסּוֹת הָאָרֶץ:
הַמְשַׁלֵּחַ מַעְיָנִים בַּנְּחָלִים בֵּין הָרִים יְהַלֵּכוּן:
יַשְׁקוּ כָּל־חַיְתוֹ שָׂדָי יִשְׁבְּרוּ פְרָאִים צְמָאָם:
עֲלֵיהֶם עוֹף־הַשָּׁמַיִם יִשְׁכּוֹן מִבֵּין עֳפָאיִם יִתְּנוּ־קוֹל:
מַשְׁקֶה הָרִים מֵעֲלִיּוֹתָיו
מִפְּרִי מַעֲשֶׂיךָ תִּשְׂבַּע הָאָרֶץ:
מַצְמִיחַ חָצִיר ׀ לַבְּהֵמָה וְעֵשֶׂב לַעֲבֹדַת הָאָדָם
לְהוֹצִיא לֶחֶם מִן־הָאָרֶץ:
וְיַיִן ׀ יְשַׂמַּח לְבַב־אֱנוֹשׁ לְהַצְהִיל פָּנִים מִשָּׁמֶן
וְלֶחֶם לְבַב־אֱנוֹשׁ יִסְעָד:

He makes grass grow for the cattle, and vegetation for the labor of man, for bringing forth bread from the earth,

and wine, which gladdens man's heart, making the face glisten from oil; and bread, to sustain man's heart.

The trees of the Lord sate themselves, the cedars of Lebanon that He planted,

where birds make their nests; the stork has its home in the cypresses.

The high mountains are for the ibex, the crags a shelter for the hyrax.

He made the moon for appointed times; the sun knows its setting.

You bring darkness and it becomes night, when all the beasts of the forest are astir.

The young lions roar for prey, asking the Almighty for their food.

When the sun rises they withdraw, and crouch in their dens.

Man goes out to his work and to his labor until evening.

Lord, how manifold are Your deeds, in wisdom have You made them all. The earth is full of Your possessions.

There is the sea, vast and broad; an innumerable swarm is in it, creatures both great and small.

There ships go; and the leviathan, which You created to frolic with.

They all fix their hopes on You to give them their food at the proper time.

When You give it to them, they gather it; when You open Your hand, they are sated with good.

When You hide Your face, they take fright; when You take away their spirit, they die and return to their dust.

When You send forth Your spirit, they are created; You renew the face of the land.

May the glory of the Lord endure forever; may the Lord rejoice in His works,

He who looks at the earth, and it trembles; who touches the mountains, and they smoke.

I will sing to the Lord as long as I live; I will sing praise to my God as long as I am able.

May my utterance please Him; I rejoice in the Lord.

May sinners be removed from the earth, and may the wicked be no more. Bless the Lord, my soul. Halleluya.

יִשְׂבְּעוּ עֲצֵי יְהֹוָה אַרְזֵי לְבָנוֹן אֲשֶׁר נָטָע:

אֲשֶׁר־שָׁם צִפֳּרִים יְקַנֵּנוּ חֲסִידָה בְּרוֹשִׁים בֵּיתָהּ:

הָרִים הַגְּבֹהִים לַיְּעֵלִים סְלָעִים מַחְסֶה לַשְׁפַנִּים:

עָשָׂה יָרֵחַ לְמוֹעֲדִים שֶׁמֶשׁ יָדַע מְבוֹאוֹ:

תָּשֶׁת־חֹשֶׁךְ וִיהִי לָיְלָה בּוֹ־תִרְמֹשׂ כָּל־חַיְתוֹ־יָעַר:

הַכְּפִירִים שֹׁאֲגִים לַטָּרֶף וּלְבַקֵּשׁ מֵאֵל אָכְלָם:

תִּזְרַח הַשֶּׁמֶשׁ יֵאָסֵפוּן וְאֶל־מְעוֹנֹתָם יִרְבָּצוּן:

יֵצֵא אָדָם לְפָעֳלוֹ וְלַעֲבֹדָתוֹ עֲדֵי־עָרֶב:

מָה־רַבּוּ מַעֲשֶׂיךָ ׀ יְהֹוָה כֻּלָּם בְּחָכְמָה עָשִׂיתָ

מָלְאָה הָאָרֶץ קִנְיָנֶךָ:

זֶה ׀ הַיָּם גָּדוֹל וּרְחַב יָדָיִם

שָׁם־רֶמֶשׂ וְאֵין מִסְפָּר חַיּוֹת קְטַנּוֹת עִם־גְּדֹלוֹת:

שָׁם אֳנִיּוֹת יְהַלֵּכוּן לִוְיָתָן זֶה־יָצַרְתָּ לְשַׂחֶק־בּוֹ:

כֻּלָּם אֵלֶיךָ יְשַׂבֵּרוּן לָתֵת אָכְלָם בְּעִתּוֹ:

תִּתֵּן לָהֶם יִלְקֹטוּן תִּפְתַּח יָדְךָ יִשְׂבְּעוּן טוֹב:

תַּסְתִּיר פָּנֶיךָ יִבָּהֵלוּן תֹּסֵף רוּחָם יִגְוָעוּן

וְאֶל־עֲפָרָם יְשׁוּבוּן:

תְּשַׁלַּח רוּחֲךָ יִבָּרֵאוּן וּתְחַדֵּשׁ פְּנֵי אֲדָמָה:

יְהִי כְבוֹד יְהֹוָה לְעוֹלָם יִשְׂמַח יְהֹוָה בְּמַעֲשָׂיו:

הַמַּבִּיט לָאָרֶץ וַתִּרְעָד יִגַּע בֶּהָרִים וְיֶעֱשָׁנוּ:

אָשִׁירָה לַיהֹוָה בְּחַיָּי אֲזַמְּרָה לֵאלֹהַי בְּעוֹדִי:

יֶעֱרַב עָלָיו שִׂיחִי אָנֹכִי אֶשְׂמַח בַּיהֹוָה:

יִתַּמּוּ חַטָּאִים ׀ מִן־הָאָרֶץ וּרְשָׁעִים ׀ עוֹד אֵינָם

בָּרְכִי נַפְשִׁי אֶת־יְהֹוָה הַלְלוּיָהּ:

30   A song of ascents. Out of the depths I call to You, Lord.

Lord, hear my voice; let Your ears be attentive to the sound of my pleas.

If You hold fast, Lord, to iniquities, my Lord, who can stand?

Yet forgiveness is with You, that You might be feared.

I hope, Lord, my soul hopes; I long for His word.

My soul awaits the Lord, more than watchers for the morning, watchers for the morning.

Await the Lord, Israel, for kindness is with the Lord, and abundant redemption is with Him.

And He will redeem Israel from all its iniquities.

After reciting the initial seven psalms, above, it is customary to spell out the name of the deceased by reciting the verses of Psalm 119 that correspond to the letters of the name.

ALEF

119   Happy are those whose path is blameless, who follow the teaching of the Lord.

Happy are those who uphold His precepts and seek Him wholeheartedly.

They do not engage in wrongdoing, but rather walk in His ways.

You commanded Your edicts to be diligently observed.

It is my wish that my ways be firmly set to observe Your statutes,

for then I would not be ashamed when looking upon all Your commandments.

I give thanks to You with a sincere heart as I study Your righteous laws.

I follow Your statutes; do not utterly forsake me.

BEIT

How can a young man bring merit to his path? By following it as befits Your word.

I seek You with all my heart; let me not stray from Your commandments.

I store Your saying in my heart, so as not to sin against You.

Blessed are You, Lord; teach me Your statutes.

With my lips I recount all the laws of Your mouth.

I rejoice in the path of Your precepts as over all riches.

I speak about Your edicts and look upon Your ways.

I delight in Your statutes; I do not forget Your word.

קל

שִׁיר הַמַּעֲלוֹת מִמַּעֲמַקִּים קְרָאתִיךָ יְהוָה:
אֲדֹנָי שִׁמְעָה בְקוֹלִי תִּהְיֶינָה אָזְנֶיךָ קַשֻּׁבוֹת לְקוֹל תַּחֲנוּנָי:
אִם־עֲוֹנוֹת תִּשְׁמָר־יָהּ אֲדֹנָי מִי יַעֲמֹד:
כִּי־עִמְּךָ הַסְּלִיחָה לְמַעַן תִּוָּרֵא:
קִוִּיתִי יְהוָה קִוְּתָה נַפְשִׁי וְלִדְבָרוֹ הוֹחָלְתִּי:
נַפְשִׁי לַאדֹנָי מִשֹּׁמְרִים לַבֹּקֶר שֹׁמְרִים לַבֹּקֶר:
יַחֵל יִשְׂרָאֵל אֶל־יְהוָה כִּי־עִם־יְהוָה הַחֶסֶד וְהַרְבֵּה עִמּוֹ פְדוּת:
וְהוּא יִפְדֶּה אֶת־יִשְׂרָאֵל מִכֹּל עֲוֹנוֹתָיו:

After reciting the initial seven psalms, above, it is customary to spell out the name of the deceased by reciting the verses of תהלים קיט that correspond to the letters of the name.

א

קיט

אַשְׁרֵי תְמִימֵי־דָרֶךְ הַהֹלְכִים בְּתוֹרַת יְהוָה:
אַשְׁרֵי נֹצְרֵי עֵדֹתָיו בְּכָל־לֵב יִדְרְשׁוּהוּ:
אַף לֹא־פָעֲלוּ עַוְלָה בִּדְרָכָיו הָלָכוּ:
אַתָּה צִוִּיתָה פִקֻּדֶיךָ לִשְׁמֹר מְאֹד:
אַחֲלַי יִכֹּנוּ דְרָכָי לִשְׁמֹר חֻקֶּיךָ:
אָז לֹא־אֵבוֹשׁ בְּהַבִּיטִי אֶל־כָּל־מִצְוֹתֶיךָ:
אוֹדְךָ בְּיֹשֶׁר לֵבָב בְּלָמְדִי מִשְׁפְּטֵי צִדְקֶךָ:
אֶת־חֻקֶּיךָ אֶשְׁמֹר אַל־תַּעַזְבֵנִי עַד־מְאֹד:

ב

בַּמֶּה יְזַכֶּה־נַּעַר אֶת־אָרְחוֹ לִשְׁמֹר כִּדְבָרֶךָ:
בְּכָל־לִבִּי דְרַשְׁתִּיךָ אַל־תַּשְׁגֵּנִי מִמִּצְוֹתֶיךָ:
בְּלִבִּי צָפַנְתִּי אִמְרָתֶךָ לְמַעַן לֹא אֶחֱטָא־לָךְ:
בָּרוּךְ אַתָּה יְהוָה לַמְּדֵנִי חֻקֶּיךָ:
בִּשְׂפָתַי סִפַּרְתִּי כֹּל מִשְׁפְּטֵי־פִיךָ:
בְּדֶרֶךְ עֵדְוֹתֶיךָ שַׂשְׂתִּי כְּעַל כָּל־הוֹן:
בְּפִקֻּדֶיךָ אָשִׂיחָה וְאַבִּיטָה אֹרְחֹתֶיךָ:
בְּחֻקֹּתֶיךָ אֶשְׁתַּעֲשָׁע לֹא אֶשְׁכַּח דְּבָרֶךָ:

GIMMEL

Grant kindness to Your servant, that I might live and keep Your word.

Uncover my eyes so I might perceive the wonders of Your teaching.

I am but a sojourner on earth; do not hide Your commandments from me.

My soul longingly partakes of Your laws at all times.

You rebuke the accursed, insolent ones who stray from Your commandments.

Remove disgrace and abuse from me, for I have upheld Your precepts.

Even when princes sit and talk about me, Your servant reflects on Your statutes.

Also Your precepts are my delight, my counselors.

DALET

My soul cleaves to the dust; revive me as Your word.

I told of my ways, and You answered me. Teach me Your statutes.

Make me understand the way of Your edicts, and I will speak about Your wonders.

My soul is dripping with anguish; sustain me, as befits Your word.

Remove the path of falsehood from me; grant me Your teaching.

I have chosen the path of faith; I have placed Your laws.

I cleave to Your precepts; Lord, do not shame me.

I run in the path of Your commandments, for You widen my heart.

HEH

Teach me, Lord, the way of Your statutes, and I will uphold it to the end.

Give me understanding, so I might uphold Your teaching and follow it wholeheartedly.

Guide me in the path of Your commandments, for in it is my desire.

Incline my heart toward Your precepts and not toward material gain.

Avert my eyes from seeing falsehood; through Your ways give me life.

Fulfill the promise You made to Your servant, which is for those who fear You.

Remove my disgrace, which I dread, for Your laws are good.

How I long for Your edicts! In Your righteousness give me life.

ג

גְּמֹל עַל־עַבְדְּךָ אֶחְיֶה וְאֶשְׁמְרָה דְבָרֶךָ:

גַּל־עֵינַי וְאַבִּיטָה נִפְלָאוֹת מִתּוֹרָתֶךָ:

גֵּר אָנֹכִי בָאָרֶץ אַל־תַּסְתֵּר מִמֶּנִּי מִצְוֹתֶיךָ:

גָּרְסָה נַפְשִׁי לְתַאֲבָה אֶל־מִשְׁפָּטֶיךָ בְכָל־עֵת:

גָּעַרְתָּ זֵדִים אֲרוּרִים הַשֹּׁגִים מִמִּצְוֹתֶיךָ:

גַּל מֵעָלַי חֶרְפָּה וָבוּז כִּי עֵדֹתֶיךָ נָצָרְתִּי:

גַּם יָשְׁבוּ שָׂרִים בִּי נִדְבָּרוּ עַבְדְּךָ יָשִׂיחַ בְּחֻקֶּיךָ:

גַּם־עֵדֹתֶיךָ שַׁעֲשֻׁעָי אַנְשֵׁי עֲצָתִי:

ד

דָּבְקָה לֶעָפָר נַפְשִׁי חַיֵּנִי כִּדְבָרֶךָ:

דְּרָכַי סִפַּרְתִּי וַתַּעֲנֵנִי לַמְּדֵנִי חֻקֶּיךָ:

דֶּרֶךְ־פִּקּוּדֶיךָ הֲבִינֵנִי וְאָשִׂיחָה בְּנִפְלְאוֹתֶיךָ:

דָּלְפָה נַפְשִׁי מִתּוּגָה קַיְּמֵנִי כִּדְבָרֶךָ:

דֶּרֶךְ־שֶׁקֶר הָסֵר מִמֶּנִּי וְתוֹרָתְךָ חָנֵּנִי:

דֶּרֶךְ־אֱמוּנָה בָחָרְתִּי מִשְׁפָּטֶיךָ שִׁוִּיתִי:

דָּבַקְתִּי בְעֵדְוֹתֶיךָ יְהוָה אַל־תְּבִישֵׁנִי:

דֶּרֶךְ־מִצְוֹתֶיךָ אָרוּץ כִּי תַרְחִיב לִבִּי:

ה

הוֹרֵנִי יְהוָה דֶּרֶךְ חֻקֶּיךָ וְאֶצְּרֶנָּה עֵקֶב:

הֲבִינֵנִי וְאֶצְּרָה תוֹרָתֶךָ וְאֶשְׁמְרֶנָּה בְכָל־לֵב:

הַדְרִיכֵנִי בִּנְתִיב מִצְוֹתֶיךָ כִּי־בוֹ חָפָצְתִּי:

הַט־לִבִּי אֶל־עֵדְוֹתֶיךָ וְאַל אֶל־בָּצַע:

הַעֲבֵר עֵינַי מֵרְאוֹת שָׁוְא בִּדְרָכֶךָ חַיֵּנִי:

הָקֵם לְעַבְדְּךָ אִמְרָתֶךָ אֲשֶׁר לְיִרְאָתֶךָ:

הַעֲבֵר חֶרְפָּתִי אֲשֶׁר יָגֹרְתִּי כִּי מִשְׁפָּטֶיךָ טוֹבִים:

הִנֵּה תָּאַבְתִּי לְפִקֻּדֶיךָ בְּצִדְקָתְךָ חַיֵּנִי:

VAV

Let Your kindness reach me, Lord, as well as Your deliverance, as befits
Your promise.
And I will answer those who revile me, for I trust in Your word.
Do not withhold the word of truth altogether from my mouth,
for I trust in Your laws.
May I follow Your teaching always and forever.
Let me walk in a wide, expansive place, for I have sought Your edicts.
I will recount Your precepts before kings and not be ashamed.
I will delight in Your commandments, which I love.
I will lift my hands to Your commandments, which I love, and I will reflect
on Your statutes.

ZAYIN

Remember the word to Your servant, with which You gave me hope.
This is my comfort in my affliction: That Your saying revives me.
Evildoers mock me greatly, but I do not veer from Your teaching.
I have always remembered Your laws, Lord, and I am comforted.
Great distress has seized me because of the wicked
who have forsaken Your teaching.
Your statutes were songs to me in the house of my sojourning.
Lord, I remember Your name in the night, and I follow Your teaching.
This became mine, because I upheld Your precepts.

ḤET

I have declared that the Lord is my portion, to follow Your words.
I plead for Your countenance with a whole heart; be gracious to me, as
befits Your promise.
I consider my ways, and I turn my feet toward Your precepts.
I hasten, I do not delay, in following Your commandments.
The pains of the wicked contorted me, but I did not forget Your teaching.
At midnight, I rise to give thanks to You for Your righteous laws.
I am a friend to all who fear You, to those who follow Your edicts.
The earth is full of Your kindness, Lord; teach me Your statutes.

ו

וִיבֹאֻנִי חֲסָדֶךָ יהוה תְּשׁוּעָתְךָ כְּאִמְרָתֶךָ:

וְאֶעֱנֶה חֹרְפִי דָבָר כִּי־בָטַחְתִּי בִּדְבָרֶךָ:

וְאַל־תַּצֵּל מִפִּי דְבַר־אֱמֶת עַד־מְאֹד כִּי לְמִשְׁפָּטֶךָ יִחָלְתִּי:

וְאֶשְׁמְרָה תוֹרָתְךָ תָמִיד לְעוֹלָם וָעֶד:

וְאֶתְהַלְּכָה בָרְחָבָה כִּי פִקֻּדֶיךָ דָרָשְׁתִּי:

וַאֲדַבְּרָה בְעֵדֹתֶיךָ נֶגֶד מְלָכִים וְלֹא אֵבוֹשׁ:

וְאֶשְׁתַּעֲשַׁע בְּמִצְוֹתֶיךָ אֲשֶׁר אָהָבְתִּי:

וְאֶשָּׂא־כַפַּי אֶל־מִצְוֹתֶיךָ אֲשֶׁר אָהָבְתִּי וְאָשִׂיחָה בְחֻקֶּיךָ:

ז

זְכֹר־דָּבָר לְעַבְדֶּךָ עַל אֲשֶׁר יִחַלְתָּנִי:

זֹאת נֶחָמָתִי בְעָנְיִי כִּי אִמְרָתְךָ חִיָּתְנִי:

זֵדִים הֱלִיצֻנִי עַד־מְאֹד מִתּוֹרָתְךָ לֹא נָטִיתִי:

זָכַרְתִּי מִשְׁפָּטֶיךָ מֵעוֹלָם ׀ יהוה וָאֶתְנֶחָם:

זַלְעָפָה אֲחָזַתְנִי מֵרְשָׁעִים עֹזְבֵי תּוֹרָתֶךָ:

זְמִרוֹת הָיוּ־לִי חֻקֶּיךָ בְּבֵית מְגוּרָי:

זָכַרְתִּי בַלַּיְלָה שִׁמְךָ יהוה וָאֶשְׁמְרָה תּוֹרָתֶךָ:

זֹאת הָיְתָה־לִּי כִּי פִקֻּדֶיךָ נָצָרְתִּי:

ח

חֶלְקִי יהוה אָמַרְתִּי לִשְׁמֹר דְּבָרֶיךָ:

חִלִּיתִי פָנֶיךָ בְכָל־לֵב חָנֵּנִי כְּאִמְרָתֶךָ:

חִשַּׁבְתִּי דְרָכָי וָאָשִׁיבָה רַגְלַי אֶל־עֵדֹתֶיךָ:

חַשְׁתִּי וְלֹא הִתְמַהְמָהְתִּי לִשְׁמֹר מִצְוֹתֶיךָ:

חֶבְלֵי רְשָׁעִים עִוְּדֻנִי תּוֹרָתְךָ לֹא שָׁכָחְתִּי:

חֲצוֹת־לַיְלָה אָקוּם לְהוֹדוֹת לָךְ עַל מִשְׁפְּטֵי צִדְקֶךָ:

חָבֵר אָנִי לְכָל־אֲשֶׁר יְרֵאוּךָ וּלְשֹׁמְרֵי פִּקּוּדֶיךָ:

חַסְדְּךָ יהוה מָלְאָה הָאָרֶץ חֻקֶּיךָ לַמְּדֵנִי:

TET

You dealt well with Your servant, Lord, as befits Your word.

Teach me good discernment and understanding, for I believe in Your commandments.

Before I discussed it, I would go astray, but now I follow Your saying.

You are good, and do good; teach me Your statutes.

Evildoers pin falsehoods on me; I uphold Your edicts with a whole heart.

Their hearts are dulled, as if covered with fat; I delight in Your teaching.

It is good for me that I was afflicted, so I might learn Your statutes.

The teaching of Your mouth is better for me than thousands of gold and silver pieces.

YOD

Your hands made me and set me in place. Give me understanding, so I might learn Your commandments.

May those who fear You see me and be glad, because I hope for Your word.

I know, Lord, that Your rulings are just, and that You afflicted me in faithfulness.

May Your kindness comfort me, as You promised Your servant.

May Your mercy come to me, so I might live; Your teaching is my delight.

May the evildoers be shamed for contorting me with lies;

I will reflect on Your edicts.

May those who fear You and who know Your precepts turn to me.

May my heart be blameless in Your statutes, lest I be ashamed.

KAF

My soul goes out in yearning for Your salvation; I await Your word.

My eyes pine for Your promise, saying: When will You comfort me?

Even when I am like a wineskin in steam, I do not forget Your statutes.

How many are the days of Your servant?

When will You pass judgment on my pursuers?

Evildoers dig pits that are meant for me;

they do not act as befits Your teaching.

All Your commandments are truth, yet they pursue me with lies; help me.

They nearly rid the earth of me; I do not forsake Your edicts.

Give me life, as befits Your kindness, so I might follow

the precept of Your mouth.

ט

טוֹב עָשִׂיתָ עִם־עַבְדְּךָ יְהוָה כִּדְבָרֶךָ:
טוּב טַעַם וָדַעַת לַמְּדֵנִי כִּי בְמִצְוֹתֶיךָ הֶאֱמָנְתִּי:
טֶרֶם אֶעֱנֶה אֲנִי שֹׁגֵג וְעַתָּה אִמְרָתְךָ שָׁמָרְתִּי:
טוֹב־אַתָּה וּמֵטִיב לַמְּדֵנִי חֻקֶּיךָ:
טָפְלוּ עָלַי שֶׁקֶר זֵדִים אֲנִי בְּכָל־לֵב ׀ אֶצֹּר פִּקּוּדֶיךָ:
טָפַשׁ כַּחֵלֶב לִבָּם אֲנִי תּוֹרָתְךָ שִׁעֲשָׁעְתִּי:
טוֹב־לִי כִי־עֻנֵּיתִי לְמַעַן אֶלְמַד חֻקֶּיךָ:
טוֹב־לִי תוֹרַת־פִּיךָ מֵאַלְפֵי זָהָב וָכָסֶף:

י

יָדֶיךָ עָשׂוּנִי וַיְכוֹנְנוּנִי הֲבִינֵנִי וְאֶלְמְדָה מִצְוֹתֶיךָ:
יְרֵאֶיךָ יִרְאוּנִי וְיִשְׂמָחוּ כִּי לִדְבָרְךָ יִחָלְתִּי:
יָדַעְתִּי יְהוָה כִּי־צֶדֶק מִשְׁפָּטֶיךָ וֶאֱמוּנָה עִנִּיתָנִי:
יְהִי־נָא חַסְדְּךָ לְנַחֲמֵנִי כְּאִמְרָתְךָ לְעַבְדֶּךָ:
יְבֹאוּנִי רַחֲמֶיךָ וְאֶחְיֶה כִּי־תוֹרָתְךָ שַׁעֲשֻׁעָי:
יֵבֹשׁוּ זֵדִים כִּי־שֶׁקֶר עִוְּתוּנִי אֲנִי אָשִׂיחַ בְּפִקּוּדֶיךָ:
יָשׁוּבוּ לִי יְרֵאֶיךָ וְיֹדְעֵי עֵדֹתֶיךָ:
יְהִי־לִבִּי תָמִים בְּחֻקֶּיךָ לְמַעַן לֹא אֵבוֹשׁ:

כ

כָּלְתָה לִתְשׁוּעָתְךָ נַפְשִׁי לִדְבָרְךָ יִחָלְתִּי:
כָּלוּ עֵינַי לְאִמְרָתֶךָ לֵאמֹר מָתַי תְּנַחֲמֵנִי:
כִּי־הָיִיתִי כְּנֹאד בְּקִיטוֹר חֻקֶּיךָ לֹא שָׁכָחְתִּי:
כַּמָּה יְמֵי־עַבְדֶּךָ מָתַי תַּעֲשֶׂה בְרֹדְפַי מִשְׁפָּט:
כָּרוּ־לִי זֵדִים שִׁיחוֹת אֲשֶׁר לֹא כְתוֹרָתֶךָ:
כָּל־מִצְוֹתֶיךָ אֱמוּנָה שֶׁקֶר רְדָפוּנִי עָזְרֵנִי:
כִּמְעַט כִּלּוּנִי בָאָרֶץ וַאֲנִי לֹא־עָזַבְתִּי פִקֻּדֶיךָ:
כְּחַסְדְּךָ חַיֵּנִי וְאֶשְׁמְרָה עֵדוּת פִּיךָ:

LAMED

Forever, Lord, does Your word stand in the heavens.
Your faithfulness is for all generations; You established the earth,
and it stands.
They stand today for Your judgment, for all are Your servants.
Had Your teaching not been my delight,
I would have perished in my affliction.
I will never forget Your edicts, for through them You gave me life.
I am Yours; save me, for I have sought Your edicts.
The wicked wish to destroy me; I ponder your precepts.
I see an end to all great things, but Your commandments are
exceedingly wide.

MEM

How I love Your teaching! It is what I speak of all day.
Your commandments make me wiser than my enemies,
for they are always mine.
I have gained discernment beyond that of all my teachers, for Your precepts
are my conversation.
I gain insight from the elders, for I uphold Your edicts.
From all evil paths I bar my feet, so I might follow Your word.
I have not turned away from Your laws, for You Yourself have taught me.
How sweet is Your saying to my palate, more than honey to my mouth.
I gain insights from Your edicts; therefore, I hate every path of falsehood.

NUN

A lamp to my feet is Your word, and a light for my path.
I have sworn and will fulfill my oath, to follow Your righteous laws.
I am exceedingly afflicted; give me life, Lord, as befits Your word.
Please, Lord, accept the offerings of my mouth, and teach me Your laws.
My life is always in my hand, but I do not forget Your teaching.
The wicked set a snare for me, but I do not veer from Your edicts.
Your precepts are my possession forever, for they are the joy of my heart.
I incline my heart to carry out Your statutes forever, to the end.

ל

לְעוֹלָם יְהוָה דְּבָרְךָ נִצָּב בַּשָּׁמָיִם:

לְדֹר וָדֹר אֱמוּנָתֶךָ כּוֹנַנְתָּ אֶרֶץ וַתַּעֲמֹד:

לְמִשְׁפָּטֶיךָ עָמְדוּ הַיּוֹם כִּי הַכֹּל עֲבָדֶיךָ:

לוּלֵי תוֹרָתְךָ שַׁעֲשֻׁעָי אָז אָבַדְתִּי בְעָנְיִי:

לְעוֹלָם לֹא אֶשְׁכַּח פִּקּוּדֶיךָ כִּי בָם חִיִּיתָנִי:

לְךָ אֲנִי הוֹשִׁיעֵנִי כִּי פִקּוּדֶיךָ דָרָשְׁתִּי:

לִי קִוּוּ רְשָׁעִים לְאַבְּדֵנִי עֵדֹתֶיךָ אֶתְבּוֹנָן:

לְכָל תִּכְלָה רָאִיתִי קֵץ רְחָבָה מִצְוָתְךָ מְאֹד:

מ

מָה אָהַבְתִּי תוֹרָתֶךָ כָּל הַיּוֹם הִיא שִׂיחָתִי:

מֵאֹיְבַי תְּחַכְּמֵנִי מִצְוֹתֶךָ כִּי לְעוֹלָם הִיא לִי:

מִכָּל מְלַמְּדַי הִשְׂכַּלְתִּי כִּי עֵדְוֹתֶיךָ שִׂיחָה לִי:

מִזְּקֵנִים אֶתְבּוֹנָן כִּי פִקּוּדֶיךָ נָצָרְתִּי:

מִכָּל אֹרַח רָע כָּלִאתִי רַגְלָי לְמַעַן אֶשְׁמֹר דְּבָרֶךָ:

מִמִּשְׁפָּטֶיךָ לֹא סָרְתִּי כִּי אַתָּה הוֹרֵתָנִי:

מַה נִּמְלְצוּ לְחִכִּי אִמְרָתֶךָ מִדְּבַשׁ לְפִי:

מִפִּקּוּדֶיךָ אֶתְבּוֹנָן עַל כֵּן שָׂנֵאתִי ׀ כָּל אֹרַח שָׁקֶר:

נ

נֵר לְרַגְלִי דְבָרֶךָ וְאוֹר לִנְתִיבָתִי:

נִשְׁבַּעְתִּי וָאֲקַיֵּמָה לִשְׁמֹר מִשְׁפְּטֵי צִדְקֶךָ:

נַעֲנֵיתִי עַד מְאֹד יְהוָה חַיֵּנִי כִדְבָרֶךָ:

נִדְבוֹת פִּי רְצֵה נָא יְהוָה וּמִשְׁפָּטֶיךָ לַמְּדֵנִי:

נַפְשִׁי בְכַפִּי תָמִיד וְתוֹרָתְךָ לֹא שָׁכָחְתִּי:

נָתְנוּ רְשָׁעִים פַּח לִי וּמִפִּקּוּדֶיךָ לֹא תָעִיתִי:

נָחַלְתִּי עֵדְוֹתֶיךָ לְעוֹלָם כִּי שְׂשׂוֹן לִבִּי הֵמָּה:

נָטִיתִי לִבִּי לַעֲשׂוֹת חֻקֶּיךָ לְעוֹלָם עֵקֶב:

SAMEKH

I hate what is twisted, but I love Your teaching.
You are my shelter and shield; I hope for Your word.
Depart from me, evildoers, so I might uphold
the commandments of my God.
Sustain me, as befits Your word, so I might live.
Let me not be ashamed of my hope.
Support me and I will be saved, and I will always turn
my attention to Your statutes.
You turn aside all those who stray from Your statutes,
for their deception is a lie.
Like dross, You destroy the wicked of the earth;
therefore I love Your precepts.
My flesh prickles in fright because of You, for I fear Your judgments.

AYIN

I have practiced justice and righteousness; do not leave me to my
oppressors.
Vouch for Your servant, for good. Keep evildoers from oppressing me.
My eyes pine for Your salvation and Your righteous word.
Deal with Your servant as befits Your kindness, and teach me Your statutes.
I am Your servant; give me understanding, so I might know Your precepts.
It is time to act for the Lord, for they have violated Your teaching.
Indeed, I love Your commandments more than gold, more than fine gold.
Indeed, I have dealt straightly with all Your edicts; I hate every false path.

PEH

Your precepts are wondrous, therefore my soul upholds them.
Your opening words enlighten; they bring understanding to the simple.
I open my mouth wide and breathe in deep, longing for Your
commandments.
Turn to me and treat me graciously, as befits those who love Your name.
Make my footsteps firm with Your saying; let no wrongdoing rule over me.
Redeem me from the oppression of man, so I might follow Your edicts.
Shine Your face on Your servant, and teach me Your statutes.
Streams of water flow from my eyes, for those who do not follow your
teaching.

ס

סֵעֲפִים שָׂנֵאתִי וְתוֹרָתְךָ אָהָבְתִּי:

סִתְרִי וּמָגִנִּי אָתָּה לִדְבָרְךָ יִחָלְתִּי:

סוּרוּ מִמֶּנִּי מְרֵעִים וְאֶצְּרָה מִצְוֹת אֱלֹהָי:

סָמְכֵנִי כְאִמְרָתְךָ וְאֶחְיֶה וְאַל־תְּבִישֵׁנִי מִשִּׂבְרִי:

סְעָדֵנִי וְאִוָּשֵׁעָה וְאֶשְׁעָה בְחֻקֶּיךָ תָמִיד:

סָלִיתָ כָּל־שׁוֹגִים מֵחֻקֶּיךָ כִּי־שֶׁקֶר תַּרְמִיתָם:

סִגִים הִשְׁבַּתָּ כָל־רִשְׁעֵי־אָרֶץ לָכֵן אָהַבְתִּי עֵדֹתֶיךָ:

סָמַר מִפַּחְדְּךָ בְשָׂרִי וּמִמִּשְׁפָּטֶיךָ יָרֵאתִי:

ע

עָשִׂיתִי מִשְׁפָּט וָצֶדֶק בַּל־תַּנִּיחֵנִי לְעֹשְׁקָי:

עֲרֹב עַבְדְּךָ לְטוֹב אַל־יַעַשְׁקֻנִי זֵדִים:

עֵינַי כָּלוּ לִישׁוּעָתֶךָ וּלְאִמְרַת צִדְקֶךָ:

עֲשֵׂה עִם־עַבְדְּךָ כְחַסְדֶּךָ וְחֻקֶּיךָ לַמְּדֵנִי:

עַבְדְּךָ־אָנִי הֲבִינֵנִי וְאֵדְעָה עֵדֹתֶיךָ:

עֵת לַעֲשׂוֹת לַיהוָה הֵפֵרוּ תּוֹרָתֶךָ:

עַל־כֵּן אָהַבְתִּי מִצְוֹתֶיךָ מִזָּהָב וּמִפָּז:

עַל־כֵּן ׀ כָּל־פִּקּוּדֵי כֹל יִשָּׁרְתִּי כָּל־אֹרַח שֶׁקֶר שָׂנֵאתִי:

פ

פְּלָאוֹת עֵדְוֹתֶיךָ עַל־כֵּן נְצָרָתַם נַפְשִׁי:

פֵּתַח־דְּבָרֶיךָ יָאִיר מֵבִין פְּתָיִים:

פִּי־פָעַרְתִּי וָאֶשְׁאָפָה כִּי לְמִצְוֹתֶיךָ יָאָבְתִּי:

פְּנֵה־אֵלַי וְחָנֵּנִי כְּמִשְׁפָּט לְאֹהֲבֵי שְׁמֶךָ:

פְּעָמַי הָכֵן בְּאִמְרָתֶךָ וְאַל־תַּשְׁלֶט־בִּי כָל־אָוֶן:

פְּדֵנִי מֵעֹשֶׁק אָדָם וְאֶשְׁמְרָה פִּקּוּדֶיךָ:

פָּנֶיךָ הָאֵר בְּעַבְדֶּךָ וְלַמְּדֵנִי אֶת־חֻקֶּיךָ:

פַּלְגֵי־מַיִם יָרְדוּ עֵינָי עַל לֹא־שָׁמְרוּ תוֹרָתֶךָ:

TZADI

Righteous are You, Lord, and upright are Your judgments.
With Your precepts, You greatly ordain righteousness and faith.
My zealotry consumes me, for my foes have forgotten Your words.
Your saying is exceedingly pure, and Your servant loves it.
Young am I, and disdained. Yet I do not forget Your edicts.
Your righteousness is eternal. Your teaching is truth.
Trouble and distress have found me; Your commandments are my delight.
Your precepts are forever righteous. Give me understanding, so I might live.

KUF

I call out wholeheartedly; answer me, Lord. I will uphold Your statutes.
I call out to You; save me, and I will follow Your precepts.
I rise before dawn and cry for help; for Your word I do wait.
My eyes precede the night watches to reflect on Your word.
Hear my voice, as befits Your kindness; Lord, give me life when You
judge me.
Pursuers of loathsomeness draw near; they distance themselves
from Your teaching.
You are near, Lord, and all Your commandments are truth.
Your precepts, I know, are of old; You established them for eternity.

REISH

See my affliction and rescue me, for I have not forgotten Your teaching.
Plead my cause and redeem me; give me life, as befits Your promise.
Salvation is far from the wicked, for they do not seek Your statutes.
Great are Your mercies, Lord; give me life when You judge me.
Many are my pursuers and my foes, yet I do not veer from Your precepts.
I see traitors and contend with them, for they do not follow Your word.
See how I love Your edicts; Lord, give me life, as befits Your kindness.
Your word begins in truth; eternal are all Your righteous laws.

צ

צַדִּיק אַתָּה יְהֹוָה וְיָשָׁר מִשְׁפָּטֶיךָ:

צִוִּיתָ צֶדֶק עֵדֹתֶיךָ וֶאֱמוּנָה מְאֹד:

צִמְּתַתְנִי קִנְאָתִי כִּי־שָׁכְחוּ דְבָרֶיךָ צָרָי:

צְרוּפָה אִמְרָתְךָ מְאֹד וְעַבְדְּךָ אֲהֵבָהּ:

צָעִיר אָנֹכִי וְנִבְזֶה פִּקֻּדֶיךָ לֹא שָׁכָחְתִּי:

צִדְקָתְךָ צֶדֶק לְעוֹלָם וְתוֹרָתְךָ אֱמֶת:

צַר־וּמָצוֹק מְצָאוּנִי מִצְוֹתֶיךָ שַׁעֲשֻׁעָי:

צֶדֶק עֵדְוֹתֶיךָ לְעוֹלָם הֲבִינֵנִי וְאֶחְיֶה:

ק

קָרָאתִי בְכָל־לֵב עֲנֵנִי יְהֹוָה חֻקֶּיךָ אֶצֹּרָה:

קְרָאתִיךָ הוֹשִׁיעֵנִי וְאֶשְׁמְרָה עֵדֹתֶיךָ:

קִדַּמְתִּי בַנֶּשֶׁף וָאֲשַׁוֵּעָה לִדְבָרְךָ יִחָלְתִּי:

קִדְּמוּ עֵינַי אַשְׁמֻרוֹת לָשִׂיחַ בְּאִמְרָתֶךָ:

קוֹלִי שִׁמְעָה כְחַסְדֶּךָ יְהֹוָה כְּמִשְׁפָּטֶךָ חַיֵּנִי:

קָרְבוּ רֹדְפֵי זִמָּה מִתּוֹרָתְךָ רָחָקוּ:

קָרוֹב אַתָּה יְהֹוָה וְכָל־מִצְוֹתֶיךָ אֱמֶת:

קֶדֶם יָדַעְתִּי מֵעֵדֹתֶיךָ כִּי לְעוֹלָם יְסַדְתָּם:

ר

רְאֵה־עָנְיִי וְחַלְּצֵנִי כִּי־תוֹרָתְךָ לֹא שָׁכָחְתִּי:

רִיבָה רִיבִי וּגְאָלֵנִי לְאִמְרָתְךָ חַיֵּנִי:

רָחוֹק מֵרְשָׁעִים יְשׁוּעָה כִּי־חֻקֶּיךָ לֹא דָרָשׁוּ:

רַחֲמֶיךָ רַבִּים ׀ יְהֹוָה כְּמִשְׁפָּטֶיךָ חַיֵּנִי:

רַבִּים רֹדְפַי וְצָרָי מֵעֵדְוֹתֶיךָ לֹא נָטִיתִי:

רָאִיתִי בֹגְדִים וָאֶתְקוֹטָטָה אֲשֶׁר אִמְרָתְךָ לֹא שָׁמָרוּ:

רְאֵה כִּי־פִקּוּדֶיךָ אָהָבְתִּי יְהֹוָה כְּחַסְדְּךָ חַיֵּנִי:

רֹאשׁ־דְּבָרְךָ אֱמֶת וּלְעוֹלָם כָּל־מִשְׁפַּט צִדְקֶךָ:

SHIN

Princes pursue me without cause, yet my heart fears Your words.

I rejoice at Your sayings, as one who finds great spoils.

I hate and abhor falsehood; I love Your teaching.

Seven times a day do I praise You for Your righteous laws.

Those who love Your teaching know great peace; for them there is no obstacle.

I await Your salvation, Lord, and I have fulfilled Your commandments.

My soul follows Your precepts, and I love them exceedingly.

I follow Your edicts and Your precepts, for all my ways are before You.

TAV

Let my song draw near You, Lord; give me understanding, as befits Your word.

Let my plea come before You; rescue me, as befits Your promise.

Let my lips utter praise, for You teach me Your statutes.

Let my tongue declare Your saying, for all Your commandments are just.

Let Your hand be ready to help me, for I have chosen Your edicts.

I long for Your salvation, Lord, and Your teaching is my delight.

May my soul live, so I might praise You; may Your laws come to my aid.

I have gone astray like a lost sheep. Seek Your servant, for I do not forget Your commandments.

ש

שָׂרִים רְדָפוּנִי חִנָּם וּמִדְּבָרְךָ פָּחַד לִבִּי:
שָׂשׂ אָנֹכִי עַל־אִמְרָתֶךָ כְּמוֹצֵא שָׁלָל רָב:
שֶׁקֶר שָׂנֵאתִי וַאֲתַעֵבָה תּוֹרָתְךָ אָהָבְתִּי:
שֶׁבַע בַּיּוֹם הִלַּלְתִּיךָ עַל מִשְׁפְּטֵי צִדְקֶךָ:
שָׁלוֹם רָב לְאֹהֲבֵי תוֹרָתֶךָ וְאֵין־לָמוֹ מִכְשׁוֹל:
שִׂבַּרְתִּי לִישׁוּעָתְךָ יְהוָה וּמִצְוֹתֶיךָ עָשִׂיתִי:
שָׁמְרָה נַפְשִׁי עֵדֹתֶיךָ וָאֹהֲבֵם מְאֹד:
שָׁמַרְתִּי פִקּוּדֶיךָ וְעֵדֹתֶיךָ כִּי כָל־דְּרָכַי נֶגְדֶּךָ:

ת

תִּקְרַב רִנָּתִי לְפָנֶיךָ יְהוָה כִּדְבָרְךָ הֲבִינֵנִי:
תָּבוֹא תְחִנָּתִי לְפָנֶיךָ כְּאִמְרָתְךָ הַצִּילֵנִי:
תַּבַּעְנָה שְׂפָתַי תְּהִלָּה כִּי תְלַמְּדֵנִי חֻקֶּיךָ:
תַּעַן לְשׁוֹנִי אִמְרָתֶךָ כִּי כָל־מִצְוֹתֶיךָ צֶּדֶק:
תְּהִי־יָדְךָ לְעָזְרֵנִי כִּי פִקּוּדֶיךָ בָחָרְתִּי:
תָּאַבְתִּי לִישׁוּעָתְךָ יְהוָה וְתוֹרָתְךָ שַׁעֲשֻׁעָי:
תְּחִי־נַפְשִׁי וּתְהַלְלֶךָּ וּמִשְׁפָּטֶךָ יַעְזְרֻנִי:
תָּעִיתִי כְּשֶׂה אֹבֵד בַּקֵּשׁ עַבְדֶּךָ כִּי מִצְוֹתֶיךָ לֹא שָׁכָחְתִּי:

Following are the verses of Psalm 119 that spell out the word נשמה, "soul."

NUN

A lamp to my feet is Your word, and a light for my path.
I have sworn and will fulfill my oath, to follow Your righteous laws.
I am exceedingly afflicted; give me life, Lord, as befits Your word.
Please, Lord, accept the offerings of my mouth, and teach me Your laws.
My life is always in my hand, but I do not forget Your teaching.
The wicked set a snare for me, but I do not veer from Your edicts.
Your precepts are my possession forever, for they are the joy of my heart.
I incline my heart to carry out Your statutes forever, to the end.

SHIN

Princes pursue me without cause, yet my heart fears Your words.
I rejoice at Your sayings, as one who finds great spoils.
I hate and abhor falsehood; I love Your teaching.
Seven times a day do I praise You for Your righteous laws.
Those who love Your teaching know great peace; for them there is no
obstacle.
I await Your salvation, Lord, and I have fulfilled Your commandments.
My soul follows Your precepts, and I love them exceedingly.
I follow Your edicts and Your precepts, for all my ways are before You.

MEM

How I love Your teaching! It is what I speak of all day.
Your commandments make me wiser than my enemies,
for they are always mine.
I have gained discernment beyond that of all my teachers, for Your precepts
are my conversation.
I gain insight from the elders, for I uphold Your edicts.
From all evil paths I bar my feet, so I might follow Your word.
I have not turned away from Your laws, for You Yourself have taught me.
How sweet is Your saying to my palate, more than honey to my mouth.
I gain insights from Your edicts; therefore, I hate every path of falsehood.

Following are the verses of תהלים קיט that spell out the word נשמה, "soul."

נ

נֵר־לְרַגְלִי דְבָרֶךָ וְאוֹר לִנְתִיבָתִי:

נִשְׁבַּעְתִּי וָאֲקַיֵּמָה לִשְׁמֹר מִשְׁפְּטֵי צִדְקֶךָ:

נַעֲנֵיתִי עַד־מְאֹד יְהֹוָה חַיֵּנִי כִדְבָרֶךָ:

נִדְבוֹת פִּי רְצֵה־נָא יְהֹוָה וּמִשְׁפָּטֶיךָ לַמְּדֵנִי:

נַפְשִׁי בְכַפִּי תָמִיד וְתוֹרָתְךָ לֹא שָׁכָחְתִּי:

נָתְנוּ רְשָׁעִים פַּח לִי וּמִפִּקּוּדֶיךָ לֹא תָעִיתִי:

נָחַלְתִּי עֵדְוֹתֶיךָ לְעוֹלָם כִּי־שְׂשׂוֹן לִבִּי הֵמָּה:

נָטִיתִי לִבִּי לַעֲשׂוֹת חֻקֶּיךָ לְעוֹלָם עֵקֶב:

שׁ

שָׂרִים רְדָפוּנִי חִנָּם וּמִדְּבָרְךָ פָּחַד לִבִּי:

שָׂשׂ אָנֹכִי עַל־אִמְרָתֶךָ כְּמוֹצֵא שָׁלָל רָב:

שֶׁקֶר שָׂנֵאתִי וָאֲתַעֵבָה תּוֹרָתְךָ אָהָבְתִּי:

שֶׁבַע בַּיּוֹם הִלַּלְתִּיךָ עַל מִשְׁפְּטֵי צִדְקֶךָ:

שָׁלוֹם רָב לְאֹהֲבֵי תוֹרָתֶךָ וְאֵין־לָמוֹ מִכְשׁוֹל:

שִׂבַּרְתִּי לִישׁוּעָתְךָ יְהֹוָה וּמִצְוֹתֶיךָ עָשִׂיתִי:

שָׁמְרָה נַפְשִׁי עֵדֹתֶיךָ וָאֹהֲבֵם מְאֹד:

שָׁמַרְתִּי פִקּוּדֶיךָ וְעֵדֹתֶיךָ כִּי כָל־דְּרָכַי נֶגְדֶּךָ:

מ

מָה־אָהַבְתִּי תוֹרָתֶךָ כָּל־הַיּוֹם הִיא שִׂיחָתִי:

מֵאֹיְבַי תְּחַכְּמֵנִי מִצְוֹתֶךָ כִּי לְעוֹלָם הִיא־לִי:

מִכָּל־מְלַמְּדַי הִשְׂכַּלְתִּי כִּי עֵדְוֹתֶיךָ שִׂיחָה לִי:

מִזְּקֵנִים אֶתְבּוֹנָן כִּי פִקּוּדֶיךָ נָצָרְתִּי:

מִכָּל־אֹרַח רָע כָּלִאתִי רַגְלָי לְמַעַן אֶשְׁמֹר דְּבָרֶךָ:

מִמִּשְׁפָּטֶיךָ לֹא־סָרְתִּי כִּי־אַתָּה הוֹרֵתָנִי:

מַה־נִּמְלְצוּ לְחִכִּי אִמְרָתֶךָ מִדְּבַשׁ לְפִי:

מִפִּקּוּדֶיךָ אֶתְבּוֹנָן עַל־כֵּן שָׂנֵאתִי ׀ כָּל־אֹרַח שָׁקֶר:

HEH

Teach me, Lord, the way of Your statutes, and I will uphold it to the end.
Give me understanding, so I might uphold Your teaching and follow it
wholeheartedly.
Guide me in the path of Your commandments, for in it is my desire.
Incline my heart toward Your precepts and not toward material gain.
Avert my eyes from seeing falsehood; through Your ways give me life.
Fulfill the promise You made to Your servant, which is for
those who fear You.
Remove my disgrace, which I dread, for Your laws are good.
How I long for Your edicts! In Your righteousness give me life.

ה

הוֹרֵנִי יְהוָה דֶּרֶךְ חֻקֶּיךָ וְאֶצְּרֶנָּה עֵקֶב:

הֲבִינֵנִי וְאֶצְּרָה תוֹרָתֶךָ וְאֶשְׁמְרֶנָּה בְכָל־לֵב:

הַדְרִיכֵנִי בִּנְתִיב מִצְוֹתֶיךָ כִּי־בוֹ חָפָצְתִּי:

הַט־לִבִּי אֶל־עֵדְוֹתֶיךָ וְאַל אֶל־בָּצַע:

הַעֲבֵר עֵינַי מֵרְאוֹת שָׁוְא בִּדְרָכֶךָ חַיֵּנִי:

הָקֵם לְעַבְדְּךָ אִמְרָתֶךָ אֲשֶׁר לְיִרְאָתֶךָ:

הַעֲבֵר חֶרְפָּתִי אֲשֶׁר יָגֹרְתִּי כִּי מִשְׁפָּטֶיךָ טוֹבִים:

הִנֵּה תָּאַבְתִּי לְפִקֻּדֶיךָ בְּצִדְקָתְךָ חַיֵּנִי:

Memorial Prayer

אָנָּא Lord and King, full of compassion, God of the spirits of all flesh, in whose hand are the souls of the living and the dead, receive, we pray You, in Your great love the soul of

For a man, say:

(*name* son of *father's name*) who has been gathered to his people. Have mercy on him, pardon all his transgressions, for there is no *Eccl. 7:20* righteous man upon the earth who does good and does not sin. Remember the righteousness that he did, and let his reward be with him, his recompense before him. Shelter his soul in the shadow of Your wings. Make known to him the path of life. In Your presence is fullness of joy, at Your right hand bliss for evermore. Bestow upon him the great goodness that is stored up for the righteous.

For a woman, say:

(*name* daughter of *father's name*) who has been gathered to her people. Have mercy on her, pardon all her transgressions, for there *Eccl. 7:20* is no righteous man upon the earth who does good and does not sin. Remember the righteousness that she did, and let her reward be with her, her recompense before her. Shelter her soul in the shadow of Your wings. Make known to her the path of life. In Your presence is fullness of joy, at Your right hand bliss for evermore. Bestow upon her the great goodness that is stored up for the righteous.

For a boy, say:

(*name* son of *father's name*) who has been gathered to his people. Remember the righteousness that he did, and let his reward be with him, his recompense before him. Shelter his soul in the shadow of Your wings. Make known to him the path of life. In Your presence is fullness of joy, at Your right hand bliss for evermore. Bestow upon him the great goodness that is stored up for the righteous.

For a girl, say:

(*name* daughter of *father's name*) who has been gathered to her people. Remember the righteousness that she did, and let her reward be with her, her recompense before her. Shelter her soul in the shadow of Your wings. Make known to her the path of life. In Your presence is fullness of joy, at Your right hand bliss for evermore. Bestow upon her the great goodness that is stored up for the righteous.

אזכרה

אָנָּא יהוה מֶלֶךְ מָלֵא רַחֲמִים, אֱלֹהֵי הָרוּחוֹת לְכָל בָּשָׂר, אֲשֶׁר בְּיָדְךָ נַפְשׁוֹת הַחַיִּים וְהַמֵּתִים, אָנָּא קַבֵּל בְּחַסְדְּךָ הַגָּדוֹל אֶת נִשְׁמַת

For a man, say:

(פלוני בֶּן פלוני) אֲשֶׁר נֶאֱסַף אֶל עַמָּיו. חוּס וַחֲמֹל עָלָיו, סְלַח וּמְחַל לְכָל פְּשָׁעָיו. כִּי אָדָם אֵין צַדִּיק בָּאָרֶץ, אֲשֶׁר יַעֲשֶׂה־טּוֹב וְלֹא יֶחֱטָא: זְכֹר לוֹ צִדְקָתוֹ אֲשֶׁר עָשָׂה, וִיהִי שְׂכָרוֹ אִתּוֹ, וּפְעֻלָּתוֹ לְפָנָיו. אָנָּא הַסְתֵּר אֶת נִשְׁמָתוֹ בְּצֵל כְּנָפֶיךָ, הוֹדִיעֵהוּ אֹרַח חַיִּים, שֹׂבַע שְׂמָחוֹת אֶת פָּנֶיךָ, נְעִימוֹת בִּימִינְךָ נֶצַח, וְתַשְׁפִּיעַ לוֹ מֵרֹב טוּב הַצָּפוּן לַצַּדִּיקִים. **קהלת ז:כ**

For a woman, say:

(פלונית בַּת פלוני) אֲשֶׁר נֶאֶסְפָה אֶל עַמֶּיהָ. חוּס וַחֲמֹל עָלֶיהָ, סְלַח וּמְחַל לְכָל פְּשָׁעֶיהָ. כִּי אָדָם אֵין צַדִּיק בָּאָרֶץ, אֲשֶׁר יַעֲשֶׂה־טּוֹב וְלֹא יֶחֱטָא: זְכֹר לָהּ צִדְקָתָהּ אֲשֶׁר עָשְׂתָה, וִיהִי שְׂכָרָהּ אִתָּהּ, וּפְעֻלָּתָהּ לְפָנֶיהָ. אָנָּא הַסְתֵּר אֶת נִשְׁמָתָהּ בְּצֵל כְּנָפֶיךָ, הוֹדִיעָהּ אֹרַח חַיִּים, שֹׂבַע שְׂמָחוֹת אֶת פָּנֶיךָ, נְעִימוֹת בִּימִינְךָ נֶצַח, וְתַשְׁפִּיעַ לָהּ מֵרֹב טוּב הַצָּפוּן לַצַּדִּיקִים. **קהלת ז:כ**

For a boy, say:

(פלוני בֶּן פלוני) אֲשֶׁר נֶאֱסַף אֶל עַמָּיו. זְכֹר לוֹ צִדְקָתוֹ אֲשֶׁר עָשָׂה, וִיהִי שְׂכָרוֹ אִתּוֹ, וּפְעֻלָּתוֹ לְפָנָיו. אָנָּא הַסְתֵּר אֶת נִשְׁמָתוֹ בְּצֵל כְּנָפֶיךָ, הוֹדִיעֵהוּ אֹרַח חַיִּים, שֹׂבַע שְׂמָחוֹת אֶת פָּנֶיךָ, נְעִימוֹת בִּימִינְךָ נֶצַח, וְתַשְׁפִּיעַ לוֹ מֵרֹב טוּב הַצָּפוּן לַצַּדִּיקִים.

For a girl, say:

(פלונית בַּת פלוני) אֲשֶׁר נֶאֶסְפָה אֶל עַמֶּיהָ. זְכֹר לָהּ צִדְקָתָהּ אֲשֶׁר עָשְׂתָה, וִיהִי שְׂכָרָהּ אִתָּהּ, וּפְעֻלָּתָהּ לְפָנֶיהָ. אָנָּא הַסְתֵּר אֶת נִשְׁמָתָהּ בְּצֵל כְּנָפֶיךָ, הוֹדִיעָהּ אֹרַח חַיִּים, שֹׂבַע שְׂמָחוֹת אֶת פָּנֶיךָ, נְעִימוֹת בִּימִינְךָ נֶצַח, וְתַשְׁפִּיעַ לָהּ מֵרֹב טוּב הַצָּפוּן לַצַּדִּיקִים.

As it is written: How great is the goodness You have in store for those   *Ps. 31:20*
who fear You, which You have created for those taking refuge in You, to
be bestowed openly.

אָנָּא May the Lord who heals the brokenhearted and binds up their
wounds, grant consolation to the mourners.

For a young boy, add:

May the death of this boy
mark the end of all anguish and sorrow for his parents.

For a young girl, add:

May the death of this girl
mark the end of all anguish and sorrow for her parents.

If the mourners have children, add the words in parentheses:

חַזֵּק Strengthen and support them in the day of their sadness and grief;
and remember them (and their children) for a long and good life. Put into
their hearts love and reverence for You, so that they may serve You with
a perfect heart; and let their end be peace. Amen.

כְּאִישׁ Like a man whose mother comforts him,   *Is. 66:13*
so will I comfort you;
and in Jerusalem you will be comforted.
Your sun will no longer set   *Is. 60:20*
and your moon will not be gathered in,
as the Lord will be for you an eternal light;
the days of your mourning will be completed
He will eliminate death forever,   *Is. 25:8*
and the Lord God will wipe tears from all faces,
and He will remove the disgrace of His people from upon the
entire earth, for the Lord has spoken.

תהלים לא:כ כְּמוֹ שֶׁכָּתוּב: מָה רַב טוּבְךָ אֲשֶׁר־צָפַנְתָּ לִּירֵאֶיךָ, פָּעַלְתָּ לַחוֹסִים בָּךְ נֶגֶד בְּנֵי אָדָם:

אָנָּא יהוה, הָרוֹפֵא לִשְׁבוּרֵי לֵב וּמְחַבֵּשׁ לְעַצְּבוֹתָם, שַׁלֵּם נִחוּמִים לָאֲבֵלִים.

For a young boy, add:

וּתְהִי פְּטִירַת הַיֶּלֶד הַזֶּה קֵץ לְכָל צָרָה וְצוּקָה לְאָבִיו וּלְאִמּוֹ.

For a young girl, add:

וּתְהִי פְּטִירַת הַיַּלְדָּה הַזֹּאת קֵץ לְכָל צָרָה וְצוּקָה לְאָבִיהָ וּלְאִמָּהּ.

If the mourners have children, add the words in parentheses:

חַזְּקֵם וְאַמְּצֵם בְּיוֹם אָבְלָם וִיגוֹנָם, וְזָכְרֵם (וּזְכֹר אֶת בְּנֵי בֵיתָם) לְחַיִּים טוֹבִים וַאֲרֻכִּים. תֵּן בְּלִבָּם יִרְאָתְךָ וְאַהֲבָתְךָ לְעָבְדְּךָ בְּלֵבָב שָׁלֵם, וּתְהִי אַחֲרִיתָם שָׁלוֹם, אָמֵן.

ישעיה סו:יג כְּאִישׁ אֲשֶׁר אִמּוֹ תְּנַחֲמֶנּוּ
כֵּן אָנֹכִי אֲנַחֶמְכֶם
וּבִירוּשָׁלַֽם תְּנֻחָֽמוּ:
ישעיה ס:כ לֹא־יָבוֹא עוֹד שִׁמְשֵׁךְ, וִירֵחֵךְ לֹא יֵאָסֵף
כִּי יהוה יִהְיֶה־לָּךְ לְאוֹר עוֹלָם
וְשָׁלְמוּ יְמֵי אֶבְלֵךְ:
ישעיה כה:ח בִּלַּע הַמָּוֶת לָנֶצַח
וּמָחָה אֲדֹנָי יֱהֹוִה דִּמְעָה מֵעַל כָּל־פָּנִים
וְחֶרְפַּת עַמּוֹ יָסִיר מֵעַל כָּל־הָאָֽרֶץ
כִּי יהוה דִּבֵּר:

Mourner's Kaddish

The following prayer, said by mourners, requires the presence of a minyan.

Mourner: יִתְגַּדַּל Magnified and sanctified
may His great name be,
in the world He created by His will.
May He establish His kingdom
in your lifetime and in your days,
and in the lifetime of all the house of Israel,
swiftly and soon –
and say: Amen.

All: May His great name be blessed for ever and all time.

Mourner: Blessed and praised,
glorified and exalted,
raised and honored,
uplifted and lauded
be the name of the Holy One,
blessed be He,
beyond any blessing,
song, praise and consolation
uttered in the world –
and say: Amen.

May there be great peace from heaven,
and life for us and all Israel –
and say: Amen.

Bow, take three steps back, as if taking leave of the Divine Presence, then bow, first left, then right,
then center, while saying:

May He who makes peace in His high places,
make peace for us and all Israel –
and say: Amen.

קדיש יתום

The following prayer, said by mourners, requires the presence of a minyan.

אבל: יִתְגַּדַּל וְיִתְקַדַּשׁ שְׁמֵהּ רַבָּא (קהל: אָמֵן)
בְּעָלְמָא דִּי בְרָא כִרְעוּתֵהּ
וְיַמְלִיךְ מַלְכוּתֵהּ
בְּחַיֵּיכוֹן וּבְיוֹמֵיכוֹן וּבְחַיֵּי דְכָל בֵּית יִשְׂרָאֵל
בַּעֲגָלָא וּבִזְמַן קָרִיב, וְאִמְרוּ אָמֵן. (קהל: אָמֵן)

קהל
ואבל: יְהֵא שְׁמֵהּ רַבָּא מְבָרַךְ לְעָלַם וּלְעָלְמֵי עָלְמַיָּא.

אבל: יִתְבָּרַךְ וְיִשְׁתַּבַּח וְיִתְפָּאַר
וְיִתְרוֹמַם וְיִתְנַשֵּׂא וְיִתְהַדָּר וְיִתְעַלֶּה וְיִתְהַלָּל
שְׁמֵהּ דְּקֻדְשָׁא בְּרִיךְ הוּא (קהל: בְּרִיךְ הוּא)
לְעֵלָּא מִן כָּל בִּרְכָתָא
/בעשרת ימי תשובה: לְעֵלָּא לְעֵלָּא מִכָּל בִּרְכָתָא/
וְשִׁירָתָא, תֻּשְׁבְּחָתָא וְנֶחָמָתָא
דַּאֲמִירָן בְּעָלְמָא, וְאִמְרוּ אָמֵן. (קהל: אָמֵן)

יְהֵא שְׁלָמָא רַבָּא מִן שְׁמַיָּא
וְחַיִּים, עָלֵינוּ וְעַל כָּל יִשְׂרָאֵל, וְאִמְרוּ אָמֵן. (קהל: אָמֵן)

Bow, take three steps back, as if taking leave of the Divine Presence, then bow, first left, then right, then center, while saying:

עֹשֶׂה שָׁלוֹם/בעשרת ימי תשובה: הַשָּׁלוֹם/ בִּמְרוֹמָיו
הוּא יַעֲשֶׂה שָׁלוֹם עָלֵינוּ וְעַל כָּל יִשְׂרָאֵל
וְאִמְרוּ אָמֵן. (קהל: אָמֵן)

God, Full of Mercy

For a male close relative:

אֵל מָלֵא רַחֲמִים God, full of mercy, who dwells on high, grant fitting rest on the wings of the Divine Presence, in the heights of the holy and the pure who shine like the radiance of heaven, to the soul of (*name* son of *father's name*) who has gone to his eternal home, and to this I pledge (without formal vow) to give charity in his memory, may his resting place be in the Garden of Eden. Therefore, Master of compassion, shelter him in the shadow of Your wings forever and bind his soul in the bond of everlasting life. The Lord is his heritage; may he rest in peace, and let us say: Amen.

For a female close relative:

אֵל מָלֵא רַחֲמִים God, full of mercy, who dwells on high, grant fitting rest on the wings of the Divine Presence, in the heights of the holy and the pure who shine like the radiance of heaven, to the soul of (*name* daughter of *father's name*) who has gone to her eternal home, and to this I pledge (without formal vow) to give charity in her memory, may her resting place be in the Garden of Eden. Therefore, Master of compassion, shelter her in the shadow of Your wings forever and bind her soul in the bond of everlasting life. The Lord is her heritage; may she rest in peace, and let us say: Amen.

For the Israeli soldiers:

אֵל מָלֵא רַחֲמִים God, full of mercy, who dwells on high, grant fitting rest on the wings of the Divine Presence, in the heights of the holy, the pure and the brave, who shine like the radiance of heaven, to the souls of the holy ones who fought in any of Israel's battles, in clandestine operations and in Israel's Defense Forces, who fell in battle and sacrificed their lives for the consecration of God's name, for the people and the land, and for this we pray for the ascent of their souls. Therefore, Master of compassion, shelter them in the shadow of Your wings forever, and bind their souls in the bond of everlasting life. The Lord is their heritage; may the Garden of Eden be their resting place, may they rest in peace, may their

אל מלא רחמים

For a male close relative:

אֵל מָלֵא רַחֲמִים, שׁוֹכֵן בַּמְּרוֹמִים, הַמְצֵא מְנוּחָה נְכוֹנָה עַל כַּנְפֵי
הַשְּׁכִינָה, בְּמַעֲלוֹת קְדוֹשִׁים וּטְהוֹרִים, כְּזֹהַר הָרָקִיעַ מַזְהִירִים,
לְנִשְׁמַת (פלוני בֶּן פלוני) שֶׁהָלַךְ לְעוֹלָמוֹ, בַּעֲבוּר שֶׁבְּלִי נֶדֶר אֶתֵּן צְדָקָה
בְּעַד הַזְכָּרַת נִשְׁמָתוֹ, בְּגַן עֵדֶן תְּהֵא מְנוּחָתוֹ. לָכֵן, בַּעַל הָרַחֲמִים
יַסְתִּירֵהוּ בְּסֵתֶר כְּנָפָיו לְעוֹלָמִים, וְיִצְרוֹר בִּצְרוֹר הַחַיִּים אֶת נִשְׁמָתוֹ,
יהוה הוּא נַחֲלָתוֹ, וְיָנוּחַ בְּשָׁלוֹם עַל מִשְׁכָּבוֹ, וְנֹאמַר אָמֵן.

For a female close relative:

אֵל מָלֵא רַחֲמִים, שׁוֹכֵן בַּמְּרוֹמִים, הַמְצֵא מְנוּחָה נְכוֹנָה עַל כַּנְפֵי
הַשְּׁכִינָה, בְּמַעֲלוֹת קְדוֹשִׁים וּטְהוֹרִים, כְּזֹהַר הָרָקִיעַ מַזְהִירִים,
לְנִשְׁמַת (פלונית בַּת פלוני) שֶׁהָלְכָה לְעוֹלָמָהּ, בַּעֲבוּר שֶׁבְּלִי נֶדֶר אֶתֵּן
צְדָקָה בְּעַד הַזְכָּרַת נִשְׁמָתָהּ, בְּגַן עֵדֶן תְּהֵא מְנוּחָתָהּ. לָכֵן, בַּעַל
הָרַחֲמִים יַסְתִּירָהּ בְּסֵתֶר כְּנָפָיו לְעוֹלָמִים, וְיִצְרוֹר בִּצְרוֹר הַחַיִּים אֶת
נִשְׁמָתָהּ, יהוה הוּא נַחֲלָתָהּ, וְתָנוּחַ בְּשָׁלוֹם עַל מִשְׁכָּבָהּ, וְנֹאמַר אָמֵן.

For the Israeli soldiers:

אֵל מָלֵא רַחֲמִים, שׁוֹכֵן בַּמְּרוֹמִים, הַמְצֵא מְנוּחָה נְכוֹנָה עַל כַּנְפֵי
הַשְּׁכִינָה, בְּמַעֲלוֹת קְדוֹשִׁים טְהוֹרִים וְגִבּוֹרִים, כְּזֹהַר הָרָקִיעַ
מַזְהִירִים, לְנִשְׁמוֹת הַקְּדוֹשִׁים שֶׁנִּלְחֲמוּ בְּכָל מַעַרְכוֹת יִשְׂרָאֵל,
בַּמַּחְתֶּרֶת וּבַצָּבָא הַהֲגַנָּה לְיִשְׂרָאֵל, וְשֶׁנָּפְלוּ בְּמִלְחַמְתָּם וּמָסְרוּ
נַפְשָׁם עַל קְדֻשַּׁת הַשֵּׁם, הָעָם וְהָאָרֶץ, בַּעֲבוּר שֶׁאָנוּ מִתְפַּלְּלִים
לְעִלּוּי נִשְׁמוֹתֵיהֶם. לָכֵן, בַּעַל הָרַחֲמִים יַסְתִּירֵם בְּסֵתֶר כְּנָפָיו
לְעוֹלָמִים, וְיִצְרוֹר בִּצְרוֹר הַחַיִּים אֶת נִשְׁמוֹתֵיהֶם, יהוה הוּא נַחֲלָתָם,

merit stand for all Israel, and may they receive their reward at the End of Days, and let us say: Amen.

For the Holocaust victims:

אֵל מָלֵא רַחֲמִים God, full of mercy, Justice of widows and Father of orphans, please do not be silent and hold Your peace for the blood of Israel that was shed like water. Grant fitting rest on the wings of the Divine Presence, in the heights of the holy and the pure who shine and radiate light like the radiance of heaven, to the souls of the millions of Jews, men, women and children, who were murdered, slaughtered, burned, strangled, and buried alive, in the lands touched by the German enemy and its followers. They were all holy and pure; among them were great scholars and righteous individuals, cedars of Lebanon and noble masters of Torah, may the Garden of Eden be their resting place. Therefore, Master of compassion, shelter them in the shadow of Your wings forever, and bind their souls in the bond of everlasting life. The Lord is their heritage; may they rest in peace, and let us say: Amen.

בְּגַן עֵדֶן תְּהֵא מְנוּחָתָם, וְיָנְוּחוּ בְשָׁלוֹם עַל מִשְׁכְּבוֹתֵיהֶם וְתַעֲמֹד לְכָל יִשְׂרָאֵל זְכוּתָם, וְיַעַמְדוּ לְגוֹרָלָם לְקֵץ הַיָּמִין, וְנֹאמַר אָמֵן.

For the Holocaust victims:

אֵל מָלֵא רַחֲמִים, דִּין אַלְמָנוֹת וַאֲבִי יְתוֹמִים, אַל נָא תֶחֱשֶׁה וְתִתְאַפַּק לְדַם יִשְׂרָאֵל שֶׁנִּשְׁפַּךְ כַּמָּיִם. הַמְצֵא מְנוּחָה נְכוֹנָה עַל כַּנְפֵי הַשְּׁכִינָה, בְּמַעֲלוֹת קְדוֹשִׁים וּטְהוֹרִים, כְּזְהַר הָרָקִיעַ מְאִירִים וּמַזְהִירִים, לְנִשְׁמוֹתֵיהֶם שֶׁל רִבְבוֹת אַלְפֵי יִשְׂרָאֵל, אֲנָשִׁים וְנָשִׁים, יְלָדִים וִילָדוֹת, שֶׁנֶּהֶרְגוּ וְנִשְׁחֲטוּ וְנִשְׂרְפוּ וְנֶחְנְקוּ וְנִקְבְּרוּ חַיִּים, בָּאֲרָצוֹת אֲשֶׁר נָגְעָה בָּהֶן יַד הַצּוֹרֵר הַגֶּרְמָנִי וּגְרוּרָיו. כֻּלָּם קְדוֹשִׁים וּטְהוֹרִים, וּבָהֶם גְּאוֹנִים וְצַדִּיקִים, אַרְזֵי הַלְּבָנוֹן אַדִּירֵי הַתּוֹרָה. בְּגַן עֵדֶן תְּהֵא מְנוּחָתָם. לָכֵן, בַּעַל הָרַחֲמִים יַסְתִּירֵם בְּסֵתֶר כְּנָפָיו לְעוֹלָמִים, וְיִצְרֹר בִּצְרוֹר הַחַיִּים אֶת נִשְׁמָתָם, יהוה הוּא נַחֲלָתָם, וְיָנְוּחוּ בְשָׁלוֹם עַל מִשְׁכָּבָם, וְנֹאמַר אָמֵן.

Psalms for Special Occasions

The following psalms may be said on special occasions:

On the day of one's wedding	Psalm 19
On the birth of a child	Psalms 20, 139
For someone who is ill	Psalms 23, 121, 130, 139
For security of Israel	Psalms 20, 120, 121, 125
On recovery from illness	Psalms 6, 30, 103
Thanksgiving	Psalms 95, 116
For guidance	Psalm 139
For success	Psalm 121
For repentance	Psalm 90
For help in difficult times	Psalms 20, 130
When traveling	Psalm 91
In thanksgiving for being saved	Psalm 124

List of Psalms by Theme

Supplication and thanksgiving for victory and salvation: 2, 17, 18, 20, 21, 30, 35, 40, 46, 60, 61, 64, 74, 76, 83, 86, 107, 108, 124, 128, 129, 140, 141, 143, 144

Request for healing, and thanksgiving for recovery: 6, 41, 71, 103, 107, 147

Hymns and songs of praise: 8, 11, 22, 24, 31, 44, 46, 48, 60, 63, 65, 67, 69, 74, 81, 84, 85, 87, 91, 92, 95, 96, 98, 102, 103, 104, 105, 106, 107, 111, 112, 113, 114, 115, 117, 118, 128, 133, 134, 135, 136, 145, 146, 147, 148, 149, 150

Reflection and contemplation: 1, 8, 14, 15, 16, 19, 25, 34, 36, 37, 49, 50, 53, 62, 73, 90, 101, 112, 127

Revelation: 24, 29, 47, 66, 68, 93, 97, 99

Confession and requests for forgiveness: 32, 51, 130

Eschatological visions: 72, 126, 138, 150

The Davidic dynasty: 89, 110, 132

The people of Israel: History, requests, etc.: 44, 73, 74, 77, 78, 80, 83, 100, 105, 106, 114, 129, 133, 134, 135, 136, 137

Faith and trust in God: 3, 4, 9, 13, 16, 21, 22, 25, 26, 27, 31, 32, 33, 37, 40, 41, 52, 56, 57, 59, 62, 65, 71, 84, 86, 112, 115, 119, 121, 125, 135, 143

Devotional passages: 23, 63, 84, 119, 131, 139

Thanksgiving for various events: 8, 9, 16, 18, 28, 30, 40, 67, 74, 75, 76, 84, 85, 96, 100, 116, 124, 138

Requests and supplications for various matters: 5, 7, 8, 9, 17, 26, 28, 31, 32, 38, 39, 42, 43, 54, 55, 56, 57, 58, 59, 64, 69, 70, 71, 74, 79, 80, 86, 88, 89, 91, 115, 123, 140, 143

The righteous and the wicked, on the wicked and evil in the world: 1, 5, 10, 14, 35, 36, 37, 52, 53, 54, 55, 58, 62, 64, 70, 73, 75, 94, 109, 137, 140, 141, 149

Zion and Jerusalem: 2, 9, 14, 20, 50, 51, 53, 65, 68, 69, 74, 76, 78, 79, 84, 87, 97, 99, 102, 110, 116, 122, 125, 126, 128, 129, 132, 135, 137, 146, 147, 149

Reproof: 82, 95, 102

Prayer of the persecuted, the sick, and the sufferer: 4, 6, 7, 12, 13, 20, 22, 30, 38, 42, 64, 69, 70, 71, 74, 79, 83, 88, 91, 102, 107, 109, 123, 137, 140, 141, 142, 143, 146

רשימה של פרקי התהלים
לפי ענייניהם

בקשה ותודה על ניצחון וישועה ב, י, יח, כ, כא, ל, לה, מ, מו, ס, סא, סד, עד, עו, פג, פו, קו, קח, קכד, קכח, קכט, קמ, קמא, קמג, קמד

בקשה לרפואה ותודה על החלמה ו, מא, עא, קג, קו, קמז

המנוני תהילה ושירי הלל ח, יא, כב, כד, לא, מד, מו, מח, ס, סג, סה, סו, סט, עד, פא, פד, פה, פו, צא, צב, צה, צו, צח, קיד, קטו, קיז, קיח, קכח, קלג, קלד, קלה, קלו, קמה, קמו, קמז, קמח, קמט, קן

התבוננות והגות א, ח, יד, טו, טז, יט, כה, לד, לו, לז, מט, נ, נג, סב, עג, צ, קא, קיב, קכו

התגלות כד, כט, מז, סח, צג, צו, צט

וידוי ובקשת סליחה לב, נא, קל

חזון אחרית הימים עב, קכו, קלח, קן

מלכות בית דוד פט, קי, קלב

עם ישראל: תולדות, בקשות וכו׳ מד, עג, עד, עו, עח, פ, פג, ק, קה, קו, קיד, קכט, קלג, קלד, קלה, קלו, קלז

פרקי ביטחון ג, ד, ט, יג, טז, כא, כב, כה, כו, כז, לא, לב, לג, לז, מ, מא, נב, נו, נז, נט, סב, סה, עא, פד, פו, קיב, קטו, קיט, קכא, קכה, קלה, קמג

פרקי דבקות כג, סג, פד, קיט, קלא, קלט

פרקי תודה על עניינים שונים ח, ט, טז, יח, כח, ל, מ, סו, עד, עה, עו, פד, פה, צו, ק, קטו, קכד, קלח

פרקי תפילה, בקשה ותחינה בנושאים שונים ה, ז, ח, ט, יז, כו, כח, לא, לב, לח, לט, מב, מג, נד, נה, נו, נז, נח, נט, סד, סט, ע, עא, עד, עט, פ, פו, פח, פט, צא, קטו, קכג, קם, קמג

צדיק ורשע, על הרשע והרשעים שב־עולם א, ה, ט, יד, לה, לו, לז, נב, נג, נד, נה, נח, סב, סד, ע, עג, עד, צד, קט, קלו, קם, קמא, קמט

ציון וירושלים ב, ט, יד, כ, נ, נא, נג, סה, סח, סט, עד, עז, עח, עט, פד, פו, צו, צט, קב, קי, קטו, קכב, קכה, קכו, קכח, קכט, קלב, קלה, קלו, קלז, קמו, קמז, קמט

תוכחה פב, צה, קכ

תפילת הנרדף, החולה, הסובל והנתון בצרה ד, ו, ז, יב, יג, כ, כב, ל, לח, מב, סד, סט, ע, עא, עד, עט, פג, פו, פח, צא, קב, קו, קטו, קכב, קלו, קם, קמא, קמב, קמג, קמורשימת הנושאים של פרקי התהלים

List of Psalms by Chapter

רשימת הנושאים של פרקי התהלים
לפי סדר הפרקים

Notes

BOOK ONE (PSALMS 1–41)

1. See Habakkuk 3:1.
2. Genesis 1:27.
3. See *Makkot* 24a.
4. See also Exodus 20:18.
5. See Exodus 25:18.
6. See also Deuteronomy 29:28: "The concealed are for the Lord our God, but the revealed are for us and for our children."
7. Deuteronomy 3:9.
8. See, for example, Psalm 68; see Exodus 19:18.
9. See 1 Samuel 21:11–22:1.
10. See Isaiah 62:6.
11. See 1 Chronicles 16:41.

BOOK TWO (PSALMS 42–72)

1. See Exodus 23:17, 34:23.
2. 1 Chronicles 29:23.
3. See 1 Kings 9:28.
4. See 1 Kings 19:11–12.
5. Exodus 20:2.
6. See *Vayikra Rabba* 22:10.

7. II Samuel 12:13.
8. See Leviticus 14:4.
9. See Numbers 19:18.
10. See I Samuel 22:9.
11. See commentary on 32:1 for an explanation of this term.
12. See I Samuel 23:19–28.
13. See Numbers 16.
14. See I Samuel 27:1–4.
15. See I Samuel 24:3–4.
16. See Psalms 57, 58.
17. See I Samuel 19.
18. See II Samuel 8.
19. See also Judges 5:4–5, which contains similar wording.
20. See Jeremiah 49:19, where the enemy is compared to a lion prowling the banks of the Jordan River.

BOOK THREE (PSALMS 73–89)

1. See I Chronicles 7:20–22.
2. See Exodus 16:2–3.
3. See Exodus 16 and 17, and Numbers 11.
4. See Numbers 11:31.
5. See Numbers 11:33–34.
6. See Numbers 14:22–23.
7. See Genesis 10:6.
8. See I Samuel 4.
9. See introduction to Psalms 45.
10. Deuteronomy 14:1.
11. As in verse 1 of this psalm.
12. See Judges 6–7.
13. See Judges 4.
14. See Judges 7:25.
15. See Judges 8.
16. See II Samuel 5:22–24.
17. Almost identical wording appears in Exodus 34:6.

18. See Isaiah 30:7.
19. See I Chronicles 6:18.
20. See I Chronicles 2:6.
21. See I Chronicles 2:6.
22. See I Chronicles 6:29.
23. Genesis 1:21.
24. See I Samuel 16:13.

BOOK FOUR (PSALMS 90–106)

1. See also *Bereshit Rabba* 68:9: "He is the place of the world, but His world is not His place."
2. See Exodus 32:12.
3. See *Tamid* 33b.
4. Leviticus 19:18.
5. Nahum 1:2.
6. Deuteronomy 32:35.
7. Exodus 17:7; Numbers 20:13.
8. Exodus 17:7.
9. Exodus 34:5–7.
10. See Genesis 1:7: "The water that was above the firmament."
11. See Genesis 1:9.
12. Genesis 1:9.
13. See also the words *mapelya* in Jeremiah 2:31 and *shalhevetya* in Song of Songs 8:6.
14. See Exodus 20:6, 34:7; Deuteronomy 5:10.
15. See Genesis 17:17–19.
16. See Genesis 20:3.
17. See Genesis 20:7.
18. Genesis 10:6.
19. Exodus 5:22–23.
20. See Exodus 7:29.
21. See Exodus 9:24.
22. See, e.g., Genesis 49:3.
23. See Exodus 12:33.
24. Exodus 17:1–7.

25. Exodus 14:10–12.
26. Exodus 15:1–19.
27. Numbers 11:33.
28. Numbers 16.
29. Numbers 16:1.
30. Numbers 16:35.
31. *Ta'anit* 29a.
32. Numbers 25:6–15.
33. Numbers 20:2–12.
34. See Numbers 20:10.
35. See, e.g., Obadiah 1:20.

BOOK FIVE (PSALMS 107–150)

1. See II Samuel 13–18, specifically 15:5–8.
2. See II Samuel 16:10, David's remark regarding Shimi son of Gera: "He curses because the Lord said to him: Curse David."
3. I Chronicles 29:23.
4. See also II Samuel 8:18, where David's sons are called *kohanim*.
5. See Genesis 14:18, where Malkitzedek is mentioned as "king of Shalem," which is identified as Jerusalem (see 76:3).
6. Genesis 14:18.
7. Exodus 15:2.
8. See also Isaiah 17:12.
9. See II Samuel 24:18–25.
10. See Numbers 10:35–36.
11. I Samuel 24:3.
12. See *Berakhot* 4b for a discussion of the reasons for this omission.

MW00834395